REPRESSION AND DISSOCIATION

The John D. and Catherine T. MacArthur Foundation
Series on Mental Health and Development

REPRESSION AND DISSOCIATION

Implications for Personality
Theory, Psychopathology, and Health

Edited by

Jerome L. Singer

THE UNIVERSITY OF CHICAGO PRESS / CHICAGO AND LONDON

Jerome L. Singer is professor of psychology at Yale University, where he is director of graduate studies in psychology, director of the graduate program in clinical psychology, and co-director of the Family Television Research and Consultation Center.

The University of Chicago Press, Chicago 60637
The University of Chicago Press, Ltd., London
© 1990 by the University of Chicago
All rights reserved. Published 1990
Printed in the United States of America

99 98 97 96 95 94 93 92 91 90   5 4 3 2 1

Library of Congress Cataloging-in-Publication Data

Repression and dissociation : implications for personality theory,
    psychopathology, and health / edited by Jerome L. Singer.
        p.   cm. — (The John D. and Catherine T. MacArthur Foundation
    series on mental health and development)
      Includes bibliographical references.
      ISBN 0-226-76105-3
      1. Repression (Psychology)   2. Dissociation (Psychology)
    3. Personality.   I. Singer, Jerome L.   II. Series.
    BF175.5.R44R47   1990
    150.19′5—dc20   89-39012
                                                                      CIP

The University of Chicago Press gratefully acknowledges a subvention from the
John D. and Catherine T. MacArthur Foundation in partial support of the costs of
production of this volume.

♾ The paper used in this publication meets the minimum requirements of the
American National Standard for Information Sciences—Permanence of Paper for
Printed Library Materials, ANSI Z39.48-1984

Contents

Contributors

Keith J. Alexander   University of Pennsylvania School
    of Medicine
Sidney J. Blatt   Yale University
George A. Bonanno   Yale University
Gordon H. Bower   Stanford University
Kenneth S. Bowers   University of Waterloo
Paul Crits-Christoph   University of Pennsylvania School of
    Medicine
Penelope J. Davis   University of Sydney and Harvard University
Marshall Edelson   Yale University, School of Medicine
Matthew Hugh Erdelyi   Brooklyn College and the Graduate
    School of the City University of New York
Bram Fridhandler   University of California, San Francisco,
    School of Medicine
Jess H. Ghannam   University of California, San Francisco,
    School of Medicine
David S. Holmes   University of Kansas
Mardi J. Horowitz   University of California, San Francisco,
    School of Medicine
Irene P. Hoyt   University of Wisconsin
John F. Kihlstrom   University of Arizona
Helen Block Lewis   Yale University
Lester Luborsky   University of Pennsylvania School of Medi-
    cine
Henry C. Markman   University of California, San Francisco,
    School of Medicine
Gary E. Schwartz   University of Arizona
Howard Shevrin   University of Michigan Medical Center
Julie Sincoff   Yale University
Jerome L. Singer   Yale University

David Spiegel   Stanford University School of Medicine
Charles H. Stinson   University of California, San Francisco,
    School of Medicine
George E. Vaillant   Dartmouth University Medical School
Daniel A. Weinberger   Stanford University

Foreword

MARDI J. HOROWITZ, M. D.

This book is the second in a series from the Program on Conscious and Unconscious Mental Processes of the John D. and Catherine T. MacArthur Foundation. The first volume is *Psychodynamics and Cognition,* edited by Mardi J. Horowitz (Chicago: University of Chicago Press, 1988). It concluded with a statement of the useful directions for future theory formation and research. One direction concerned schemas and the other individual mental control of ideas and feelings.

The cornerstone of the theory of intrapsychic control in psychodynamics uses the construct of defense mechanisms, and central to that construct is the unconscious regulatory process called repression. This volume deals with repressive control both as a current defense mechanism and as a habitual personality style or coping operation. Coverage, broadly, of one defense such as repression lays the groundwork for a revised theory of control of ideas and feelings that may converge psychodynamic and cognitive science points of view. It sets the stage for explorations of other more complex defense mechanisms such as dissociation. Indeed, it may point the way to a new, general psychology of how thought relates to emotion and intentionality.

Preface: A Fresh Look at Repression, Dissociation, and the Defenses as Mechanisms and as Personality Styles

JEROME L. SINGER

Repression: A Key Concept in Psychodynamic Theory

The concept of psychological defenses is central to any examination of the relation of conscious to unconscious mental processes. If there is any single formulation that encompasses the complex features of psychoanalysis and related psychodynamic theories, it is that a considerable portion of human thought, communication, social behavior, or psychological symptomatology involves more or less successful efforts to ward off from consciousness or from observation by others a variety of threatening conflictual cognitive contents or emotional reactions. The term Sigmund Freud used most often to represent such warding-off processes was "repression"—or, in its most frequent variants, "suppression", "dissociation," or "inhibition" (Erdelyi 1985; see also Erdelyi, in this volume). His earliest use of the concept of suppression was in describing a case in which a conflictual set of "intentions" led to a mother's dissociation from awareness of the painful thoughts, resulting in symptoms of poor lactation or vomiting when attempting to breast-feed her child. The condition was relatively successfully treated by hypnotism (Freud [1892–93] 1966).

Thirty-four years later, after much use of terms such as "defense" and "repression" relatively interchangeably, Freud ([1926] 1959) revised his anxiety theory. He sought to distinguish "repression" from "defense" by attempting the preliminary listing of specific defenses such as isolation, denial, undoing, and repression, which he linked to particular neurotic syndromes such as anxiety neurosis, conversion hysteria, and obsessional neurosis. In the new anxiety theory, it is not the process of repression that evokes symptomatology or the manifestations of anxiety but rather the threat of emergence of conflictual ideation or affect that arouses anxiety. The defenses then operate to repress (in general terms) those thoughts or affects by forgetting (the specific use of repression) or by isolation, undoing, intellectualization, or other mechanisms. But Freud continued to use "repression" as the most general form of warding off as well as identifying it as a specific defense linked to forgetting (Erdelyi 1985).

Repression has therefore often been called the "queen of the defenses," the most general form of avoidance of conscious representation of frightening memories, wishes, or fantasies or of the unwanted emotions. The specific defense mechanisms of isolation, denial, rationalization, projection, reaction formation, intellectualization, or sublimation all serve to repress thought or affect.

In its general form, repression proves to be more of a metapsychological principle rather than a testable hypothesis about human behavior. It is not surprising, therefore, that psychologists interested in finding a "handle" for testing psychoanalytic theory have focused attention more on the specific use of repression as a defense. During the 1930s and 1940s, many experiments sought to test the perhaps oversimplified view that pleasant memories would be more easily recalled than unpleasant ones (the "PU" studies) or that electric shock–associated words or socially unacceptable words would be harder to learn and, if learned, harder to retrieve.

This extensive laboratory literature was reviewed by David Rapaport in his remarkable book *Emotions and Memory* (Rapaport [1942] 1952). Rapaport's great talent as a scholar and synthesizer of psychoanalytic theory led him to conclude that most of the research was irrelevant to the psychoanalytic model of repression. He wrote, "Repression is twofold. While primal-infantile-repression expels and keeps out of consciousness *an instinct representation,* repression proper affects the derivatives of instinct representations. To keep material out of consciousness means to deprive it of its preconscious verbal images or its energy-cathexis, or both. . . . The effect of repression consists not only in expelling and keeping a memory out of consciousness, but also of displacing its 'affect-charge' to another idea or in suppressing it entirely" (Rapaport [1942] 1959, 168–69).

Rapaport went on to argue that the widespread notion that "Freud taught the forgetting of the disagreeable" is fallacious. Rather, he suggested, Freud's discovery was of a function that prevented an unconscious idea, potentially conflictual, from emerging into conscious awareness: "This function, called repression, proved to be a specific and variable one, hardly amenable to the statistical treatment adopted by experimentalists" (Rapaport [1942] 1959, 169). Forgetting must be regarded as just one of what we would call today those cognitive disruptions that occur when there is a conflict between a "censor" and "prohibited unconscious tendencies" striving for expression. When one analyzes such cognitive disturbances, one finds that particular mechanisms have been active to produce (1) "screen memories" in the place of forgotten early childhood experiences, (2) the flow of free associations, and (3) dream structures. Thus, repression leads to conscious content by displacing, condensing, substituting, symbolizing, or secondarily elaborating the (presumed) underlying unconscious ideas and their affective charge.

Rapaport's presentation of the classic psychoanalytic model and his denigration of "statistical," nonclinical efforts to capture the operation of repression (either in its "primal" more general or in its specific form) poses a serious challenge to investigators. In the present volume, the chapters by Marshall Edelson and by David S. Holmes reflect two sharply contrasting responses to that challenge, Edelson by embracing the classic psychoanalytic stance and carrying it to what some might consider an extreme, Holmes by dismissing the psychoanalytic position out of hand and putting the burden of proof on its proponents. Other contributors to this volume choose perhaps a more middle course, focusing attention on the "motivated forgetting" characteristic of repression or on some effort to link repression to more general aspects of cognitive processing (see the chapters by Mardi J. Horowitz et al.; Matthew Hugh Erdelyi; Lester Luborsky, Paul Crits-Christoph, and Keith J. Alexander; and Penelope Davis as well as those on hypnotic dissociation and forgetting by David Spiegel; Kenneth S. Bowers; and John F. Kihlstrom and Irene P. Hoyt).

One implication of Rapaport's critique of laboratory research is that the operation of defenses is continuous and that the complexity of ongoing thought may preclude capturing the phenomena involved in one cross-sectional experimental manipulation or in one set of risqué versus neutral stimuli. His advocacy of the clinical approach or of qualitative observations of subjects' extended reactions obtained from a laboratory experiment (cf. Sharp 1930, 1938) implies a methodological strategy of studying not just an outcome in a learning experiment but also the process of attempted learning, attempted retrieval, and attempted communication of conflictual material. Sharp's (1930) thesis was conducted in an era of much greater sensitivity about profanity and sacrilege. Subjects were required to learn paired nonsense syllables like "jeh-sus, god-dum." They could be observed mispronouncing the component syllables of a pair, trying to disconnect them and learn them in vertical order, struggling in various ways to perform the task as required but not to accept or expose the embarrassing connection. Such observations of ongoing behavior, as Rapaport implies, appear to capture the continuing active process of defenses better than outcome data on relative recall of pleasant, unpleasant, or neutral words.

In this same sense of defense as a continuing process, one can consider the possibility that persisting reliance on a specific defense or a related group of defenses may lead to a crystallized pattern that emerges, as Freud suggested early in his paper on "Character and Anal Eroticism" (Freud 1908), in a personality style or, as outlined in more detail in the later book on the anxiety theory (Freud [1926] 1959), in a specific neurosis such as the obsessional or hysterical forms. Thus, it may often be difficult to capture a defense as it operates in a specific instance with a specific unwanted thought. One can, however, observe the consequences of recurrent, habitual reliance on particular defenses since these may be reflected in particular lifelong mannerisms or even in identifiable personality "types." Sullivan (1956) sought to capture this patterning in his discussion of "clinical entities," and Shapiro (1965) used the term "neurotic styles" to link recurrent specific defensive manifestations to a particular personality organization. More recently, Horowitz (1976) has proposed that the tie between defense and neurotic style implies different intervention strategies or therapeutic "counters" for the patients' typical means of warding off distress. He has outlined specific ways for a therapist to treat a patient with a posttraumatic stress reaction depending on whether the crystallized neurotic style is obsessive (with its characteristic defenses of intellectualization or isolation) or hysterical (with characteristic defenses repression, inattention, global thinking, etc.). The longitudinal research conducted by Vaillant has pointed to intriguing implications of such crystallized defensive patterns (see the chapter by George Vaillant in this volume) as they unfold over a long life span. The chapters in this book by Helen Block Lewis, Sidney J. Blatt, Penelope Davis, Daniel A. Weinberger, Gary E. Schwartz, and George A. Bonanno and Jerome L. Singer represent approaches that emphasize the presumed implications of defenses that work together to lead specifically to a repressor personality organization.

Why Study Repression, and Why Now?

While the concept of repression is central to psychoanalytic theory, we need not limit the importance of the phenomenon of motivated forgetting or of selective inattention to a particular historical trend within psychology or behavior theory. Any attempt at formulating a modern theory of human cognition or motivation, or of personality more generally, needs to consider the special role played by the necessity for selective filtering of complex information and for controlling through a variety of devices such as inattention, distraction, dissociation, or avoidance the dysphoric consequences either of information overload or of threatening information for which no immediate remedy exists. As a child, well before I had ever heard of psychology or Freud, I often used to hear people apply a Yiddish or German phrase rather scornfully to someone, "Er macht sich nicht wissendich" (He makes himself unknowing). I read of the famous incident of the twelfth-century murder of Archbishop Thomas Becket in Canterbury Cathedral by knights who had earlier heard King Henry II exasperatedly cry, "Who will rid me of this man?" But, of course, the king later could assert that he knew nothing of the actual murder conspiracy, having spoken only rhetorically. Seven centuries later, we heard the doctrine of "plausible deniability" clearly enunciated by Vice-Admiral Poindexter before the congressional committee investigating the Iran-Contra scandal in 1987. Indeed, President Reagan repeatedly asserted that he could not remember certain alleged memoranda or that he had ever given explicit orders for many of the activities carried out by his national security adviser or by Lieutenant Colonel North.

Whether manifested on the stage of national foreign policy or in the privacy of one's consciousness, the effort at "disassociating" oneself from potential culpability or "dissociating" two incompatible experiences or wishes in one's personal life seems to be critical to understanding human psychology. In any effort to build new models for conceptualizing thought and behavior, repression and its closely linked defenses (or, if one prefers the less psychoanalytically linked term, "coping" or "filtering processes") merit a careful reexamination. In any project that seeks to examine the links between conscious and unconscious mental processes, we are bound to consider the question, What are the consequences of selective attention or inattention, of motivated forgetting, or of developing a style of information processing in which a significant portion of the potentially negative experiences we might confront in thought or action are systematically relegated to procedures that keep them out of conscious awareness? Ultimately, any theory of personality has to confront the major individual difference variable, so well emphasized by Carl Jung, that some people devote only a small portion of their waking time to conscious thought and rumination, preferring instead physical or social interactions that preclude opportunities for extended reminiscences and mental rehearsals of potentially frightening or challenging events, while others welcome opportunities for conscious elaboration of all manner of experience.

The repressor personality style seems especially intriguing in recent years with the emergence of the fields of behavior medicine and health psychology. Persons who are characterized by much systematic avoidance (whether consciously or unconsciously controlled is an issue still to be studied) seem, from a host of clinical reports as well as from some well-controlled studies, to be at great risk for physical health problems. The discovery by Weinberger, Schwartz, and Davidson that persons who report on questionnaires that they are minimally anxious but who also fill out a questionnaire in a defensive or "socially desirable" manner prove to be physiologically more aroused than even self-reported high-anxious persons has opened a new vein of exploration (see Weinberger, Schwartz, and Bonanno and Singer, all in this volume). Such a finding suggests a potential link between a personality style that emphasizes an avoidant or repressor pattern and a bodily response pattern of autonomic stress that could lay the basis for some of the findings that have associated the repressor with psychosomatic or more general physical illness.

In effect, then, we can identify two major objectives of this volume. The first, as part of a broader reexamination of conscious and unconscious phenomena and of the so-called defense mechanisms, is to take a careful look at the phenomenon or process of repression from the perspective of theory and empirical research. The second objective is to review the much more recent and newly emerging data on the repressor personality style and its near cousins such as the field dependent personality (see Lewis, in this volume) and the anaclitic depressive (see Blatt, in this volume). There is a special area of clinical and experimental research that has associated hypnosis with repression or dissociation. We have also tried to examine more carefully whether the special phenomena of hypnosis studied in the laboratory or the clinic can clarify the relation between repression and forgetting. Is dissociation a separate process, related generally to the underlying avoidant function of repression but not really the same, or is the process just another manifestation of a basic avoidant coping style or process? (see Spiegel, Kihlstrom and Hoyt, and Bowers, all in this volume). Generally, the use of hypnosis focuses more on the process of repression or dissociation of specific events rather than on personality style, although it is possible that an avoidant pattern may make some patients more susceptible to hypnosis. At any rate, we cannot consider the current state-of-the-art research of avoidant defense without examining the special properties of the "splitting" of human consciousness that seems especially possible under the interpersonal conditions created in a hypnotic atmosphere.

The Organization of This Volume

While this volume is derived from a conference on "Repression, Dissociation, and the Warding off of Conflictual Cognitive Contents" convened at Yale University under MacArthur Foundation sponsorship, it is not a conference "proceedings" in the narrow sense. At the conference itself, a number of additional participants were present throughout (see the list in the preface). There were discussion periods and much talk during lunch, dinner, and coffee breaks. A number of potential projects or proposed collaborative researches between specific participants actually developed in that atmosphere. The conference might therefore be termed a success for the small group of specific participants.

This volume makes no pretense of attempting to capture the give and take or personal interactions of the meetings since even the audiotapes of the discussion periods lose much in transcription. Instead, the people who made formal presentations were asked to provide scholarly chapters expanding on their remarks and, if they chose, incorporating some of their reactions from the meeting or even new material. Since the list of contributors includes so many of the active researchers or scholars in the field, I believe that this approach may yield a very thorough review of the current state of theory and knowledge on the subject of repression and that it may also be an important introduction to a potential series addressing the general issue of defenses.

The structure of the volume follows that of the original conference closely. The volume opens with a contribution by Matthew Hugh Erdelyi, whose research on memory and whose fine book *Psychoanalysis: Freud's Cognitive Psychology* (1985) was a major stimulant for the reexamination of the role of defense mechanisms in cognition. Erdelyi sets the work on repression and forgetting into a historical perspective and provides a scholarly review of Freud's use of the term. The links between the psychoanalytic concept and early studies of memory more generally by Ebbinghaus and Bartlett are identified. Finally, Erdelyi presents some of his own stimulating research and challenges the reader to a fresh look at the notion of selective forgetting and retrieval.

The contribution from Marshal Edelson, a distinguished scholar of psychoanalysis and the author most recently of *Hypothesis and Evidence in Psychoanalysis* (1984), throws down the gauntlet to those investigators who seek to understand or to research defense mechanisms outside the medium in which they were discovered, the psychoanalytic process itself. Adopting a stance that some may feel is extreme in his use of a cinematographic model, he proposes psychosexual fantasy as the central issue for psychoanalytic theory, calling for a new type of research on private mental processes, an investigative method perhaps best carried out by idiographic methodologies rather than the nomothetic ones represented by the other contributors. Readers can decide for themselves whether Edelson's position casts serious doubt on the entire effort to conduct empirical research on psychoanalytic propositions outside the individual analysis.

The chapter by Mardi J. Horowitz and the Conscious-Unconscious Mental Processes Research Group represents an alternative approach that also stems from an initially psychoanalytically informed model. Derived from the Langley Porter Psychiatric Institute's Center for the Study of Neurosis and the work there on treatment of posttraumatic stress responses, Horowitz and his coauthors seek actively to relate clinically derived observations and concepts to broader issues in the psychology of personality and current cognitive research.

While some may see Edelson as a psychoanalytic conservative and Horowitz as a psychoanalytic reformer pushing to integrate psychoanalysis into general behavior theory, David S. Holmes represents himself in the next chapter as a Diogenes looking for a data-based theory and as a "dust-bowl empiricist." In effect, he seems to say to Edelson and Horowitz, "A plague on both your houses," calling for a new, more thoroughly research-based approach to selective cognitive processing. Again, readers may decide whether the subsequent chapters and the empirical work described therein address the challenge cast by Holmes.

The next section of this volume introduces a series of approaches to identifying the process of repression or related phenomena by studying subliminal perception and hypnosis. These methods (in contrast to the earlier efforts at laboratory research on forgetting reviewed in Rapaport's ([1942] 1959) classic volume and brought up to date in Holmes's chapter) seek to retain some of the flavor of the psychoanalytic atmosphere in which repression was "discovered." Howard Shevrin's chapter, based on his distinguished career of research in this area, provides a psychoanalytically derived rationale for the importance of studying defensive phenomena through the subliminal perception paradigm. Indeed, this methodology, often scorned in the 1960s and 1970s, has been reviving recently in the work of general cognitive and social cognition researchers (Kihlstrom 1987). The three subsequent chapters examine the phenomenon of hypnosis as a model for understanding conscious and unconscious processes and the whole question of dissociated experiences and motivated or "suggested" forgetting.

Kenneth S. Bowers provides a wide-ranging review of the phenomenon of hypnosis and its properties and focuses on the empirical evidence of unconscious or out-of-awareness processes that influence hypnotic performance. Here we see the impressive achievements of and further possibilities for systematic empirical research using the hypnotic paradigm in studying defensive or filtering processes in human cognition and emotion. The chapter by David Spiegel, a distinguished clinical investigator of hypnosis, assays an imaginative exploration of the special properties of the dissociation mechanism (a form or variant of repression). Of particular importance is Spiegel's effort to cast the phenomenon into the perspective of important new theoretical developments in psychology such as the "global workspace" conception of Baars and the exciting new concepts of parallel distributed processing of Rumelhart and McClelland and their group, very recent ideas that are reshaping a good deal of current cognitive psychology. At the conference itself, Spiegel showed a remarkable film of a depressed Vietnam War veteran who, under hypnosis, retrieves a horrifying, apparently previously forgotten memory of a bombardment in which an orphan boy shortly to be adopted by the narrator was killed.

The next chapter of this section, contributed by John F. Kihlstrom and Irene P. Hoyt, now brings together hypnosis and dissociation with repression. Kihlstrom and Hoyt put these phenomena into a contemporary information-processing perspective, introduce further empirical research beyond that reviewed by Bowers and Spiegel, and seek to make a careful distinction between dissociation and repression. This section concludes with a chapter (originally more informal discussion) by the distinguished cognitive theorist and experimentalist Gordon H. Bower, who attempts to reexamine the questions raised in the papers on memory, hypnosis, and repression. He proposes, for example, a distinction between types of awareness that involves separating the ability to describe or to communicate an experience or wish from the ability to take such an experience into account for subsequent action. With Bower's chapter, we have rounded out the first major portion of this volume and have explored the theory and empirical research on the repressive *process*. Readers can decide how well the attempts of the contributors of most of the chapters in this section meet the goals of suggesting whether defense concepts such as repression and dissociation derived originally from psychoanalytic therapy (1) retain their unique properties, (2) fit well into broader conceptual schemes based on current forms of information-processing theory, and (3) provide inspiration for future empirical study.

We turn next to the second major way of examining repression—as a crystallized or habitual style of dealing with thought and action that leads to a dispositional or trait-like characteristic and, indeed, to a personality style that has implications for mental and physical health. This section opens with a chapter by the late Helen Block Lewis, one of the pioneers in the empirical study of cognitive style and of the study of shame. This chapter, completed on Lewis's deathbed just six months after her vigorous participation in the Yale conference, addresses the question of what impels a defensive process such as repression. She proposes that emotions such as shame, guilt, and humiliated fury are the experiences that people seem to wish to forget or to dissociate and reviews empirical and clinical literature relevant to this proposition. The pattern of such a continuous defense process becomes organized into a cognitive style such as field dependence.

Also in this section, the contribution by Lester Luborsky and his collaborators describes some of the earliest attempts to devise measures of a repressor personality style. A consideration of the relations between some of these earlier measures is based on a recent reanalysis of data available in previous studies. The chapter by George E. Vaillant, known for his longitudinal follow-up studies of Harvard graduates, reexamines the various definitions of defense. He proposes a somewhat different interpretation of repression and dissociation and then provides evidence from his research on the long-term implications for mental and physical health of regular reliance on separate defenses of repression, dissociation, suppression, and reaction formation.

All the chapters in the section thus far reflect to some degree an acceptance of certain fundamental psychoanalytic propositions, even though Lewis tries to move to new ground in her theory of emotion. The chapter by Sidney J. Blatt, while still reflecting an adherence to psychoanalytic object representation propositions, offers a sweeping new personality distinction, between the anaclitic and the introjective, for ordering style variations that relate to defenses. A distinction between classes of defense, avoidant versus counteractive, is also included, and these are linked to the anaclitic (avoidant) versus introjective (counteractive) types. New empirical data relevant to this proposal are reviewed.

Daniel A. Weinberger may well be considered a key person whose work stimulated this conference. Along with Gary Schwartz, he identified a group of persons who report very low levels of distress or anxiety but who also score high on a measure of defensiveness (repressors) and who concomitantly show high levels of physiological arousal. Weinberger's chapter reviews a very extensive literature and his own recent research pointing to the correlates in social behavior, mental and physical health of the repressor style. Penelope Davis's chapter follows close on Weinberger's position with examples of specific studies that deal with emotional memory. So, in a way, we come full circle from Erdelyi's chapter to these demonstrations that repressor personalities do show the kind of difficulty, especially with negative affective memory, that stimulated Freud's original insight about repression as selective forgetting.

Two final chapters extend the concept of repressor personality further into the field of psychophysiology and health. Gary E. Schwartz provides a broadranging system view that seeks to show how repression functions within the regulatory structures linking thought, behavior, and physiology. Very recent research on repressors and immune system functioning is described. Finally, George A. Bonanno and I seek to outline a general model of the human personality forever seeking to balance the needs for individuality, autonomy, and privacy with the desire for affiliation and communion. Within such a framework (already touched on earlier by Blatt), the functions of attention to one's own thoughts, memories, and fantasies must be brought into relation with the need for bodily attention and for attention to cues from others. We have proposed that repression as a defensive style emerges from an imbalanced shift toward affiliation and an avoidance of internal sensibility. We review an extensive literature linking the repressor personality style to various aspects of physical health. A brief closing chapter points up the main points of agreement and contradiction that emerge from this lengthy exploration, and some needed new research is outlined.

In summary, I have sought in this introduction to provide the reader with a Baedeker through a lengthy and challenging terrain. Our human eagerness for novelty, for gathering new information, and for assigning meanings and creating ever-widening and differentiated cognitive schemata and scripts is matched by a need for selection and control or regulation and filtering of new input or of the associative replay of stored information. The process of repression, systematic avoidance of potentially threatening material in thought or social experience, was first described by Freud as a source of anxiety and neurosis. The evidence for such a defensive process, the ways in which it can be explored in a variety of clinical and research paradigms, and, finally, some of the implications of a crystallized avoidant style for mental and physical health are presented herewith in the hope that our formulations will stimulate new thinking about theory and research in personality, psychopathology, and behavioral medicine.

References

Edelson, Marshall. 1984. *Hypothesis and evidence in psychoanalysis.* Chicago: University of Chicago Press.

Erdelyi, M. H. 1985. *Psychoanalysis: Freud's cognitive psychology.* New York: Freeman.

Freud, S. [1892–93] 1966. A case of successful treatment by hypnotism: With some remarks on the origin of hysterical symptoms through "counter-will." In *The standard edition of the complete psychological works of Sigmund Freud,* ed. J. Strachey, vol. 1. London: Hogarth.

———. [1908] 1959. Character and anal eroticism. In *The standard edition of the complete psychological works of Sigmund Freud,* ed. James Strachey, vol. 9. London: Hogarth.

———. [1926] 1959. Inhibitions, symptoms and anxiety. In *The Standard edition of the complete psychological works of Sigmund Freud,* ed. James Strachey, vol. 20. London: Hogarth.

Horowitz, M. J. 1976. *Stress response syndromes.* New York: Aronson.

Kihlstrom, S. 1987. The cognitive unconscious. *Science* 237, no. 1445:1452.

Rapaport, D. [1942] 1959. *Emotions and memory.* New York: International Universities Press.

Shapiro, D. 1965. *Neurotic styles.* New York: Basic.

Sharp, A. A. 1930. The influence of certain emotional inhibitions on learning and recall. Ph.D. diss., University of Chicago.

———. 1938. An experimental test of Freud's doctrine of the hedonic tone to memory revival. *Journal of Experimental Psychology* 22:395–418.

Sullivan, H. S. 1956. *Clinical studies in psychiatry.* New York: Norton.

Acknowledgments

In the early summer of 1986, a conference on Repression and Dissociation was held at Yale University. It was organized by the editor of this volume in connection with the evolving Program on Conscious and Unconscious Mental Processes located at the Langley Porter Psychiatric Institute under the direction of Mardi J. Horowitz, professor of psychiatry at the School of Medicine of the University of California, San Francisco. The program and the conference were supported by a grant from the John D. and Catherine T. MacArthur Foundation.

Attending the conference, in addition to the contributors to this volume, were Walter Mischel of Columbia University, who served as a discussant for some papers, and members of the staff of the consciousness-unconsciousness program, including Jesse Ghannam, Sandra Tunis, Charles Stinson, Daniel Weiss, and Henry Markman. John Conger represented the MacArthur Foundation at our meetings. Through the three days of meetings and pleasant lunches and dinners, there was a remarkable degree of lively discussion on both theoretical issues and potential research directions. The present volume reflects not only papers prepared in advance of the conference but also reactions to the interactions in the meeting, which are generally incorporated by the authors into their chapters. Specific research has already emerged from the meeting and is incorporated into the current activities of the Program on Conscious and Unconscious Mental Processes. The foreword by Mardi Horowitz and the introductory chapter by the editor set the issues of the conference into perspective with the conscious-unconscious processes program.

Assistance in clerical preparation of the manuscript material for the book came from Virginia Hurd, Frances DeGrenier, and Louise Koch. Julie Sincoff helped with preparation of the tables in the final chapter. Editorial assistance from two unidentified scholarly reviewers is gratefully acknowledged. Peter Nathan of the MacArthur Foundation played a useful liaison role in the development of this book.

One of our participants, Dr. Helen Block Lewis, professor emerita in the Department of Psychology at Yale University, took an active role throughout the conference. Tragically, she died just six months afterward in January 1987. Her revised chapter was completed literally on her deathbed. It is only fitting that we dedicate this volume to Dr. Helen Block Lewis.

JEROME L. SINGER

1 Repression, Reconstruction, and Defense: History and Integration of the Psychoanalytic and Experimental Frameworks

MATTHEW HUGH ERDLEYI

Repression and Amnesia

I shall begin not with Sigmund Freud but with Hermann Ebbinghaus. I wish to propose that in 1885, about a decade before Freud introduced the concept of repression into modern psychology—strictly speaking, reintroduced it since Johann Herbart had used the concept as well as the term more than half a century before—Ebbinghaus published the first experimental study of repression, demonstrating that repression produces amnesia. Thus viewed, Ebbinghaus's research may be thought of as the first laboratory demonstration of what is commonly known today as "directed" or "intentional forgetting" (Freud used the latter expression in 1894; cf. Bjork 1972; Epstein 1972; Freud [1894] 1962; Geiselman, Bjork, and Fishman 1983; Roediger and Crowder 1972; Weiner 1968).

It hardly needs to be said that this is not the mainstream view, in or out of experimental psychology; indeed, it may be the first time that such a view has been advanced. I hope the reader will not dismiss it on that account.

To probe the matter further, let us examine Ebbinghaus's work on forgetting. From experiments he conducted on himself, Ebbinghaus obtained data showing that the retention of to-be-remembered materials declines over time. These retention levels, when plotted against time, yield the familiar Ebbinghaus "curve of forgetting" (see fig. 1). These results seem commonsensical enough—we forget over time. Yet they may be misleading, as another retention function, this one obtained only a decade ago, suggests (Erdelyi and Kleinbard 1978; see fig. 2).

Paradoxically, although the Erdelyi and Kleinbard function resembles an upside-down version of Ebbinghaus's curve, it too seems commonsensical—we remember over time. What then is the truth? Does retention decrease or increase over time? The answer, of course, is that both may be right—or

This work was supported in part by grant 6-64345 from the City University of New York PSC-CUNY Research Award Program.

1

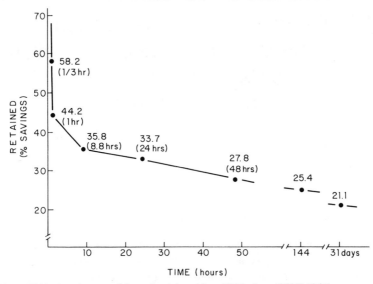

Fig. 1. Ebbinghaus's curve of forgetting (plotted from Ebbinghaus [1885] 1964).

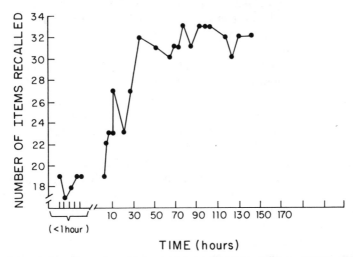

TIME (hours)

Fig. 2. Level of recall over time with repeated testing (Erdelyi and Kleinbard 1978, study 1).

wrong. Retention may decrease, increase, or stay constant over time (Ballard 1913; Erdelyi 1984, 1987; Erdelyi and Kleinbard 1978; Payne 1987; Roediger and Payne 1982). Retention at any time, as Ballard (1913) demonstrated in his seminal monograph "Oblivescence and Reminiscence," is the balance between two contradictory tendencies of memory, reminiscence and oblivescence (forgetting). A variety of factors can cause this balance (retention) to be

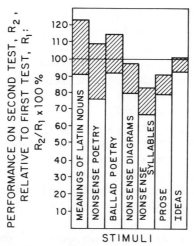

Fig. 3. Ballard's summary of his data for several types of stimulus materials, showing *hypermnesia* ("improvement") (when top of bar graph exceeds 100 percent of initial recall level); *reminiscence* (hatched segment of bar graph); and *forgetting* ("oblivescence") (distance between top of white section of bar graph and 100 percent initial recall level).

either negative, in which case amnesia is observed, or positive, in which case hypermnesia (improvement) is obtained (see fig. 3). Thus, the contradiction between the Ebbinghaus and the Erdelyi and Kleinbard functions has to do not with reliability—both are easily replicated—but with differences in methods and materials used, each of which differentially affect the relative contribution of oblivescence and reminiscence in retention.

Summarized below are the major differences between the Ebbinghaus and the Erdelyi and Kleinbard experiments (also Erdelyi and Becker 1974):

Ebbinghaus used nonsense syllables, whereas Erdelyi and Kleinbard used meaningful pictures;

Ebbinghaus used percent savings as his index of retention, whereas Erdelyi and Kleinbard used recall;

Ebbinghaus's initial retention levels were at ceiling (100 percent retention), Erdelyi and Kleinbard's below 50 percent;

Ebbinghaus used a between-stimulus procedure in which he retested himself only once on equivalent lists of different stimuli, at different time intervals; Erdelyi and Kleinbard, instead, used a multiple testing procedure in which the subjects recalled the same stimulus list successively over repeated recall trials;

finally, and most important, Ebbinghaus avoided thinking about the to-be-remembered materials (they were "left to themselves" [(1885) 1964, 4, 65], precluded from "review" [4]), whereas Erdelyi and Kleinbard's subjects actively thought about (and sought for) the items in memory.

Without being drawn unduly into a detailed consideration of these various factors, it may be asserted that the last factor—thinking versus not-thinking—is the crucial variable: this is so because, excepting for the thinking factor, amnesic functions can be readily obtained using the whole package of Erdelyi and Kleinbard methods and materials (pictorial stimuli, recall as the retention test, imperfect initial retention levels, and repeated testing for the same to-be-remembered materials).

We see, then, that there are two contradictory trends in (accessible) memory over time, a down function (oblivescence/forgetting) and an up function (reminiscence), and that we can intentionally determine which one will hold sway by thinking or not-thinking of the to-be-remembered materials. By thinking of the to-be-remembered materials—rehearsing the remembered and searching for the inaccessible—we cause reminiscence to exceed oblivescence, and hypermnesia results; by inhibiting thinking about the to-be-remembered materials, we cause oblivescence to exceed reminiscence, and amnesia results (Ballard 1913; Erdelyi 1987).

I shall try to demonstrate that intentional not-thinking of some target material is what Freud meant by "repression" and that, therefore, Ebbinghaus's experiment was actually one on repression and the psychogenic amnesia it can produce. It is true, of course, that Ebbinghaus's "repression" study had nothing to do with defense, but for the moment the discussion concerns the mechanism component of the "mechanism of defense." As I have suggested elsewhere (Erdelyi and Goldberg 1979), psychologists and psychoanalysts have tended to confuse the psychological mechanism with the purpose for which it is deployed. Repression—intentional not-thinking of some matter—can be used for defense, in which case it is a mechanism of defense, but it can also be used for a variety of other purposes (as Ebbinghaus did), in which case it remains the same mechanism but not a mechanism of defense. This is such an obvious point that it is almost hard to make.

There are other matters, however, that must surely concern the reader in this unexpected comingling of Ebbinghaus and Freud. Ebbinghaus's "repression" was not unconscious; need not Freud's be? Is not the repressed of Freud subject to recovery? Need it not cause symptoms? Does it not require the continuous expenditure of psychic energy? And so forth. I wish to postpone these questions for the moment to take note of the role of thought inhibition in post-Freudian (including non-Freudian) approaches to defense and some implications of thought inhibition that have not been sufficiently probed.

The notion that thought inhibition might be analogous or equivalent to repression and produce the effects adduced to repression has been variously proposed since Freud. For example:

> Harry Stack Sullivan's (1956) emphasis of "selective inattention," which, in the context of memory, amounts to a notion of thought avoidance (the

approach seems to be an elaboration of Freud's attention-withholding concept in the *Interpretation of Dreams* [(1900) 1953, chap. 7]);

Dollard and Miller's (1950) neo-Freudian, neobehavioristic treatment of "thought stopping";

Eriksen and Pierce's (1968) notion of "cognitive avoidance" (which may start, according to them, as a conscious act but which, through routine deployment, may become automatized and, therefore, unconscious; and

Walter Mischel's (1986) similar espousal of "cognitive avoidance" as the mechanism corresponding to repression.

The equivalence of "cognitive avoidance" (selective not-thinking, inattention, etc.) and repression has not, however, taken serious hold in the modern experimental or clinical literatures—perhaps because such proposals originated before the full blooming of cognitive psychology—and some theoretical aspects of cognitive avoidance have not been sufficiently developed.

First, there has been a failure to draw a rather obvious distinction between two kinds of inaccessibility or forgetting. There is the well-known availability-accessibility distinction of Tulving and Pearlstone (1966) in which inaccessible (but available) memories are inaccessible owing to retrieval failure, despite reasonable retrieval effort. The cognitive-avoidance notion suggests, however, another type of inaccessibility, one brought about not by retrieval failure but by retrieval recalcitrance; the subject fails to access some memory complex not because he or she cannot in principle access it but because he or she refuses to access it. Note that this latter type of inaccessibility, which is as foreign to the experimental laboratory as it is commonplace in the clinic—let us term it "inaccessibility due to retrieval avoidance" to distinguish it from the traditional inaccessibility due to retrieval failure—is not a response-bias effect. Because of the subject's refusal to access the memory complex, the material remains genuinely outside awareness. Thus, we have here "processing bias," not merely "response bias" (Erdelyi 1985; Erdelyi, Finks, and Feigin-Pfau, 1989; Erdelyi and Goldberg 1979). If, somehow, the repression/cognitive avoidance could be abrogated, then the repressed material should suddenly become accessible.

Or should it? Not to the extent that Ebbinghaus applies, for, as we have seen, Ebbinghaus established in his classic work that cognitive avoidance/not-thinking of some recently learned material produces amnesia. Note that one need not even set out to forget something; all that needs to be done is to exclude some target material from conscious thought—not to think about it—and Ebbinghaus takes over automatically.

Thus, the retrieval failure associated with repression need not occur because of repression at the time of formal testing/querying (in an experiment or a therapy session); the retrieval failure may occur as a result of a chronic disposition to repress the material in the interval before formal testing. For example, when Ebbinghaus tried to remember his heretofore repressed (intentionally left-to-themselves) nonsense syllables seven days later—when he intentionally stopped repressing/not-thinking of them and tried actively to retrieve them—his retention was highly amnesic despite the sudden abrogation of repression (see fig. 1). Chronic, prolonged retrieval avoidance/thought inhibition/cognitive avoidance (or whatever verbal formula one adopts) inexorably produces amnesia.

We see, therefore, that the abrogation of repression need not yield the return of the repressed material (Erdelyi 1974; see also Freud [1926] 1959, 143). Does it follow, therefore, that the repressed cannot be recovered? This is tantamount to asking whether "forgetting" (in the usual sense of inaccessibility due to retrieval failure) implies permanent information loss. The modern memory literature suggests otherwise. Interestingly, however, the question has not been put to the Ebbinghaus function directly: with the resumption of protracted thinking/retrieval effort, would the bottomed-out Ebbinghaus curve start to rise again?

I have some data on this issue (Erdelyi and Halberstam 1987), involving not nonsense syllables but the story "The War of the Ghosts" (see fig. 4). After some ten weeks of (mostly) not-thinking of the story (the subjects did not expect to be tested on it again), considerable amnesia was evinced. However, active thinking over the next several days produced hypermnesia for a significant portion of the material forgotten in the interim (net recall level increased by some 30 percent).

To summarize, (1) not-thinking about the to-be-remembered material produces amnesia, by which is not necessarily meant the permanent loss of the target information, and (2) active thinking (retrieval effort, rehearsal, etc.), even after amnesia has taken place, produces hypermnesia. Thus, by intentionally controlling our allocation of conscious thinking, we can, for whatever reasons (including presumably defense), control the accessibility to conscious memory of past events. Given the recent emphasis on the distinction among different kinds of memories (e.g., between declarative and procedural knowledge; Anderson 1983; Squire 1986; Tulving 1983), it should be added that the effects of repression might apply to some types of memory but not to others. It might thus be the case, for example, that recall of some declarative knowledge may be forgotten without knowledge of a different type (skills, symptoms, etc.) being comparably affected. As I have suggested elsewhere (Erdelyi 1985), Freud's famous formula, "Hysterics suffer mainly from reminiscences" (Breuer and Freud [1895] 1955, 7), may be profitably aligned with modern notions of memory dissociation or "remembering without awareness" (Jacoby and Witherspoon 1982).

We are, it seems, ready to turn to Freud and his concept of repression. Before proceeding with the task, however, two caveats. Bartlett (1932), whose work will also figure in what follows, taught modern cognitive psy-

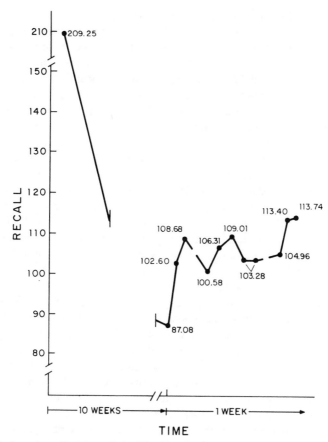

Fig. 4. Amnesia and hypermnesia for "The War of the Ghosts" (from Erdelyi and Halberstam 1987).

chologists how pervasively memories of the past are subject to a variety of reconstructions, if not outright fabrications; now, the reader must be warned that Freud's writings on repression and defense have themselves been over-taken by the types of revisions and distortions to which far simpler stories, such as "The War of the Ghosts," are prone. Also, it is worth underscoring that Sigmund Freud's psychological theorizing spanned a very long time inter-val: a full half century. Even a timid, careful, circumscribed theorist—which Freud was not—could be expected to modify his thinking to some extent over the years, let alone half a century. Consequently, it is worth keeping in mind that we contend with a temporally far-flung, shifting text that is immeasurably more complex than "The War of the Ghosts" and that our problem is one not merely of remembering it right but of reading it right.

The treatment of repression as thought inhibition or avoidance best fits

Freud's earlier formulations on the topic, roughly the first quarter century of psychoanalysis (say, 1893–1915), when Freud was more focally interested in memory processes than he was later. His first treatment of the problem precedes psychoanalysis. In a clinical paper on a woman who could not breast-feed her child, in which he reports a successful treatment by hypnotic suggestion (a technique antedating both psychoanalysis and its forerunner, the cathartic technique of Breuer), Freud ([1892–93] 1966) sets forth the essential elements of his theory of repression and defense: he proposes that the patient was ambivalent about breast-feeding her child, that she was in deep conflict about it, without, however, being aware of her conflict. According to Freud, her reluctance to breast-feed her child would have been unduly distressing to her, and she dealt with the "distressing antithetic ideas" (those involving her disinclination to breast-feed the child) by "suppressing"/"inhibiting"/"excluding"/"dissociating" them from consciousness. Freud adds that "the distressing antithetic idea, which has the appearance of being inhibited . . . continues to exist as a disconnected idea, often unconsciously to the patient" and can "put itself into effect through the agencies of the somatic inervations" (Freud [1892–93] 1966, 122).

This early, prepsychoanalytic paper provides, in a nutshell, Freud's theory of repression, even though Freud does not use the term. It did not take him long to do so, however. In the same year, in his "Preliminary Communication" with Breuer (Breuer and Freud [1893] 1955), which was to become the first section to the *Studies on Hysteria* (Breuer and Freud [1895] 1955), Freud makes use for the first time of the term "repression"—*verdrängt* (repressed)—characteristically intermixing it with a number of synonyms: "It was a question which the patient wished to forget, and therefore intentionally repressed from his conscious thought and inhibited and suppressed" (10). In the English translation of the *Studies on Hysteria,* translated and edited by James Strachey in collaboration with Anna Freud, there appears an important—and in my opinion revisionistic—footnote in connection with this passage, in which it is suggested that the repression in question is unconscious. I shall return to this footnote presently. For the moment, I wish to emphasize that the notion of repression was articulated in more or less analogous fashion over the next two decades of Freud's writings.

In *The Interpretation of Dreams,* for example, Freud states: "This effortless and regular avoidance by the psychical process of the memory of anything that had once been distressing affords us the prototype and the first example of *psychical repression*" (Freud [1900] 1953, 600). In 1915, in his article "Repression," Freud formulated the concept as clearly as it is possible: "The essence of repression lies simply in turning something away and keeping it at a distance from the conscious" ([1915] 1957a, 147). This, presumably, is what Ebbinghaus did with his nonsense syllables in "leaving them to themselves" and avoiding "reviewing" them. These formulations correspond to what I have variously termed "cognitive avoidance," "thought inhibition," and "not-thinking." Freud himself, as I have emphasized elsewhere (Erdelyi 1985; Erdelyi and Goldberg 1979), communicates the idea through a vast sprawl of more or less interchangeable rubrics throughout his writings. Below, in alphabetical order, are listed some of the more frequently encountered terms or formulas:

"after-pressure [after-expulsion]"	Freud [1915] 1957a, 148
attention "neglect"/"withdrawal"	Freud [1900] 1953, 594
"effortless and regular avoidance of the memory"	Freud [1900] 1953, 600
"avoidance of thought"	Breuer and Freud [1895] 1955, 156
"banish" from consciousness	Breuer and Freud [1895] 1955, 118
"censorship of consciousness"	Freud [1915] 1957a, 149–50
"conscious rejection"	Breuer and Freud [1895] 1955, 134
"debar the thoughts"	Freud [1901] 1960, 4
"defense"	Breuer and Freud [1895] 1955; Freud [1894] 1962, [1926] 1959, etc.
"dissociation"	Freud [1892–93] 1966, 122
"exclusion"	Freud [1892–93] 1966, 121
"exclusion from thought activity"	Breuer and Freud [1895] 1955, 133
"fending off" the incompatible idea	Breuer and Freud [1895] 1955, 157
"attempt at flight"	Freud [1926] 1959, 92; Freud [1940] 1964, 185
"inhibition of thought"	Breuer and Freud [1893] 1955, 10
"intentional forgetting"	Freud [1894] 1962, 48
"intentional repression from conscious thought"	Breuer and Freud [1893] 1955, 10; Breuer and Freud [1895] 1955, 116
"keeping away from consciousness"	Freud [1926] 1959, 142
"laborious suppression"	Breuer and Freud [1893] 1955, 12; Freud [1892–93] 1966, 51
"not thinking of the unbearable idea"	Freud [1894] 1962, 48
"not to think about it anymore"	Freud [1894] 1962, 52
"preventing . . . from becoming conscious"	Freud [1915] 1957b, 166
"pushing the [unbearable idea] away"	Freud [1894] 1962, 47

"repression," "intentional repression"	Breuer and Freud [1893] 1955, 10; Breuer and Freud [1895] 1955, 116
"repudiation"	Freud [1900] 1953, 594
"resistance"	Breuer and Freud [1895] 1955, 154; Freud [1940] 1964, 185; etc.
"suppression"	Breuer and Freud [1893] 1955, 10; Freud [1892–93] 1966, 126; Freud [1894] 1962, 47; Freud [1940] 1964, 166
"splitting" of the mind/ego	Freud [1940] 1964, 202
"splitting-off of a group of ideas"	Breuer and Freud [1893] 1955, 12
to "thrust . . . out of one's thoughts"	Freud [1894] 1962, 48
"keeping something out of consciousness"	Freud [1915] 1957a, 105
"withdrawal of cathexis [attention/ processing resources]"	Freud [1915] 1957b, 180, 181

The terms are numerous but the meaning (with a few semantic drifts here and there) the same. Because of the impalpability of the referents, it is difficult not to resort to multiple modes of expression and alternative metaphors—as I have done in much less than a half century ("not-thinking," "cognitive avoidance," "thought inhibition," "biased allocation of attention" [Erdelyi 1974; Erdelyi and Goldberg 1979]; "biased processing" [Erdelyi 1985; etc.]).

We may now turn to some of the questions about repression raised earlier as well as a few new ones.

Dissociation and Repression

Note Freud's use of the terms "dissociation," "disconnection," and "splitting." Given the apparent interest among some (see Bowers and Meichenbaum 1984; Horowitz 1988, in this volume) to consider a distinction between repression and dissociation, it is worth emphasizing that the distinction did not operate in Freud's thinking—he often used "dissociation" synonymously with "repression." Freud actually addressed this issue directly: "Moreover, I should like at this point to express a doubt as to whether splitting of consciousness . . . is really different from one due to conscious rejection" (Breuer and Freud [1895] 1955, 134).

Freud's disagreement with Janet over dissociation was not about the term ("dissociation" vs. "repression") but over what brings about repression/dissociation: "According to the theory of Janet . . . the splitting of consciousness is a primary feature of the mental change in hysteria. It is based on an innate weakness of the capacity for psychical synthesis, on the narrowness of the 'field of consciousness (*champ de la conscience*)' which in the form of a psychical stigma, is evidence of the degeneracy of hysterical individuals" (Freud [1894] 1962, 46). Freud does not agree with Janet that dissociation/repression is strictly a psychopathological condition absent in normal people or that it results from poverty of psychological energy (*misère psychologique*) that gives rise to a failure of mental synthesis, hence dissociation. Instead, Freud holds that repression/dissociation is a motivated act: "I repeatedly succeeded in demonstrating that the splitting of the contents of consciousness is the consequence of a voluntary act on the part of the patient; that is to say, it is instituted by an effort of will, the motive of which is discernible" (Freud [1894] 1963, 69). The motive, according to Freud, is to avoid (consciousness of) some unbearably distressing memory or impulse: "These patients whom I have analyzed had enjoyed good mental health up to the time at which an intolerable idea presented itself within the content of their ideational life; that is to say, until their ego was confronted by an experience, an idea, a feeling, arousing an affect so painful that the person resolved to forget it. . . . The patients can recollect with the most satisfactory minuteness their efforts at defence—their resolution to 'push the thing out,' not to think of it, to suppress it" (Freud [1894] 1963, 69–70).

The point I wish to establish is not that Freud was right and Janet wrong but, rather, that they were arguing about theory and not terms. The distinction between dissociation and repression resides in the theoretical conceptualization that one imposes on the terms; there is no formal distinction—unless one deliberately wishes to impose one (see Erdelyi 1988). My own predilection is to avoid distinctions unless they are absolutely necessary.

Ebbinghaus—for reasons of neither psychological poverty nor defense—chose to dissociate/repress his just-memorized nonsense syllables from conscious thought. Amnesia was the result. The essential point is that not-thinking/repressing/dissociating/cognitively avoiding/leaving to itself/warding off some to-be-remembered material for whatever reason—psychological poverty, defense, experimental exigencies, or what have you—can result in amnesia.

Suppression and Repression

Having attempted to level one incipient distinction, I now turn to a long-established and, in my opinion, pernicious one: that between suppression and repression. The distinction is so well entrenched, so endlessly repeated in both introductory texts as well as scholarly monographs, that it is almost unthinkable that one should wish to lay challenge to it. However, I have tried to show (Erdelyi and Goldberg 1979) that Freud—Sigmund, not Anna—used suppression and repression interchangeably, from his earliest writings (e.g., Freud [1892–93] 1966) to his last (Freud [1940] 1964). As far as I know, the only hint in Freud's own writings of such a distinction occurs in a footnote in *The Interpretation of Dreams* in which he suggests that repression "lays more stress" than suppression "upon the fact of attachment to the unconscious" (Freud [1900] 1953, 5:606). It does not seem reasonable to erect a theoretical edifice on such a passing hint, which Freud consistently ignores in the rest of his work.

Conscious and Unconscious Repression

Let us turn to the revisionist footnote of James Strachey and Anna Freud, which deals with the fundamental question on which the suppression-repression distinction hinges. Freud's first use of the concept of repression is so much at variance with the later established orthodoxy of repression being of necessity unconscious—which Anna Freud ([1936] 1946), perhaps more than any other figure, foisted on the field—that an attempt is made in the footnote—or so I claim—to realign Freud's description of repression with the future orthodoxy.

The critical passage goes as follows: "It was a question of things which the patient wished to forget, and therefore intentionally repressed from his conscious thought and inhibited and suppressed" (Breuer and Freud [1893] 1955, 10). The footnote argues that "the word 'intentionally' merely indicates the existence of a motive and carries no implication of *conscious* intention" (10). However, the immediate as well as broader context of the passage tends to belie the claim. In a later section of *The Studies* (the Case of Katharina), Freud uses the formula "conscious rejection" (134). Twenty years later, in his article "Repression," Freud ([1915] 1957a) speaks of the "censorship of the conscious" (149–50) and feels obliged to warn the reader not to assume that repression is always a conscious undertaking ("it is a mistake to emphasize only the repulsion which operates from the direction of the conscious upon what is to be repressed" [148]). In the Case of the Psychotic Dr. Schreber, Freud states that repression "emanates from the highly developed systems of the ego—systems which are capable of being conscious" (Freud [1911] 1958, 67). In a footnote added in 1914 to *The Interpretation of Dreams,* Freud remarks, "In any account of the theory of repression it would have to be laid down that a thought becomes repressed as a result of the continued influence upon it of two factors: It is pushed from the one side (by the censorship of

Cs.) and from the other (by the *Ucs.*)" ([1900] 1953, 547). In his article "The Unconscious," Freud ([1915] 1957b) states, "Consciousness stands in no simple relation . . . to repression" (192).

Not until his late "structural" theorizing (e.g., Freud [1933] 1964)—perhaps under the influence of Anna Freud—does repression appear to become a characteristically unconscious process, and, by this time (see Erdelyi 1985), the concept stood not for the old repression ("repression in the narrow sense") but for defense mechanisms in general ("repression in the general sense"). Thus, the earlier ("narrow") sense of "repression," which is what we have been dealing with thus far, is only one of a compendium of specific mechanisms of defense. To these others we shall turn presently. For now it is enough to emphasize that, for the first quarter century of his theorizing, Freud did not take a strong stand (or interest) on whether repression was conscious or unconscious, and, even in his later writings (e.g., Freud [1920] 1955, [1923] 1961), his position is by no means that clear; he seems to be suggesting that complex ego processes such as defense mechanisms *can* be unconscious, not that they are invariably unconscious. For example, "We have evidence that even subtle and difficult intellectual operations which ordinarily require strenuous reflection can equally be carried out preconsciously and without coming into consciousness. . . . [T]he example of resistance remaining unconscious during analysis is therefore by no means unique" (Freud [1920] 1955, 26–27). It does not follow, however, that resistance is necessarily unconscious or that it ceases to be resistance when it is conscious; Freud seems to be asserting only that resistance can be unconscious—thus his expression, in this context, "the resistance of the conscious and the unconscious ego" (Freud [1920] 1955, 20).

Unfortunately, Freud's position is never completely unambiguous because of his tendency toward self-contradiction—a few lines before the preceding quotation, he says, "The resistances themselves are unconscious at first" (19)—and even in his earlier writings he sometimes did suggest that the defenses were unconscious (e.g., Freud [1896] 1962). However, until past 1915, and then arguably, there is no coherent position that repression needed to be unconscious, even if it often was unconscious. Actually, it does not appear that the issue was ever that salient for Sigmund Freud. It is Anna Freud's book *The Ego and the Mechanisms of Defense* ([1936] 1946) that established the diktat, followed ever since, inside and outside psychoanalysis, that defense mechanisms are necessarily unconscious. Ironically, in a posthumous publication, Anna Freud seems to reverse herself at one juncture, at least in regard to the defense mechanism of reaction formation (Sandler and Freud 1985, 22–23):

> *Anna Freud:* Heinz Hartmann would say that it can become automatic.

Joseph Sandler: . . . I still think that there must be an awareness of the impulse to evoke the response.
Anna Freud: Hartmann and I discussed it at the time, in 1936 and 1937. There must be a momentary awareness.
Joseph Sandler: An unconscious awareness?
Anna Freud: It could even be a conscious momentary awareness.

The reconstructive distortion of the original repression-defense concept of Sigmund Freud is brought to a culminating point in DSM-III-R (American Psychiatric Association 1987) in what amounts, in some ways, to a 180 degree redirection of terminology. "Defense," which had been conceived of by Freud as a voluntary ("intentional") act, is now rendered as "relatively involuntary" (DSM-III-R, 393). "Suppression" is defined in DSM-III-R the way "repression" (along with "suppression") had been rendered by Freud in the *Studies* ("suppression [is] a mechanism in which the person intentionally avoids thinking about disturbing problems, desires, feelings, or experiences" [DSM-III-R, 394]). "Repression," in a vague rendering that touches neither on the question of "intention" nor on the conscious-unconscious nature of the process, is defined by its putative consequence (identical to suppression's)—amnesia ("repression [is] a mechanism in which the person is unable to remember or be cognitively aware of disturbing wishes, feelings, thoughts, or experiences" [DSM-III-R, 394]).

I make a big fuss about the terminological issue not merely to make a historical point—hardly that important—but because I think that the assumption that repression needs to be unconscious has done tremendous harm by preventing the integration of psychoanalysis and experimental psychology. If repression (defensive or otherwise) can be conscious, then suddenly it becomes an obvious and ubiquitous device. Indeed, Ebbinghaus becomes a pioneer in the study of nondefensive repression, which is my claim.

Anna Freud and post-Freudians notwithstanding, the fiat that defense mechanisms need be unconscious does violence to Freud's basic scientific strategy toward psychology (Erdelyi 1985). Freud decried the "philosophers'" (e.g., Wundt's) insistence that—by definition—the psychological was perforce conscious and that anything that was not conscious was not psychological. Freud relentlessly exposed this stance as point begging. It too would be point begging—or an exercise in semantic dictation—to demand that repression, defensive or otherwise, needs to be unconscious.

This does not mean, of course, that defensive repression does not take place unconsciously. I am simply suggesting that defense mechanisms *can* also be deployed consciously and add, not incidentally, that they are much easier to study experimentally in their conscious manifestation. The latter methodological point is a crucial one. For, even if defense mechanisms such as repression were endemically deployed unconsciously, as clinical experience suggests, it

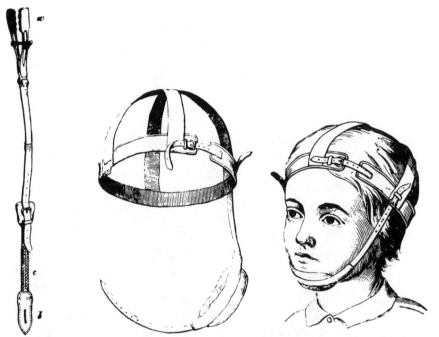

Fig. 5. The *Kopfhalter* and chin band with helmet of Dr. Daniel Gottlieb Moritz Schreber, father of the psychotic Dr. Daniel Paul Schreber (adapted from Schreber 1853, 199, 220).

would forget repeated exposures to stimuli such as stories, newspaper articles—or Claperède. At one meeting, Claparède hid a pin between his fingers and pricked her with it while shaking hands. Within minutes she forgot the incident. But when Claparède reached out for her hand, she pulled it back in a reflexive fashion, not knowing why. When asked about this behavior, she said in a flurry, "Doesn't one have the right to withdraw her hand?" When Claparède queried her further, she finally expressed the suspicion that a pin might be hidden in his hand. When asked why she would think that, she said that it was just an idea that went through her mind, adding, "Sometimes pins are hidden in people's hands" (Claparède [1911] 1951, 69–70).

A richer example, provided by the psychoanalytic literature, is the relation between the delusions and hallucinations of the psychotic Dr. Schreber and the grotesque physical experiments to which he was subjected as a child by his eminent physician father (Niederland 1959; Schatzman 1973; see also Erdelyi 1985). Schreber's father, author of books (all too well received) such as *The Harmful Body Positions and Habits of Children* (1853), introduced numerous bizarre orthopedic inventions. He devised, for example, a chin band and helmet contraption (see fig. 5) which he forced his son to wear "to ensure proper growth of the jaw and teeth" (Schreber [1903] 1955, in Schatzman

1973, 49). He invented a supplementary device, the *Kopfhalter* (head holder), to force the child to maintain a properly erect head. The *Kopfhalter* was a strap that was clamped at one end onto the child's hair and on the other onto his underwear so that the child's hair would be pulled with any slackening of erect posture. It served, in the father's words, as a "reminder": "The consciousness that the head cannot lean forward past a certain point soon becomes a habit. . . . This instrument can similarly be used against a sideways posture of the head" (Schreber 1853, 198–99, in Schatzman 1973, 49).

The psychotic son, a doctor of jurisprudence and formerly a prominent judge, who was writing his delusional autobiography in an insane asylum, seemed to be "remembering" the helmet decades later when he wrote: "This was perhaps the most abominable of all miracles. . . . The expression used for it if I remember correctly was "the-head-compressing-machine. . . . The little devils . . . *compressed my* head as though in a vise by turning a kind of screw, causing my head temporarily to assume an elongated almost pear-shaped form. It had an extremely threatening effect, particularly as it was accompanied by severe pain" (Schreber [1903] 1955, 138, in Schatzman 1973, 46–47). Elsewhere, he seems to be remembering the pain associated with the *Kopfhalter:* "I suffer from uninterrupted headaches of a kind certainly unknown to other human beings, and hardly comparable to ordinary headaches. They are *tearing* and pulling pains" (Schreber [1903] 1955, 201, in Schatzman 1973, 49). "[The] sensation of pain is like a sudden *pulling* inside my head which calls forth a very unpleasant feeling . . . and may be combined with the tearing off of a part of the bony substance of my skull—at least that is how it feels" (Schreber [1903] 1955, 164, in Schatzman 1973, 49–50).

There are numerous other examples of this sort in Schreber's autobiography, involving delusional or hallucinatory allusion to other contraptions, to justify Schatzman's conclusion: "Schreber suffers from reminiscences. His body embodies his past. He retains memories of what his father did to him as a child; although part of his mind knows they are memories, he does not" (Schatzman 1973, 52). Schatzman, who is critical of Freud for writing a case study of the psychotic Dr. Schreber (Freud [1911] 1958) without reading the famous works of his father, nevertheless emerges with Freud's conclusion of 1893: patients "suffer from reminiscences." Symptoms, in the contemporary parlance of Jacoby and Witherspoon (1982), are a form of "remembering without awareness."

From this approach, which holds open the possibility of repression producing amnesia for only aspects of memory, arises a somewhat new perspective on Freud's (and Janet's) insight that hysterics/neurotics suffer from "reminiscences." It may be incorrect that the symptoms are "conversions" of the once-conscious memory complex; rather, the symptoms may be the procedural-memory component of the original memory complex that, in contrast to the

> ory. . . . We unwittingly become creative artists; and the tale, if
> it is repeated from time to time, imposes itself on its author's own
> belief, and he ends by offering it in good faith as an authentic fact
> duly and legitimately established.

The quotation is not from Bartlett (1932). It is not from Freud either,
though it appears in *The Interpretation of Dreams* ([1900] 1953, p. 46) in the
section where Freud reviews the widespread opinion of the time that memory
is revisionistic in nature. (The passage is from Jessen [1855].) This constructivist conception of memory, as William Brewer (1984) has demonstrated in
an insightful chapter on schemas, was the prevalent Continental view; it was
apparently Bartlett's achievement to transplant successfully this Continental
tradition into the arid soil of Anglo-American associationist psychology.
Freud unmistakably incorporated the constructivist position into his thinking,
both on dreams and on cognition in general:

> It [is] highly probable that the psychical function which carries
> out what we have described as the secondary revision of the con-
> tent of dreams is to be identified with the activity of our waking
> thought. . . . It is the nature of our waking thought to establish
> order in material of that kind, to set up relations in it and to make
> it conform to our expectations of an intelligible whole. . . . In
> fact, we go too far in this direction. . . . In our effort at making
> an intelligible pattern of the sensory impressions that are offered
> to us, we fall into the strangest errors or even falsify the truth
> about the material before us. [Freud (1900) 1953, 499]

Freud devotes his important article "Screen Memories" ([1899] 1962) to a
discussion of the revisionistic nature of memory. He, like Bartlett, speaks of
"omissions" (306) in "fragmentary recollections" (303); like Bartlett, emphasizes importations ("I cannot help concluding that what I am dealing with is
something that never happened at all but has been unjustifiably smuggled in"
[318]); and makes clear that, in general, past memories are "remodelled"
(318) and subjected to "falsification" (318): "Not that they are complete inventions; they are false in the sense that they have shifted an event to a place
where it does not occur . . . or that they have merged two people into one or
substituted one for the other, or the series as a whole give signs of being combinations of two separate experiences" (322).

So Freud, already before the turn of the century, is very Bartlettian. There
is, however, one major difference in his position, as I have emphasized in
Psychoanalysis (1985): not all the revisions that Freud has in mind are intellective in nature, that is, produced by considerations of coherence, cultural
expectations, literary conventions, and the like. Freud makes clear that, at
least in some cases, "these falsifications of memory are tendentious, that is,
they serve the purposes of repression and replacement of objectionable or disagreeable impressions" (Freud [1899] 1962, 322).

The reader may now perceive my thrust: I wish to propose that the reconstructive processes of memory—which, incidentally, occur unconsciously, or often unconsciously, according to Bartlett ("schemata are active, without any awareness at all" [1932, 200]; "though . . . active," they are "not conscious" [20]; "first there was the process, in all instances witting during its early stages, but later producing unwitting transformations" [87])—may be harnessed for defensive purposes and supplement repression with a variety of distorting reconstructions and constructions, which have come to be known collectively in psychoanalysis as the mechanisms of defense. I am, in effect, applying my approach to repression to reconstructive processes in general. The mechanisms of reconstruction, as with repression, need not be defensive in intent; it is when the mechanisms are deployed in the service of defense that they become *defense* mechanisms.

I present below some research on "The War of the Ghosts" (Erdelyi and Halberstam 1987) that may reveal some defensive reconstructions at work in a nine-and-a-half-year-old child, Karina. The finding was serendipitous. It had not occurred to me that "The War of the Ghosts" could be an unsettling story; for adults it is not, but, evidently, it may be for some children. Karina had been tested along with a number of adult subjects in connection with an unrelated experimental issue—whether it might be possible to reverse Bartlettian reconstructions in the recall of the "The War of the Ghosts." She produced the usual Bartlettian distortions but, unlike any of the adults, exhibited a novel kind.

Table 1 presents the original text of "The War of the Ghosts" and table 2 Karina's initial mastery of it (R_1) after two readings of the story and an intervening recall effort. (On R_1, the first postlearning recall trial, Karina performed like the other adults in the study.) Table 3 presents Karina's recall of the story some twelve weeks later. Since it was her second postlearning recall effort, it is designated R_2.

This delayed recall, R_2, is noteworthy in several respects. First, it shows a very substantial amount of forgetting, consistent with Ebbinghaus. (Although average on R_1, Karina evinced more forgetting on R_2 than any of the adults.) Further, despite its brevity, the recall narrative instantiates a number of Bartlett-type effects (e.g., "hunting for seals" becomes "fishing"; the "men" or "warriors" become "Soiixx Indians"; the "river" becomes a "lake"; etc.). Also, an important set of omissions should be noted: the complete disappearance of all the scary parts of the story; the Indians are even asserted to be *not* on the warpath.

In two additional recall efforts right after R_2 (R_3 and R_4), there is a recovery of the Indians' war footing, but the rest of the unpleasant business remains inaccessible (for R_4, see table 4). There is a peculiar emphasis on the log ("It was a very mossy log"), and there may be here some kind of "displacement of accent."

Table 1. "The War of the Ghosts": The Text of the Original Story

One night two young men from Egulac went down to the river to hunt seals, and while they were there it became foggy and calm. Then they heard war-cries, and they thought: "Maybe this is a war-party." They escaped to the shore, and hid behind a log. Now canoes came up, and they heard the noise of paddles, and saw one canoe coming up to them. There were five men in the canoe, and they said:

"What do you think? We wish to take you along. We are going up the river to make war on the people."

One of the young men said: "I have no arrows."

"Arrows are in the canoe," they said.

"I will not go along. I might be killed. My relatives do not know where I have gone. But you," he said, turning to the other, "may go with them."

So one of the young men went, but the other returned home.

And the warriors went on up the river to a town on the other side of Kalama. The people came down to the water, and they began to fight, and many were killed. But presently the young man heard one of the warriors say: "Quick, let us go home: that Indian has been hit." Now he thought: "Oh, they are ghosts." He did not feel sick, but they said he had been shot.

So the canoes went back to Egulac, and the young man went ashore to his house, and made a fire. And he told everybody and said: "Behold I accompanied the ghosts, and we went to fight. Many of our fellows were killed, and many of those who attacked us were killed. They said I was hit, and I did not feel sick."

He told it all, and then he became quiet. When the sun rose he fell down. Something black came out of his mouth. His face became contorted. The people jumped up and cried.

He was dead.

Source: Bartlett (1932, 65).

Table 2. Karina's First Recall (R₁) of "The War of the Ghosts" after Two Presentations of the Story

One day two young men went down to the river to hunt for seals. Suddenly they heard war cries. They heard the sound of paddles splashing in the water. The young men thought this was a war party and hid themselves behind a log. Soon they saw a canoe coming towards them. There was five Indians in the canoe. One of them asked the young men "What do you think",? Will you join us? We are going to war on the people. One of the young men said, "I have no arrows"! The Indian replied "we have arrows in the canoe". Then one of the young men said, "I cannot go for my family does not know where I am; but you can go". Soon they departed one to war and one to his family. The soon arrived at a village further south than Kalama. The villager soon came to the waterfront and started a battle. Many people from both sides died. Soon the young man heard an Indian warrior say, "We better leave that man got hit", So they left for Egulac. The young man then went home and lit a fire and told his story when he was done he sat there to sunrise and then fell down. Something black came out of his mouth. His face was twisted. He was dead

Note: No corrections of any sort were made on Karina's written recall.

Table 3. Karina's Second Recall (R_2) of "The War of the Ghosts," Some Twelve Weeks after the First (R_1)

Two men went fishing. They saw some Soiixx Indians. The were not on the warpath. There were canoes full of Indians. One of the canoes came near the log where they were hiding. It was a very mossy log. The canoe that went by them didn't see them. This all happened out in the woods. The two men were fishing in a lake.

Note: No corrections of any sort were made on Karina's written recall.

Table 4. Karina's Fourth Recall (R_4) of "The War of the Ghosts"

One day two men went fishing. They went to a lake in the forest. When they were in the middle of fishing some Souixx Indians on the warpath came along. The two men hid from the Indians behind an old mossy log. There were canoes full of Indians. One of these canoes went by the old, mossy log were the two men were hiding. But the Indians did not see the two men.

Note: No corrections of any sort were made on Karina's written recall.

Table 5. Karina's "Last" Recall (R_n)

One day two men went fishing. While in the middle of fishing some Souixx Indians on the warpath came along. The two frightened men hid behind an old mossy log. One of the canoes went past the log but the Indians didn't see the two men.

Note: No corrections of any sort were made on Karina's written recall.

For the next week, Karina (like the adult subjects) produced several additional recall attempts of the original story. The last recall effort, R_n (see table 5), revealed neither hypermnesia nor any recovery of the unpleasant events: the warriors never see the two young men; the young man never accompanies the warriors; there is no fighting, no wounding of the young man, no black thing coming out of his mouth, no death. Unlike Karina, none of the adults failed to include on subsequent recall trials the fighting and the death of the young man.

We decided to retest Karina's recall of the original story some six months later. She produced three successive recall efforts, R_{n+1}, R_{n+2}, and R_{n+3}, which are presented in tables 6–8. Note that, after these six months, the story is substantially reconstructed and elaborated. Yet, at the same time, the recall narrative recovers not only some of the facts but also some of the distressing emotion that had been excluded in the earlier attempts. Thus, in R_{n+1}, in contrast to R_n, not only do the warriors see the two young men, despite their hiding behind "an old rotten moldy log," but one of the young men is actually persuaded to go with the warriors, as in the original story. The emotional impact is softened, however, by the omission of all references to fighting. Nevertheless, the heartbreak that results is undone, in a happy variant of the

Table 6. Karina's Recall R_{n+1}, Some Nine Months After R_1

There were two men and they went fishing one day. They went to a pond. They caught some fish, then an indian war canoe came and both men hid behind an old rotten moldy log. The indian chief said, "do any of you want to join the trib". Then one man got up and said yes it was, it was his friend. But the other man knew that he had children and a wife and they would be heartbroken if he left them. The other man seemed out of his mind his friend thought. Then he went to his friends home and told them what happened. The wife and children were very heartbroken. Then the friend said, "I'll go join the indian chief and try to get your husband back the friend", said. So the friend went back to pond where he had been fishing recently and found the indian chief still there and joined the tribe. He found his friend and told him and then he decided he would miss his wife so he went with his friend and lived quite happily ever on and erased this from memory.

Note: No corrections of any sort were made on Karina's written recall.

Table 7. Karina's Recall R_{n+2}

There were two men who went fishing one day at the swamp. Then suddenly an Indian war canoe came down the stream of the swamp. The two men hid behind an old rotting log for they were scared. The chief asked if anyone wanted to join his tribe knowing people were there because they were always there. One of the two men said yes. But the other man persued him out of it saying that he would break his wifes and childrens hearts so the man didn't go. His friend the husbands story and told them never to mention it (the story) to him. So they his family did theat, and the family lived happily ever after and never mentioned it again.
The End.

Note: No corrections of any sort were made on Karina's written recall.

Table 8. Karina's Recall R_{n+3}

One day two peasant farmers went fishing in a swamp. They had caught a couple of fish. Then suddenly an indian war canoe came. The two men hid behind an old rotting moldy log. The chief knowing people were there asked if anyone wanted to join his tribe. One of the men was about to say yes but his friend peursued him not too by telling him how heartbroken his wife and children would be if he joined the tribe. The friend told the family and told them not to mention the incident again to him, so they never did and they lived happily ever after and never mentioned the incident to him scared he might actually leave them and they would all be heartbroken. They all lived *happily* ever after.
The End.

Note: No corrections of any sort were made on Karina's written recall.

Orpheus legend, by the rescue and safe return of the young man to his home. The ending of R_{n+1} is striking (at least for this student of repression): they "lived quite happily ever on and erased this from memory."

In R_{n+2} and R_{n+3}, the action of the young man in R_{n+1} is softened into a mere (though still disturbing) impulse: he is dissuaded by his friend from joining the Indian tribe. Here there is an emphasis on never mentioning the story again, presumably in line with the goal of "erasing" the events or impulses "from memory."

These data, as suggestive as they may be, do not, of course, provide decisive evidence for defensive repression and revisions. For one, they are based on a single subject, and it is not clear how replicable the pattern may be. Then, too, there is a base-rate issue: since a great deal of detail was forgotten, it may be mere chance that the forgotten material happened to include all the frightful elements. Finally, the question may be raised whether the distortions attributed to defense may not be the products of story schemas (or scripts) to which young children are accustomed (e.g., ". . . and they lived happily ever after"). This question points to another, more basic question, however. May it not be that such story schemas/scripts are the very mechanisms that, when deployed for defensive purposes, as in repression, are defense mechanisms?

Once we get into complex, real-life memories, as when reviewing clinical transcripts, it is even more difficult, perhaps impossible, to determine when a particular distortion of past experience is the result of intellective or emotional factors. Indeed, the "new look" in perception, which foreshadowed the triumph of the Bartlettian approach to memory, subsumed both (e.g., the effects of "set" as well as "defense"). Further, it is difficult, if not impossible, to demarcate in practice one distortion from another (Erdelyi 1985). This holds as much for Bartlett as it does for Freud. In our laboratory work on "The War of the Ghosts" (Erdelyi and Halberstam 1987), we were surprised at how difficult it was to define for scoring purposes what, beyond omissions, distinct Bartlettian transformations constitute, for they all are ultimately one form or another of "intrusions" or "importations." Not coincidentally, the same problem applies to defense mechanisms, and for the same reason, for they are the same mechanisms.

What I am proposing, then, is that, in addition to already overlapping terminologies in Bartlett and Freud—"omission," "rationalization," "symbolization," misplacements of "emphasis," "falsification," "condensation," "transference," "elaboration," "importation," "intrusion"—Freud's defense mechanisms are nothing other than frequent types of reconstructions observed in the clinic. The only difference between the two is that Freud's reconstructions and omissions are, rightly or wrongly, assumed to play a defensive role. Regardless, they are the same mechanisms. All the standard defense mechanisms—repression, isolation, projection, reaction formation, displacement, rationalization, and so on—can be conceptualized as simple transformations or reconstructions (Freud [1909] 1955; Suppes and Warren 1975).

My claim, then, is that schemas need not be merely intellective; they may also deal with the emotionally invested side of our mental structures, our self-esteem, our notions of morality, our fears, our wishes. Thus, schemas transform memories not merely into the more reasonable but also into the more palatable. I see absolutely no theoretical barrier to this generalization. Bartlett, the academic psychologist, was apparently not interested in emotionally laden schemas, but there is nothing intrinsic in his theory that excludes them. Freud, the clinician, focused on defensive schemas and underplayed the merely intellective schemas. In psychoanalysis, an effort has been made to remedy this excessive stress on the defensive by the positing of "conflict-free" spheres of cognitive functioning. It is perhaps time that academic psychology similarly correct the overemphasis of the merely intellective and incorporate into its corpus "conflict-fraught" spheres of cognitive functioning.

I claim that Freud, with his defense mechanisms, provides the neglected defensive side of the pervasive operation of schemas in our lives.

References

American Psychiatric Association. 1987. *Diagnostic and statistical manual of mental disorders.* 3d ed., rev. Washington, D.C.: American Psychiatric Press.

Anderson, J. R. 1983. *The architecture of cognition.* Cambridge, Mass.: Harvard University Press.

Ballard, P. B. 1913. Oblivescence and reminiscence. *British Journal of Psychology: Monograph Supplements* 1, no. 2:1–82.

Bartlett, F. C. 1932. *Remembering.* Cambridge: Cambridge University Press.

Bjork, R. A. 1972.Theoretical implications of directed forgetting. In *Coding processes in human memory,* ed. A. W. Melton and E. Martin. Washington, D.C.: Winston.

Bowers, K. S., and D. Meichenbaum. 1984. *The unconscious reconsidered.* New York: Wiley.

Breuer, J., and S. Freud. [1893] 1955. On the psychical mechanism of hysterical phenomena: Preliminary communication. Trans. A. Strachey and J. Strachey. In *The standard edition of the complete psychological works of Sigmund Freud,* ed. J. Strachey, vol. 2. London: Hogarth.

———. [1893–95] 1955. *Studies on hysteria.* Trans. A. Strachey and J. Strachey. In *The standard edition of the complete psychological works of Sigmund Freud,* ed. J. Strachey, vol. 2. London: Hogarth.

Brewer, W. F. 1984. The nature and function of schemas. In *Handbook of social cognition,* ed. R. S. Wyer, Jr., and T. K. Srull, vol;. 1, pp. 119–60. Hillsdale, N.J.: Erlbaum.

Byrne, D. 1964. Repression-sensitization as a dimension of personality. In *Progress in experimental personality research,* ed. B. A. Maher, vol. 1. New York: Academic.

Cermak, L. S. 1982. *Human memory and amnesia.* Hillsdale, N.J.: Erlbaum.

Claparède, E. [1911] 1951. Recognition and "me-ness." In *Organization and pathology of thought,* ed. D. Rapaport, 58–75. New York: Columbia University Press.

Dollard, J., and N. Miller. 1950. *Personality and psychotherapy.* New York: McGraw-Hill.

Ebbinghaus, H. [1885] 1964. *Memory.* Trans. H. A. Ruger and C. E. Bussenius. New York: Dover.

Epstein, W. 1972. Mechanisms of directed forgetting. In *The psychology of learning and motivation,* ed. G. Bower, vol. 6. New York: Academic.

Erdelyi, M. H. 1974. A new look at the new look: Perceptual defense and vigilance. *Psychological Review* 81:1–25.

———. 1984. The recovery of unconscious (inaccessible) memories: Laboratory studies of hypermnesia. In *The psychology of learning and motivation: Advances in research and theory,* ed. G. Bower. New York: Academic.

———. 1985. *Psychoanalysis: Freud's cognitive psychology.* New York: Freeman.

———. 1986. Experimental indeterminacies in the dissociation paradigm of subliminal perception. *Behavioral and Brain Sciences* 9:30–31.

———. 1987. On the distinction between reminiscence and hypermnesia (and that between cumulative recall and recall), with some theoretical consequences. Department of Psychology, Brooklyn College, City University of New York. Typescript.

———. 1988. Some issues in the study of defense processes: Discussion of Horowitz's comments, with some elaborations. In *Psychodynamics and cognition,* ed. M. J. Horowitz. Chicago: University of Chicago Press.

Erdelyi, M. H., and J. Becker. 1974. Hypermnesia for pictures: Incremental memory for pictures but not words in multiple recall trials. *Cognitive Psychology* 6:159–71.

Erdelyi, M. H., J. Finks, and M. B. Feigin-Pfau. 1989. The effect of response bias on recall performance, with some observations on processing bias. *Journal of Experimental Psychology: General* 118:245–54.

Erdelyi, M. H., and B. Goldberg. 1979. Let's not sweep repression under the rug: Toward a cognitive psychology of repression. In *Functional disorders of memory,* ed. J. F. Kihlstrom and F. J. Evans. Hillsdale, N.J.: Erlbaum.

Erdelyi, M. H., and M. Halberstam. 1987. Hypermnesia for "The War of the Ghosts": Preliminary report, with observations on a collapse of memory phenomenon and a Freudian Bartlett effect in a child. Department of Psychology, Brooklyn College, City University of New York. Typescript.

Erdelyi, M. H. and J. Kleinbard. 1978. Has Ebbinghaus decayed with time? The growth of recall (hypermnesia) over days. *Journal of Experimental Psychology: Human Learning and Memory* 4:275–89.

Eriksen, C., and J. Pierce. 1968. Defense mechanisms. In *Handbook of personality theory and research,* ed. E. Borgatta and W. Lambert. Chicago: Rand McNally.

Freud, A. [1936] 1946. *The ego and the mechanisms of defense.* Trans. C. Baines. New York: International Universities Press.

Freud, S. [1892–93] 1966. A case of successful treatment by hypnotism: With some remarks on the origin of hysterical symptoms through "counter-will." Trans. J. Strachey. In *The standard edition of the complete psychological works of Sigmund Freud,* ed. J. Strachey, vol. 1. London: Hogarth.

———. [1894] 1962. The neuro-psychoses of defence. Trans. J. Rickman. In *The standard edition of the complete psychological works of Sigmund Freud,* ed. J. Strachey, vol. 3. London: Hogarth.

———. [1894] 1963. The defense neuro-psychoses. Trans. J. Rickman. In *Sigmund Freud: Early psycho-analytic writings,* ed. P. Rieff. New York: Collier.

———. [1896] 1962. Further remarks on the neuro-psychoses of defence. Trans. J. Rickman. In *The standard edition of the complete psychological works of Sigmund Freud,* ed. J. Strachey, vol. 3. London: Hogarth.

————. [1899] 1962. Screen memories. Trans. J. Strachey. In *The standard edition of the complete psychological works of Sigmund Freud*, ed. J. Strachey, vol. 3. London: Hogarth.

————. [1900] 1953. *The interpretation of dreams.* Trans. J. Strachey. In *The standard edition of the complete psychological works of Sigmund Freud*, ed. J. Strachey, vols. 4, 5. London: Hogarth.

————. [1901] 1960. *The psychopathology of everyday life.* Trans. A. Tyson. In *The standard edition of the complete psychological works of Sigmund Freud*, ed. J. Strachey, vol. 6. London: Hogarth.

————. [1909] 1955. Notes upon a case of obsessional neurosis. Trans. A. Strachey and J. Strachey. In *The standard edition of the complete psychological works of Sigmund Freud*, ed. J. Strachey, vol. 10. London: Hogarth.

————. [1911] 1958. Psycho-analytic notes on an autobiographical account of a case of paranoia (dementia paranoides). Trans. A. Strachey and J. Strachey. In *The standard edition of the complete psychological works of Sigmund Freud*, ed. J. Strachey, vol. 12. London: Hogarth.

————. [1914] 1958. Remembering, repeating and working-through (further recommendations in the technique of psycho-analysis II). Trans. J. Riviere and J. Strachey. In *The standard edition of the complete psychological works of Sigmund Freud*, ed. J. Strachey, vol. 12. London: Hogarth.

————. [1915] 1957a. Repression. Trans. C. M. Baines and J. Strachey. In *The standard edition of the complete psychological works of Sigmund Freud*, ed. J. Strachey, vol. 14. London: Hogarth.

————. [1915] 1957b. The unconscious. Trans. C. M. Baines and J. Strachey. In *The standard edition of the complete psychological works of Sigmund Freud*, ed. J. Strachey, vol. 14. London: Hogarth.

————. [1920] 1955. *Beyond the pleasure principle.* Trans. J. Strachey. In *The standard edition of the complete psychological works of Sigmund Freud*, ed. J. Strachey, vol. 18. London: Hogarth.

————. [1923] 1961. *The ego and the id.* Trans. J. Riviere and J. Strachey. In *The standard edition of the complete psychological works of Sigmund Freud*, ed. J. Strachey, vol. 19. London: Hogarth.

————. [1926] 1959. *Inhibitions, symptoms and anxiety.* Trans. A. Strachey and J. Strachey. In *The standard edition of the complete psychological works of Sigmund Freud*, ed. J. Strachey, vol. 20. London: Hogarth.

————. [1933] 1964. *New introductory lectures on psycho-analysis.* Trans. J. Strachey. In *The standard edition of the complete psychological works of Sigmund Freud*, ed. J. Strachey, vol. 22. London: Hogarth.

————. [1940] 1964. *An outline of psycho-analysis.* Trans. J. Strachey. In *The standard edition of the complete psychological works of Sigmund Freud*, ed. J. Strachey, vol. 3. London: Hogarth.

Geiselman, R. E., R. A. Bjork, and D. L. Fishman. 1983. Disrupted retrieval in directed forgetting: A link with posthypnotic amnesia. *Journal of Experimental Psychology: General* 112:58–72.

Grünbaum, A. 1984. *The foundations of psychoanalysis.* Berkeley: University of California Press.

Haley, J. 1976. *Problem solving therapy.* New York: Harper & Row.

Holender, D. 1986. Semantic activation without conscious identification in dichotic listening, parafoveal vision, and visual masking: A survey and appraisal. *Behavioral and Brain Sciences* 9:1–66.

Horowitz, M. J., ed. 1988. *Psychodynamics and cognition.* Chicago: University of Chicago Press.

Jacoby, L. L., and L. Witherspoon. 1982. Remembering without awareness. *Canadian Journal of Psychology* 32:300–324.

Janis, I., G. F. Mahl, J. Kagan, and R. R. Holt. 1969. *Personality: Dynamics, development, and assessment.* New York: Harcourt, Brace & World.

Jessen, P. 1855. *Versuch einer Wissenschaftlichen Begründung der Psychologie.* Berlin.

Lazarus, R. S. 1983. The costs and benefits of denial. In *The denial of stress,* ed. S. Breznitz, 1–30. New York: International Universities Press.

Lewinsohn, P. M., W. Mischel, W. Chaplin, and R. Barton. 1980. Social competence and depression: The role of illusory self-perception? *Journal of Abnormal Psychology* 89:203–12.

Mischel, W. 1986. *Introduction to personality: A new look.* 4th ed. New York: Holt, Rinehart & Winston.

Niederland, W. G. 1959. Schreber: Father and son. *Psychoanalytic Quarterly* 28:151–69.

Parkin, A. J. 1987. *Memory and amnesia: An introduction.* Oxford: Blackwell.

Payne, D. G. 1987. Hypermnesia and reminiscence: A historical and empirical review. *Psychological Bulletin* 101:5–27.

Posner, M. I. 1973. *Cognition: An introduction.* Glenville, Ill.: Scott, Foresman.

Roediger, H. L., and R. G. Crowder. 1972. Instructed forgetting: Rehearsal control or retrieval inhibition (repression)? *Cognitive Psychology* 3:255–67.

Roediger, H. L., and D. G. Payne. 1982. Hypermnesia: The role of repeated testing. *Journal of Experimental Psychology: Learning, Memory, and Cognition* 8:66–72.

Sackeim, H. A., and R. C. Gur. 1978. Self-deception, self-confrontation and consciousness. In *Consciousness and self-regulation: Advances in research,* ed. G. E. Schwartz and D. Shapiro, vol. 2. New York: Plenum.

Sandler, J., and A. Freud. 1985. *The analysis of defense: The ego and the mechanisms of defense revisited.* New York: International Universities Press.

Schachter, D. L. 1987. Implicit memory: History and current status. *Journal of Experimental Psychology: Learning, Memory, and Cognition* 13:501–18.

Schatzman, M. 1973. *Soul murder: Persecution in the family.* New York: Random House.

Schreber, D. G. M. 1853. *Die schadlichen Korperhaltungen und Gewohnheiten der Kinder nebst Angabe der Mittel dagegen* (The harmful body positions and habits of children, including a statement of counteracting measures). Leipzig: Fleischer.

Schreber, D. P. [1903] 1955. *Memoirs of my nervous illness.* Ed. and trans. I. Macalpine and R. A. Hunter. London: Dawson.

Shiffrin, R. M., and W. Schneider. 1977. Controlled and automatic human information processing. II. Perceptual learning, automatic attending, and general theory. *Psychological Review* 84:127–90.

Squire, L. 1986. Mechanisms of memory. *Science* 232:1612–19.

Sullivan, H. S. 1956. *Clinical studies in psychiatry.* New York: Norton.

Suppes, P., and H. Warren. 1975. On the generation and classification of defense mechanisms. In *International Journal of Psychoanalysis* 5:405–14.

Tulving, E. 1983. *Elements of episodic memory.* Oxford: Clarendon.

Tulving, E., and Z. Pearlstone. 1966. Availability versus accessibility of information in memory for words. *Journal of Verbal Learning and Verbal Behavior* 5:381–91.

Weinberger, D., G. Schwartz, and R. Davidson. 1979. Low-anxious, high-anxious and repressive coping styles: Psychometric patterns and behavioral and physiological responses to stress. *Journal of Abnormal Psychology* 88:369–80.

Weiner, B. 1968. Motivated forgetting and the study of repression. *Journal of Personality* 36:213–34.

2 Defense in Psychoanalytic Theory: Computation or Fantasy?

MARSHALL EDELSON

A Question about the Conceptualization of Defense in Psychoanalytic Theory

I shall be concerned here with an explication of the theory of defense in psychoanalysis and with questions about that theory, especially some suggested by conceptual work in cognitive psychology.[1]

1. Psychoanalysis as a body of knowledge is, most generally, a psychology of mind—not a general psychology, a psychology of behavior, a psychology of interpersonal interactions, or a theory of personality.[2]

2. More specifically, psychoanalysis is an intentional psychology of mind. That is to say, it is concerned with generating knowledge about the nature, causal interrelations, and causal powers of such entities as wishes and beliefs, which may be either mental dispositions or occurrent mental states. Psychoanalysis is not concerned, as a general psychology of mind would be, with generating knowledge about those aspects of mental capacities and processes that are not influenced by wishes and beliefs (some aspects of reality-accommodated perception, e.g.).

There is a widely held view that talk of wishes and beliefs is not causal or scientific, that it is talk of reasons rather than causes, and that it inevitably commits one to a view of psychoanalysis as hermeneutics. Not so.

A different version of material in this chapter appears in "Imagination, Fantasy, and Defense," chapter 9 of my recent *Psychoanalysis: A Theory in Crisis* (1988). Many issues and topics, and the implications of a number of distinctions, mentioned here are given far fuller treatment in that book, where I also attempt to justify that which here is, for reasons of space, just asserted.

1. The depiction of psychoanalytic theory in this chapter is a revised version, and in some cases a paraphrase, of material in Edelson (1988, 1989). In those works, I drew implications from this particular depiction of the theory for research methodology. Space limitations prevent me from going into these implications in this chapter.

2. A psychoanalyst carrying out a psychoanalysis as a treatment uses a great deal of knowledge about human beings that does not belong to the core of psychoanalytic theory (my focus here). By *core* I mean what is most distinctive, central, and essential about psychoanalysis as a body of knowledge, not what is peripheral in it or merely consistent with it.

33

3. Mental states are entities in the domain of psychoanalysis. The mental states of a person include (*a*) that person's mental representation of an object, state of affairs, event, or sequence of states of affairs or events and (*b*) a relation between him and his own mental representation.[3] Relations between persons and mental representations include "wishes that," "wishes for," or "wishes to"; "believes that"; "perceives that"; "remembers that"; and "imagines that."

Mental states have properties. Some of these have to do with the relations, and in particular the causal relations, that they are capable of forming with other mental states—for example, the capacity of a perception to produce a belief or the capacity of a combination of desire and belief to produce a voluntary willing of an act.

4. Mental representations are symbolic representations. They symbolize objects, states of affairs, events, or sequences of states of affairs or events. These are the contents of mental states.

5. The mind operates on such symbolic representations, transforming them and therefore producing changes in mental states. Mental operations—such as those variously designated by such terms as "dream work," "primary process," and "defense mechanisms"—link mental states causally to one another. Operations that operate on symbolic representations as these mental operations do are symbolic operations.

6. It is an open question how best to conceptualize defenses, defense mechanisms, or defensive strategies. Are these more fruitfully considered to be contentless operations or computations on contents (rule-governed deletions, transpositions, combinations, substitutions, etc.)? Repression, for example, might be treated as an operation of deletion. Or are defenses more fruitfully considered to involve mental contents? Such mental contents, for example, might be constituents of mental representations of the mind's own workings, as when a "defense mechanism" such as repression, for example, is considered to be a person's fantasy that his mind, conceived to be corporeal, carries out an act of swallowing and so makes mental contents disappear.

In this chapter, I shall focus on this question. Are defenses computations or fantasies? Are they rule-governed operations on mental states—which are sensitive or responsive to the symbolic-semantic contents of those states—or are they themselves particular kinds of symbolic-semantic contents belonging to a particular kind of mental state?

Which of these alternative conceptualizations of defense in psychoanalytic theory is most perspicuous or fruitful?

3. *Man, he, his, him,* and *himself* are used in their generic sense unless the context indicates otherwise, in order to avoid the repeated use of such phrases as *he or she.*

Psychoanalytic Theory

1. Psychoanalysis is a theory about mental contents. In particular, psychoanalysis attempts to explain the contents of mental states—neurotic symptoms, dreams, and parapraxes—that seem inexplicable, given the contents of other mental states and presupposing that some sort of rule-governed sequence of operations generates new mental states according to a principle of rationality.

Rational action as a concept depends on relating beliefs and desires to intended actions. The principle of rationality can be stated as a rule-governed transformation. If you desire a state of affairs X and you believe that a state of affairs Y is necessary to produce X, then produce the intention to bring about Y. More concisely:

(Desire-that $[X]$ &
Believe-that $[X$ only if $Y]$), THEN
(Act to bring about Y)

Here, X and Y are mental representations or components of mental representations. (X and Y are components of the mental representation "X only if Y," which is part of the mental state "believes-that X only if Y.") Such computations can be carried out only if they are sensitive or respond to, or take into account, semantic or symbolic contents of the mental states involved. To carry out the rule, an agent must know, and the rule must be so formulated, that (a) the mental representation X, which is a constituent of his mental state of desire, is the same X appearing in the mental representation that is a constituent of his mental state of belief and (b) the Y appearing in the mental representation that is a constituent of that state of belief is the same mental representation Y that is a constituent of his intention to act.

Notice that the mental states are causally related by virtue of the continuity, the sameness, of their constituent mental representations. If there is no such continuity, we have a causal gap between or among mental states. The psychoanalytic theory of both defense and dream work can be viewed as explaining the contents of such inexplicable mental states by postulating rule-governed operations on mental representations rather than on mental states in toto. Such operations as these would lead to the production of one mental state from another by effecting transformations on the form or the symbolic contents of mental representations.

If so, there is a critical difference between the way cognitive psychologists use a representational theory of mind to explain rational action and the way psychoanalysts use it to explain neurotic symptoms, dreams, and parapraxes. For, as should be clear from the example given in explicating the principle of rationality, the computations generated mental states from other mental states. They did not alter mental contents as such.

2. Psychoanalysis accords causal priority to the links among the contents of various mental states that are forged by such symbolic operations as condensation, displacement, translation into imagery, and iconic or metaphoric symbolization. This distinguishes it from a cognitive psychology of mind. A cognitive psychology of mind accords causal priority to the links among various mental states created by truth-conserving symbolic operations. Examples of such truth-conserving symbolic operations are those belonging to logic or to reality-accommodated reasoning, which move a person from one mental state to another by transforming mental representations in processes of cognitive inference.

The distinction just drawn is a distinction psychoanalysis marks by the terms "primary process" and "secondary process." Primary processes are distinguished in part by the primacy they accord such symbolic operations as condensation, displacement, translation into imagery, and iconic or metaphoric symbolization.

3. Interest in mental representations and in the symbolic operations that form and transform them identifies psychoanalysis as a representational and computational psychology of mind.[4] But it does not have things to say about every kind of mental representation and operation.

4. A nonpsychoanalytic but representational and computational psychology of mind takes as of central importance rational action (caused by desire and belief acting together) and irrational action (beliefs are in error, or relevant beliefs are missing). Psychoanalysis, on the other hand, takes as of central importance the relation between wishes and imagination, in particular sexual wishes, and especially as imagination is implicated in the vicissitudes of wish fulfillment.[5]

Moreover, psychoanalysis is primarily concerned not with the functioning of imagination in reality-oriented anticipations but rather with the functioning of imagination under special conditions. These conditions make possible the construction of wish fulfillments that give pleasure without regard to reality considerations. They ultimately make possible the construction of elaborate unconscious fantasies, which are wish fulfillments in the shadow of imagined threat. (Fantasy refers here not only to fantasies about external objects and their doings but to fantasies about internal objects and their doings as well. Internal objects are imagined to inhabit, to be located inside, the mind.)

5. Psychoanalysis focuses on the causal efficacy of unconscious fantasies as mental dispositions. Manifestations of such mental dispositions (occurrent

4. In referring to a representational psychology of mind, I more or less follow Fodor (1981). For one formulation by him of the characteristics of a representational theory of mind, see Fodor (1981, 26). See also Dennett (1978), Fodor (1968, 1975, 1983), Pylyshyn (1985), and Searle (1983) as well as Edelson (1988, chaps. 6, 7).

5. For an account of the role of imagination in psychoanalytic theory, see Wollheim (1969, 1974, 1979, 1982, 1984).

mental states, including desires, beliefs, intentions in action, conscious fantasies, or dreams) may be evoked in several ways.

a) Such manifestations of an unconscious fantasy may be evoked periodically and spontaneously. The unconscious fantasy as a mental disposition may have a characteristic intrinsic propensity to manifest itself, which is independent of situational objects or events.

b) Such manifestations of an unconscious fantasy may be evoked by situational objects or events, which might be said through resemblance or metaphoric relations to "remind" the person of the unconscious fantasy (without his being aware of the connection) and therefore evoke manifestations of it, including affects such as excitement and anxiety that may be associated with it.

c) Manifestations of an unconscious fantasy may be evoked by the willed mental activity of the person. He wants and intends to activate a conscious fantasy, which is a derivative of the unconscious fantasy, in order to experience, for example, excitement or desire and its satisfaction in a wish fulfillment or in order to master anxiety.

6. Psychoanalysis distinctively raises questions about the contents of mental states. It wants to explain mental contents. Not how is someone able to remember, or to believe, or to dream, but why does he remember, believe, or dream just that? Not how is he able to form or carry out intentions, but why does he intend doing, or why does he carry out the intention to do, just that?

Metapsychology may be regarded as an attempt to replace a causal representational intentional psychology with a nonsemantic theory. Such a nonsemantic theory would involve no reference to and assign no causal role to mental contents—much as learning theory tries to formulate laws using such concepts as conditioning, reinforcement, and stimulus generalization without regard to the content of what is learned. Metapsychology so regarded must fail as a psychoanalytic theory.[6]

7. Psychoanalysis especially raises questions about causal gaps, that is, about the inexplicability of the contents of particular mental states. These contents are inexplicable (*a*) sometimes because they do not seem to have any causal links to the contents of other mental states to which a person has access (e.g., they do not seem to be caused by any wishes and beliefs the person is aware of); (*b*) sometimes because the objects, states of affairs, or events in external reality, which are their putative cause, or which would be the right kind of cause of them, do not seem to exist or ever to have existed (e.g., dreams, hallucinations, and nonveridical memories); and (*c*) sometimes because mental states with particular contents do not seem to produce the other mental states or the actions one might expect, given the nature of the contents

6. On the inadequacy of a contentless theory, such as learning theorists propose, for dealing with the kind of questions psychoanalysis raises about its domain, see Stoller (1985, 105–6).

and the particular mental state to which they belong (e.g., a person is unable to form the right kind of intention to act, or the intention, once formed, does not result in action, or an effort to remember certain contents fails, although the capacity of memory is unimpaired). Neurotic symptoms, dreams, and parapraxes are paradigmatic of the kind of causal gaps in which psychoanalysis takes an interest.

What is distinctive about any causal gap in which psychoanalysis takes an explanatory interest is that it cannot be explained as the result of (a) impairments in neuropsychological systems or innate defects in psychological capacities, (b) intrinsic features of situations or social contexts to which a person is exposed, or (c) departures from rationality due simply to error or ignorance.

8. Psychoanalysis is guided by a powers or generative rather than a successionist or correlation account of causality. It is interested in the causal power of an entity (such as a mental disposition) to produce effects by virtue of the nature of and interrelations among its internal constituents. Investigating the causal efficacy of an unconscious fantasy poses theoretical and methodological problems similar to those posed by an investigation of the causal efficacy of a virus. These problems are quite different from those that arise in discovering, testing, and applying mathematical-functional relations or correlations among quantitative variables such as are exemplified, for example, by the laws of mechanics.

The psychoanalyst wishes to demonstrate (a) that unconscious fantasies exist; (b) what their constituents (contents) are; (c) how these are structured, organized, or related to one another; and (d) how such a fantasy—given the kind of mental state it is as well as what its contents are—is capable of being activated and capable in turn of activating causal mechanisms to produce its effects. These causal mechanisms are mental operations such as are designated by the terms "primary process," "dream work," and "defense mechanisms."

9. The phenomenology of a mental state is given by what kind of mental state it is, what it is like to be in that kind of mental state, and the contents of that mental state. It is these properties of a mental state that produce its effects. Occurrent mental states have causal powers by virtue of their phenomenology. They are caused by mental dispositions (unconscious fantasies, e.g.), mental activity (attention, e.g.), or other occurrent mental states. In turn, they cause still other occurrent mental states or new mental dispositions, or they strengthen existing mental dispositions.

Unconscious fantasies are especially suitable to be fundamental causes in psychoanalysis, for then, like all mental states and dispositions in our commonsense intentional psychology (e.g., desires and beliefs), they possess their causal powers by virtue of their phenomenology. As mental dispositions, their causal power is manifested by the occurrent mental states that are their immediate or remote effects. How immediate or remote these effects are depends on (*a*) what causal mechanisms—mental operations—such fantasies activate; (*b*) the effects of causal powers in opposition to them; and in general then (*c*) how short and direct or long and tortuous the causal path from latent contents to manifest contents is.

10. The causal powers of unconscious fantasies are not always manifest (just as a virus may exist in a host and have causal powers without their being on a particular occasion manifest). There are times when nothing exists to activate them. Even when they are activated, for example, by various ad hoc or unlawful external events or states of affairs—as these are interpreted (represented) by the person who "has" the fantasy—they may not succeed in manifesting themselves. The effect actually produced depends on what other causal powers are at work. Psychoanalysis is especially interested in negative causes—for example, those causal powers that oppose the manifestations of unconscious fantasies insofar as these are sexual wish fulfillments. The usual outcome to be explained is explained as a compromise among different, and different kinds of, causal powers.

The Psychoanalytic Theory of Defense

The Target of Defense

The target of defense is the content of a fantasy that is a sexual wish fulfillment.

Starting from Breuer and Freud's *Studies on Hysteria* ([1893–95] 1955), and from Freud's work in particular, where his attempt is to explain neurotic symptoms, we may emphasize, as he did there, unconscious mental states, conflict, and defense. But, starting from *The Interpretation of Dreams* ([1900] 1953) and the very important later paper "Formulations on the two principles of mental functioning" ([1911] 1958a), where Freud's attempt is to explain dreams, neurotic symptoms, and a wide range of other mental phenomena as well, we may emphasize, as he did there, wish fulfillment and the difference between primary and secondary process.

Taking conflict as a point of departure tends to lead to the assimilation of the phenomena of primary interest to psychoanalysis—neurotic symptoms, parapraxes, and dreams—to the principle of rationality. Given this point of departure, we believe that, once we grasp what the person's unconscious desires and beliefs are, we shall see that mental operations on mental states have been governed by a principle of rationality after all. Whatever irrationality the phenomena that psychoanalysis investigates manifest results from the fact that—because the person's beliefs were formed in childhood or unconscious mental states have been rendered inaccessible to the corrections or influences of experience—the person holds mistaken or false beliefs (the person is in error) or has insufficient knowledge (the person is ignorant). If I am not mistaken, this perspective on the phenomena of interest to psychoanalysis permeates ego psychology and the way it influences what is viewed as the therapeutic action of psychoanalysis. It is especially attractive to those who wish to integrate psychoanalysis and cognitive psychology. The difference made by taking wish fulfillment, fantasy, and primary process instead as a point of departure will be suggested by what follows in this chapter.

The Motive for Defense

The motive for defense is ultimately the quest for pleasure, when that quest takes place under conditions of threat. The motive for defense is not just a matter of a quest for security or an attempt to avoid pain. A defense is an attempt to solve a problem: how to achieve gratification under conditions of threat (Schafer 1968).

The Means of Defense

The means of defense are primary processes. That is, defenses are typically symbolic operations on mental representations of a certain kind—fantasies, which are both constructed and, in the interests of defense, revised by means of primary processes.

Indications of Defense

A manifest indication of defense is resistance. A defense is primarily a strategy for achieving gratification under conditions of threat; such a strategy may involve, in part, the expulsion of the contents of mental states or the significance of such contents from consciousness. A person will resist efforts to make him aware of such contents or their significance, and this "fighting off" constitutes evidence for the existence and causal role of a defensive strategy of the kind in which psychoanalysis is interested, just as antibodies constitute evidence for the presence and causal role of a virus. However, resistance is not a fight directed against the original noxious agent (the conditions of threat); rather it involves both anticipation of attempts to interfere—or anticipation of events or circumstances that might interfere—with a defensive strategy and the prevention or circumvention of these. Resistance and defense should be differentiated, then, as often they are not even in psychoanalytic clinical work. The terms "defense" and "resistance" are not synonyms. Psychoanalysis also differentiates between "repression" and "countercathexis"—between ways of expelling something from awareness and ways of ensuring that what has been expelled is permanently prevented from returning to awareness.

Either the contents of a mental state or the significance of the contents of a mental state may be the target of repression or countercathexis. What is denoted by "avoiding awareness of the *significance* of the contents of a mental state?" One may avoid awareness of (*a*) experience of the phenomenology of a mental state (what it is like to be in that state) rather than merely knowledge of the contents of that mental state, (*b*) what the connection is between the contents of different mental states (these mental states may be contemporaneous or precede or follow one another), (*c*) what the connection is between some remembered mental state and what one is doing or saying now, (*d*) knowledge of what being in a mental state having certain contents implies about oneself or another or about the likelihood that various other mental states will occur, and (*e*) knowledge of the causal efficacy of a mental state or set of mental states (that it is causally related, e.g., to ego-alien symptoms or ego-syntonic character traits).

Some Characteristics of Defensive Strategies

Defense is not something that happened once in the past. It is possible to observe the results of a currently active process of defense in vivo, in the present—as an analysand, for example, reports not only amnesia for whole periods of his life ("I can't remember anything before age twelve") but amnesia for everything said in the session of the day before or later in a session for what he said earlier in that session.

How does repression occur? Erdelyi (1985, 149ff.) speaks of omissions, of ellipses, of attenuations, of displacements of accent. If an analysand does not remember or is not aware of a fantasy and struggles against becoming aware of it, we speak confidently of what is unconscious and repression. What about the analysand who mentions something casually without apparent awareness of its significance, in the manner of the miscreant who hides the stolen letter by crumpling it up and throwing it down in plain view so that whoever sees it will say, "But that couldn't be what I'm looking for!"? Here the analysand enacts both detective and thief. How do we identify the rule-governed operation called "the defense of the purloined letter"? What about the analysand who buries a significant utterance under an avalanche of worries, busy thoughts, and preoccupations? What about the analysand who allocates his attention in such a way that he just does not notice certain things? What about the analysand who, when something is called to his attention, says, "Oh yes, I was thinking about that when I came in, but I forgot about it!"? What about the analysand who can go for years beginning each day's session with, "I can't remember anything about yesterday's session," but who has no difficulty remembering if the psychoanalyst tells him what happened during it? What about the analysand who blurts things out in an altered state of consciousness, in a trance-like state, but acts almost immediately as if he had never said them at all, although he has no trouble remembering saying them when reminded by the psychoanalyst of what he said? (Did Freud give up the notion of the etiological role of hypnoidal states in favor of the notion of defense too readily?)

We seem to have a vast number of ways to keep things "out of mind" and a vast number of different states called "out of mind." I am not satisfied that order can be introduced into all this by introducing, as metapsychologists are wont to do, abstract gatekeepers or filters—devoid of content—between unconscious and preconscious, between preconscious and conscious, between what is conscious and the communication of what is conscious.

When we study repression or countercathexis, we study a continuously active process that inexorably extends its sphere of influence. Repression takes in or encompasses more and more. If something is a target of repression, then anything connected to it, and anything connected to anything that is connected to it, and so on and on, may become a target of defense. Repression "swallows" more and more—in fact, repression may be an imagined swallowing, a fantasy rather than a contentless operation on mental contents. The inability to remember, then, is the effect of a fantasy in which contents have been swallowed and disappeared. Here is a strategy that can be used to mitigate conditions of threat at the same time that it is a wish-fulfilling fantasy gratifying "oral" wishes. The linkages between the various contents swallowed are determined by primary, not secondary, process, a supposition often ignored by those who wish to assimilate psychoanalytic theory to learning theory or cognitive psychology. That is, the links are formed in fantasy, in the world of imagination.

Similarly, a countercathexis becomes ever more elaborate. It is put together from, and propped up by, whatever is at hand. The problem solver uses whatever material is at hand as a bricoleur or handyman does to construct his bricolage. A bricolage (Edelson 1988, chap. 2) is not constructed according to known rules, operations, or procedures. Defensive strategies are improvisatory and jerry-rigged from whatever is at hand. What the analysand is doing in relation to his own mental states (in bringing them about and in responding to them) often appears to be a perfect jumble of ad hoc tactics and strategies, taking opportunistic advantage of whatever is at hand, whatever is found, whatever material is available.[7]

Usual formulations of defense mechanisms do not seem to capture this quality of improvisational inventive problem solving. Erdelyi (1985) speaks of the ego as the seat of "*sophisticated psychological strategies* for avoiding or distorting reality" (130; my emphasis). Are these strategies really concerned with reality or with the products of imagination—wish fulfillments? He also speaks of "makeshift stratagems" (132). If we wish to consider fantasies attempts at problem solving, at dealing with unattainable wishes, con-

---

7. See, e.g., Freud ([1900] 1953, 4:237). Also, from evolutionary theory, "Adaptations [are] contrivances jerry-rigged from parts available" (Gould 1986, 63–64).

flicts, and dilemmas, then Schafer (1968) has stated one problem that a fantasy is produced to solve: ensuring "the maximum of instinctual gratification possible under conditions of danger" (55).

What strategies for achieving gratification under conditions of threat are possible? One may as well ask, What are the limits of human imaginativeness and inventiveness? These may turn almost any object, event, or state of affairs that exists or occurs in the nonlawful ad hoc circumstances in which such a problem may be repeatedly encountered into a resource that can be used in attempts to solve it.

These comments suggest problems for theory and research. If defensive strategies are improvisatory and jerry-rigged from whatever is at hand, "defense" denotes a difficult-to-delimit set of mental activities. One cannot simply tell from "looking at it" that something observable is a manifestation of defense or what defense it is a manifestation of. And how does one predict what will happen to be "at hand"?

Perhaps, it will turn out that different defensive strategies, broadly conceived, can be characterized by their position on six dimensions: repression, other defenses, type of threat, resistance and countercathexis, gratification, and scope.[8]

a) To what extent is repression a part of a defensive strategy? Just what is repressed? How extensive is the realm swallowed by repression?

b) What measures other than repression are employed to mitigate conditions of threat?

c) What kinds of threat are mitigated?

d) How are attempts to interfere with the defensive strategy, or events or circumstances that might interfere with the defensive strategy, anticipated, and prevented or resisted, or forestalled or circumvented? How is what has been expelled from consciousness prevented from returning to consciousness?

e) To what extent does the defensive strategy make gratification possible? How does it make gratification possible? Just what kind of gratification does it make possible?

f) To what extent is a defensive strategy occasionally activated, in response to specific kinds of threat, and to what extent maintained permanently in place?

Defenses as Computations

Might it be fruitful to conceptualize defenses as contentless mechanisms—symbolic operations or computations on mental representations (including fantasies)?

Such a conceptualization is exemplified by Suppes and Warren's (1975)

8. For a similar formulation, see Waelder (1960), who mentions three coordinates: repression, countercathexis, and gratification.

attempt to generate and classify defense mechanisms in terms of a set of elementary operations and combinations of elementary operations on propositions (standing for unconscious ideas or impulses and conscious or preconscious thoughts or feelings).[9]

Suppes and Warren define defense mechanisms as transformations of propositions: "By a transformation we mean a function that maps unconscious propositions (thoughts or impulses) into conscious propositions; a transformation may also be thought of as a process that takes unconscious propositions and changes them in specific ways into conscious propositions" (1975, 405–6). They also assume that propositions are all in the form "actor-action-object" and that the action carries the impulse or feeling. Their goal is to replace arbitrary lists of defense mechanisms by a way of systematically generating possible defense mechanisms from a small set of elementary transformations and the possible combinations of these. They introduce three types of transformations: on actor, on action, and on object. Their list of elementary transformations consists of two actor transformations, four action transformations and two object transformations.

The two actor transformations are (1) change self as actor to other as actor and (2) change other as actor to self as actor. The first gives the elementary defense of projection, the second the elementary defense of identification.

The four action transformations are (1) change action to opposite of action, (2) change action to denial of action, (3) change action to intellectualization of action, and (4) change action to intensification of action. The first gives the elementary defense of reaction formation, the second the elementary defense of denial, the third the elementary defense of intellectualization, and the fourth the elementary defense of affectualization.

The two object transformations are (1) change object x to self as object and (2) change object x to object y, where y is an object other than x and other than self. The first gives the elementary defense of turning against the self, the second the elementary defense of displacement.

Assuming that at most one transformation is applied to each constituent of the proposition, the possible number of defense mechanisms that can be generated if the unconscious proposition is self-action-object is twenty-nine; an additional twenty-nine defense mechanisms can be generated if the unconscious proposition is other-action-object. The latter group includes fifteen defense mechanisms involving identification.

I too was once entranced by the possibility of formulating psychoanalytic theory in a canonical formal language for the sake of rigor and explicitness (Edelson 1977). In particular, I thought for some time that it might be possible

9. Suppes and Warren, in justifying their transformational calculus, quote Waelder's (1960) call for "an alphabet of defense mechanisms, i.e., a description of simple forms out of which the more complex mechanisms are composed" (183).

to apply the notion of rule-governed transformations (like those used in Chomsky's linguistic theory) acting on latent or unconscious propositions (or, in the present context, unconscious fantasies), however these are mentally represented, to produce manifest or preconscious or conscious propositions, however these are mentally represented (Edelson 1972, 1975, 1977, 1978).[10]

My analogy ran something like this.

a) The operations of the dream work are like linguistic operations insofar as they are transformational operations.

b) Unconscious ideas or impulses (I now would say unconscious fantasies) are like deep structures insofar as they are the objects of such transformations.

c) The manifest content of the dream—images under a linguistic descriptions—are like surface structures insofar as they are the results of such transformations.

d) The person's capacity to dream is like language capacity insofar as the difference between knowledge of the dream work and the performance of making a particular dream is like the difference between knowledge of transformational-generative grammar and making a particular sentence.

e) The creativity of dreaming is like the creativity of language in that with finite means an infinite set of novel forms can be generated.

As part of a justification for such an approach, I referred (Edelson 1972) to some comments by Freud in the Schreber case (Freud [1911] 1958b, 63–64):[11] "Freud represented the familiar principal forms of paranoia as contradictions or transformations of the proposition 'I (a man) *love him* (a man).' Delusions of persecution assert: 'I do not *love* him—I *hate* him, because HE PERSECUTES ME.' Erotomania involves the transformation: 'I do not love *him*—I love *her,* because SHE LOVES ME.' Delusions of jealousy represent the contradiction: 'It is not *I* who loves the man—*she* loves him' " (Edelson 1972, 208–9). Freud concludes with the proposal that negation of the entire proposition results in megalomania, where "I do not love at all—I do not love any one" is taken to be equivalent to "I love only myself." Each of these propositions is an imagined state of affairs, a fantasy.

I continue to believe that this "transformational-generative model" is important for the psychoanalytic theory of defense, despite the reservations I have and am about to express.

In Freud's formulation, the agent recruits beliefs to justify propositions resulting from a single transformation. Suppes and Warren (1975) suppose that "I love him" becomes "he hates me" by three different transformations. They

10. This was an analogy. Though I referred to Chomsky's linguistic theory, no one should suppose that I intended to suggest that transformations operated on syntactic categories in the unconscious.

11. As did Suppes and Warren somewhat later, in a somewhat different context, but for similar reasons (1975, 406).

do not consider the relation between the mental state (a feeling) "I hate him" and the mental state (a justificatory belief) [because] "I believe he hates me." They go no further than a single transformation in explaining how "I love him" becomes "I love her." Again, they do not consider the relation between the mental state "I love her" and the justificatory belief [because] "(I believe) she loves me."

But then Suppes and Warren make no differentiation between "she loves me," a mental representation, which is part of a mental state of an agent ("I believe she loves me"), and "I love her," which is a mental state of an agent; in that mental state, "her" is a mental representation, to which the agent is related by the psychological activity "love." Nor, similarly, do they make a differentiation between "I love him," which is a mental state, and "he hates me," which is a mental representation, to which the agent is related by the psychological activity "believe."

For the transformational-generative approach, it seems to me it should make a difference whether what is to be transformed by an operation is (*a*) a mental representation that is part of a mental state ("I believe *he hates me*" or "I hate *him*"), (*b*) a mental state ("*I believe he hates me*" or "*I love him*"), or (*c*) a mental state in which the mental representation to which an agent is related is a mental representation of one of his own mental states ("*I do believe that I believe he hates me*—that I have such a belief upsets me").[12]

It seems to me either that such distinctions as these are trivial or that they will turn out to be critical in solving some problems associated with the trans-formational-generative approach to conceptualizing the defense mechanisms within a representational psychology of mind. If the latter, a departure from the transformational-generative model may be required. For example, the psychoanalytic theory of defense may require more focus on the different roles beliefs play in relation to wishes than this model can easily provide.

Suppes and Warren themselves recognize that assimilating unconscious contents to the form actor-action-object is a simplification, likely to result in serious inadequacies. Boden (1974) comments, "The enormous complexity and perverse idiosyncrasy of human personal belief systems prevent opera-tionalization of 'defensive' concepts except at a relatively coarse or trivial level" (269). Counting against a predictable outcome of a repeatedly used simple transformation is the fact that the analysand's associations so often lead to the unexpected; the analysand's responses are so often surprising not just to himself but to the psychoanalyst as well (Edelson 1984, 136–37). Freud, of course, has made the same point, for example, in the Wolf Man case (see, e.g., Edelson 1988, chap. 13).

Furthermore, the list of forty-four elementary and combinations of elemen-

---

12. If we were not able to represent our own mental states as wishes or beliefs, then we should not be able to reflect on or change them.

tary transformations has no obvious correspondence to many of the lists or descriptions of defense mechanisms psychoanalysts provide (see, e.g., Bibring et al. 1961). As a practicing psychoanalyst, I find it difficult to connect various ones of these to actual clinical observations, although it is always possible that this failure is due to imaginative or conceptual deficiencies of my own.

Suppes and Warren imagine that regression may be managed by introducing an explicit formal machinery for temporal reference; I doubt it.

In what is for purposes of this chapter a key confession, in comparing their attempt with Holland's (1973), they "emphasize that by making our own analysis completely formal and explicit we had to sacrifice suggestive but informal developments relating our ideas to those of primary process" (Suppes and Warren 1975, 413).

Just consider the complicated transformations Freud uses in his explanations in "A Child Is Being Beaten" ([1919] 1955). Freud traces the vicissitudes of the historical development of the fantasy "A child is being beaten" (see esp. 185–91). The first phase of the beating fantasy, in a case of a female child, is represented by the phrase, "My father is beating the child whom I hate." The content and meaning of the fantasy is, "My father does not love this other child, he loves only me." The next phase of the beating fantasy (as constructed in the psychoanalysis) is represented by the phrase, "I am being beaten by my father." The content and meaning of this fantasy, which is an expression of the child's guilt, is, "No, he does not love you, for he is beating you." This fantasy is not only a punishment for forbidden genital wishes but a regressive substitute for a genital relation with father. In the third phase, accompanied by sexual excitement, the content becomes, "Strange and unknown boys are being beaten by someone, perhaps a teacher, and if I am there at all, I am probably looking on." The child is now identified with the boys who are being beaten, and the gratification is, therefore, masochistic rather than—as in the first phase—sadistic.

What I want to emphasize here is that it is clear that Freud is *not* thinking in terms of rule-governed operations that are themselves not mental states, representations, or contents but only mechanisms that simply operate on mental states, representations, or contents. He is thinking rather of the kind of changes in a fantasy that are like those an author might make in a script. What we have here is like a theme and variations, with each variation motivated by different considerations, or, in other words, different wishes and beliefs, and often providing in the imagination both protection and gratification simultaneously.

Defenses as Fantasies

Are defense mechanisms as a kind of mental process actually different from what is being defended against? At least, I am not so confident that I can distinguish them in the clinical situation. Defenses are primitive, magical, and "inappropriate" and function according to the primary process (Gill 1963, 105), just as forbidden wish fulfillments are and do. Could it be that defenses are fantasies, too? "Whistling in the dark" (Bibring et al. 1961), which is typical of the way analysand and psychoanalyst talk about "defense," is a fantasy, not a computation. An analysand does not simply set a "mechanism" into motion. He is imagining doing something. He is imagining doing something to mental states or contents. He is imagining what sorts of things he is doing and what sorts of things these are he is doing them to.

How can one separate the anxiety-reducing and wish-fulfilling aspects of a mental phenomenon? Any mental phenomenon seems to function both to gratify and to make secure, is an expression of both impulse and defense, provides discharge for what it also provides protection from. It rarely if ever makes sense to interpret a mental phenomenon as if here were a disembodied "mechanism of defense," pure and simple, no more than it makes sense to interpret a mental phenomenon as if here were a pure manifestation of impulse uncorrupted by defensive aims. In fact, there often appears to be a hierarchy or layering, such that what is defense at one level (or from one point of view) is what is defended against at another (Gill 1963, 120–27). Homosexuality may defend against the dangers of heterosexuality, and then heterosexuality in turn may defend against the dangers of homosexuality. Where is the wish fulfillment, and where is the defense? In the same fantasy.

Another way, perhaps, of expressing this problem is to note that a mental phenomenon such as a neurotic symptom may seem to be the product of a wish, a fear, and what the analysand does to gratify the wish and at the same time to reduce the fear. But at the same time, a complex or network of wishes and beliefs, of different kinds, and in different kinds of relations to one another, seems to be implicated—seems to constitute the structure of the phenomenon (Wollheim 1971, 144–47).

Alas, for the theorist and therapist, there is no easy way to classify or separate wishes, fears, and what the analysand does about his fears. If an analysand says, "I am a guinea pig or dog, stretched out on this couch, and you are probing my mind, and it hurts, and I hate you for doing this to me," the analysand's fear is his wish, his wish is his fear, and what he does about his fear, which is also his wish, is to produce a fantasy so that he gratifies his wish and avoids what he fears simultaneously, without letting himself quite know what he accomplishes in the world of his imagination.

The view of the defenses as fantasies has been anticipated by others; I mention Schafer (1968) as an example. He conceptualizes the mechanisms of defense as wishes—that is, as "dynamic tendencies having mental content" (51). Isolation is an effective imagining of keeping certain things from touching—"the intrapsychic enactment of not touching, hence not engaging in the anal-sadistic acts of masturbating, soiling, killing, playing, observing the primal scene, making babies, and so forth" (54). Undoing is an enactment of "blowing away": " 'To blow away' I take to include a reference to fantasies about the creative, curative and annihilating powers of flatus, breath and wind in general" (54). Projection (imagining oneself as attacked by an outside force) gratifies the wish to be penetrated. Fantasies of spitting out, defecation, and being devoured may also be implicated in projection. Schafer adds to this account of projection "the patient's search for his emotional life in the therapist's; the passive experience of his impulses; the relation of anxiety and guilt to both his active and passive experiences; the oral, anal and homosexual significance of the shift of emphasis [from one's own impulse, thought, or feeling to the other's]; and the pleasure and dread of merging with the therapist" (56). Denial is a psychic act involving an assault on oneself, on another, and on the relation between the two. Introjection "realizes the wishful fantasy of incorporating the object orally for purposes of regaining omnipotence and effecting destruction or preservation of the object" (57). Repression may be a fantasy about swallowed ideas. Gaps in memory may be a fantasy about female genitalia. A sense of defect, of incompleteness, of a need to have the psychoanalyst fill something in, of voids in the mind, all may be fantasies of being a woman or of castration. To repress a name or memory of a person may be a killing of the person in fantasy.[13]

Imagination, Fantasy, and Defense in Psychoanalytic Theory

What is the role of imagination in the core theory of psychoanalysis? How are imagination and defense related?

Wishing and Imagining

The mental process of interest begins with a sexual wish. The sexual wish results in a fantasy, which fulfills the wish.

There is a special relation between wishing and imagination that does not hold for wishing and action.[14] Rational action is explained by citing a combination of wish and belief that are concurrently efficacious. For carrying out an action, a wish is necessary, but also, given that wish, belief is necessary, and, other things being equal, the two together will suffice to produce an intention to act.

For imagining an action, wishing is enough. This is true even for those wishes that, in conjunction with belief, might lead to intentions to act. It is

13. Holland (1973) is aware of this way of looking at the defenses; it certainly keeps, as Suppes and Warren (1975) noted, his "ego's algebra" from being as neat and mathematical as he might have wished it to be.

14. For a beautiful statement about the relation of wish and imagination, see Wollheim (1979, 58–60).

also true for those wishes that are in conflict with, or that compete with, other wishes. But, most important to psychoanalysis, it is true for wishes that would not ordinarily or could not lead to action, wishes that some unalterable condition, for example, were changed—that you were different, or that I were different, or that something that has happened in my past had not happened. Without any particular belief coming into the matter at all, I can still imagine you being different, or my being different, or that what has happened has not happened at all.

Wishes and beliefs produce intentions to act, and actions lead to change in the external world. But wishes and imagination may not be connected or connected immediately with any change in the external world at all. That, of course, is why psychoanalysis poses such conundrums for the philosophy of science and for most conceptions of scientific methodology.

Fantasy, Primary Process, and the Truth of Beliefs

That the fantasies of interest to psychoanalysis are produced by primary process distinguishes them from anticipatory reality-oriented imaginings.

For rational action, it is essential for a person to have some conception of truth. That the person considers, more or less justifiably, that his belief is true determines that, together with his wish, it produces an intention to act. Imagination, however, may be quite comfortable with beliefs not only in whose truth the person has no confidence but about the truth of which he has no concern. It is not simply that considerations of truth do not influence imagination but that "imagination has *the power* to reject such considerations: the considerations are not influential, but this is because they are not permitted to be influential" (Wollheim 1979, 52).

Wishes and Beliefs

What are possible relations between wishes and beliefs?[15]

a) In rational action, the content of an instrumental belief determines whether an action that will satisfy a wish is possible and, if possible, what action will lead to its satisfaction. Psychoanalysis is not distinctively concerned with instrumental beliefs.

b) In attempting to understand action, we may say that a causative belief gives rise to a wish ("I believe he wishes to hurt me, and therefore I wish him dead").

c) A presuppositional belief stands as presupposition to a wish—"I wish to revenge myself on my father, but I can do that only if he is alive." (When the Rat Man permitted truth to matter, he believed his father dead, but, under the

---

15. Here I make use of Wollheim's explication of the relation between wishes and beliefs as the internal constituents of neurotic symptoms (1971, 144–47).

influence of primary process, he believed him—imagined him—alive and therefore available for purposes of revenge.)

d) Wish fulfillments support and sustain presuppositional and instrumental beliefs. "This must be so because I have this wish." The Rat Man held on to wishes directed to his father in his imagination so that he could maintain his belief that his father was still alive. "He must be alive because I imagine this wish fulfilled." Freud thought that Dora wished to be pregnant and that she imagined that she was pregnant so that she could maintain her belief that she really did have intercourse with K, the friend of her father.

Of course, the beliefs that are maintained are "themselves the objects, and the products, of desire; of, that is, further and more fundamental desires" (Wollheim 1971, 147).

Can such relations among wishes, beliefs, and imaginings be explained by the kinds of theories that appeal to cognitive psychologists, which give primacy to rule-governed computations on mental states? The answer to this question is crucial in determining to what extent psychoanalysis is the same kind of representational theory of mind formulated by cognitive psychologists such as Fodor (1968, 1975, 1981, 1983) and Pylyshyn (1985).

Wish Fulfillments and Effective Imagination:
A Cinematic Model

Wish fulfillments, of the kind that dreams are thought to be, are not hallucinations but the products of effective imagination. There are degrees of imagining. Wish fulfillments are products of effective imagination, the extreme degree of imagination.[16]

The closest that one can come to this idea is in remembering what it was like to watch a movie as a child. It is a mistake to think that the child does not know he watches a movie or that he does not know who he is. But he inhabits the movie and usually some central character in it with such completeness that he feels what that character feels, or perhaps he inhabits some secondary character, judging the central character favorably or unfavorably, and responds as that character does to the hero or heroine.

It is like a long swoon into an inner world. Questions of the truth of this or that fact or circumstance or of the reality of the whole spectacle are not permitted to disturb his immersion in it or to interrupt his open-mouthed trance. The effects are enormous. The child laughs hysterically, yearns, despairs, cries, trembles in terror, is unbearably excited, joyful, fulfilled, exultant, triumphant, stirred to new effort.

16. The concept of effective imagination is Wollheim's. Wollheim, in works I have previously cited, has also explicated effective imagination in terms of theater (rather than film). I have found his explication useful, and have borrowed from it, in developing the cinematic model described in the text.

The next closest that one can come to the idea of effective imagination is to remember the vividness, peremptoriness, power, and effects of the sexual fantasies of adolescence. Thinking of the child in the movie and the adolescent in the grip of his own created excitement, one accepts the description of dreams as the products of effective imagination.

The cinematic model is particularly persuasive to me because as a psychoanalyst I have often felt that I was being assigned a part to play in some script I only gradually came to know. Both psychoanalyst and analysand are imagining, and each is in the imagination of the other. The power of the imagination come home to me as I find myself with each analysand saying things—especially saying things in a certain way or with a certain intonation, with shifts in position, hesitations, and even gestures—things different from analysand to analysand, which, although ambiguous, of course, are capable of being interpreted by each analysand in such a way that they fit right in with that analysand's script. I often have the experience that something the analysand is saying or doing is conveying a scene to me, or a series of scenes, as if I were indeed watching the screen on which his fantasy unfolds. Is the psychoanalyst's state of mind such that he imagines himself into the internal audience of the analysand's effective imaginings?

So-called countertransference also testifies to the power of the imagination, whether the term refers to the psychoanalyst's incorporation of the analysand in some fantasy of his own—rather independently of, and perhaps distracting him from, the objectives of the psychoanalysis—or to the psychoanalyst's awareness of the mental states the analysand's activity arouses in him, which for the psychoanalyst are clues to the content of the inner drama of the analysand in which he, like it or not, plays a part and to which, at the same time, he bears witness.

Effective Imagination and a Corporeal Conception of Mind

Of great interest to psychoanalysis, as a representational psychology of mind, is that persons are able to represent symbolically their own mental states and in particular are able to represent symbolically their own psychological activities (thinking, feeling, perceiving, remembering, believing, and wishing). In other words, a person is able to form a higher-order mental representation of himself (the person) carrying out a psychological activity that in turn is directed to a mental representation of an object or state of affairs. Of even greater interest perhaps to psychoanalysis is that a person is able to represent symbolically not only his own body (and, as we know, that representation need not correspond to the facts of anatomy) but his own mind as well—what Wollheim refers to as "the mind's image of itself" (1969).

It is part of effective imagination that the fact that we are merely imagining is suppressed; the dream is an example (Wollheim 1979, 54). It is also a part of effective imagination that it is governed by a corporeal concept of the mind itself.

The analysand, in fantasizing, may have a spatial or corporeal concept of his mind something like the following. "My mind is a place, in a geography." "My mind is a house, where things are put and kept, and where things happen in different rooms." "My mind is a body, with a gastrointestinal tract or a gastrointestinal-urinary tract, that takes things in from the world, digests them, keeps them inside, excretes and loses them. These things inhabit my mind, and do things in and to it, or are extruded and lost to it." "My mind is a penis, which throbs and pounds, can't wait to shoot things out, 'takes off,' penetrates incisively, wilts or can't get anywhere."

The corporeal concept of the mind is a concept of the mind as possessing powers; its states and contents have an exaggerated efficacy, adjusting "the world so that it conforms to its objects" (Wollheim 1979, 54). Given a corporeal concept of mind, we have, for example, "omnipotence of thoughts," belief in the magical powers of the mind, and what Freud calls "the overvaluation of psychic phenomena."

A New Look at Primary and Secondary Process

This entire description of effective imagination and its differences from rational action corresponds to descriptions of primary process and its differences from secondary process. In short, primary process might be defined as (*a*) the construction of wish-fulfilling mental representations (wish fulfillment has primacy compared to any other end for such a process) by means of condensation, displacement, pictorialization, and iconic symbolization and (*b*) effective imagining, in which the truth of beliefs is not permitted to matter, in which the fact that one is merely imagining is suppressed, and which is dominated by a corporeal concept of mind that results in an overvaluation of psychic phenomena (the belief that thoughts are omnipotent and that the mind has magical powers). If action is a manifestation of primary process, it is an enactment, an exteriorization of an inner drama, not a rational act resulting from a conjunction of wish and reality-accommodated instrumental belief.

Affects and the Cinematic Model

In the cinematic model, an internal scriptwriter-director determines or initiates what it is that we imagine; we feel that we determine or initiate it. To say that there is an internal audience is to say that what we imagine has an effect on us that is intrinsic to the imagining itself and not merely a consequence of it. The adolescent's sexual excitement is *in* the fantasy.

It is important to distinguish between affects that are in a fantasy and affects resulting from reflecting on a fantasy. Reflecting on the content of the fantasy, which is the fulfillment of a sexual wish, and on the excitement the internal audience experienced in response to this content, leads to evaluative judgments. Insofar as the judgments themselves are made under the influence of primary process, they too are embodied in fantasies.

One may think of anxiety, guilt, or shame as responses to the fantasy but outside it. "How could I get excited by something as yukky as that!?" "What does that imply about me?" Postfantasy evaluative responses may themselves be expressed in fantasies, constructed by primary process. "What, in the light of what I believe, would happen to me if I actually did something like that?" (So the Wolf Man as a child, in the light of his sexual researches and his preoccupation with castration, interpreted a scene of his parents copulating as implying that having such passive pleasure with his father would necessarily entail his being castrated.) "What if my father had come in while I was doing that?" "How would my mother react if she knew what went on in my mind?"

But it is also possible that the internal audience identifies with the central character, the hero of the fantasy, as he reacts to another actor, who responds unfavorably to him. So, in a scene in which the hero takes pleasure in exhibiting himself, one of the other actors turns away in disgust, belittles him, or mocks him. In this case, the wish fulfillment and the conditions of threat are both part of the same fantasy, with the effects of the fantasy shifting as an internal audience identifies empathically first with the central character's pleasure and then with his response to another actor who regards him unfavorably.

The adolescent's guilt, anxiety, or shame, as he notices or reflects that he had this fantasy, or that he became sexually excited in it, or both, are a consequence of his imaginative activity but also a part of it. The adolescent's guilt, anxiety, or shame may be *in* his sexual wish-fulfilling fantasy and not a simple reaction to that fantasy, separate from it. Guilt may be the feeling that the central character, with whom the internal audience identifies, has as he is scolded or shunned by another actor in a fantasy that is otherwise a wish fulfillment; anxiety the feeling he has as he is threatened with harm by another actor in a fantasy that is otherwise a wish fulfillment; and shame the feeling he has as he is laughed at, belittled, or ridiculed by another actor in a fantasy that is otherwise a wish fulfillment.

Emotions are mental states in which feeling is a relation to a mental representation, just as wishing and believing and perceiving are. Emotions are not simply contentless physiological reactions to stimuli. It is of course the case that, just as intentions to act may cause actions, so emotional states may cause physiological changes (both are mental-representation-to-world causal relations). If an emotion appears without contents in a psychoanalysis, the contents are somewhere; it is a matter of discovering what the analysand has done with them.

Is there a tendency in psychoanalysis ("affects are discharge phenomena") and cognitive psychology to regard emotions as analogous to action rather than as mental states? "Emotional states can be caused by cognitive states, just as the movements of my fingers as I type this sentence are caused by my thoughts and intentions" (Pylyshyn 1984, 269).

More typically, in cognitive psychology emotions are bypassed. "The structural model [in psychoanalysis] is not easily accommodated to modern information-processing models of cognition, which typically (as one would expect of models based on the computer metaphor) avoid the problems of emotions and morality" (Erdelyi 1985, 131).

Effective Imagination, Fantasy, and Defense

Psychoanalysis has its raison d'être in an important fact about human beings. A human being has, at any one time, and at one and the same time, multiple wishes—and some of these are in principle incapable of gratification. But, even among those that are in principle capable of gratification, strains are inevitable. Simultaneous wishes may conflict. The desired states of affairs, even if in principle attainable, may be logically incompatible. Also, the desired states of affairs, while in principle attainable and logically compatible, may compete for the same resources (organismic and environmental), and these resources, of course, are never unlimited. Certainly, then, at the least, it is unlikely (*a*) that the gratification of conflicting or competing wishes can all be maximized simultaneously; (*b*) that any attempt at resolution of conflicts or dilemmas can be effected without some cost in frustration, pain, or misery; or (*c*) that all wishes can be gratified.

A solution to such a conflict or dilemma may involve awareness of the problem and may have been effected by conscious thought, governed by the principle of rationality. It may involve conscious rejection or renunciation of an unattainable wish or assignment of priorities to conflicting or competing wishes as well as deliberate voluntary implementation of plans and decisions following from rational thought and assignment of priorities. Then we consider whatever misery accrues—as a result of failures of gratification of wishes following from error (mistaken beliefs) or ignorance (lack of necessary knowledge) or as a result of the choice to frustrate some wishes in favor of others—normal misery—the normal lot of mankind.

But what if the venue changes from rational action to effective imagination as a way of gratifying wishes, including wishes to avoid painful states? Here, the objective is to gratify wishes through effective imagination, that is, by imagining them as gratified. In order to gratify as many as possible, such devices as condensations are employed by the scriptwriter, where one element in the script can simultaneously allude to many events or objects because, for example, it has played a part in each of them or resembles each of them in some way.

As I have noted, evaluative judgments, as a response to a wish fulfillment, may be expressed in a fantasy outside the fantasy that is a wish fulfillment, but such a judgment also may occur in the fantasy that is a wish ful-

fillment. For example, the internal audience in the fantasy that is a wish fulfillment identifies with the central character's reaction to being regarded
unfavorably by another actor who has a necessary part in the scenario of wish
fulfillment. Just as the internal audience's identification with a sexually excited central character has the power to create pleasurable sexual excitement
in the person who has the fantasy, so its empathic identification with the central character when he is made to feel anxious, guilty, or ashamed by another
actor has the power to create anxiety, guilt, or shame in the person who has
the fantasy.

If the response to a wish fulfillment in fantasy is anxiety, guilt, or shame,
which are painful affects, then the person, who seeks both to experience pleasure and to avoid the experience of pain, faces the problem of fulfilling wishes
under conditions of threat. He may attempt to solve this problem in fantasy,
governed by primary process, so that some degree of wish fulfillment is possible while the threat is to some extent mitigated.

These painful affects will motivate the person to carry out defensive strategies—for example, to revise the fantasy in various ways to mitigate the painful affects and at the same time safeguard a measure of pleasurable wish fulfillment.

These revisions may have external manifestations since fantasies, as dispositional mental states, have the power to cause conscious mental states of various kinds, including intentions to act. An imagined undoing in a fantasy, for
example, may cause an actual enactment (such as the Rat Man's clearing the
path so that his lover will not be hurt by what he imagines his anger at her has
placed in the path to hurt her). But the symbolic operations on such a mental
representation as a fantasy will not necessarily be observable by the research
investigator from a mere scrutiny of the person's actions. Both fantasy and
symbolic operations on it may have to be inferred. That psychoanalytic theory
refers to hypothetical mental states and processes, which cannot be observed,
does not make it unusual, as scientific theories go, but does pose some difficulties for research.

I shall not attempt to enumerate the inexhaustible supply of strategies and
devices available to the scriptwriter in his rewriting. He may keep the story
but attempt to tone down (defense: make it less exciting!) or otherwise change
the response of the internal audience. He may draw the audience away from
an emphatic feeling with the central character or induce it to sympathize instead with the feelings of an actor responding favorably to the central character. He may do something about an actor who regards the central character
unfavorably. He may also abandon the script, locking it up in an attic or safe
(repression as an act of effective imagining!). He may instead close the movie
house, or allow the film to unfold before an empty house, or refuse admittance
to critics of any kind (repression as an act of effective imagining!).

The Unanticipated Consequences of Defensive Strategies

A frequent mistake in both research and clinical work is to regard all the consequences of a defensive strategy as motivated, that is, as something sought in using the defensive strategy.[17] Sometimes the consequence of a defensive strategy is an unanticipated consequence of it, a "side effect," so to speak. Effective imagination results in changes in the person, in the phenomenology of his mental states, in his dispositions, and therefore in his actions.

Michelangelo, according to Freud, defending himself against loss of his mother, incorporates her. She is now inside him. As is the way with effective imagination, she is capable there of doing things to him, pleasant and unpleasant, and he is also capable of becoming her. Becoming her—and it is part of his imagining that he now possesses her beliefs and wishes—he loves boys as she loved him. It was no necessary part of what he intended that he now becomes homosexual in his life—an unanticipated and perhaps not altogether welcome to him effect of the efficacy of his imagined gratification of his wish to hold on to her (Wollheim 1974).

Similarly the student who imagines that when he writes he excretes. When, of course, he imagines closing the sphincter and becoming constipated, he is simply managing internal contents, which for one reason for another he enjoys holding on to or controlling. He may indeed want to avoid killing his teacher with noxious matter. He does not necessarily self-punitively intend that he should flunk the course because he could not get a paper in on time.

The Pathological Effects of Defensive Strategies

A person may fear his own imagination and treat it like a beast to be tamed, caged, or destroyed. (Indeed, sad to say, there are treatises on psychoanalytic theory and technique and the objectives of psychoanalytic therapy that appear to take the same attitude toward the "id.") Analysands may report inner emptiness—the screen of imagination is what stands blank, without script, scene, or character. Analysands may report being trapped before the screen of imagination, enthralled, unable to leave the movie theater, going through the same scenes over and over, the world outside the movie theater pallid and unreal, the world inside the movie theater intense, colorful, the only reality. Analysands may report that they are no longer in control of the actors or the play: scenes flash into their minds that they have not determined or initiated; the action takes a surprising turn; an actor appears in search of a part; an actor refuses to perform his role as directed, forgets his lines, does not appear on cue; the projector breaks down; the screen is rent by an ugly distracting tear.

17. A similar mistake is made by those who, because some anatomical structure has a present function or a use, regard it as necessarily having been selected in the process of evolution because of the adaptive value of that function or use. On this point, see Gould (1977, 1980, 1983).

We may, of course, under some frightful circumstances, want to live in fantasy alone. Then the world cannot reach or hurt us. Then we can have the world we want. We can express feelings without danger of rebuff or ridicule, gratify wishes without obstacle or attack, even communicate what we want to communicate to anyone without that one knowing what we have communicated and hurting us in response. Here it seems we might live without risk.

But we cannot rid the imagination of the demons that we introduce into it. In addition, fantasies, which have causal power, have unexpected and unwelcome consequences. Also, of course, we sacrifice the gratification of wishes that we might sometimes otherwise achieve by acting in and changing the actual world.

If it is effective imagination that solves the problem of achieving wish fulfillment under conditions of threat, we should not then regard defense as some sort of well-defined contentless computation, from a finite list of such computations, operating on a mental state. Effective imagination does its work by means of primary process. So it makes our dreams—and, it would seem, our defenses as well. It is primary process, and the ubiquity and power of primary process, rather than unconscious conflict or infantile sexuality, which are its progeny, that may turn out after all to be Freud's single greatest discovery.

Conclusion

It is possible that defenses are effective in reducing anxiety (or guilt or shame), at the same time permitting some degree of gratification, just because they are, as wish fulfillments are, effectively imagined doings.

References

Bibring, G. L., T. F. Dwyer, D. S. Huntington, and A. F. Valenstein. 1961. A study of the psychological processes in pregnancy and of the earliest mother-child relationship. *Psychoanalytic Study of the Child* 16:9–72.

Boden, M. A. 1974. Freudian mechanisms of defence: A programming perspective. In *Freud: A collection of critical essays*, ed. R. Wollheim, 242–70. New York: Anchor.

Breuer, J., and S. Freud. [1893–95] 1955. *Studies on hysteria*. In *The standard edition of the complete psychological works of Sigmund Freud*, ed. J. Strachey, vol. 2. London: Hogarth.

Dennett, D. C. 1978. *Brainstorms: Philosophical essays on mind and psychology.* Montgomery, Vt.: Bradford.

Edelson, M. 1972. Language and dreams: *The interpretation of dreams* revisited. *Psychoanalytic Study of the Child* 27:203–82.

———. 1975. *Language and interpretation in psychoanalysis.* New Haven, Conn.: Yale University Press. Reprint. Chicago: University of Chicago Press, 1984.

———. 1977. Psychoanalysis as science. *Journal of Nervous and Mental Disease* 165:1–28.

———. 1978. What is the psychoanalyst talking about? In *Psychoanalysis and language,* ed. J. Smith, 99–170. New Haven, Conn.: Yale University Press.

———. 1984. *Hypothesis and evidence in psychoanalysis.* Chicago: University of Chicago Press.

———. 1988. *Psychoanalysis: A theory in crisis.* Chicago: University of Chicago Press.

———. 1989. The nature of psychoanalytic theory: Implications for psychoanalytic research. *Psychoanalytic Inquiry* 9(2):169–192.

Erdelyi, M. H. 1985. *Psychoanalysis: Freud's cognitive psychology.* New York: Freeman.

Fodor, J. A. 1968. *Psychological explanation: An introduction to the philosophy of psychology.* New York: Random House.

———. 1975. *The language of thought.* New York: Crowell.

———. 1981. *Representations: Philosophical essays on the foundations of cognitive science.* Cambridge, Mass.: MIT Press.

———. 1983. *The modularity of mind: An essay on faculty psychology.* Cambridge, Mass.: MIT Press.

Freud, S. [1900] 1953. *The interpretation of dreams.* in *The standard edition of the complete psychological works of Sigmund Freud,* ed. J. Strachey, vols. 4, 5. London: Hogarth.

———. [1911] 1958a. Formulations on the two principles of mental functioning. In *The standard edition of the complete psychological works of Sigmund Freud,* ed. J. Strachey, vol. 12, pp. 218–26. London: Hogarth.

———. [1911] 1958b. Psycho-analytic notes on an autobiographical account of a case of paranoia (dementia paranoides). In *The standard edition of the complete psychological works of Sigmund Freud,* ed. J. Strachey, vol. 12, pp. 9–82. London: Hogarth.

———. [1919] 1955. "A child is being beaten": A contribution to the study of the origin of sexual perversions. In *The standard edition of the complete psychological works of Sigmund Freud,* ed. J. Strachey, vol. 17, pp. 175–204. London: Hogarth.

Gill, M. M. 1963. Topography and systems in psychoanalytic theory. *Psychological Issues* Monograph no. 10. New York: International Universities Press.

Gould, S. J. 1977. *Ever since Darwin.* New York: Norton.

———. 1980. *The panda's thumb.* New York: Norton.

———. 1983. *Hen's teeth and horse's toes.* New York: Norton.

———. 1986. Evolution and the triumph of homology, or why history matters. *American Scientist* 74:60–69.

Holland, N. N. 1973. Defence, displacement, and the ego's algebra. *International Journal of Psycho-Analysis* 54:247–57.

Pylyshyn, Z. W. 1985. *Computation and cognition: Toward a foundation for cognitive science.* 2d ed. Cambridge, Mass.: MIT Press.

Schafer, R. 1968. The mechanisms of defence. *International Journal of Psycho-Analysis* 49:49–62.

Searle, J. R. 1983. *Intentionality: An essay in the philosophy of mind.* Cambridge: Cambridge University Press.

Stoller, R. 1985. *Observing the erotic imagination*. New Haven, Conn.: Yale University Press.

Suppes, P., and Warren, H. 1975. On the generation and classification of defence mechanisms. *International Journal of Psycho-Analysis* 56:405–14.

Waelder, R. 1960. *Basic theory of psychoanalysis*. New York: International Universities Press.

Wollheim, R. 1969. The mind and the mind's image of itself. In *On art and the mind*. Cambridge, Mass.: Harvard University Press.

———. 1971. *Sigmund Freud*. New York: Viking. Reprint. Cambridge: Cambridge University Press, 1981.

———. 1974. Identification and imagination. In *Freud: A collection of critical essays*, ed. R. Wollheim, 172–95. New York: Anchor.

———. 1979. Wish-fulfillment. In *Rational action: Studies in philosophy and social science*, ed. R. Harrison, 47–60. Cambridge: Cambridge University Press.

———. 1982. The bodily ego. in *Philosophical essays on Freud*, ed. R. Wollheim and J. Hopkins, 124–38. Cambridge: Cambridge University Press.

———. 1984. *The thread of life*. Cambridge, Mass.: Harvard University Press.

3 A Classification Theory of Defense

Mardi J. Horowitz, Henry C. Markman, Charles H.
Stinson, Bram Fridhandler, and Jess H. Ghannam

The theory of defense contains a conundrum involving the anticipation of ideas and feelings becoming conscious. For a defensive process to be inferred, at least three elements have to be postulated. The first is a motivational force aimed at conscious representation or action. The second is a capacity to process the motives into forms accessible to conscious representation. The third is an anticipation of the consequences of conscious representation or action. Defensive motives or purposes are based on such anticipation. The conundrum is, How can anticipation occur if the warded-off contents do not become conscious because of defensive processes?

The question is solved in either of two circumstances. One is that the consequences of conscious representation can be anticipated without any conscious representation. Residues of memory of past associations and sensitizations could operate entirely in unconscious information processing, for example. The second way out of this conundrum is that small amounts or periods of conscious representation could occur, but with feedforward inhibitions as a result of assessing these episodes. Whichever way out might be relevant, both assume unconscious assessment of threat and selection of control operations likely to reduce the threat. This assumption is integral to the psychodynamic theory of defense.

There may be many defensive purposes. Among the most common is to avoid painful emotions, self-criticism, and others' hostility, disapproval, and withdrawal of love. There may also be many defensive processes by which ideas and emotions are controlled. That is where a classification theory may focus to take advantage of the recent advances in understanding cognition.

This paper was prepared for the workshop on defense of the Program on Conscious and Unconscious Mental Processes supported by the John D. and Catherine T. MacArthur Foundation, 23–25 June 1986, at Yale University.

Background

Josef Breuer and Sigmund Freud ([1893–95] 1955) described hysteria as a consequence of repression of traumatic memories. Freud went on to describe other defense mechanisms ([1916–17] 1963), but it was not until 1936, with the publication of Anna Freud's *The Ego and the Mechanism of Defense,* that a systematic exposition and categorization were put together. Abraham ([1924] 1948) developed an earlier list, attempting a hierarchy of defense mechanisms according to developmental periods such as the oral, anal, and phallic psychosexual phases. The work was popular among clinicians but was not fully supported by subsequent clinical studies of character-based defensive styles (Shapiro 1965; Kernberg 1975; Horowitz 1986; Horowitz et al. 1984).

Several investigators since Anna Freud expanded on her list, with increasing methodological sophistication in terms of conceptual clarity and operational definition (Bibring et al. 1961; Hartmann, Kris, and Loewenstein 1964; Bellack, Hurvich, and Gediman 1973; Bond et al. 1983; Perry and Cooper 1986; Vaillant 1977; and Vaillant and Drake 1985). Various defenses suggested are defined in alphabetical order in an appendix to this chapter derived from a more extensive review elsewhere (Horowitz 1988a). Perhaps the most influential work along these lines was that by Vaillant (in this volume). His studies used the vocabulary of Anna Freud, operationally defined the mechanisms, and found reliability in ratings of broad sweeps of information. Vaillant successfully related type of habitual defense mechanisms to longitudinal variables such as health.

We add to these approaches for the following reasons.

1. The issue of adaptiveness remains unclear and difficult to study. The defenses as defined describe large-scale patterns of outcome and are very similar to what are called coping strategies in psychosocial research on stress, except that the outcomes of coping strategies are more adaptive and those of the defenses less adaptive. Even so, some of the defenses are regarded as adaptive (humor, sublimation, and suppression) and some more maladaptive (splitting, pathological denial, projection, and acting out).

2. The A. Freud and Vaillant classification scheme does not conceptually differentiate the defense mechanisms by relating them to control processes, with the result that highly complex behavioral outcomes such as undoing stand side by side with more simple outcomes such as suppression. The labels of defense used can be successfully applied to reports of life history (Vaillant 1977; Vaillant and Drake 1985). We have found, however, that direct observation of psychotherapy videotapes leads to recognition of phenomena hard to describe in these terms. This suggests that the classic defense mechanisms are outcomes that may emerge in histories reported by patients but that what is now needed is an additional and supplementary cognitive model for how the

defenses are accomplished as seen in shorter-order patterns. These cognitive operations may be regarded as the processes leading to the classical mechanisms (Haan 1977).

Another empirical line of research on classification theory of defense mechanisms that incorporates a distinction between processes and outcomes was developed by Haan (1977), who grounded her classification in a theory of cognitive development and the earlier work of Kroeber (1963). Where Vaillant was concerned with adaptation over a long stretch of time, Haan focused her research on more immediate details of processing of internal and external information. She described generic processes and various possible outcomes of each process. The processes were different modes of mental function, including cognition, attention focusing, regulation of affect, and control of impulses to act. Haan includes in her classification of processes such categories as discrimination, detachment, means-ends symbolization, delayed response, sensitivity to other people, time reversion, selective awareness, diversion, transformation, and restraint. The outcomes of each category of process are classed as defense, coping, or fragmentation. Coping is the least pathological, fragmentation is the most pathological, and defense occupies the middle position as having both adaptive and maladaptive value.

Take, for example, interpersonal sensitivity as a process. Haan defined "empathy" as a coping outcome of this process, "projection" as its defensive outcome, and "delusional ideation" as a fragmenting outcome to sensitivity to others. We found the process and outcome classification devised by Haan useful and so preserved it. Fragmentation phenomena, however, may result from dysregulation or failure of several processes, not just one. Also, the generic processes described by Haan have not been widely accepted by other investigators. Thus, we have changed this in the proposed classification system.

Suppes and Warren (1975) also viewed defense mechanisms as the outcome of several process variables. Unconscious propositions approaching conscious representation may be translated, according to their theory, in terms of three possible transformations. These transformations involve the actor, the action that may be taken, and the object of the proposition. For example, if the proposition "I hate my brother" were threatening to contemplate, it could be transformed into "I hate myself" by transformation of the object of the action. It could be changed to "I love my brother" by transformation of the action to "My brother hates me" by transformation of the actor and object. We followed this object-relations approach as one of our three main levels of examining defensive processes and outcomes.

Our Approach to Classification Theory

The present classification theory of defensive processes stems from research on the psychological effects of stressful life events (Horowitz 1986). Posttrau-

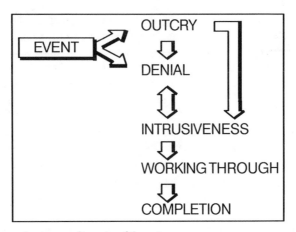

Fig. 1. Phases of responses after a stressful event.

matic stress disorders are marked by extreme experiences suggesting excessive control as well as failures of control. One type of experience is avoidant: the person may deny the implications of the event and may feel emotionally numb. Another type of deflection from ordinary conscious experience after a traumatic life event is intrusive: the person may be flooded with unwanted ideas, images, and intense pangs of emotion. Phases of denial and intrusion often follow an initial phase of outcry, as shown in figure 1. The initial outcry phase is often an undercontrolled expression of intense feelings with many ideas that cannot be fully processed. The phase of denial, in which there seems to be a very high level of regulation of conscious experience, commonly follows outcry. After that, there is a phase in which there is once again a less controlled manifestation of ideas and feelings. The transition from the denial to an intrusive phase seems to be one in which there is an unconscious reduction of control. At other times, the entry into an intrusive phase can be precipitated by a reminder of the stressful experiences. The denial phase is characterized by omissions of some topics that might be expected after the stressful event and that will indeed be conscious during the phase of intrusion or working through reactions to the serious life event. Empirical evidence for these phases has been found with use of our Impact of Event Scale, which shows coherent clustering of intrusive items and avoidant items at different times in the reaction of persons to a particular serious life event (Horowitz et al. 1979; Zilberg, Weiss, and Horowitz 1982).

Both types of deflections from ordinary experience—intrusions and omissions—seem to indicate the presence or failure of regulatory processes. In states characterized by extremes of denial, relatively successful defenses ward off conscious representation and emotion about the traumatic event. The very

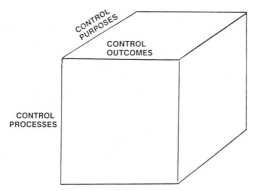

Fig. 2. Conceptual domains in the control of ideas and feelings.

nature of the loss of volitional control in episodes of intrusive imagery with searingly strong emotions suggests that aims at control have failed.

Periods of not thinking about a recent traumatic event suggest regulation of themes for conscious representation and communication of topics as a level of controls for a first consideration. In our classification scheme, mental set— that is, the control of what theme will be contemplated and in what way— forms the first level of control of ideas and feelings.

We will consider the regulation of topic, the regulation of schemas for organizing thought about a topic, and then the sequence of thought about a topic in a series of tables to be presented later in this paper. First, however, it is important to differentiate the purpose, process, and outcome of defensive operations (Horowitz 1980; Sandler and Freud 1985; Wallerstein 1983).

In order to do this, we will for the moment leave the definition of "defense" rather diffuse. Instead, we will use the term "control" to imply various ways in which incipient topics, schemas, and thoughts and feelings might be inhibited or facilitated. In the following tables that organize the classification according to regulation of mental set, regulation of schemas, and regulation of the sequence of conscious representations, we will relate various processes to different outcomes. That is, along one dimension we will list various control processes and along the other dimension various control outcomes.

A third dimension to take into consideration, the consideration of control purposes, is shown in figure 2. The reason it is necessary to consider control purposes is that a given outcome might be judged as adaptive or maladaptive depending on the purpose of the control. For example, in the denial phase that might follow reaction to a serious life event, one purpose might be to maintain emotional intensity within tolerable limits, to avoid out-of-control states of mind. A heavy dose of inhibition of topics might accomplish this purpose and might be adaptive to it. At the same time, another purpose might be to arrive at a decision about the meaning of the life event to the self and what to do about it. Warding off the topic from conscious representation might be maladaptive to this purpose. The same inhibitory efforts, not to think of memories of the stressful event, might be adaptive in relation to one purpose and maladaptive in relation to another (Wegner et al. 1987).

The most common purpose of controls is to avoid entry into states that are flooded with emotion, states in which the person is cognitively disrupted, or states in which the person might express feelings and ideas or act in ways that he or she anticipates will meet with social disapproval.

The control processes under central consideration will concern ways of regulating representation of ideas and feelings so that they may gain conscious awareness. Thus, the controls under question are those that concern the conscious experience of ideas and emotions as well as those that will concern the expression to others of ideas and feelings and communication. The cornerstone of psychodynamic theory concerns not the inhibition of communication so much as the inhibition of ideas and feelings before they can gain or be maintained in conscious representation. Conscious representation includes verbal and nonverbal modes, such as motoric enactions.

The Regulation of Mental Set

Mental set is a specific state of preparedness for processing a constellation of ideas and emotions. It includes a determination of the next theme for conscious representation and how this theme will be processed. A person cannot contemplate every theme or bit of unfinished business at once. Choices are made consciously or unconsciously.

We assume that there is unconscious motivation toward the conscious representation of certain mental contents such as traumatic memories. Such memories are "active"; that is, they contend to find a high place in an intentional hierarchy that selects the next theme for conscious thought or social communication.

Controls might inhibit active memories of a traumatic event from gaining a high place in the hierarchy of potential topics for conscious thought. In table 1, there are several types of outcome that may occur as the result of the interaction of such control processes and the intrinsic property of such active memories. One is adaptive regulation.

In adaptive regulation as an outcome, the person might use inhibitions of a theme to effectively dose emotional remembrance. He or she might have periods of time in which he or she is dealing with a traumatic event, that is, periods dealing with its memory and reactions to it, and other periods of time in which he or she could recuperate while not thinking about the injury or loss suffered and so have reductions in levels of emotional and physiological arousal.

Table 1. Regulation of Mental Set

Processes: Types of Control	Outcomes		
	Regulation		
	Adaptive	Maladaptive	Dysregulation
Intentional hierarchy: Selection of next theme for thought	Dosing (periods of time on and off stressful theme)	Forgetting of stressful themes	
Temporal set: Short or long orientation	Looking at only one step at a time, relating the event to a life span	Denial or urgency of threat, disavowal of long-range implications of changes	
Sequential set: Problem solving or reverie	Planning, restorative fantasies	Work obsession during relaxation (a form of undoing); autistic fantasy	
Representational set: Words, images, enactions in isolation or with cross translation	Intellectual analysis: Solving problems in words because images evoke too many emotions	Numbing of emotional responses by words without images, images without words; isolation	Chaotic intrusion of stressful topics; distraught states such as panic, confusion, exhaustion
Locus of attention toward thought or action	Restorative changes between activity and contemplation	Compulsive action to avoid thought; remembrance and fantasy to avoid action	
Activation level: Regulating rate of information flow in various systems of representation	Excitation and rest cycles	Hypervigilance; avoidant sleeping	

Source: Horowitz (1988a).

It is possible that the control processes may be overused to the point where the outcome could be said to be maladaptive regulation. Complete forgetting of stressful topics, so that the person does not deal with them and remains frozen in denial, appears to be such an outcome.

It is also possible that the person may be relatively unable to use the control process of carefully selecting the next topic of thought. This may involve chaotic intrusion of memories of the traumatic event or other stressful topics, with distraught states of mind such as panic, confusion, or exhaustion. These are listed as dysregulation in table 1.

These same headings of either adaptive or maladaptive regulation and of dysregulation will be used in other tables that cover control of person schemas and the sequence of thoughts within a topic. Across these tables a generalization can be made: the adaptive levels of regulatory outcome are marked by flexibility, as in using both reality-based and fantasy-based modes of thinking in examining propositions about a topic, whereas the maladaptive level of regulatory outcome is marked by rigidity, as when the person cannot switch out of a fantasy-based mode because it is too important as a defense and so cannot adequately and realistically appraise propositions about a topic. The dysregulatory levels of outcome from use of a control process are marked by loss of volition. That is, the person cannot decide to use a control process effectively to reduce emotional intensity and level of arousal. A decision to carry out to a conclusion a line of thought also cannot be implemented.

Below intentional hierarchy as a control process in table 1, the reader will find controls that include the setting of the temporal mode, sequential mode, and representational mode for the topic. The selection of temporal mode refers to whether the person will take a short or long frame of reference in viewing points to be made about a topic. In a short frame of reference, one will look at points having to do with how to take one step at a time in terms of what next actions might be taken in the immediate moments. In a long-range time set, one might relate the stressful life event to the entire life span of the person, both in the past and in the inner map of the potential future.

Either a short or a long view can lead to an adaptive outcome, depending on the situation and the individual's emotional reactions to it. Most often, an adaptive outcome of control of this aspect of mental set is characterized by flexibility, taking short and long views alternatively. A maladaptive outcome may be from rigid use of controls so that a short view is never left or a long view is taken at the expense of executing useful short-run actions. For instance, the person may deny the urgency of the threat or disavow its long-range implications. Other consequences of inability to use these control processes may be confusing jumbles of short- and long-run views or a state of dysregulation in which there are chaotically intrusive experiences and distraught states such as panic.

For example, when floodwaters are rising, someone who stacks sandbags is acting adaptively. Later, when the flood has been controlled, an individual might continue to put up sandbags as a ritual and at the expense of planning for long-range hygiene and food supplies. The same short-run view that was at first adaptive to the purpose of survival is now maladaptive. The defensive action of continuing to stack unnecessary sandbags is perhaps adaptive to some other purpose, perhaps to reduce the highly intense emotional excitations that otherwise might lead to distraught states. The maladaptive level of regulation may still be more adaptive than the outcome of dysregulation.

The third item of table 1 refers to controls of sequential mode. These controls determine the kind of flow from one active concept or idea to another. For example, problem-solving thought is a sequential mode in which activated concepts are arranged by principles of logic and by fidelity to real circumstances or probabilities. A quite different mode may be used in activating a sequence of concepts during fantasy reveries on a topic. A concept can be associatively linked to a preceding one by sensory similarities between them or by congruencies to desire or fear rather than by reasoning. Such modes are also called primary-process thinking.

Controls of representational mode represent another way to modulate expression of thought and arousal of emotion. These controls determine whether the flow of concepts will proceed in lexical, image, or enactive (motoric) representation. By using such controls, a person might remember a serious life event, such as a car accident, only in words. He might block recollection in visual images to avoid emotional arousal from more sensory depictions of memories and reactive thoughts.

Table 1 also describes outcomes for control of attention and control of activation level of various mental systems. The former refers to the direction of attention toward the inner or outer worlds, which in the adaptive case leads to fruitful variation between constructive action or factual thinking and inner contemplation and in the maladaptive case results in compulsive action or avoidant thought. The latter—control of activation—refers to the adjustment of the amount of activity throughout the mental system: high and low levels of overall mental activity would tend to be accompanied by corresponding levels of physiological arousal.

Regulation of Person Schemas

Table 1 concerned the control processes that affected what theme would be next in conscious thought and the setting for how the successive points on that theme might be developed and represented. The organization of information within a mental set is by schemas. Table 2 is an effort to model these processes and their outcomes. It concerns how some schemas from a larger repertoire are activated or inhibited. The most important schemas to consider from a psychodynamic perspective are those at a high level, ones that involve self-organization and views of others. These may be called person schemas (Horowitz 1987, 1988a, 1988b).

Person schemas are information structures that are presumed important in representation of features and regulation of thought and action regarding the self and others. Like lower-level schemas, schemas of person afford tremendous advantages. They can represent complicated feature constellations including sensory representations, emotions, motives, wishes, or memories. They allow recognition of individuals by filling in missing details of partial representations, organization or anticipation of behavior patterns, and generalization of attitudes and expectations to similar people.

A role-relationship model (RRM) is a still more complex type of schema, an interpersonal schema, composed of embedded and interacting person sche-

Table 2. Regulation of Person Schemas and Role-Relationship Models

| Processes: Types of Control | Outcomes | | |
| | Regulation | | Dysregulation |
	Adaptive	Maladaptive	
Altering self person schema	Flexible adaptation; enriched self identity	Omnipotent disregard of personal vulnerability; "as if" self-concepts; regression to earlier self-concepts; passive self-concept to avoid responsibility; dissociation	Depersonalization; chaotic lapse of identity; annihilation anxiety; panic on separations; derealization
Altering other person schema	Flexible adaptation; enriched perception of others	Disregard of the nature of the other; "as if" concepts of the other; projection; regression to earlier or stereotypic concepts of the other	Chaotic or gross misperception of the identification, intentions, emotions or actions of others
Altering role relationship models	Resilient changes to maintain coherence between mental working model and actual situation; creation of new mature interpersonal action patterns, such as sublimation, succorance, nurturance, altruism	Role reversals; projective identification; dissociations and splitting; altruistic surrender; use of others as self-extensions; idealization; passive-aggression; displacement	Chaotic or grossly distorted interpersonal patterns with disturbances in perceptions of self and other

mas (Horowitz 1987). In addition to providing the features of the contained individual person schemas, a role-relationship model organizes information about and regulates the nature of interaction of two or more person schemas (other-other, self-other, or self-self interactions). Thus, a self schema including representation of a desire or goal (e.g., to be intelligent or talented) and a schema of an authority might be embedded in a role-relationship model. Emergent characteristics manifested by the role-relationship model containing the associated embedded schemas might include script-like sequences of interpersonally directed desires, actions, and intentions (e.g., wishes or actions with the aims of being perceived by the other as intelligent or talented).

Large numbers of self and other schemas may exist in potential or in various levels of activation within the brain, depending on past and current situations. The complex stimuli of an event elicit into activation the best fitting of the schemas. In a sense, these compete for primacy in determining perception of present experience and consequent action. Defensive purposes may be a concomitant feature of this competition in that certain schemas may inhibit others. A dreaded state of mind associated with the activation of an unpleasant self schema might be reflexively inhibited before significant activation by a competing, more acceptable self schema.

The concept of person schemas and role-relationship models can be clarified by considering how a person will work through a stressful life experience such as the death of a loved one. Memories of the life and death of the person, as related to the self, are reviewed during mourning. Different states of mind occur during this passage through grief. Sometimes the death is viewed as a loss; a desired person who wanted to stay was taken away by illness or accident. At other times, the death is viewed as an abandonment, according to a role-relationship model in which the self is needy, the other a deliberate deserter. At still other times, the status of the deceased as dead is not recognized, and current life plans are organized by expectations of reunion. The latter role-relationship model produces a mood of hope that can protect against the former ones of sad despair or anger, just as anger can protect against sadness, and vice versa.

Furthermore, sometimes a self schema as strong and liberated may be used as the referent for considering a theme. At other times, a self schema as weak and vulnerable may be operative. The same life event, the death, has different meanings in different states of mind because different self schemas are active and influencing its perception and interpretation. If one interpretation begins to cause excessive painful and out-of-control emotional responses, more tolerable alternate schemas may be activated, shifting perceptions and accompanying mood.

Table 2 gives examples of three types of control processes, involving alteration of (1) the active self person schema, (2) the active other person schema, and (3) the active role-relationship model within which the two person schemas are embedded. Regulatory and dysregulatory outcomes for these control processes are listed in the table. For example, the person may have a usual state of mind organized by a view of the self as an ordinary person. An extraordinary challenge may then occur. The person may organize responses by shifting to a stronger, more competent and effective self schema than used in an ordinary state of mind. The sense of mastery and the mood organized by this resilient self-concept may allow the excitement of the stress events and stress response to have a positive aspect. This could be an adaptive regulatory outcome.

To defend against the threat of succumbing to stress and feeling overwhelmed, the person might activate a grandiose self schema. This could support reassuring but risky beliefs in nonvulnerability to threat. This might be a maladaptive regulatory outcome with reference to the purpose of avoiding risks to the self. Similarly, regression to a view that one is a protected child who need not remain alert to a threat would be reassuring and also a maladaptive regulatory outcome because it would not match the actual fact that one is unprotected by another.

In failures to stabilize a coherent self schema, only fragmentary self schemas might be available for organizing experience. The outcome would be a state of dysregulation, including states of experiencing a chaotic loss of identity or a sense of depersonalization.

Problematic emotions and intentions that are related to the self may be shifted from the self schema and projected as properties of the other. This process may have an adaptive origin in the detection of emotionally induced somatic cues (perhaps in response to subtle pheromone, vocal prosodic, or facial expression signals) that are then appropriately projected onto the other, such as for early detection of fear or anger. Although this adaptive and defensive process may regulate preparedness, reduce emotional pain, prevent depersonalization, or stave off identity crisis, it can be carried to irrational and maladaptive extremes.

Stressful, conflictual situations may elicit a sequence or variety of different schemas or role-relationship models until the most suitable or stable one, or ones, is found. This may occur as an automatic sequence or under some degree of volitional control. When an adaptive outcome is not possible, the person may use such control processes to arrive at defensive outcomes. For example, the person who has been placed in a victim role may reverse roles so that he or she acts out an aggressor role, a kind of role reversal, converting passivity to activity.

Dissociations and splitting are also outcomes in which the person may separate views so that there are all-good role-relationship models and all-bad role-relationship models (Kernberg 1975). While this separation may relieve an ambivalent relationship by reducing hostility, the all-good view of the relationship sets the person up for a catastrophic shift when signs of "badness" are noted in the self or other. Nonetheless, in very stressful situations, such all-good, all-bad views are a useful defense. Sometimes, for example, patients in an accident situation divide health care attendants into those who were gallant heroes and those who were horrible villains. The gallant heroes reduced pain and suffering; the villains were incompetents who caused anxious waiting or pain during examination. As the memory of the accident is gradually worked through, all the parties involved maybe become more realistic from these all-good and all-bad extremes.

Other irrational or unrealistic views may be constructed from control processes and be considered as defensive outcomes. These involve seeing others as self-extensions, excessively idealizing other people so that the self seems less vulnerable, or displacing blame from one person to another so that the person on whom one is dependent is not blamed. For example, a doctor may have made a mistake in the treatment of the subject of a traumatic injury. The subject may blame the nurse because it seems more necessary to emotional well-being to idealize and trust the doctor; to avoid fright, the subject has to see the doctor as perfect. Thus, a role-relationship model of the self in relationship with a perfect healer is used as a working model in order to preserve emotional stability.

Controls of Conscious Representations and the Sequence of Points on a Topic

Table 3 lists controls that primarily regulate the temporal flow of ideas or propositions of a theme. It includes control processes that arrange sets of propositions into decision trees, revise working models, and rehearse new modes of thinking and acting.

The central topic of this book is repression. Repression is listed near the top of table 3 as a potentially maladaptive outcome of the process of controlling conscious representation of certain propositions in a specific theme. Repression may also be considered to be the inhibition of the whole theme or the inhibition of a set of actions based on a role-relationship model, which contains a script for the interaction between self and others. In all these instances, repression—like many other defensive outcomes, such as denial, projection, displacement, and so on—seems to involve unconscious anticipation of aversive consequences of impending conscious representations, followed by inhibition. Anxiety may play an important role in this anticipatory process.

Staying for the moment at the level of the inhibition of the conscious representation of an element in a theme, a further discussion of conscious and unconscious operations in repression will be undertaken, as it is the central thread through this book.

In classic psychoanalytic theory, the inhibition of the processes leading to conscious representation of an idea is hypothesized to occur before conscious representation of that point (Freud [1900] 1938). Freud ([1915] 1957) differentiated between primal repression (ideas that had never been consciously represented) and secondary repression (derivatives of primarily repressed contents, which had been consciously represented, ought to be consciously represented, could be consciously represented, and would be consciously represented were it not for unconsciously instituted inhibitions). Both types of repression might require anticipation of consequences of conscious representation. Primal repression would quite clearly require such anticipation because the repressed ideas theoretically are never conscious, whereas secondary repression could operate through brief consciousness of the derivative idea,

Table 3. Regulation of Conscious Representations and Sequencing

Processes: Types of Control	Outcomes		
	Regulation		Dysregulation
	Adaptive	Maladaptive	
Controlling representation by:			
Facilitation of associations	Contemplation of implications	Rumination and doubting	
Inhibition of associations	Dosing; selective inattention; careful choice of what is expressed; suppression	Denial; disavowal; repression; isolation; numbing; communicative reluctance; somatization; acting out	
Sequencing ideas by:			
Seeking information	Understanding; learning new skills	Intellectualization	
Switching concepts	Emotional balancing	Undoing; reaction formation; displacement	Intrusion of ideas; emotional flooding; indecision; paralysis of action
Sliding meanings and valuations	Humor; wisdom	Exaggeration; devaluation; reaction formation	
Arranging information into decision trees	Problem solving	Rationalization	
Revision working models	Adaptation; identifications; acceptance	Externalization; introjection	
Practicing new modes of thinking and acting	Replace previous automatic reactions with new ways of responding	Counterphobic rehearsals	

Source: Horowitz (1988a)

coupled with some mechanism, perhaps involving anxiety, for "recognizing" the danger that consciousness of the derivative could lead to consciousness of the primally repressed idea.

Inhibition of representation may take place at the entry of information to enactive, image, or lexical modes of representation as well as sites of transformation from one mode to another (Horowitz 1983, 1988a). Thus, consciousness can be restricted not only by nonrepresentation but also by nontransformation of information from one mode to another. A usual episode of consciousness, for example, might combine visual images, words, and motoric tensions around a theme. Constriction of the theme could involve an episode of conscious representation with only visual images, without simultaneous transformation of meanings to lexical representations of meanings. "Lifting" this latter form of inhibition might involve facilitation of such transformations.

Repression should be distinguished from suppression. Suppression is not quite what William James ([1890] 1983) meant when he was referring to the instant forgetting of a representation, but it is quite close.

Suppression is the result achieved when ideas that have, at least momentarily, been consciously represented in the current state of mind are inhibited because they are pushed from awareness. The inhibitory process might be associated with an act of will—fully intentional conscious aim—or with less or no conscious aim. In any case, alternative ideas are facilitated and occupy the limited channels of conscious representation.

Suppression and repression may both be distinguished from a reluctance to reveal to others what one is aware of in conscious self-reflection. Communicative reluctance is an outcome of inhibition in which the person is consciously representing some ideas but aims to avoid expressing these points to another person. It differs from suppression in that it assumes not an aim to avoid continued conscious representation but rather an aim to avoid certain communications. Communicative reluctance in one modality, such as verbal communication, may be associated with leakage of the information in another, such as through prosodic expression of emotion in the face, in bodily posture, gesture, and voice.

Other defensive outcomes that are closely related to repression, suppression, and communicative reluctance include disavowal and denial. In the outcome of control processes that is called disavowal, representation of some aspects of the warded-off ideas occurs with co-occurrence of disclaimers in consciousness as well as in expression to others. In disavowal, the internal representation of the situation and the currently instantiated self schema interact to make the perception of the situation—that is, its final schematic instantiation—more bland, more distant, and less problematic than the features of the actual external situation. Dislocation of the proposition from the self schema organizing the current state of mind reduces emotional response. In effect, the person believes, "It is happening, but not really in the here-and-now to me, and doesn't really matter that much."

Denial is closely related to disavowal and, like disavowal, concerns an external situation and its internal implications. It is a blanket term describing a status determined by many mechanisms (Bresnitz 1983). In its most specific form, the term "denial" refers to a state of warding off the conscious representation of perceptual information by selective inhibition. It is a more global, or extreme, outcome than disavowal in that it is characterized by a perception that is sharply at variance with the actual external situation, to such an extent that a more objective observer of the same situation would regard the perception as untenable.

An attempt will be made below to link these theoretical constructs and terms to a fragment of clinical material. The subject was a patient in clinical research who gave informed consent to the study of his records by multiple scientists.

Case Illustration

A man in his mid-thirties came to treatment five years after his brother committed suicide, complaining of anxiety and depression related to the death. Past history of importance includes a childhood injury that left him with a visible deformity. He subsequently channeled his energies into intellectual activity while admiring his brother for his perfect body. The patient had success in his work despite significant anxiety over failure. He was less happy in his relationships with women, where he felt uncertain about making a commitment.

He experienced intrusive images of the living and handsome body of his dead brother accompanied by waves of intrusive sadness and ideas of longing that the brother was about to visit him, still alive. With respect to the intrusive images of his brother as alive, the absence of images of his brother's body as dead might be a salient omission, a partial denial of his death accomplished by repression and suppression. Clearer episodes of omission included disavowal of the importance of the suicide of the brother to himself and disavowal of the connection of that death to other recent symptomatic phenomena such as his own uncertainty with women and his repeated entry into anxious states of mind. He also had as a complaint an extensive communicative reluctance to disclose to close friends that his brother had died. Such clusters of defenses are common: one rarely sees a single defense in a person using controls to modify his or her level of current stress.

After an evaluation period in which the patient emphasized the importance of his brother's death to his problems, he began to disavow the relevance of the death in therapy. He also depreciated the therapist's efforts to help him. In addition to these defensive avoidances, he experienced various intrusions and omissions such as an intrusive image related to memories of himself at age five. He wondered why these occurred at this time.

In this intrusive image, he saw himself as five years old, falling down in the street because of his injury and being shamed by his father's angry, accusatory voice because his father felt socially embarrassed by having a handicapped son, a form of selfishness on his father's part. This memory was associated with the conscious and communicated idea that his father ought to have been more helpful. An omissive aspect of this intrusive memory is found in the fact that this image emerged at a time when he was becoming more aware in therapy of the importance to himself of his brother's death and his remorse over not helping his brother "up" when his brother called him one week before his suicide. His brother had then "fallen down" in terms of being found prone on the floor after the suicide. The patient omitted the association between the childhood memory and the recent stressor events.

This fragment of a case will now be considered in terms of the types of control processes and regulatory outcomes shown in tables 1–3.

His Defensive Operations at the Level of Mental Set

When the patient entered states characterized by reverie, absorption, and the use of visual modes of representation, more ideas and emotions about his brother occurred. He would then change the theme of his contemplation to rouse himself from the absorbed state of mind. The theme selected was his current work. He would enter a state of worry about his projects in order to facilitate suppression (see table 3) of intrusively sad moods induced by the theme of his brother's death. The suppression involved a process of shifting in sequential mode from reverie to problem solving and in representational mode from visual images to lexical representations (control processes listed in table 1).

His Defensive Operations at the Level of Self Schemas and Role-Relationship Models

In order to model the patient's defensive processes as they may involve person schemas, it is necessary to infer possible elements of such schemas, including traits and rules of self, traits and rules of other, wishes, scripts of action, emotion of self toward other, scripts of responses of object, scripts of reactions of self, and self-estimation for the schematized actions (e.g., guilt) (see Horowitz 1987, 1988a, 1988b). Role-relationship model configurations depict an interaction of desired, dreaded, problematic, and compromise role-relationship models activated from a repertoire. Defensive outcomes stabilize compromise or problematic role-relationship models to avoid use of dreaded role-relationship models.

The dreaded role-relationship model we infer was one in which he was a capable man and his brother was in the role of handicapped man. The patient believed that the brother committed suicide because of despair about overcoming a perceived mental handicap. As it happens, our patient had a physical handicap and compensated by developing his mind. Before the suicide, the brother called the patient, as already mentioned. In the role-relationship model in question, there was a script, a sequence of interaction in which (1) the handicapped man (brother) asked (1) the competent man (self) for help, (2) the self ignored the plea for self-enhancing reasons, (3) the brother signaled that he had been harmed by neglect, (4) the self expressed no remorse but (5) estimated the self as bad, and the brother estimated himself as bad. The stress event, the brother's suicide, matched the model of this dreaded role-relationship model. The patient did not take up his brother's invitation to visit him shortly before the brother killed himself because the patient wanted instead to do his own work and spend time with his girlfriend.

As a defense against feeling too selfish and guilty, he activated another schema described by another role-relationship model in which he himself was not capable but vulnerable and handicapped. This role-relationship model organized and was supported by the memory of falling in the street as a weak child and blaming his father for selfishly neglecting him. The defensive process is alteration of which schemas organize mental life, and the defensive outcome is role reversal.

His Defensive Operations at the Level of Sequencing Conscious Representations

This patient felt that working despite his brother's plea for help was bad. This approximation of the idea of working and the enduring attitude that selfishness was bad because it harmed others led him to feel guilty. To avoid the danger of being flooded with remorse, he inhibited each element in this sequence, leading to an outcome of repression.

The defensive inhibition of ideas and the role reversal already described can be modeled in figure 3. The defensive purpose shown is to exit from a state of remorseful rumination and to avoid the arousal of guilt feelings. The defensive process is to inhibit the ideas that evoke remorse and to facilitate ideas of anger that can reciprocally inhibit guilt. This set of defensive processes includes a shift in role of self from aggressor to victim by activating a different schema of relationships (represented by a different role-relationship model) as well as a shift in temporal mode from recent events to remote childhood ones. The defensive outcome is a shift from a guilty state into a state of mildly angry resignation—that his father was the same way and nothing can now be done about it.

Summary

The defense mechanisms, derived from the writings of Sigmund Freud ([1926] 1959) and first systematized by Anna Freud (1936), have been widely regarded as fundamental processes. In this chapter, however, we regarded the traditional defense mechanisms as defensive outcomes of regulation, efforts

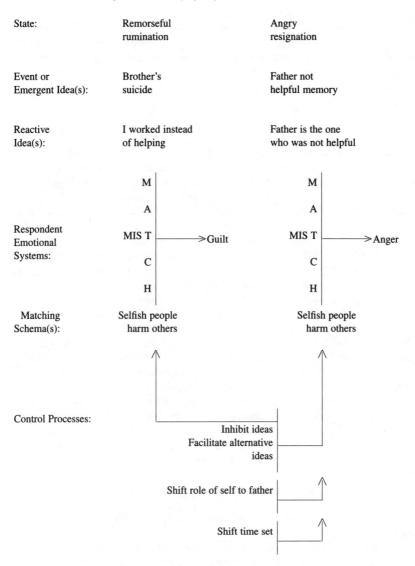

State: Remorseful   Angry
                         rumination   resignation

Event or   Brother's   Father not
Emergent Idea(s):   suicide   helpful memory

Reactive   I worked instead   Father is the one
Idea(s):   of helping   who was not helpful

Respondent   M   M
Emotional   A   A
Systems: MIS T ──────►Guilt   MIS T ──────►Anger
                         C   C
                         H   H

Matching   Selfish people   Selfish people
Schema(s):   harm others   harm others

Control Processes:
                                          Inhibit ideas
                              Facilitate alternative
                                                 ideas
                         Shift role of self to father
                                     Shift time set

Fig. 3. Thematic progression of ideas, schemas, emotional response potentials, and control processes.

that might, in varied circumstances, also have outcomes that would be labeled either as adaptive regulation or as dysregulation, the latter being defined as succumbing to stress.

   In this classification, we proposed the fundamental divisions of regulatory processes into those controls that affect (1) the overall thematic content of thought as well as the modes for conscious representation, (2) the schemas that organize the thoughts and feelings within a state of mind, and (3) the association of linkages between sequences of ideas and feelings that may be consciously represented.

Appendix

The following list of defense mechanisms is from Horowitz (1988a, 191–96).

Altruism.—In altruism, one deals with emotional conflicts, or internal or external stress, by dedicating oneself to fulfilling the needs of others instead of one's own.

Conversion of passive to active.—To defend against the threat of a weak and vulnerable position, the person may conceptually place self in the active role. Identification with an aggressor is one form of this defense.

Denial.—The most frequent defense is denial: the avoidance of awareness of some painful external reality. It is accomplished by withholding conscious understanding of the meaning and implications of what is perceived—especially by refusing to take in the extended significance of new information. Magical thinking ("Pay no attention and it will go away") also plays a powerful role in denial. Within limits, denial is a normal process used to slow down the response to bad news. Persons with myocardial infarctions treated in coronary care units persist in telling themselves and others that their pain is due to "indigestion." Physicians may ignore the early warning signs of cancer in themselves on the grounds that "it means nothing." While denial is considered a "normal" defense because it may allow a graded acceptance of bad news, it is maladaptive if it interferes with rational action.

Devaluation.—In devaluation, one deals with emotional conflicts, or internal or external stress, by attributing exaggerated negative qualities to self and others.

Disavowal.—To avoid stressful news or its implications, the person may assert that the situation does not matter to him or her, and, to cover over unwanted inner fears, wishes, or feelings, the person may say that these emotions are not important to the self.

Displacement.—In displacement, the avoided ideas and feelings are transferred to some other person, situation, or object. For example, hypochondriacal patients may displace worry and ward off a concern that their minds are failing, focusing concern instead on a body part.

Dissociation.—In dissociation, one deals with emotional conflicts, or internal or external stress, by a temporary alteration in the integrative functions of consciousness or identity.

Distortion.—Various forms of altering meanings and sliding evaluations can be used to distort a stressful topic. Devaluation, disavowal, exaggeration, and minimization are all forms of distortion.

Exaggeration.—In order to protect self-esteem or emotional balance, certain meanings can be given exaggerated value. For example, personal strength can be appraised in an exaggerated way to avoid fear before a fight.

Humor.—One may deal with emotional conflicts, or internal or external stress, by using humor and emphasizing the amusing or ironic aspects of the conflict or stress.

Idealization.—In idealization, one deals with emotional conflicts, or internal or external stress, by attributing exaggerated positive qualities to self and others.

Intellectualization.—In intellectualization, the person avoids the emotional implications of a topic by dealing with it on a purely ideational level. In a related defense, *generalization,* the person deals with the topic at an abstract rather than a personal level to avoid excessive emotion.

Isolation.—The process of isolation consists of splitting of ideas and feelings, as in having the obsessive idea or image of "killing" without feeling anger or hostility toward the object. This defense leads to flatness of affect or seeming indifference.

Minimization.—As a maneuver to reduce stress, the person undervalues a topic. For example, the degree to which the self was to blame for an accident could be minimized to avoid shame and guilt.

Omnipotent control.—In using omnipotent control to defend against the stress of having others abandon or fail to attend properly to the self, the person acts from an attitude of having total control of the object. Sometimes, when the stress is fear that the environment will be overwhelming, the defense of omnipotent control includes attitudes of an irrational nature, in which the person believes that wishes, rituals, or incantations will bend environmental forces to his or her will.

Passive aggression.—In passive aggression, one deals with emotional conflicts, or internal or external stress, by indirectly and unassertively expressing aggression toward others.

Projection.—In projection, a warded-off impulse or idea is attributed to the external world. For example, people who struggle with their own hatred may develop a delusion that others are out to get them. This gives one an acceptable rationale for hating and allows one to avoid recognition of one's own destructive impulses.

Projective identification.—In projective identification, an aspect of the self that one does not wish to acknowledge is placed not in the working model of the self but in that of another to whom the self is closely related. Although the other is then seen as having a bad attribute, the self remains closely affiliated with the other. Instead of distancing the self from the other, who may now be viewed as being angry at the self (rather than vice versa), one may provoke the other person to behave in a hostile manner—thus providing a reality basis for locating the anger of the self as if it were in the other person.

Rationalization.—Rationalization consists of proclaiming logical reasons for actions actually performed for other reasons, usually to avoid stress or self-blame. Rationalization is also used to justify avoiding unpleasant duties.

Reaction formation.—In reaction formation, a warded-off idea or feeling is replaced by an unconsciously derived but consciously felt emphasis on its opposite. For example, an older boy is jealous of a baby brother and has a fantasy that, if the baby were to die, he would again be the center of his parents' attention. Having such a fantasy, he realizes, is "bad" because he has been "ordered" to love the baby. Reaction formation consists of replacing the wish to be rid of the brother with an exaggerated concern for the baby's welfare. If the defense works adaptively, he cares for the brother even though he wishes, occasionally, for the restoration of his only-child status. If the conflict is intense, the reaction formation may lead to symptoms. For instance, such a boy might have a compulsion to check up on the baby to make sure it is all right, not suffocated or kidnapped.

Regression.—Regression consists of turning back the maturational clock and returning to earlier modes of dealing with the world. Some persons confronted with the stress and environmental cues of hospitalization become, for example, "regressively" childlike in terms of demands, demeanor, and dependence on others.

Repression.—Repression consists of withholding from conscious awareness an idea or a feeling. Conscious expulsion of thoughts from the mind is *suppression*. Repression differs from suppression in being an involuntary rather than a voluntary process. It may operate to exclude from awareness what was once experienced as inability to remember an important but traumatic event (e.g., amnesia) or to curb ideas and feelings that have not yet reached consciousness but would emerge were it not for the defensive process. For example, one may repress the awareness of erotic arousal by a person inappropriate for sexual love or may repress hatred for someone who "ought to love."

Somatization.—In somatization, one deals with emotional conflicts, or internal or external stress, by preoccupation with physical symptoms disproportionate to any actual physical disturbance.

Splitting.—In splitting, one deals with emotional conflicts, or internal or external stress, by viewing oneself or others as all good or all bad, failing to integrate the positive or negative qualities of self and others into cohesive images; often the same person will be alternately idealized and devalued.

Sublimation.—Sublimation is the process whereby one replaces an unacceptable wish with a course of action that is similar to the wish but does not conflict with one's value system. For example, aggressive wishes may be sublimated into working hard to fight against and solve social problems.

Suppression.—In suppression, one deals with emotional conflicts, or internal or external stress, by intentionally avoiding thinking about disturbing problems, wishes, feelings, or experiences.

Turning against the self.—In the defense of turning against the self, an inappropriate impulse directed outward is redirected at the self. The guilt that would follow from aggression against an object of hatred can be avoided by hurting oneself (as by self-mutilation).

Undoing.—Undoing expresses both the impulse and its opposite, as in being very domineering one minute and then offering obsequiously to defer to another. In rapid repetition, undoing may lead to indecisiveness.

References

Abraham, K. [1924] 1948. A short study of the development of libido, viewed in light of mental disorder. In *Selected papers*. London: Hogarth.

Bellack, L., M. Hurvich, and H. Gediman. 1973. *Ego functions in schizophrenics, neurotics, and normals*. New York: Wiley.

Bibring, G., T. Dwyer, D. Huntington, and A. Valenstein. 1961. A study of the psychological process in pregnancy and of the earliest mother child relationship. II. Methodological considerations. *Psychoanalytic Study of the Child* 16:62–72.

Bond, M., S. Gardner, J. Christian, and J. S. Sigal. 1983. Empirical study of self-rated defense styles. *Archives of General Psychiatry* 40:333–38.

Bresnitz, S., ed. 1983. *Denial of stress.* New York: International Universities Press.

Breuer, J., and S. Freud. [1893–95] 1955. *Studies on hysteria.* In *The standard edition of the complete psychological works of Sigmund Freud,* ed. J. Strachey, vol. 2. London: Hogarth.

Freud, A. 1936. *The ego and the mechanisms of defense.* London: Hogarth.

Freud, S. [1900] 1938. *The interpretation of dreams.* In *The basic writings of Sigmund Freud,* ed. A. A. Brill. New York: Random House.

———. [1915] 1957. Repression. In *The standard edition of the complete psychological works of Sigmund Freud,* ed. J. Strachey, vol. 14, pp. 141–58. London: Hogarth.

———. [1916–17] 1963. *Introductory lectures on psycho-analysis.* In *The standard edition of the complete psychological works of Sigmund Freud,* ed. J. Strachey, vols. 15, 16. London: Hogarth.

———. [1926] 1959. Inhibitions, symptoms and anxiety. In *The standard edition of the complete psychological works of Sigmund Freud,* ed. J. Strachey, vol. 20, pp. 77–178. London: Hogarth.

Haan, N. 1977. *Coping and defending.* New York: Academic.

Hartmann, H., E. Kris, and R. M. Lowenstein. 1964. *Papers on psychoanalytic psychology.* New York: International Universities Press.

Horowitz, M. J. 1980. Psychological response to serious life events. In *Human stress and cognition: An information processing approach,* ed. V. Hamilton and D. Warburton. New York: Wiley.

———. 1983. *Image formation and psychotherapy.* New York: Appleton-Century-Crofts.

———. 1986. *Stress response syndromes.* 2d ed. Northvale, N.J.: Aronson.

———. 1987. *States of mind.* 2d ed. New York: Plenum.

———. 1988a. *Introduction to psychodynamics.* New York: Basic.

———, ed. 1988b. *Psychodynamics and cognition.* Chicago: University of Chicago Press.

Horowitz, M. J., N. Wilner, and W. Alvarez. 1979. Impact of event scale: A study of subjective stress. *Psychosomatic Medicine* 41(3):209–18.

Horowitz, M. J., C. Marmar, J. Krupnick, N. Wilner, N. Kaltreider, and R. Wallerstein. 1984. *Personality styles and brief psychotherapy.* New York: Basic.

James, W. [1890] 1983. *Principles of psychology.* Cambridge, Mass.: Harvard University Press.

Kernberg, O. 1975. *Borderline conditions and pathological narcissism.* Northvale, N.J.: Aronson.

Kroeber, T. C. 1963. The coping functions of the ego mechanisms. In *The study of lives,* ed. R. White. New York: Atherton.

Perry, C., and S. Cooper. 1986. A preliminary report on defenses and conflicts associated with borderline personality disorder. *Journal of the American Psychoanalytic Association* 34, no. 4:863–94.

Sandler, J., and A. Freud. 1935. *The analysis of defense.* New York: International Universities Press.

Shapiro, D. 1965. *Neurotic styles.* New York: Basic.

Suppes, P., and H. Warren. 1975. On the generation and classification of defense mechanisms. *International Journal of Psycho-Analysis* 50:404–14.

Vaillant, G. E. 1977. *Adaptation to life.* Boston: Little, Brown.

Vaillant, G., and R. Drake. 1985. Maturity of ego defenses in relation to DSM III Axis II personality disorder. *Archives of General Psychiatry* 42:597–601.

Wallerstein, R. 1983. Defenses, defense mechanisms, and the structure of the mind. *Journal of the American Psychoanalytic Association* 31, no. 5, suppl.:201–25.

Wegner, D. M., D. J. Schneider, S. R. Carter III, and T. L. White. 1987. Paradoxical effects of thought suppression. *Journal of Personality and Social Psychology* 53, no. 1:5–13.

Winston, A., J. Pollack, L. McCullough, et al. 1988. Patient-therapist interaction related to outcome. Paper presented at the meeting of the American Psychiatric Association, Montreal, May.

Zilberg, N., D. Weiss, and M. Horowitz. 1982. Impact of event scale: A cross-validation study and some empirical evidence. *Journal of Consulting and Clinical Psychology* 50:407–14.

4 The Evidence for Repression: An Examination of Sixty Years of Research

DAVID S. HOLMES

At the outset, it might be helpful if I described briefly the role I played in the conference on "Repression, Dissociation, and the Warding off of Conflictual Cognitive Contents." When Jerome Singer called and invited me to partici- pate, I was impressed with the topic and the participants, but I wondered, "Why invite me?" The question arose because some years earlier I had pub- lished a review in which I concluded that there was no reliable evidence for the existence of repression (Holmes 1974), and since then I had not seen any- thing new in the literature to change that conclusion. Singer replied that it was his hope to include within the conference the entire spectrum of points of view concerning repression and that my point of view was certainly "different" from those of most of the other participants. Furthermore, he suggested that it was important to have a critic at the conference. The role of "nonbeliever" and "critic" can be difficult, but it is one with which I had had some experi- ence (e.g., Holmes 1968a, 1968b, 1974, 1978, 1981a, 1981b, 1983, 1984, 1985b). Indeed, a colleague once likened me to Diogenes, who walked through the night with a lantern looking for an honest man. I, he suggested, have walked through the dark night of psychology looking for a concept in which I could believe. My lantern has been a textbook on research methodol- ogy, and, unfortunately, it has often revealed more flaws than facts and more errors than insights. My role in the conference, then, was to balance theory with data and to focus a critical light on the data.

Definition

The definition of "repression" is of course essential to studying the phenom- ena. Unfortunately, defining "repression" presents a thorny problem because Freud used the term differently at different times, and Erdelyi (in this volume) has aptly demonstrated that, by referring to different citations, one can include or exclude almost any behavior from Freud's umbrella of repression. What is one to do in this situation? From my perspective, the most practical, pragmatic, and prudent thing to do is to use a definition of "repression" that matches as closely as possible the conventional use of the term. In other words, in the absence of an authoritative definition, we should use the definition held by most individuals. This may be heretical, but exactly what Freud did or did not mean by the term "repression" may be irrelevant now anyway. Arriving at the conventional usage is not a problem-free process, however, and my pen poised over a pile of texts and journals does not serve as an objective and infallible divining rod. However, examination of a variety of texts and the amalgam of laboratory research that has been published over the past sixty years does lead to what appears to be a widely held definition.

It is my belief that in its general use the concept of repression has three elements: (1) repression is the selective forgetting of materials that cause the individual pain; (2) repression is not under voluntary control: and (3) repressed material is not lost but instead is stored in the unconscious and can be returned to consciousness if the anxiety that is associated with the memory is removed (Freud [1915] 1957). The assertion that repression is not under voluntary control differentiates repression from suppression and denial, with which it is sometimes confused or which some theorists choose to consider as types of repression (Erdelyi, in this volume). It should be noted that there are two types of repression. On the one hand, there is what Freud called "repression proper" or "after expulsion," in which an individual consciously recognizes something as threatening (anxiety provoking) and then represses the thought to avoid the anxiety (Freud [1915] 1957). On the other hand, there is "primary repression," in which threatening material is relegated to the unconscious before it is consciously recognized as stressful. Unless it is explicitly stated otherwise, in my discussion of repression I will focus on "after expulsion." Having defined "repression," we can now go on to consider the ways in which it has been traditionally studied in the laboratory.

Approaches to Studying Repression

Five approaches have been used to study repression in the laboratory, and in this section I will briefly consider the methods, findings, and weaknesses of each approach along with the conclusions that can be drawn.

Differential Recall of Pleasant and Unpleasant Experiences

In an early attempt to study repression, investigators asked subjects to make lists of their pleasant and unpleasant experiences. Later, the subjects were unexpectedly asked to recall the experiences they had recorded. The investigators then compared the two lists to determine whether subjects were less likely to recall (i.e., repress) unpleasant than pleasant experiences. In most studies, it was found that unpleasant experiences were less likely to be re-called, and the findings were taken as evidence for repression (e.g., Jerslid 1931; Meltzer 1931; Stagner 1931).

These results were initially appealing, but two sets of related findings raised questions about whether the differential recall was due to repression. First, subsequent investigators reported data demonstrating that the recall of per-sonal experiences was due to the intensity of affect rather than the type of affect (pleasant vs. unpleasant) associated with the experiences (e.g., Menzies 1936; Waters and Leeper 1936). In other words, emotionally intense experi-ences were more likely to be recalled than less intense experiences regardless of whether they were pleasant or unpleasant.

The second set of findings stemmed from an attempt to reconcile the con-flicting findings concerning the influence of intensity versus type of affect on recall. In 1970, I proposed that (*a*) the recall of experiences is determined by the intensity of affect associated with experiences at the time of recall, (*b*) the intensity of the affect associated with experiences declines over time, and (*c*) the affect associated with unpleasant experiences is more likely to decline or will decline faster than the affect associated with pleasant experiences (Holmes 1970). If the affect associated with unpleasant experiences showed more or faster declines, at the time of the second recall the unpleasant experi-ences would be less intense, and, if intensity determines recall, the unpleasant experiences would be less likely to be recalled. To test these hypotheses, col-lege students were first asked to keep a diary of their pleasant and unpleasant experiences for seven days and to score each experience for pleasantness-unpleasantness on a nine-point scale. Each experience was recorded on a card, and the affect score for the experience was recorded on the back of the card. A week later, the subjects were unexpectedly asked to write down all the ex-periences they had recorded on their diary cards. When that task was com-pleted, the subjects were given their diary cards and asked to read each expe-rience and to give the experience a score on a nine-point scale in terms of how pleasant-unpleasant it was at that time. (Note that the original scores for affect were on the backs of the cards and thus could not influence the subjects' sec-ond scoring.) With this procedure, it was possible to measure differential re-call and to measure changes in affect for pleasant and unpleasant experiences that were and were not recalled. The results indicated that unpleasant experi-ences showed greater declines in affective intensity than pleasant experiences and as a consequence were less likely to be recalled. These results indicate that reduced recall of unpleasant experiences is due to a reduced affective intensity associated with the unpleasant experiences rather than to repression. These results are presented schematically in figure 1.

One caveat concerning these results must be noted. This investigation did not indicate why there were greater declines in the affective intensity asso-ciated with unpleasant than pleasant experiences. It could be argued that the

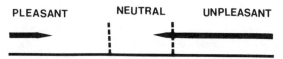

Fig. 1. Schematic representation of how the differential decline of the affective intensities associated with pleasant and unpleasant experiences influences subsequent recall of the experiences. Vertical lines represent intensity thresholds that determine whether an experience will be recalled. Evidence indicates that the affect associated with unpleasant experiences is more likely to decline to points below the threshold necessary for recall.

declines were due to repression of the unpleasant affect, thus reintroducing repression as an explanation. There are, however, two alternative (and I think better) explanations for the decline in intensity of unpleasant experiences. First, given the lapse of time between the occurrence and the recall of the experiences, a subject may discover that the experience did not result in the dire consequences that were expected (failing a test in French is not the end of the world), or a subject may take some remediative action that alters the nature of the experience (studying harder may improve future performance in French). The absence of dire consequences or the use of remediative action could serve to reduce the original negativity of the experience and in turn reduce the likelihood of its recall. The second explanation is based on the findings that subjects think more about intense experiences than neutral experiences (D'Zurilla 1965; Menzies 1936; Waters and Leeper 1936) and that repeated exposure results in more positive attitudes toward stimuli (Zajonc 1968). It then may be that the attention given to unpleasant experiences results in their becoming less unpleasant and therefore less intense.

It might also be noted that, if the decline in affect or reduction in recall of unpleasant experiences was due to repression, it would be expected that individual differences in personality would be associated with the changes in affect/recall (e.g., it would be expected that "hysterics" would be more likely to show the effect than "nonhysterics"). To test that possibility, I conducted a second investigation using the same procedures, but I also collected a wide variety of measures of personality from the subjects (Holmes 1973b). The results of that investigation replicated the earlier findings in terms of declines in affect and recall but failed to reveal any relation between declines in affect or recall and personality. Overall, then, it appears that the differential recall of pleasant and unpleasant experiences cannot be used to support the concept of repression.

I have dealt with these findings in some detail not only because they are interesting and relevant in terms of the laboratory research but also because they appear to be particularly relevant to nonlaboratory instances of forgetting that are interpreted as being due to repression. If a client were unable to recall an unpleasant experience, and if with some prompting the experience was recalled but stripped of its original negative affect, it is likely that this would be interpreted as an instance of repression or at least denial. However, there is no evidence for that interpretation, and the behavior can be more easily and parsimoniously accounted for in terms of the normal differential decline of affect associated with pleasant and unpleasant experiences and the effects those declines have on recall. Because this line of research does not provide evidence for repression, we must go on to consider the results generated by another approach.

Differential Recall of Completed and Incompleted Tasks

A second approach of studying repression involved having subjects work on a series of tasks that were constructed so that some tasks could be completed and others could not. Later, the subjects were asked to recall the completed and incompleted tasks. If incompletions are interpreted by subjects as stressful failures, it would be expected that incompletions would be more likely to be repressed and therefore recalled less well than completions.

Paradoxically, this line of research originally was begun to test the Gestalt notion that incompletions create "tension systems" and thus will be *more* likely to be recalled (Butterfield 1964; Lewin 1940; Prentice 1944). In the early tests of that prediction, it was generally found that subjects recalled more incompletions than completions, but there were notable exceptions. These exceptions were sometimes explained by suggesting that "embarrassment" over failure to complete a task led the subject to repress the recall of the task (Lewis and Franklin 1944; Zeigarnik 1927). Experimenters then seized on the completed/incompleted task procedure as a technique for manipulating stress and testing for repression, and there followed a long series of experiments (Eriksen 1952a, 1952b; Forest 1959; Gilmore 1954; Glixman 1948; Green 1963; Rosenzweig 1943; Rosenzweig and Mason 1934; Sanford and Risser 1948; Smock 1957; Tudor and Holmes 1973). When testing for repression, the completable and incompletable tasks were usually represented as parts of an intelligence test so as to heighten the stress associated with incompletions.

In the six most methodologically refined experiments in this group, subjects participated under conditions of high stress (tasks were presented as an intelligence test) and low stress (no importance was attached to the tasks). It was predicted that under high stress fewer incompletions than completions would be recalled (i.e., incompletions would be repressed because they were threatening) and that under low stress there would not be a difference in the recall of incompletions and completions. This was found to be the case in all six experiments, thus apparently providing considerable evidence for the existence of repression (Eriksen 1952a, 1952b; Gilmore 1954; Glixman 1948; Lewis and Franklin 1944; Smock 1957; Tudor and Holmes 1973).

There is, however, an alternative explanation for the findings. Specifically, the differences in the recall of completed and incompleted tasks may be due to differences in the degree to which the tasks were originally learned. In other words, in these experiments differential learning may have been misinterpreted as differential forgetting (repression). Fortunately, data are available that enable us to disentangle differential learning from differential forgetting.

In one experiment (Caron and Wallach 1957), subjects in a "continued stress" condition were exposed to the completed and incompleted tasks under stress (they were led to believe that the task was an intelligence test), and then they were tested for recall under stress, as had been done in most of the research. In contrast, subjects in a "relief" condition were exposed to the tasks under the stress, were then debriefed concerning the deception so that the stress was eliminated, and then were tested for recall. If recall were influenced by repression, subjects in the continued stress group should recall fewer incompletions than subjects in the relief group because the stress had not been eliminated in the continued stress group and therefore the subjects in that group would still have reason to repress. On the other hand, if recall were a function of original learning, no differences in the recall of incompletions would be expected between the groups because the conditions under which they had learned the materials were identical. The results indicated that the subjects in the continued stress and relief groups did not differ in recall, and the authors concluded that "recall tendencies in the present study are due to a *selective learning* rather than a selective remembering mechanism" (Caron and Wallach 1957, 378 emphasis added). Similar results were produced in my laboratory (Holmes 1973a). It appears that what originally looked like repression was in fact differential learning. Overall, then, the differential recall of completed and incompleted tasks has not provided evidence for the concept of repression, and therefore we must go on to consider the results of yet another approach to studying repression.

Changes in Recall Associated with the Introduction and Elimination of Stress: Repression and the Return of the Repressed

In the third approach to studying repression in the laboratory, not only did investigators seek to demonstrate repression following a stress, but they also attempted to demonstrate that the repressed material could be returned to consciousness when the stress was removed (the "return of the repressed"). Furthermore, the investigators introduced procedures that ensured that the material for which recall was to be tested was equally learned by both experimental and control subjects prior to the experimental manipulation of stress, thereby eliminating the problem found in the differential recall of completions and incompletions.

In these experiments, subjects in the experimental and control conditions were first tested for their ability to recall a set of neutral materials (nonsense syllables, words, etc.). This was done to make sure that all the subjects actually knew the materials for which recall would be tested later. The subjects in the stress condition were then exposed to a stress (e.g., failure, negative personality feedback). The stress was associated with the materials to be recalled (e.g., the materials were part of a test that the subject was led to fail, or the stress occurred in the same situation in which the materials had been presented) so that the previously neutral materials were then "painful" or anxiety provoking. The subjects in the control condition were not exposed to the stress. After the experimental manipulation of stress, the subjects were tested for recall. It was typically found that subjects in the stress condition recalled fewer of the previously neutral materials than subjects in the control condition, a finding that was interpreted as evidence for repression.

After stress had been manipulated and recall tested, the stress was eliminated so that the return of the repressed material could be tested. Stress was eliminated by exposing subjects to success (e.g., good performance on a test or positive personality feedback, depending on how stress had been induced), or the subjects were debriefed about the deception that was used to induce the stress. All the subjects were then tested again for their recall of the material. Typically, recall improved after the stress was eliminated ("return of the repressed"), and, consequently, there were no longer differences in recall between the stress and the control groups. This patterning of findings has been reported in numerous experiments, and in many cases it was concluded that the findings provided evidence for repression and the return of the repressed (Zeller 1950, experiments 1, 2; Zeller 1951; Merrill 1954; Flavell 1955; Holmes 1972; Holmes and Schallow 1969; Penn 1964; Aborn 1953; Truax 1957; D'Zurilla 1965). (Findings that are typical of this group of experiments are represented by the "neutral feedback" and "threatening feedback" conditions in fig. 2.)

These results were very impressive, and they were widely cited as evidence for repression. Unfortunately, however, there is a serious interpretative problem with this research. Although the performance of the subjects in these experiments is consistent with what would be expected on the basis of repression, most of these experiments did not offer evidence concerning the process that was responsible for the performance. It was assumed that the decrement in recall was due to repression, but it is also possible that the decrement in recall was due to the interfering effects of stress (Russell 1952; Truax 1957). As early as 1952, it was pointed out that "it is possible also that failure situations may produce a drive state (frustration, anxiety, or insecurity) which affects behavior in this case through the elicitation of *competing* responses" (Russell 1952, 214; emphasis added). Consistent with this possibility, postexperimental interviews revealed that subjects in the stress condition thought more about the stress to which they had been exposed than subjects in the

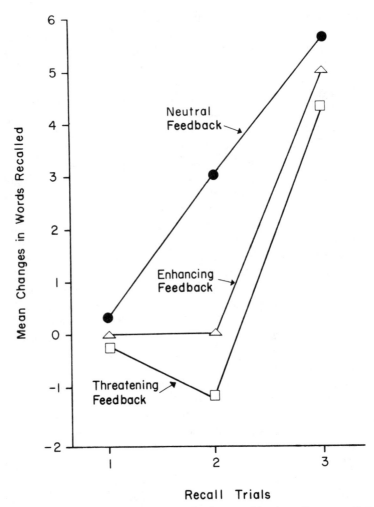

Fig. 2. Ego-enhancing personality feedback has the same deleterious effect on recall as does ego-threatening personality feedback, thus suggesting that declines in recall are due to interference rather than repression. (The differences between the "enhancing" and the "threatening" conditions in this figure are not statistically reliable.) When the deception is revealed and the interference is thereby eliminated, differences in recall among conditions are eliminated. Recall that trial 1 occurred before the stress/interference manipulation, trial 2 occurred after the stress/interference manipulation, and trial 3 occurred after the deception was revealed. (Figure adapted from Holmes 1970.)

control condition thought about the neutral experience to which they had been exposed (D'Zurilla 1965). This is exactly the opposite of what would be expected on the basis of repression and lends credence to the possibility that decrements in recall were due to stress-related interference rather than to repression.

To test the hypothesis that the decrements in recall following stress were due to interference rather than repression, I conducted two experiments in which subjects were exposed to either stressful, interfering, or neutral conditions (Holmes 1972; Holmes and Schallow 1969). In one experiment, the subjects first had their recall tested for a group of nouns. They then took a "multiple-choice Rorschach test" in which the words from the recall list were the response alternatives. During the test, the subjects in stress ("threatening feedback") condition received bogus feedback indicating that six of their ten responses were signs of serious pathology. Subjects in an interference ("enhancing feedback") condition received bogus feedback that their responses indicated that they were very creative and showed signs of leadership (i.e., something to think about that was not stressful). Finally, subjects in a control ("neutral feedback") condition received neutral personality feedback (Holmes 1972). After taking the bogus test, the subjects were again tested for their recall of the words. Finally, the subjects were debriefed concerning the deception, and their recall for the words was then tested again. The results indicated that, after the stress/interference manipulation, the subjects in the stress and interference conditions showed comparable levels of recall that were poorer than those of the subjects in the control condition. After being debriefed concerning the deception, the subjects in all the conditions showed comparable levels of recall. These results are presented in figure 2. From these results, it was concluded that decreased recall following stress was due to interference rather than to repression.

It could be argued that the comparable patterns of recall that were found in the stress and interference conditions were due to different processes. Specifically, it is possible that repression was operating in the stress condition and that interference was operating in the interference condition. It is impossible to demonstrate conclusively that identical processes were operating in the two conditions, but some data suggestive of that possibility are available (Holmes 1972). Specifically, if repression were operating, it would be expected that the decrement in recall would be greater for stimulus words that were directly associated with the stress (words used as responses that led to negative feedback) than for words that were not directly associated with the stress. That was not found to be the case; words that were not associated with the stress were just as likely to be forgotten as words that were associated with the stress. That effect could be accounted for better by interference than by repression. Once again, what originally appeared to be positive findings concerning repression were in fact due to another process, and therefore we must approach the study of repression in yet another way.

Individual Differences and the Search for Repression

Because there are numerous defense mechanisms (Holmes 1985a), it is not realistic to expect all individuals to use repression when exposed to stress. In some respects, that poses a problem for studying repression, but it also offers an opportunity because we can test for the existence of repression by comparing the recall patterns of individuals who are or are not expected to use repression. There are three lines of research in which this approach has been used. The most notable of these involves the use of the Repression-Sensitization Scale (R-S scale; Byrne, Barry, and Nelson 1963) to identify individuals who are expected to use repression. The R-S scale is made up of items from the Minnesota Multiphasic Personality Inventory (MMPI) that ask about the presence of symptoms. Individuals who do not acknowledge many symptoms are said to be "repressors," whereas individuals who acknowledge a high number of symptoms are said to be "sensitizers." This scale has been used in hundreds of studies of differential recall. Unfortunately, there is a very serious logical problem associated with the use of the R-S scale: there is no way to distinguish between individuals who actually have symptoms and do not report them ("repressors," or more likely deniers) and individuals who do not have symptoms and therefore cannot report them (nonrepressors). In other words, individuals without symptoms are falsely classified as repressors. Obviously, this scale cannot be used to support the notion that some individuals are more likely to use repression than others, and the use of the scale by researchers who did not consider the logic of the test has served only to add irrelevant data and erroneous conclusions to this body of literature.

The second line of research in which investigators attempted to link individual differences to the use of repression revolved around the complete/incomplete task recall paradigm (see the previous section). In this research, investigators examined the potential interaction between differential recall and personality factors such as ego strength, hysteria, hypnotizability, and need for achievement (Alper, 1946, 1948, 1957; Atkinson 1953; Atkinson and Raphelson 1956; Caron and Wallach 1957, 1959; Coopersmith 1960; Eriksen 1954; Jourard 1954; Petrie 1948; Rosenzweig and Sarason 1942; Tamkin 1957; Tudor and Holmes 1973; Weiner 1965; Weiner, Johnson and Mehrabian 1968). The only consistent finding in this line of research was that subjects with high need for achievement recalled more incompletions under high stress than low stress. It appears that, when subjects with high need for achievement were confronted with unsolvable problems in ego-involving situations, they persisted in working on or thinking about their failures rather than repressing them (Coopersmith 1960; Weiner 1965). Not only do these findings fail to provide support for the concept of repression, but they are the opposite to what would be predicted on the basis of repression.

The third line of research in this area was introduced by Schwartz, and it involves using measures of social desirability and anxiety (e.g., Davis and Schwartz 1987; Weinberger, Schwartz, and Davidson 1979; and see reviews by Davis and Weinberger, both in this volume). In these studies, subjects who had high scores on the Marlow-Crown Social Desirability Scale and low scores on the Taylor Manifest Anxiety Scale were identified as "repressors," and it was found that these subjects were less likely than other subjects to report stressful or unpleasant events. The problem is that individuals who are high on social desirability may be upset by and less willing to report undesirable events, but that does not mean that they are not aware of them. Indeed, the investigators reported that, although "repressors" did not report undesirable events, they showed higher physiological arousal than other subjects. If they had actually repressed the material and were unaware of it, they would not have been aroused. It is noteworthy that Schwartz and his colleagues were aware of the problem. In a footnote in one of their early articles, they wrote: "Although we propose retaining the term *repression* because of its use in the literature, the extent to which this defensive style is characterized by the use of repression relative to other defenses such as denial, negation and suppression is not currently known" (Weinberger, Schwartz, and Davidson 1979, 370). It is unfortunate that this important qualification concerning terminology was obscured in a footnote because many readers may have misinterpreted the evidence for denial as evidence for repression. Furthermore, Davis and Weinberger (both in this volume) were aware of the problem I have raised before they wrote their reviews but unfortunately elected not to address the problem. Overall, then, this research provides interesting documentation concerning the use of denial, but it does not provide evidence for the existence of repression. Once again, we are left without evidence for repression.

Perceptual Defense

Thus far, this discussion has been focused on "repression proper" or "after expulsion," but, before concluding, some brief attention should be given to "primary repression."

Theoretically, with primary repression the stressful materials are relegated to the unconscious before the individual even becomes aware of their existence. In studying primary repression, investigators have generally sought to determine whether subjects were less likely to perceive stressful than nonstressful material (see the review in Eriksen and Pierce 1968). For example, stressful and nonstressful words were flashed on a screen for very short periods of time, and it was the subjects' task to read the words. In most of the early research, it was found that the stressful words had to be on the screen for longer periods of time than nonstressful words before the subjects were able to read them, and it was therefore concluded that the subjects were defending against (repressing) the recognition of the stressful words by simply not seeing them. Unfortunately, subsequent research indicated that the difference in the time required for recognition of the two types of words was due to factors other than repression. For example, it turned out that the stressful words were less familiar than the nonstressful words, and familiarity influences recognition. It was also found that subjects were less willing to say the stressful ("dirty") words until they were absolutely sure that it was those words that were being flashed and that hesitancy rather than lack of recognition influenced their reporting of words. When familiarity was equated across the two types of words, and when social constrains were eliminated from the situation, the perceptual defense or repression effect disappeared.

About ten years ago, interest in perceptual defense was revived by Erdelyi, who proposed a variety of interesting cognitive theories to explain primary repression or perceptual defense (Erdelyi 1974; Erdelyi and Goldberg 1979). The problem is that, although Erdelyi offered explanations for the phenomenon, he did not provide controlled evidence that the phenomenon existed but instead relied on anecdotal clinical evidence. In other words, he offered an elegant and compelling explanation for a phenomenon that has not been demonstrated. Despite the lapse of over ten years, that situation has not changed, and therefore we are still without evidence supporting the existence of primary repression.

Conclusions

In conclusion, I want to make three points. First, I want to point out that, despite over sixty years of research involving numerous approaches by many thoughtful and clever investigators, at the present time there is no controlled laboratory evidence supporting the concept of repression. It is interesting to note that even most of the proponents of repression agree with that conclusion. However, they attempt to salvage the concept of repression by derogating the laboratory research, arguing that it is contrived, artificial, sterile, and irrelevant to the "dynamic processes" that occur in the "real world." That is an interesting argument, and I want to comment on it briefly before moving on.

With regard to its relevance, it is interesting to note that, when the laboratory research was initially published and appeared to provide support for repression, most theorists embraced the laboratory procedures as appropriate and cited the data as evidence for repression. Only when more refined research demonstrated that the data did not necessarily support repression did the advocates of repression turn their backs on the procedures. Note that the procedures had not changed, only the results. (It might be mentioned that Freud was a notable exception to the group that embraced the early laboratory demonstrations. When Rosenzweig wrote to him about his research on repression, Freud replied with disinterest, indicating that the concept did not need empirical support [see MacKinnon and Dukes 1964].)

Furthermore, by defining as irrelevant the many situations and stresses that have been employed in the laboratory investigations, the advocates of repression have severely limited the domain in which repression can supposedly operate. It is possible that we might someday find evidence for repression, but, because of the restrictions that have been imposed to protect the concept, it appears that the range of situations in which the concept can be applied will be so limited that it will be virtually useless.

After dismissing the laboratory research, the clinicians retreat to their consulting rooms for evidence for repression, but what evidence have they produced there? The "evidence" they offer consists only of impressionistic case studies, and, in view of the data concerning the reliability and validity of clinical judgments, those observations cannot be counted as anything more than unconfirmed clinical speculations—certainly not as "evidence" for repression. For a review of the reliability and validity of such clinical observations, I refer you to the excellent work of Mischel (1968). However, we need not go to that research because during this conference we had a dramatic demonstration of the unreliability of clinical judgments concerning repression when we watched the videotapes presented by Mardi J. Horowitz. The tapes were presented as a means of illustrating the use of repression by a client in therapy, but there was no agreement between the conferees concerning when, or even if, repression had occurred. Such unreliability is especially noteworthy in this group of individuals, who, by virtue of being invited to participate in this prestigious conference, must be defined as experts on repression. This is a serious blow to the clinical evidence.

It is important to note that my conclusion that there is no evidence for repression must *not* be interpreted as suggesting that repression does not exist because of course we cannot prove the null hypothesis. Those who choose to continue using the concept of repression may do so, but they must do so with the knowledge that, despite sixty years of research, there is no evidence for the concept. I think that our current regulations concerning "truth in packaging" and "protective product warnings" should be extended to the concept of repression. The use of the concept might be preceded by some such statement as, "Warning. The concept of repression has not been validated with experimental research and its use may be hazardous to the accurate interpretation of clinical behavior."

The second major point I wish to make is that, although there is no evidence for repression, it should not be concluded that there is not selectivity in perception and recall. Indeed, there is good evidence that transient and enduring factors such as cognitive sets, emotional states, and the availability of labels can influence what we perceive, store, and recall. The excellent work by Bower is clear testimony to the existence of such processes (Bower 1981). The important point here is that the processes underlying those effects are very different from the process of repression, and they lead to very different interpretations of the behavior.

It is important that we not misinterpret the evidence for those other processes as evidence for repression. The importance of making clear distinctions and discriminating between bodies of data is illustrated in the case of another defense mechanism, projection. For many years, evidence that individuals who were consciously aware of their traits and projected those traits onto others was mistakenly used as evidence for the projection of unconscious traits (see the reviews in Holmes 1968a, 1978, 1981a). The work of Schwartz and his colleagues has led to a parallel confusion in the area of repression (Davis and Schwartz 1987; Weinberger, Schwartz, and Davidson 1979). Their work on the influence of social desirability on recall and physiological responsiveness is fascinating and provides support for denial, but, as I pointed out earlier, it is not relevant to repression, and using it to support the concept of repression is erroneous and misleading.

In seeking evidence for repression, one could take the position of Humpty Dumpty, who pointed out, "When I use a word, it means just what I choose it to mean—neither more nor less" (Carroll 1960), and then simply define as "repression" the various processes that have been demonstrated to result in differential recall. That saves the term, but most of the important connotative features of the concept would have to be stripped away. It is better to keep the concept as it is but recognize that in its present form it is without empirical support.

Third, and finally, I would like to address briefly the question, Where do we go from here? It has been pointed out that in most cases "a theory is not overthrown by data but by a better theory" (Conant 1948). I agree, but I think that a distinction should be made between overthrowing a theory and abandoning a theory. We do not have another theory with which to overthrow repression, but despite numerous tests neither do we have data to support the theory, and therefore it might be appropriate to abandon the theory. From a practical standpoint, data provide the "bottom line." They are the test of the theory. If the data have been adequately collected but are inconsistent with what is predicted by the theory, then we must ask serious questions about the theory, elegant as it may be. The time has come to ask whether we should continue to pursue evidence for repression and whether we should now file the theory under "interesting but unsupported." The research on repression has been the preface to a larger area of research on factors that influence selective recall. From my perspective, the time has come to turn the page and begin focusing our attention and efforts on what may be more exciting and more productive lines of research related to information processing. One cannot prove the null hypothesis, and therefore we cannot conclude that repression does not exist, but, after sixty years of research has failed to reveal evidence for repression, it seems reasonable to question whether continued expenditure of effort on this topic is justified. Regardless of how fascinating the repression hypothesis is, the time may have come to move on. With regard to that possibility, a citation from Mischel is of interest. In his recent text, Mischel commented on Erdelyi's paper "Let's Not Sweep Repression under the Rug," which involves a defense of repression (Erdelyi and Goldberg 1979). However, Mischel "accidentally" cited the title as "Let's *Now* Sweep Repression under the Rug" (Mischel 1986, 534). That "Freudian slip" may very well have been prophetic. The time may very well have come for us to get repression behind us (or under the rug) so that we can move on.

References

Aborn, M. 1953. The influence of experimentally induced failure on the retention of material acquired through set and incidental learning. *Journal of Experimental Psychology* 45: 225–31.

Alper, T. 1946. Memory for completed and incompleted tasks as a function of personality: An analysis of group data. *Journal of Abnormal and Social Psychology* 41:403–20.

———. 1948. Memory for completed and incompleted tasks as a function of personality: Correlation between experimental and personality data. *Journal of Personality* 17:104–37.

———. 1957. Predicting the direction of selective recall; its relation to ego strength and *N* achievement. *Journal of Abnormal and Social Psychology* 55: 149–65.

Atkinson, J. 1953. The achievement motive and recall of interrupted and completed tasks. *Journal of Experimental Psychology* 46: 381–90.

Atkinson, J., and A. Raphelson. 1956. Individual differences in motivation and behavior in particular situations. *Journal of Personality* 24: 349–63.

Bower, G. H. 1981. Mood and memory. *American Psychologist* 36: 129–48.

Butterfield, E. 1964. The interruption of tasks: Methodological, factual, and theoretical issues. *Psychological Bulletin* 62:309–22.

Byrne, D., J. Barry, and D. Nelson. 1963. The revised repression-sensitization scale and its relationship to measures of self-description. *Psychological Reports* 13:323–34.

Caron, A., and M. Wallach. 1957. Recall of interrupted tasks under stress: A phenomena of memory or learning? *Journal of Abnormal and Social Psychology* 55:372–81.

———. 1959. Personality determinants of repressive and obsessive reactions to failure stress. *Journal of Abnormal and Social Psychology* 59:236–45.

Carroll, L. 1960. *The annotated Alice: Alice's adventures in Wonderland and through the looking glass.* New York: Potter.

Conant, J. 1948. *On understanding science: An historical approach.* New Haven, Conn.: Yale University Press.

Coopersmith, S. 1960. Self-esteem and need achievement as determinants of selective recall and repetition. *Journal of Abnormal and Social Psychology* 60:310–17.

Davis, P. J., and G. E. Schwartz. 1987. Repression and the inaccessibility of affective memories. *Journal of Personality and Social Psychology* 52:155–62.

D'Zurilla, T. 1965. Recall efficiency and mediating cognitive events in "experimental repression." *Journal of Personality and Social Psychology* 3:253–56.

Erdelyi, M. H. 1974. A new look at the new look: Perceptual defense and vigilance. *Psychological Review* 81:1–25.

Erdelyi, M. H., and B. Goldberg. 1979. Let's not sweep repression under the rug: Toward a cognitive psychology of repression. In *Functional disorders of memory,* (ed. J. F. Kihlstrom and F. J. Evans, 355–402. Hillsdale, N.J.: Erlbaum.

Eriksen, C. 1952a. Defense against ego threat in memory and perception. *Journal of Abnormal and Social Psychology* 47: 231–36.

———. 1952b. Individual differences in defensive forgetting. *Journal of Experimental Psychology* 44: 442–43.

———. 1954. Psychological defenses and "ego strength" in recall of completed and incomplete tasks. *Journal of Abnormal and Social Psychology* 49:45–50.

Eriksen, C., and J. Pierce. 1968. Defense mechanisms. In *Handbook of personality theory and research,* ed. E. Borgatta and W. Lambert. Chicago: Rand McNally.

Flavell. J. 1955. Repression and the "return of the repressed." *Journal of Consulting Psychology* 19:441–42.

Forest, D. 1959. The role of muscular tension in the recall of interrupted tasks. *Journal of Experimental Psychology* 58:181–84.

Freud, S. [1915] 1957. Repression. In *The standard edition of the complete psychological works of Sigmund Freud,* ed. Jo Strachey, vol. 14. London: Hogarth.

Gilmore, J. 1954. Recall of success and failure as a function of subjects' threat interpretations. *Journal of Psychology* 38:359–65.

Glixman, A. 1948. An analysis of the use of the interruption technique in experimental studies of repression. Psychological Bulletin 45:491–506.

Green, D. 1963. Volunteering and the recall of interrupted tasks. *Journal of Abnormal and Social Psychology* 66:392–401.

Holmes, D. S. 1968a. Dimensions of projection. *Psychological Bulletin* 69:248–68.

———. 1968b. The search for closure in a visually perceived pattern. *Psychological Bulletin* 70:296–312.

———. 1970. Differential change in affective intensity and the forgetting of unpleasant personal experiences. *Journal of Personality and Social Psychology* 15:234–39.

———. 1972. Repression or interference: A further investigation. *Journal of Personality and Social Psychology* 22:163–70.

———. 1973a. Differential recall of completed and incompleted tasks: Forgetting or learning. Psychology Department, University of Kansas. Typescript.

———. 1973b. Differential recall of pleasant experiences and personality. Psychology Department, University of Kansas. Typescript.

———. 1974. Investigations of repression: Differential recall of material experimentally or naturally associated with ego threat. *Psychological Bulletin* 81:632–53.

———. 1978. Projection as a defense mechanism. *Psychological Bulletin* 85:677–88.

———. 1981a. Existence of classical projection and the stress-reducing function of attributive projection: A reply to Sherwood. *Psychological Bulletin* 90:460–66.

————. 1981b. The use of biofeedback for treating patients with migraine headaches, Raynaud's disease and hypertension: A critical evaluation. In *Medical psychology: A new perspective,* ed. L. Bradley and C. Prokop, 423–37. New York: Academic.

————. 1983. An alternative perspective concerning the differential physiological responsiveness of persons with Type A and Type B behavior patterns. *Journal of Research in Personality* 17:40–47.

————. 1984. Meditation and somatic arousal reduction: A review of the experimental evidence. *American Psychologist* 39:1–10.

————. 1985a. Defense mechanisms. In *Encyclopedia of psychology,* ed. R. J. Corsini, 347–350. New York: Wiley.

————. 1985b. Self-control of somatic arousal: An examination of meditation and biofeedback. *American Behavioral Scientist* 28:486–96.

Holmes, D. S., and J. R. Schallow. Reduced recall after ego threat: Repression or response competition? *Journal of Personality and Social Psychology* 13:145–52.

Jerslid, A. 1931. Memory for the pleasant as compared with the unpleasant. *Journal of Experimental Psychology* 14:284–88.

Jourard, S. 1954. Ego strength and the recall of tasks. *Journal of Abnormal and Social Psychology* 49:51–58.

Lewin, K. 1940. Formalization and progress in psychology: Studies in topological and vector psychology. *University of Iowa Studies, Studies in Child Welfare* 16:9–44.

Lewis, H., and M. Franklin. 1944. An experimental study of the role of the ego in work. II. The significance of task-orientation in work. *Journal of Experimental Psychology* 34:195–215.

MacKinnon, D., and W. Dukes. Repression. In *Psychology in the making,* ed. L. Postman. New York: Knopf.

Meltzer, H. 1931. Sex differences in forgetting pleasant and unpleasant experiences. *Journal of Abnormal Psychology* 25:450–64.

Menzies, R. 1936. The comparative memory value of pleasant, unpleasant, and indifferent experiences. *Journal of Experimental Psychology* 18:267–79.

Merrill, R. 1954. The effect of pre-experimental and experimental anxiety on recall efficiency. *Journal of Experimental Psychology* 48:167–72.

Mischel. W. 1968. *Personality and assessment.* New York: Wiley.

————. 1986. *Introduction to personality.* 4th ed. New York: Holt, Rinehart & Winston.

Penn. N. 1964. Experimental improvements on an analogue of repression paradigm. *Psychological Record* 14:185–96.

Petrie, A. 1948. Repression and suggestability as related to temperament. *Journal of Personality* 16:445–58.

Prentice, W. 1944. The interruption of tasks. *Psychological Review* 51:329–40.

Rosenzweig, S. 1943. An experimental study of "repression" with special reference to need-persistive and ego-defensive reactions to frustration. *Journal of Experimental Psychology* 32:64–74.

Rosenzweig, S., and G. Mason. 1934. An experimental study of memory in relation to the theory of repression. *British Journal of Psychology* 24:247–65.

Rosenzweig, S., and S. Sarason. 1942. An experimental study of the triadic hypothesis: Reactions to frustration, ego-defense, and hypnotizability. I. Correlational approach. *Character and Personality* 11:1–19.

Russell, W. 1952. Retention of verbal material as a function of motivating instructions and experimentally induced failure. *Journal of Experimental Psychology* 43:207–16.

Sanford,R., and J. Risser. What are the conditions of self-defensive forgetting? *Journal of Personality* 17:244–60.

Smock, C. 1957. Recall of interrupted or non-interrupted tasks as a function of experimentally induced anxiety and motivational relevance of the task stimuli. *Journal of Personality* 25:589–99.

Stagner, R. 1931. The reintegration of pleasant and unpleasant experiences. *American Journal of Psychology* 43:463–68.

Tamkin, A. 1957. Selective recall in schizophrenia and its relation to ego strength. *Journal of Abnormal and Social Psychology* 55:345–49.

Truax, C. B. 1957. The repression response to implied failure as a function of the hysteria-psychasthenia index. *Journal of Abnormal and Social Psychology* 55:188–93.

Tudor, T. G., and D. S. Holmes. Differential recall of successes and failures: Its relationship to defensiveness, achievement motivation, and anxiety. *Journal of Research in Personality* 7:208–24.

Waters, R., and R. Leeper. 1936. The relation of affective tone to the retention of experiences in everyday life. *Journal of Experimental Psychology* 19:203–15.

Weinberger, D. A., G. E. Schwartz, and R. J. Davidson. 1979. Low-anxious, high-anxious, and repressive coping styles: Psychometric patterns and behavioral and physiological responses to stress. *Journal of Abnormal Psychology* 88: 369–80.

Weiner, B. 1965. The effects of unsatisfied achievement motivation on persistence and subsequent performance. *Journal of Personality* 33:428–42.

Weiner, B., P. Johnson, and A. Mehrabian. 1968. Achievement motivation and the recall of incompleted and completed examination questions. *Journal of Educational Psychology* 59:181–85.

Zajonc, R. D. 1968. Attitudinal effects of mere exposure. *Journal of Personality and Social Psychology Monograph Supplement* 9:2–27.

Zeigarnik, B. 1927. Uber das Behalten von erledigten und underledigten Handlungen. *Psychologische, Rorschung* 9:1–85.

Zeller, A. 1950. An experimental analogue of repression. II. The effect of individual failure and success on memory measured by relearning. *Journal of Experimental Psychology* 40:411–22.

———. 1951. An experimental analogue of repression. III. The effect of induced failure and success on memory measured by recall. *Journal of Experimental Psychology* 42:32–38.

5 Subliminal Perception and Repression

HOWARD SHEVRIN

In this chapter, I will be describing a narrowly circumscribed body of research bearing on the nature of repression. The boundaries of this body of research are defined by the use of subliminal stimulation for investigating unconscious processes. For my purposes here, I define "subliminal stimulation" as the presentation of a stimulus, usually visual, so quickly at the given levels of illumination that the viewer can either report seeing only a small portion of the stimulus or none of it.

After a brief presentation of the psychoanalytic concept of repression, a series of subliminal studies will be described purporting to investigate the nature of unconscious processes bearing on repression, followed by an assessment of these studies and ending with some suggestions for the future.

The Psychoanalytic Conception of Repression

Repression refers to the motivated forgetting of a particular mental content (referred to in psychoanalytic terminology as an "idea") related to a conflictual and objectionable wish. It might be more correct to refer to repression as a motivated inhibition of recall for two reasons: (1) we do not usually learn about repression until there is an attempt to recall a particular mental content, (2) according to the psychoanalytic theory of repression, the content is in fact not forgotten but remains unconscious and active, may undergo a variety of changes, and can influence other mental contents or actions. One might say that a repressed content is gone but *not* forgotten.

As an example of a clinical instance of repression, I cite the case of a young woman in analysis who in one session started to describe in great detail her sexual feelings for the analyst and her sexual anxieties, in particular about childbirth, which were disturbing to her. On the following day, she announced at the beginning of the session that she would like to continue talking about what she had been discussing the day before because she knew it had been important but that she could not remember any of it. As the session progressed, she found herself thinking of the novel *The Good Earth* and in particular of one scene in which the heroine goes out into the fields and gives birth. Although the analyst was fully expecting that at this point the patient would recall the previous session, the patient remained oblivious to the connection. Trying hard as she might, she could not recall what she knew to have been so important.

We see in this clinical example the inhibition of recall even when consciously desired and in the presence of an awareness of related or derivative contents (the heroine giving birth), but no awareness of their relationship to the repressed content. Nor is it reasonable to account for the failure of recall as caused by an absence of appropriate retrieval cues—the heroine giving birth would need to be considered a powerful retrieval cue. We can, however, also see the difficulty in the psychoanalytic conception of repression because the motivation for the repression, the key defining characteristic distinguishing it from ordinary forgetting, must be inferred. In the example, it is presumably the patient's conflict over her transference feelings toward the analyst, in particular her forbidden erotic feelings for him. Although clinically this may be persuasive, as Erdelyi has noted, "psychology has yet to develop a methodology of purpose" (1985, 259).

A much more frequent and commonplace form of repression, perhaps experienced by everyone at least several times a day, is to find oneself following a line of thought until one comes across a painful topic, at which point the topic is dropped and one thinks of something else. Up to this point, one can be said to be avoiding a painful thought, but it is not yet repression, one might be able to retrieve the painful content in a moment or two (for a study of momentary forgetting as an instance of repression, see Luborsky 1979). But, once avoided, it frequently happens that the content falls prey to repression, disappears from consciousness, and cannot thereafter be voluntarily recalled. Presumably, the initially avoided idea is drawn in more closely within the sphere of more deeply repressed material once attention is withdrawn from it. We see in this latter point another important factor in repression—the pull from underneath—from the direction of the repressed wishes.

The "why" of repression is presumed to be the motive, and, even though this "why" must usually be inferred, the "how" of repression—the processes by which it takes place—is equally difficult to establish. In his paper on repression, Freud ([1915] 1957) developed an attentional model for the "how" of repression, in which he reasoned that repression began with the withdrawal of attention, the initial avoidance previously described, but that this avoidant act is in itself not sufficient to maintain a repression because the repressed content is closely affiliated with a powerful wish or drive that exerts a pressure to become conscious. Put differently, the repressed content is closely allied with disavowed but important aspects of the person's affect life that do not cease their activity even though unconscious. Therefore, a more or less permanent counterforce must be conjectured to exist that goes beyond the initial withdrawal of attention. However, this counterforce is not uniformly effective, and certain derivatives or compromise formations emerge that are related to the repressed content, like the heroine giving birth, but are not consciously experienced as related.

It would follow from this understanding of repression that at least three different processes would need to be investigated: (1) the underlying unconscious wish actively pressing toward consciousness, (2) the initial withdrawal of attention from a derivative of this wish, and (3) an ongoing process of inhibition. I might tell you beforehand that no study to my knowledge meets these three criteria and to that extent it cannot be said that repression has been fully investigated. There are various approximations in which one or another of these three criteria are compromised or ignored. Nevertheless, these efforts constitute a series of halting steps in the right direction. Erdelyi (1985) has come to the same conclusion, stressing that, although all the necessary components of repression have been separately identified in the laboratory, their conjoint activity has not. I would add to this that the tendency of repressed wishes to strive toward consciousness and participate in producing derivatives or compromise formations is not sufficiently stressed in the experimental literature or in Erdelyi's otherwise excellent exegesis of the problem. His second criterion, that aversive stimuli tend to be avoided, comes close, but he does not ascribe to these aversive stimuli the active property of striving toward consciousness.

Subliminal Perception and Repression: Early Studies

The original subliminal technique developed by Poetzl ([1917] 1960) during World War I emerged from the confluence of two different streams: (1) the sensory neurology of brain-injured patients, and (2) Freud's psychoanalytic theory of dreaming. Thus, at the very beginning of subliminal research, we see a combination of the neurophysiological and the psychodynamic that was to disappear for some fifty years until the work of Libet et al. (1967) and Shevrin (e.g., Shevrin and Rennick 1967; Shevrin and Fritzler 1968a). Of further interest is the fact that this early work of Poetzl's and much of the subsequent work of Fisher (1956, 1957, 1960; Fisher and Paul 1959) did not focus narrowly on the operation of defenses as such but on demonstrating the existence of unconscious processes subject to various visual and symbolic transformations occurring during the course of recapturing the subliminal stimulus in dreams, images, and free associations.

These transformations were related by Poetzl and subsequently by Fisher to primary process changes affecting the subliminal stimulus. Poetzl hypothesized that these visual transformations of a primary process nature were caused by (1) primitive perceptual processes disinhibited either by damage to the visual cortex or by the brevity of exposure to normal subjects and (2) the impact of symbolic processes of psychodynamic relevance. Poetzl tacitly assumed that these symbolic transformations were a function of defenses because Freud, in *The Interpretation of Dreams* ([1900] 1953), had made out a strong case for primary process transformations resulting from the operation of defensive disguises. At the same time, Freud had carefully allowed for the role of sleep and dreaming as altered states to play a role in defining the nature of these nighttime thought processes. In fact, one could argue that in *The Interpretation of Dreams* Freud had attempted to combine his own dynamic, motivational theory with his older colleague Breuer's theory of altered states.

Breuer (Breuer and Freud [1893–95] 1955) had posited that hysterics fell prey to symptoms, in particular conversions, because they went into so-called hypnoid states more readily than others or because circumstances favored such alterations (i.e., nursing a sick father for hours on end). In these hypnoid states, dramatic distortions could take place, as, for example, seeing a hand as a snake. The symbolic transformations presumed to be characteristic of the altered state were then walled off from waking daytime consciousness and contributed to symptom formation. In effect, Breuer favored a dissociation theory, while Freud's theory was dynamic or motivational. As with Janet, one could not speak of a motive for the dissociated hypnoid state but rather of circumstances, either internal or external, producing the alteration in state: Janet posited a constitutional weakness in integrated consciousness, while Breuer favored both situational (e.g., fatigue) and dispositional factors. Breuer noted that these hysterical patients, for example, were very easily hypnotized. Indeed, Anna O. (Breuer and Freud [1893–95] 1955) was fully capable of hypnotizing herself. In the joint work with Breuer, Freud minimized the importance of altered states in favor of a motivational explanation.

However, in *The Interpretation of Dreams,* Freud acknowledged that there is a normal alteration of state of consciousness that is not motivated, certainly not defensively motivated. I refer to the radical shift in consciousness from waking to sleeping and back to waking, to which one must add the recent knowledge contributed by sleep-dream research about even more subtle shifts in consciousness within sleep itself that again cannot be accounted for on a motivational basis. Freud posited that the shift to dreaming sleep, a notable alteration in consciousness, resulted in a lessening of the repressive barrier, presumably because access to action was blocked, and thus in the more likely emergence in dream consciousness of blatantly repressed wishes (e.g., dreams of frankly oedipal gratifications) or, as is more frequently the case, of primary process disguises of such wishes in the form of condensations, displacements, and symbolic transformations. It was left unclear to what extent these transformations were a function of the emergence of powerful, unconscious, infantile wishes due to the lessening of repression and how much they were a function of the changed state of sleep. Both were clearly at work, and in this sense we can say that in *The Interpretation of Dreams* Freud tacitly incorporated Breuer's hypnoid hypothesis along with his own dynamic views.

This digression into Freud's dream theory was necessary because the early work on subliminal perception focused on dream recoveries of subliminal registrations (see Shevrin 1986). These early investigations drew on Freud's dream model, which incorporated states of consciousness and dynamic variables. Thus, Poetzl demonstrated that what was not consciously perceived in the briefly flashed picture (usually at one one-hundredth of a second) would emerge subsequently in reported dreams in some symbolically transformed manner that presumably would occur as a complex function of state changes and repressed wishes. But these two different factors were not disentangled.

In Fisher's pioneering work, the Poetzl technique was adopted to study not only the nature of primary process transformations but also the vicissitudes of the transference relationship to the experimenter and its bearing on the subject's past and current conflicts. Fisher's early studies were models of inventive empirical work closely linked to clinical observations and insightfully elaborated theoretically. Fisher's subliminal research provides a rich inventory of findings displaying the range and depth of subliminal effects that have been only partly exploited in subsequent more rigorous investigations. Among these findings, several stand out in particular: (1) confirmation of Poetzl's finding that subliminally registered aspects of the stimulus enter into dreams; (2) the apparent, immediate transformation of the *consciously* perceived aspects of the stimulus in the light of personal, symbolic meaning (more about this later); (3) the apparent immediate transformation of the registered, *preconscious* pictorial elements in various forms and their emergence in such responses as dreams, images, and free associations; and (4) the necessity to assume, as Poetzl had, that the stimulus registered in exquisite detail, almost photographically, although little of it was conscious at the time (this assumption was made necessary by the recovery of small, concrete details of the picture involving, for example, reversals of figure and ground and seemingly arbitrary fragmentation of the visual gestalts rarely occurring in waking consciousness).

Let me cite one example from Fisher's work. Following the tachistoscopic exposure of a photograph of two Siamese cats with a parakeet perched between them, one subject thought that she had seen two animals resembling dogs or pigs. In her drawing, the animals emerged as vaguely bird-like creatures with four legs (Fisher 1956, 23). In one of her images elicited by a word association procedure (to the word "dog" she had associated "house"), this subject drew a watchdog with a remarkably bird-like form, which she could not draw otherwise even though she was critical of her drawing, became confused, and could not understand why she continued to draw a bird, stating that she knew very well how to draw a dog and had done so many times. When the subject saw the bird on full reexposure, she immediately noticed the resemblance between the bird-dog and the parakeet, which she referred to as a "pigeon"—a designation that elicited a series of associations to her father, who apparently was cruel to animals and kept a large vicious dog that at one time bit the patient.

Fisher made note of the fact that, in the initial representation of the picture, a visual condensation of the consciously perceived animals and the bird was already present that had been registered but not consciously perceived. Moreover, these condensations appeared very quickly, in a matter of minutes, already influenced by significant early memories (e.g., father's vicious dog, etc.). Fisher hypothesized that the patient was struggling against revived unconscious anal sadistic wishes and that, despite her conscious "laundering" of the percept, it was therefore heavily tinged with these derivatives. Fisher argued that something like dream work had already begun at the moment that the picture was originally flashed. The registration did not simply remain unchanged until nighttime. Rather, the same unconscious forces were already at work in the daytime.

The logic of Fisher's argument is as follows. Primary process transformations of great personal significance are present almost instantaneously; these primary process transformations (e.g., condensations) are due to defensive efforts; therefore, the defensive process is already at work in the initial preconscious registration of the briefly flashed stimulus. The repressive process is not a delayed event occurring as a result of the changed state of sleep; rather, it is operating instantaneously with the exposure of the picture. Fisher's empirical approach and way of accounting for his findings have the merit of being quite close to the way a psychodynamic clinician functions; they have the disadvantage of not separating out independently the manifestations of defensive operations from the motives for them or the role that changes in states of consciousness might play. It should also be recalled that Poetzl had hypothesized that various visual transformations (e.g., figure-ground reversals) were due to the nature of vision and were not necessarily defensive in origin, although they might be put to defensive use.

Of particular relevance to the investigation of defenses with subliminal stimuli was Poetzl's original observation that a so called law of exclusion was at work. According to this law, items of the subliminally presented picture seen consciously were unlikely to be recovered in the dream, and, conversely, items not initially seen consciously would more likely appear in subsequent dreams. Shevrin and Luborsky (1958) were able to confirm this law of exclusion by collecting several repeated conscious recalls of the subliminal stimulus and to compare what was subsequently recalled consciously with what was recovered in the dream. They did, indeed, find that items recalled in subsequent conscious recalls were less likely to appear in dreams, and vice versa. The law of exclusion would appear to refer to a state-of-consciousness variable—the difference between waking and dreaming consciousness—and not directly to defenses.

However, Shevrin and Luborsky also found that, the more items recovered in the dream, the more unpleasant the dream was as rated by judges, suggesting that the recovered items became part of some anxiety-arousing defensive operation. This finding was still highly circumstantial and at some psychological remove from any concrete, individual act of repression. Further support for the law of exclusion was provided by Paul and Fisher's (1959) finding that subjects with a higher threshold for recognizing the subliminal stimulus recovered more of the stimulus in their dreams. The higher threshold finding calls to mind perceptual defense studies, although these studies were limited insofar as they did not show what happened to the defended against stimuli that are apparently available for subsequent recall in dreams. The subliminal studies based on the Poetzl technique demonstrated that what is not consciously perceived may then be drawn into dynamically unconscious processes, undergo various primary process transformations, and become part of dreams, images, or free associations.

These early studies drew heavily on psychodynamic theory to explain their findings, which certainly encouraged such interpretations. In retrospect, and in the light of hundreds of studies done subsequently (see Dixon 1981), the basic findings of these early studies have stood the test of time: much more registers of the stimulus during a brief flash than can be consciously reported; moreover, what is not reported can be recovered in dreams as well as in other forms. Recent masking studies such as those of Marcel (1983) have also found that registration is greater than conscious perception and that unreported stimuli effect subsequent responses, although the nature of these responses, selected solely on the basis of neutral cognitive characteristics, have limited relevance to psychodynamic hypotheses. In principle, this need not be the case; the masking technique can be adapted and used to explore such hypotheses.

Later Studies

The problem in the early Poetzl-type studies remained as to how to separate the factor of state from that of the dynamic operation of defenses. These early studies were also not characterized by systematic controls or reliability estimates. Subsequent studies by Fisher himself and others rectified this situation. A series of studies by Shevrin and colleagues (Shevrin and Fritzler, 1968b; Shevrin, Smith, and Fritzler 1969, 1970, 1971; Shevrin 1973) investigated defenses separately by including an assessment of individual repressiveness based on certain diagnostic characteristics. At the heart of this diagnostic assessment were assumptions about the long-term effects of a defense on thinking, reality testing, and character formation. A person who relies mainly on repression will show a pervasive lack of interest in ideation, know less about the world than his general level of intelligence would lead one to expect, and show a readiness to respond overemotionally to circumstances. When we have evidence for these traits on psychological tests, we infer that the person characteristically relies on repression as a defense.

It is important to stress that rarely do we have direct evidence of actual repression, that is, individual instances of repression. In effect, we make the inference on the basis of a probability model: given these characteristics, it is highly likely that the person relies on repression more often than on other defenses and more often than do people who are dissimilar in these respects. For this reason it is better to talk about *repressiveness,* that is, a tendency to repress, than about repression, referring to actual instances of repression (as apparently happened in the clinical example cited earlier). This is in principle no different from what any experienced clinician does in the course of a clinical examination. Tests make it easier to compare different people because they are administered and scored in a uniform and systematic manner.

In the Shevrin experiments, visual subliminal stimuli were related for the first time to the event-related potential (ERP), and, in addition, the design of the studies included individual assessments of repressiveness. Several of these studies had the further advantage of using twins, some of whom had discrepant repressiveness ratings and some of whom did not. The main findings emerging from these studies can be summarized as follows: high-repressive subjects as compared to low-repressive subjects responded with (1) a *smaller* ERP amplitude to a subliminal stimulus, (2) a *greater* ERP amplitude to the same stimulus when supraliminal, and (3) a *smaller* number of stimulus-related associations recovered in free associations.

The paradoxical reversal between the sub- and supraliminal amplitudes may be accounted for by the operation of two different tactics serving the same strategic goal. When the stimulus is subliminal, it is hypothesized that it is more likely to enter into a dynamically relevant repressive organization (see Poetzl [1917] 1960; Fisher 1956, 1957, 1960; Shevrin and Luborsky 1958), and thus a smaller response serves the strategic end of keeping awareness of the stimulus and its related ideas out of consciousness. When the stimulus is supraliminal, it is less likely to enter into such a dynamic, repressive organization, and thus increasing attention to it can serve to keep attention from being turned inward. When the stimulus was subliminal, a repressive act was more likely in progress. When it was supraliminal, an avoidant act was likely being used.

This formulation finds support in another study in which it was found that, when a subject had a greater ERP response to a subliminal stimulus, the subject showed a smaller response to a supraliminal stimulus presented simultaneously. The subliminal stimulus was visual, the supraliminal stimulus tactile (Shevrin and Rennick 1967). It was also found in that study that, when subjects free associated or did serial sevens while the tactile stimulus was being delivered and they were instructed to pay attention to time intervals between tactile stimulations, the amplitude of the ERPs was reduced to the tactile stimulus. This finding would fit with both Rapaport's (1967) and Kahneman's (1973) hypotheses that, at any given time, there is a limited reservoir of attention available and that, when a portion is devoted to one task, it is less available for another. I would add to this formulation that this shift in attention deployment may be motivated defensively and can involve a subliminal stimulus.

The subliminal studies that included repressiveness as a factor appeared to go beyond the earlier studies insofar as they separated out a defensive factor from a state factor. The concept of repressiveness itself, however, was inherently limited. It was, as already stated, based on a probability model involving certain assumptions relating cognitive and affective factors to character formation, which, it was assumed, determined the likelihood of using a particular defense like repression. These studies did not examine specific acts of repression. Freud's theory, as illustrated in my clinical example, dealt with individual defensive acts based on the conflictual significance of the material. Certainly, Freud would accept the proposition that there were dispositional elements involved in repression, but having the disposition and actually repressing at a particular time are not the same thing. The theory would appear to require that the personal conflictual relevance of the material be established, which thus far only a clinical assessment can provide.

Silverman's large body of research on subliminal psychodynamic activation might be considered as an effort in this general direction (see Silverman 1983), although Silverman was not interested specifically in repression or in defenses as such but in testing certain clinical hypotheses about the nature of psychopathology. Implicit in these hypotheses were the full range of dynamic defensive issues. Thus, in his research on aggression in schizophrenia (Silverman and Silverman 1967; Silverman and Candell 1970; Silverman et al. 1971), he hypothesized that an aggressive subliminal stimulus would tend to produce more thought pathology, presumably as a consequence of a further breakdown in defenses against such a cognitive regression. The "Mommy and I are one" message improved performance in a variety of diagnostic groups, presumably because it strengthened defenses, although here again the evidence is indirect and inferential. In the Silverman research, the subliminal stimuli were generic words or phrases selected to characterize a conflict applicable to an entire diagnostic group (e.g., schizophrenics) or indeed to anybody ("Mommy and I are one"). I will take up the problem posed by generic stimuli in the discussion section below (for a review and evaluation of Silverman's research, see Balay and Shevrin 1988).

In my own recent work (Shevrin 1988), I have attempted to base the experimental approach on a thorough clinical assessment of the patient. Words are selected from interview and test protocols that in the judge's mind capture the patient's conscious experience of a symptom (e.g., a phobia), are words that are considered to be related to the patient's unconscious conflict producing the symptom. These words, along with suitable controls, are presented both subliminally and supraliminally. Event-related potentials are obtained and the information content of the ERP's related to the pathological and control categories determined.

The main finding to emerge thus far is that, when presented subliminally, the pathological words are discriminated early (within four hundred milliseconds), but that, when they are presented supraliminally, they are discriminated later (between four hundred and seven hundred milliseconds) as compared to the control words. Additionally, the words related to the hypothesized unconscious conflict produce an even greater delay as compared to the words related to the conscious experience of the symptom, regardless of stimulus duration. These findings suggest that some kind of inhibitory process is operating when the pathological words are presented supraliminally and that this inhibition is greater for the conflict-related words even when they are presented subliminally, although subliminally the effect overall is still present earlier for all the words (Shevrin 1988). As long as the words are outside consciousness (i.e., presented subliminally), the pathological words can be discriminated early, much as is the case for the control words.

This finding is consistent with the cognitive hypothesis that preconsciously multiple codes are quickly activated, usually within several hundred milliseconds (Posner and Boies 1971). It is only when the words are presented supraliminally and thus emerge directly in consciousness that some inhibitory process appears to be at work affecting category discrimination for the pathological words. It maybe that this delay of approximately five hundred milliseconds is a function of the selective search for preconsciously activated codes that are not anxiety arousing. In terms of the psychodynamic model of repression cited earlier, this would mean that the delay was a function of the search for more distant derivatives of the conflict that can be permitted into consciousness. By the same token,this explanation would imply that the conflictual meaning of the words remains in a state of repression and could not readily enter consciousness. Interestingly, the similarity in direction of findings for the conscious symptom words and the unconscious conflict words, although different in degree, supports the psychoanalytic theory that symptoms are compromise formations in which significant derivatives of unconscious conflicts are present.

With research of this kind, we may be a step closer to investigating an actual repressive process insofar as the stimuli had been judged to be related to unconscious conflicts bearing on symptom formation; but we do not as yet have a clear look at the inner workings of that process in terms of either attentional or neurophysiological events related to consciousness. On the basis of much subliminal research, it can be said with some certainty that consciousness as such is a later and optional step (Shevrin and Dickman 1980). A considerable amount of cognitive and affective activity goes on prior to consciousness itself, and some of this cognitive activity may be much delayed in reaching consciousness or may do so in highly transformed ways—or may not reach consciousness at all. It would thus be very helpful to know something about the nature of consciousness itself as a system quite apart from the particular state in which it is activated.

Libet's work on the time parameters involved in activating consciousness for a tactile stimulus is of special importance in this regard (Libet 1965, 1966). He found that a certain critical time interval is necessary for the cortical recruitment involved in the act of becoming conscious. This time period averages about five hundred milliseconds poststimulus, although Libet discovered a considerable amount of individual variation—anywhere from two hundred to one thousand milliseconds. Could a portion of this individual variance be due to repressiveness as a predispositional factor? Would subjects rated high on repressiveness have a longer time interval before consciousness was activated?

Shevrin, Ghannum, and Libet (1987) have undertaken to answer this question. In a preliminary study based on six subjects, we did find encouraging results. Clinical judges basing judgments of repression on the Wechsler Adult Intelligence Scale (WAIS), Rorschach, and Early Memories tests could successfully predict the amount of time taken for cortical recruitment. The Hysteroid-Obsessoid Questionnaire (Caine and Hawkins 1963) also predicted the amount of time taken for cortical recruitment and thus provided an independent line of convergent evidence supporting the clinical judgments. These results suggest that Libet's finding may point to a neurophysiological factor predisposing some people to develop repression as a defense, much as a high IQ may predispose other people to develop intellectualization as a defense.

Discussion

In the classic psychoanalytic view of repression as originally described by Freud, the clearest examples were those of "after expulsion." An unwelcome thought or memory entered consciousness, the person withdrew attention from it (a fully conscious act), and then the thought or memory was further inhibited, in part by a so-called countercathexis and in part by being further drawn into more deeply repressed contents closer to the repressed wish. In other words, there were two forces at work simultaneously: (1) the conscious withdrawal of attention (avoidance) and (2) the pull from the direction of the dynamic unconscious.

In a certain sense, it is paradoxical that something repressed should appear in any form at all in consciousness. One would need to argue that repression was to a degree unsuccessful so that in any act of "after expulsion" one could say that initially repression must have failed. But the problem is more complex than that. At any given time, there must exist a complex balance or interaction of forces made up of the repressed wish, derivatives of that wish, environmental activations, and vicissitudes of attention. From this vantage point, it might be correct to say that there is never a fully repressed content, but rather a constant shifting among these forces with derivatives of greater or lesser distance from the repressed wish entering consciousness. When we add to this a set of transformations due to altered states of consciousness such as are induced by sleep and dreaming, the balance between the expressive and the repressive forces is always shifting.

The concept of altered state itself may be in need of further extension if we include the states of mind Horowitz (1979) and his coworkers have been exploring. Shifts in states of mind may be motivated but may also be the result of certain set patterns of self-other relationships that have become part of the individual's character structure and are in this sense attitudinal or dispositional but that nevertheless contribute to the balance of forces that at any given time determine whether an act of repression happens. Indeed, it is the "wiggle" in these shifts that the analytic process takes advantage of in free associations, slips, and symptoms.

Where does subliminal perception fit as an investigative tool in the exploration of repression? Its one main strength is that it can be used as a means for probing the nature of unconscious processes. If the probe itself is neutral, as in the Shevrin, Smith, and Fritzler (1970), twin study, then dispositional or personality factors such as repressiveness can be introduced to see how a neutral unconscious probe is affected by a repressive personality disposition. As we have seen, the evidence suggests that a repressive person responds less fully to the neutral subliminal probe, in terms of both a diminished brain response and fewer stimulus-related associations. If the subliminal probe is selected to be related to an unconscious conflict in a state of repression, then the brain process appears to reflect a significant delay supraliminally in discriminating the category belongingness of the probe, suggesting an inhibitory process perhaps related to a selective search for less anxiety-arousing derivatives.

Implicit in this hypothetical account of the results from subliminal research is an assumption concerning the key role of preconscious processes. In an earlier paper (Shevrin 1985), I ventured the thought that the psychoanalytic concept of the preconscious would serve as the bridge between cognitive science and psychodynamic theory, in particular as it has been developed by ego psychologists. Fisher developed a quite useful model for defining the role of the preconscious and subliminal stimulation. As early as 1957, he posited that every external stimulus first entered the psychic apparatus at a preconscious level, which meant that all incoming stimuli must go through a descriptively unconscious phase. When in this preconscious phase, links are made to memory, thus resulting in recognition.

With most supraliminal stimuli, the input is quickly delivered to consciousness, but not before a number of activations occur, some of which may in fact be influenced by dynamically unconscious forces. This model accounts for the possibility that even an ordinary supraliminal stimulus may fail to enter consciousness if the influence of dynamically unconscious forces is strong enough. For example, Brakel (1989) has reported some interesting clinical instances of patients in psychotherapy in which such actions as the psychotherapist falling asleep briefly are not noticed at all but are then dreamt about. Although the dreams reveal the preconscious registration of the sleeping therapist, the patient remains totally ignorant of the link to the actual stimulus, even when this is forcefully pointed out by the therapist.

With respect to a subliminal input, according to Fisher's model a complex interaction occurs preconsciously with memory traces and dynamically unconscious influences. In the early Poetzl work, when the stimulus was flashed at one one-hundredth of a second, it was possible for some of it to enter consciousness immediately and for the rest of it to be recovered later in images, free associations, and dreams. As in the Fisher example cited earlier, we saw how even the initial conscious perception of the subliminal stimulus can already be influenced by dynamically unconscious forces.

In Fisher's model, the repressive process begins preconsciously and is a function of the extent to which the preconsciously registered subliminal input is influenced by dynamically unconscious forces. Subliminal perception provides us with examples of a repressive process withdrawing a content from the *preconscious* rather than from *consciousness*. The input is no longer capable of entering waking consciousness directly as an item related to the stimulus, but it can be delivered in an indirect and unacknowledged form in dreams, images, and free associations. Parts of the subliminal stimulus enter consciousness for the first time as belonging to some other memory system or organization (see Shevrin, 1986, 1987 for extended discussion of subliminal stimulation, consciousness, and memory). In this way of understanding subliminal processes, it is strongly suggested that repression may be at work continuously and effects in particular the range of natural subliminal inputs that occur normally throughout the day. As Fisher pointed out, in addition to the day residues present briefly in consciousness and then later dreamt about, subliminal research has shown that countless more day residues may be present preconsciously than ever enter consciousness at all until they enter dream consciousness during the night.

What light does subliminal research throw on the manner in which repressed material is organized? As Balay and Shevrin (1988) point out in their review of Silverman's work, this issue is central to understanding the nature of dynamic unconscious organizations. Earlier I spoke of neutral stimuli and stimuli designed to be related to uniquely individual unconscious conflicts. In Silverman's research, a generic form of a conflict, or conflict resolution, is presented, the best-known example being, "Mommy and I are one." Can such generic representations of conflict work?

Freud in his paper on the unconscious ([1915] 1957) described the double registration of memories, by which he had in mind the patient who had a keen intellectualized understanding of his own Oedipus complex that he could describe to the analyst in great detail (perhaps with accuracy) but without any hint of benefit. Freud reasoned that the actual oedipal experiences had to be activated in the transference before resolution and change was possible. The first registration is generic, the second concrete and idiosyncratic. In cognitive science terms, we might say that the first form is related to semantic memory and the second to episodic, autobiographical memory (Tulving 1983).

If generic, subliminal stimuli work as well or better than concrete, specific ones, it might in fact tell us something about the way in which repressed memories are organized. The evidence from the Silverman work is ambiguous at best in this respect, and he himself appears to argue on both sides, as if he assumes that the "Mommy and I are one" message is at one and the same time general across people and uniquely relevant to each. Nevertheless, when told that in Virginia people say "Momma" and not "Mommy," he advised the researchers in Virginia to change the word to "Momma." But what of the rest of the message, in particular the "are one"? Is that beyond such individual modification?

Balay and I (1988) suggest that the inconsistencies in Silverman's results and the failure to replicate in other laboratories may in part derive from this generic approach to highly individual experiences organized at the level of episodic, autobiographical memories. In a recently completed study, Balay (1987) found that aggressive words, selected across a wide range of meanings so that one or more words might touch on some episodic memory, when presented subliminally to bipolar patients in remission, produced, as compared to normals, a significant reduction in form level of the Holzman ink blot test presented one card at a time immediately after a subliminal presentation as well as a significant increase in both aggressive and sexual content. These results fit with the psychoanalytic hypothesis that bipolar patients have special difficulty with aggression even during periods of remission and that activation of these feelings results in greater loss in reality testing and control over both aggressive and sexual derivatives of defended-against conflicts.

In future work, the effort needs to be made to combine careful clinical assessment with the refined use of sub- and supraliminal stimuli so that individual acts of repression can be directly identified. These individual acts can best be hypothesized as involving attentional processes, conflictual material of unique personal significance, linked to the individual's history. The proper investigation of these hypotheses must await the development of methods for independently identifying the influence of specific motives.

References

Balay, J. S. 1987. The role of aggression in bipolar affective disorder: A subliminal approach. Ph. D. diss. University of Michigan, Ann Arbor.

Balay, J., and H. Shevrin. 1988. The subliminal psychodynamic activation method: A critical review. *American Psychologist* 43, no. 3:161–74.

Brakel, L. A. W. 1989. Understanding negative hallucinations: Toward a developmental classification of disturbances in reality awareness. *Journal of the American Psychoanalytic Association* 37:2, 437–63.

Breuer, J., and S. Freud [1893–95] 1955. *Studies on hysteria.* In *The standard edition of the complete psychological works of Sigmund Freud,* ed. J. Strachey, vol. 2. London: Hogarth.

Caine, T. M., and T. G. Hawkins. 1963. Questionnaire measure of hysteroid-obsessoid components of personality: HOQ. *Journal of Consulting Psychology* 27:3.

Dixon, N. F. 1981. *Preconscious processing.* New York: Wiley.

Erdelyi, M. H. 1985. *Psychoanalysis: Freud's cognitive psychology.* San Francisco: Freeman.

Fisher, C. 1956. Dreams, images, and perception: A study of unconscious-preconscious relationships. *Journal of the American Psychoanalytic Association* 4:5–48.

———. 1957. A study of the preliminary stages of the construction of dreams and images. *Journal of the American Psychoanalytic Association* 5:5–60.

———. 1960. Subliminal and supraliminal influences on dreams. *American Journal of Psychiatry* 116:1009–17.

Fisher, C. and I. H. Paul. 1959. The effect of subliminal visual stimulation on imagery and dreams: A validation study. *Journal of the American Psychoanalytic Association* 7:35–83.

Freud, S. [1900] 1953. *The interpretation of dreams.* In *The standard edition of the complete psychological works of Sigmund Freud,* ed. J. Strachey, vols. 4, 5. London: Hogarth.

———. [1915] 1957. The unconscious. In *The standard edition of the complete psychological works of Sigmund Freud,* ed. J. Strachey, vol. 14, pp. 159–215. London: Hogarth.

Horowitz, M. J. 1979. *States of mind: Analysis of change in psychotherapy.* New York: Plenum.

Kahneman, D. 1973. *Attention and effort.* Englewood Cliffs, N.J.: Prentice-Hall.

Libet, B. 1965. Cortical activation in conscious and unconscious experience. *Perspectives in Biology and Medicine* 9:77–86.

———. 1966. Brain stimulation and the threshold of conscious experience. In *Brain and conscious experience,* ed. J. C. Eccles, 165–81. New York: Springer.

Libet, B., W. W. Alberts, E. W. Wright, and B. Feinstein. 1967. Responses of human somato-sensory cortex to stimuli below the threshold of conscious sensation. *Science* 518:1597–1600.

Luborsky, L., H.Sackeim, and P. Christoph. 1979. The state conducive to momentary forgetting. In *Functional disorders of memory*, ed. J. Kihlstrom and F. Evans, 325–53. Hillsdale, N.J.: Erlbaum.

Marcel, A. J. 1983. Conscious and unconscious perception: An approach to the relations between phenomenal experience and perceptual processes. *Cognitive Psychology* 15, no. 2:218–300.

Paul, I. H., and C. Fisher. 1959. Subliminal visual stimulation: A study of its influence on subsequent images and dreams. *Journal of Nervous and Mental Disease* 29, no. 4:315–40.

Poetzl, O. [1917] 1960. The relationships between experimentally induced dream images and indirect vision. In *Preconscious stimulation in dreams, associations and images: Classical studies*, ed. C. Fisher. *Psychological Issues*, vol. 2, no. 5, monograph 7. New York: International Universities Press.

Posner, M., and S. Boies. 1971. Components of attention. *Psychological Review* 78:391–408.

Rapaport, D. 1967. The theory of attention cathexis: An economic and structural attempt at the explanation of cognitive processes. In *The collected papers of David Rapaport*, ed. M. M. Gill, 778–94. New York: Basic Books.

Shevrin, H. 1973. Brain wave correlates of subliminal stimulation, unconscious attention, primary- and secondary-process thinking, and repressiveness. Monograph no. 30. *Psychological Issues* 8, no. 2:56–87.

———. 1985. The Freudian unconscious and the cognitive unconscious: Identical or fraternal twins? Paper presented at an invitational workshop at the Center for Advanced Study in the Behavioral Sciences sponsored by the John D. and Catherine T. MacArthur Foundation, Stanford, California, 14–17 July.

Shevrin, H. 1986. Subliminal perception and dreaming. *Journal of Mind and Behavior* 15, nos. 2–3:379–96.

———. 1988. Unconscious conflict: A convergent psychodynamic and electrophysiological approach. In *Psychodynamics and cognition*, ed. M. J. Horowitz. Chicago: University of Chicago Press.

Shevrin, H., and S. Dickman. 1980. The psychological unconscious: A necessary assumption for all psychological theory? *American Psychologist* 34:421–34.

Shevrin, H., and D. Fritzler. 1968a. Visual evoked response correlates of unconscious mental processes. *Science* 161:295–98.

———. 1968b. Brain response correlates of repressiveness. *Psychological Reports* 23:887–92.

Shevrin, H., J. H. Ghannam, and B. Libet. 1987. A neural correlate of consciousness related to repression. Typescript.

Shevrin, H., and L. Luborsky. 1958. The measurement of preconscious perception in dreams and images: An investigation of the Poetzl phenomenon. *Journal of Abnormal and Social Psychology* 56, no. 3:285–94.

Shevrin, H., and P. Rennick. 1967. Cortical response to a tactile stimulus during attention, mental arithmetic and free associations. *Psychophysiology* 3:381–88.

Shevrin. H., W. H. Smith, and D. Fritzler. 1969. Repressiveness as a factor in the subliminal activation of brain and verbal responses. *Journal of Nervous and Mental Disease* 149:261–69.

———. 1970. Subliminally stimulated brain and verbal responses of twins differing in repressiveness. *Journal of Abnormal Psychology* 76:39–46.

———. 1971. Average evoked response and verbal correlates of unconscious mental processes. *Psychophysiology* 8, no. 2:149–62.

Silverman, L. H. 1983. The subliminal psychodynamic activation method: Overview and comprehensive listing of studies. In *Empirical studies of psychoanalytic theories,* ed. J. Masling, vol. 1. Hillsdale, N.J.: Erlbaum.

Silverman, L. H., and P. Candell. 1970. On the relationship between aggressive activation, symbiotic merging, intactness of body boundaries, and manifest pathology in schizophrenics. *Journal of Nervous and Mental Disease* 150:387–99.

Silverman, L. H., P. Candell, T. F. Pettit, and E. Blum. 1971. Further data on effects of aggressive activation and symbiotic merging on ego functioning of schizophrenics. *Perceptual and Motor Skills* 32:93–94.

Silverman, L. H., and S. E. Silverman. 1967. The effects of subliminally presented drive stimuli on the cognitive function of schizophrenics. *Journal of Projective Techniques and Personality Assessment* 31:78–85.

Tulving, E. 1983. *Elements of episodic memory.* Oxford:Clarendon.

6 Hypnosis, Dissociation, and Trauma: Hidden and Overt Observers

DAVID SPIEGEL

As a phenomenon illustrating certain aspects of human consciousness, hypnosis has attracted theoretical attention for more than a century and has been a tool in the development of theories of mind as diverse and influential as Freud's psychoanalysis and Janet's dissociation theory. The persistence of interest in the phenomenon despite the varied uses to which it has been put attests to the possibility that hypnosis represents something fundamental about human consciousness that deserves examination in the light of current theories of cognition.

Hypnosis has been described in terms of the prevailing science of its day for two centuries, starting with the notion that psychological influence at a distance was linked to invisible forces such as magnetism, electricity, and gravity that were of great contemporary scientific interest (Ellenberger 1970). This association was similar to Freud's use of the hydraulic model in describing the psychic economy (Freud 1923). While these historical analogies are not always flattering, they point to the possible fertility of using models derived from current science in exploring the meaning of the transformation into the hypnotic state. Recently, there has been renewed interest in the hypnotic state as cognitive psychology has rediscovered the unconscious and has in turn been influenced by information-processing theory linked to computer systems (Kihlstrom 1987; Bowers 1976).

Computational Models of Consciousness

Parallel Distributed Processors

In a relatively simple computing system composed of a single processor and various storage units, work is done on information only when it gains

The preparation of this manuscript was supported by the John D. and Catherine T. MacArthur Foundation. The author also wishes to thank Bernard Baars and David Galin for their thoughtful critiques.

121

access to the processor: there it may be relabeled, transformed, or merged with other information. An analogy between such a central processing unit and consciousness will be explored below. However, by themselves, such systems are rather inflexible, using binary digital logic, which approximates human mental function poorly. This is where modeling using parallel distributed processing (PDP) systems has proved more fruitful. In such systems, a variety of processors can work on stored information simultaneously, creating patterns of interaction among networks of information that allow for approximate and pattern-recognition type response rather than a simple *yes* or *no* (Rumelhart and McClelland 1986).

The connectionist viewpoint holds that learning and memory can be successfully modeled on the basis of a pattern of interrelations or weightings among various elements of a network (McClelland and Rumelhart 1986). Input of given fixed values (i.e., a specific perceptual input) has the effect of activating the net by clamping components of it at a certain level of mutual excitation and inhibition. Given the history of relations between these and the remaining elements of the net or weightings, cycles of adjustment start to reverberate through the net, which assimilates the new information and leads to both a certain output from the net and to an accommodation in the relative weightings in the net; that is, it changes on the basis of the new input and thereby "learns." This model is interesting because it can respond to partial information with activation of related elements of a pattern. Thus, in a system like this, a miss is not as good as a mile. Partial information becomes extremely useful, so, for example, pattern recognition is possible when the input pattern is similar to but not identical to the pattern that has been previously stored (McClelland, Rumelhart, and Hinton 1986). Furthermore, from the point of view of dissociation, the model is interesting because it provides a mechanism for local learning via changes in connection weights without overarching global knowledge: "These learning rules are completely local, in the sense that they change the connection between one unit and another on the basis of information that is locally available to the connection rather than on the basis of global information about overall performance. The model thus stands as an alternative to the view that learning in cognitive systems involves the explicit formulation of rules and abstractions under the guidance of some explicit overseer" (McClelland and Rumelhart 1986, 214).

This connectionist view of memory is composed of a kind of bottom-up contentiousness; that is, interacting excitatory and inhibitory elements compose the net, and networks of nets can in turn excite and inhibit one another. More important, the parallel and distributed nature of these processors makes clear in the model something that must of course go on in the brain—that multiple decision tasks are conducted simultaneously. Thus, the model itself is both contentious and dissociated: its elements function autonomously and produce outputs that may form competitive relations with one another in other nets. Obviously, some hierarchical system must be developed to reduce these myriad simultaneous tasks to the reasonably, if not absolutely, sequential flow that we experience as consciousness. That is, we construct a sense of personal continuity through the maintenance of a consistent stream of memory and a kind of smoothing function under which we subsume disparate experiences under a common heading of personal identity (Kihlstrom 1987).

From this point of view, it is not remarkable that there are breaks in the continuity of personal identity, for example, in various dissociative and post-traumatic stress disorders (Spiegel, 1984, Spiegel, Hunt, and Dondershine 1988; Kluft 1984a, 1984b). Given the multiplicity of processors and occasions in which self-identity is designated, it is a complex network indeed that can integrate these disparate inputs, which are the outputs of other processors, and produce an apparently consistent, albeit subtly changing, self-concept. If memories are parallel and distributed, they are not automatically unitary, and therefore in structure they are dissociated. They function more or less autonomously, even though they may be integrated by some higher processor. McClelland and Rumelhart (1986) note that the distributed memory model fits traumatic amnesia well, for two reasons: (1) the fact that content learned may persist despite dense amnesia to the episode in which it was learned can be accounted for by the activation of weightings in the net despite the loss of the weightings associated with the episode itself, (2) large changes in connection strengths analogous to the effect of one traumatic experience do not always assist learning. Such memories are kept out of consciousness and yet exert effects that can be modeled using PDPs. The point is that such memories need not be integrated, and, if they involve self-concept, they may indeed be mutually exclusive of one another and/or compete with one another, yielding in the aggregate a dissociative disorder in which there is a discontinuity in personal identity and memory. It is the distributed nature of memory and its context dependence that makes dissociation potentially the rule rather than the exception.

Global Workspace

One other cognitive science model of consciousness that has intriguing application to the understanding of hypnosis is the global workspace model proposed by Baars (1988). In this model, an analogy is drawn between the structure of the conscious and unconscious mind and two major components of computer systems. Baars's analogy identifies consciousness with the processor in a simple computer, where the work of processing stored information occurs in rapid but clearly serial sequence, one operation at a time. Unconscious processes can be thought of as analogous to parallel distributed processors (PDPs), where numerous files, directories, and programs are available for use and are processed in a special purpose network with limited access to total data. Baars (1988) postulates in his global workspace theory that the domain of consciousness is defined by an interaction between the global workspace and parallel specialty processors that exert influence on one another, creating a context influencing the selection of certain files for activation and incorporation into the global workspace. He likens this to the competition among various factions in a legislature for access to the rostrum to address the entire body. While no computer analogy for human consciousness will be perfect, this theory holds certain attractions in accounting for hypnotic experience.

Absorption

Three major aspects of the hypnotic state that have been widely held to be defining characteristics are absorption (Tellegen and Atkinson 1974; Tellegen 1981), dissociation (Hilgard 1977), and suggestibility (Spiegel and Spiegel [1978] 1987). The *absorption* construct has been described as *"a disposition for having episodes of single 'total' attention that fully engage one's representational (i.e., perceptual, enactive, imaginative, and ideational) resources"* (Tellegen and Atkinson 1974). The typical experience employed in the questionnaire is that of the person who becomes so absorbed in a movie or a novel that he loses awareness of his surrounding environment and becomes fully engaged in the imagined world, experiencing himself, for example, as in the movie rather than in the audience. This concept built on earlier work by As (1962) and Shor (1960) on the correlation of the frequency of hypnotic-like experiences with hypnotizability and by Josephine Hilgard (1970) demonstrating a connection between imaginative involvements in early life and later high hypnotizability. According to this theory, the hypnotic experience is primarily one of intense absorption. The focal idea is attended to at the expense of any peripheral or contrasting experience.

From this point of view, the hypnotic experience is something like entering one directory in a simple DOS-type computer program without a path command linking it to the contents of other directories. Once one directory has been entered, the computer becomes frustratingly obtuse to the existence of needed programs in any other directory. The program that ran beautifully a minute ago simply will not function because the computer protests ignorance of the existence of DOS files stored elsewhere, for example. The absorption model of the trance experience is quite similar. A subject becomes so fully involved in the hypnotic metaphor, for example, floating in a warm bath, that the fact that he is actually sitting in a chair at ambient temperature disappears from awareness. The logical incongruity of feeling a pleasant, warm, floating sensation or picturing pleasant surroundings recedes from awareness, facilitated by the reduction or suspension of the need to analyze the realities of the situation logically and critically. After all, the body is not really floating or any warmer than it was a moment before. Rather, the hypnotized individual affiliates intensely with a metaphor involving mental and associated physical changes.

Further, such a hypnotized individual seems to lack metaconsciousness, awareness of being aware. Indeed, it has often been observed clinically that highly hypnotizable performers, such as actors and musicians, dissociate their ordinary awareness of themselves when they are performing and feel a reduced sense of agency. They often are embarrassed to take credit for a good performance. A highly hypnotizable pianist reported that her only memory of her graduation recital was of floating above the piano admiring the grain of the wood. She had to ask a stagehand whether she had in fact completed her program, which she had performed extremely well. A well-known author described the act of writing his novels as "taking dictation from a muse." The common hypnotic distortion of time perception and its link to absorption is clearly related to normal experience, well described by William James: "In general, a time filled with varied and interesting experiences seems short in passing, but long as we look back. On the other hand, a tract of time empty of experiences seems long in passing, but in retrospect short" (James 1890, 624).

Many experiences involve this narrowing of focus to the point at which the awareness of being aware is restricted. In hypnosis, multiple channels of information may be accessed, but there is awareness of only one of them being accessed: such trance experiences often seem short both in passing and in retrospect. A Vietnam veteran who spent forty-five minutes intensely reliving his combat experiences, in hypnotic age regression, recalled nothing of the session beyond two visual images immediately after (Spiegel 1981).

The absorption model is a powerful one and has been influential in the field, especially in the last decade, despite the fact that the studies of its association with measured hypnotic responsivity demonstrate a relation that is moderate at best. The correlation is on the order of .3 (Tellegen and Atkinson 1974), accounting for only 10 percent of the variance in hypnotizability scores, suggesting a significant but hardly complete contribution to the phenomenon of hypnotizability. However, one reason may be that it is hard to be both absorbed and aware of being absorbed, so self-reports may systematically underrepresent the true occurrence of absorption.

Dissociation

A second major component of the hypnotic experience is *dissociation*. This has been a classical component of the hypnosis literature from its very inception (Nemiah 1985) and has included major work done almost a century ago, for example, the study of intriguing cases of multiple personality disorder by

Morton Prince (1905), who founded the *Journal of Abnormal Psychology.* This work involved, among others, William James (1890) and Sidis (Sidis and Goodhard 1905), who were strongly influenced by Janet (1920).

One factor that distinguishes dissociation from repression is what happens to the material held out of consciousness. While Freud's first two topographies provide general rules of organization of unconscious material, they are vague at best: the material is either simply unconscious or perhaps associated more closely with id than superego. Dissociation as a model of defense, on the other hand, carries with it the implication of two or more incompatible mental contents that are structured so as to exclude one another from consciousness. This formulation implies that the unconscious material is stored in a certain form— specific contents associated with specific affects—with rules of interaction among various dissociated subunits. During his early period of interest in dissociation, Freud underscored the importance of conflict in the etiology of dissociative symptoms:

> It seems to me that the concept of a "defense hysteria" in itself implies that at least *one* moment of this kind must have occurred. Consciousness, plainly, does not know in advance when an incompatible idea is going to crop up. The incompatible idea, which, together with its concomitants, is later excluded and forms a separate psychical group, must originally have been in communication with the main stream of thought. Otherwise the conflict which led to their exclusion could not have taken place. (It is otherwise in hypnoid hysteria, where the content of the separate psychical group would never have been in the ego-consciousness.) It is these moments, then, that are to be described as "traumatic": it is at these moments that conversion takes place, of which the results are the splitting of consciousness and the hysterical symptom. [Breuer and Freud [1893–95] 1955, 167]

The ways in which different personality states in a multiple personality patient interact with one another are an example. Some personalities form alliances against others, for instance. This mental structure is reminiscent of PDPs, in which related sets of information are stored and processed independently of other sets. Stimulation of a certain personality state will tend to activate some and suppress others. A simpler example of such cohesive subunits is state-dependent memory, in which content and affect are stored interwoven and therefore retrieved together (Bower 1981). Thus, the attractiveness of the dissociation theory is that it provides a model for understanding unconscious interaction among dissociated subunits, a model that fits at least some clinical cases of dissociation. It is not that material that is simply repressed cannot also be active while unconscious. However, the rules of such interaction among repressed fears and wishes are more generic assumptions about the system as a whole than about the structure of any particular subunit and its relation to other particular subunits.

The concept of dissociation implies some kind of divided or parallel access to awareness. Several systems may co-occur, seemingly independently. This may take the form of a physical sense of dissociation in which, for example, a hypnotized individual experiences one hand as being not as much a part of his body as the other hand. The altered sensation, for example, lightness, tingling, and numbness, makes the hand seem to be constituted in a different relation to the rest of the body than the other hand, as though two separate systems for interpreting somatic perception were occurring simultaneously rather than one that incorporates similar sensations from all parts of the body. Clinical extremes of dissociation, which involves the spontaneous mobilization of hypnotic experience, include fugue states, in which an individual experiences a discrete and reversible but rather profound change of personal identity. For hours, days, or weeks, a person in a fugue functions as an individual who lacks memory of his usual personal identity. Such individuals may wander to a different city and get a new job. They sometimes stumble into a hospital emergency room, complaining that they cannot remember who they are. These fugues are usually quickly reversible with guidance under hypnosis. The formal induction of the hypnotic state with a structured reorientation in time, such as age regression to an earlier time, can help the person regain access to his or her normal personal identity memory stores. Another example is traumatic amnesia. A rape victim may lose all memory for events of the rape despite no actual loss of consciousness during the event. Nonetheless, these memories do not disappear and may be reaccessed, either through repeated interrogation or formal use of hypnosis (Wagstaff, Traverse, and Milner 1982; Spiegel 1980).

Perhaps the most extreme clinical form of dissociation is multiple personality disorder. These individuals experience themselves as dissociated into two or more distinct personalities, generally with different names, often of different ages, different predominant emotions, and different degrees of memory of what occurs when other personality states emerge: asymmetrical amnesia. Many of these personalities maintain rather distinct individual histories, engaging in certain kinds of activity with a distinct memory for what they did in the previous state but often unaware of what other personalities have done in the interim. One personality, for example, may be sexually provocative and physically self-destructive, while others of the personalities may consider themselves responsible, austere, and sexually celibate. These personalities often give the appearance of functioning quite independently or of being actively hostile to one another. Issues of control among them are major therapeutic problems. Some personalities designate themselves as protectors and try to organize and integrate the functioning of the various personalities, often with some difficulty (Kluft 1984a; Braun 1984). Most of these patients are extremely hypnotizable (Spiegel et al. 1987), and the dissociation can be viewed as a mobilization of spontaneous hypnotic ability in the service of defending against extreme environmental stress. These patients not infrequently have histories of severe physical, sexual, and emotional abuse (Spiegel 1984; Wilbur 1984; Kluft 1984b).

An analogy can be drawn between these dissociated mental states in multiple personality disorder and separate nets in a PDP model. This theoretical approach presupposes a pattern of storage of information organized into coherent subunits. The coherence of these subunits may include networks of meaning or connections between affect and content. The activation of one network tends to inhibit the activation of another competing network. Dissociation fits this model neatly in that it postulates the organization of stored information into coherent subunits that have their own rules of organization and interaction with other subunits. Thus, an analogy can be drawn between PDP nets and the extreme dissociation seen in multiple personality disorder, for example, in which each personality has a fairly exclusive store of memories, experiences, and identities that become manifest as a given personality obtains access to consciousness. Furthermore, each personality has a series of usually strong opinions about the other personalities. They experience themselves as in a battle for access to consciousness, and many of the personalities will often actively struggle to keep other personalities out of consciousness and thereby limit the ability of the latter to control what the patient does.

Similarly, this can be viewed as one complex network of nodal activation that tends to perpetuate and reinforce its own activation and access to the processor or global workspace while at the same time sending inhibitory commands to competing networks. Being in a dissociated state is analogous to working in one directory of a computer without being able to access the main menu indicating the presence of other directories and without path commands enabling the directory to find information needed from another directory. The presence of the material in one directory makes the computer act as though the other material does not exist. As long as it operates, it can be seen as actively inhibiting the expression of the content of other directories, and, without path commands or a menu, the dominant directory keeps the other programs out of the user's awareness. While most theories of human cognition account in some way for the fact that the majority of material is out of awareness, the rules for access to awareness vary greatly, depending on one's theoretical orientation (e.g., psychoanalytic, cognitive behavioral, social learning, etc). What is attractive about the dissociationist viewpoint is that rules of access of information into consciousness can be encoded into the content and affect of the unconscious material itself. A network encoding condiments is relatively more receptive to salt than it is to rocks when it is looking for sugar. The rules of interaction are thus diverse and distributed among the networks processing information: hence the virtue of a PDP model in which numerous interactions among dissociated subunits can occur, leading to a hierarchy of access to the central processor, the global workspace, or consciousness.

In this model, part of the power of consciousness is its ability to straddle and merge otherwise disparate and even conflicting networks. In a central processing unit, a computer can take information from any of a variety of directories, use a program to sort it and compute with it, and return it altered to its original files or create new ones. The central unit can bypass or change the usual rules of interaction: it can merge files that previously had no contact with one another. Likewise, in consciousness, previously unconnected strands of a person's life history may come together in a new way. A word may acquire a new meaning that stimulates the development of a different associational network than existed previously, for example, on its appearance in a new or different context; or, in psychotherapy, a patient with a dissociative disorder may learn to see dissociated elements of self as aspects of one broader self that need not conflict intensely. From this point of view, the psychotherapy of dissociation is like writing path commands in a computer—broadening simultaneous access to otherwise incompatible information. For example, Vietnam veterans have benefited from hypnotic imagery that allows them to grieve the loss of friends in combat in conjunction with happy earlier times with them. One such patient commented, "I had not allowed myself to think of those good times ever since his death" (Spiegel 1981).

Hilgard (1977) has expanded on the concept of hypnotic dissociation by developing neodissociation theory, built on Janet's description of the mind rather than Freud's. Hilgard emphasizes a horizontal rather than a vertical depiction of the relation between conscious and unconscious states. Rather than viewing access to consciousness as archaeological, with unconscious material more deeply buried and harder to access, Janet's and Hilgard's theories postulate that there exists a series of available but unused aspects of consciousness near the surface. In the hypnotic state, two or more of these are activated, possibly without awareness. As evidence for this theory, Hilgard cites his work on the "hidden observer" (Hilgard, Morgan, and MacDonald 1975). He discovered this phenomenon while using hypnosis to eliminate pain among experimental subjects. After demonstrating that one highly hypnotizable subject was able to eliminate the discomfort in a hand immersed in a circulating ice water bath by simply making it numb, he said to the subject, still in trance, "Perhaps there is some part of you that is aware of some discomfort," then instructed the subject to signal how much pain he really felt by moving his finger. Using this method, the subject indicated that in fact he felt a considerable amount of pain. Hilgard labeled this portion of the subject's experience the *"hidden observer."* His and other work has shown that approximately one-third of highly hypnotizable subjects capable of these extreme perceptual alterations demonstrate the hidden observer phenomenon.

The essence of dissociation and neodissociation theory is that the unconscious subunits have organized structures and rules governing their interaction. Cognition, emotion, and action may be combined (Kihlstrom 1984) and therefore express certain organized function, seemingly autonomously and to the blissful exclusion of other organized subunits. Hilgard (1984) draws a tentative analogy between his and others' laboratory observations of the hidden observer phenomenon and clinical observations of multiple personality disorders. He refers to a controversial but interesting study by Watkins and Watkins (1979–80) in which patients with different ego states were given hidden observer instructions with regard to pain. They observed that some but not all of the alternative ego states demonstrated the hidden observer phenomenon.

The hidden observer theory has been criticized as an artifact (Spanos and Hewitt 1980; Spanos 1983). However, Lawrence and Perry (1981) found that a similar proportion of high hypnotizables undergoing hypnotic age regression, that is, reliving aspects of their past as though they were occurring in the present, demonstrate similar hidden observer phenomena. They relive the past as though it were occurring in the present but maintain a hidden consciousness that in fact they are adults reliving earlier life experiences. Yet two-thirds of these high hypnotizables do not maintain this observing consciousness. The proportions are puzzling. Why is it that some do and some do not demonstrate this hidden observer phenomenon?

The problem is even bigger, in that it is not immediately obvious what the relation between absorption and dissociation is. While both are clearly associated with hypnotic experience, neither phenomenon seems able to account fully for the other. Is it possible to develop some theory that can incorporate both in a systematic description of hypnotic experience? The reader will not be surprised to discover below a modest proposal.

Neoabsorption Theory and the Hidden Observer

Using the global workspace model, for the purposes of this discussion consciousness is represented as a serial processor accessing several competing parallel systems, perhaps five to nine at any one time, analogous to Miller's (1956) description of "The Magical Number Seven, Plus or Minus Two," as a limit on the "amount of information that we are able to receive, process, and remember" (233). In ordinary consciousness, one has metaconsciousness, that is, the awareness of sampling among all these processes, whereas, in hypnotic consciousness, one is *aware* of only one of the parallel systems or contexts. Although several other systems may be active in immediate memory available to the global workspace, one experiences them as dissociated, hence the automaticity and amnesia associated with hypnosis. Thus, the range of access of consciousness to parallel systems may be the same in trance and nontrance conditions, but the experience is one of being hooked into only *one* of the parallel systems or contexts. This could account for the trance experience of absorption as being in only one "directory" and unaware of the existence of other "directories," the non–hidden observer kind of hypnotic regression. The hidden observer may be someone who is less thoroughly hypnotized, with conscious access to *two* parallel systems rather than *one*—however, not five to nine as in ordinary awareness.

Thus, the theory postulates that in normal consciousness the global workspace is roughly but not exactly analogous to a serial processor in that more than one but a limited number of parallel processors are available for utilization and operating in consciousness at any one time—for the sake of argument, somewhere between five and nine, with rapid cycling among them. This is congruent with our ordinary experience: we are aware of physical sensations, such as body position, as well as hunger or sexual interest while at the same time thinking about a particular problem, planning the contiguous day's activities, and feeling some lingering sadness over a friend's recent illness. There is a long tradition in the psychoanalytic movement of utilizing the concept of preconscious to differentiate materials out of immediate awareness but instantly available to it from deeply repressed memories and fantasies, and this seems to be a useful distinction. We experience ourselves as being able simultaneously to process at least two or three and possibly as many as nine different concepts, emotions, and perceptions. Thus, it makes sense to think of consciousness as a window to parallel programs accessible to the global workspace. Self-consciousness is the awareness of processing them.

Consider, then, that what may happen in the transition into a hypnotic state is that while the actual window of consciousness remains the same size, that is, it is processing the same seven plus or minus two bits of information, the hypnotized individual experiences the window as if it were smaller, as though it were processing only one bit of information. This would fit the absorption aspect of hypnosis perfectly. The hypnotized person is aware of only one percept, memory, or experience. He relives the past as though it were occurring in the present, disconnecting it from his ordinary historical perspective, for example.

How, then, can this model account of dissociation? It would postulate that the window remains the same size but that the experience of the window is restricted. The same number of parallel programs, perhaps five to nine, are actively sampled and processed in the global workspace, but the hypnotized individual has only one of them as an object of consciousness. Dissociation fits rather nicely into this model. Other experiences continue to be processed, but out of awareness: they are not objects of consciousness. For example, dissociation of the left hand experienced in the Hypnotic Induction Profile protocol (Spiegel and Spiegel 1978) implies that the hand is connected under a different and unclear set of rules than that applicable to the rest of the body.

It is not that the ordinary experience of the hand is unavailable—it is simply not accessed. Indeed, the phenomenon of discussion becomes apparent when the subject is asked to *compare* two different experiences, as in the hidden observer paradigm. Also, the dissociated awareness of identity in the fugue state is in theory accessible at any time but is experienced as unavailable. Patients with multiple personality disorder can in fact switch in seconds to awareness of most if not all of their dissociated personalities, albeit in sequence. Yet at any one time their consciousness is limited to one or perhaps two. This is different from the ordinary waking experience of the normal person or nondissociated patient, who may, in fact, be very different in mood, cognition, and behavior in different states of mind (Horowitz 1979), but the differences are not reinforced by amnesia for experience in the various states. Thus, in the hypnotic state, the serial processor *seems* more limited than it *is* because the choice among available competing contexts is restricted. Thus, what would be processed as a request to perform a certain activity in ordinary awareness becomes compulsive compliance and suggestibility in the hypnotic state. The source of the instruction may be forgotten (Evans 1980), and the compliance is experienced as automatic because it is disconnected from the source (Spiegel and Spiegel 1978).

This theory holds that the hidden observer phenomenon is not so much the essence of hypnotic dissociation as it is less than complete dissociation. So far, this position has not been supported by examination of correlations between the hidden observer phenomenon and standardized scales of hypnotic responsivity; that is, the theory might receive support were hidden observers to score lower on hypnotizability scales than nonhidden observers. Such has not proven to be the case (E. R. Hilgard, personal communication, 1988). However, this may simply be a reflection of the limitations of the scales and the items employed to distribute scores at the extreme upper end of the scales. The measures may not be able to discriminate these fine gradations of response. Another test of the theory might be in the performance of a specific hypnotic task. In theory, it should be possible to demonstrate whether the hidden observer is capable in fact of a complete and independent description of a hypnotically dissociated experience. It is very difficult to test this problem reliably in the paradigms that have previously been used, pain and hypnotic age regression (Hilgard, Morgan, and MacDonald 1975; Hilgard 1984; Lawrence and Perry 1981), since subjects can report that they were in a great deal of pain, whether or not they actually were. Similarly, they can report that they were aware of their ordinary age and orientation during hypnotic age regression whether or not this was the case. Thus, an experimental design should involve using a task in which retrieval of content is necessary to validate the hidden observer's reports of awareness.

Per se, this window theory of hypnotic dissociation could allow for separate nonconscious complete parallel processing of all perception, which is simply isolated from awareness via amnesia, according to Hilgard (Hilgard and Hilgard 1975), and yet retrievable by a hidden observer. If our inferences about the data are correct, they would suggest that the narrowing of the awareness of the size of the window actually affects the way in which the percepts are processed. This is consistent with recent evoked potential studies demonstrating that hypnotic visual hallucinations that should obstruct perception of stimuli on a television monitor in fact reduce the amplitude of the late components of the cortical evoked response to the visual stimuli (Spiegel et al. 1985). This study, and a more recent replication using somatosensory perceptual alteration (Spiegel, Bierre, and Rootenberg 1989), provide evidence that a hypnotically dissociated percept is not completely processed out of conscious awareness; rather, cortical processing of it is reduced as its perception is reduced. Given this evidence and the fact that the hidden observer phenomenon occurs only in about one-third of highly hypnotizable subjects (Hilgard 1977), the hidden observer phenomenon can be viewed as only a partial explanation of hypnotic dissociation, but a useful one to illustrate the broader phenomenon.

Many experiences involve this narrowing of focus to the point at which the awareness of being aware is restricted. In hypnosis, multiple channels of information may be accessed, but the awareness is that only one of them is being accessed. The window remains the same size, but it seems smaller. The global workspace remains global but is perceived as regional. The hidden observer may be a compromise between the pure dissociated and unitary awareness of the extremely highly hypnotizable patient and the ordinary awareness of multiple or conflicting experiences that we might call the "*overt observer.*"

The Experience of Self: The Overt Observer

It is no accident that the issue of dissociation is often raised in conjunction with the concept of self. Kihlstrom's (1984) theory postulates that the difference between co-consciousness and consciousness, in Prince's and Janet's term, is the assignment of "self" as a label applied to the network of associations or memories. Those that include a representation of self, or a metaconsciousness, are conscious; those that function without such an association are co-conscious or unconscious. The problem is that, as Kihlstrom (1984, 196) notes, people in dissociated states "lose themselves," for example, in movies. Thus, the absorption in a unitary dissociated state seems to involve not a recognition of self-attribution but rather the suspension of it or, indeed, the lack of self-*awareness* as a monitoring function. The self-schema may exist more in the relation among elements than as a content of any particular element. Indeed, in multiple personality disorder, the differing "selves" may in part be related to the asymmetrical amnesia. That is, each cluster of dissociated elements carries with it a different self that emerges from its role in regulating its own subset of elements. Each personality in such a patient has a complex structure of relations among elements that involve a subgroup rather than the totality of the person. The awareness of self, as in the hidden observer, is colored by selective choice of memories, experiences, and desires. One personality may be the perennial pathetic victim, another sexually demonstrative, a third self-destructive. The self is not generic but rather derives from the process of mediating elements and the particular set of elements that is mediated. However, the intriguing point about neodissociation theory is that it suggests that subunits of the whole can function semiautonomously rather than requiring the whole structure for any one piece to manifest its meaning. The functioning of the whole may be influenced by a misperception of the number of elements influencing it, especially when the structure of these elements is such that they pretend to autonomous functioning by being able to link memory, affect, intention, and action. One or more parts act as if each were the whole.

This notion of the self as a mediating function rather than a collection of attributes means that awareness of self emerges from processing, from choosing among experiences. In this sense, self is not an ordinary object of consciousness but rather a subject of consciousness. The self is seen as a relation to objects rather than an object in itself, reminiscent of the dialectical models of Hegel ([1841] 1931) and certain phenomenologists (Kierkegaard [1849] 1954; Bergson [1889] 1960). Intense absorption involves active processing with the suspension of self-awareness because of the narrow focus of awareness on the content of the experience. This applies for brief periods during normal absorption, for example, while watching a good movie or in a performance. In more pathological situations such as spontaneous fugue states, the individual loses ordinary awareness of self and may experience a change in self in fugues or competing selves in multiple personality disorder. Dissociation emerges because the sense of integration that comes from awareness of mediating among several cognitive and perceptual functions at once is lost. These functions still occur, but awareness of mediating among them does not. In patients, this may serve important defensive purposes. For example, during and after a trauma, the awareness of self becomes extraordinarily painful. The rape victim who was made into an object to be humiliated during the assault finds the notion of self contaminated by fear and pain. Suspension of this view of self becomes a welcome rather than a frightening experience. One patient with a previous history of dissociative disorder experienced a rape in her early twenties. She dissociated to a person named "No One" during the rape and then had repeated spontaneous experiences of the emergence of this alternative personality. The name itself was fascinating. She was made to feel like a "nobody" during the rape, and at the same time the defensive purpose of this dissociation was served by her retrospective view that "No One" was raped.

Indeed, many patients with multiple personality disorder have one or more personalities that are identified as "regulator" personalities with responsibility for ordering the contents of consciousness, that is, deciding which personality is "out" at any one time. The fragmentation comes in that the regulation function is somehow separated from the remainder of self or selves. There is not the continual reinforcement of self-concept that emerges from the management of conflicting desires, perceptions, thoughts, and interaction. Rather, selfhood is experienced as something asserted intermittently and periodically, usually to resolve power struggles among competing selves.

The connection between hypnotic dissociation and trauma has received support from an apparently minor unexpected finding of Josephine Hilgard's (1970) in her retrospective study of childhood experiences that were correlated with later high hypnotizability. Her major findings were that a history of imaginative involvement and identification with the opposite-sex parent was associated with higher hypnotizability, providing general support for her theory that a well-developed capacity to trust was a prerequisite for high hypnotizability. However, the third correlate with hypnotizability as measured by Form C of the Stanford Hypnotic Susceptibility Scales (Weitzenhoffer and Hilgard 1962) $(r = .30, N = 187)$ was severity of punishment in childhood. This punishment variable was negatively correlated with parental warmth. Hilgard speculated at the time that "a possible tie between punishment and hypnotic involvement might come by way of dissociation. . . . Although we have no direct evidence, some of our case material . . . suggests that reading or other involvements may sometimes be an escape from the harsh realities of a punitive environment" (Hilgard 1970, 220). This finding emerged despite the fact that the sample consisted of nonpatient students at a private university. Indeed, when Frischholz (1985) reanalyzed Hilgard's data, he found that a multiple correlation combining imaginative involvement and punishment yielded a significantly higher correlation with later hypnotizability $(r = .44)$ than either alone. It is important to note that this was a retrospective study, subject to possible biases in recollection of early life events. That is, people who differ in hypnotic capacity may also differ in the way in which they experience and later recall events.

More recently, two studies have shown a significant positive correlation between hypnotizability and the symptoms of posttraumatic stress disorder among Vietnam combat veterans (Stutman and Bliss 1985; Spiegel, Hunt, and Dondershine 1988). These findings suggest that dissociation serves as a defense during trauma, allowing some individuals to experience painful events as though they had happened to a different "self" (Spiegel 1986). This defense trades awareness of immediate physical helplessness during trauma for a subsequent sense of psychological helplessness, with intrusive recollection of the events (absorption), the loss of pleasure in usually enjoyable activities (dissociation), and extreme sensitivity to stimuli reminiscent of the trauma (suggestibility), as described in DSM-III-R (American Psychiatric Association 1987). This suggests a strong dissociative component to the symptomatology of posttraumatic stress disorder.

Thus, absorption in a special state and suspension of self-consciousness can be a normal "regression in the service of the ego" (Gill and Brenman 1959), to optimize concentration and performance, or it can be defensive, to eliminate the contamination of the self-concept with memories of a traumatic experience.

At the same time, dissociation carries with it the implication of association, of the other personality states warded off. Fugue, amnesia, and multiple personality patients usually carry with them an uneasy awareness that something is wrong, that there lurks some hidden truth about them that is frightening, demeaning, or demoralizing. At the least, they are troubled by episodes of lost time, accusations that they have done or said things they cannot remember, awakening in a strange bed. They are not uncommonly depressed, as though they were somehow aware of the arbitrary boundaries of their own self-definitions and the reason for such limitation of self. There is a certain comfort that comes from the continuity of self, the awareness of ongoing mediation despite the diversity of stimuli. In normal awareness, security of the self-concept in fact facilitates dissociation for specific purposes, such as intense concentration in performing. To experience a continuity of self, one needs to be not only performer but also audience. In formal and spontaneous trance experience, these functions are separated. Subjects may be totally absorbed in one or the other role and lose the continuity of selfhood associated with mediation of these various functions.

This model of consciousness postulates that the development of stable and unitary self-consciousness is an achievement, not a given. Mental contents are processed in a complex and relatively independent fashion, making it possible, if not probable, that more than one self may emerge (Jaynes 1976; Galin 1974). What is surprising is not that strange syndromes such as multiple personality disorder occur but rather that they do not occur more often.

The hidden observer can be understood as self-consciousness of less than total absorption. It emerges because of Hilgard's ability to elicit comparison of two types of pain experience, one with and one without benefit of hypnotic analgesia, or rather one that focuses on the pain perception itself and one that focuses on the competing hypnotic metaphor of tingling numbness or warmth. The overt observer is the unified self-concept that emerges out of the mediation of experiences, perceptions, thoughts, and emotions. It does not exist in any one state of absorption in perception or memory, but it emerges from the ability to contrast and compare among them. The capacity to observe oneself is suspended in the narrow focus of hypnotic absorption, begins to emerge in the comparison of two states, as in the hidden observer condition, and exists more fully in ordinary awareness. The fullest overt self-observation is nondissociated and emerges out of the interaction of various contents of perception and experience with the process of selecting among them. The main point is that the experience of self is not simply another mental content but rather emerges out of the comparative assessment of the self's management of mental contents. Descartes's self-concept (and ours of him) emerged when he *compared* thinking to being, not from his thinking alone. When these processes are isolated, as in extremes of dissociation such as fugue and multiple personality, the experience of self is similarly fragmented. As Kierkegaard ([1849] 1954) put it, "The self is a relation which relates itself to its own self. . . . the self is not the relation but [consists in the fact] that the relation relates itself to its own self" (146).

Suggestibility

"The absence of criticism in auto-hypnotic states is the reason why auto-suggestions so frequently arise from them" (Breuer and Freud [1893–95] 1955, 216]—some of the commonly observed suggestibility in hypnosis can be accounted for in this way. It is not that the hypnotized person is unable to say no—but that it does not occur to him to do so. The metaphor presented becomes all absorbing, and any implied action is a natural consequence.

The compulsive tendency among patients with dissociative disorders referred to in the earlier literature as "suggestibility" is interwoven with instability in the Self-concept. Firm direction applied by an outsider is not countered by an internal orientation: the input mediation function is limited and awareness of it restricted. Such patients often rationalize their compulsive compliance with an inner sense of inferiority. "Who am I to decide when he seems to know what to do?" The structuring attempts of the outside supplant rather than struggle with internal direction. One such patient described herself as a "disciple in search of a teacher." Hypnotic suggestibility can thus be understood as a limitation in the ability to conceive of alternatives (Spiegel 1974). Not only does the intense absorption of the trance state make a suggested action, for example, "Your hand will feel light and float up in the air like a balloon," seem to be the only obvious choice, restricting the range of perceived alternative actions, both for that hand and for any other kind of physical activity, but it also suspends the range of perceptions about sources of the idea for such activity; that is, the *content* enters consciousness via the hypnotic instruction shorn of its context. The *source* of the instruction is not fully attended to as a separate piece of information. Instead of then saying, "This person wants me to let my hand float up in the air," the hypnotized person experiences the instruction as though it were self-, rather than other, generated: "My hand feels light." The self-other distinction suffers from the lack of competing contexts, and so any instruction for action, any ideomotor stimulus, is identified as self-generated, even though it is in fact generated by someone else.

William James (1890) conceived ideas to be invitations to action rather than mere imprints of perception. Why then, he wondered, do we not act on every idea we have? Lying in bed on a cold morning, he observed how he prolonged his stay there. Each image of his getting up, lighting a fire, and getting dressed was edited by competing ideas reminding him of the cold and the hours before he was required to appear at the university. Consider what happens in a hypnotically absorbed state. With only one idea in mind, the editing function is reduced or eliminated. Thus, such individuals are prone to act rather than consider and hence are "suggestible."

Keeping this model in mind, in hypnosis, unlike ordinary awareness, the same processes of perception and choices about attending to internal versus external stimuli continue, but conscious awareness is narrowed to the *content* of the instruction, not its source, or other competing instructions. Therefore, the performance of the instruction comes to *seem* automatic. The subject is responsive to a source and yet strangely unaware of it. He experiences the levitated hand as dissociated, as though it were responding to a different set of commands than the rest of his body, not because it is, but because the context of that hand's activity has been isolated from the context of the remainder of the body's activity, which has not been the object of an ideomotor instruction. This is related to the often observed phenomenon of posthypnotic source amnesia, in which an individual will comply with an instruction but forget where the instruction came from (Evans 1980). The absorption in the content restricts awareness of the source of the information. In the absence of this information, the person tends later to attribute it to self, to act as though it were something he *wanted* to do. In order to understand and act on the thought that a competing idea is in somebody else's best interests rather than his own, it is necessary to maintain awareness that the instruction comes from outside the self. The narrowed focus of awareness makes that more difficult. This becomes a serious problem in living for high hypnotizables, who tend too easily to identify as *self*-generated instructions from *others* that are not uncommonly not in the patient's best interest (Spiegel, 1974).

Conclusion

In summary, dissociation and absorption are seen as complementary and essential aspects of hypnosis. The guiding premise is that the processor in the global workspace is engaged in a reasonably uniform and continuous task of processing competing contexts, allowing certain of them into consciousness, and that ordinary awareness involves a broader awareness of competing contexts that have access to the work of this processor than does hypnotic consciousness. In hypnosis, the processor continues as usual, but awareness of its work is restricted. Absorption in one aspect of the work makes the carrying out of the remaining tasks seem more automatic than it is and hence more dissociated. Dissociation is compatible with a PDP analysis of mental function, modeling in consciousness the function of distributed nets that process information in parallel. Furthermore, the conception of self is understood as arising out of an awareness of the executive task of mediating among distributed processors. Anything restricting the domain of nets being processed will therefore alter the self-concept. Among the psychiatric disorders, those most commonly presenting with a disturbance of self-awareness (i.e., fugue states and multiple personality disorder) are those that involve hypnotic dissociative phenomena and alterations in the continuity of memory. Clinically, dissociation involves a fragmentation of consciousness and automaticity, usually for defensive purposes. Theoretically, dissociation is the logical consequence of absorption in a mental system that processes far more information than the absorbed, hypnotized, individual can maintain in consciousness or be aware of processing.

References

American Psychiatric Association. 1987. *Diagnostic and statistical manual of mental disorders* 3d ed., rev. Washington, D.C.: American Psychiatric Press.

As, A. 1962. Nonhypnotic experiences related to hypnotizability in male and female college students. *Scandinavian Journal of Psychology* 3:47–64.

Baars, B. J. 1988. *A cognitive theory of consciousness.* Cambridge: Cambridge University Press.

Bergson, H. [1889] 1960. *Time and free will: An essay on the immediate data of consciousness.* Trans. F. L. Pogson. New York: Harper & Row.

Bower, G. H. 1981. Mood and memory. *American Psychologist* 36:129–48.

Bowers, K. S. 1976. *Hypnosis for the seriously curious.* Monterey, Calif.: Brooks-Cole.

Braun, B. G. 1984. Towards a theory of multiple personality and other dissociative phenomena. *Psychiatric Clinics of North America* 7:171–93.

Breuer, J., and S. Freud. [1893–95] 1955. *Studies on hysteria.* In *The standard edition of the complete psychological works of Sigmund Freud* ed. J. Strachey, vol. 2. London, Hogarth.

Collins A. M. and E. F. Loftus. 1975. A spreading-activation theory of semantic processing. *Psychological Review* 82:407–28.

Ellenberger, H. F. 1970. *The discovery of the unconscious.* New York: Basic.

Evans, F. J. 1980. Phenomena of hypnosis. II. Posthypnotic amnesia. In *Handbook of hypnosis and psychosomatic medicine,* ed. G. D. Burrows and L. Dennerstein. New York: Elsevier/North-Holland.

Freud, S. [1895] 1966. Project for a scientific psychology. In *The standard edition of the complete psychological works of Sigmund Freud,* ed. J. Strachey, vol. 1.

――――. [1923] 1961. The ego and the id. In *The standard edition of the complete psychological works of Sigmund Freud*, ed. J. Strachey, vol. 19. London, Hogarth.

Frischholz, E. J. 1985. The relationships among dissociation, hypnosis, and child abuse in the development of multiple personality disorder. In *Childhood antecedents of multiple personality,* ed. R. P. Kluft. Washington, D.C.: American Psychiatric Press.

Galin, D. 1974. Implications for psychiatry of left and right cerebral specialization: A neurophysiological context for unconscious processes. *Archives of General Psychiatry* 31:572–83.

Gill, M. M., and M. Brenman. 1959. *Hypnosis and related states: Psychoanalytic studies in regression.* New York: International Universities Press.

Hegel, G. W. F. [1841] 1931. *The phenomenology of mind.* Trans. J. B. Baillie. New York: Macmillan.

Hilgard, E. R. 1977. *Divided consciousness: Multiple controls in human thought and action.* New York: Wiley.

――――. 1984. The hidden observer and multiple personality. *International Journal of Clinical and Experimental Hypnosis* 32:248–53.

Hilgard, E. R., and J. R. Hilgard. 1975. Hypnosis in the relief of pain. Los Altos, Calf.: Kaufmann.

Hilgard, E. R., A. H. Morgan, and H. MacDonald. 1975. Pain and dissociation in the cold pressor test: A study of hypnotic analgesia with "hidden reports" through automatic key pressing and automatic talking. *Journal of Abnormal Psychology* 84:280–89.

Hilgard, J. R. 1970. *Personality and hypnosis: A study of imaginative involvement.* Chicago: University of Chicago Press.

Horowitz, M. J. 1979. *States of mind: Analysis of change in psychotherapy.* New York: Plenum.

James, W. 1890. The consciousness of self. In *Principles of psychology,* vol. 1. New York: Holt.

Janet, P. 1920. *The major symptoms of hysteria.* New York: Macmillan.

Jaynes, J. 1976. *The origins of consciousness in the breakdown of the bicameral mind.* Boston: Houghton Mifflin.

Kierkegaard, S. [1849] 1954. *Fear and trembling and the sickness unto death.* Trans. W. Lowrie. New York: Doubleday.

Kihlstrom, J. F. 1984. Conscious, subconscious, unconscious: A cognitive perspective. In *The unconscious reconsidered,* ed. K. S. Bowers and D. Meichenbaum. New York: Wiley.

――――. 1987. The cognitive unconscious. *Science* 237:1445–52.

Kluft, R. P. 1984a. Multiple personality in childhood. *Psychiatric Clinics of North America* 7:121–34.

――――. 1984b. Treatment of multiple personality disorder. *Psychiatric Clinics of North America* 7:9–29.

Lawrence, J. R. and C. Perry. 1981. The "hidden observer" phenomenon in hypnosis: Some additional findings. *Journal of Abnormal Psychology* 90:334–44.

Marcel, A. J. 1983. Conscious and unconscious perception: An approach to the relations between phenomenal experience and perceptual processes. *Cognitive Psychology* 15:238–300.

McClelland, J. L., and D. E. Rumelhart. 1985. Distributed memory and the representation of general and specific information. *Journal of Experimental Psychology* 114:159–88.

———. 1986. A distributed model of human learning and memory. In *Parallel distributed processing: Explorations in the microstructure of cognition*, vol. 2, *Psychological and biological models*, ed. D. E. Rumelhart and J. L. McClelland. Cambridge, Mass.: MIT Press.

McClelland J. L. D. E. Rumelhart, and G. E. Hinton. 1986. The appeal of parallel distributed processing. In *Parallel distributed processing: Explorations in the microstructure of cognition*, vol. 1, *Foundations,* ed. D. E. Rumelhart and J. L. McClelland. Cambridge, Mass.: MIT Press.

Miller, G. A. 1956. The magical number seven, plus or minus two: Some limits on our capacity for processing information. *Psychological Review* 63:81–97.

Nemiah, J. C. 1985. Dissociative disorders. In *Comprehensive textbook of psychiatry,* 4th ed., vol. 1, ed. H. I. Kaplan and B. J. Sadock. Baltimore: Williams & Wilkins.

Prince, M. 1905. *The dissociation of a personality.* London: Longmans, Green.

Rumelhart, D. E., and J. L. McClelland, eds. 1986. *Parallel distributed processing Explorations in the microstructure of cognition.* Vol. 1, *Foundations.* Cambridge, Mass.: MIT Press.

Seidenberg, M. S., M. K. Tanenhaus, J. M. Leiman, and M. Bienkowski. 1982. Automatic access or the meanings of ambiguous words in context: Some limitations of knowledge-based processing. *Cognitive Psychology* 14:489–537.

Shor, R. E. 1960. The frequency of naturally occurring "hypnotic-like" experiences in the normal college population. *International Journal of Clinical and Experimental Hypnosis* 8:151–63.

Sidis, B., and S. P. Goodhart. 1905. *Multiple personality.* New York: Appleton-Century-Crofts.

Spanos, N. P. 1983. The hidden observer as an experimental creation. *Journal of Personality and Social Psychology* 44:170–76.

Spanos, N. P., and E. C. Hewitt. 1980. The hidden observer in hypnotic analgesia: Discovery or experimental creation? *Journal of Personality and Social Psychology* 39:1201–14.

Spiegel, D. 1981. Vietnam grief work using hypnosis. *American Journal of Clinical Hypnosis* 24:33–40.

———. 1984. Multiple personality as a posttraumatic stress disorder. *Psychiatric Clinics of North America* 7:101–10.

———. 1986. Dissociating damage. *American Journal of Clinical Hypnosis* 29:123–31.

Spiegel, D., P. Bierre, and J. Rootenberg. 1989. Hypnotic alteration of somatosensory perception. *American Journal of Psychiatry* 146:749–54.

Spiegel, D., S. Cutcomb, C. Ren, and K. Pribram. 1985. Hypnotic hallucination alters evoked potentials. *Journal of Abnormal Psychology* 94:249–55.

Spiegel, D., E. J. Frischholz, L. S. Lipman, and N. Bark. 1989. Dissociation, hypnotizability and trauma. Paper presented at the annual meeting of the American Psychiatric Association, San Francisco, 8 May.

Spiegel, D., E. J. Frischholz, H. Spiegel, L. S. Lipman, and N. Bark. 1987. Hypnotizability and dissociative psychopathology. Paper presented at the annual meeting of the Society for Clinical and Experimental Hypnosis, Los Angeles, 29 October.

Spiegel, D., T. Hunt, and H. F. Dondershine. 1988. Dissociation and Hypnotizability in posttraumatic stress disorder. *American Journal of Psychiatry* 145:301–5.

Spiegel, H. 1974. The grade 5 syndrome: The highly hypnotizable person. *International Journal of Clinical and Experimental Hypnosis* 22:303–19.

———. 1980. Hypnosis and evidence: Help or hindrance? *Annals of the New York Academy of Sciences* 347:73–85.

Spiegel, H., and D. Spiegel. [1978] 1987. *Trance and treatment: Clinical uses of hypnosis*. Washington, D.C.: American Psychiatric Press.

Stutman, R. K., and E. L. Bliss. 1985. Posttraumatic stress disorder, hypnotizability, and imagery. *American Journal of Psychiatry* 142:741–43.

Tellegen, A. 1981. Practicing the two disciplines for relaxation and enlightenment: Comment on "Role of the feedback signal in electromyograph biofeedback: The relevance of attention" by Qualls and Sheehan. *Journal of Experimental Psychology: General* 110:217–26.

Tellegen, A., and G. Atkinson. 1974. Openness to absorbing and self-altering experiences ("absorption"), a trait related to hypnotic susceptibility. *Journal of Abnormal Psychology* 83:268–277.

Wagstaff, G. J., J. Traverse, and S. Milner. 1982. Hypnosis and eye-witness memory—two experimental analogues. *IRCS Medical Sciences: Psychology and Psychiatry* 10:894–95.

Watkins, J. G., and H. H. Watkins. 1979–80. Ego states and hidden observers. *Journal of Altered States of Consciousness* 5:3–18.

Weitzenhoffer, A. M., and E. R. Hilgard. 1962. Stanford Hypnotic Susceptibility Scale, Form C. Palo Alto, Calif.: Consulting Psychologists Press.

Wilbur, C. B. 1984. Multiple personality and child abuse. In *Multiple personality*, ed. B. G. Braun, Psychiatric Clinics of North America, vol. 7. Philadelphia: Saunders.

7 Unconscious Influences and Hypnosis

KENNETH S. BOWERS

The scientific investigation of hypnosis has always been fraught with methodological and conceptual hazards (see, e.g., Hull 1933; Bowers 1984a; Spanos 1986). The same can be said of the scientific investigation of unconscious processes (see, e.g., Bowers and Meichenbaum 1984; Erdelyi 1985). Clearly, anyone who has the audacity to explore both domains is subject to double jeopardy.

Wisely or not, I have been actively engaged in both areas (Bowers 1984a, 1984b), though, until now, I have had the good sense to maintain them as more or less separate and distinct domains of inquiry. The integration of hypnosis and of unconscious processes seems to be my present mandate, however, so I will attempt in a very preliminary way to place hypnotic phenomena in a broader frame of reference—one that emphasizes the role of unconscious influences on thought and behavior.

I will proceed by first introducing what I call Type I unconscious influences. Type I influences determine thought and behavior in a manner that is unnoticed, subtle, inexplicable, and/or disavowed by the ordinary, intact person trying to understand his or her behavior. I will argue that Type I influences are not very important for understanding hypnosis, even though some people argue (erroneously, I think) that indirect and subtle forms of suggestion are the apotheosis of hypnotic influence. Type I influences are important, however, for understanding ordinary attitude and behavior change that social psychologists have studied in the laboratory for years, and they often have a profound effect in psychotherapy (Frank 1973) and in the marketplace (Cialdini 1985).

Type II unconscious influences, on the other hand, involve changes or discontinuities in how ordinary information is processed. For the most part, Type

This manuscript was prepared with the help of a grant from the Spencer Foundation. I would like to thank Patricia Bowers, Debra Hughes, and Mark Zanna for their comments on an earlier draft. Portions of this chapter were presented as an invited address, entitled "Suggestion and Subtle Control," on 24 August 1982, at the annual convention of the American Psychological Association, Washington, D.C.

143

II influences are not typically addressed by social psychologists, but I will argue that full-blown hypnotic responsiveness requires elucidation in terms of them. As well, Type II unconscious influences are likely to operate while a person is asleep, drugged, fatigued, or in a state of high arousal.

I should emphasize, however, that hypnotic behavior is a complex and subtle phenomenon that is multidetermined by exogenous (e.g., role-prescribed) as well as endogenous factors (e.g., Kihlstrom 1986). So, in emphasizing the effect of Type II influences on hypnosis, I am not denying the effect of situational cues and demands on hypnotic behavior (e.g., Orne 1959; Bowers 1973; Evans and Orne 1971). I am, however, denying that such task and role demands are entirely sufficient to account for hypnotic phenomena. Thus, my position is distinct from the social psychological theory of hypnosis proposed by Spanos (1986). According to this theory, hypnosis is reducible to acting in accordance with various unambiguous demands to behave and experience in accordance with hypnotic suggestions. The last sections of this chapter will detail some conceptual and empirical reasons why I think such a social psychological position is inadequate to a complete understanding of hypnosis.

One caveat is in order at this point. Hypnosis, is not, per se, very concerned with the issue of defense. Defenses typically involve a threatening impulse or perception that the person avoids representing in conscious experience. The dissociations involved in and revealed by hypnosis (Hilgard 1977) for the most part are not operating as a defense against such threats.

Nevertheless, hypnotic dissociations can function to keep certain kinds of information out of consciousness—a state of affairs that is most evident when posthypnotic amnesia is suggested. Further, when dissociative-type defenses have been mobilized to keep unpleasant information and impulses out of awareness, hypnosis may occasionally be helpful in disinterring such "forgotten" material. Finally, hypnosis has occasionally been used to study artificially induced conflict and psychopathology (e.g., Reyher 1967). But, for the most part, hypnosis per se can be viewed as a relatively conflict-free domain of investigation, which can nevertheless teach us a great deal about how information can be unconscious, conflict free, and influential, all at the same time.

Type I Unconscious Influences

Two previous articles (Bowers 1984, 1987) are for the most part devoted to an analysis of Type I unconscious influences (though I am introducing the present typological notation for the first time here). I will briefly summarize the basic position that is treated at greater length in those papers.

Perception without Noticing

An unreconstructed behaviorist would surely insist that a stimulus must be perceived in order to reinforce and shape behavior but just as surely reject any claim that a perceived stimulus must be consciously represented in order to be an effective mover and shaper of behavior. In the worldview of such a Skinnerian-type behaviorist, consciousness of a stimulus is not implied by the perception of it but is instead considered to be only one of its possible effects (e.g., Skinner 1963).

Accordingly, all that is required to document perception is discriminative behavior. However, even very low-level organisms are capable of perception thus indexed, and I assume that there is really no question of awareness or consciousness ever playing a role in the discriminative behavior of say, worms or ants. It is for this reason that I think that Dennett's (1969) reference to such discriminative behavior as reflecting awareness$_2$ is misleading (for a summary of Dennett's nomenclature, see Bower, in this volume). I prefer to speak of such simple discriminative behavior as reflecting perception without noticing (Bowers 1984). It is one of the ironies of contemporary cognitive psychology that perception without noticing (unconscious perception, if you will) is subject to continuous challenges when the discriminative behavior of humans is at issue (e.g., Holender 1986). The assumption seems to be that, once consciousness has emerged, we are incapable of discriminative behavior that does not involve it. I find this assumption quite unlikely on a priori grounds, and recent experimental work has challenged it with ever more methodological sophistication (e.g., Cheesman and Merikle 1986).

First-Order Consciousness

Given sufficient grey matter for selective attention to emerge as a biological possibility and sufficient stimulus energy impinging on sensory receptors to be selectively attended, we have the necessary conditions for what I refer to as first-order consciousness (Bowers 1987). In effect, first-order consciousness implies that selective attention has transformed something perceived into something noticed. Thus, we can speak of "perceived information" when referring to information that simply engenders discriminative responsiveness and reserve the term "noticed information" for perceived information that is, in addition, selectively attended and therefore consciously perceived. Humans can typically verbalize noticed information, so first-order consciousness corresponds reasonably well to Dennett's awareness$_1$. However, I am perfectly willing to assume that many animals are capable of selective attention—and hence of first-order consciousness—even though they are not capable of verbalizing the contents of consciousness.

In a very insightful paper that deserves more attention than it has received, Lundh (1979) emphasizes the difference between perception and noticing, though casting the distinction in his own terminology. He asserts that "the failure to distinguish clearly between perceptions . . . on the one hand, and introspective awareness of these perceptions . . . on the other hand, is a major source of confusion in psychology" (227). For example, it is precisely the lack of such a distinction that has made it impossible for many investigators to take subliminal perception seriously. Thus, in a manner that Dennett (1969) would doubtless approve, Eriksen (1959, 1960) argued that a discriminative response to a stimulus reflected conscious perception of it. In doing so, however, Eriksen thereby rendered subliminal (i.e., unconscious) perception a logical impossibility since there was then no conceivable way to index subliminal perception empirically. (For a more thorough analysis of Eriksen's position on subliminal perception, see Bowers 1984b, 231–34.) The current literature on subliminal perception, though more methodologically sophisticated than the earlier work, continues to be saddled with similar conceptual and definitional problems (see Holender [1986] and the various commentaries thereto). However, recent investigations by Marcel (1983) and Cheesman and Merikle (1986) have taken the perception/noticing distinction seriously. Their analyses and findings have begun to legitimize the concept of subliminal perception and to clarify why this controversy has taken so long to resolve (e.g., Dixon 1971).

Research on subliminal perception is not the only experimental research relevant to the distinction between perception and noticing. Investigations of dichotic listening (MacKay 1973), blindsight (Weiskrantz et al. 1974), parafoveal vision (Rayner and Bertera 1979), and split-brain patients (Sperry 1968) are other domains of inquiry that address very similar conceptual issues, and all of them remain controversial (e.g., Holender 1986; Campion, Latto, and Smith 1983). As indicated earlier, unconscious perception has never achieved consensus status in cognitive psychology. Nevertheless, there are now very good conceptual and empirical reasons to assume that thought and behavior are in fact subject to influences that are not represented in first-order consciousness (Lundh 1979; Bowers 1984; Kihlstrom 1984; Marcel 1983; Cheesman and Merikle 1986).

Second-Order Consciousness

Whereas first-order consciousness involves noticing something perceived, second-order consciousness involves beliefs, theories, and understandings of information represented in first-order consciousness. Insofar as one's own action is concerned, second-order consciousness involves understanding how one's thought, feeling, and behavior are influenced by a variety of factors accessible to observation or introspection. However, it is at precisely this point that we run into some formidable obstacles.

It is philosophically well established that observations do not entail a particular understanding of them (Lakatos 1970). In other words, what we see, even under highly controlled laboratory conditions, does not completely constrain what we can legitimately say about the phenomenon observed (Bowers

1984b). This general limitation on induction is no less true when our own behavior, rather than some impersonal event in nature, is the target of inquiry and observation.

Introspection is also a very fallible source of information about the causes and influences operating on one's thought and behavior (Nisbett and Ross 1980; Lyons 1986). For example, when people in one study were asked to select which of four pairs of stockings was superior, they had little introspective access to the fact that their (typical) selection of the rightmost pair of stockings was probably due to a position effect rather than to considerations of quality or color, which were ordinarily proffered as the justification for choosing it (Nisbett and Wilson 1977).

In general, then, introspection has no special or privileged access to the causal connections linking behavior to its determinants (Bowers 1984b, 1987). There are several reasons for this. First, as we saw in the previous section, some determinants of thought and behavior are either never selectively attended in the first place or immediately forgotten and unavailable to first-order consciousness. Second (a related point), some influences have an automatic effect on thought and action that is very difficult to monitor and notice (Shiffrin and Schneider 1977; Bargh 1984). In either case, influences that are not represented in first-order consciousness cannot be invoked to explain one's action.

Third, while introspection often refers simply to things noticed in first-order consciousness, it sometimes refers as well to implicit, commonsense theories and beliefs that are brought to bear on the contents of first-order consciousness (Wegner and Vallacher 1977). Unfortunately, such theories and beliefs, though often a source of solace, comfort, and conviction, are as often misleading or simply wrong (Nisbett and Ross 1980). Partly, theories can be wrong because they cannot include reference to unnoticed but actual influences on thought and behavior (see above). Partly, they can be wrong because they are often dominated by various cognitive heuristics, such as availability and representativeness (Nisbett and Ross 1980; Tversky and Kahneman 1974), which can be very misleading when inappropriately applied. Finally, the accounts that people give of their own behavior are themselves determined—motivated by the need to maintain one's self-esteem (Sullivan 1953), self-concept (Rogers 1959), or assumptive world (Frank 1973). Whether such explanations are also sensitive to and incorporate the actual determinants of behavior is not something that can simply be assumed but is subject to doubt, examination, and verification.

In effect, self-understanding is like understanding anything else—first there is a hypothesis, and then there is some attempt to validate it. Such attempts are often limited, tiresome, and onerous and can be circumvented simply by assuming the validity of one's conscious experience—an assumption that may or may not be warranted. Insofar as the assumption is unwarranted, I think it is fair to regard the person as ignorant and/or self-deceived. In either case, it makes sense to regard the person's thought and behavior as unconsciously determined—that is, determined by factors that are not well represented in second-order consciousness.

Since neither observation nor introspection can deliver an indubitable account of own's own action, and since theories always remain provisional and subject to doubt, I have argued (Bowers 1984b, 1987) that human action is *necessarily* subject to unconscious influences. By way of clarifying the "logically necessary unconscious," consider the following. Thought and behavior are unconsciously influenced until such time as a valid account of them is forthcoming; however, thought and behavior are logically prior to valid theories about them. Practically speaking, rendering a valid account of one's action typically requires more and different kinds of information than was necessary to engender the action in the first place. For example, a person in Nisbett and Wilson's (1977) "consumer survey" of stocking preferences might be considerably helped in identifying an important if previously unsuspected influence on his or her choice by knowing that almost 80 percent of the participants chose the rightmost pair of stockings. This knowledge would not of course prove the effect of position on choice of stocking; but surely such an account is far more likely to surface as plausible than it would if a person knew only that his or her own preferred pair of stockings just happened to occupy the rightmost position.

To summarize, since neither observation nor introspection confer indubitable knowledge about the whys and wherefores of thought and behavior, we are left with implicit or explicit beliefs, theories, attitudes, and so on to provide plausible accounts in this regard. However, theories about one's own thought and behavior are as provisional and subject to error as any other theory. Until one's action has been validated against a broad range of additional evidence and information, it makes sense to claim that unconscious influences have been partly responsible for the action in question. Ultimately, of course, it is the very nature of a theory to be incomplete vis-à-vis the phenomena it explains (e.g., Popper 1979). Since an account of one's action is necessarily incomplete, the action in question is subject to unconscious influences that are logically necessary. By the same token, it is doubtless true that, for practical purposes, the quality and kind of unconscious influences operating on a particular action are often trivial and "safe" to disregard. However, it is not always easy to know when we are confronting such a benign set of circumstances and when not. The difficulties inherent in such a decision make it possible—even tempting—to assume that each and every action is transparently everything and only what it appears to be. Indeed, the temptation to so regard an action may be greatest when there is a defensive need to disavow influences that have a high likelihood of influencing the action in question.

One implication of the above comments is that conscious experience has unconscious determinants. In other words, second-order consciousness, which is composed of implicit and/or explicit beliefs, theories, and related cognitions (see, e.g., Meichenbaum and Gilmore 1984), is itself subject to influences that are not themselves well represented in first- or second-order consciousness. Indeed, conscious experience can help hide from view the very determinants that have generated it. The authority of conscious experience, however errant or bizarre (paranoid delusions, e.g.), can be so subjectively compelling that it brooks no questioning of its source or testing of its validity. Thus, people can be responsive to influences that they overlook or disavow in second-order consciousness. When second-order consciousness represents the actual determinants of thought and behavior reasonably well, we often speak of a person having good reality testing; when this is not the case, various kinds of difficulties are imputed to the person—from a mild and perhaps even endearing defection from good judgment ("love is blind," e.g.) to flagrant psychosis.

Another implication of this general position is that people can have first-order consciousness of influences without having second-order consciousness that they are influential. This implication can be illustrated by several issues or controversies in psychology, of which I can mention only a few. Dulany (1962) and others (e.g., Spielberger 1962) long ago argued that people must be aware of the response-reinforcement contingencies in a verbal conditioning paradigm in order to show conditioning effects. Other investigators have denied the role of such awareness (e.g., Verplanck 1962). My hunch is that part of the controversy, at least, may be due to the fact that different notions of consciousness are implied by participants in the debate.

Consider, for example, a pilot subject that I ran in a conditioning task several years ago (Bowers 1975). The subject in fact showed a clear conditioning effect. Moreover, she later revealed under questioning awareness of her response, of my reinforcement, and of the response/reinforcement contingencies. However, when subsequently asked whether my reinforcement had anything to do with her responses, she replied rather emphatically in the negative. She argued that my reinforcement always came after her response, so the former could not possibly have influenced the latter. Clearly, the subject's working theory of interpersonal influence mistakenly assumed that trials are independent. Nonetheless, she noticed in first-order consciousness everything that Dulany (1962) insists is important for conditioning to occur, she simply remained unaware in second-order consciousness of how influential these noticed events were. I therefore think that it is legitimate to argue that this woman was in a very important sense unconsciously influenced by the contingent reinforcement of which she was clearly aware.

In a delightful book, Cialdini (1985) has documented many different ways in which people are subject to subtle but powerful influence techniques. Most of them are effective not because they are subliminal (i.e., unrepresented in first-order consciousness) but because the nature of the influence attempts, while perfectly noticeable, makes them nonetheless far more powerful movers and shapers of behavior than ordinary lay theories appreciate (Kruglanski 1980).

Finally, the notion of demand characteristics—which, incidentally, came to conceptual fruition in the hypnosis literature (Orne 1959)—is profitably understood in terms of first- and second-order consciousness. As Orne (1969) has noted, demand characteristics "change the subject's behavior in such a way that he is often not clearly aware of their effect. In fact, demand characteristics may be less effective or even have a paradoxical action if they are too obvious. With the constellation of motives that the usual subject brings to a psychological experiment, the 'soft sell' works better than the 'hard sell'. Rosenthal (1963) has reported a similar finding in experimenter bias: the effect is weakened, or even reversed, if the experimenter is paid extra to bias his results" (148). I have also emphasized the important difference between unrecognized and recognized demand characteristics (Bowers 1973). In our current terminology, if demand characteristics are simply noticed in first-order consciousness, they can be implicit but powerful shapers of experimental behavior. However, when a person interprets such demand characteristics in second-order consciousness as an obvious attempt to coerce compliance, subjects may demonstrate considerable reactance (Brehm 1966).

To summarize, a common variant of Type I unconscious influences is operative when a person's implicit theory of social influence does not sufficiently represent the actual power of an intervention to alter thought and behavior. This insufficiency presumably occurs under a variety of circumstances, only two of which need be mentioned by way of illustration: (a) a person of exceptional naïveté is subjected to an influence attempt that most people of average sophistication would immediately recognize and perhaps resist; (b) a person of reasonable sophistication does not recognize an exceptionally subtle influence attempt for what it is and so cannot resist it. The notions of "exceptional subtlety" and "exceptional naïveté" are clearly underspecified at present, and I must rely on the reader's common sense and imagination to appreciate my intent here. What I wish to emphasize is that, in both cases, the intervention may well be noticed in first-order consciousness but not appreciated in second-order consciousness as influential.

Most social psychological research, especially the branch of it concerned with attitude change, exploits Type I unconscious influences. It involves cleverly contriving experimental conditions so as to alter subjects' attitudes and beliefs without their appreciating the coerciveness of the intervention. Kelley (1973), for example, has pointed out that successful experiments in cognitive dissonance and attribution depend on constraining behavior without subjects recognizing the constraints for what they are. It is precisely under conditions of unrecognized constraint (or perceived freedom) that internal experience is most likely to be consistent with outward behavior and that the behavior will be self- or internally attributed (Ross and Fletcher 1985). This strategy of influence may require considerable finesse and cleverness on the part of the perpetrator.

A good illustration of the subtlety involved in getting from external influence to internal attribution of it is provided in Ronald Clark's (1971) definitive biography of Albert Einstein. Clark reports that the propagandist Kurt Blumenfeld carefully plotted the conversion of Einstein to Zionism: "Utilizing [Einstein] for publicity purposes was thus a delicate matter and was only successful if I was able to get under his skin in such a way that eventually he believed that the words had not been put into his mouth, but had come forth from him spontaneously" (380). The trick is to generate behavioral change without mobilizing the person's appreciation or comprehension of what is happening (Bowers 1973). Not only social psychologists and propagandists but gifted clinicians and advertisers intuitively practice the art and craft of Type I influence (Cialdini 1985), sometimes without quite realizing it (Bowers 1987).

Implications of Type I Unconscious for the Freudian Unconscious

It is clear that the emphasis so far has been on unconscious influences that are external to the perceiver. However, the unconscious that Freud introduced with such vigor clearly refers to the effect of endogenous information— thoughts, feelings, and fantasies—of which the person remains unaware. The question naturally emerges as to whether the analysis I have submitted for the unconscious effect of external influences is at all relevant to a Freudian or psychoanalytic account of the unconscious. I have addressed this issue elsewhere (Bowers 1984b, 1987) and will only briefly summarize my position here.

I assume that endogenous information can be processed without being selectively attended. Perhaps the most accessible illustration of this possibility involves what I have called the reading reverie, in which someone reading a book suddenly "comes to" with the realization that nothing on the page just "read" has been processed. Under these circumstances, people will often have difficulty remembering what they were thinking about instead of reading (see Varendonck 1921). My argument is that often people do not selectively attend to their interpolated reading reveries when they occur and so can have difficulty retrieving them later. This scenario seems to hold for one of Freud's ([1908] 1959) patients, who suddenly burst out crying without at first knowing why. However, after a few moments reflection, she was able to recover an organized and morose daydream in which she was seduced, impregnated, and finally abandoned by a local pianist, whom she had never met in reality. Her reverie was indeed sad, and, to the extent that it was originally unattended as well, she seemed to have less control over its affective consequences.

Erdelyi (1985, in this volume; Erdelyi and Goldberg 1979) has emphasized that avoidance of or inattention to information is sufficient to account for Freud's notion of repression, at least as he initially formulated it (Breuer and Freud [1893–95] 1974). So have I (Bowers 1984b). Frankly, however, I have my doubts whether such a thought avoidance concept of repression can easily account for Freud's later embellishments of the concept, wherein repressed content "develops in a more unchecked and luxuriant fashion if it is withdrawn by repression from conscious influence. It ramifies like a fungus, so to speak, in the dark and takes on extreme forms of expression, which when translated and revealed to the neurotic are bound not merely to seem alien to him, but to terrify him by the way in which they reflect an extraordinary and dangerous strength of instinct" (Freud [1915] 1959, 90). Whether this "fungus hypothesis" of repression is valid is perhaps a moot point. Even if some dangerous ideas do proliferate better in the dark, so to speak, it is not clear that this follows from or is implied by "the essence [of repression, which] lies simply in the function of rejecting and keeping something out of consciousness" (Freud [1915] 1959). Some kind of collateral assumptions seem required to permit the so-called essence of repression to include the proliferation of an unconscious associative network; clearly, such a proliferation goes considerably beyond the initial exclusion of a painful idea.

Implications of Type I Unconscious Influences for Hypnosis

Many years ago, Boris Sidis (1898), a well-known psychopathologist and friend of William James, opined that "in the normal state a suggestion is more effective the more indirect it is" (52); in hypnosis, on the other hand, "the more direct we make our suggestion the greater the chance of its success" (79). There is no doubt that modern social psychologists (e.g., Kelley 1973; Cialdini 1985) recognize the wisdom inherent in the first of these two quotations and regularly employ more or less subtle and/or indirect influences that people do not understand or appreciate as having powerful effects on behavior. As well, the second of Sidis's two comments seems confirmed in common practice because the typical hypnotic suggestion is administered in a direct, straightforward manner that permits without coercing a response. However, the conventional views of influence as espoused almost one hundred years ago by Sidis are currently being challenged.

The Challenge of Indirect Hypnotic Suggestion

Several well-known clinical hypnotists emphasize the importance of indirect and subtle suggestive communications to maximize the likelihood of producing hypnotically suggested effects (Erickson and Rossi 1980; Barber 1977). Without explicitly invoking social psychological principles of interpersonal influence, the strong implication in their view is that, by giving permissive, indirect suggestions, people who might otherwise balk at responding hypnotically will in fact do so. In other words, the advocates of subtle or indirect suggestion seem to imply that such techniques succeed at least in part because of their Type I unconscious effect on thought and behavior. Moreover, it is argued that indirect suggestions, by circumventing resistances and defenses of the subject/patient, will minimize or even eliminate individual differences in hypnotic ability insofar as treatment outcome is concerned (e.g., Barber 1980).

The fact is, however, that controlled laboratory studies do not sustain the position of those who advocate the peculiar power of indirect hypnotic suggestion. McConkey (1984b), for instance, demonstrated that truly hypnotized subjects administered an indirect suggestion for a positive visual hallucination were highly variable in their response to it. This was true even though all of them had just demonstrated a similar hallucination to a direct suggestion. Moreover, there was no question that demand characteristics for the indirect hallucination were operative since most of the control subjects who were simulating hypnosis in fact reported the visual hallucination, which they did not in fact experience (for an account of the simulation paradigm in hypnosis research, see Sheehan and Perry 1976; and Orne 1979). According to McConkey, postexperimental inquiry revealed that "the indirect suggestion was perceived by some real Ss as an illegitimate request for an experiential alteration; that is, for these Ss, the indirect suggestion was not embedded in the appropriate verbal framework to allow them to respond" (311). Thus, in a hypnotic context, indirect suggestions seem to have the paradoxical effect of engendering reactance for some otherwise hypnotically responsive subjects.

Another investigation experimentally evaluated Barber's (1977) "rapid induction analgesia" (Van Gorp, Meyer, and Dunbar 1985). This technique was devised to capitalize on the supposed advantages of indirect and permissive hypnotic suggestions to reduce clinical pain. In the experiment, cold pressor pain was employed in a comparison of direct and indirect hypnotic analgesia suggestions. The reductions from baseline pain reports were far greater when hypnotized subjects received direct suggestions for analgesia than when they received rapid induction analgesia. Moreover, the reported reductions in the group receiving direct suggestions for hypnotic analgesia were much greater for high- than they were for low-hypnotizable subjects—a differential effect that did not occur in the rapid analgesia condition.

This pattern of results from the Van Gorp, Meyer, and Dunbar (1985) investigation must be understood in the light of the following observation: the effect of hypnotic ability on responsiveness to hypnotic suggestion is so ubiquitous in the hypnosis literature that "the effects of a treatment intervention are *not* due to suggestion *unless* treatment outcome is correlated with hypnotic ability" (Bowers 1984a, 444). Consequently, whatever reductions were achieved in the rapid analgesia condition were probably not due to hypnotic suggestion per se. While there is little doubt that considerable reductions in pain can be achieved by means other than hypnosis (e.g., Turk, Meichenbaum, and Genest 1983), unless the reductions are correlated with hypnotic ability they cannot reasonably be attributed to hypnotic suggestion per se (Miller and Bowers 1986).

A third investigation of indirect suggestion (Matthews et al. 1985) indicated no difference between direct and indirect suggestions on subjects' performance on two standard assessments of hypnotic ability. Evidently, the use of indirect suggestion does not necessarily impair hypnotic performance or eliminate the effect of individual differences in hypnotic ability. By the same token, there is no indication in any of these three studies that indirect, subtle suggestions constitute an irresistible elixir of Type I unconscious influences.

The Spanosian Challenge

Nicholas Spanos is currently the most prolific investigator of hypnosis, and, since most of his publications report experimental findings, his views have considerable appeal to researchers unacquainted with the domain of hypnosis. A thorough review of Spanos's work is not feasible here, but it is important to convey the thrust of his position, the better to contrast it with a dissociative view of hypnosis to be introduced later.

The essence of Spano's view seems to be as follows: the way a person interprets a hypnotic suggestion is the final common pathway for a host of attitudinal and expectational variables, and, when the attitudes and expectations of a person are optimized in various ways, it dramatically increases the hypnotic responsiveness of a person who would otherwise demonstrate low hypnotic ability. An important implication of Spanos's view is that high hypnotic ability is due largely to a " 'talent' for interpreting test items in a way that leads to high test scores" (Spanos 1986, 493) and that individual differences in hypnotic ability are due largely to differences in how people interpret ambiguously worded hypnotic suggestions. Consequently, one very important way to encourage a proper interpretation of a particular suggestive communication is thoroughly to disambiguate it. Under these circumstances, individual differences are said to be minimized (Gorasinni and Spanos 1986).

An illustration of treatment-enhanced responsiveness to hypnotic suggestions may help convey the gist of Spanos's views. In one recently reported experiment, subjects were given four practice suggestions and told, for example, that the suggestion

> will specifically tell you that your arm is like a hollow balloon
> being pumped up with helium . . . and that it's rising into the air

by itself. . . . you must do everything that is required of someone making believe such a thing. You must lift your arm up and you must imagine that the arm is really a hollow balloon that is being pumped full of helium, rising by itself. You must . . . actually make it seem real. . . . Rivet your attention on the hollow arm, the lightness, the fact it's going up by itself and so on. Don't imagine anything or pay attention to anything that is unrelated to the make-believe situation. [Spanos et al. 1986, 351]

Other aspects of the training for heightened responsiveness to hypnotic suggestions include exposing subjects to information that demystifies hypnosis, having them view a videotape of a model responding successfully to various practice suggestions while verbalizing appropriate imaginings and sensations, seeing the model interviewed regarding his or her experiences, and being encouraged in the proper interpretation of the suggested phenomena. Finally, subjects are exposed to four new practice suggestions. As a result of these interventions, Spanos and his colleagues report quite substantial increases in hypnotic responsiveness—people who were initially chosen for their low hypnotic ability were, after training, scoring in the moderate and even high range of hypnotic ability.

All in all, there is an important sense in which Spanos's view of hypnosis agrees with that expressed by Sidis nearly one hundred years ago: the more direct and explicit hypnotic suggestions are, the more likely they are to succeed. In another sense, however, Spanos's view seems out of phase with the more traditional account since an avowedly social psychological explanation of hypnotic behavior ought to be more concerned with perpetrating subtle and indirect forms of influence. I will amplify on this curious inconsistency below. For now, several general comments on Spanos's procedures and claims for them are in order.

At first blush, there is a great deal in Spanos's position to command our attention and respect. If in fact hypnotic interventions can be made effective for a large number of individuals who would ordinarily be unaffected by them, this is surely something to celebrate, especially in a treatment context in which pain control (e.g., Hilgard and Hilgard 1975; Hilgard and LeBaron 1984) or the hypnotic treatment of various allergies (e.g., Black 1969) and other vegetative symptoms (Bowers and Kelly 1979) is at issue. However, Spanos's claims should also awaken our skepticism. A great deal of research has indicated that hypnotic ability is a very stable, trait-like feature of people (Bowers 1979b; Hilgard 1965; Morgan, Johnson, and Hilgard 1974). Further, two hundred years of clinical observation and fifty years of laboratory investigations strongly converge on a conclusion that profound, hypnotically produced alterations in cognition and somatic responsiveness have, for the most part, been confined to people who demonstrated high hypnotic ability (Black 1969; Perry and Laurence 1983; Bowers and Kelly 1979). On due consideration, then, it seems unlikely that individual differences in hypnotic ability can be (*a*) conceptually reduced to relatively malleable differences in how hypnotic suggestions are interpreted and (*b*) empirically dispatched simply by getting subjects to interpret the suggestions appropriately.

Second, it is well known that, in experimental contexts, clear directives to behave in a particular manner may well lead to extremely high degrees of overt compliance (e.g., Orne 1962; Milgram 1963). Such near-universal compliance would disallow any correlation of the behavior with hypnotic ability. However, as indicated earlier, the absence of such a correlation makes it extremely unlikely that near-universal compliance is a specifically hypnotic effect. Thus, if Spanos were able to get virtually everyone in his experiments to behave in accordance with the implicit and explicit demands of the experiment, it would strongly suggest "that something besides hypnosis [had] unwittingly become the focus of investigation" (Bowers and Davidson 1986, 469). (It should be noted that Spanos seems to regard the elimination of individual differences in hypnotic ability as a potentially realizable ideal; his actual findings, however, come nowhere close to demonstrating this state of affairs. Consequently, his research is saved from being irrelevant vis-à-vis the domain of hypnosis to the extent that he continues to find robust and ineradicable individual differences in hypnotic ability.)

Third, as indicated earlier, expectation and attitude are thought by Spanos and his followers to be powerful and manipulable determinants of hypnotic performance. It is therefore interesting to note that the data reported by various other investigators show such factors to have no (e.g., Ashford and Hammer 1978) or low (e.g., Shor et al. 1984) effect on hypnotic responsiveness. The latter study is a particularly well-balanced account of the issues under consideration. The investigators assessed subjects' expectations of how they would perform on each item of the Harvard Group Scale of Hypnotic Susceptibility (Shor and Orne 1962). These expectations predicted performance on each item less well than did hypnotic ability, as assessed by subjects' performance on all of the other scale items. As the authors neatly summarize their findings, "Expectations do have some effect on response to hypnosis, . . . but they are far from self-fulfilling prophecies" (Shor et al. 1984, 383).

As implied by Shor et al. (1984), one possible mechanism of positive attitudes and expectation on the enhancement of hypnotic performance is that they encourage fully motivated and cooperative participation in hypnosis. Indeed, Kidder (1972) earlier documented how subtle social influences operative in the hypnotic context mobilize subjects' cooperation and belief in the hypnotic nature of their experience, and it may well be that some of the effect of indirect hypnotic suggestion is similarly effective in bringing people to a point of maximum cooperation and belief in the hypnotic nature of their experiencing (cf. Orne 1961). Implied here is the possibility that Type I unconscious influences may be operative in helping convince people that they are hypnotized.

Enlisting the subject's full cooperation and belief may thus catalyze hypnotic responsiveness, but it is not a substitute for genuine hypnotic talent. This conclusion is supported by a sophisticated statistical (spectral) analysis of hypnotic ability recently completed in our laboratory by Balthazard and Woody (1985). Their analyses indicate that social compliance may contribute in an important way to successful performance on relatively easy motor items of a standardized hypnotic susceptibility scale. However, performance on more difficult scale items (such as negative visual hallucinations) demands considerable alteration and distortion in perception and memory. Responsiveness of this kind seems to require a genuine talent for absorptive involvement in the suggested state of affairs (Tellegen and Atkinson 1974) that is quite distinct from social compliance. Tellegen (1978–79) had earlier made a quite similar distinction.

To summarize, in a specifically hypnotic context, Type I influences may subtly engender cooperation and belief in one's behavior as hypnotically inspired. Insofar as this is true, a hypnotist may indeed exercise real if subtle control over the person being hypnotized. However, as we have already mentioned, Spanos argues that hypnotic responsiveness is maximized when suggestive communications are very explicit and unambiguous. According to conventional wisdom in social psychology, however, such explicit and direct communications are ill advised if the goal is not merely overt compliance with suggestive communications but subjective experience that is consistent with the outward behavior.

In the context of hypnosis, the lack of consistency between outward behavior and inward experience of it would be critical since hypnotic responsiveness is interesting only when and if the hypnotized person not only behaves in accordance with the suggested state of affairs but subjectively experiences it as well (Orne 1966; Bowers 1979b). Thus, if a hypnotized person only says that he feels no pain of cold pressor while inwardly writhing in agony, nothing much of interest has been demonstrated—at least insofar as hypnosis is concerned.

While Spanos clearly advocates unambiguously explicit suggestive communications, he is also on record as affirming the subjectively genuine effect of hypnotic suggestions (e.g., Spanos et al. 1979; Spanos and Radtke-Bodorik 1980)—though, as Kihlstrom (1986) notes, he sometimes seems to equivocate in this regard. In terms introduced earlier, Spanos's position seems to be that hypnotized subjects simply do not appreciate in second-order consciousness the power of various hypnotic communications—this despite the fact that they are very direct and explicit demands to behave in a particular way. As I have already indicated, however, such direct demands to behave in a particular manner seem to operate at cross-purposes with the conventional wisdom in social psychology, which implies that explicit and unambiguous suggestive communications should mitigate against the internal attribution and experience of the suggested state of affairs.

The apparent contradictions raised by an exclusively social psychological account of hypnosis can be finessed by assuming that something more than Type I influences is involved in producing the distortions of behavior and experience reported by deeply hypnotized persons. It is therefore time to examine Type II unconscious influences, which I think are thoroughly implicated in hypnotic phenomena.

Type II Unconscious Influences

Whereas Type I unconscious influences are effective by some combination of message subtlety and receiver naïveté, Type II unconscious influences are a result of alterations in how information is received and processed. A prototype example of Type II influence has recently been reviewed by Bennett (1988). Surgical patients were administered a suggestive communication while under general anesthesia. Essentially, patients were told to pull on their ear lobes in a subsequent postoperative interview with the investigator. On the average, patients in this experimental group manifested the suggested response six times more often than did a control group of surgical patients who did not receive the suggestive communication. Moreover, none of the patients in the experimental condition were later able to recall the suggestive communication, even when hypnosis was employed to aid recall (Bennett, Davis, and Giannini 1981).

Evans (1979) reviewed a somewhat similar series of studies not employing surgical patients. Subjects in alpha-free, Stage I sleep were provided suggestions for particular responses, together with a cue that was to trigger their subsequent occurrence. When the cue was administered later that night or on a subsequent night up to five months later, it elicited an appropriate response a reasonably high proportion of the time; irrelevant cues, however, were ineffective in this regard (Evans et al. 1966, 1970). All this transpired without any evident waking memory for the original, sleep-administered suggestions.

Both the Bennett (1988) and the Evans et al. (1966, 1970) investigations speak to the possibility for state-specific learning and memory, which remains inaccessible to conscious recall (Swanson and Kinsbourne, 1979). Additionally, the research establishes rather persuasively that directed and discriminative behavior does not require either the perpetrator's consciousness (in any ordinary sense) or awareness of the behavior's initiating conditions and/or activating cues. This is worth stressing because advocates of the social psychological approach to hypnosis argue that responses of a hypnotized person to suggestive communications are strategically and therefore consciously enacted. While it is clearly the case that hypnotized subjects are neither drugged nor sleeping (Evans 1979), the question remains whether they are simply engaging in strategic behavior in accordance with suggestive communications or whether something more complex is going on.

Before addressing this issue, however, it should be noted that the way in which information is processed can be altered by means having little to do with sleep or drugs. Extreme stress, sensory isolation, high or low arousal, and fatigue are several distinctly psychological factors that can separately and interactively affect how information is processed—rendering it especially influential because it is not submitted to the critical reality testing of a fully alert human being (see Breuer and Freud [1893–95] 1974, esp. the first two parts of sec. 3; Zuckerman 1964; Bower 1981; Morris and Singer 1966). Various cult groups engender such state-specific effects, the better to help induce profound conversion experience (Conway and Siegelman 1978; Delgado 1977), and I know from personal experience that college fraternities do too. What is perhaps more surprising is that none of these rather extreme psychological factors need to be present in order to generate a Type II alteration in the way information is processed—for it can also be induced by hypnotic suggestions.

My argument is that hypnosis generates a significant discontinuity in the way information is processed and that an important condition of this discontinuity involves a loss of generalized reality orientation (GRO) (Shor 1979). According to Shor,

> In all of our waking life we carry around in the background of our awareness a kind of frame of reference or orientation to generalized reality which serves as a context or arena within which we interpret all of our ongoing conscious experiences. Under certain conditions—of which hypnosis is just one—this wide frame of reference or orientation to generalized reality can fade into the very distant background of our minds so that ongoing experiences are isolated from their usual context. When that happens the distinction between imagination and reality no longer exists for us. [1970, 91]

The reduction in GRO helps to increase the ratio of primary to secondary process thinking (Gill and Brenman 1959; Fromm 1979; Hammer, Walker, and Diment 1978) and to alter the relations among various levels of cognitive control—with subsystems of control being less embedded in or guided by overarching conscious plans and intentions than is ordinarily the case (Miller, Galanter, and Pribram 1960; Hilgard 1977, 1979; Kihlstrom 1984).

In sum, I am arguing that hypnosis involves Type II unconscious influences, which implies that hypnosis significantly alters how information is received and processed. As indicated earlier, the social psychological account implies that hypnosis may well involve Type I influences, which alter only what information is attended and how it is understood. But it denies that Type II unconscious influences are involved in the production of hypnotic phenomena. The remainder of this chapter is devoted to a closer examination of the relative merits of these two distinct views.

A Neodissociative Account of Hypnosis

Type II unconscious influences alter how information is processed, and, according to Hilgard's (1973, 1977) neodissociation model of hypnosis, that is precisely what occurs when a person is hypnotized and responds to various suggestive communications (see also Kihlstrom 1984). This model assumes a hierarchical system of cognitive control. The highest level of control involves executive and monitoring functions, the exercise of which is ordinarily experienced as awareness, initiative, and volition. When a person is hypnotized, the relations among various levels of control are altered in a manner that (a) changes how a person experiences his or her behavior and (b) reduces the extent to which the highest levels of control initiate and monitor the suggested state of affairs (cf. Miller, Galanter, and Pribram 1960). It is thus convenient to speak of dissociated experience and of dissociated control as two complementary aspects of hypnotic responsiveness. While these two aspects of dissociation can be treated as if they were distinct, it should be emphasized at the outset that expositional convenience more than theoretical necessity has inspired this distinction.

Dissociated Experience

A hypnotically suggested response is ordinarily experienced as peculiarly automatic, compulsive, or nonvolitional. This experience of nonvolition that accompanies hypnotic responsiveness has been termed the "classic suggestion effect" (Weitzenhoffer 1978, 1980). Notice that the emphasis on how a suggested response is experienced focuses our attention on an important effect of a suggestive communication rather than on the communication itself. According to this emphasis, any communication could theoretically engender a classic suggestion effect in the receiver, regardless of the intentions of the sender. There is a relatively high correspondence between communications that are intended and received as suggestions; however there can be exceptions to this rule. For example, Weitzenhoffer (1974) has shown that ordinary instructions can occasionally engender a suggestion effect, and people will sometimes respond volitionally to intended suggestions (Spanos, Rivers, and Ross 1977; Bowers 1981; Bowers 1982). Combining such exceptions with those many instances in which persons do not respond overtly to an intended suggestion argues against overidentifying the concept of suggestion with the specific procedures and communications intended to produce it.

Distinguishing between a suggested effect and the means of inducing it has an important consequence: it permits us to understand how a classic suggestion effect can be produced with no intention or forethought whatsoever and even in the total absence of an explicit communication. To illustrate, Mesmer probably never gave explicit suggestions for the dramatic crises that characterized the behavior of his clientele (Bailly et al. 1784; Tinterow 1970). Yet there can be little doubt that these crises were in fact suggested effects, which were engendered by a context of heightened expectations that the patients would experience them. Similarly, Orne (1959) demonstrated that dominant arm catalepsy occurred only in hypnotized subjects who had earlier been misinformed (in a lecture about hypnosis) that such catalepsy was an invariant feature of deep hypnosis. A control group that was not misinformed in this way showed no such effect. The point here is that classic suggestion effects need not be immediately preceded by an explicit, suggestive communication but can instead be triggered by previous and/or implicit communications, expectations, and ideas that can be difficult to identify independently of their effects.

This difficulty in identifying the idea behind the suggested effect is most problematic when the idea itself is hidden or dissociated from consciousness, as is often the case in hysterical disorders as described by Pierre Janet ([1929] 1965). According to Janet, suggestion was the invariant "stigmata" or central feature of hysteric disorders, and dissociated ideas were the basis for suggestion. The reason that hysteric symptoms could take so many forms was a simple extention of the fact that the ideas behind them were limitless. As we know, Janet's concepts of suggestion and dissociation were soon superseded by Freud's emphasis on repression of affect and ideas (see Perry and Laurence 1984), with the variety of symptomatology being more in the service of hiding the nature of the underlying problem than directly expressing it.

Because dissociation was displaced by repression, the very notion of suggestion has become more and more identified with hypnosis rather than psychopathology. And, in the context of hypnosis, a certain ambiguity has arisen with respect to the term "suggestion." On one hand, it has come to mean a specific and explicit communication intended to have a classic suggestion effect. Thus, items on the various standardized scales of hypnotic ability (e.g., the Stanford Scale of Hypnotic Susceptibility, form C, Weitzenhoffer and Hilgard 1962) are typically referred to as suggestions, irrespective of whether a subject responds to them in the classic, nonvolitional manner. On the other hand, the term "suggestion" often refers precisely to the nonvolitional response engendered by a hypnotic communication. For purposes of clarity, I prefer, whenever possible, to use the term "suggestive communications" for scale items appearing on standardized scales of hypnotic ability (and for other similar communications intended to produce a suggested effect) and to reserve the term "suggestion" for the classic effects of such communications.

It is important to be explicit about what is gained and lost by identifying suggestions with their effects rather than with the procedures used to engender them. What we lose is a certain operational precision that accrues when we identify suggestion with the explicit procedures for producing it. What we gain, however, is conceptual clarity. That is, identifying suggestion with the nonvolitional way overt responsiveness is experienced promotes the recognition that suggestion is distinct from a host of other influences that depend on persuasion, social compliance, advice taking, and so on. These latter influences are typically experienced as something that the person actively does, volitionally, even if he or she does so under duress.[1]

It should be emphasized that a deeply hypnotized subject ordinarily remains aware of both the suggestive communication and of his or her response to it. What is not well represented in consciousness is the psychological connection linking the activating idea and the person's subsequent enactment of it. Because this link is dissociated from consciousness, the hypnotized person does not feel as though he or she is actively producing the suggested state of affairs; rather, the suggested effect is experienced as happening on its own—nonvolitionally, as it were.

The experience of nonvolition that is part and parcel of hypnotic responding means that the hypnotized subject remains for the most part unaware that a good deal of effort may have been exercised in order to produce the suggested state of affairs. For example, Orne (1959) instructed deeply hypnotized subjects to hold a kilogram weight up in the air at arm's length, followed by a suggestive communication that the weight was resting on a table and that their arms would not get tired. The main finding of this experiment was that the subjects did not hold the weight up as long under these hypnotic conditions as they subsequently did under highly motivated, waking conditions. However, in the waking condition, the effort and discomfort involved was experienced quite vividly, whereas, in the hypnotic condition, the subjects did not spontaneously report the pain and discomfort that would ordinarily accompany such an effort (M. T. Orne, personal communication, 19 January 1987). Presumably, the effort that the subjects expended was simply dissociated from consciousness.

Sometimes the effort involved in producing the suggested effect is more cognitive than physical. Thus, hypnotic pain analgesia frequently seems to be aided by supporting images—either suggested or spontaneously occurring. For example, one young woman in an experiment on hypnotic pain analgesia spontaneously imagined herself as the Venus de Milo, with no arm to feel the painful stimulus (Hilgard and Hilgard 1975). Such fantasies may indeed be important, at least for some people, in achieving hypnotic analgesia; however,

---

1. A useful distinction here might be made between volitional and voluntary acts. Volition implies an experience of initiative and participation vis-à-vis one's actions. A voluntary act, on the other hand, is one that is not coerced by circumstances. Thus, if a person is asked at the point of a gun to hand over all his or her money, he or she may do so volitionally, but involuntarily.

the fantasies or imaginings are not always experienced as effortfully produced and/or instrumental to the analgesic effects achieved (Spanos et al. 1979; Miller and Bowers 1986). In other words, the experience of actively and effortfully producing the fantasy and the reduction in pain that results are simply not represented in conscious awareness.

Despite the fact that hypnotically suggested effects and hysteric symptoms both involve dissociation, they differ in terms of what dissociation typically renders unconscious. As we have seen, the hypnotized subject ordinarily remains aware of the activating idea—that is, of the suggestive communication. Such a person thus retains the possibility for low-level monitoring of the proceedings and for calling a halt to them if they begin to infringe on his or her sense of propriety (e.g., Gill and Brenman 1959). The situation is different in important ways for people suffering various hysteric symptoms. In this case, as noted earlier, the activating idea is itself dissociated from consciousness and therefore cannot easily be subjected to critical appraisals or modified in the light of reality considerations. It is precisely the inability to deal realistically with unconscious (i.e., dissociated) ideas that renders them less tractable in the context of hysteria than suggestive communications are in a hypnotic context.

The situation with hypnosis may become more like hysteria when suggestions for posthypnotic amnesia are administered. However, a truly dense amnesia, in which a person can remember absolutely nothing from the hypnotic episode, is rather rare—occurring in less than 5 percent of university students (e.g., Bowers and Brenneman 1981). Even the most difficult items on the Stanford C Scale—the hallucinated voice and a negative visual hallucination—are passed by twice as many people as demonstrate total posthypnotic amnesia. (The amnesia item does not require complete amnesia in order to pass it; rather, it is passed when three or fewer of the C Scale items are recalled, and 27 percent of the normative sample meet this criterion; Hilgard 1965, 238.) There may be a good reason for this relatively low success rate in generating complete amnesia. In my experience, people often find dense amnesia disquieting since it is perceived as representing a more complete loss of control than is typically the case for other hypnotic responses. After all, if a person can remember nothing that he or she has done, then he or she could have done anything.

In sum, dissociated experience in the context of hypnosis refers to the fact that the suggested state of affairs seems to occur nonvolitionally—which is to say that the physical and/or cognitive initiative and effort involved in the production of suggested effects is not well represented in conscious experience. This so-called classic suggestion effect occurs when the subsystem of control activated by the suggestive communication is relatively less embedded in and guided by high-level executive controls. Notice that, at one level, control is in fact being exercised by the hypnotized person, who may exercise considerable cognitive and physical work to accomplish the suggested state of affairs. However, the control being exercised is not consciously experienced. Consequently, hypnotic responsiveness to suggestive communications may be experienced as a loss of personal control—a state of affairs that can be exacerbated when posthypnotic amnesia for suggested effects is also suggested. This perceived loss of personal control may well prove threatening for some people and serve to limit the completeness of their participation in the hypnotically suggested state of affairs.

It is important to reemphasize at this juncture that, in the context of hypnosis, the entire issue of control refers primarily to the shift in the relations among various levels of cognitive control. The degree of actual control that is achieved by hypnosis and by the hypnotic context is a somewhat different issue and may vary from miniscule to considerable, depending on the circumstances and the personalities involved (see, e.g., Perry 1979). Under ordinary circumstances, however, it is clear that hypnosis is a very poor means of establishing a powerful controlling relationship over another person—Svengali myths to the contrary notwithstanding (Coe, Kobayashi, and Howard 1973). According to Marks (1979), for example, the CIA flirted with hypnosis but ultimately gave it up as totally insufficient to achieve their rather unsavory plans for hypnotically programmed assassination. By comparison to "basic training" of the military, hypnosis is virtually hapless. For example, Gwynne Dyer (1985), in his book *War,* cites William Manchester's first "kill," a sniper who had already begun shooting Manchester's comrades. Nonetheless, after Manchester shot and killed the sniper, he "felt remorse and shame. I can remember whispering foolishly, 'I'm sorry' and then just throwing up. . . . I threw up all over myself. It was a betrayal of what I'd been taught since a child" (101).

Dyer comments:

> Like all the other tens of millions of soldiers who had been
> taught from infancy that killing was wrong, and had then been
> sent off to kill for their countries, he was almost helpless to dis-
> obey, for he had fallen into the hands of an institution so power-
> ful and so subtle that it could quickly reverse the moral training
> of a lifetime. . . . [T]he armed forces of every country can . . .
> take almost any young male civilian and turn him into a soldier
> with all the right reflexes and attitudes in only a few weeks. Their
> recruits usually have no more than twenty years' experience of
> the world, most of it as children, while the armies have had all of
> history to practice and perfect their techniques. [1985, 102]

There is absolutely no reason to believe that hypnosis could achieve anything like this degree of control over the ordinary person. The effectiveness of basic training derives from the fact that it exploits (Type I) influence techniques that are for the most part quite noticeable but whose power to change and transform thought and behavior is, as Dyer avers, quite subtle—that is, not well understood by the recruits. Partly for this reason, the techniques are virtually impossible to resist. The fact that societies endorse rather than question basic training provides formidable sanctions that can intimidate those rare individuals who are not seduced.

The alteration in control produced by hypnosis is altogether different; it refers primarily to shifts in cognitive control structures rather than to the dominance of one's behavior by subtle external influences, the power of which is simply unrecognized and difficult to resist. As we have seen, the shift in the balance of cognitive controls that characterizes hypnosis engenders suggested responses that are experienced as nonvolitional. However, there are indications that we overlook some important aspects of hypnosis if we concentrate solely on the extent to which it promotes nonvolitional experiencing of the suggested effects. Hence, it is time to concern ourselves with the issue of dissociated control.

Dissociated Control

When I was on sabbatical at Stanford's Hypnosis Laboratory in 1977–78, I was working with an extraordinarily talented hypnotic virtuoso who failed to show up one day for his session—a most unusual defection from his ordinary reliability. When I phoned him to make another appointment, I discovered the reason for his absence: a very bad case of poison oak that he had contracted four days earlier. Not only was he extremely uncomfortable from the infection, but the drugs he had taken to relieve the itching had also made him quite groggy and sleepy. Despite several years of participating in various hypnosis projects and demonstrations in the Stanford laboratory, it had not occurred to him that he might have the cognitive wherewithal to deal with the discomfort hypnotically.

When I saw the young man the next day, I could see why he was miserable. The infection extended from the inside of his left forearm, up through his armpit, across his chest almost to his other armpit, and halfway down his stomach. I told him to hypnotize himself and to let me know when he was ready for my help. When he conveyed his readiness, I gave him suggestions for the itching and discomfort to stop and for the healing time to accelerate.

On alerting no more than three or four minutes after the entire procedure had begun, he informed me that the itching had stopped almost instantly when the suggestions had been delivered to switch it off. I followed the case for a week or so, and by the tenth day after the original infection, his skin was almost normal—certainly all the swollen, weeping skin had long since completely disappeared. It is of course difficult to say without the necessary controls whether this rate of healing was exceptional. However, the patient reported no further return of the itching and discomfort.

This brief clinical vignette exemplifies a general observation of some considerable interest to an understanding of hypnosis: it seems to be effective in treating symptoms that are not under the direct control of the central nervous system. Moreover, the benefits deriving from direct suggestion under hypnosis are more apt to be directly correlated with hypnotic ability when the complaint concerns a vegetative symptom—for example, pain (Hilgard and Hilgard 1975), skin allergies (Black 1969), asthma (Maher-Loughnan 1970; Collison 1975), severe burns (Chapman, Goodell, and Wolff 1959), migraine (Cedercreutz 1978), and even congenital skin disorders (Mason 1952)—than when the complaint concerns habit disorders such as smoking and overeating (Wadden and Anderton 1982). The latter problems seem more responsive to motivational and expectational effects mobilized by hypnotic and other forms of treatment (Perry, Gelfand, and Marcovitch 1979; Wadden and Anderton 1982; McConkey 1984a), and successful treatment of them with hypnosis is far less likely to correlate with hypnotic ability (though, for a counterexample, see Andersen 1985).

Notice that, if hypnotically enhanced motivation and expectations for success were alone sufficient to ameliorate or eliminate various vegetative disorders, then, as in the case with habit disorders, everyone who submitted to hypnotic treatment for such problems should have a good chance at success—regardless of how hypnotizable they were. The only conceivable advantage of high hypnotizability would thus be a very limited one: patients high in hypnotic ability would be more able than their low-hypnotizable counterparts to dissociate from consciousness any special effort or motivation involved in achieving treatment success. Thus, high- but not low-hypnotizable subjects would experience the successful remission of their symptoms as occurring effortlessly and nonvolitionally. As already indicated, however, the evidence seems to suggest that, the higher the patient's hypnotic ability, the more likely he or she is to obtain significant relief from various vegetative disorders as a result of direct suggestions under hypnosis. So it is not merely how the relief is experienced but its occurrence that seems correlated with hypnotic ability.

The above comments imply that the mental mechanisms underlying successful hypnotic treatment of vegetative disorders differ from those operative in the successful treatment of habit disorders. Insofar as the latter are particularly responsive to enhanced motivation and expectations for healing, there is some reason to think that placebo effects are in fact operative (Frank 1973). However, there is very good evidence that the mechanisms operative in hypnotic analgesia are not due to placebo effects (McGlashen, Evans, and Orne 1969; Stern et al. 1977), and it is highly unlikely that many of the reports in the literature regarding hypnotic treatment of warts (Sinclair-Gieben and Chalmers 1959), of skin allergies (Black 1969), and of burns (Chapman, Goodell, and Wolff 1959) can be explained as a placebo effect (Bowers 1979a). For example, in many of the articles cited above, there was compelling evidence that the treatment effects were, per suggestion, unilateral—that is, confined to one arm or one side of the body. It seems highly improbable that a generalized expectation of healing could account for such "zone-specific" healing (Bowers 1979a). My assumption is that appropriate suggestive communications under hypnosis directly and selectively activate lower centers of cognitive control, thereby circumventing the initiative and/or interference of the executive control center. Indeed, many hypnotically achieved treatment effects, such as unilateral inhibition of allergic reactions, seem difficult and even impossible to achieve by a conscious, willful effort, and some concept of dissociated control therefore seems implicated.

The Example of Hypnotic Analgesia

By way of documenting the notion of dissociated control, I would like to summarize a dissertation recently conducted in my laboratory by Mary Miller (1986; the first half was published as Miller and Bowers 1986). This investigation proceeded on the assumption—confirmed by many previous investigations (e.g., Hilgard 1967; McGlashen, Evans, and Orne 1969; Spanos et al. 1979)—that the degree of hypnotic analgesia would correlate with hypnotic ability. What was novel about her experiment was the inclusion of subjects carefully selected for their hypnotic ability but exposed to nonhypnotic treatment interventions. The prediction was that these latter subjects would successfully reduce pain but that the amount of pain reduction would not correlate with hypnotic ability. This pattern of findings would suggest that mechanisms responsible for generating hypnotic analgesia are different from those generating pain reduction by nonhypnotic means. In sum, Miller addressed directly the difference between hypnotic phenomena conceptualized as a dissociative (Type II) process, on one hand, and as reducible to deliberately enacted cognitive strategies that were simply misattributed as nonvolitional, on the other.

In one study, Miller ran high- medium- and low-hypnotizable subjects in one of three treatment groups. The first group was hypnotized and administered standard suggestions for pain analgesia. A second group was administered a treatment known as stress inoculation, which is based on a cognitive-behavioral model of pain control (Turk, Meichenbaum, and Genest 1983). Subjects were informed that how they thought about and coped with the sensation of pain could modify their experience of it, and they were then trained in a variety of cognitive strategies designed to aid them in their coping efforts. The third treatment group was handled in exactly the same way as the stress inoculation condition, with one exception: at the last minute, subjects in this group were told that people who minimized pain by hypnosis did so by invoking cognitive strategies—"so what you will be doing involves hypnotic reduction of pain." In other words, this last-minute addendum established a hypnotic context (Gruenewald 1982) that might potentiate whatever pain reduction resulted from stress inoculation.

The ten high- and ten low-hypnotizable subjects in each of the three treatment groups had twice experienced hypnosis—once on the Harvard Group Scale of Hypnotic Susceptibility (Shor and Orne 1962) and once on a group version of the Standard Scale of Hypnotic Susceptibility, form C (Weitzenhoffer and Hilgard 1962). In addition they had all been exposed to a pretreatment immersion of cold pressor and then provided with one of three treatment interventions for the control of pain. Consequently, subjects were all well prepared for the posttreatment exposure to cold pressor. However, they were not informed of this second exposure until after completing the first cold pressor immersion. As in the pretreatment immersion, subjects here gave pain ratings from 0 to 10 once every ten seconds, and the pain ratings for the first fifty seconds of the cold pressor constituted the data for analysis. The experimenter was blind regarding the subject's hypnotic ability and did not know which treatment he or she was to receive until after the first immersion was completed.

The findings revealed that the expected correlation between pain reduction and hypnotic ability occurred in the hypnotic analgesia condition (point biserial $r = .48$, $p < .02$) but not in the stress inoculation condition (point biserial $r = .04$) or in the stress inoculation condition when defined as hypnosis (point biserial $r = .18$, NS). Moreover, an analysis of the cognitive strategies reported after the posttreatment immersion indicated that sixteen out of eighteen people in the stress inoculation condition reported thoughts and fantasies that were later judged (by two independent judges) to be strategic enactments for reducing pain. When the stress inoculation condition was defined as hypnotic, seventeen out of eighteen subjects reported such thoughts and fantasies. However, only three out of eighteen subjects in the hypnotic analgesia condition reported thoughts and fantasies that were later judged to be strategic enactments instrumental to pain reduction. There was a significant correlation of .36 between strategy use and the reduction in pain ratings from pre- to posttreatment cold pressor immersions. Cognitive strategies did therefore seem to counter pain in direct proportion to the extent of their use. However, they were used very little in the hypnotic analgesia condition, and only in this condition did pain reduction correlate with hypnotic ability. As summarized by Miller and Bowers (1986), "The use of cognitive strategies and one's hypnotic responsiveness each play a powerful role in potentiating treatment effects, but they seem to operate quite distinctly and independently from one another. Cognitive strategy use leads to pain reductions only in the nonhypnotic treatments, whereas hypnotic ability potentiates pain reduction only in the hypnotic treatment" (11–12).

In this first of two studies, Miller had to rely on a differing pattern of correlates from hypnotic to nonhypnotic conditions to infer differing mechanisms underlying the two different kinds of pain reduction. In her second study, however, she tried to establish this fact more directly.

The deliberate enactment of cognitive strategies to reduce pain presumably involves conscious effort, and this effort should in turn interfere with a simultaneously performed task that requires conscious processing of information. According to Spanos (1986) and other advocates of a social psychological interpretation of hypnosis, hypnotic analgesia consists precisely of various strategic enactments that successfully minimize the experience of pain. The strategies are actively and consciously deployed; subjects' later reports to the contrary are presumably due to misattributing the analgesic effect to fantasies and to the hypnotic context in which the reduced pain is experienced.

If Spanos is right, that is, if hypnotic analgesia is achieved by the same kind of cognitive strategies that subjects use in cognitive-behavioral treatments of pain control, then hypnotic analgesia should interfere with the performance of a simultaneous task that requires conscious attention. Indeed, hypnotic analgesia should interfere with such a task to the same extent as cognitive strategies not performed under the aegis of hypnosis. Miller (1986) set out to test this hypothesis in her second experiment.

The Nelson-Denny Reading Test (1973) was used to compete with hypnotic analgesia and with a stress inoculation strategy of pain control. This test adopts a multiple-choice format, in which the subject is given a word to define and five alternative choices, only one of which is a synonym (e.g., "A quandary is a: a) quarrel, b) foundry c) predicament d) guest e) factory"). For purposes of the experiment, three separate vocabulary tests were composed by drawing thirty-seven items randomly from forms A and D of the Nelson-Denny Reading Test. The first of the three versions thus created served as a baseline assessment of a subject's vocabulary. The second version was administered during the subject's pretreatment assessment of cold pressor pain, and the third version was administered during the posttreatment assessment of cold pressor pain. This procedure permitted Miller to covary out the subject's baseline vocabulary from both his or her pre- and posttreatment vocabulary performance.

Subjects were eighteen high- and eighteen low-hypnotizable subjects (here, as in the first experiment, identified on the Harvard Group Scale of Hypnotic Susceptibility and on a group adaptation of the Stanford Scale of Hypnotic Susceptibility). After the initial vocabulary assessment, subjects were all administered a pretreatment assessment of cold pressor pain. During the period of immersion, subjects took the second version of the vocabulary test, reporting their answers orally, just as they had done on the first assessment. Unlike the first experiment, the pain ratings were not provided during the actual immersion. Instead, subjects were asked immediately after the immersion to rate from 0 to 10 the pain levels that they had experienced at the beginning, middle, and end of the immersion.

After completing the pretreatment, subjects were for the first time informed of the second phase of the experiment; half the high and half the low hypnotizables were then assigned to either a hypnotic analgesia or to a stress inoculation treatment condition. After the treatment intervention, subjects were exposed to a second (posttreatment) immersion, which proceeded in the same way as the first one had. The experimenter was blind throughout the experiment regarding the hypnotic ability of the subjects and did not know until after the pretreatment immersion which treatment the subject would eventually receive.

As expected, the pain ratings during the posttreatment trials (adjusted for corresponding pretreatment ratings) indicated that the high hypnotizables experienced significantly less pain and distress than did low hypnotizables in the hypnotic analgesia condition. Unexpectedly, superior analgesic effects in high relative to low hypnotizables also emerged in the stress inoculation condition. That is, the anticipated subjects by treatment interaction was not forthcoming.

The main question for this study of course concerns the effect of pain and of the two kinds of pain reduction on the vocabulary test performance. From its baseline assessment, vocabulary performance declined by 25–45 percent during the first (pretreatment) immersion in cold pressor. Clearly, the pain of cold pressor adversely affected subjects' ability to perform a cognitively demanding task. What, then, is the effect of the two different pain control treatments on vocabulary performance during the posttreatment cold pressor immersion? For the high hypnotizables in the stress inoculation condition, there is an additional 31 percent drop in their vocabulary performance from pre- to posttreatment immersion in the cold pressor. The comparable reduction for the low hypnotizable subjects in the stress inoculation condition is 30 percent. This reduction in the subjects' vocabulary scores transpired despite the fact that they successfully reduced pain—presumably through the use of cognitive strategies that interfered with their ability to deal with the vocabulary test.

The situation in the hypnotic analgesia condition was quite different. The low hypnotizables show only a slight (8 percent) decrease in their vocabulary performance from the pre- to the posttreatment immersion in the cold pressor; the high hypnotizables, on the other hand, show a slight (10 percent) increase in their vocabulary performance from the pre- to the posttreatment cold pressor immersion. In other words, despite the fact that hypnotic analgesia is quite effective in reducing the pain of high-hypnotizable subjects, it does not lead to any further deterioration in a simultaneously performed task; indeed, it permits a modest recovery of the cognitive functioning that is badly impaired by the pain of cold pressor. Presumably, this recovery is due to the fact that hypnotic analgesia makes the cold pressor less painful and does so in a manner that does not require diverting conscious effort from the vocabulary task.

The pattern of findings in Miller's two investigations strongly suggests that the reductions in pain achieved by hypnotic analgesia are not mediated by the deliberate enactment of cognitive strategies. Such strategies are clearly effective in reducing pain. However, in the first study, when they were the principle basis for an analgesic effect, the degree of pain reduction did not correlate with hypnotic ability.[2] Moreover, the second study indicated that reducing pain by the effortful enactment of cognitive strategies interferes with a simultaneously performed task that also demands high-level processing of information. The extent of hypnotic analgesia, on the other hand, is invariably characterized by its correlation with hypnotic ability, and we now have direct evidence indicating that hypnotic analgesia does not seem to require executive initiative and/or the sustained effort of higher, conscious processes. Rather, lower levels of cognitive (pain) control seem to be activated more or less directly by the suggestions for hypnotic analgesia. This is precisely what is meant by dissociated control, which I think characterizes hypnotic responding and distinguishes it from other forms of responsiveness to social influence.

Conclusion

When the complexities of unconscious influence intersect with the complexities of hypnosis, there is bound to be some difficult intellectual terrain to travel. Historically, it has been easy to over-emphasize the unconscious effect of specific content variables—such as sex and aggression—and to exaggerate beyond all plausibility the properties and powers of hypnosis. The legacy of skeptical inquiry has doubtless served a very useful purpose in both areas, making us more critical and cautious in our claims. Moreover, the fact that both domains of inquiry now have established research traditions means that healthy doses of empiricism can be brought to bear on flights of fancy that have often characterized work in these two areas. With time, however, it has become clear that we simply cannot make due with a psychology that does not incorporate a well-conceived notion of unconscious influences. Nor, I would argue, can a well-turned theory of hypnosis—one that is sensitive to clinical as well as experimental evidence—evolve without regard to unconscious influences.

As is well known, Freud in his writings referred repeatedly to hypnosis—

2. The fact that such a correlation did appear in the second study probably reflected the fact that high hypnotizables were more able than their low counterparts to become effortlessly absorbed in the strategies. Recall that in the second investigation, unlike the first one, subjects were not required to provide pain reports every ten seconds; this lack of interruption may well have been conducive to the high hypnotizable subjects' becoming thoroughly and uninterruptedly involved in the strategies, even though they had not been hypnotized (Miller 1986). Whether this somewhat ad hoc explanation really accounts for the unexpected correlation between pain reduction and hypnotic ability in the stress inoculation condition remains to be seen.

particularly to posthypnotic amnesia—as an example of how ideas could be both unconscious and influential (cf. Erdelyi 1985). There is a sense in which the current chapter returns the favor, examining how a descriptive model of unconscious influences might help clarify hypnosis. It will take time to see whether the intersection between these two phenomena maps out terrain too steep for the conventional traveler or whether it will now begin to pique the interest of psychologists anxious for some exciting and challenging intellectual scenery that too few of us have enjoyed.

References

Andersen, M. S. 1985. Hypnotizability as a factor in the hypnotic treatment of obesity. *International Journal of Clinical and Experimental Hypnosis* 33:150–59.

Ashford, B., and A. G. Hammer. 1978. The role of expectancies in the occurrence of posthypnotic amnesia. *International Journal of Clinical and Experimental Hypnosis* 36:281–91.

Bailly, J. S., et al. [1784] 1965. Secret report on mesmerism, or animal magnetism. In *The nature of hypnosis,* ed. R. E. Shor and M. T. Orne. New York: Holt, Rinehart & Winston.

Balthazard, C. G., and E. Z. Woody. 1985. "The spectral analysis of hypnotic performance with respect to 'absorption.'" Department of Psychology, University of Waterloo. Typescript.

Barber, J. 1977. Rapid induction analgesia: A clinical report. *American Journal of Clinical Hypnosis* 19:138–47.

———. 1980. Hypnosis in the unhypnotizable. *American Journal of Clinical Hypnosis* 23:4–9.

Bargh, J. A. 1984. Automatic and conscious processing of social stimuli. In *Handbook of social cognition,* vol. 3, ed. R. S. Wyer and T. K. Srull. Hillsdale, N.J.: Erlbaum.

Bennett, H. L. 1988. Perception and memory for events during adequate general anesthesia for surgical operations. In *Hypnosis and memory,* ed. H. Pettinati. New York: Guildford.

Bennett, H. L., H. S. Davis, and J. A. Giannini. 1981. Nonverbal response to intraoperative conversation. *British Journal of Anaesthesia* 57:174–79.

Black, S. 1969. *Mind and body.* London: Kimber.

Bower, G. 1981. Mood and memory. *American Psychologist* 35:129–48.

Bowers, K. S. 1973. Hypnosis, attribution, and demand characteristics. *International Journal of Clinical and Experimental Hypnosis* 21:226–38.

———. 1975. The psychology of subtle control: An attributional analysis of behavioral persistence. *Canadian Journal of Behavioral Science* 7:78–95.

———. 1979a. Hypnosis and healing. *Australian Journal of Clinical and Experimental Hypnosis* 7:261–77.

———. 1979b. *Hypnosis for the seriously curious.* New York: Norton.

————. 1981. Do the Stanford Scales tap the "classic suggestion effect"? *International Journal of Clinical and Experimental Hypnosis* 29:42–53.

————. 1984a. Hypnosis. In *Personality and the behavioral disorders.* 2d ed., ed. N. S. Endler and J. McV. Hunt. New York: Wiley.

————. 1984b. On being unconsciously influenced and informed. In *The unconscious reconsidered,* ed. K. S. Bowers and D. Meichenbaum. New York: Wiley.

————. 1987. Revisioning the unconscious. *Canadian Psychology* 28:93–104.

Bowers, K. S., and H. A. Brenneman. 1981. Hypnotic dissociation, dichotic listening, and active versus passive modes of attention. *Journal of Abnormal Psychology* 90:55–67.

Bowers, K. S., and T. M. Davidson. 1986. On the importance of individual differences in hypnotic ability. *Behavioral and Brain Sciences* 9:468–69.

Bowers, K. S., and P. Kelly. 1979. Stress, disease, psychotherapy and hypnosis. *Journal of Abnormal Psychology* 88:490–505.

Bowers, K. S., and S. LeBaron. 1986. Hypnosis and hypnotizability: Implications for clinical interventions. *Hospital and Community Psychiatry* 37:457–67.

Bowers, K. S., and D. Meichenbaum. 1984. *The unconscious reconsidered.* New York: Wiley.

Bowers, P. G. 1982. The classic suggestion effect: Relationships with scales of hypnotizability, effortless experiencing, and imagery vividness. *International Journal of Clinical and Experimental Hypnosis* 30:270–79.

Brehm, J. W. 1966. *A theory of psychological reactance.* New York: Academic.

Breuer, J., and S. Freud. [1893–95] 1974. *Studies on hysteria.* Harmondsworth: Penguin.

Campion, J., R. Latto, and Y. M. Smith. 1983. Is blindsight an effect of scattered light, spared cortex, and near-threshold vision? *Behavioral and Brain Sciences* 6:423–48.

Cedercreutz, C. 1978. Hypnotic treatment of 100 cases of migraine. In *Hypnosis at its bicentennial,* ed. F. H. Frankel and H. S. Zamansky. New York: Plenum.

Chapman, L. F., H. Goodell, and H. G. Wolff. 1959. Changes in tissue vulnerability induced during hypnotic suggestion. *Journal of Psychosomatic Research* 4:99–105.

Cheesman, J., and P. M. Merikle. 1986. Distinguishing conscious from unconscious processes. *Canadian Journal of Psychology* 40:343–67.

Cialdini, R. 1985. *Influence: Science and practice.* Glenview, Ill.:Scott-Foresman.

Clark, R. 1971. *Einstein: The life and times.* New York: World.

Coe, W., K. Kobayashi, and M. I. Howard. 1973. Experimental and ethical problems of evaluating the influence of hypnosis in antisocial conduct. *Journal of Abnormal Psychology* 82:476–82.

Collison, D. A. 1975. Which asthmatic patients should be treated by hypnotherapy. *Medical Journal of Australia* 1:776–81.

Conway, F., and J. Siegelman. 1978. *Snapping.* New York: Delta.

Delgado, R. 1977. Religious totalism: Gentle and ungentle persuasion under the first amendment. *Southern California Law Review* 51:1–98.

Dennett, D. C. 1969. *Content and consciousness.* London: Routledge & Kegan Paul.

Dixon, N.F. 1971. *Subliminal perception: The nature of a controversy.* London: McGraw-Hill.

Dulany, D. E. 1962. The place of hypotheses and intentions: An analysis of verbal control in verbal conditioning. In *Behavior and awareness,* ed. C. W. Eriksen. Durham, N.C.: Duke University Press.

Dyer, G. 1985. *War.* New York: Crown.

Erdelyi, M. H. 1985. *Psychoanalysis: Freud's cognitive psychology.* New York: Freeman.

Erdelyi, M. H., and B. Goldberg. 1979. Let's not sweep repression under the rug: Toward a cognitive psychology of repression. In *Functional disorders of memory,* ed. J. F. Kihlstrom and F. J. Evans. Hillsdale, N.J.: Erlbaum.

Erickson, M. H., and E. L. Rossi. 1980. The indirect forms of suggestion. In *The collected papers of Milton H. Erickson on hypnosis,* vol. 1, *The nature of hypnosis and suggestion,* ed. E. L. Rossi. New York: Irvington.

Eriksen, C. W. 1959. Unconscious processes. In *Nebraska Symposium on Motivation, 1958,* ed. M. R. Jones. Lincoln: University of Nebraska Press.

———. 1960. Discrimination and learning without awareness: A methodological survey and evaluation. *Psychological Review* 67:279–300.

Evans, F. J. 1979. Hypnosis and sleep: Techniques for exploring cognitive activity during sleep. In *Hypnosis: Developments in research and new perspectives,* ed. E. Fromm and R. E. Shor. New York: Aldine.

Evans, F. J., L. A. Gustafson, D. N. O'Connell, M. T. Orne, and R. E. Shor. 1966. Response during sleep with intervening waking amnesia. *Science* 152:666–67.

———. 1970. Verbally induced behavioral responses during sleep. *Journal of Nervous and Mental Disease* 150:170–87.

Evans, F. J., and M. T. Orne. 1971. The disappearing hypnotist: The use of simulating subjects to evaluate how subjects perceive experimental procedures. *International Journal of Clinical and Experimental Hypnosis* 19:277–96.

Frank, J. 1973. *Persuasion and healing.* Baltimore: Johns Hopkins University Press.

Freud, S. [1908] 1959. Hysterical phantasies and their relation to bisexuality. In *Sigmund Freud: Collected Papers,* Vol. 2, ed. E. Jones. New York: Basic.

———. [1915] 1959. Repression. In *A general selection from the works of Sigmund Freud,* ed. J. Rickman and C. Brenner. Garden City, N.Y.: Doubleday.

Fromm, E. 1979. The nature of hypnosis and other altered states of consciousness: An ego psychological theory. In *Hypnosis: Developments in research and new perspectives,* ed. E. Fromm and R. E. Shor. New York: Aldine.

Gill, M. M., and M. Brenman. 1959. *Hypnosis and related states: Psychoanalytic studies in regression.* New York: International Universities Press.

Gorassini, D. R., and N. P. Spanos. 1986. A social-cognitive skills approach to the successful modification of hypnotic susceptibility. *Journal of Personality and Social Psychology* 50:1004–12.

Gruenewald, D. 1982. Some thoughts on the distinction between the hypnotic situation and the hypnotic condition. *American Journal of Clinical Hypnosis* 25:46–51.

Hammer, A. G., W-L. Walker, and A. D. Diment. 1978. A nonsuggested effect of trance induction. In *Hypnosis at its bicentennial,* ed. F. Frankel and H. S. Zamansky. New York: Plenum.

Hilgard, E. R. 1965. *Hypnotic susceptibility.* New York: Harcourt, Brace & World.

———. 1967. A quantitative study of pain and its reduction through hypnotic suggestion. *Proceedings of the National Academy of Sciences, U.S.* 57:1581–86.

————. 1973. A neo-dissociation interpretation of pain reduction in hypnosis. *Psychological Review* 80:396–411.

————. 1977. *Divided consciousness: Multiple controls in human thought and action.* New York: Wiley.

————. 1979. Divided consciousness in hypnosis: The implications of the hidden observer. In *Hypnosis: Developments in research and new perspectives,* ed. E. Fromm and R. E. Shor. New York: Aldine.

Hilgard, E. R., and J. R. Hilgard. *Hypnosis in the relief of pain.* Los Altos, Calif.: Kaufmann.

Hilgard, J. R., and S. LeBaron. *Hypnotherapy of pain in children with cancer.* Los Altos, Calif.: Kaufmann.

Holender, D. 1986. Semantic activation without conscious identification. *Behavioral and Brain Sciences* 9:1–23.

Hull, C. L. 1933. *Hypnosis and suggestibility: An experimental approach.* New York: Appleton-Century-Crofts.

Janet, P. [1929] 1965. *The major symptoms of hysteria.* New York: Hafner.

Kelley, H. H. 1973. The process of causal attribution. *American Psychologist* 28:107–28.

Kidder, L. 1972. On becoming hypnotized: How skeptics become convinced: A case study of attitude change? *Journal of Abnormal Psychology* 80:317–22.

Kihlstrom, J. F. 1984. Conscious, subconscious, unconscious: A cognitive perspective. In *The unconscious reconsidered,* ed. K. S. Bowers and D. Meichenbaum. New York: Wiley.

————. 1986. Strong inferences about hypnosis. *Behavioral and Brain Sciences* 9:474–75.

Kruglanski, A. 1980. Lay epistemo-logic–process and contents: Another look at attribution theory. *Psychological Review* 87:70–87.

Lakatos, I. 1970. Falsification and the methodology of scientific research programmes. In *Criticism and the growth of knowledge,* ed. I. Lakatos and A. Musgrave. Cambridge: Cambridge University Press.

Lundh, L-G. 1979. Introspection, consciousness, and human information processing. *Scandinavian Journal of Psychology* 20:223–38.

Lyons, W. 1986. *The disappearance of introspection.* Cambridge, Mass.: MIT Press.

McConkey, K. M. 1984a. Clinical hypnosis: Differential impact on volitional and nonvolitional disorders. *Canadian Psychology* 25:79–83.

————. 1984b. The impact of an indirect suggestion. *International Journal of Clinical and Experimental Hypnosis* 32:307–14.

McGlashan, T. H., F. J. Evans, and M. T. Orne. 1969. The nature of hypnotic analgesia and the placebo response to experimental pain. *Psychosomatic Medicine* 31:227–46.

MacKay, D. 1973. Aspects of the theory of comprehension, memory and attention. *Quarterly Journal of Experimental Psychology* 25:22–40.

Maher-Loughnan, G. P. 1970. Hypnosis and autohypnosis for the treatment of asthma. *International Journal of Clinical and Experimental Hypnosis* 28:1–14.

Marcel, A. J. 1983. Conscious and unconscious perception: An approach to the relations between phenomenal experience and perceptual processes. *Cognitive Psychology* 15:238–300.

Marks, J. 1979. *The search for the "Manchurian candidate" : The CIA and mind control.* New York: Times Books.

Mason, A. A. 1952. A case of congenital ichthyosiform erythrodermia of Brocq treated by hypnosis. *British Medical Journal,* 23 August, 422–23.

Matthews, W. J., H. Bennett, W. Bean, and M. Gallagher. 1985. Indirect versus direct hypnotic suggestions—an initial investigation: A brief communication. *International Journal of Clinical and Experimental Hypnosis* 33:219–23.

Meichenbaum, D., and J. B. Gilmore. 1984. The nature of unconscious processes: A cognitive-behavioral perspective. In *The unconscious reconsidered,* ed. K. S. Bowers and D. Meichenbaum. New York: Wiley.

Milgram, S. 1963. Behavioral study of obedience. *Journal of Abnormal and Social Psychology* 67:371–78.

Miller, G. A., E. Galanter, and K. H. Pribram. 1960. *Plans and the structure of behavior.* New York: Holt.

Miller, M. E. 1986. "Hypnotic analgesia and stress inoculation in the reduction of cold-pressor pain." Ph.D. diss., University of Waterloo.

Miller, M. E., and K. S. Bowers. 1986. Hypnotic analgesia and stress inoculation in the reduction of pain. *Journal of Abnormal Psychology* 95:6–14.

Morgan, A. H., D. L. Johnson, and E. R. Hilgard. 1974. The stability of hypnotic susceptibility: A longitudinal study. *International Journal of Clinical and Experimental Hypnosis* 22:249–57.

Morris, G. O., and M. T. Singer. 1966. Sleep deprivation: The context of consciousness. *Journal of Nervous and Mental Disease* 143:291–304.

Nelson-Denny Reading Test. 1973. Chicago: Houghton-Mifflin.

Nisbett, R., and L. Ross. 1980. *Human inference: Strategies and shortcomings of social judgment.* Englewood Cliffs, N.J.: Prentice-Hall.

Nisbett, R., and T. D. Wilson. 1977. Telling more than we can know: Verbal reports on mental processes. *Psychological Review* 84:231–54.

Orne, M. T. 1959. The nature of hypnosis: Artifact and essence. *Journal of Abnormal and Social Psychology* 58:277–99.

———. 1961. The potential uses of hypnosis in interrogation. In *The manipulation of human behavior,* ed. S. D. Biderman and H. Zimmer. New York: Wiley.

———. 1962. On the social psychology of the psychological experiment: With particular reference to demand characteristics and their implications. *American Psychologist* 17: 776–83.

———. 1966. Hypnosis, motivation, and compliance. *American Journal of Psychiatry* 122:721–26.

———. 1969. Demand characteristics and the concept of quasi-controls. In *Artifact in behavioral research,* ed. R. Rosenthal and R. L. Rosnow. New York: Academic.

———. 1979. On the simulating subject as a quasi-control group in hypnosis research: What, why, and how. In *Hypnosis: Developments in research and new perspectives,* 2d ed., ed. E. Fromm and R. E. Shor. New York: Aldine.

Perry, C. 1979. Hypnotic coercion and compliance to it: A review of evidence presented in a legal case. *International Journal of Clinical and Experimental Hypnosis* 27:187–218.

Perry, C., R. Gelfand, and P. Marcovitch. 1979. The relevance of hypnotic susceptibility in the clinical context. *Journal of Abnormal Psychology* 88:592–603.

Perry, C., and J-R. Laurence. 1983. Hypnosis, surgery, and mind-body interaction: An historical evaluation. *Canadian Journal of Behavioral Science* 15:351–72.

———. 1984. Mental processing outside of awareness: The contributions of Freud and Janet. In *The unconscious reconsidered,* ed. K. S. Bowers and D. Meichenbaum. New York: Wiley.

Popper, K. 1979. *Objective knowledge: An evolutionary approach.* Rev. ed. Oxford: Oxford University Press.

Rayner, K., and J. H. Bertera. 1979. Reading without a fovea. *Science* 206:468–69.

Reyher, J. 1967. Hypnosis in research on psychopathology. In *Handbook of clinical and experimental hypnosis,* ed. J. Gordon. New York: Macmillan.

Rogers, C. R. 1959. A theory of therapy, personality, and interpersonal relationships, as developed in the client-centered framework. In *Psychology: A study of science,* ed. S. Koch. New York: McGraw-Hill.

Rosenthal, R. 1963. On the social psychology of the psychological experiment: The experimenter's hypothesis as unintended determinant of experimental results. *American Scientist* 51:268–83.

Ross, M., and G. J. O. Fletcher. 1985. Attribution and social perception. In *The handbook of social psychology,* ed. G. Lindzey and E. Aronson, 3d ed., vol. 2. New York: Random House.

Schafer, D. W. 1975. Hypnosis on a burn unit. *International Journal of Clinical and Experimental Hypnosis* 23:1–14.

Sheehan, P. W., and C. W. Perry. 1976. *Methodologies of hypnosis: A critical appraisal of contemporary paradigms of hypnosis.* Hillsdale, N.J.: Erlbaum.

Shiffrin, R. M., and W. Schneider. 1977. Controlled and automatic human information processing. II. Perceptual learning, automatic attending, and a general theory. *Psychological Review* 84:127–90.

Shor, R. E. 1970. The three-factor theory of hypnosis as applied to the book-reading fantasy and to the concept of suggestion. *International Journal of Clinical and Experimental Psychology* 28:89–98.

———. 1979. A phenomenological method for the measurement of variables important to an understanding of the nature of hypnosis. In *Hypnosis: Developments in research and new perspectives,* ed. E. Fromm and R. E. Shor. New York: Aldine.

Shor, R. E., and E. C. Orne. 1962. *Harvard Group Scale of Hypnotic Susceptibility, form A.* Palo Alto, Calif.: Consulting Psychologists Press.

Shor, R. E., D. D. Pistole, R. D. Easton, and J. F. Kihlstrom. 1984. Relation of predicted to actual hypnotic responsiveness, with special reference to posthypnotic amnesia. *International Journal of Clinical and Experimental Hypnosis* 32:376–87.

Sidis, B. 1898. *The psychology of suggestion.* New York: Appleton.

Sinclair-Gieben, A. H. C., and D. Chalmers. 1959. Evaluation of treatment of warts by hypnosis. *Lancet,* 3 October, 480–82.

Skinner, B. F. 1963. Behaviorism at fifty. *Science* 140:951–58.

Spanos, N. P. 1986. Hypnotic behavior: A social-psychological interpretation of amnesia, analgesia, and "trance logic." *Behavioral and Brain Sciences* 9:449–67.

Spanos, N. P., and L. Radtke-Bodorik. 1980. Integrating hypnotic phenomena with cognitive psychology: An illustration using suggested amnesia. *Bulletin of British Society of Experimental and Clinical Hypnosis* 3:4–7.

Spanos, N. P., L. Radtke-Bodorik, J. D. Ferguson, and B. Jones. 1979. The effects of susceptibility, suggestions for analgesia and the utilization of cognitive strategies on the reduction of pain. *Journal of Abnormal Psychology* 88:282–92.

Spanos, N. P., S. M. Rivers, and S. Ross. 1977. Experienced involuntariness and response to hypnotic suggestions. In *Conceptual and investigative approaches to hypnosis and hypnotic phenomena,* ed. W. R. Edmonston, Jr. *Annals of the New York Academy of Sciences* 296:208–21.

Spanos, N. P., L. A. Robertson, E. P. Menary, and P. J. Brett. 1986. *Journal of Abnormal Psychology* 95:350–57.

Sperry, R. W. 1968. Hemisphere disconnection and unity in conscious awareness. *American Psychologist* 23:723–33.

Spielberger, C. D. 1962. The role of awareness in verbal conditioning. In *Behavior and awareness,* ed. C. W. Eriksen. Durham, N.C.: Duke University Press.

Stern, J. A., M. Brown, G. A. Ulett, and I. Sletten. 1977. A comparison of hypnosis, acupuncture, morphine, valium, aspirin, and placebo in the management of experimentally induced pain. In *Conceptual and investigative approaches to hypnosis and hypnotic phenomena,* ed. W. R. Edmonston, Jr. *Annals of the New York Academy of Sciences* 296:175–93.

Sullivan, H. S. 1953. *The interpersonal theory of psychiatry.* New York: Sullivan.

Swanson, J. M., and M. Kinsbourne. 1979. State dependent learning and retrieval: Methodological cautions and theoretical considerations. In *Functional disorders of memory,* ed. J. F. Kihlstrom and F. J. Evans. Hillsdale, N.J.: Erlbaum.

Tellegen, A. 1978–79. On measures and conceptions of hypnosis. *American Journal of Clinical Hypnosis* 21:219–37.

Tellegen, A., and G. Atkinson. 1974. Openness to absorbing and self-altering experiences ("absorption"), a trait related to hypnotic susceptibility. *Journal of Abnormal Psychology* 83:268–77.

Tinterow, M. M. 1970. *Foundations of hypnosis: From Mesmer to Freud.* Springfield, Ill.: Thomas.

Turk, D., D. Meichenbaum, and M. Genest. 1983. *Pain and behavioral medicine: A cognitive-behavioral perspective.* New York: Guilford.

Tversky, A., and D. Kahneman. 1974. Judgment under uncertainty: Heuristics and biases. *Science* 185:1124–31.

Van Gorp, W. G., R. G. Meyer, and K. D. Dunbar. 1985. The efficacy of direct versus indirect hypnotic induction techniques on reduction of experimental pain. *International Journal of Clinical and Experimental Hypnosis* 33:319–28.

Varendonck, J. 1921. *The psychology of daydreams.* New York: Macmillan.

Verplanck, W. 1962. Unaware of where's awareness: Some verbal operants—notates, monents, and notants. In *Behavior and awareness,* ed. C. W. Eriksen. Durham, N.C.: Duke University Press.

Wadden, T. A., and C. H. Anderton. 1982. The clinical use of hypnosis. *Psychological Bulletin* 91:215–43.

Wegner, D. M., and R. R. Vallacher. 1977. *Implicit psychology.* New York: Oxford University Press.

Weiskrantz, L., E. K. Warrington, M. D. Sanders, and J. Marshall. 1974. Visual capacity in the hemianopic field following a restricted occipital ablation. *Brain* 97:709–28.

Weitzenhoffer, A. M. 1974. When is an "instruction" an "instruction?" *Internal Journal of Clinical and Experimental Hypnosis* 22:258–69.

————. 1978. Hypnotism and altered states of consciousness. In *Expanding dimensions of consciousness,* ed. A. A. Sugarman and R. E. Tarter. New York: Springer.

————. 1980. Hypnotic susceptibility revisited. *American Journal of Clinical Hypnosis* 22:130–46.

Weitzenhoffer, A. M., and E. R. Hilgard. 1962. *Stanford Hypnotic Susceptibility Scale, form C.* Palo Alto, Calif.: Consulting Psychologists Press.

Zuckerman, M. 1964. Perceptual isolation as a stress situation: A review. *Archives of General Psychiatry* 11:255–76.

8 Repression, Dissociation, and Hypnosis

JOHN F. KIHLSTROM AND IRENE P. HOYT

Since the time of Janet and Freud, hypnosis has been regarded as a valuable medium for the investigation of unconscious processes. However, these processes have been described in different terms by different authorities. Janet thought that the mechanism responsible for denying conscious access to certain mental contents was dissociation (his term was actually *desagregation*), while Freud postulated the concept of repression. Both processes were held to deny certain mental contents to phenomenal awareness and voluntary control. Both assume the existence of a psychological unconscious, by which percepts, memories, and thoughts denied to conscious awareness could nevertheless exert a palpable effect on ongoing experience and action. Yet it is also clear that the two concepts are different—at least, they were different in the minds of Janet and Freud. Janet seems to have believed that repression was a special form of dissociation, in which the denial to consciousness was motivated by considerations of defense. Freud, for his part, seemed to believe that dissociation was utterly trivial and that repression was a separate process with its own ontological status.

In fact, about all that Janet and Freud agreed on, or so it would seem, was that nonconscious mental processes were psychologically important and that the phenomena of hypnosis illustrated them. The purpose of this chapter is briefly to survey the application of repression and dissociation concepts to the phenomena of hypnosis, in the hopes of achieving some conceptual and empirical distinctions between them. Because dissociation has received a great deal of attention in recent years (e.g., Hilgard 1977; Kihlstrom 1984, 1985,

The point of view represented in this chapter is based on research supported in part by grant MH-35856 from the National Institute of Mental Health and in part by an H. I. Romnes Faculty Fellowship from the University of Wisconsin and a visiting fellowship (research scholar) from Macquarie University. We thank Joseph Chorny, Jacquelyn Cranney, William Fleeson, Ellen M. Grigorian, A. Gordon Hammer, Lucy Cantor Kihlstrom, Kevin M. McConkey, Robert M. Nadon, Laura Otto, Patricia A. Register, Daniel L. Schacter, Douglas J. Tataryn, Betsy A. Tobias, Ian K. Waterhouse, and James M. Wood for their comments at various stages.

181

1987a, 1987b), we begin with an examination of the literature, inspired by psychoanalytic theory, on repression and hypnosis.

Transference in Hypnosis

Freud's own earliest writings on hypnosis contain little reference to repression. From 1888 to 1892, Freud published a number of papers on hypnosis, reflecting the period (1885–86) he had spent with Charcot in Paris, supported by a traveling fellowship. The intellectual consequences of this visit were apparently profound for Freud (Ellenberger 1970; Macmillan 1986). In a real sense, Freud went to Paris a neurologist and returned a psychologist—albeit a biologically oriented psychologist (Sulloway 1979). Macmillan (1986) has shown just how much of Freud's early psychopathological theory (as reflected, e.g., in the *Studies on Hysteria* [Breuer and Freud (1893–95) 1955]) was derived from Charcot ([1887] 1889) and his pupil Janet (1889). This debt extends to Freud's conceptualization of hypnosis as well.

The classic psychoanalytic approach to hypnosis probably had its beginnings in the *Three Essays on the Theory of Infantile Sexuality* ([1905] 1953), in which Freud drew attention to the subject's stance of credulity and submissiveness with respect to the hypnotist (for a review, see Gill and Brenman 1959). Later, in *Group Psychology and the Analysis of the Ego* ([1921] 1955), Freud asserted that hypnosis was similar to love, with the single difference that hypnosis excluded sexual satisfaction. Further, he argued that "the hypnotist awakens in the subject a portion of his archaic heritage which had also made him compliant towards his parents and which had experienced an individual re-animation in his relation to his father; what is thus awakened is the idea of a paramount and dangerous personality, towards whom only a passive-masochistic attitude is possible, to whom one's will has to be surrendered—while to be alone with him, 'to look him in the face', appears a hazardous enterprise" (p. 127). Interestingly, no hint of this characterization appears in Freud's ([1891] 1966) essay on hypnosis for Bum's *Therapeutic Lexicon,* apparently written under the influence of Charcot, Janet, and Bernheim and republished without revision in the second and third editions of 1893 and 1900.

Schilder and Kauders (1927) went even further than Freud and denied the essential erotic difference between hypnosis and love. They write, "The hypnotist can often detect an expression of sexual excitement in the eyes of women before they fall asleep and after awakening. Trembling occurs similar to that accompanying erotic stimulation" (85). On the other hand, Kubie and Margolin (1944) argued that transference was incidental to hypnosis, an artifact of the hypnotist's technique. If a transference relationship was established before induction, it was carried over into hypnosis. If this could be prevented somehow, as by a purely mechanical means of induction, then no transference would occur.

intentions of the hypnotist is taken by Sheehan as an objective index of the subject's personal involvement with the hypnotist. Interestingly, it is not highly correlated with hypnotizability. More important in the present context, however, the archaic flavor of the psychoanalytic concept of transference is missing in these studies, just as it is from Hilgard's (1971, 1979) interview data. While it is clear that hypnotic subjects have a special relationship with their hypnotist, that relationship is more appropriately characterized by rapport than by transference.

Repression in Posthypnotic Amnesia

Although the psychoanalytic theory of hypnosis has received little support, the dominant position of psychoanalysis within personality and clinical psychology has often led to interpretation of certain hypnotic phenomena in terms of repression. At a descriptive level, for example, the concept is well applied to hypnotic analgesia, in which the subject appears unaware of painful stimulation impinging on his or her sensory surfaces. In psychoanalytic terms, such a phenomenon might seem to be analogous to primal repression, in which certain percepts, thoughts, memories, and impulses are denied entry into consciousness. Similarly, posthypnotic amnesia might be considered analogous to repression proper, or after expulsion, in which percepts once accessible to awareness are subsequently denied to consciousness. But, while a painful stimulus is by definition noxious, the events of hypnosis are typically benign, if not downright pleasant. What, then, is the motivation for repression?

From a psychoanalytic point of view, posthypnotic amnesia may be seen as resulting from the repression by the subject of memories associated with the hypnotic experience. This hypothesis was alluded to by Freud himself, formally proposed by Schilder and Kauders (1927), and cited favorably by Rappaport (1942) and Stengel (1966). According to Schilder and Kauders, the motive for the amnesia lies in the subject's transference relationship with the hypnotist: "Obviously, the hypnotized is ashamed of his infantile-masochistic adjustment and denies the hypnosis in order to conceal the adjustment. Very frequently, therefore, we find hypnotized subjects indignantly denying that they have been hypnotized" (1927, 60). According to Rappaport (1942, 176), recovery of these memories occurs when the subject accepts his or her masochistic relationship, an affective change that is instigated by the hypnotist's further suggestions.

Thus, hypnotic events are repressed not because they are intrinsically threatening but because the transference relationship in which they occur makes them so. The repression theory of amnesia is troubled, of course, by the general lack of evidence for these sorts of transference processes in hypnosis. We still seem to be missing the motive for repression. Nevertheless, a number of investigators have assumed that posthypnotic amnesia is somehow analogous to repression, and it is this assumption that we must confront.

Posthypnotic Amnesia as a Repression-like Process

In fact, there are three different empirical approaches to the study of repression in posthypnotic amnesia. In one, which involves the hypnotic induction of laboratory analogues of the clinical psychopathology (a form of artificial neurosis), the assumption that posthypnotic amnesia involves a repression-like process is central to the experimental paradigm. In the others, which involve "complex indicators" and selective recall, repression is less an assumption and more a hypothesis to be tested.

Amnesia in the Induction of Artificial Conflict

Nowhere is that assumption more visible than in the large body of research employing hypnotic suggestion to induce in nonpatient subjects the kinds of intrapsychic conflicts assumed by psychoanalytic theory to be at the heart of neurosis. The technique was introduced by Luria (1932), coming from outside psychoanalysis, in his *Nature of Human Conflict*. Luria's method was to suggest to a normal subject, during hypnosis, that he or she had committed a crime too terrible to contemplate. This suggested paramnesia was covered by amnesia along with the other events and experiences of hypnosis. Thus, according to Luria's reasoning, the subjects' posthypnotic behaviors should be influenced by these conflictual, threatening (but not consciously accessible) memories. Later, when the subjects were asked to perform a simple psychomotor task, the effects of the paramnesia were clearly visible in their behavior. For example, the subjects rested their hands on separate tambours and were instructed to press with their preferred hand whenever they gave a free association to the items in a word list. Critical works extracted from the paramnesia were then presented along with neutral, unrelated words. Luria reported that subjects responded to the critical words with irrelevant movements, as recorded by the tambour under their nonpreferred hand. Luria's findings were essentially replicated by Huston, Shakow, and Erickson (1934), again using hypnosis as the vehicle for inducing both paramnesia and amnesia. The apparent success of these efforts directly stimulated at least three different lines of research.

In one, Levitt and his colleagues (e.g., Levitt 1967; for an overview, see Levitt and Chapman 1979) directly administer suggestions for anxiety to hypnotized subjects. These are then followed by suggestions for amnesia covering the induction of anxiety. In a series of studies, Levitt and his colleagues observed a number of effects of the anxiety suggestion on subsequent test behavior, even though the subjects were unaware of the source of their emotional state—or, for that matter, even of being anxious. Thus, hypnotic amnesia seemed to function in a manner analogous to repression, by denying the subjects' awareness of unpleasant material that nonetheless influenced their behavior.

A variant on this technique has been adopted by Bower (1981) and his colleagues to permit controlled studies of mood effects on memory. Some mood, positive or negative, is suggested to subjects, who are then asked to study or remember some material. It is common in these experiments to cover the mood induction with amnesia, but the intent here is not to create an experimental analogue of repression. Rather, it is to prevent the subject from consciously recognizing the experimental source of his or her mood so that he or she experiences it in a more lifelike manner. Because these studies do not bear directly on the status of posthypnotic amnesia as a repression-like process (if for no other reason than that half the subjects are experiencing positive moods), they are not further considered here.

A second line of research, devised by Blum (1979), suggests that hypnotized subjects will relieve some experience from early childhood that is of a conflictual, ego-threatening nature. The content of the experience is then covered by an amnesia suggestion, leaving the subject in a free-floating emotional state. Again, Blum has observed a variety of effects of these emotions on psychological functioning, and, again, amnesia appears to serve as an analogue of repression—in this case, by isolating the content of the memory from its associated affect.

Yet a third approach has followed Luria more closely in using suggested paramnesias rather than direct suggestion of memory revivification. That is, a memory is fabricated that would have certain emotional consequences, and the fabrication procedure is covered by amnesia. Finally, the subject is given a posthypnotic suggestion to feel certain sexual or aggressive emotions whenever certain cues are presented. Reyher (1967) and his colleagues have reported that these procedures produce a variety of somatic and emotional symptoms, including feelings of nausea, guilt, and shame, headaches, and perspiration. Here again, the suggestion for amnesia seems to be operating in a manner analogous to repression.

Unfortunately, the results of other investigations shed doubt on the repressive effects of the suggestion for amnesia. Sheehan (1969) performed a study based on Reyher's paradigm, but including a comparison group of insusceptible subjects instructed to simulate hypnosis. The real-simulator design was invented by Orne (1959) in order to determine which effects, commonly attributed to hypnosis, might rather be attributable to the presence of subtle cues in the experimental procedure indicating the hypothesis of the experiment and the manner in which it is to be tested. If an experimental situation contains such cues, then subjects who are highly motivated to comply with the experimenter's wishes might simply act on them rather than behave in accordance with hypnotic suggestions.

In Sheehan's experiment, reals and simulators behaved in substantially the same manner. Now, the logic of the real-simulator paradigm is as follows: if reals and simulators behave differently, then the behavior of the reals cannot be attributed merely to the demand characteristics of the experiment. However, if they behave similarly, no conclusions can be drawn. Perhaps the reals picked up on, and behaved in accordance with, the same demand characteristics noticed by the simulators; on the other hand, it may be that the behavior of the reals is genuine and that the simulators' performances are fortuitously correct. Sheehan's results do not allow us to choose between these two possibilities. Until an experiment can be designed in which reals and simulators behave differently in Reyher's paramnesia paradigm, it is impossible to determine whether posthypnotic amnesia has effects analogous to repression (see also Reyher 1969; Sheehan 1971b).

Amnesia for Complex Indicators

A second approach to the study of repressive processes in amnesia is based on Jung's work with word associations (e.g., Jung and Ricklin [1906] 1973). As is well known, Jung presented patients and subjects with a series of stimulus words and asked them to report the first word that came to mind in response to each. Jung considered certain response characteristics, such as abnormally long reaction times or electrodermal responses, repetition of the stimulus, and perseveration of the response to be "complex indicators"—that is, related to some kind of conflict or threat, conscious or unconscious. When the series was later repeated, with the subject instructed to give the identical response as he or she had on the first occasion, Jung noticed that the complex indicators tended to produce errors.

Clemes (1964) adapted Jung's technique, administering a word-association test to a number of subjects. On the basis of the individual subjects' response latencies, word lists were idiographically constructed that consisted of half complex indicators and half neutral words. The subjects then memorized their lists while hypnotized. After a suggestion of partial amnesia, to the effect that they would remember only half the words, hypnosis was terminated. Clemes found that recall favored the neutral items over the complex indicators, indicating that a repression-like process had been invoked by the suggestion for posthypnotic amnesia. There was no differential recall shown by a control group who studied the list in the normal waking state. However, a recent attempt at replication failed to produce similar results (Stam, Radtke-Bodorik, and Spanos 1980). Thus, Clemes's evidence for a repression-like process in posthypnotic amnesia must be considered equivocal.

Selective Recall for Success and Failure

The most productive line of research was begun by Hilgard and Hommel (1961), who drew their inspiration from Zeigarnik's (1927) work on memory for interrupted tasks (the paper, originally published in German, is reprinted in Rapaport 1960). Zeigarnik engaged normal (nonpatient) subjects in a series of fairly simple tasks. For each subject, half the tasks were interrupted before they could be completed; the remainder were allowed to be finished. On a later test of incidental memory, she found that recall favored interrupted over completed tasks, a result that has since been christened the Zeigarnik effect. Zeigarnik, a student of Kurt Lewin, argued that brain systems involved in task performance remained activated until the tasks were completed, thus rendering memory traces of task performance more accessible to retrieval—a process we would now call a kind of priming effect.

However, Zeigarnik also noted that under certain conditions her effects were reversed. When the subjects construed task interruption as a sign of failure or lack of ability, memory favored completed tasks as opposed to interrupted ones. Zeigarnik interpreted this as a kind of repression of ego-threatening material. Her study, which has been called "a methodological milestone in the study of experimental psychodynamics" (MacKinnon and Dukes 1964, 676), set in motion a line of inquiry that has lasted more than fifty years (e.g., Blaney 1986; Butterfield 1964; Holmes 1974; Weiner 1966). For example, Rosenzweig and his colleagues experimentally controlled task perception and again reversed Zeigarnik's effect under conditions of ego threat (e.g., Rosenzweig 1938, 1952). Rosenzweig also produced the first link to hypnosis, demonstrating that the selective forgetting of uncompleted tasks under conditions of ego threat—repression—was significantly correlated with hypnotic susceptibility (Rosenzweig and Sarason 1942; Sarason and Rosenzweig 1942; see also Brenman 1947; Petrie 1948). This formed the basis for Rosenzweig's "triadic hypothesis" that hypnotizable individuals prefer repressive defenses and tend to gloss over or rationalize frustration (Rosenzweig and Saranson 1942; Sarason and Rosenzweig 1942).

In many ways, the standardized procedures used to assess individual differences in hypnotizability constitute an ideal medium for the study of Zeigarnik's effects (for reviews, see Hilgard 1965; Kihlstrom 1985). Here, a group of unselected volunteer subjects is administered a hypnotic induction accompanied by suggestions for a representative set of hypnotic phenomena. For example, it might be suggested that there is a fly buzzing annoyingly around the subject's head. The subjects, presumably all positively motivated for hypnosis (by virtue of their volunteer status), are asked to try to experience each suggested effect. In the conventional forms of these scales, response to each suggestion is indexed by an objective, behavioral criterion. To continue the example, the subject would be scored as "passing" the fly hallucination if he

or she made any observable acknowledgment of the presence of the fly—
perhaps by brushing the face or shaking the head. However, only a very few
subjects, about 10 percent are "hypnotic virtuosos" who will experience all
(or virtually all) the suggestions. Most subjects will experience a mix of successes and failures (only very rarely are subjects so insusceptible to hypnosis
that they will have none of the experiences at all). So, following the logic of
Zeigarnik and Rosenzweig, it should be possible to examine the subject's recall for these test items after hypnosis has been terminated and determine
whether recall favors passed or failed items.

At the very least, this would tell us whether Zeigarnik's Gestalt effect, or
its repressive reverse, can be obtained in the hypnotic domain as well as in the
sorts of tasks typically used in the Zeigarnik-Rosenzweig tradition. But there
is more because the standardized scales usually end with a suggestion of amnesia. As with any other hypnotic suggestion, response to amnesia varies
widely and is highly correlated with hypnotizability. Therefore, if posthypnotic amnesia involves a repression-like process, the reverse Zeigarnik effect
should be especially prominent in those highly hypnotizable subjects who are
most responsive to amnesia suggestions—and in those hypnotizable subjects
who actually show amnesia.

The initial experiment along these lines was performed by Hilgard and
Hommel (1961), employing data gathered in the standardization of the Stanford Hypnotic Susceptibility Scale. Those few insusceptible subjects who
failed all the items, as well as those hypnotizable subjects who passed all the
items, were excluded from analysis. The remaining subjects, 97.6 percent of
the entire group, showed a general tendency to favor passed over failed items.
On the average, these subjects recalled 60.2 percent of the items they had
passed but only 49.0 percent of those they had failed. The difference was
highly significant and represents a reverse Zeigarnik effect indicative of
repression. It seems plausible to conclude that failure to respond positively to
hypnotic suggestions is generally disappointing, at least for subjects who are
positively motivated for hypnosis, and that those items that are failed are also
repressed.

When the sample was stratified into three levels of hypnotizability (high,
medium, and low), however, somewhat different results were obtained (see
table 1). The differential recall of passed over failed items was not significant
for the hypnotizable subjects. Hilgard and Hommel (1961) suggested that this
might be a statistical artifact of the very low levels of recall displayed by these
subjects during posthypnotic amnesia. They also examined selective recall
after the amnesia suggestion was canceled by the prearranged reversibility
cue. Under these circumstances, the hypnotizable subjects recalled considerably more material than they had previously, but there remained a residual
pool of items that remained unrecalled despite the reversal of the amnesia.
This pool contained a disproportionate share of failed items. Thus, Hilgard

Table 1. Extent of Selective Recall during Posthypnotic Amnesia

Study	N	Hypnotizability		
		High	Medium	Low
Hilgard and Hommel (1961)	124	.06	.19	.15
O'Connell (1966):				
Sample A	100	.07	.12	.43
Sample B	152	.11	.15	.33
Sample C	54	.18	.27	.40
Sample D	86	− .02	.27	.44
Sample E	94	.10	.20	.05
Coe et al. (1976)	29			
Objective		− .22	− .03	.08
Subjective		− .08	− .10	.17
Pettinati and Evans (1978)	88	.10	.20	.20
Pettinati et al. (1981)	278	.14	.16	.23
Chorny et al. (1988):	501			
Objective		.08	.13	.26
Subjective		.09	.12	.23

Note: Positive values indicate that recall favors passed items over failed ones; negative values indicate that recall favors failed items.

and Hommel (1961) concluded that the repressive process represented by the reverse Zeigarnik effect, if indeed that is what it is, is largely independent of hypnosis and amnesia.

Hilgard and Hommel (1961) also considered an alternative to the repression hypothesis, one based on salience effects. As is well known, salient events are more accessible in memory (Von Restorff 1933; Tversky and Kahneman 1973). The argument is that suggestions that are successful are highly salient for hypnotic subjects—the more so for insusceptible subjects, who after all have relatively few of them. However, it would seem that the salience hypothesis would predict a Von Restorff-type contrast effect—that recall would favor passed items among insusceptible subjects, which it does, and failed items among hypnotizables, which it does not. On these grounds, repression is probably to be preferred over salience.

On further examination, however, the finding of the reverse Zeigarnik effect in and of itself does not permit us to distinguish between a selective repression of failed items and a selective enhancement of passed items. The two processes are not the same. The difference between them may be seen by considering what is missing in the Hilgard and Hommel (1961) study (and in all subsequent studies employing their paradigm): an untreated control group. Suppose that we recruited a representative sample of subjects and simply read them the hypnotizability scale items, without asking them to experience the suggested effects or to have amnesia, and that, later on, we asked them simply to recall the items. In this case, memory cannot be selectively affected by repression or enhancement, for the simple reason that the subjects have had no experiences of success and failure.

Suppose, then, that we determined that under these circumstances the average subject recalls 60 percent of the items. This figure would then establish a baseline representing the proportion of passed and failed items a subject would be expected to remember. With an expected value of 60 percent, then, the Hilgard and Hommel (1961) data would provide evidence of repression, not enhancement, because the proportion of failed items recalled is lower than expected. On the other hand, if the baseline were 50 percent, the same data would provide evidence for enhancement, not repression, because the proportion of passed items recalled is greater than expected. Just such data has been collected by Cooper (1979) from a fairly large sample of college student subjects. He estimated that the average subject recalls about 64 percent of critical items. Assuming that his baseline is generalizable across samples, then, the results of Hilgard and Hommel (1961) may be taken as evidence of repression—the selective and disproportionate forgetting of failure.

O'Connell (1966) replicated the Hilgard and Hommel (1961) procedure on five new samples of subjects who had received various standardized hypnotizability scales, with similar results (see table 1). Again omitting subjects who either passed or failed all the items and thus could not show selective recall, there was a significant overall tendency for recall to favor passed over failed items. Again, this reverse Zeigarnik effect in recall was most pronounced among those who were relatively insusceptible to hypnosis. On the assumption that most hypnotic subjects are positively motivated to experience the suggestions, O'Connell (1966) interpreted these results as providing evidence of a repression-like process operating independently of hypnosis and amnesia. In addition, he argued that insusceptible subjects also experienced an enhancement of memory for those few items that they successfully experienced, leading to the observed difference in selective recall among hypnotizability groups.

The next foray into this area was by Coe and his colleagues (Coe et al. 1976). They argued, correctly, that repression could not be studied adequately without considering the subject's subjective emotional responses to the suggestions. Investigators can *assume* that subjects are disappointed when they fail items and pleased when they pass them, but this is not necessarily so. (In fact, unpublished research in our laboratory provides considerable evidence that, for individual suggestions, the subjective feeling of success is not highly correlated with behavioral response.) Accordingly, Coe et al. asked subjects to rate their emotional responses to each item on a five-point scale, with the poles marked "pleasant" and "unpleasant." In fact, objective pass-fail status was not correlated with emotional valence. Coe's differential recall results, summarized in table 1, reversed those of Hilgard and Hommel and of O'Connell. Overall, recall favored failed over passed items (using objective indices of item response) and unpleasant over pleasant ones (using subjective ratings). This effect was strongest for hypnotizable subjects; insusceptible subjects showed a somewhat weaker preference for failed items. This study provides no evidence for repression, though the trends have the flavor of Von Restorff-type contrast effects. However, owing to the small number of subjects involved, none of the differences were statistically significant.

Most recently, Pettinati and Evans (1978; Pettinati et al. 1981) analyzed two new samples of subjects, using only behavioral pass-fail ratings, and replicated the findings of Hilgard and Hommel (1961) and O'Connell (1966). In general, recall favored passed items. Although the difference was not statistically significant, the reverse Zeigarnik effect was greatest in subjects of low and moderate hypnotizability (see table 1). Pettinati and Evans (1978) also analyzed the data with an alternative index of selective recall designed to remove the artifactual influence of the total number of times remembered. The old and new indices were in fact highly correlated, suggesting that the artifact was not a serious one. The difference in selective recall between hypnotizable and insusceptible subjects remained constant. A second study, reanalyzing data originally collected by Kihlstrom et al. (1980), yielded similar results (Pettinati et al. 1981). Overall, recall favored passed over failed items. Further, there was a nonsignificant trend for this difference to be reduced among the highly hypnotizable subjects, and, for those highs who met a criterion for posthypnotic amnesia, it was reduced virtually to zero.

In our laboratory, Chorney followed the lead of Coe et al. (1976) in examining the effects of both objective and subjective success on memory for scale items (Chorney et al. 1988). A total of 501 subjects completed HGSHS:A, evaluating their responses to the various suggestions in terms of both the standard behavioral criteria and their subjective impressions of success. Preliminary analysis indicates that selective recall tended to favor passed over failed times, regardless of whether item status was determined in objective or subjective terms, and the degree of selectivity was highest among insusceptible, nonamnesic subjects. Thus, Chorny's results generally confirmed the findings of Hilgard and Hommell (1961), O'Connell (1966), and Pettinati (Pettinati and Evans 1978; Pettinati et al. 1981) and contradicted those of Coe et al. (1976): selective recall generally favors passed or successful items.

In an attempt to distinguish between repression and enhancement effects, Chorny et al. (1988) administered the HGSHS:A to a control sample of 103 subjects under conditions that precluded the experience of success or failure. The average control subject recalled 5.83 items (64.8 percent) during a test of initial recall, compared to an average of 3.37 items (37.4 percent) for the experimental subjects on the comparable test of posthypnotic amnesia. Thus, the recall bias exhibited by hypnotic subjects seems more closely akin to repression than enhancement. Nevertheless, because the degree of selectivity was negatively correlated with hypnotizability, this repression-like tendency is unrelated to either hypnosis or posthypnotic amnesia. Rather, the mechanism of posthypnotic amnesia appears to be superimposed on ordinary selective recall effects.

With the exception of the small sample collected by Coe et al. (1976), then, all the studies reviewed here agree that hypnotic subjects show a general tendency to recall passed over failed items during posthypnotic amnesia. Assuming that the reverse Zeigarnik effects reflects repression, it appears that there is a general tendency for hypnotic subjects to repress their failures. This tendency is not magnified in those who are most highly hypnotizable and thus most responsive to amnesia suggestions. In fact, if anything, it is reduced, so it cannot be said to constitute part of the mechanism by which posthypnotic amnesia takes place—or, indeed, to have anything to do with hypnosis per se. In summary, then, it is difficult to see in posthypnotic amnesia either the motive to avoid unpleasant, threatening, and conflict-laden memories or the selective impairment in retrieval of these memories that are part and parcel of the classic concept of repression.

Dissociation in Posthypnotic Amnesia

Although Hilgard initiated the formal study of repression-like processes in posthypnotic amnesia (in addition to his collaboration with Hommel, the Clemes study was also done under his supervision), he himself has always favored an interpretation in terms of dissociation (Hilgard 1966, 1977, 1979). The prima facie evidence suggesting a dissociative mechanism for posthypnotic amnesia is the same as that indicating a repressive one. The phenomenon presents us with a set of memories, denied to conscious awareness (as reflected in the subject's inability to recall them) but remaining stored in memory (as reflected by the recovery of memory that occurs when the reversibility cue is given to cancel the amnesia suggestion). Both dissociation and repression require this continued availability of inaccessible memories.

Both concepts also require that the memories remain dynamically active— that is, although they are outside the scope of phenomenal awareness, they exert a demonstrable influence on ongoing experience, thought, and action. This is what dissociation means in the descriptive (as opposed to the explanatory) sense: posthypnotic amnesia affects some aspects of memory function but not others. As defined by Tulving (1983), the dissociation paradigm in psychological research involves the differential effects of an experimental manipulation on two dependent variables. Dissociation occurs when the manipulation affects one variable but not the other or effects the two variables in different ways (i.e., positive and negative). An extremely powerful example of this paradigm is found in cases of "double dissociation," where there are two manipulations that are found to affect two variables differently. Tulving (1983) has also proposed two other variants on the dissociation paradigm: pathological dissociation, in which the experimental manipulation is replaced by two or more patient groups, and developmental dissociation, in which it is replaced by two or more age levels.

In this descriptive sense, at least, posthypnotic amnesia certainly can be described in terms of dissociation (see the comprehensive reviews in Kihlstrom 1977, 1984, 1985, 1987a, 1987b; Kihlstrom and Evans 1979). For example, posthypnotic amnesia exerts a profound effect on free recall, but it exerts considerably less effect on recognition (e.g., Kihlstrom and Shor 1978) and relearning (Hull 1933) measures of memory. It does not appear to affect either proactive or retroactive inhibition (e.g., Dillon and Spanos 1983; Graham and Patton 1968). Nor does it appear to affect the subject's use of factual knowledge acquired during the hypnotic session (e.g., Evans 1979) or the priming effects that occur when subjects are asked to perform some processing task on material covered by the amnesia suggestion (e.g., Kihlstrom 1980; Spanos, Radtke, and Dubreuil 1982). All these dependent variables are measures of memory: the fact that posthypnotic amnesia affects some but not others is indicative of dissociation in its limited, descriptive sense. But what is dissociated?

Steps toward a Description of Dissociation

Gregg (1979, 1980) has suggested that the dissociation is between optional and obligatory memory processes. Obligatory processes are those that occur automatically, without any conscious intention or control on the part of the subject; optional processes, by contrast, are those whose deployment and operation can be deliberately controlled by the individual. There is some evidence favoring Gregg's hypothesis: obligatory processes are perhaps best represented by the sorts of interference, savings, and transfer effects familiar from the literature on paired associated learning (Crowder 1976) and by the priming effects that lie at the core of spreading activation models of memory retrieval (Anderson 1983). The persistence of these effects in the face of a failure of free recall would, indeed, seem to indicate that amnesia affects the optional, but not the obligatory, aspects of memory processing. At the same time, however, there are some troubling anomalies in the application of the optional-obligatory distinction to research on posthypnotic amnesia. Chief among these is the finding that recognition is relatively unaffected in amnesic subjects. There is nothing obligatory about performance on recognition tests: subjects can choose to withhold a positive recognition response just as easily as they can choose to withhold a free-recall report (for a detailed critique, see Kihlstrom 1985).

Another potential dissociation is between declarative and procedural memory. Declarative memories represent factual knowledge about the nature of the physical and social world; by contrast, procedural memory represents the cognitive processes—the rules, skills, and strategies—by which declarative knowledge may be manipulated and transformed. The limited evidence available suggests that posthypnotic amnesia has no effect on the acquisition or retention of either cognitive or motor skills (for a detailed review, see Kihlstrom 1985, 1987a, 1987b), suggesting that the dissociation is between declarative memory (which is impaired) and procedural memory (which is spared). But there are certain aspects of declarative memory that are relatively unimpaired in posthypnotic amnesia. For example, in the phenomenon of posthypnotic source amnesia, subjects may remember factual information acquired while they were hypnotized but forget the circumstances under which they learned it (Evans 1979). Alternatively, amnesic subjects may forget the contents of a word list memorized during hypnosis but retain the words in their vocabulary. In these experiments, both variables involve declarative memory, yet amnesia affects one but not the other.

Kihlstrom (1980, 1985, 1987a, 1987b; see also Kihlstrom and Evans 1979) and Tulving (1983) have suggested that these findings illustrate a dissociation between the episodic and the semantic forms of declarative memory. Episodic memory is autobiographical memory, concerning one's own past experiences and referring to the spatiotemporal and organismic context in which those experiences occurred; semantic memory may be thought of as the mental lexicon of categorical world knowledge stored without reference to the episodic context in which it has been acquired and used. In fact, the episodic-semantic distinction organizes a large portion of the empirical literature on posthypnotic amnesia (for a review, see Kihlstrom 1985). Posthypnotic amnesia impairs performance on episodic memory tasks such as free recall but spares performance on semantic memory tasks such as word association (e.g., Kihlstrom 1980; Williamsen, Johnson, and Eriksen 1965). This dissociation between episodic and semantic memory is a feature that this experimentally induced temporary amnesia shares with certain permanent pathologies of memory observed in the neuropsychological clinic, such as the amnesic (Korsakoff's) syndrome (Schacter and Tulving 1982).

But even here there are some anomalous findings, due in large part to the fact that some memory tasks are not easily classified as either declarative or procedural, episodic or semantic, in nature. For example, McKoon and her colleagues (McKoon, Ratcliff, and Dell 1986) have pointed out that retroactive inhibition—in which memory for one word list impairs retrieval of another list learned previously—is an effect of episodic memory but is not impaired by posthypnotic amnesia (for a reply, see Tulving 1986). Similarly, relearning and priming may be classified as episodic memory effects because they reflect the residual activity of memory traces encoded during some previous event. While this is true, there appear to be qualitative differences between, say, recall and relearning or priming. The difference is that recall, almost by definition, requires conscious awareness of a previous experience, whereas relearning and priming do not. For example, Nelson (1978) has shown that savings in relearning can occur even for items that are neither recalled nor recognized. Also, patients displaying anterograde amnesia due to lesions in the medial temporal lobe and associated areas show unimpaired repetition priming effects of words that they cannot recall or recognize (e.g., Schacter 1985).

Explicit and Implicit Memory

Thus, comparison of various forms of episodic memory effects reveals a further distinction between memory with and without awareness (Eich 1984; Jacoby 1986; Jacoby and Witherspoon 1982) or between implicit and explicit memory (Graf and Schacter 1985; Schacter 1987). As defined by Schacter (1987), explicit memory requires the conscious recollection of a previous episode, whereas implicit memory is revealed by a change in task performance (facilitation or interference) that is attributable to information acquired during that episode. An increasingly large body of literature from both normal and patient populations indicates that these two forms of memory are dissociable and that people can display implicit memory (e.g., savings or priming effects) without having any conscious recollection of the episode on which these effects are based). In many ways, the implicit-explicit distinction subsumes the distinctions drawn earlier between optional and obligatory, procedural and declarative, and episodic and semantic memory. Certainly explicit memory, which involves the conscious recollection of the details of a prior experience, comes very close to what Tulving originally meant by episodic memory (Tulving 1985).

Just as the explicit-implicit memory distinction more accurately characterizes the dissociations observed in normal remembering and the amnesic syndrome, so it appears to capture the dissociations observed in posthypnotic amnesia (Kihlstrom 1987a). Consider, for example, two experiments by Kihlstrom (1980), originally presented as bearing on the episodic-semantic distinction. In the first experiment, subjects classified as low, medium, high, and very high in hypnotizability memorized a list of fifteen unrelated words to a criterion of two correct recitations. After reaching criterion, they received a suggestion of posthypnotic amnesia—that they would not be able to remember the words they learned, or that they learned any words at all, until administration of the reversibility cue. Note that the suggestion is directed toward episodic memory—the amnesia covers a particular episode in the subject's experience. On an initial test of recall, the subjects of very high hypnotizability (who, following Hilgard, might be called hypnotic virtuosos; Register and

Table 2. Dissociation between Explicit and Implicit Memory in Posthypnotic Amnesia (after Kihlstrom 1980)

Experiment	Index of Memory Performance	Hypnotizability	
		Insusceptible	Virtuoso
1	Free recall	13.90	.20
	Word association:		
	Critical	10.80	12.20
	Neutral	8.40	10.40
2	Free recall	15.83	1.25
	Category instances:		
	Critical	10.83	9.42
	Neutral	7.83	7.08

Note: Priming effects are reflected by the difference between response to critical and neutral probes in the word association and category instances tasks.

Kihlstrom 1986) remembered virtually none of the words they had previously memorized, showing a very dense posthypnotic amnesia—a deficit in episodic memory. The insusceptible subjects, by contrast, showed virtually perfect memory for the word list.

At this point, the subjects were asked to give word association to various probes; half of these, called critical stimuli, were selected because they had a high a priori probability of eliciting the items from the previously memorized word list; the remainder, called neutral stimuli, targeted items that the subjects had not learned. The critical and neutral lists were carefully matched in terms of stimulus-response probabilities, and learning of the two lists was counterbalanced across subjects. Three results were of special interest (see table 2). First, posthypnotic amnesia did not disrupt the word-association performance of the hypnotic virtuosos: the items from the memorized word list remained available for use in their vocabulary. More important, there was a semantic priming effect observed in the word-association performance, such that the subjects were more likely to give the targeted response to critical as opposed to neutral stimuli. Most important, there was no difference in priming between virtuoso and insusceptible subjects, despite the fact that the virtuosos displayed a dense posthypnotic amnesia on the initial recall test. These findings were confirmed in a conceptual replication in which subjects memorized a categorized word list and were asked during amnesia to provide instances of critical and neutral taxonomic categories.

The dissociation between free recall and word-association performance is, as Kihlstrom (1980) and Tulving (1983) noted, a dissociation between episodic and semantic memory. But the dissociation between free recall and semantic priming is somewhat more difficult to interpret in those terms. Clearly, priming is an effect of episodic memory on a semantic memory task, but, just as clearly, priming does not require awareness of the learning experience that is the source of the facilitation in word-association or category-instantiation performance. In Schacter's terms, then, these experiments show a dissociation between explicit and implicit forms of episodic memory—the former impaired, the latter spared—in the effects of posthypnotic amnesia. The results of experiments on relearning and retroactive and proactive inhibition would also appear to illustrate this dissociation, although it may be necessary to repeat the experiments now that the explicit-implicit distinction has been formally articulated.

But even here there is an anomaly: under some circumstances at least, recall is impaired by posthypnotic amnesia, but recognition is not—at least not to the same degree. The problem is that recall and recognition are both measures of explicit memory, so we should not observe any dissociation between them. One possible resolution of this anomaly is to argue that recognition is generally easier than recall and thus less likely to show amnesic effects. However, there are reasons to think that recognition can be mediated by implicit as well as explicit memory. A number of investigators (e.g., Jacoby and Dallas 1981; Mandler 1980) have suggested that recognition of an item can be mediated by two qualitatively different processes: (*a*) respecification of the context in which an event occurred or (*b*) the feeling that an item is familiar. The former process is closer to the ordinary meaning of the word "remembering" because it involves conscious recollection of the spatiotemporal context in which the event took place as well as the role of the self as agent or experiencer of the event. The second process is more like an inference or a judgment of prior occurrence and resembles the experience in which a face or name "rings a bell."

In some cases, the "bell ringing" or feeling of familiarity may reflect the residual activation of the trace encoded by the prior experience—the same residual activation that underlies repetition and semantic priming effects. Thus, recognition by respecification might be construed as explicit memory, while recognition by familiarity might be construed as implicit memory. Unfortunately, most comparisons of recall and recognition do not permit a distinction between the respecification and familiarity components of recognition. However, ongoing research in our laboratory appears to reveal a dissociation, predicted by the explicit-implicit memory distinction, between them during posthypnotic amnesia. That is, amnesic and nonamnesic subjects may not differ in recognition by familiarity, but they may well differ in recognition by respecification (Kihlstrom 1985).

Repression and Dissociation in Cognitive Theory

Freud and Janet were continually at odds over the question of repression versus dissociation as the mechanism underlying unconscious mental processes of the kind observed in clinical psychopathology. They and their seconds also disagreed about the conceptual relation between the two processes. The First and Second Dynamic Psychiatries divided over the relation between the two concepts (Ellenberger 1970). At the same time, other theorists, contemporary with Freud and Janet, refused to choose between the two approaches, seeing value and utility (as well as unfortunate vagueness) in both concepts. For example, Sears (1936) suggested that both concepts were necessary to account for the functional disorders of memory observed in the clinic. More recently, Hilgard (1977), in reviving the theory of dissociation, saw no need to revive as well the ancient battle between Janet and Freud. Instead, he attempted to show how repression and dissociation might be related to each other. Adopting the topographic language of depth psychology, he described the repressive barrier as horizontal, with the function of preventing direct access to the contents of the unconscious system. In terms of contemporary memory theory (Kihlstrom 1984), the contents of the system covered by the horizontal, repressive barrier would be described as unavailable to introspective access or voluntary control under any circumstances. The contents of this system can be known only indirectly, through their effects on publicly observable behavior, and they are not amenable to conscious, voluntary control.

On the other hand, following Prince's use of the term "co-conscious," the dissociative barrier is depicted as vertical, segregating some contents of the conscious and preconscious systems from others. This barrier prevents conscious access to percepts, memories, and thoughts that nonetheless remain available, in principle, to introspective awareness (Kihlstrom 1984, 1987a, 1987b). A physical model (if perhaps an overly literal one) for this vertical division is cerebral commissurotomy, which effectively prevents the two hemispheres of the brain from communicating with each other, even though their individual operations remain unimpaired. Although the contents of dissociated memory systems are in principle available to direct introspection and voluntary control, they are temporarily denied access to these executive functions.

Because repression and dissociation are both postulated mechanisms for denying introspective access to certain mental contents, it would seem useful to conclude with some comments about how these processes could be conceptualized in terms of contemporary information-processing approaches to memory (see also Erdelyi 1985; Erdelyi and Goldberg 1979; Hilgard 1977; Hoyt 1987; Kihlstrom 1984, 1985, 1987a). For this purpose, let us assume that repression and dissociation are not mutually exclusive and that it would be possible to construct a cognitive system in which both were possible. Let us further assume, for purposes of exposition, that repression, like dissociation, operates on declarative knowledge, factual knowledge about the self or the outside world. The postoedipal child who is unaware that he loves his mother desperately and the rape victim who blocks out all memory for her assault have both lost access to some piece of declarative knowledge—some empirical or believed-in fact about the world. Both concepts—repression and dissociation—would permit unconscious procedural knowledge, differing qualitatively (i.e., in terms of its representational format) from declarative knowledge and inaccessible in principle, under any circumstances, to direct introspective access. Within the domain of declarative knowledge, then, it remains to make further distinctions between conscious, preconscious, dissociated, and repressed mental contents (Kihlstrom 1987a, 1987b).

Let us now identify the conscious system with working memory, that portion of declarative memory that contains activated representations of the organism in its immediate environment as well as of the organism's current processing goals and goal-relevant memory structures activated by perceptual processing or memory retrieval (Anderson 1983). In these terms, as I have argued elsewhere (Kihlstrom 1984, 1985, 1987a, 1987b), the essential distinction between what is conscious and what is not is that conscious mental contents are both activated (by perception or thought) and linked with activated representations of the self, its goals, and its local environment. Preconscious mental contents are latent: not activated (or, more properly, not activated above some threshold) and perforce not linked to the activated mental representation of the self. Dissociated, subconscious mental contents, while fully activated, are not linked with either an active mental representation of the self or the active mental representation of the context, or both (Kihlstrom 1984, 1985, 1987a, 1987b).

One approach to repression may begin with the reminder that Freud used the terms "repression" and "suppression" interchangeably throughout his writings on the subject (Erdelyi and Goldberg 1979). Perhaps, then, repression is a close kin of conscious, deliberate denial. Recently, Wegner and his colleagues have developed an interesting paradigm for the study of conscious, deliberate thought suppression that may be of use in understanding repression (Wegner et al. 1987). In their experiments, subjects are asked not to think about a white bear but to indicate if they should happen to do so. Three findings are of interest: (*a*) subjects were generally unable to suppress the target thought completely—even though, under ordinary conditions, they would have been extremely unlikely to have entertained it in the first place; (*b*) when they were subsequently asked to think about the bear deliberately, they produced more target thoughts than a control group that had not been asked to suppress them at the outset; and (*c*) this rebound effect was reduced when subjects are given something else to think about, as a distraction from white bears.

The thought suppression paradigm of Wegner et al. (1987) deserves further exploration as a vehicle for the experimental study of repression. However, as they themselves note, conscious suppression is not the same as repression—precisely because repression, in order effectively to defend the individual against threatening ideas and impulses, must be unconscious. Hoyt (1987) has suggested that one mechanism for transforming conscious thought suppression into unconscious repression is afforded by recent information-processing analyses of attention (Egeth 1977; Kahneman 1973; Kahneman and Triesman 1984) and the acquisition of cognitive skills (e.g., Anderson 1982; Schneider and Shiffrin 1977; Shiffrin and Schneider 1977). Attention is construed as the allocation of processing resources to some object or activity; these resources are limited, placing constraints on the number of objects or activities that can be attended simultaneously. At the same time, paying attention is also construed as a cognitive skill. The ability to divide attention among two or more simultaneous tasks, as required by dissociative processes, may be one such skill (Spelke, Hirst, and Neisser 1976). Deploying attention away from unpleasant cognitive contents that would otherwise attract it, as required by repression, may be another (Wegner et al., 1987).

While attentional capacity may wax and wane with maturational changes over the life cycle (producing, e.g., at least some of the memory deficits associated with childhood and old age), attentional skills—like other cognitive and motoric abilities—develop over time, with practice. At the initial stages of their acquisition, such skills demand the allocation of considerable attention, but, with practice, they become automatized (Anderson 1982; Hasher and Zacks 1979; LaBerge and Samuels 1975; Logan 1980; Posner and Snyder 1975; Schneider and Shiffrin 1977; Shiffrin and Schneider 1977, 1984). Some theorists hold that automatization of a cognitive process appears to change its representational format, from declarative to procedural in form (Anderson 1982). Automatic procedures are so named because they are inevitably engaged by the presentation of specific stimulus inputs, regardless of any intention on the part of the subject; in addition, they consume little or no cognitive resources. Thus, automatized processes are unconscious in that the person has no introspective access to their operation (Kihlstrom 1987a, 1987b, in press).

In most cases, of course, the person has direct introspective access to the final products of cognitive processing—the particular percept, memory, image, thought, or goal that appears in consciousness. But the goal of dissociative and repressive procedures, if indeed they exist, is quite different: their purpose is to allow the person to remain unaware of what is being processed. Thus, both the operation of dissociative and repressive skills and the products of their operation may be inaccessible to consciousness. It is an open question whether dissociation and repression ever become fully automatized in this sense; in fact, there seem to be cognitive costs associated with both processes (for further discussion of these issues, see Hoyt 1987; Kihlstrom 1987a, 1987b). Nevertheless, the information-processing approach to attention and cognitive skills suggests a mechanism by which the act of repression itself could be rendered unconscious—as Freud required it to be and, indeed, as it must be to serve as an effective defense.

References

Anderson, J. R. 1982. Acquisition of cognitive skill. *Psychological Review* 89:369–406.

————. 1983. *The architecture of cognition.* Cambridge, Mass.: Harvard University Press.

Blaney, P. H. 1986. Affect and memory: A review. *Psychological Bulletin* 99:229–46.

Blum, G. S. 1979. Hypnotic programming techniques in psychological experiments. In *Hypnosis: Developments in research and new perspectives,* ed. E. Fromm and R. E. Shor. New York: Aldine.

Bower, G. H. 1981. Mood and memory. *American Psychologist* 36:129–38.

Brenman, M. 1947. The use of hypnotic techniques in a study of tension systems. In *Hypnotherapy: A survey of the literature,* ed. M. Brenman and M. Gill. New York: International Universities Press.

Breuer, J., and S. Freud. [1893–95] 1955. *Studies on hysteria.* In *The standard edition of the complete psychological works of Sigmund Freud,* ed. J. Strachey, vol. 2. London: Hogarth.

Butterfield, E. C. 1964. The interruption of tasks: Methodological, factual, and theoretical issues. *Psychological Bulletin* 62:309–22.

Charcot, J. M. [1887] 1889. *Clinical lectures on diseases of the nervous system.* London: New Sydenham Society.

Chorney, J. C., I. P. Hoyt, P. A. Register and J. F. Kihlstrom. 1988. Selective recall of hypnotic experiences. University of Wisconsin. Typescript.

Clemes, S. R. 1964. Repression and hypnotic amnesia. *Journal of Abnormal and Social Psychology* 69:62–69.

Coe, W. C., R. J. Baugher, W. R. Krimm, and J. A. Smith. 1976. A further examination of selective recall following hypnosis. *International Journal of Clinical and Experimental Hypnosis* 24; 13–21.

Cooper, L. M. 1979. Hypnotic amnesia. In *Hypnosis: Developments in research and new perspectives,* ed. E. Fromm and R. E. Shor. New York: Aldine.

Crowder, R. S. 1976. *Principles of learning and memory.* Hillsdale, N. J.: Erlbaum.

Dillon, R. F., and N. P. Spanos. 1983. Proactive interference and the functional ablation hypothesis: More disconfirmatory data. *International Journal of Clinical and Experimental Hypnosis* 31:47–56.

Dolby, R. M., and P. W. Sheehan. 1977. Cognitive processing and expectancy behavior in hypnosis. *Journal of Abnormal Psychology* 86:334–45.

Egbeth, H. 1977. Attention and preattention. In *The psychology of learning and motivation,* ed. G. H. Bower. vol. 11, pp. 277–320. New York: Academic.

Eich, J. E. 1984. Memory for unattended events: Remembering with and without awareness. *Memory and Cognition* 12:105–11.

Ellenberger, H. F. 1970. *The discovery of the unconscious: The history and evolution of dynamic psychiatry.* New York: Basic.

Erdelyi, M. H. 1985. *Psychoanalysis: Freud's cognitive psychology.* San Francisco: Freeman.

Erdelyi, M. H., and B. Goldberg. 1979. Let's not sweep repression under the rug: Toward a cognitive psychology of repression. In *Functional disorders of memory,* ed. J. F. Kihlstrom and F. J. Evans. Hillsdale, N. J.: Erlbaum.

Evans, F. J. 1979. Contextual forgetting: Posthypnotic source amnesia. *Journal of Abnormal Psychology* 88: 556–63.

Freud, S. [1891] 1966. Hypnosis. In *The standard edition of the complete psychological works of Sigmund Freud*, ed. J. Strachey, vol. 1. London: Hogarth.

———. [1905] 1953. *Three essays on the theory of sexuality.* In *The standard edition of the complete psychological works of Sigmund Freud*, ed. J. Struchey vol. 7. London: Hogarth.

———. [1921] 1955. *Group psychology and the analysis of the ego.* In *The standard edition of the complete psychological works of Sigmund Freud*, ed. Strachey, vol. 18. London: Hogarth.

Gill, M. M., and M. Brenman. 1959. *Hypnosis and related states: Psychoanalytic studies in regression.* New York: International Universities Press.

Graf, P., and D. L. Schacter. 1985. Implicit and explicit memory for new associations in normal and amnesic subjects. *Journal of Experimental Psychology: Learning, Memory, and Cognition* 11:501–18.

Graham, K. R., and A. Patton. 1968. Retroactive inhibition, hypnosis, and hypnotic amnesia. *International Journal of Clinical and Experimental Hypnosis* 16:68–74.

Gregg, V. H. 1979. Posthypnotic amnesia and general memory theory. *Bulletin of the British Society of Experimental and Clinical Hypnosis,* no. 2:11–14.

———. 1980. Posthypnotic amnesia for recently learned material: A comment on the paper by J. F. Kihlstrom (1980). *Bulletin of the British Society of Experimental and Clinical Hypnosis,* no. 2:11–14.

Hasher, L., and R. T. Zacks. 1979. Automatic and effortful processes in memory. *Journal of Experimental Psychology: General* 108:365–88.

Hilgard, E. R. 1965. *Hypnotic susceptibility.* New York: Harcourt, Brace & World.

———. 1966. Posthypnotic amnesia: Experiments and theory. *International Journal of Clinical and Experimental Hypnosis* 14:104–11.

———. 1977. *Divided consciousness: Multiple controls in human thought and action.* New York: Wiley-Interscience.

———. 1979. Divided consciousness: The implications of the hidden observer. In *Hypnosis: Developments in research and new perspectives,* ed. E. Fromm and R. E. Shor. New York: Aldine.

Hilgard, E. R., and L. S. Hommel, 1961. Selective amnesia for events within hypnosis in relation to repression. *Journal of Personality* 29:205–16.

Hilgard, J. R. 1971. How the subject perceives the hypnotist. Frieda Fromm-Reichman Lecture presented at the Department of Psychiatry, Stanford Medical School, Stanford, California, October.

———. 1979. *Personality and hypnosis: A study of imaginative involvement.* 2d ed. Chicago: University of Chicago Press.

Holmes, D. S. 1974. Investigations of repression: Differential recall of material experimentally or naturally associated with ego threat. *Psychological Bulletin* 81:632–53.

Hoyt, I. P. 1987. Dissociation, repression, disconnection: Toward a "neo-repression" theory of affect without awareness. University of Wisconsin. Typescript.

Hull, C. L. 1933. *Hypnosis and suggestibility: An experimental approach.* New York: Appleton.

Huston, P. E., D. Shakow, and M. H. Erickson. 1934. A study of hypnotically induced complexes by means of the Luria technique. *Journal of General Psychology* 11:65–97.

Jacoby, L. L. 1986. Memory observed and memory unobserved. In *Real events remembered: Ecological approaches to the study of memory*, ed. U. Neisser and E. Winograd. Cambridge: Cambridge University Press.

Jacoby, L. L., and M. Dallas. 1981. On the relationship between autobiographical memory and perceptual learning. *Journal of Experimental Psychology: General* 3:306–40.

Jacoby, L. L., and D. Witherspoon. 1982. Remembering without awareness. *Canadian Journal of Psychology* 36:300–324.

Janet, P. 1889. [*Psychological automatisms*]. Paris: Alcan.

Jung, C. G., and F. Ricklin. [1906] 1973. The associations of normal subjects. In *The collected works of C. G. Jung*, ed. W. McGuire, vol. 2. Princeton, N. J.: Princeton University Press.

Kahneman, D. 1973. *Attention and Effort*. Englewood Cliffs, N. J.: Prentice-Hall.

Kahneman, D., and A. Triesman. 1984. Changing views of attention and automaticity. In *Varieties of attention*, ed. R. Parasuraman and D. R. Davies, 29–61. New York: Academic.

Kihlstrom, J. F. 1977. Models of posthypnotic amnesia. In *Conceptual and investigative approaches to hypnosis and hypnotic phenomena*, ed. W. E. Edmonston. *Annals of the New York Academy of Sciences* 277:284–301.

———. 1980. Posthypnotic amnesia for recently learned material: Interactions with "episodic" and "semantic" memory. *Cognitive Psychology* 12:227–51.

———. 1984. Conscious, subconscious, unconscious: A cognitive perspective. In *The unconscious reconsidered*, ed. K. S. Bowers and D. Meichenbaum. New York: Wiley.

———. 1985. Posthypnotic amnesia and the dissociation of memory. In *The psychology of learning and motivation*, ed. G. H. Bower. New York: Academic.

———. 1987a. The cognitive unconscious. *Science* 237: 1445–52.

———. 1987b. What this discipline needs is a good ten-cent taxonomy of consciousness. *Canadian Psychology* 28:116–18.

———. 1989. Cognition, unconscious processes. In *Neuroscience year: The yearbook of the Encyclopedia of Neuroscience*. Boston: Birkhauser Boston.

Kihlstrom, J. F., and F. J. Evans. 1979. Memory retrieval processes during posthypnotic amnesia. In *Functional disorders of memory*, ed. J. F. Kihlstrom and F. J. Evans. Hillsdale, N. J.: Erlbaum.

Kihlstrom, J. F., F. J. Evans, E. C. Orne, and M. T. Orne. 1980. Attempting to breach posthypnotic amnesia. *Journal of Abnormal Psychology* 89:603–16.

Kihlstrom, J. F., and R. E. Shor. 1978. Recall and recognition during posthypnotic amnesia. *International Journal of Clinical and Experimental Hypnosis* 26:330–49.

Kubie, L. S. and S. Margolin. 1944. The process of hypnotism and the nature of the hypnotic state. *American Journal of Psychiatry* 100:611–22.

Laberge, D., and S. J. Samuels. 1975. Toward a theory of automatic information processing in reading. *Cognitive Psychology* 6:293–323.

Levitt, E. E. 1967. *The psychology of anxiety*. Indianapolis: Bobbs-Merrill.

Levitt, E. E., and R. H. Chapman. 1979. Hypnosis as a research method. In *Hypno-*

sis: Developments in research and new perspectives, ed. E. Fromm and R. E. Shor. New York: Aldine.

Logan, G. D. 1980. Attention and automaticity in Stroop and priming tasks. Cognitive Psychology 12:523–53.

Luria, A. R. 1932. The nature of human conflict. New York: Liveright.

McConkey, K. M., and P. W. Sheehan. 1976. Contrasting interpersonal orientations in hypnosis: Collaborative versus contractual modes of response. Journal of Abnormal Psychology 85:390–97.

McDermott, D., and P. W. Sheehan. 1976. Interpersonal orientations in hypnosis: Toward egalitarian interaction in the hypnotic test situation. American Journal of Clinical Hypnosis 19:108–15.

MacKinnon, D., and W. Dukes. 1964. Repression. In Psychology in the making, ed. L. Postman. New York: Knopf.

McKoon, G., R. Ratcliff, and G. S. Dell. 1986. A critical evaluation of the semantic-episodic distinction. Journal of Experimental Psychology: Learning, Memory, and Cognition 12:295–306.

Macmillan, M. 1986. Souvenir de la Salpetriere: M. le Dr. Freud à Paris, 1885. Australian Psychologist 21:3–29.

Mandler, G. 1980. Recognizing: The judgment of previous occurrence. Psychological Review 87:252–71.

Mischel, W. 1973. Towards a cognitive social learning reconceptualization of personality. Psychological Review 80:252–83.

Nelson, T. O. 1978. Detecting small amounts of information in memory: Savings for nonrecognized items. Journal of Experimental Psychology: Human Learning and Memory 4:453–68.

O'Connell, D. N. 1966. Selective recall of hypnotic susceptibility items: Evidence for repression or enhancement? International Journal of Clinical and Experimental Hypnosis 14:150–61.

Orne, M. T. 1959. The nature of hypnosis: Artifact and essence. Journal of Abnormal Psychology 58:277–99.

Petrie, A. 1948. Repression and suggestibility as related to temperament. Journal of Personality 11:1–19.

Pettinati, H. M., and F. J. Evans. 1978. Posthypnotic amnesia: Evaluation of selective recall of successful experiences. International Journal of Clinical and Experimental Hypnosis 26:317–29.

Pettinati, H. M., F. J. Evans, E. C. Orne, and M. T. Orne. 1981. Restricted use of success cues in retrieval during posthypnotic amnesia. Journal of Abnormal Psychology 90:345–53.

Posner, M. I., and C. R. R. Snyder. 1975. Attention and cognitive control. In Information processing and cognition, ed. R. Solso. Hillsdale, N. J.: Erlbaum.

Rappaport, D. 1942. Emotions and memory. Baltimore: Williams & Wilkins.

———, ed. 1960. The organization and pathology of thought. New York: Columbia University Press.

Register, P. A., and J. F. Kihlstrom. 1986. Finding the hypnotic virtuoso. International Journal of Clinical and Experimental Hypnosis 34:84–97.

Rehyer, J. 1967. Hypnosis in research on psychopathology. In Handbook of clinical and experimental hypnosis, ed. J. E. Gordon. New York: Macmillan.

———. 1969. Comment on "Artificial induction of posthypnotic conflict." *Journal of Abnormal Psychology* 74:420–22.

Rosenzweig, S. 1938. The experimental study of repression. In *Explorations in personality,* ed. H. A. Murray. New York: Oxford University Press.

———. 1952. The investigation of repression as an instance of experimental idiodynamics. *Psychological Review* 59:339–45.

Rosenzweig, S., and S. Sarason. 1942. An experimental study of the triadic hypothesis: Reaction to frustration, ego defense, and hypnotizability. I. Correlational approach. *Character and Personality* 11, no. 2:1–19.

Sarason, S, and S. Rosenzweig. 1942. An experimental study of the triadic hypothesis: Reaction to frustration, ego defense, and hypnotizability. II. Thematic apperception approach. *Character and Personality* 11, no. 2:150–65.

Sarbin, T. R., and W. C. Coe. 1972. *Hypnosis: A social psychological analysis of influence communication.* New York: Holt, Rinehart & Winston.

Schacter, D. L. 1985. Priming of old and new knowledge in amnesic patients and normal subjects. *Annals of the New York Academy of Sciences* 444:41–53.

———. 1987. Implicit memory: History and current status. *Journal of Experimental Psychology: Learning, Memory, and Cognition* 13:501–18.

Schacter, D. L., and E. Tulving. 1982. Memory, amnesia, and the episodic-semantic distinction. In *The expression of knowledge,* ed. R. L. Isaacson and N. E. Spear. New York: Plenum.

Schilder, P., and O. Kauders. 1927. *Hypnosis.* New York: Nervous and Mental Disease Publications.

Schneider, W., and R. M. Shiffrin. 1977. Controlled and automatic human information processing. I. Detection, search, and attention. *Psychological Review* 84:1–66.

Sears, R. R. 1936. Functional abnormalities of memory, with special reference to amnesia. *Psychological Bulletin* 33:229–74.

Sheehan, P. W. 1969. Artificial induction of posthypnotic conflict. *Journal of Abnormal Psychology* 74:16–25.

———. 1971a. Countering preconceptions about hypnosis: An objective index of involvement with the hypnotist. *Journal of Abnormal Psychology* 78:299–322.

———. 1971b. An explication of the real-simulating model: A reply to Reyher's comment on "Artificial induction of posthypnotic conflict." *International Journal of Clinical and Experimental Hypnosis* 19:46–51.

———. 1980. Factors influencing rapport in hypnosis. *Journal of Abnormal Psychology* 89:263–81.

———. In press. Towards understanding the variability of hypnotic response. In *What is hypnosis?* ed. P. L. N. Naish. Oxford: Open University Press.

Sheehan, P. W., and R. M. Dolby. 1975. Hypnosis and the influence of most recently perceived events. *Journal of Abnormal Psychology* 84:331–45.

———. 1979. Motivated involvement in hypnosis: The illustration of clinical rapport through dreams. *Journal of Abnormal Psychology* 88:573–83.

Sheehan, P. W., and K. M. McConkey. 1982. *Hypnosis and experience: The exploration of phenomena and process.* Hillsdale, N. J.: Erlbaum.

Shevrin, H. 1979. The wish to cooperate and the temptation to submit: The hypnotized subjects' dilemma. In *Hypnosis: Developments in research and new perspectives,* ed. E. Fromm and R. E. Shor. New York: Aldine.

Shiffrin, R. M., and W. Schneider. 1977. Controlled and automatic human information processing. II. Perceptual learning, automatic attending, and a general theory.
Psychological Review 84:127–90.

———. 1984. Automatic and controlled processing revisited. *Psychological Review*
91:269–76.

Shor, R. E. 1962. Three dimensions of hypnotic depth. *International Journal of Clinical and Experimental Hypnosis* 10:23–38.

———. 1979. A phenomenological method for the measurement of variables important to an understanding of hypnosis. In *Hypnosis: Developments in research and
new perspectives*, ed. E. Fromm and R. E. Shor. New York: Aldine.

Spanos, N. P. 1986. Hypnotic behavior: A social-psychological interpretation of amnesia, analgesia, and "trance logic." *Behavioral and Brain Sciences* 9:449–502.

Spanos, N. P., H. L. Radtke, and D. L. Dubreuil. 1982. Episodic and semantic memory in posthypnotic amnesia: A reevaluation. *Journal of Personality and Social Psychology* 43:565–73.

Spelke, E. S., W. Hirst, and U. Neisser. 1976. Skills of divided attention. *Cognition*
4:215–30.

Stam, H. J., H. L. Radtke-Bodorik, and N. P. Spanos. 1980. Repression and hypnotic
amnesia: A failure to replicate and an alternative formulation. *Journal of Abnormal
Psychology* 89:551–59.

Stengel, E. 1966. Psychogenic loss of memory. In *Amnesia*, ed. C. W. M. Whitty and
O. L. Zangwill. London: Butterworths.

Sulloway, F. J. 1979. *Freud: Biologist of the mind*. New York: Basic.

Tulving, E. 1983. *Elements of episodic memory*. Oxford: Oxford University Press.

———. 1985. Memory and consciousness. *Canadian Psychology* 26:1–12.

———. 1986. What kind of a hypothesis is the distinction between episodic and semantic memory? *Journal of Experimental Psychology: Learning, Memory, and
Cognition* 12:307–11.

Tversky, A., and D. Kahneman. 1973. Availability: A heuristic for judging frequency
and probability. *Cognitive Psychology* 5:207–32.

Von Restorff, H. 1933. Uber die Wirkung von Bereichsbildungen im Spurenfeld. *Psychologie Forschung* 18:299–342.

Wegner, D. M. D. J. Schneider, S. R. Carter, and T. L. White. 1987. Paradoxical
effects of thought suppression. *Journal of Personality and Social Psychology* 53:5–
13.

Weiner, B. 1966. Effects of motivation on the availability of memory traces. *Psychological Bulletin* 65:24–37.

White, R. W. 1941. A preface to the theory of hypnotism. *Journal of Abnormal and
Social Psychology* 36:477–505.

Williamsen, J. A., H. J. Johnson, and C. W. Eriksen. 1965. Some characteristics of
posthypnotic amnesia. *Journal of Abnormal Psychology* 70:123–31.

Zeigarnik, B. 1927. Das Behalten von erledigten und unerledigten Handlungen. *Psychologie Forschung* 9:1–85.

9 Awareness, the Unconscious, and Repression: An Experimental Psychologist's Perspective

GORDON H. BOWER

I am an experimental/cognitive psychologist, and the topics of this conference and volume—unconscious processes, repression, and dissociation—are of great interest to cognitive psychologists, However, we rarely talk about such topics in our technical writings—for instance, none of these terms are even mentioned in standard textbooks of cognitive psychology. Since they have been out of favor for some time, I shall be treading on unfamiliar ground for my credentials. I will begin my contribution by discussing the topics of awareness, consciousness, and the sorts of behavior that most psychologists would agree are unconscious in a noncontroversial sense. I will end with a discussion of the concept of repression and different interpretations of the recovery of forgotten memories.

A Philosophical Distinction

As everyone knows, discussions of consciousness, awareness, and unconscious processes are rife with semantic confusions, ill-defined terms that cover multiple phenomena, and many inconsistencies of language. Psychologists and philosophers of mind have invested major efforts in trying to analyze several serviceable terms to use in such discussions. My discussion will borrow heavily from the philosopher Dan Dennett's treatise *Content and Consciousness* (1969), especially chapter 6 (see also Dennett, 1981). Although similar distinctions were proposed by psychologists Charles Eriksen (1960) and Matthew Erdelyi (1974), it is Dennett's arguments that have been very helpful in clarifying my thinking about consciousness and awareness.

Dennett's first move is to recast the notion of consciousness into awareness in the sense that "being conscious" becomes a synonym for "having the capac-

The author is supported by research grant MH-13950 from the National Institutes of Mental Health. He also acknowledges support from a MacArthur Foundation grant to Mardi Horowitz for studies of unconscious processes.

ity to be aware of" things. This is the sense of the word "consciousness" that we identify with being awake or alert as contrasted to being in a coma. Dennett's second move is to recast the use of the phrase "aware of something" into a phrase involving a propositional attitude, into "aware that some proposition is true." Thus, a sentence such as "I am aware of a car in the road" would be rephrased as "I am aware that a car is in the road." Thus, if we let p stand for the proposition "A car is in the road," the general frame of such statements is "I am aware that p." These are relatively innocuous rewritings of ordinary usage.

Dennett next observes that the common mental language of the layman runs together and confuses two distinct senses of awareness. Let us suppose that a person or organism A is aware of the contents of some proposition p; then the two distinct senses of awareness, denoted by subscripts, are expressed as follows by Dennett: "(1) A is aware$_1$ that p at time t if and only if p is the content of the input state to A's 'speech center' at time t; (2) A is aware$_2$ that p at time t if and only if p is the content of an internal event in A at time t that is effective in directing current behavior" (Dennett 1969, 118–19). Roughly speaking, people are aware$_1$ of some proposition (about themselves or the world) if they would be able to talk about it and are aware$_2$ of some other proposition if they behave in such manner that an observer could claim with justification that they are "taking account of" that belief (proposition) in their behavior, even though they may not be able to talk about it.

Typically, people are aware of a fact in both senses, and these form the ordinary cases, but it is the discrepancies that are interesting. Dennet's distinction is compelling to me and seems to illuminate a number of cases to which it may be applied. Let us consider several illustrations.

Some Illustrative Applications of the Distinction

If a person drives a car for several minutes while concentrating on a radio program or a conversation with a passenger, he may later say that he was unaware of most of the highway during the trip. Yet he obviously used the visual cues of the highway to steer his car around curves and avoid traffic. So a more appropriate description of the driver's mental state would say that he was aware$_1$ of the radio program but not of the highway; on the other hand, he was aware$_2$ of the curves along the highway at the same time as he was aware$_1$ of the radio program.

By definition, nonverbal animals can be only aware$_2$ of their environment. In the sense of being awake and alert, animals can be "conscious" and have the capacity for being aware$_2$ of happenings around them, but they would not be aware$_1$. If primates were taught to communicate their desires (say, for food), as in the primate language projects, we would be tempted to say that they are aware$_1$ of (some of) their inner states.

By the same criteria, self-regulating machines that respond to their environment may be said to be aware$_2$ of it. Thus, a computer program that plays creditable chess is clearly aware$_2$ of the chessboard, its actions and those of its opponent, and the state of the game. If a chessplaying program were to be hooked up to a speech-generating machine (several are available), allowing it to describe the gameboard, its moves, and its goals, one would be tempted to say that the program would be aware$_1$ of these facts. Clearly, however, the contents of working memory of the chess program would still differ considerably from that of human chess players if only because the humans might be thinking fleetingly about many things besides chess while they are playing.

The two measures of the contents of a person's experience disagree in many cases; these cases can be reformulated in terms of awareness$_1$ versus awareness$_2$. A simple experiment by Sperling (1960) illustrates the difference between one's perceptual experience and the ability to report it verbally. If one quick-flashes a three by four visual matrix of twelve letters in a tachistoscope, the perceiver has the impression of having seen most of the letters, but the iconic memory of the matrix fades rapidly, long before the subject can "read off" more than four to six letters from the fading icon. By special techniques of cuing and partial report, Sperling discovered that subjects indeed perceived and were aware$_2$ immediately of nearly all the letters in the display despite their inability to name all of them (in the sense of aware$_1$). That illustrates a discrepancy between our two measures of awareness of an experience.

Another example comes from studies of psychophysical judgments of near-threshold stimuli, such as those used in studies of "subliminal perception." It is widely acknowledged that subjects may verbally report no awareness$_1$ of (and no confidence in) having seen a near-threshold stimulus like a word. Yet, when forced to choose in a two-alternative test, they can nonetheless show significant above-chance detection or recognition of it. So that is a case where a person shows awareness$_2$ (by the forced-choice criterion) but not awareness$_1$ (by his confidence) of experiencing a weak signal.

Such "dissociations" between different indices of perceptual experience have been frequently reported. As one example, Weiskrantz et al. (1974) and Weiskrantz (1980) described patients with brain injury in the right occipital lobe who seemed to be blind in their left visual field. Such patients report no subjective experience (no awareness$_1$) of pictures that were quick-flashed to their left visual field; yet, when forced to choose between two pictures, they were likely to select the flashed picture. In a similar vein, Sackheim, Nordlie, and Gur (1979) tested hypnotic subjects who had been instructed to behave as though they were functionally blind. While reporting no subjective experience of perceiving the pictures flashed at them, these subjects nonetheless avoided the target picture to a significant degree when forced to indicate which one of three alternatives presented auditorially had been flashed. Clearly, these hypnotically blind subjects had to be aware$_2$ of the flashed picture in order to avoid it. This experiment illustrates also how one indicator of awareness ("verbal reports") can be controlled by social variables (the hypnotist's suggestion) in a manner independent of the variables controlling the other indicator of awareness.

More celebrated cases of perceptual dissociation occur with the "split brain" patients studied by Sperry (1968) and Gazzaniga (1970). These patients have had a commissurotomy to disconnect the two cerebral hemispheres in order to ameliorate frequent epileptic seizures. If one quick-flashes a pair of works like "key ring", one on either side of a central fixation point, these patients will in effect "see" "ring" in their left, talking hemisphere and see "key" in their right, nontalking hemisphere. If asked what they saw, they will verbally report the word "ring", with no awareness$_1$ of the "key" stimulus. But, if requested to use their left hand (guided by their right hemisphere) to reach under a blanket and pick out by touch the object corresponding the flashed stimulus, they will pick up a key. So we could claim that the left hemisphere is aware$_1$ of what it saw, whereas the right hemisphere is only aware$_2$ of what it saw. Marks (1980) provides an excellent discussion of the implications of such split-brain findings for the question of the unitariness of consciousness.

A minor indeterminacy with Dennett's distinction is that people have differing degrees of detail information available about a stimulus event and that different response indicators can be sensitive to different degrees of detail. A common example arises from our impoverished skills of verbal description. Thus, a person may notice and be aware of a face or abstract painting and be able subsequently to select that face or painting from a lineup. Yet he might be unable to describe accurately the face or painting in sufficient detail so that any other person could pick it out. Our skills of verbal description here are very poor since we have had so little practice in using discriminative concepts to describe such stimuli. Such cases raise questions about what "proposition" the subject might be aware of, in Dennett's sense. A given stimulus like a person's face has several levels of description, each with different degrees of completeness. This illustration shows that different indicators sometimes allow us to infer that different amounts of discriminative information about the same stimulus are available to awareness.

Unconscious Processes in Cognitive Psychology

It is appropriate to comment on the notion of unconscious processes from the perspective of cognitive psychology. If by unconscious processes we refer to bodily and psychological events of which we are not aware$_1$, then such processes are assumed to play a major role in all modern theories of cognition.

On Becoming Aware$_1$

As a first observation, everyone accepts the fact that infants and preverbal children are quite aware$_2$ of their environment, although they have not yet acquired the linguistic skill necessary to describe it (or to be aware$_1$ of it). Children appear to acquire considerable knowledge about objects, people, actions, spatial relations, and locations long before they learn to talk about these things.

How, then, do children learn to talk about their internal states, to become aware$_1$ of them? Just as the verbal community teaches children to discriminate and label dogs from cats, so does it also teach children to discriminate and label bodily stimuli, internal states, and thoughts. Different bodily states differ enormously in how visible they are to external observers. For instance, the trainers or parents can easily teach a child to label the pain caused by a stubbed toe or bruised elbow because the parent can see the injury or its causal antecedent. The training becomes more difficult for the parent when the child has internal pains such as stomachaches, headaches, or toothaches because the sore spot is not visible to the trainer. It is harder still for parents to train children to label their mood states, emotional feelings, and internal thought sequences. As an external observer the parent can only infer the child's internal state from noting what went just before (e.g., turning off his favorite television cartoon) and noting the child's overt reactions (e.g., crying, or pouting, or striking out at the parent). Such occasions provide an opportunity for parents to teach children a label for their inferred mental states, by saying something like, "What you're feeling now is anger." Our skill as trainers in such cases is just an extension of our everyday skill of "reading" the emotions of the people we interact with everyday. As children become acculturated, they acquire more complex discriminations of the verbal labels for describing their external and internal situations.

From this perspective, then, it is proper to say that in the beginning all psychological processes in children are unconscious since they are at most only aware$_2$ of them. Acquiring awareness$_1$ for some processes thus requires the attainment of a hard-won repertoire of discriminative abilities, verbal labeling skills, and general linguistic competence in which our social-language community plays a crucial role. This may be why anthropologists tell us that different cultures have considerably different concepts and vocabularies for describing internal states.

A second important point is that the training of children to label their internal states is especially difficult, sometimes inaccurate, and that the results are often confusing, even tragically chaotic. People are often uncertain how to label their internal states; therefore, they often look to their external conditions, to what is going on around them, to infer (just as their trainer-parent had to do) what they are probably feeling. This account of how we label our feelings was bolstered by the classic study of Schachter and Singer (1962). They showed that people who were psychologically aroused by an injection of adrenalin labeled their internal feelings in two compatible ways—as either euphoria or anger—depending on the behavior of a like-injected partner who displayed either euphoria or anger in the experimental situation.

This experiment and its follow-ups demonstrated how strong external social situations are in determining the specific emotion a person feels and how weak and unstable are the internal contributors to the specificity of our feelings. It is almost as though the person uses an emotion word to label the evoking situation rather than his specific internal state. He says, "I'm angry," when he might have said with more accuracy, "I'm in what I consider an anger-provoking situation, and I'm physiologically aroused."

The ambiguity of emotional states and people's generally poor ability to label them fosters an especially acute difficulty for psychiatric patients. Neurotic patients may be those among us who are especially poorly attuned to their emotions or to appropriate ways to interpret the autonomic arousal patterns characteristic of different emotions. This could result from being raised in a dysfunctional family that punished bodily displays of particular emotions or reinforced verbal formulaic expressions of love and respect. Owing to an unusual training environment, patients' verbal descriptions of past emotional scenes may be seriously "out of synch" with their bodily displays of emotion. On the one hand, patients may profess feeling joy, sadness, or anxiety over some remembered event yet reveal no such emotion in their body and expressiveness. On the other hand, patients may verbally deny feeling angry or anxious over some upsetting event while their body may reveal extreme agitation and anxiety (see Weinberger, Schwartz, and Davidson 1979). The "repressor" style may result from a family life that reinforced children for denying or blocking negative emotions. Such discrepancies of different emotion indicators are to be expected for reports of emotional experiences given outside their original situational context wherein different contingencies of reinforcement prevail for the different response systems.

Types of Unconscious Processes

Having noted the child's difficulty of achieving awareness$_1$, let me now note several obvious examples that most cognitive psychologists would agree involve unconscious processes. First, all our rapid, routine information processes involved in pattern recognition, speech perception, speech production, fantasy generation, rapid motor skills, and so forth are assumed to occur so rapidly that they are effectively unconscious. Most modern cognitive theories analyze such skills into a number of components, each performing some small function (such as feature extraction for pattern recognition). It is assumed routinely that people have no awareness$_1$ of any of these millisecond-range stages in the process; at best, people are aware$_1$ of some of the *products* of the process. Second, we recognize that people are typically unaware$_1$ of most internal physiological reflexes and homeostatic adjustments. For example, our pancreas releases more or less insulin depending on the glucose level in our bloodstream; but we are blissfully unaware$_1$ of the many hundreds of such homeostatic happenings within us. Biofeedback training of our internal organs holds out the prospect of teaching us to become aware$_1$ of the grosser aspects of these physiological reflexes, but, for the most part, they carry out their adjustments outside our awareness.

Third, and moving to our overt activities, experimental psychologists recognize a number of instances in which it is proper to say that a person is unaware$_1$ of various behavioral happenings. Some of these were noted by B. F. Skinner in his *Science and Human Behavior* (1953, 288–90), and I will summarize them here.

First, people may be unaware$_1$ that they have just carried out some action. A typical example would be an unnoticed slip of the tongue or slip of action in which the behavior deviates from the person's dominant intention. People typically skip right past such slips without noticing them.

Second, people may be unaware$_1$ that they are in the midst of carrying out some action. Included here would be tics and absent-minded mannerisms (e.g., beard stroking, mustache twirling, fingernail biting). Such mechanical habits are likely when the person is concentrating on something else. A first step in helping people overcome such mannerisms (if they are offensive) is to give them feedback training so that they can be made aware$_2$ of when they are performing the act. A person may have trouble noticing what he is doing if the act involves minimal proprioceptive feedback. For example, a person may be unaware$_1$ of tension in his neck muscles or of a continual scowl on his face because feedback from the neck and facial muscles may be too weak to notice.

Third, people may not notice that they tend to behave in a certain way in a given situation—that is, if left to their own devices, they would never arrive at this inductive generalization about themselves. For example, a man may engage in serious business discussions only with other men in his office but engage in joking banter only with his women colleagues at work. Or a teacher may treat all and only students in a bored, diffident manner. Such persons may not notice such generalizations about their behavior and may even deny them.

Such examples raise the important point that there are different descriptions of the same behavioral episode, especially interpersonal actions; in particular, the person may describe his own behavior in ways that differ significantly from the way observers describe it. What one person considers sarcasm or a practical joke an observer (or the victim) may take to be a hostile act. What one person considers aggressive actions another considers assertive. What is reckless behavior for one is considered bold or courageous by another. One person's self-assured confidence is another person's arrogant egotism. More generally, we can say that an actor may be aware$_1$ of his action under one interpretation but not aware$_1$ of it under an alternative, less-flattering interpretation.

It would seem that such differing interpretations constitute a major source of what psychoanalysts view as the client's "denial" or "warding off" of certain impulses or conflicts that the analyst interprets as "latent" in the client's behavior. The client claims he is doing one thing, whereas the analyst interprets his actions as having an alternative intention. The difference is similar to that between the "manifest" versus the alleged "latent" content of a dream. The difference here trades on the truly "interpretive" nature of our vocabulary for social actions. We interpret social actions, even simple ones, by inferring the plans and goals behind them, and people who use different frameworks, who begin with different inferences about underlying motives, such as a therapist versus a client, may categorize an action quite differently, seeing it as conveying quite different "meanings."

Fourth, to continue listing common types of unawareness, people may be unaware$_1$ of the fact that their behavior or attitude has changed since an earlier occasion. This was a familiar result in experiments on cognitive dissonance and attitude change (e.g., Bem 1965). A typical experiment was one conducted by Goethals and Reckman (1973), who first measured high school students' opinions toward busing of schoolchildren to achieve racial integration. Two weeks later, each subject engaged in a three-person discussion in which a student confederate of the experimenter presented strong, persuasive arguments contrary to the earlier opinion of the subject. Following that discussion, most subjects changed the reports of their current opinion to a large degree toward the opposing viewpoint. Moreover, when asked to recall what their original opinion had been (knowing that the experimenter would check their records), they "recalled" that they had had an original opinion very close to their current one. For instance, an originally anti-busing student who had had his opinion changed to be pro-busing was likely to remember his original opinion as more pro-busing (or less anti-busing) than it had been. Furthermore, the subjects seemed unaware$_1$ of the change: they reported that the discussion had merely supported and articulated clearly their original position and that it had had no effect in altering their opinion. Needless to say, control students not subjected to the counterarguing discussions did not change their opinion about busing, and they remembered accurately how they had answered the earlier opinion questionnaire. Such demonstrations support the general point that people may not be aware$_1$ that their behavior or opinion has changed.

Fifth, people are often not aware$_1$ of the variables that are influencing their behavior. A man may say that he goes to the beach for his health, but we may notice that he goes only to the beach where beautiful women in bikinis congregate. An interesting paper by Nisbett and Wilson (1977) reviews a large sample of similar cases to illustrate the inaccuracy of introspective reports about causal factors in certain circumstances (but, for a reply, see Ericsson and Simon 1980).

As one example, Latané and Darley (1970) have shown that people are less likely to help a person in distress the greater is the number of other bystanders in that situation who are not helping. For instance, the more people who overhear a person in another room having what sounds like an epileptic seizure or heart attack, the lower the probability that any given individual will rush to get help for that person. Yet, in extensive interviews, subjects persistently claimed that their own lack of helping had nothing to do with the presence of other bystanders. Further, when the experiment was described to others, they all predicted that their own behavior would not in the least be influenced by the presence of others. So, people are quite unaware$_1$ of the strong social determinants of their behavior in such situations.

A second example may be taken from the experiments by Maier (1931) on the role of subtle hints in problem solving. Maier demonstrated that hints had an enormous influence on whether a solution to his insight puzzles would "occur" to subjects, even though they were rarely aware$_1$ of the hint. To illustrate, faced with the problem of tying together two strings hanging from the ceiling more than two arms' lengths apart, a subtle hint would be for Maier, while casually walking about the room, to brush by one of the strings, setting it into pendular motion. Although such hints influenced the likelihood that subjects solved the problem in the next few minutes (by making a pendulum of the strings), they had no awareness$_1$ of the relation. Subjects often believed that their insights arose spontaneously; they often either forgot the hint or denied ever noticing it.

Included in this subtype are the many recent demonstrations in which subjects learn about and use covariations among subtle, incidental stimulus features, despite the fact that they cannot (accurately) verbally describe what they have learned (Lewicki 1986). For example, subjects may view photographs of women, with some said to be friendly and others highly competent. The experimenter arranges the trait attributions to be correlated with a subtle, non-obvious feature such as whether the woman has long or short hair. Subjects will learn this covariation as indicated by their later appropriate classification of new women with long or short hair. Yet, when questioned in detail, subjects almost never mention the test figures' length of hair as a reason for their judgment—rather, they fabricate stories about culturally relevant attributes such as soft eyes, dimples, warm smile, and so on. In such examples, we can say that a part of the subject's brain is registering the relevant covarying feature and later using it to guide ratings, even though the person's verbal explanations are primarily being controlled by his or her (incorrect) theories of what facial features should be correlated with friendliness or competence. Lewicki (1986) cites a number of cases of such nonconscious learning of covariations.

People can fail to notice variables controlling their behavior for many reasons. The relevant cues or controlling stimuli may be to subtle or buried in the mosaic of our social environment. As an example, people's mood of well-being is demonstrably influenced by the weather; they are happier on sunny days, gloomier on rainy, overcast days. Yet they fail to appreciate (or are not typically aware₁ of) this influence of the weather on them. I am told that close analyses reveal that patients with alleged "free-floating anxiety" can often be found (by persistent self-monitoring) to have their panic attacks triggered by certain dreadful thought sequences. although the result may be so delayed that they had not been aware₁ of this causal sequence. As another illustration, a person may be so distracted by salient stimuli that he is unable to pay much attention to relevant cues, even those from his own behavior. Thus, he would be "unconscious" of certain things he is doing. For instance, a person who has a dysfluent speech mannerism (e.g., interjecting "ah" frequently) could not be expected to monitor and suppress that habit for the first time as he delivers an important speech extemporaneously before a critical audience. His primary task there would simply be too attention demanding. As a third reason, people may have a particular theory about what variable should control their behavior, and this theory blinds them to noticing and labeling the relevant controlling variable (see Nisbett and Wilson 1977).

The above listing is long but hardly exhaustive of cases in which cognitive (or behavioral) psychologists are quite content to say that people are unaware₁ (or unconscious) of what they are doing or why they are doing it. We may disagree among ourselves regarding the import of such observations or how to train people to be more aware₁ of these happenings, but there is little disagreement over accepting such phenomena as "real" despite being unconscious. Now, I suppose that most of the phenomena I have mentioned above would not be considered by psychoanalysts as interesting manifestations of the "Freudian Unconscious" (with the capital U) since these phenomena are not especially related to the repression of taboo wishes and/or memories of traumatic events. Let me now turn to a discussion of repression, the interpretation of forgetting, and the recovery of formerly inaccessible memories.

Repression and the Recovery of Forgotten Memories

Repression is alleged to be the foundation on which psychoanalysis rests. Experimental psychologists have for many years been interested in repression, interpreting it as "motivated forgetting" of wishes and/or events. As a memory theorist, I would try to analyze motivated failures to remember as occurring at one of several possible states—during initial learning, during storage over the retention interval, or during the retrieval phase.

Motivated Nonlearning

To begin at the beginning, we know that people can consciously control the *initial registration* of an event—how much attention they give to it, how they categorize the event, and how they relate it to their other knowledge (so-called elaborative processing). Also they can control the extent to which the event is rehearsed, in the sense of its being thought about and repeated internally in their working memory. In many experiments on the "directed forgetting" of target items in a learning task (see Bjork 1978), subjects indeed use such strategies to reduce their initial learning of items that they are told they need not remember.

People may sometimes use such strategies to avoid thinking about and learning about certain events that cast them in an unflattering light, that make them feel ashamed or anxious. But avoidance of a topic does not imply a "continual effort to suppress" thinking about it, as Freud suggested, any more than the fact that I get absorbed in a movie means that I am working hard to avoid doing my income taxes at home. Activities can simply be absorbing in themselves, and doing one activity need not involve "effortful suppression" of others.

If whenever I begin to think of an embarrassing event I consciously instruct myself to stop it and think instead of a pleasant activity, I thereby deny rehearsal time to that avoided memory so that it will not be strengthened as much as more pleasant memories that might have begun as the same initial strength in memory. We might call this "motivated nonlearning" or "motivated nonrehearsal" rather than motivated forgetting.

Are people aware$_1$ of what they are doing in such cases? They probably are in most cases: the thought stopping (or thought deflection) is often a quite deliberate act to which people have introspective access. Perhaps with practice, the thought deflection (or anticipation of the unpleasant idea) becomes faster and almost "automatic," occurring with less introspective access. For example, married couples assuredly learn to avoid particular topics of conversation (such as the death of a child, past infidelities, financial losses) that they know will prove especially disruptive to their current happiness. This could be a variant of repression. Dollard and Miller (1950, chap. 12) long ago gave a plausible learning-theory account of such a mechanism.

Unfortunately, the process of nonlearning described above has a major flaw: it does not differentiate between cases in which the process works successfully and those in which it fails. Not all our negative events are forgotten. We know that people generally remember huge numbers of emotionally upsetting and unpleasant events—insults, frustrations, rejections, failures—many of which are personally humiliating and are direct assaults on their self-esteem. People also remember all varieties of sad, depressing events, too, such as personal losses or the deaths of loved ones. In fact, Holmes (1970) and Dutta and Kanungo (1967, 1975) have found in autobiographical (diary) recall studies and in laboratory studies of recall that people are more likely to remember emotionally arousing events in proportion to their intensity, regardless of whether the events are pleasant or unpleasant.

The status of motivated nonlearning can be summarized by saying that learning theorists have several plausible, mechanistic explanations of it, such as lack of attention, nonrehearsal, automatized avoidance of unpleasant thoughts, and so on. However, we confront a major problem in specifying the conditions under which any of these mechanisms comes into operation. That is, we cannot predict when unpleasant events will be remembered better or worse then neutral events. We need an acceptable account of when motivated nonlearning will occur. Dan Weinberger (personal communication, 1987) proposed that repression operates not on "unpleasant or painful" thoughts but only on those highly charged ideas (of oneself) or wishes that are "intolerable to one's self-concept." Thus, a person may well remember an unpleasant divorce or job layoff because those events are not a serious threat to his or her self-concept. While this is a useful beginning, in characterizing ideas or event memories likely to suffer repression, the hypothesis is still relatively vague and needs to be operationalized. Needless to say, given the ethical safeguards protecting experimental subjects from undue distress, acceptance of such a hypothesis practically prevents our testing it in the laboratory.

Motivated Overwriting of Memories

To return to the general analysis, I have argued that people may not remember something either because they did not learn it very well, or because the learned material gets overwritten or destroyed while in storage, or because the cues in the retrieval environment fail to rearouse the memory trace. Having discussed motivated nonlearning as an analogue of repression, let me turn now to the processes of overwriting and retrieval failure. Overwriting is another name for learning different associations to the same cues. Thus, if a man suffered a humiliation from his boss, he may later record in memory new, more pleasant experiences with him (or mentally review earlier ones). The result of such interpolated learning is that the worker will become increasingly likely to forget the humiliating experience when he thinks of his boss. This is just a form of retroactive interference, which is a familiar cause of forgetting (e.g., Crowder 1976). In effect, one can "bury" a particular association to a given person by covering it with many more (and different) associations to that person. Such interference may work especially well if the recent associations are affectively incompatible with the to-be-buried association so that they do not automatically remind the person of that earlier, humiliating experience. I mention this type of overwriting as a theoretical possibility, but it is unclear how much it contributes to clinical cases of repression. It might be a likely cause of forgetting of childhood events that we experienced with family members whom we have since seen in many other, friendlier contexts.

Retrieval Failures

I save for last the discussion of retrieval failure because I believe it is the largest contributor to forgetting. Let me place memory retrieval in its proper perspective. For understanding memory, I am a dedicated associationist. Associationists conceive of a memory trace as an associative configuration of concepts describing the event in question. The trace also includes "descriptions" of one's thoughts and feelings during the original event, linkages to preceding causes and subsequent events caused by the target event, and so on. Thus, a memory of a single event is an internal representation comprising a large constellation of event descriptors including feelings, attributes, properties, and causal sequences of scenes, each of which can serve as an "index cue" for recalling more or less of the constellation. Once stored, a memory is likely to be rearoused by presenting a partial description of the event to the learner, for example, "Tell me about the time in 1976 when your father took you to the circus." We may think of such question as specifying index cues (e.g., father, me, circus, 1976) that the person uses to search for a memory record that fits this specification (for a detailed description of this process, see Norman 1982; Norman and Bobrow 1979). Of course, not all memories are deliberately cued by outsiders' questions. We may question ourselves (as in, "Where did I leave my keys?"), and, in idle reverie or fantasy, we are continually retrieving the "next thought" in a sequence as the current idea or image in working memory triggers the next associated idea to which it is linked. This is the familiar method of free association or stream-of-consciousness reporting, and we can understand that some patients may be motivated to avoid certain lines of self-cues, to not think about certain painful or conflicted topics.

An implication of a retrieval view of memory is that some cues will fail whereas others will succeed in retrieving one and the same memory trace. At the conference, we carried out an elementary demonstration of this contrast. In the morning, using a cover story, I asked the conference participants to write down in random order their first, second, or third free association to each of twenty category names, such as a bird, a city, a weapon, and so on. In the afternoon during my talk, I asked them to free recall the twenty words that they had written that morning. After much mental struggling and blank staring, the participants averaged about six items recalled of the twenty. I then read them the original category cues (bird, city, etc.), with the result that they were now able to recall about 19.5 of the original twenty items that they had produced that morning. The participants were "genuinely remembering," too, since they always gave the appropriate associate (first, second, or third as originally requested).

The demonstration dramatized the difference between an effective cue (the category) and a relatively ineffective cue ("the words you wrote this morning"). A proponent of the Freudian theory of mind, when confronted with the earlier failure to recall, is prone to ask, "Where did all those memories go? Were they repressed?" The answer is that they were not repressed and they did not "go" anywhere; memories are simply dispositions that can be actualized in certain circumstances (or retrieval environments) and not in others. They are like "responses" waiting for the right "stimulus" to release them.

On Recovering Old Memories

Such a perspective gives a memory theorist a somewhat different slant on claims that a client in therapy has just "recovered a repressed memory." Clients on the analytic couch may indeed eventually remember many events from their childhood that they had not thought of for a long time. But the skeptical associationist always asks, How hard or persistently did the client try to recall those events on previous occasions? What cues did the therapist force the client to think about? What range of index prompts were tried? What feelings, moods, images, or mental states in the client did the therapist recreate to combine with descriptive cues in order to promote recall?

Memory for life events is like a sausage chain. If you retrieve one, its linkages prompt you to retrieve another, and so you pull one memory after another out of your biographical storehouse. I would guess the memory recoveries of patients on the analytical couch are not so extraordinary that they always require explanation in terms of a "lifting of repression." I think that most of us can remember many events from our childhood (after about four years old) if we relax, take our time, free associate, systematically probe ourselves with context cues ("Where did I live? Who were my friends? What were my toys like? etc.). Also, we must jump in after any retrieved memory to relentlessly follow up its associations and their associations in turn. Several experimental reports (Erdelyi and Kleinbard 1978; Williams and Hollon 1981) show that such procedures can be quite effective in slowly retrieving "lost memories" over a period of hours or days of the person struggling to recall. The point is that the very fact that a client in therapy comes out with a memory that he had not thought of for a long time cannot be taken as presumptive evidence that the memory was repressed.

A related problem with a patient's claim of remembering long-repressed memories is that the therapist has only inexact ways to determine the accuracy of the memories (and veracity is necessary for the repression hypothesis). Memories of remote events are notoriously subject to all manners of distortion. To mention just the common memory distortions: we may mislocate where or when an event occurred; we may confuse and fuse together aspects from two different events; we may confuse a heard-of or imagined event with an actual witnessed event; we may fill in its gaps by completing the story fragment in a conventional, schematized way; and our memory is often "self-serving," assigning ourselves greater power and responsibility than we deserve for good outcomes and less blame than we deserve for bad outcomes (Greenwald 1980). Given such possibility for distortions, the analyst who recovers an "alleged" memory should be cautious in claiming its veracity, no matter what affect is attached to the memory.

Motivated Retrieval Failures

Turning to motivated failures to retrieve a memory, the current evidence on this topic (reviewed in Holmes 1974, and in this volume) is that, depending on how repression is defined, it is either a well-known phenomenon (called "conscious suppression") or an extremely weak, evanescent phenomenon in the laboratory. Motivated suppression of the reporting of memories is, of course, commonplace. It occurs in the everyday little lies that we tell others out of politeness; it occurs more dramatically whenever a spy or criminal withholds answers under interrogation; and so on. On the other hand, obtaining reliable evidence for unconscious repression of memories in the laboratory has proved difficult despite years of conscientious experimentation by sympathetic investigators. In concluding his review of the research literature relevant to repression, Holmes (1974, 649) wrote, "There is no consistent research evidence to support the hypothesis derived from the theory of repression. The lack of evidence for the theory is especially notable in view of the wide variety of approaches which have been tried and the persistent effort which has been made during the last half century to find support for the theory." In his paper at the conference, Holmes (in this volume) claims to have found no new evidence to cause him to revise his negative conclusion about repression.

To summarize my discussion of repression, I have indicated several places in the causal chain, from encoding through storage to retrieval, at which motivational factors could enter. The evidence for motivated nonlearning and motivated suppression of memory reporting is both extensive and commonplace. But reliable evidence for unconscious repression, which is automatic with principal parts of it occurring outside awareness, is extremely meager, and its few apparent demonstrations are subject to alternative interpretations.

The Statistical Nature of Remembering

Part of the problem in demonstrating repression is that there are so many perfectly ordinary reasons why people forget, reasons documented by years of investigations of forgetting of unemotional material. So a theorist who claims that repression is an additional factor causing forgetting of traumatic emotional material has to control for or rule out these garden-variety causes of memory failures. Adding to the difficulty is the view of most memory theorists that remembering is inherently a probabilistic, unreliable process that may still occasionally fail even when all the proper factors are in place. This probabilistic view of remembering motivates our use of many subjects and many items in typical memory experiments. Whether a given subject recalls a given item in a given retrieval environment at a particular moment is still largely a "statistical matter." The laws in the psychology of memory are statistical in nature. We can make the probability of recall very large or small, but we seem unable to make it perfectly determinable in all cases.

The probabilistic view clashes with what I take to have been Freud's view espoused in his treatise *The Psychopathology of Everyday Life* (Freud 1915). He seems to have claimed that nearly every instance of forgetting (or slips of the tongue or slips of action), no matter how trivial, can be viewed as determinately caused by a specific repressed wish. While that strikes me as a fitting hope for a psychoanalyst (or any scientist) to adopt, it would be charitable in the extreme to believe that there is much evidence in its favor. Freud's "evidence" in this respect was to take certain key concepts surrounding the forgotten item (e.g., a person's name), to have the client freely associate to them, and then to interpret these in analytic terms. Freud followed the same method in interpreting slips of the tongue.

The problem with this method is that it is essentially "proof by imagination" (namely, Freud's). Given the lack of constraints on psychoanalytic interpretations of "unconscious, primary process thinking," it is possible to move from one set of concepts (the slip or forgotten name) to almost any other set of concepts by "predicative thinking." In Freud's view, all roads lead back to the client's unconscious conflicts, which Freud either knew about or could guess. An acceptable control condition would have been for the patient to free associate about any slip (or forgetting event) made by someone else: would Freud's interpretations have ended at the same destination? I suspect so.

In a postconference note, Ken Bowers (in this volume) took a deterministic position similar to Freud's. To use Bowers's illustration, suppose that, while introducing a familiar person, you suddenly block on his or her name. Bowers claims that (1) there must be a principled explanation for the block at this moment and (2) motivated retrieval failure is probably that explanation. The statistical view of memory denies both claims; if memory performance is inherently a probabilistic matter, then the "must" obligation in 1 is rejected. Since I have seen many hundreds of such recall blocks by subjects trying to recall unemotional laboratory materials, I have little reason to accept his point 2. I realize that the philosophical issue of whether the behavioral sciences are inherently statistical or deterministic has been debated for decades without significant resolution. The reader should not equate the deterministic position with the scientific approach and the statistical view with flabby intuitionism. Recall that the most rigorous, quantitative theories of learning are stochastic in nature (e.g., see Atkinson, Bower, and Crothers 1965).

Is Posthypnotic Amnesia a Model of Repression?

In discussing repression as a kind of dissociation, Kihlstrom and Spiegel (both in this volume) introduce the topic of posthypnotic amnesia. Posthypnotic amnesia seems to be a case of the subject having several kinds of awareness$_2$ without awareness$_1$ of the learned material covered by amnesia. Let us review several illustrations of this discrepancy. An early experiment by Bitterman and Marcuse (1945) gave hypnotized subjects a posthypnotic suggestion to forget certain key words in a word list they were studying. Later, when tested for recognition memory, subjects said that they did not remember having studied those key words; nonetheless, they gave an enhanced galvanic skin reaction (GSR) to these key words in comparison to truly novel words included in the test series. So, these subjects were not aware$_1$ of remembering earlier presentations of these words, but their GSR showed awareness$_2$ of memory for these events.

A related study by Coe et al. (1976) demonstrated that learned material covered by hypnotic amnesia was nonetheless completely effective in causing retroactive interference and forgetting of related learning material. Coe et al. taught their subjects a list of A-B paired associates, hypnotized them and taught them a list of interfering A-C pairs, and then suggested amnesia for that second list. On arousal from hypnosis, a test for recall of the original A-B associations found poorer A-B recall, a standard retroactive interference effect; in fact, the amnesic subjects forgot the A-B associates to the same degree as did control subjects whose hypnotically learned second list was not covered by suggested amnesia. Thus, the amnesia suggestion did not produce the "functional ablation" of the second-list memories that one would naively expect from the subjects' conscious inability to recollect the second-list events; quite the contrary, the second list, which amnesic subjects were told to forget, continued to exert strong interference on recall of the first list.

A related finding by Dillon and Spanos (1983) was that hypnotically suggested amnesia to forget items presented on earlier trials in Brown-Peterson short-term memory task did not reverse the usual cumulative proactive interference that develops in this task; on the other hand, a shift in the taxonomic category from which the items were drawn (e.g., from animals to games) caused the normally expected "release from proactive interference" for all subjects whether or not amnesia for prior items had been suggested.

Another case of memory without awareness$_1$ for hypnotically amnesic subjects has been reported by Huesmann, Gruder, and Dorst (1987). Huesmann, Gruder, and Dorst had their subjects under hypnosis solve a series of "three-water-jug" problems that required a common pouring solution (e.g., to get the target amount of water in jug A, first fill jug A, emptying it out twice into jug B and once into jug C). After suggesting amnesia for these problems and awakening their subjects from hypnosis, the experimenters gave them some more water-jug problems. While professing not to remember having ever seen such problems, the amnesic subjects nonetheless persisted with the old "set" method, $A - 2B - C$, despite the fact that it failed on the test problem and a far simpler solution was possible. Thus, the persistence of the maladaptive set (so-called "Einstellung") illustrates that these hypnotic subjects were aware$_2$ of what they had learned but were not aware$_1$ of it because it was covered by an amnesia suggestion.

Another kind of dissociation was described by Kihlstrom (personal communication, 1985), who found that his hypnotic subjects nonetheless showed strong priming in word-fragment completion for items covered by hypnotic amnesia. In priming demonstrations, subjects first read a list of words (such as "steel"), and several minutes later are given a test on which they are to fill in the missing letters of the word fragments (like "st – – l") to make the first word that comes to mind. Typically, several completions are possible ("steal," "still," "stall"), but the primed word (presented earlier) occurs as a completion far above its baseline or unprimed frequency. Kihlstrom's hypnotically amnesic subjects showed good priming memory (in the sense of awareness$_2$) for the studied words, while at the same time showing many failures of awareness$_1$ of having studied these items because they were covered with amnesia. A further related finding by Jacoby and Dallas (1981) is that priming effects on word identification are statistically independent of subjects' conscious recollection or nonrecollection of having seen that word in the study list.

Such dissociations between different indices of remembering under hypnotic amnesia have sometimes been discussed in terms of obligatory versus optional memory performances (Cofer, Chmielewski, and Brockway 1976; Gregg 1979). Thus, conscious recall, reconstruction, and recognition memory tasks are said to involve an optional component: the person can decide to alter or suppress his best performance, just as a spy during interrogation may avoid revealing answers to sensitive questions. On the other hand, measures of perceptual priming, GSR, retroactive interference, and persisting set are obligatory, almost "automatic," features of memory over which the person has little voluntary control. An alternative rendering of these differences is in terms of Dennett's aware$_1$ versus aware$_2$ distinction: hypnotically amnesic subjects are aware$_2$ of certain memories for which they lack awareness$_1$ because those are covered by amnesia.

How Complete Is the Dissociation of Posthypnotic Amnesia?

We may inquire whether posthypnotic amnesia provides a good paradigm for the concept of dissociative memory, as Kihlstrom suggests (1985, in this volume). Indeed, the phenomenon appears compelling: subjects at first are unable to recall certain material (say, events during hypnosis) after amnesia for these is suggested, but then, on the subjects receiving a releasing signal (the hypnotist saying, e.g., "Now you can remember everything"), the "amnesia lifts," and the subject is able to recall a normal amount of these events. The problem, as Kihlstrom clearly recognizes, is that various skeptical interpretations of posthypnotic amnesia are plausible. Let me recount several of these skeptical arguments so that the reader can catch their drift.

First, posthypnotic amnesia is an uncommon phenomenon. I gather (from Coe 1978) that about two-thirds of the unselected adult population do not respond at all to suggestions for posthypnotic amnesia. Of the one-third of subjects who show some degree of suggested amnesia, about half of them appear to achieve their nonrecall by conscious suppression of overt recall. Spanos and Bodorik (1977) intensively interviewed their subjects who revealed some suggested amnesia and pressured them with challenges and demands to try to break through (or breach) the amnesia. In different experiments, in between 40 and 63 percent of the subjects, either the amnesia could be breached by forceful commands to recall, or subjects would admit that they had deliberately suppressed reporting the items they did remember.

What about the other one-sixth of the subjects who show "true amnesia"? We have to rely entirely on their introspective reports. According to Spanos and Bodorik (1977), the nonrecallers may be classified into several types. (1) Some subjects may think of the items but not be able to say them overtly, as though their mouths were locked shut. (2) Some subjects report simple lack of motivation to recall items; for instance, they may say that they were too drowsy or relaxed to make the effort to search for the to-be-remembered items. (3) Some subjects are motivated deliberately to avoid searching for the to-be-remembered items; they use a strategy of deliberately concentrating on some distracting thought or image. It is as though the request to "recall session items" is internally countermanded as "think about some other topic." (4) Finally, some subjects report "really trying" to search for and retrieve the to-be-remembered items, but the ideas just seem to elude their grasp. Of these four subcategories of nonrecallers, the first three are using some conscious strategy to reduce the search required by the typical recall task. One is hesitant to say that such subjects are demonstrating "true amnesia." Only the fourth category of subjects comprises the genuine article, and they are a tiny minority.

How are we to interpret this fourth category of amnesic subjects? It is not their overt lack of recall but their phenomenology and subjective explanation of it that distinguishes them. In the role-playing theory of hypnosis advanced by Sarbin and Coe (1972) and Coe (1978), subjects are interpreted as becoming deeply involved in playing the role of the "hypnotic subject in trance." They behave according to the hypnotist's suggestions and their expectations about what the role requires of them.

Sarbin and Coe hypothesize that the greater the subjects' degree of involvement in their role and in the imaginings suggested by the hypnotist, the greater will be their tendency to believe their imaginings to be real. In this perspective, asking subjects to report their phenomenology under hypnosis is akin to asking them to play a role and to "keep secret" the fact that they are role-playing.

In this role theory, the interesting question becomes, How is it that the subjects persuade themselves that they really cannot recall? Partly it may be a matter of retrospective self-delusion (see Bem 1965 on self-persuasion); looking back over their failure to recall (for one of the first three reasons above), subjects may explain or rationalize their failure by citing the indicated amnesic role rather than the thought deflections they employed to play that role. Coe (1978) discusses several other interpretations of how suggested non-recallers could persuade themselves that they were truly amnesic.

The role-playing theory also implies that "amnesics" will nonetheless show normal memory for the amnesic material if the tests bypass common conceptions of what "remembering" implies. In particular, obligatory or nondeliberate indices of memory, such as perceptual priming, interference, persisting set, or GSR arousal to the amnesic material, are beyond voluntary control and so will occur regardless of the subjects' role expectations.

The conclusion from these skeptical considerations is that posthypnotic amnesia cannot be taken as a laboratory-pure model of dissociation or repression. It may be the best model we have, but it carries its own baggage of interpretive problems.

Summary

This chapter discussed the views of a cognitive psychologist towards the topics of conscious awareness, unconscious wishes and behaviors, repression, and the recovery of repressed memories. I began by citing Dennett's distinction between two senses of awareness: people are aware$_1$ of a fact (wish, proposition) if they can talk about it and are aware$_2$ of it if their behavior indicates that they are taking account of it. Awareness$_1$ depends on a self-descriptive, speech repertoire, and I briefly traced its development and the obstacles children encounter in learning to describe their internal states. I discussed a number of puzzling behavioral discrepancies or dissociations whose nature is clarified by recasting them as a contrast between awareness$_1$ and awareness$_2$. In particular, the contents of the Freudian Unconscious are said to be in awareness$_2$ but not in awareness$_1$ under normal circumstances.

I then discussed the notion of unconscious processes (in contrast to the Unconscious) in cognitive psychology and listed several illustrations of unconscious behaviors of which the actor is unaware$_1$. An important point is that a person may be aware$_1$ of his social behavior under one description (or interpretation), whereas an observer or analyst may infer that the person's behavior has a different goal (of which the subject is unaware$_1$), thus creating a different interpretation and explanation of the behavior. Another important point is that people are often unaware₁ of the powerful situational variables determining their behavior.

I then discussed the concept of repression and noted the three logical stages of a remembering episode at which motivational factors could exert their influence—either during initial registration, retentive storage, or retrieval. There is evidence for conscious, deliberate forms of motivated nonlearning and for motivated nonreporting of memories. A hypothetical process of automatizing "stopping thinking about a given topic" was described (see Dollard and Miller 1950), but the exact conditions under which such a mechanism might operate remain obscure.

In discussing the recovery of memories during psychotherapy, the differing potencies of different retrieval cues was noted. I suggested that long-lost memories can be retrieved by using systematic strategies involving associative retrieval cues and that clinical anecdotes are not especially persuasive for claiming that recovered memories were formerly repressed. I ended by citing the failures to demonstrate repression in laboratory settings, which evidence is also reviewed by Holmes (in this volume).

I then discussed posthypnotic amnesia as a model for studying dissociative phenomena and repression. I outlined the skeptical view of posthypnotic amnesia: it is relatively rare in the general population; the "amnesia" can often be breached by pressure for honest reporting; the "amnesia" is often due to deliberate strategies that subjects follow to prevent, deflect, or distract from recall of the target material. I then discussed how amnesic subjects might delude themselves into the belief that they were really trying to recall. Finally, I discussed several involuntary, obligatory measures of memory that demonstrated that, in these respects, the material covered by amnesia had its normal mnemonic influence. Thus, the allegedly amnesic material acted to cause interference on other material, perceptual priming, persistent set, and GSR arousal, all despite the subject consciously reporting an inability to recollect the material. These discrepancies again illustrated the distinction between the differing senses of awareness outlined in the beginning of the chapter.

References

Atkinson, R. C., G. H. Bower and E. J. Crothers. 1965. *An introduction to mathematical learning theory.* New York: Wiley.

Bem, D. J. 1965. An experimental analysis of self-persuasion. *Journal of Experimental Social Psychology* 1:199–218.

Bitterman, M. E. and S. L. Marcuse. 1945. Autonomic response in post-hypnotic amnesia. *Journal of Experimental Psychology* 35:248–52.

Bjork, R. A. 1978. The updating of human memory. In *The psychology of learning and motivation,* ed. G. H. Bower, 235–60. New York: Academic.

Coe, W. C. 1978. The credibility of posthypnotic amnesia: A contextualist's view. *International Journal of Clinical and Experimental Hypnosis* 26:218–45.

Coe, W. C., B. Basden, D. Basden, and C. Graham. 1976. Posthypnotic amnesia: Suggestions of an active process in dissociative phenomena. *Journal of Abnormal Psychology* 85:455–58.

Cofer, C. N., D. L Chmielewski, and J. F. Brockway. 1976. Constructive processes and structure of human memory. In *The structure of human memory,* ed. C. N. Cofer, 190–203. San Francisco: Freeman.

Crowder, R. G. 1976. *Principles of learning and memory.* Hillsdale, N. J.: Erlbaum.

Dennett, D. 1969. *Content and consciousness.* London: Routledge and Kegan Paul.

———. 1981. Towards a cognitive theory of consciousness. In *Brainstorms,*ed. D. Dennett, 149–73. Cambridge, Mass.: MIT Press.

Dillon, R. F. and M. P. Spanos. 1983. Proactive interference and the functional ablation hypothesis: More disconfirmatory data. *International Journal of Clinical and Experimental Hypnosis* 32:47–56.

Dollard, J., and N. E. Miller. 1950. *Personality and psychotherapy.* New York: McGraw-Hill.

Dutta, S., and R. Kanungo. 1967. Retention of affective material: A further verification of the intensity hypothesis. *Journal of personality and Social Psychology* 5:476–80.

———. 1975. *Affect and memory: A reformulation.* New York: Pergamon.

Erdelyi, M. H. 1974. A new look at the new look: Perceptual defense and vigilance. *Psychological Review* 81, no. 1:1:25.

Erdelyi, M. H., and J. Kleinbard. 1978. Ebbinghaus decayed with time? The growth of recall (hyperamnesia) over days. *Journal of Experimental Psychology: Human Learning and Memory* 1:275–89.

Ericsson, K. A., and H. A. Simon. 1980. Verbal reports as data. *Psychological Review* 87:215–51.

Eriksen, C. W. 1960. Discrimination and learning without awareness: A methodological survey and evaluation. *Psychological Review* 67, no. 5:279–300.

Freud, S. 1915. *The psychopathology of everyday life.* New York: Macmillan.

Gazzaniga, M. S. 1970. *The bisected brain.* New York: Appleton-Century-Crofts.

Goethals, G. R. and R. F. Reckman. 1973. The perception of consistency in attitudes. *Journal of Experimental Social Psychology* 9:491–501.

Greenwald, A. G. 1980. The totalitarian ego: Fabrication and revision of personal history. *American Psychologist 35:* 603–18.

Gregg, G. 1979. Posthypnotic amnesia and general memory theory. *Bulletin of the British Society of Experimental and Clinical Hypnosis* 2:11–14.

Holmes, D. S. 1974. Investigations of repression: Differential recall of material experimentally or naturally associated with ego threat. *Psychological Bulletin* 81:632–53.

Huesmann, L. R., C. L. Gruder, and G. Dorst. (1987). A process model of posthypnotic amnesia. *Cognitive Psychology* 19:33–63.

Jacoby, L. l., and M. Dallas. 1981. On the relationship between autobiographical memory and perceptual learning. *Journal of Experimental Psychology: General* 110:306–40.

Kihlstrom, J. F. 1985. Post-hypnotic amnesia and the dissociation of memory. In *The *psychology of learning and motivation: Advances in research and theory,* ed. G. H. Bower, 132–78. New York: Academic.

Latané, D., and J. N. Daley. 1970. *The unresponsive bystander: Why doesn't he help?* New York: Appleton-Crofts.

Lewicki, P. 1986. *Nonconscious social information processing.* Orlando, Fla.: Academic.

Maier, N. R. F. 1931. Reasoning in humans. II. The solution of a problem and its appearance in consciousness. *Journal of Comparative Psychology* 12:181–94.

Marks, C. E. 1980. *Commissurotomy, consciousness, and unity of mind.* Montgomery, Vt.: Bradford.

Nisbett, R. E., and T. D. Wilson. 1977. Telling more than we can know: Verbal reports on mental processes. *Psychological Review* 84:231–59.

Norman, D. A. 1982. *Learning and memory.* San Francisco: Freeman.

Norman, D. A. and D. G. Bobrow. 1979. Descriptions: An intermediate state in memory retrieval. *Cognitive Psychology* 11:107–23.

Sackheim, J. A., J. W. Nordlie, and R. C. Gur. 1979. A model of hysterical and hypnotic blindness: Cognition, motivation, and awareness. *Journal of Abnormal Psychology* 88:474–89.

Sarbin, T. R. and W. C. Coe. 1972. *Hypnosis: A social and psychological analysis of influence and communication.* New York: Holt, Rinehart & Winston.

Schachter, S., and J. E. Singer. 1962. Cognitive, social, and physiological determinants of emotional states. *Psychological Review* 69:379–99.

Skinner, B. F. 1953. *Science and human behavior.* New York: Macmillan.

Spanos, N. P., and H. L. Bodorik. 1977. Suggested amnesia and disorganized recall in hypnotic and task-motivated subjects. *Journal of Abnormal Psychology* 86:295–305.

Sperling, G. 1960. The information available in brief visual presentations. *Psychological Monographs* 74, whole no. 498.

Sperry, R. W. 1968. Hemispheric disconnection and unity in conscious awareness. *American Psychologist* 23:723–33.

Weinberger, D. A., G. E. Schwartz, and R. J. Davidson. 1979. Low-anxious, high-anxious, and repressive coping styles: Psychometric patterns and behavioral and physiological responses to stress. *Journal of Abnormal Psychology* 88: 369–80.

Weiskrantz, L. 1980. Varieties of residual experience. *Quarterly Journal of Experimental Psychology* 32:365–86.

Weiskrantz, L., E. K. Warrington, M. D. Sanders, and J. Marshall. 1974. Visual capacity in the hemianopic field following a restricted occipital ablation. *Brain* 97:709–28.

Williams, M. D., and J. D. Hollon. 1981. The process of retrieval from very long-term memory. *Cognitive Science* 5:87–119.

10 Shame, Repression, Field Dependence, and Psychopathology

HELEN BLOCK LEWIS

Shame, the "Sleeper" in Psychopathology

If we ask ourselves just what it is that is being warded off by repression (and other defenses), one self-evident answer is states of shame and guilt. For reasons not yet altogether clear in the history of psychoanalysis, the centrality of these two principal moral emotions has never been emphasized in psychopathology, even though a theoretical link between psychopathology and a malfunctioning or archaic superego has been established since Freud's *The Ego and the Id* ([1923] 1961).

Over the past forty years as a practicing psychoanalyst, much of this time coinciding with ongoing research with H. A. Witkin, I have been slowly pushed to the realization that undischarged shame is implicated in the "archaic" or "irrational" guilt that evokes neurotic and psychotic symptoms. What I can now describe that was not apparent to me when I began analytic work in 1945 is a lightning-speed sequence from an evoked state of shame almost simultaneously into humiliated fury and thence into guilt for what is processed by the person as forbidden anger—unjust, wrong, or inappropriate anger. My observations about the role of shame connect with Freud's ([1923] 1961) concept of unconscious archaic or irrational guilt as the source of neurosis and psychosis. The patient "does not feel guilty," he wrote; "he feels ill" (50). But I specifically add undischarged shame as emotional force fueling guilt over "unjust" anger. My observations dovetail with Horowitz's (1981) demonstration of the difficulty of separating righteous from self-righteous indignation and with Horowitz's (1982) empirical finding that discomfort over "vulnerability" (shame), and rage at the source of the vulnerability, is the most frequent theme of "intrusive," repetitive thoughts.

Shame appears to create its own "feeling trap." It forbids the "unjust" expression (or sometimes even the feeling) of retaliatory hostility ("turning the tables," "getting even") at the same time that it presses toward this discharge. There seem to be two components in this inhibition of discharge. The first inheres in the experience of shame, which tends to evoke the shame of being ashamed. The second component derives from our attachment to others, which evokes guilt for harming them by retaliatory shaming.

Let us look first at the way the experience of shame evokes more shame. When shame is overt, it is an acute experience, in which the self is at the center of experience. Shame catches the self "at the quick," as Helen Lynd (1958) put it. Darwin (1872) was, in fact, the first scientist to discuss the psychology of shame. He observed that it is a state of acute, painful self-consciousness, especially involving the face. He also observed that "under the press of shame there is a strong desire for concealment" (321). The paradox of shame is thus an acute, painful self-consciousness, occurring together with an acute momentary need for unconsciousness, a "turning away" from the experience. Adults who introspect shame tell us that, along with the blushing, sweating, and palpitations that signal it and the impulse to avoid shame, there is the simultaneous realization that these are "excessive" or "irrational" responses and beyond self-control. This creates a sense of incongruity or childishness about the experience of being ashamed. Adults are ashamed of being ashamed. People often automatically disclaim or deny that they are in a state of shame because they are ashamed of being ashamed. Their disclaimer or denial often reflects their own recognition of the irrationality or incongruity of the shame response.

Second, the humiliated fury that is being evoked almost simultaneously with shame (signaled perhaps by the flushing and increased heartbeat) is in response to some experience of rejection ("loss of love") by a significant attachment figure. Humiliated fury is blocked, however, by the person's attachment (love), which has rendered the person vulnerable to shame to begin with. Guilt automatically accompanies the impulse to retaliate or hurt the other in revenge. The more psychologically sophisticated among us now say, "Don't get mad, get even." But this is not an easy proposition if one really cares about one's lover, one's child, one's parent, or one's therapist.

Thus, shame exerts its almost lethal momentary effect on the self because it is being processed as shameful, while its natural push for rageful retaliation is being processed as forbidden (guilty). We have thus connected with one of the observations about which there is much agreement in psychiatry, namely, that forbidden anger somehow produces symptoms. The sequence I have observed—shame, rage, guilt—is also congruent with another reasonably established psychiatric observation, namely, that low self-esteem is characteristic of neurotic and psychotic populations. Shame-rage may be the "sleeper" in both forbidden anger and low self-esteem. If this line of reasoning is correct, there should be a correlation between shame and self-directed hostility, a hypothesis for which there is some empirical evidence (Witkin, Lewis, and Weil 1968; Safer 1975; Lindsay-Hartz 1984; Wicker, Payne, and Morgan 1983;

Miller 1985). While low self-esteem and self-directed hostility are not synonymous, they are two ways of describing cognitions in the shame experience. That low self-esteem is a central feature of pathological depression is a proposition about which both psychoanalysts—particularly Bibring (1953), in disagreement with Freud ([1917] 1957)—and the behaviorists (Seligman, Beck) agree. (For a fuller treatment of this point, see Lewis 1981). There is also some empirical evidence for a shame model of paranoia (Colby 1977) as well as recent clinical evidence for a role of shame in schizophrenia (Morrison 1985, 1987). Recent clinical accounts have also called attention to the role of shame in so-called narcissistic disorders (Wurmser 1981; Broucek 1982; Morrison 1983). Most recently, Silberstein, Streigel-Moore, and Rodin (1988) have called attention to shame as a possible factor in bulimia. Silberstein, Streigel-Moore, and Rodin also suggest that shame plays an important role in women's "normative discontent" with their weight.

A brief word is in order at this point about my use of the term "undischarged" shame and guilt as the primary force producing symptoms. I am following the assumptions of Tomkins (1962) and Izard (1979) that emotions are a central force in human behavior. In the case of guilt, discharge is by making amends—doing or undoing something—or else by appropriate punishment. In the case of shame, which is about the self, the immediate discharge seems to be at least temporary oblivion of the self. As I shall indicate a bit later on in this chapter, I have begun to think of shame as a kind of "primary repression."

I have also lately begun to understand, with the help of my colleagues Thomas Scheff and Suzanne Retzinger (see Scheff and Retzinger in press), that laughter relieves shame. Retzinger (1985) has already offered some empirical evidence for this point. That shared laughter dissolves humiliation is an observation that Freud ([1905] 1960) first made in his much-neglected book on jokes. (For a fuller treatment of this point, see Lewis 1983). For example, ridicule easily evokes shame and shame-rage if it is perceived as hostile, while it can also easily relieve shame if the ridicule is perceived as good humored, that is, accepting of the person. It is just this human capacity to convey opposite emotional messages in the same cognitive content that can create crazy-making ambiguities.

Scheff and Retzinger (in press) have also suggested that both shame and laughter are unique to the human species, and, following Nietzsche, they suggest that laughter arises out of the relief of shame. Children's delighted laughter when they have mastered some task that they were not sure was within the grasp of their competence might be considered an illustration of this point. Finally, it has been suggested that shame can be discharged in renewed dignity (Lynd 1958) and ambition (Izard 1979).

Research Base

Let us step back now from these speculations to take a look at the research base out of which my focus on the sequence shame-rage-guilt has evolved. There is no room in this chapter for a full description of the roundabout way my attention was called to shame, except to say that it involved a felicitous combination of psychoanalytic practice and research on the construct field dependence (Witkin et al. 1954), which I helped to develop.

Clinical Observations

As I have indicated elsewhere (Lewis 1971), I was troubled by the few cases of apparently successful completed analyses that surprised me when the patients returned as failures. These experiences, as it turned out in retrospect, were quite parallel with Kernberg's (1975) and Kohut's (1971) descriptions of their surprisingly difficult patients, for which the diagnostic categories of "borderline" or "narcissistic" personality were invoked (Lewis, 1987). Quite independently of their work, which surfaced at about the same time as mine (Lewis 1971), I was drawn to the hypothesis that some failure of psychoanalytic understanding or technique was at issue. Specifically, my hypothesis was that unanalyzed shame in the transference and in the patient-therapist interaction was complicated in therapeutic failure. At the time that I was speculating about the reasons for therapeutic failure, I was busy speculating, together with Witkin and Edmund Weil, on how field-dependent and field-independent people might differ with respect to shame and guilt.

From observations of an embarrassed four-year-old child patient, a little girl who watched me vigilantly and continuously during our sessions, I suggested (Lewis 1963) that shame functions particularly as a protection against the loss of self-boundaries. Especially during states of absorbed sexual fantasy, that is, in states of longing for attachment figures, shame preserves self-boundaries. My little patient suffered from an emotional coldness that neither of her parents could conceal. She was vigilantly defending against the shame of rejection. My patient was a clear example, as well, of the fact that shame is the response to rejection, a fact for which we have, as yet, no adequate theoretical explanation.

Research on Field Dependence

Ironically, it was as a researcher rather than as a psychoanalyst that I first became involved in studying the nature of human nature and, thus indirectly, the nature of shame and guilt. When Max Wertheimer, the founder of Gestalt psychology, came to the New School's University in Exile in New York in 1938, I had the good fortune to become his student.

Wertheimer was interested in refuting the narcissistic nature of human nature. (Forgive my updating of language: he spoke of the issue as egotism.) Specifically, Wertheimer hypothesized that even so apparently an egotistical function as the perception of one's own body in space is governed by the organization of the field.

Under Wertheimer's influence, and on a somewhat different track, I undertook a series of experiments (Lewis 1944; Lewis and Franklin 1944) with the hypothesis that, under conditions of cooperative work, the Zeigarnik effect of remembering uncompleted tasks would disappear. Our hypothesis was confirmed; when subjects were working cooperatively, there was no difference in recall between those tasks that the person had personally brought to a close and those completed by the partner. We did, of course, have some subjects who were not so task oriented and apparently experienced their partner's task completion as a personal failure. For these people, the Zeignarik effect held. At the time of these experiments, although I knew I was dealing with personal failure, I had not yet formulated the idea that failure is the cognitive component of shame.

It also became apparent to me that, while it correctly predicted the major effect, Wertheimer's theory made no room for individual differences. Similarly, while Wertheimer's theory yielded evidence that, on the average, the organization of the field does influence perception of the upright in space, it could not account for individual differences. Witkin's observation of striking individual differences in the extent to which judgment is influenced by the organization of the field and his discovery that there were remarkably congruent personality characteristics correlated with perceptual performance started our line of research into these personality correlates (Witkin et al. 1954). We considered our hypothesis well within the psychoanalytic framework since we were assuming that even so stable a product of the "ego apparatus" (again, forgive my outmoded terminology) as space perception might be influenced by the emotional vicissitudes in personality development. Our work was part of the 1940s and 1950s "new look" in perception and cognition that Erdelyi (1974, 1985) has reviewed for us.

Our demonstration of field dependence as a perceptual cognitive/personality style has yielded more than three thousand studies, at last count, and has turned out to have many clinical implications (Witkin 1965; Lewis 1984). What was apparent at once was that the extent of field dependence is related not to the extent of pathology but rather to the form of pathology (Witkin et al. 1954; Witkin 1965; Lewis 1971, 1985). Field dependence is robustly related to depression (Witkin et al. 1954; Witkin 1965; Crouppen 1976; Levenson and Neuringer 1974; Newman and Hirt 1983; Patsioskas, Clum, and Luscomb 1979), while field independence is connected, as one might intuitively predict, to the apparent self-centeredness of paranoia (Schooler and Silverman 1969; Johnson 1980; Witkin et al. 1954; Witkin 1965).

During the 1960s, Witkin, Weil, and I planned and executed a study in which we predicted that field-dependent patients would be more prone to shame than guilt in their first two therapy sessions, whereas field-independent patients would be more prone to guilt than shame. The transcripts of the first two psychotherapy session of "pairs" of field-dependent and field-independent patients in treatment with the same therapist were assessed for their implied affective content by Gottschalk and Gleser's (1969) method. As predicted, field-dependent patients showed significantly more shame than guilt anxiety, whereas field-independent patients showed significantly more guilt than shame. (Needless to say, all the transcripts were overflowing with both.) Our study also yielded evidence that, as one might expect on an introspective basis alone, shame and self-directed hostility occur in conjunction with each other. This finding has been subsequently confirmed (Safer 1975; Smith 1972). Guilt, in contrast, and surprisingly, occurred in our transcripts in conjunction with hostility directed both outward and inward, in about equal frequency.

Our success in predicting the occurrence of shame and guilt in therapeutic sessions helped persuade me that my focus on shame was grounded in some psychological realities. I was also encouraged to undertake my phenomenological study of the two states (Lewis 1971). The 180 transcripts that we collected in the course of our therapy study were the source material from which I worked.

Before turning to a very brief review of these phenomenological differences, it is worth noting that there is evidence for the usefulness of the distinction between shame and guilt. Blatt's (1974) contrast between anaclitic and introjective depression may overlap the categories of shame and guilt. Grinker, Werble, and Drye's (1968) description of the depression experience as characterized particularly by loneliness and emptiness may parallel both Blatt's anaclitic depression and a shame-prone superego mode.

Empirical evidence for the importance of shame in depression has been building steadily in the last two decades. Izard's (1972; Izard and Schwartz 1986) carefully developed instruments for studying the affective phenomenology of depression have continued to show that shame/shyness is an important component of the emotion profiles of depressive experience. Other direct evidence comes from a study by Smith (1972) in which patients adjudged more shame-prone were more likely to be suffering from depression. This result held more strongly for women. Hoblitzelle (1987), using her newly developed self-report measure for shame and guilt-proneness, has obtained results that show a significant correlation between her shame measures and depression. Harder and Lewis (1986) have recently shown that it is possible to differentiate shame from guilt and that shame correlates with depression. Hoblitzelle has also found a significant correlation between her shame measures and the extent to which people use internal, stable, global attributions for failure, especially blaming their own "characters." Finally, a recent empirical study of guilt and conscience in the major depressive disorders suggests that "negative self-esteem" rather than guilt "forms the cornerstone" in depressed patients of all types (Prosen et al. 1983). Shame may be understood as the affective state that accompanies low self-esteem.

The moral of this story of a serendipitous association between the psychology of space perception and the psychoanalysis of shame and guilt is the implied demonstration that all human behavior is embedded in our emotional needs, that is, in the lifelong attachment system that is our uniquely human fate.

The Phenomenology of Shame and Guilt

Before proceeding to the phenomenological distinctions between shame and guilt, it is important to emphasize that shame and guilt very often occur simultaneously, especially in the wake of a moral transgression. The position of the self in shame and guilt is, however, clearly distinguishable, especially when nonmoral shame (Ausubel 1955) occurs in the wake of failure or rejection. Since I undertook my phenomenological account (Lewis 1971), Hoblitzelle (1987) and Harder and Lewis (1986) have independently confirmed in empirical studies that shame can be distinguished from guilt.

I use the term "shame" to cover a family of feelings: humiliation, mortification, feeling ridiculous, painful self-consciousness, chagrin, shyness, and embarrassment. Each of these states differs from the others, but all have in common that the self is helpless. "Guilt," similarly, refers to a family of feelings: fault, blame, responsibility, obligation. Each of these states differs from the others, but all have in common that some thing was done or not done. In guilt, the self is able to have done or not done the guilty act.

When I began my phenomenological study of shame and guilt, psychoanalytic literature was in a phase in which the "manifest content" of experience was somewhat suspect, like the manifest content of dreams. In the literature, guilt was more often used to signify an unconscious force that motivated behavior rather than a conscious experience. Even more troublesome was the way the literature treated the term "superego." The superego, although formally acknowledged to be a theoretical construct, was nevertheless treated as an established fact or explanatory system. The superego was the "heir of the Oedipus complex." Both the superego and the Oedipus complex were regarded as established facts instead of as theoretical constructs. If women could not live through the Oedipus complex because they were already castrated, then their superegos were necessarily relatively undeveloped. The shame that they often displayed and felt was further evidence for their relatively primitive superegos. My phenomenological study of shame and guilt aimed at rectifying what was obviously faulty theory by bringing psychoanalysis back closer to experience.

I come now to the concept of the self. As I suggested thirty years ago, I use the term "self" to refer to three central aspects of experience. First, there is the registration of experience as one's own. This registration is ordinarily automatic, without requiring consciousness. But we glimpse that it is a complicated process when we observe what happens to the registration of experience as one's own when people are under the press of strong negative affect—horror, shame, or guilt. Also, many of us experience depersonalization and/or estrangement. The experiences we know to be our own seem in some way no longer ours or else very strange when they should be familiar. I assumed (Lewis 1958) that infants have an automatic registration of experience as their own rather than being born without any sense of self. The recent avalanche of information telling us about the enormous intellectual capacities of infants and of their obvious social nature indicates that my hunch at that time was right. Complicated intellectual processes, such as responding by crying to the sounds of other newborns or recognizing mother's voice, are evinced in infants one to two days old; they could not be if there were not some central registration of the infant's experience as its own, some rudimentary self.

Second, the self registers its boundaries, safeguarding its own identity. Especially when people are closely attached, however, the self often travels from its own boundaries into an empathic or vicarious experience of what is happening to the other person. Especially when one is in a state of longing or sexual arousal, one is preoccupied with what the beloved is feeling about the self. Vicarious experience of the other's emotional state involves the self in leaving its own boundaries. I think that it is possible, for example, that the shame one feels after masturbating with such longings is a sharp, painful reminder that the self has left its boundaries and should return to its (lonely) state in order to preserve its identity.

Finally, the self involves a localization of experience as occurring within the self or occurring outside the self. The experience that something has occurred outside the self is the self's own experience. After all, it is the self that is doing the localizing. Stimuli that appear to occur within the self may actually be coming from "without," while those appearing to come from without are nevertheless "within" the self. People's experience of a phantom limb after amputation is a good illustration of what I am talking about. The stimuli that appear to be still coming from the lost limb are actually "within" the self, which is an organization or reference point for stimuli, including their localization in the world. Even though a limb is gone, the organization of experience still locates it in the old way. Shame, which appears to be so other connected, is actually one's own vicarious experience of the other's scorn. Guilt, which seems so self-initiated and self-propelled, is actually often initiated by the behavior of another person in relation to the self. We know how infuriating it is when someone is "making us" feel guilty. I dwell on this point a bit because shame has so often been considered a lower-order, "other-connected" form of behavior in contrast to the self-initiated character of guilt, which appears to be more internalized.

We come now to some highlights of the phenomenology of shame and guilt. First of all, when one has committed a moral transgression, both states may be evoked simultaneously. We say to ourselves, "How could I have done *that?*" at the same time that we may be saying to ourselves, "How could *I* have done that?" With the first emphasis on the thing done, we say, "Mea culpa"; with the second emphasis on the I, we are saying, "I am ashamed of myself." Because shame and guilt so often occur together in moral transgression, they are very easy to confuse. Especially when shame is evoked by moral transgression but cannot be acknowledged, the thoughts and feelings that are carried by the shame feeling will linger long after appropriate amends have actually been made and the transgression presumably rectified.

Second, it is clear that shame is about the whole self, while guilt is about things done or undone for which the self is responsible. Guilt, being about things, is more specific. The relation of the self to the other person is thus very different in shame and guilt. In shame, the self is the focus of the experience, while, in guilt, the self, although suffering, is not the focus of angry attack. In shame, the self has fallen short of its own high ideals; it can no longer regard itself with satisfaction or pride. The self has lost its respected place not only in its own eyes but also in the eyes of others. In shame, the other is experienced as intact and scornful of the self. In guilt, the other is injured, or hurt, while the self, which is responsible for the injury, is able to repair it. In shame, the self is unable, helpless to avoid the others' scorn.

Third, it becomes clear that shame can be evoked not only by a moral transgression for which the self is responsible but also by a failure of the whole self in the nonmoral arena. Shame is evoked by failure. We can thus speak of moral and nonmoral shame (Ausubel 1955). Shame is evoked by the "loss of love," by the failure of attachment. It is evoked by sexual rebuff, or by failure in athletic competition, or by failure to get a job. All these involve one's dignity in relation to others. Shame may also be evoked by the failures of one's parents and one's children. Shame is clearly social since it so often involves the self in vicarious experience of beloved others' shortcomings as well as one's own. Of course, whenever shame is evoked by failure, it is easy to begin to think of what one might have done or not done to avoid failing or to avoid offending the person whose love is now lost. Guilt is often the immediate successor to bypassed shame because in guilt, at least, the self is not helpless but able to do something. Especially if the other person is actually unloving and one is unable to change this whatever one does or did, the shame of continued helplessness becomes compounded into an endless sequence of restless guilt—"if only I had or had not done" an endless variety of things. People suffering bereavement, a state in which the shame of loss is inevitable, are often comforted by realizing that they are plagued by an endless stream of guilty "if onlys" and by tracing these "if onlys" to their utter helplessness.

Fourth, because the self is so central in the experience of shame, shame is painfully acute. While the self is momentarily "paralyzed," painful body states occur: blushing, sweating, heart palpitations. These are painful enough in themselves; the simultaneous realization that they are "irrational" responses and beyond control makes one ashamed of being ashamed. Guilt, in contrast, involves an intact self, able to have done and to undo something. It is a more respectable state and may even involve some satisfaction, some quiet moral elevation in acknowledging that one is guilty. There is no corresponding gratification in the acknowledgment of the shame of failure to be loved or respected.

Fifth, because the self is so paralyzed in shame, it has trouble managing the rage that shame evokes. Humiliated fury evoked by the failure of attachment seeks discharge by "turning the tables" on the unloving other. But it is blocked both by the person's love for the faithless one and by the automatic guilt that accompanies the impulse to retaliate and hurt the other in revenge.

Finally, because the self is so damaged at the moment of shame, so helpless to deal with the loss of love, we can realize how close is the affinity between the experience of shame and the experience of depression. Because the self is so active in guilt in the effort to make amends, we realize that there is an affinity between the state of guilt and the symptoms of obsessional neurosis and of paranoia. In the latter illness, the person is convinced of his high moral mission to rectify evil, even if this means killing people. We have known, ever since statistics began to be collected, that women are more prone to depression than men, while men are more prone to paranoia than women. The difference between the operation of shame and guilt may be a factor in this sex difference (Lewis 1976, 1985).

Overt and Bypassed Shame

I have also found it useful to distinguish between two kinds of shame experience: overt, unacknowledged shame, and bypassed shame. It often happens that patients describe to their therapists the most acute states of overt shame. They say, "I could crawl through a hole," or, "I could die," but they do not label their own state as shame. For example, one woman patient, explaining to her male therapist how awful she felt about her facial tics, described her feelings as "a very, very, sensitive sore spot," so much so that she could not

Table 1. Summary of the Phenomenology of Shame and Guilt

	Shame	Guilt
Stimulus	Disappointment, defeat, or moral transgression	Moral transgression
	Deficiency of self	Event or thing for which the self is responsibile
	Involuntary; self unable, as in unrequited love	Voluntary; self able
	Encounter with the other or within the self	Within the self
Conscious content	Painful emotion	Affect may or may not be present
	Autonomic responses: rage, blushing, tears	Autonomic responses less
	Global characteristics of self	Specific activities of self
	Identity thoughts; internal theater	No identity thoughts
Position of self in the field	Self passive	Self active
	Self focal in awareness	Self absorbed in action or thought
	Self-imaging and consciousness; multiple functions of self ("split")	Self intact, functioning silently
	Vicarious experience of other's negative view of self	Pity; concern for injury to other
Nature and discharge of hostility	Humiliated fury	Righteous indignation
	Discharge blocked by guilt and/or love of other; self-directed	Discharge on self and other
	Discharge in good humored and/or shared laughter	Discharge in acts of reparation
Characteristic symptoms	Depression; hysteria; "affect disorder"	Obsessional; paranoia, "thought disorder"

Note: Shame variants: humiliation, mortificaton, embarassment, feeling ridiculous, chagrin, shyness, painful self-consciousness. Guilt variants: responsibility, obligation, fault, blame.

look at her boyfriend "straight in the face" while she talked about her tics. Nevertheless, during several pages of session transcript, neither she nor her therapist ever once identified her state as shame.

In bypassed shame, the person is aware of the cognitive content of shame-connected events but experiences only a "wince" or slight "blow" at the time the shame event occurred. In this pattern of bypassed shame, the person's experience proceeds smoothly, except for a peripheral, nonspecific disturbance in awareness. What does occur in awareness is ideation about the shame event, specifically thoughts (mainly doubts) about the self-image seen from the "other's" viewpoint. These sometimes escalate into an internal auditory colloquy about the shame-connected event. The person cannot seem to stop thinking (obsessing) about the shame-connected event.

The following excerpt will illustrate bypassed shame. It comes from the transcript of a twenty-one-year-old man in treatment with an experienced woman psychoanalyst. The excerpt is from the third session, and he is clearly processing a previous remark of hers that his "negative" reactions seem rather passive, "which you brought out last time." There are several long pauses, punctuated by some nonverbal encouragement from the therapist. The patient then says,

> I don't know, I'm throwing in a million things here. I don't know if I'm getting to the core of this thing.
>
> THERAPIST. Don't wrack your brains, just say anything that comes into you.
>
> PATIENT. [Long pause.]
>
> THERAPIST. What are you thinking?
>
> PATIENT. I don't know. I have this feeling that, that there's something there [mm, mm]. I felt myself almost wince a second ago and I was trying to think what it is that I'm . . . you know. I was also thinking of what I would do if I were the therapist, and I had a patient facing me [mm] and, uh, just what significance I would give to each of his reactions, each of his movements and the like. This is something that I didn't think about, uh, to my knowledge for some time—this what would I do if I were the other.
>
> THERAPIST. I wonder if you wonder what I think of you. If that isn't one thing that's interfering.
>
> PATIENT. Probably, yeah, I think so. I think so. Uh, and yet I don't think I want to know . . . I know I think if it were unfavorable it would probably bother me . . . I keep thinking, what am I trying to say. I—and I'm staring at the wall, and the sink, and, eh, I also, one other thing that's been bothering me. I think that I feel that I'm depending on you too much. And I haven't been really trying to work out my problems on my own.

There follows an insoluble dilemma of thought about whether he ought not to work harder in therapy. He then wonders whether he will or will not want to continue in therapy after the sessions are over. "I played with about four thousand shapeless doubts right now." There follows a long pause during which he ruminates about the effectiveness of psychotherapy.

> I wish I could write on a sheet of paper just what it is that might strike me during the week and come in with it.
>
> THERAPIST. How would that help?
>
> PATIENT. I don't know, I can't seem to formulate anything to say, and, eh, you say, "Don't wrack your brains," but I find myself wracking my brains . . . I could see myself skipping some questions. These thoughts that I'm blocking here and now, I would, if I could, put them down.
>
> THERAPIST. What are you skipping?

PATIENT. [Sighs.] I'm going through [slight laugh] a list of names . . . [Long pause.] I find that I have a lot of guilt feelings about masturbation. Although I realize it's normal, it still bothers me.

The patient's shift in position of the self into the position of the observing therapist watching his "movements" can be understood as a primary process transformation of the patient's bypassed shame of masturbation. Note how much obsessive thinking infuses the train of ideation. The train of ideation can also become an insoluble dilemma of guilt. Whichever way the person thinks does not turn out right. As I have suggested elsewhere (Lewis 1981), the Rat Man's obsessional states were just such insoluble dilemmas: not paying the three kronen would be cowardice, while paying them would bring the rat punishment. I have suggested also that each of the Rat Man's obsessional states was preceded by some bypassed shame.

One conclusion that may be drawn from studying the phenomenology of shame and guilt is that both states come into operation when attachment ties are threatened and that both states serve to restore and maintain the threatened affectional bonds.

Shame and the Attachment Emotions

The concept of an attachment system (Bowlby 1969–80; Harlow and Mears 1979) that is biologically grounded and necessary for species survival may now replace Freud's concept of human nature as "narcissistic." In this new theoretical framework, shame and guilt can be understood not only as "drive controls" but as the means by which we maintain our fundamental affectional ties.

Why, then, should shame be the response to "loss of love"? Vicarious emotional experience is the foundation of attachment (on both sides), and it is the price we pay for attachment. Shame is the vicarious experience of the other's rejection of the self. Shame is the state in which one "accepts" the loss of the other as if it were a loss in the self. Humiliated fury, which is the inevitable accompaniment of shame, angrily protests the loss at the same time that it demands restitution of the other's positive feeling. But being angry at and wanting the love of the other person is inherently disorganizing; it is a useful reaction only if the other person is stably affectionate. When the other person is rejecting or unable to stay stably affectionate, humiliated fury is useless. It will not effect the change in the other's feeling that is required. It leads back into shame, humiliated fury, and chronic irrational guilt.

Some recent observations about infant-mother interactions, using Ainsworth's Strange Situation techniques, suggest that something like a forerunner of shame is operating in the behavior of infants (Main and Weston 1982). Videotapes of "securely attached" infants responding to their mothers' return show that, even while they are seeking and accepting reunion, there is a brief gaze aversion or a blank facial expression. Even with secure attachment, reunion after separation is apparently experienced with a mixture of pleasure and some hint of shame.

An "insecure" infant, "when held by the mother, clings, then angrily pushes her away, then clings, then pushes her away, then clings again" (Main and Weston 1982, 52). Main and Weston tell us that this overt disorganization of behavior is very distressing to witness. Other "insecure" infants show an even more astonishing pattern. They do not show anger. Rather, they actively avoid the mother: "Picked up, they indicate in an emotionless way, a desire to be put down often pointing to a toy . . . in order to distract the mother. They are often markedly more friendly to a stranger than to the mother (which makes their behavior even more pointed)" (40).

It seems to me that these avoidant infants may be showing the forerunner of a pattern of reaction that involves bypassing the shame of being rejected. They do not directly express humiliated fury. Rather, they behave as if they were "turning the tables" on the rejecting mother by rejecting her. Main and Weston offer us an explanation of infants' avoidance of their rejecting mothers in terms of attachment theory. They grapple with the problem of how avoidance (shame?) can be "proximity seeking," as attachment theory requires. They write, "When an attached infant is subject to threats from an attachment figure, the infant is placed in a theoretically irresolvable and self-perpetuating conflict situation. The mere fact that approach is forbidden when it is most necessary should activate the attachment system even further; it should also activate angry behavior, but approach is still not possible and this should further activate the system. Vacillation between approach, avoidance, and angry behavior may be expected. There is no solution to this problem so long as the infant focuses his attention on the attachment figure. A shift of attention is the only solution—an anti-attention mechanism, something like denial or repression, is required."

"Primary repression" (Freud [1915] 1957), the primordial turning away from noxious stimuli, is the anti-attention mechanism that Main and Weston are invoking. That it needs to be reinforced by "secondary repression" in order to prevent the return of the repressed may now be understood in terms of attachment theory. Attachment is what keeps the rageful longings operating whether or not there is conscious awareness of them. That one's own humiliation may be relieved by the vicarious experience of the other's humiliation is itself a reflection of the attachment system into which we are born. The attachment system, however, in which "getting even" is a relief or even a pleasure, as in sadism, is the same one in which "getting even" is processed as wrong because it hurts the other. The temporary ablation of the self in shame thus maintains the attachment system, even at the expense of the self.

Some Excerpts from Psychotherapy Sessions Illustrating
Sequences from Overt and Bypassed Shame

Before turning to some psychotherapy sequences, it might be useful to look at one excerpt that catches the retaliatory hostility that is generated even in the midst of a shame response. The following few lines comes from a very field-independent twenty-one-year-old woman, a college student, who applied for therapy for a problem about her husband's impotence. (She herself had been sexually abused as a child by a father figure.) She is now recounting to her therapist, an experienced male psychoanalyst, how she experienced her very first therapy session with a previous male therapist.

> PATIENT. The first time I saw him I couldn't stop crying . . . I was very aware of his hairdo: and I had a nickname for him because of his hairdo like a porcupine. Because his hair stood straight up almost three inches, I never knew how his hair stood up like that . . . Even though I was hysterical, I remember that I was looking at him and what I thought.

Sequences from Overt, Unacknowledged Shame

Let us look now very briefly at some excerpts that illustrate the sequence shame-rage-guilt when the shame or humiliation is overt but unacknowledged. The patient is a twenty-one-year-old field-dependent young woman, a college student, who applied for treatment because of facial tics about which she said she felt so ashamed she "could die" and for bouts of depression. The therapist is the same senior psychoanalyst already mentioned. The excerpt comes from the session after he failed to keep his previous appointment with her, without notifying her. The patient describes her reaction to being stood up in some detail, without actually naming the words "shame" or "humiliation." In fact, to have acknowledged that she was shamed by being stood up might itself be shameful because it might be considered a "childish" response.

The patient speaks, instead, of "feeling helpless" and of "having no control over events." What is most apparent in this excerpt is her view that her frustrated anger, which she does clearly name, is not justified. Although she could not have known why the therapist failed to appear without notice, she apparently made the assumption that the therapist's lapse was not his fault. This, in turn, assumed a benign relationship between them such that he did not intend any social affront. Clearly, another interpretation, that the therapist carelessly stood her up (it was a holiday), was too hurtful for her to entertain. Indeed, if she had believed that he was careless (and there is some evidence in the transcript that she may have entertained this thought), her indignation at him would be justified but difficult for at least two reasons—it is the permissible-impermissible rage that comes with the shame of hurt feelings, and, if he were careless, she would no longer have a trustworthy therapist.

It is apparent also that her emphasis on her anger being "at the situation," not at the therapist, avoids the possibility that he was to blame. Her attempt to explain the event focuses on herself, on her "helplessness." "Just my luck," she says; "these things are always happening to me." These two phrases represent low self-esteem and self-directed hostility. She also says that she "hates the feeling of helplessness and not being able to do anything about it. I guess everybody hates that feeling" (note here that she is already apologizing for having the feeling) and that, generally, after a few days it just wears off.

The patient speaks of her anger as "ripping," a phrase that clearly articulates fury. She also says in the same breath that she was "on the verge of tears," an indication of how depressing humiliated fury can be if it is forbidden. As the excerpt progresses, she makes clear that, had she been furious at the therapist, she would have "felt guilty because I had no grounds." "But it still doesn't take away the anger, you know, the frustration." The patient is thus describing the push of humiliated fury (frustration) at the same time that this anger is unjustified, that is, forbidden by her own code.

Her exact words are worth quoting at this point: "Just things like that happen, and there's no one you can really blame, uh, . . . rationally, you know, and really feel right about blaming the person. In fact, if I had blamed you, I would have felt downright guilty because I, I feel I had no grounds. I would have no grounds to be angry with you because you couldn't help it. And yet probably, you know, I unconsciously was angry at you for not coming . . . I feel guilty if I am angry at someone, who, I feel, rationally, I have no grounds to be angry and, uh, I feel guilty and try to talk myself out of the anger . . . But still it doesn't take away the feeling of, uh, you know, the anger, or, or of the frustration."

It should be noted that, when the patient does speak about her anger, it is most often accompanied by a slight laugh, which can be interpreted as relieving her embarrassment and apologizing for being angry. The laugh also connotes that the affront she received was not so terrible since it was only about herself and that both parties need not take her anger so seriously.

Overt, Unidentified Shame and Depression

Attention to the acute, often wordless state I have called overt, unidentified shame helps to show the patient the sequence from this state into depression. Here is a sample of a sequence, selected from the transcript of a psychotherapy session (Lewis 1971). The patient is a twenty-one-year-old field-dependent man, a college student who came to treatment for excessive shyness and fear of impotence. The therapist is a man, an experienced psychiatrist.

Patient and therapist are discussing the patient's reactions to school. Shortly after remarking that his marks are only "fair," there is a very long pause, after which the patient suddenly asks the therapist if he is from the West and remarks on the therapist's accent, which is clearly different from the patient's own Brooklyn accent. Patient goes on to tell of his own interest in languages and history, but these are "too damned hard." One is competing against "brilliant people." Soon there is another very long pause.

THERAPIST. What were you thinking?

PATIENT. Mm . . . nothing . . . that I can remember anyway . . .

THERAPIST. Hm?

PATIENT. Nothing that I can remember. If I was thinking.

THERAPIST. You looked sort of depressed. Is that the way you were feeling?

PATIENT. I was . . . I have been depressed for quite a while. I don't know what I . . . [hm?] I don't know what I think when I [inaudible] like that. Sometimes I just stare at something. [Pause.] Wake up eventually. I don't know what the heck happens in between. [Pause.]

Both the patient and the therapist identify the patient's emotional response as depression, but the context, in which the patient seems to be comparing himself to "brilliant people," and the fragmentation of the patient's thought and speech (many pauses, repetitions, false starts, inaudibility) suggest that he may be feeling shame. The patient, however, apparently experienced his own state as a blank, that is, a momentary loss of self. This is a characteristic moment of unidentified shame.

When the therapist asks if the patient connects his feeling with "talking about school," the patient does not see any connection. The patient himself locates depressed feeling as occurring after he leaves a session, associating it specifically with an image of a "nosy" therapist. The patient is thus "turning the tables" on the therapist. His guilt, however, for this "unjustified" retaliation is evident in his attempt to soften it by making a joke of it. In this sequence from shame into retaliatory hostility and thence into guilt we see the patient's attempt to remain "attached" to the benign therapist. Making a joke of his image of the therapist as "nosy" could create shared laughter in which both the patient's and the therapist's humiliation would dissolve (Freud [1905] 1960).

Here is the text of this exchange:

THERAPIST. Do you think that talking about school and your problems with school, and opinions about what you'd like to do, and what you have to do . . . have caused you to feel depressed?

PATIENT. No . . . [Pause.] Frankly I was depressed before I came here so [inaudible] I'll tell you some things. The last two times I been depressed when I left here. Not that . . . when I was talking I wasn't depressed. It's after I leave. That bothers me.

THERAPIST. Have you wondered about that?

PATIENT.   Yes.

THERAPIST.   What thoughts do you have about it?

PATIENT.   I . . . I made a joke out of it to my sister. That's all. But uh . . .
[inaudible] laugh out of it. I said, I don't know what's the matter with
this guy, he's so nosy. [Laugh.] [Inaudible sentence.]

THERAPIST.   Do you think that that's the aspect of the situation that makes
you depressed?

PATIENT.   I don't know. [Pause.]

THERAPIST.   Well I know you don't know, but I wondered if that's what
you feel.

PATIENT.   I feel like an idiot sometimes. When I think what I told you.
[Mm.] [Pause.] But it has some bearing I suppose.

THERAPIST.   You say you feel like an idiot.

PATIENT.   Well yeah, I start thinking what the hell am I telling him now
. . . imagine telling him [inaudible]. It annoys me. I say why'd I tell him
that for. [Mm].

THERAPIST.   So that your feeling was somehow that you had made yourself appear in a bad light.

PATIENT.   Yeah. [Pause.]

THERAPIST.   Apparently that both annoyed you and depressed you.

PATIENT.   I wasn't . . . uh . . . [Pause.] at the . . . [Pause.] Yeah I suppose so. [Pause.]

THERAPIST.   Do you suppose that that has some relevance for your . . .
toward understanding your general feeling of depression?

PATIENT.   No. That I [inaudible] I'm not very eloquent.

THERAPIST.   So . . . the fact that you apparently felt depressed because
you had put yourself, somehow, or felt you put yourself in a bad light
. . .

PATIENT.   No, I'm not usually that concerned about what people think of
me. I just don't like to give them the edge. You know what I mean. Leave
myself open. Not that you do anything, but . . . you know . . .

THERAPIST.   You're not too sure.

PATIENT.   Well you record it for posterity down there, so . . . I'm not too
[inaudible] who hears about it anyway . . . I mean aside from the people
who are doing the research themselves.

THERAPIST.   Then it would seem from what you've said that somehow you
feel or you see the relationship as a struggle in a way.

PATIENT.   What's a struggle. Coming here?

THERAPIST.   No. Struggle that each one is somehow maneuvering to be
one up on the other.

PATIENT.   Well that's the way I see the world in general. That you have to
watch your back at all times. There's an awful lot of hypocrisy in the
world; you don't have to be . . . look hard for it. People are vicious.

[Hm.] No getting away from that. Including myself. So uh . . . I . . . you know . . . became fairly cautious. Before I let myself open. [Pause.] I . . . I never really would [?] use for anything [Hm?]. Nobody ever really used me for anything, so I don't know if I should feel . . . feel that way. But I mean, from general experience, people . . . are pretty nasty . . . that's all. [Mm.] [Pause.]

The patient is now in an insoluble dilemma about whether to believe that people are "pretty nasty." The therapist's interpretation that the patient "sees a struggle that each one is somehow maneuvering to be one up on each other" was perfectly accurate. But, because it apparently rested on the assumption that this struggle is ipso facto neurotic or transferential, it made no room for the inevitability of this reaction vis-à-vis the therapist. It thus operated to increase the patient's guilt at his own retaliatory hostility. The interpretation thus seems to assume that one-upsmanship is not a valid undercurrent of feeling in the patient-therapist relationship. If the therapist had assumed that the shame-hostility-guilt sequence is an inevitable part of all significant relationships, perhaps he could have helped the patient get out of the feeling trap. For example, an explicit assurance that it was inevitable and thus normal for the patient to feel hostile toward the therapist might have helped.

"I feel like an idiot sometimes, when I think what I told you" is an excellent phenomenological description of shameful fury, directed at the self. The imagery appears paranoid, although the patient rationally is not concerned with what people think of him. He feels ashamed and simultaneously guilty for his retaliatory hostility, so he tries to justify his feeling. He phrases it as "giving others the edge" and describes people as "vicious," including himself. He knows that the therapist is not "doing anything," except "record for posterity," and is not really concerned about that.

"Nobody ever really used me for anything so I don't know why I should feel that way" expresses one side of a conflict between the patient's awareness (guilt) that his fury is rationally unjust and inappropriate and a compelling feeling of humiliated fury at being used (for the research). Without the therapist's help in showing him the inevitability of his retaliatory feelings and the guilt they engender, the patient ends up more ashamed, depressed, and in an insoluble dilemma, without quite knowing why.

The next excerpts drawn from two sessions illustrate a patient's natural tendency to "turn the tables" on the therapist and his neglect of this aspect of the shame-rage sequence. The patient, who suffers from facial tics, opens a session by offering the therapist what she calls a "silly problem" (thereby earning a Gottschalk shame score). By some psychic alchemy, of which neither party is aware, the problem is that she feels guilty for failing to keep her standing appointment to have Thanksgiving dinner with her mother at home, without advance notice. Her boyfriend, to whose home she has decided to go, thinks she ought to discuss her irrational guilt with her therapist, and so here goes. She knows how silly it is to feel guilty, but she cannot help it. (When I was at Yale, my graduate students hung a cartoon on my door. It showed a woman patient lying on the couch, and her male analyst was saying to her, "Aren't you ashamed that you still feel guilty about that.") The therapist, perhaps responding in the spirit of minimizing mother's powers, suggests that the "patient was worrying too much in advance."

The patient opened her next session by telling the therapist, very tentatively and apologetically, with many slight laughs, that she was right and he was wrong. Her mother did make her feel guilty after all. He might have thought that she (the patient) was "making it up," but she was not. The therapist thought that he was being disputed. The patient was signaling to him by her embarrassed laughter that she was making a trivial point—one that "he might not even remember" from the last session. She was thus already feeling both ashamed and a bit guilty for her need to put him down. This aspect of the shame-rage sequence, however, went right by him. In fact, he tacitly agreed with her that she ought not to want to put him down. He obviously assumed that turning the tables is a neurotic defense.

In the midst of this exchange about wanting to prove him wrong, the therapist suddenly called attention to her facial tic. She was terribly disconcerted by his comment. She actually thought that he might be "making it up," that he had not seen a tic but might be saying he did for benign reasons. She then lost her train of thought (Luborsky 1970)—an instance of what seems like some selective inattention because she was so occupied with being disconcerted. (The dictionary lists "embarrassed" as a synonym for "disconcerted.") In a few minutes, she was off on a depressed train of thought about her many failings: lapses of memory, inability to keep things organized, and even inability to keep her appointments straight—the very lapse that the therapist made when he failed to show. In short, under the press of shame-rage-guilt, in the last of which the therapist concurred, the patient experienced an increase in her neurotic symptoms. The content of the last exchange between the therapist and the patient illustrates that the tables have been turned back on the patient:

THERAPIST. You have to keep telling yourself over and over about appointments?

PATIENT. Yeah. Because I'll forget. I mean if I don't keep on reminding myself I'm gonna forget completely. I have a terrible memory. I know it . . . Ever since this therapy has been going on.

And so we are reminded of Freud's ([1917] 1957) original, brilliant observation that, in depression, the self-reproaches are unconsciously meant for "someone the patient loves, or has loved or should love. Every time one examines the facts, this conjecture is confirmed" (248). Including the sequence of shame-rage-guilt in the dynamics of depression helps illuminate the process by which this substitution takes place.

Sequence from Bypassed Shame

The next excerpt comes from the transcript of a twenty-one-year-old college student, a field-independent man in treatment with an experienced male psychotherapist. The patient entered treatment for relief of chest pains diagnosed as functional. (His father had died about two years previously of a heart attack in the patient's presence.) The patient, in his first session, suggested to the therapist that the chest pains might have something to do with "too high an ego-ideal" that I'm setting up. (He was obviously unwittingly agreeing with Piers and Singer's [1953] idea that shame results from failure to live up to ego-ideals.) The patient was clearly in an insoluble dilemma: if he did not work hard, he felt guilty; if he did, then he might be liable, doctors say, to a stress heart attack. The patient also kept referring to the fact that he "received" his chest pains, sometimes in church, in the subway.

Throughout the patient's transcript there was little indication of overt shame, although there was much talk of the difficulty of avoiding failure. The therapist made two interventions, both of which must have evoked considerable shame. He called attention to the patient's way of saying he "received" his chest pains, an observation that quickly evoked the patient's embarrassed laughter and his saying that this was just a manner of speaking and that he knew no one was *sending* him chest pains. Second, the therapist attempted to get the patient to agree that his ego-ideals were too high by suggesting that he need not strive so hard for excellence at school. (The patient was studying to become a concert artist.) There were several rounds of this interpretation followed by the patient's familiar insoluble dilemma of guilt, with increases in the therapist's sarcasm. Finally, at the end of the session in which their quarrel had escalated, the patient suddenly inquired about the microphones (which had been explained much earlier when the patient agreed to participate in the study). It was the end of the session, and the therapist suggested bringing that up next time.

Indeed, the patient opened his next session with a fantasy, which he himself labeled as weird, illogical, and improbable but which he could not stop thinking about, namely that the therapist "out of duty" had *sent* a copy of the session transcript to the school at which the patient studies. "Well, I just thought that maybe you were drawing severe conclusions and that someone should know about it in school. And some administrative official should know about me. I thought maybe you were *sending* them out of duty or something. And what's gonna happen if he does do it . . ."

I suggest that the patient's rational sounding ideation about sending a transcript is a primary process transformation of the patient's bypassed shame. In spite of the patient's better judgment, the fantasy condensing sending and receiving is very compelling. In this obsessional, paranoic ideation, both the therapist and the patient are caught in a dilemma of insoluble guilt.

Implications for Future Research

It is obvious that I have been using Luborsky's (1970) symptom-context method in an open, unsystematic study of the sequence shame-rage-guilt. What now needs to be done is a systematic study of the sequence with all appropriate controls. Shame markers as well as guilt markers can be identified in the content of session transcripts. Shame markers could even, in future, be identified in videotapes (Izard, personal communication). We already know that there is some evidence for the co-occurrence of shame and self-directed hostility (shame-rage). Sequences into guilt ought not be too difficult to find. It should also be possible to identify the therapist's explicit and implicit role in fostering the sequence or else interrupting it to show the patient how he or she struggles to maintain attachment, even at the expense of the self.

References

Ausubel, D. 1955. Relationships between shame and guilt in the socializing process. *Psychological Review* 62:378–90.

Bibring, E. 1953. The mechanism of depression. In *Affective disorders,* ed. P. Greenacre. New York: International Universities Press.

Blatt, S. 1974. Levels of object representation in anaclitic and introjective depression. *Psychoanalytic Study of the Child* 29:107–57.

Bowlby, J. 1969–80. *Attachment and loss.* 3 vols. New York: Basic.

Broucek, J. 1982. Shame and its relationship to early narcissistic developments. *International Journal of Psycho-Analysis* 65:369–78.

Colby, K. 1977. Appraisal of four theories of paranoid phenomena. *Journal of Abnormal Psychology* 86:54–59.

Crouppen, G. 1976. Field dependence in depressed and normal males, as an indication of relative proneness to shame and guilt and ego functioning. Ph.D. diss., California School of Professional Psychology.

Darwin, C. 1872. *The expression of the emotions in man and animals.* London: Murray.

Erdelyi, M. 1974. A new look at the new look: Perceptual defense and vigilance. *Psychological Review* 81:1–26.

———. 1985. *Psychoanalysis: Freud's cognitive psychology.* New York: Freeman.

Freud. S. [1905] 1960. *Jokes and their relation to the unconscious.* In *The standard edition of the complete psychological works of Sigmund Freud,* ed. J. Strachey, vol. 8. London: Hogarth.

————. [1915] 1957. *Repression.* In *The standard edition of the complete psychological works of Sigmund Freud,* ed. J. Strachey, vol. 14. London: Hogarth.

————. [1917] 1957. *Mourning and melancholia.* In *The standard edition of the complete psychological works of Sigmund Freud,* ed. J. Strachey, vol. 14. London: Hogarth.

————. [1923] 1961. *The ego and the id.* In *The standard edition of the complete psychological works of Sigmund Freud,* ed. J. Strachey, vol. 19. London: Hogarth.

Gottschalk, L., and G. Gleser. 1969. *The measurement of psychological states through the content analysis of verbal behavior.* Berkeley: University of California Press.

Grinker, R., B. Werble, and R. Drye. 1968. *The borderline syndrome.* New York: Basic.

Harder, D., and S. Lewis. 1986. The assessment of shame and guilt. In *Advances in personality assessment,* ed. J. Butcher and C. Spielberger, vol. 6, pp. 89–114.

Harlow, H., and C. Mears. 1979. *The human model: Primate perspectives.* New York: Wiley.

Hoblitzelle, W. 1987. Distinguishing between shame and guilt and the role of shame in depression. In *The role of shame in symptom formation,* ed. H. B. Lewis. Hillsdale, N.J.: Erlbaum.

Horowitz, M. 1981. Self-righteous rage and the attribution of blame. *Archives of General Psychiatry* 38:1223–28.

————. 1982. Stress response syndromes and their treatment. In *Handbook of stress,* ed. L. Goldberger and S. Breznitz. New York: Free Press.

Izard, C. 1972. *Patterns of emotions: A new analysis of anxiety and depression.* New York: Academic.

————, ed. 1979. *Emotions in personality and psychopathology.* New York: Plenum.

Izard, C., and G. Schwartz. 1986. Patterns of emotion in depression. In *Depression in young people: Developmental and clinical perspectives,* ed. M. Rutter, C. Izard, and P. Read. New York: Guilford.

Johnson, D. 1980. Cognitive organization in paranoid and nonparanoid schizophrenics. Ph.D. diss., Yale University.

Kernberg, O. 1975. *Borderline conditional and pathological narcissism.* New York: Aronson.

Kohut, H. 1971. *The analysis of the self.* New York: International Universities Press.

Levenson, M., and C. Neuringer. 1974. Suicide and dependence. *Omega* 5:181–85.

Lewis, H. B. 1944. An experimental study of the role of the ego in work. *Journal of Experimental Psychology* 34:113–26.

————. 1958. Overdifferentiation and under-individuation of the self. *Psychoanalysis and the Psychoanalytic Review* 45:3–24.

————. 1963. A case of "watching" as a defense against an oral incorporation fantasy. *Psychoanalytic Review* 50:68–80.

————. 1971. *Shame and guilt in neurosis.* New York: International Universities Press.

————. 1976. *Psychic war in men and women.* New York: New York University Press.

————. 1981. *Freud and modern psychology.* Vol. 1, *The emotional basis of mental illness.* New York: Plenum.

————. 1983. *Freud and modern psychology.* Vol. 2, *The emotional basis of human behavior.* New York: Plenum.

————. 1984. Freud and modern psychology: The social basis of humanity. *Psychoanalytic Review* 71:7–26.

————. 1985. Depression vs. paranoia: Why are there sex differences in mental illness. *Journal of Personality* 53:150–78.

————. 1987. On shame and the narcissistic personality. In *The many faces of shame,* ed. D. Nathanson. New York: Guilford.

Lewis, H. B., and M. Franklin. 1944. The experimental study of the role of the ego in work: The significance of task orientation in work. *Journal of Experimental Psychology* 34:195–215.

Lindsay-Hartz, J. 1984. Contrasting experiences of shame and guilt. *American Behavioral Scientist* 27:698–704.

Luborsky, L. 1970. New directions in research on neurotic and psychosomatic symptoms. *American Scientist* 58:661–68.

Lynd, H. 1958. *On shame and the search for identity.* New York: Harcourt, Brace.

Main, M., and D. Weston. 1982. Avoidance of the attachment figure in infancy. In *The place of attachment in human behavior,* ed. C. Parkes and J. Hinde. New York: Basic.

Miller, S. 1985. *The shame experience.* Hillsdale, N.J.: Analytic.

Morrison, A. 1983. Shame, the ideal self and narcissism. *Contemporary Psychoanalysis* 19:295–315.

Morrison, N. 1985. Shame in the treatment of schizophrenia: Theoretical consideration with clinical illustrations. *Yale Journal of Biology and Medicine* 58:289–97.

————. 1987. The role of shame in schizophrenia. In *The role of shame in symptom formation,* ed. H. B. Lewis. Hillsdale, N.J.: Erlbaum.

Newman, R., and M. Hirt. 1983. The psychoanalytic theory of depression: Symptoms as a function of aggression and field articulation. *Journal of Abnormal Psychology* 92:42–49.

Patsioskas, A., G. Clum, and R. Luscomb. 1979. Cognitive characteristics of suicide attempters. *Journal of Consulting and Clinical Psychology* 47:478–84.

Piers, G., and M. Singer. 1953. *Shame and guilt.* Springfield, Ill.: Thomas.

Prosen, M., D. Clark, M. Harrow, and J. Fawcett. 1983. Guilt and conscience in major depressive disorders. *American Journal of Psychiatry* 140:839–44.

Retzinger, S. 1985. The resentment process: Videotape studies. *Psychoanalytic Psychology* 2:129–53.

Safer, J. 1975. The effects of sex and psychological differentiation on response to a stressful situation. Ph.D. diss., New School of Social Research.

Scheff, T., and S. Retzinger. In press. *Laughter and resentment.*

Schooler, C., and J. Silverman. 1969. Perceptual styles and their correlates among schizophrenic patients. *Journal of Abnormal Psychology* 74:459–70.

Silberstein, L., R. Striegel-Moore, and J. Rodin. 1987. Feeling fat: A woman's shame. In *The role of shame in symptom formation,* ed. H. B. Lewis. Hillsdale, N.J.: Erlbaum.

Smith, R. 1972. The relative proneness to shame or guilt as an indicator of defensive style. Ph.D. diss., Northwestern University.

Tomkins, S. 1962. *Affect, imagery, consciousness.* New York: Springer.

Wicker, F., G. Payne, and R. Morgan. 1983. Participant descriptions of guilt and shame. *Motivation and Emotion* 7:25–39.

Witkin, H. 1965. Psychological differentiation and forms of pathology. *Journal of Abnormal Psychology* 70:317–36.

Witkin, H., H. Lewis, H. Hertzman, K. Machover, P. Meissner, and S. Wapner. 1954. *Personality through perception.* New York: Harper.

Witkin, H., H. Lewis, and E. Weil. 1968. Affective reactions and patient-therapist interactions among more or less differentiated patients early in therapy. *Journal of Nervous and Mental Disease* 146:193–208.

11 Repression in College Men Followed for Half a Century

GEORGE E. VAILLANT

Definitions

It is clear from the papers in this volume that there are important semantic problems in our definition of repression. One cause for the problem is that the conventional terms for defenses that psychoanalysis has made popular (e.g., "repression," "dissociation," and "reaction formation") were devised to describe clinical experience without any intent for use in scientific investigation or consensual validation. Such terms do, however, possess the advantage of being familiar to many investigators. In contrast, the scientific terminologies for unconscious defensive operations that have been devised by investigators such as Lazarus, Moos, and Horowitz can be used in experimental investigations, but these terms are idiosyncratic and do not have wide currency.

Clearly, semantic problems must be solved if we are to meet the goals of this volume. Although Erdelyi chided Anna Freud for oversimplifying very complex issues, I suspect that, in terms of bringing order to defense mechanisms, her approach is valuable. I believe that in, solving semantic problems, simple *is* better. Therefore, in this chapter I shall depend heavily on Anna Freud's definitions. By simplifying defense mechanisms, Anna Freud (Freud 1937) did for the very complex issues of ego mechanisms of defense what DSM-III-R (American Psychiatric Association 1987) did for diagnosis. She made it possible to keep a variety of defenses in mind and also to differentiate one from another. By way of contrast, in 1926 her father (Freud [1926] 1959) described the defense of isolation, which he claimed he was describing "for the first time," and completely forgot—or repressed—that he had defined the defense quite clearly in 1894 (Freud [1894] 1962), for he had forgotten to catalog—to oversimplify—his definitions.

We found at the conference from which this volume arose that even among investigators within a single country one needs to develop a common lan-

This work was supported by research grants KO5-MH00364, MH39799, and MH42248 from the National Institute of Mental Health.

guage. In his talk, Gary Schwartz used "repression" to mean almost any kind of ego mechanism of defense; so did Sigmund Freud (Freud [1906] 1953). The example that Erdelyi gave of his daughter's use of "repression" could also be described as "sublimation." What Daniel Weinberger called "repression" Anna Freud might have called "reaction formation." Finally, the process of altered consciousness to which David Spiegel has referred can perhaps best be labeled "dissociation." Only Ebbinghaus, as described by Erdelyi, used "repression" in the narrow sense that Anna Freud (Freud 1937) defines it: to forget the idea but to retain the affect in consciousness. This difficulty in consensual definition of defenses should not surprise us. A major reason that Anna Freud's own Hampstead Clinic group never published their extensive archival studies of different examples of defense was because they could not obtain rater reliability.

In this chapter, I shall try to provide mutually exclusive definitions of the four defenses repression, reaction formation, suppression, and dissociation. I will then try to illustrate some of the real-life consequences of using one defense rather than another. Finally, I will offer several case illustrations to show rather than tell what I mean by "repression."

If we posit that the four components of conflict are the subject or ownership of the impulse, the object of the impulse, the affect associated with the impulse, and the ideational "conscious" recognition of the impulse, then each defense distorts these four components in a different way.

Repression

The "forgetting" of repression is probably qualitatively different from "normal" forgetting. In his seminar demonstration, Gordon Bower demonstrated for us that our "forgetting" most of a list of words could be undone if he offered us clues. In contrast, the "forgetting" of repression astonishes the observer and is often accompanied by highly symbolic behavior that suggests that the repressed is still "in mind." Repression often reflects seemingly inexplicable naïveté and memory lapse or frank failure to acknowledge input from selected sense organs. In Gordon Bower's example, we all "forgot" about the same percentage of words.

The amnesia that results from repression is also different from the forgetting of word lists demonstrated by Gordon Bower because the affect surrounding the idea remains in consciousness and because the repressed idea has an uncanny way of returning—albeit in disguised form. If the defense mechanism of isolation allows the idea to remain in consciousness but stripped of any affective coloring or meaning, the defense of repression allows the affect to remain in consciousness, but the idea is rendered unconscious.

As with non–conflict driven "forgetting," the user of repression can associate to what has been forgotten. At nineteen, one subject in the Study of

Adult Development said that he could remember nothing of his life before age seven. Later in the interview, however, he remarked that poetry "sometimes seems to arrive full blown from my unconscious mind." While we had no evidence whether his "lost" childhood memories returned in his poetry, it became clear with the passage of time that his poetry served as a catharsis for painful, allegedly repressed war experiences. Of another nineteen-year-old member of the Study of Adult Development, the psychiatrist had remarked, "His memory is very poor for early events," and the study internist had remarked, "I was amazed at his lack of memory and utter vagueness about dates." At thirty-two, however, the same subject was able to say, "Yes, I recollect the troubles in the family very clearly," and went on to describe, for the first time, terrible parental fights that had plagued his childhood. Later, this subject returned a questionnaire to the study with the following remark: "I found this report packed with my papers. It was sealed and ready to be mailed, but somehow it had been misplaced." The facts were that the subject had received the questionnaire two years before, at a time when his career seemed lost in a blind alley; he did not "remember" to mail it until he had once more redirected his career into a more gratifying area. Once the danger of career stagnation was averted, the repressed could return, and he could share with the study the account of his previous job dissatisfaction.

Repression differs from suppression by causing the individual to forgo, rather than just to postpone, cherished goals. Unlike psychotic denial, repression prevents the identification of conflict-laden ideas rather than preventing recognition of external reality. Repression differs from dissociation in that it alters ideational memory rather than affective state. Repression differs from reaction formation in that it "forgets" rather than reverses ideational content.

There are many psychoanalysts who would take issue with my suggestion that repression is merely one defense among many, for throughout much of his career Sigmund Freud used the terms "defense" and "repression" synonymously. "Repression," he wrote, "is the cornerstone on which the whole structure of psychoanalysis rests" (Freud [1914] 1957, 16). Yet Freud, when he chose, could define "repression" with great specificity. "Repression," he wrote, was when "the affect from which the ego has suffered remains as it was before, unaltered and undiminished, the only difference being that the incompatible idea is kept down and shut out from recollection" ([1894] 1962, 54).

Before going on to discuss three alternative defenses that are often called "repression," let me offer a hypothetical example that will quickly illustrate the distinctions that I am trying to make. If a man were weeping in a cemetery but could not recall for whom he wept, this would be repression. If he denied the existence of his tears, that would represent psychotic denial. If he got the giggles or got drunk at the wake, that would be dissociation (neurotic denial). If he said he wept from happiness, that would be reaction formation. If he brushed aside his tears, said he would think about his father's death tomorrow, and indeed remembered to grieve the next day, that would be suppression.

Dissociation

Dissociation or neurotic denial involves temporary but drastic modification of one's character or one's sense of personal identity to avoid emotional distress. This can include hypnotic trance, fugues, some hysterical conversion reactions, sudden unwarranted sense of superiority or counterphobic behavior, and of course Stanislavsky method acting. Dissociation involves a short-term refusal to perceive responsibility for one's own acts or feelings, but, unlike projection, dissociation does not attribute these feelings to someone else.

Reaction Formation

This defense reflects conscious affect and/or behavior that is diametrically opposed to an unacceptable instinctual impulse. This mechanism includes overtly caring for someone else when one wishes to be cared for one's self. It involves nine-year-old boys "hating" pretty girls and adolescent ascetics "loving" a hated rival or an unpleasant duty. The term "reaction formation" can encompass facets of both "identification with the aggressor" and "altruistic surrender" in the sense that those terms are defined by Anna Freud in *The Ego and the Mechanisms of Defense* (1937). Reaction formation is distinct from dissociation in that the cognition is turned into its exact opposite rather than being replaced by a state of altered consciousness (i.e., sex is "bad" in contrast to "funny"; money is called "dirty" rather than gambled away).

Suppression

Suppression allows the individual to hold all components of a conflict (subject, object, idea, and affect) in mind and then to postpone action, affective response, or ideational worry. Thus, suppression reflects a semiconscious decision to defer paying attention to a conscious impulse or conflict. Freud once said, "I have omitted to state whether I attribute different meanings to the words 'suppressed' and 'repressed.' It should have been clear, however, that the latter lays more stress than the former on the fact of attachment to the unconscious" (Freud [1900] 1953, 5:606). A spy who under interrogation by the enemy dissembled would represent simply lying, for there is no conflict. Neither his knowledge nor his wish to withhold knowledge from the enemy represents conflict. A person who, having realized the need to urinate during a long church service and then having successfully put the impulse out of mind until the end of the service rather than either walk out in the middle or consciously suffer until the end, would illustrate suppression.

Table 1. The Contrasting Association between Related Defensive Styles and Psychosocial Outcome Variables: Evidence That Repression Is Unrelated to Psychopathology

	Repression	Dissociation	Suppression	Reaction Formation
Diagnosis of mental illness	.00	.20**	−.36***	.07
Global mental health, age 47	−.06	−.17**	.31***	−.08
	(−.05)	(−.43**)	(.57***)	(−.02)
Global mental health, age 63	−.05	−.22**	.30***	−.10
Good physical health	−.01	−.17**	.10	−.17**
	(−.01)	(−.23***)	(.19***)	(−.06)
Maturity of psychosocial development (10)	−.07	−.09	.29***	.01
	(−.01)	(−.35***)	(.45***)	(.05)
Warm childhood	.02	−.09	.20**	.10
	(.00)	−.09)	(.13**)	(−.09)
Marriage stable	.10	−.23***	.25***	.07
	(.04)	(−.27***)	(.24***)	(.07)
Alcohol abuse	.00	.34***	−.15*	.06
	(−.04)	(.50***)	(−.15**)	(.07)

Note: Spearman correlation coefficient was the statistic used. The correlations in parentheses refer to replication of the correlations, using different raters and a sample of 307 inner-city men with low IQ and disadvantaged socioeconomic status (9, 10).
* $p < .05$.
** $p < .01$.
*** $p < .001$.

Suppression includes looking for silver linings, stoicism, minimizing acknowledged discomfort, employing a stiff upper lip, and counting to ten before expressing anger. The argument is often made that suppression is simply a conscious coping mechanism. But, if suppression were voluntary, more people would use it, for, as table 1 suggests, suppression is highly adaptive. Freud himself spoke of the postponement of gratification as being the hallmark of maturity, the end state of his goal of replacing id (and superego) with ego. But the ego is not always conscious.

Let me clarify what I mean by "suppression." It may be argued that everyone's ego is a personality system designed for the delay of gratification and for orderly and adaptive expression of needs. But some individuals are very much more adept at this relatively automatized, often out-of-awareness use of suppression than others.

I shall offer two examples. One of the study members had summed himself up by saying that he had a "strong streak of patience. I can go a long way with people before I lose my cool." I asked him about his children, and he told me that his daughter had cystic fibrosis. He said, "No one is willing to predict the course of her affliction." I asked him how he had mastered the discovery of his daughter's diagnosis. "It was a pretty rough blow to learn about it." Blowing his nose, he added, "I took it harder than my wife. We were fortunate in having an excellent doctor. He was great in showing us how to handle the disease. My wife gets all the credit. We decided not to treat it as a problem." In other words, while acknowledging the dangers and his own emotional upset and without fending off my painful questions (as members of the study often did), he had nevertheless told me the bright side. There was a treatment plan that could be followed for cystic fibrosis, and the people by his side were wonderful. He said he did not treat it as a problem, but, in fact, the way he behaved was perfectly realistic. He was at peace with his conscience, his instincts, his reality, and the people who mattered to him.

Another study member described a Navy diving accident in the following manner. He was forty feet underwater, his air valve was jammed, his radio did not work, and he knew that there was only eight minutes of air left in his diving helmet. He immediately recognized that there was nothing that he could do for himself. "I thought my end had come . . . struggling would not have helped and used maybe three times as much air. I didn't pray. I merely sat, very much like an old cow, and waited for help—very unhappy." He knew his feelings, he knew they would not help, and so he kept them inside until he was rescued. Under the same circumstances, many others would have panicked or denied the reality. Defenses come into play when reason is overwhelmed.

Empirical Evidence

Besides helping us speak a common language, a second aim of this volume is to develop methodologies for investigating phenomena that have been studied mainly within the context of psychotherapy. I have studied defenses in the Study of Adult Development using the methods of longitudinal follow-up and psychobiography (Vaillant 1976, 1977, 1986; Vaillant, Bond, and Vaillant 1986). We cannot directly measure a mountain's height from top to bottom, but, if we know the distance between our points of observation, we can assess a mountain's height through "triangulation," by integrating several indirect, oblique, but measured views of its peak. So it is with defenses. Analogous to cautious psychobiography, defenses can be identified by contrasting biographical fact with autobiographical subjective statement and with the subject's creative product. Translating from biography into clinical formulation, we can compare data in medical records and lab tests (signs of disease) with the chief complaint and the history of the present illness (the autobiographical symptoms of disease) and with the mental content and pathological behaviors (e.g., the creative products of disease). Thus, an artist's biography and a patient's old medical record correspond to one another. An artist's autobiography and a patient's account of his or her present illness correspond to each other. Third, William Blake the artist's paintings correspond to William Blake the patient's delusional constructions. By examining these three sources of information together, one can concretize defensive (adaptive) distortion as not just "chance" and thus obtain rater reliability (Vaillant, Bond, and Vaillant 1986).

A simple illustration of what I am writing about is to watch a hypnotized person as the clock strikes three go over and open a window. The symptom is irrationally opening the window of a cold room. The autobiographical statement is, "I suddenly felt hot." The biographical fact will be that the patient in hypnotic trance was commanded both to open a window on the stroke of three and to forget that such a command had been given. The behavior illustrates not "normal" forgetting but the "defense" of repression.

I will take advantage of the Study of Adult Development, a fifty-year prospective study of "normal" but gifted college men (Vaillant 1977), to illustrate how longitudinal observation can be used to obtain consensual agreement as to the nature of the defense used. Analogous to Horowitz's studies of intrusive imagery, by virtue of having three hundred pages of questionnaires and interviews it was possible for me to study defenses not by weighting individual examples but by sheer repetition of example—of inconsistency between behavior, biography, and autobiography.

In their sophomore year almost half a century ago, two hundred college students had been studied by internists, psychiatrists, psychologists, and anthropologists. Since college graduation, the men have been followed up approximately every two years by extensive questionnaires covering all aspects of their lives with both forced choice and open-ended autobiographical questions. At the ages of thirty and forty-seven to fifty-seven, the men were reinterviewed. As a comparison group, 307 inner-city men prospectively followed since age fourteen were interviewed for two hours at age forty-seven.

Identification of defensive style was assessed in the following general manner. Raters of defenses were blinded both to childhood records and to the independent adult ratings. They were given uniform definitions of fifteen defenses and trained on interview protocols that had been rated by many others. The fifteen defenses were divided into three clusters determined on the basis of prior empirical study: (*a*) mature defenses: sublimation, suppression, anticipation, altruism, and humor; (*b*) intermediate/neurotic defenses: displacement, repression, isolation (intellectualization), and reaction formation; and (*c*) immature defenses: projection, schizoid fantasy, passive aggression (turning against the self), acting out, hypochondriasis, and dissociation (neurotic denial).

Raters then reviewed each man's chart, especially autobiographical responses on the biennial questionnaires, and the twenty- to thirty-page summaries of interviews. Each man's behavior at times of crisis and conflict was recorded as a vignette. Evidence that a vignette reflected a defense mechanism sometimes depended on earlier data.

The mid-life interviews had been designed to focus on difficulties in the individual's relationships, physical health, and work. In writing the interview summary, the interviewer was instructed to elucidate but not to label the behaviors by which the individuals had coped with these difficulties. Interview protocols were prepared by the interviewer from verbatim notes taken during the interview. Numerous direct quotes were included in the interview protocols, but the methodology embodied both the scientific limitations and the advantages of journalism. The purpose was to use the interviewer's summary as the first step in data reduction and to retain·interview emphasis that is often lost in transcripts of tape recordings.

For each of the interview protocols, raters were asked to note all possible instances of each of the fifteen defensive styles. Attention was paid to concrete past behaviors, to the style of adaptation to past difficulties, and to specific vicissitudes of the interview interaction.

To control for marked variation across subjects in the frequency of identified defensive vignettes, the following quantitative strategy was adopted to force clinical judgment of the global maturity (health) of defenses into a nine-point scale. The relative proportion of defense vignettes in each of the three general categories (mature, intermediate, and immature) was determined. This ratio was used to distribute a total of eight points. Of the eight points, one to five points were assigned to each of the three general categories, but the total had to be eight. The score for overall defensive style for each man was then estimated by subtracting the rating (1–5) for immature defenses from the rating (1–5) for mature defenses. This procedure provided a nine-point range, a normal distribution of scores, and a rater reliability of .84. Global ratings by the two raters for the inner-city men differed by more than two points for twenty-one (7 percent) out of 307.

Individual Defenses

For each interview, ten to thirty instances of defensive behavior were noted, reflecting three to seven different defenses. Weighing of the salience of each individual defense was achieved through redundancy, that is, through frequency rather than certainty of identification. Each rater scored each defense as follows: 0 if absent, 1 if noted once or twice, and 2 if it was the most frequently used defense or it was noted three times or more. Reliability was only modest. The raters had more difficulty agreeing on individual defense ratings, and, depending on the defense, one rater could score a given defense 2 (major) and the other could score it 0 (absent) in 4–20 percent of cases. For this reason, the two raters' ratings were summed, providing an individual rat-

Table 2. Significant Correlations between Repression and Outcome Variables

	Repression	Dissociation	Suppression	Reaction Formation
Maturity of ego development (11, 12)	−.21*	−.08	.02	−.05
Lifetime visits to psychiatrists or psychologists	−.19**	.18**	−.13*	.12

Note: Spearman correlation coefficient was the statistic used.
* $p < .05$.
** $p < .01$.

ing for each defense that ranged from 0 (both agreed it was absent) to 4 (both agreed it was major).

Interrater reliability for reaction formation was $r = .74$, for repression $r = .63$, for suppression $r = .59$, and for dissociation $r = .01$, no better than chance (Vaillant 1976). However, when the ratings on dissociation of the blind raters were summed, they correlated with mine, $r = .55$ (Vaillant 1976), and, no matter who rated dissociation, its frequent use was negatively correlated with outcome.

Empirical Associations of Defense Choice and Outcome

Table 1 illustrates that the often-confused mechanisms of repression, dissociation, reaction formation, and suppression correlate in sharply contrasting ways with major psychosocial outcome variables. Repression, when narrowly defined (Freud [1894] 1962; Freud 1937), is uncorrelated with psychopathology or mental or physical health assessed in a variety of ways by independent raters (Vaillant 1976; Vaillant, Bond, and Vaillant 1986). Dissociation (neurotic denial) was highly correlated with psychopathology, and suppression was consistently seen as correlated with positive mental health. Both dissociation and reaction formation—comprising perhaps different facets of Jerome Singer's and Daniel Weinberger's repressive-defensive style—were correlated with poor physical health. Despite the low levels of rater reliability for individual defenses, the different association of defenses with outcomes was replicated by different raters assessing defensive style in our two very different socioeconomic samples (Vaillant 1976; Vaillant, Bond, and Vaillant 1986).

Of many variables looked at, table 2 illustrates that repression, as defined in this chapter, correlated only two variables. These were an absence of psychological mindedness (reflection on affect and conflict) as reflected by relative underutilization of psychiatrists—given an equal degree of psychopathology (table 1)—and being rated at a low ego level by Loevinger's sentence completion test (Loevinger 1976; Vaillant and McCullough 1987). This asso-

ciation may also have reflected a style of not thinking about affect-laden issues.

Case Illustrations

A third purpose of this conference was to consider how emotionally charged
personal life issues are processed and revised. Both as a way of presenting my
methods of studying ego mechanisms of defense and as a way of giving my
semantic quibbles some life, let me present three case histories. Obviously,
any single example could occur by chance alone; it is the aggregate of examples that conveys a defensive style. "Defensive style" may be read as "coping style" or as a means of altering inner and outer reality that exceeds chance
levels. I hope that the "forgetting" depicted below appears qualitatively different from the "forgetting" of simple word lists described by Gordon Bower.
But the beauty of science is that, if my "proof" fails, that is of equal interest.
The reader must judge.

The first study member illustrates both repression and dissociation. The
research psychiatrist had described the man as a college student as being "very
direct and easy in his manner. He is open and frank. He talks easily and to the
point." Selective descriptive adjectives for him were "pleasant," "easygoing,"
and "passive." The psychiatrist continued his description:

> The boy gives no history of anxiety manifestations . . . examina-
> tions do not bother him . . . he sleeps well, and his dreams are
> not well remembered . . . he describes very intense emotions
> which may be followed within two or three minutes by a com-
> plete change in the quality of his feelings . . . even distressing
> emotional reactions tend to fade quickly. . . . This boy's interest
> in the drama dwarfs other possibilities of activity. . . . He has not
> really thought about a great many of the problems which con-
> front other boys. . . . He thinks he is rather easily imposed
> upon. He was supposed to be a student in stagecraft but found
> himself taking part in a great deal of the less pleasant work, such
> as sweeping up after the show. He did not complain for about
> three weeks, and then worked up a "beautiful case of hysteria."
> He has not had other temper outbursts. . . . He says his anger
> does not need to be controlled because there is no natural ten-
> dency towards anger.

At eighteen, the boy described his dreams as not well remembered and not
unpleasant. At age nineteen, the psychiatrist commented that the boy had "not
yet begun to think of sexual experience" and that the subject denied experiencing any sexual tension. At twenty-four, when the boy brought up his con-

cern about homosexuality for the first time, the subject suggested that perhaps the study psychiatrist had known about his concerns all along. He wrote of his homosexual concerns, "I don't know whether it's psychological [*sic*] or psychological in origin." Under most circumstances, he was an excellent speller; thus, his "slip of the pen" in spelling "physiological" might suggest this latent recognition of the psychological basis of his conflict.

At age thirty-three, in response to his difficulty in returning questionnaires, he wrote, "I must have a mental block on the questionnaire. It seems to be much more than ordinary procrastination." A possible explanation was that this young man (for whom we had abundant evidence of conflict over intimacy with women) had just married. There were no further questionnaires for the next seven years. Adjustment to marriage was not easy for him, and, during the interval, he wrote a play called *Help Me, Carl Jung, I Am Drowning,* but, as suggested by the negative correlations in table 2, he never saw a psychiatrist. He just wrote plays about them.

When I interviewed him for the second time at sixty-five, he talked in a relaxed manner with multiple slips of the tongue and never completely revealed himself. But, consistent with a man who used dissociation less and sublimation more, he had learned to make his comforting daydreams come true. His inexplicable repression when young now more resembled suppression. He observed that he rarely had marital arguments. "Too much bottling up, I believe, but it's always been that way . . . we both have a tendency to keep silent when we should talk or explode." When asked his philosophy over rough spots at age sixty-five, our subject said that it was summarized by rule 7 of the Bombay Golf Club: "You play the ball where the monkey drops it." This is as good a definition of stoicism as I can imagine. If at forty-seven he could say that "sometimes make-believe and reality got mixed up," at sixty-five in retirement he was extremely effective in shaping the life of the Massachusetts town in which he lived. But his very success still led to slips of the tongue. Over the opposition of his bishop, he spoke of personally appointing the "victor—I mean vicar" to his church in the Berkshires.

Under stress, his use of repression at age sixty-five could still be identified. When I asked him about his psychiatrically troubled daughter, he replied, "The details are fuzzy; my mind is blank to things I don't want to remember." I pressed him for details. He said, "We sent her to McLean's, and heaved a sigh of relief." I asked him if he had ever found anybody with similar problems with whom to discuss his daughter, and he replied, "I can't remember." He finally admitted that he did talk to his daughter's psychiatrist, but he said that he viewed his daughter as something he had no control over. "I put my mind on other things." Suddenly, he said, "Phooey!" and we changed the subject. In short, his life illustrated a finding often observed in the maturation of adults; repression evolves into suppression, and dissociation evolves into sublimation. This is illustrated in the later productive life of Bertha Pappenheim, who as a young woman became famous as Josef Breuer's hysterical patient Anna O. (Freeman 1972).

Another subject who used repression as a dominant defensive style had been the son of a deaf mother and an emotionally labile father. His early life was filled with severe punishment and threat. Both his parents felt that they hit him too much, and from eight to eleven he was separated from his mother and lived with his father. Nevertheless, in college he was seen as a likeable albeit rather dull and uninteresting person. When he was twenty-six, the social investigator was impressed with his happiness. At age thirty-one, he was described as a bland but healthy man and, at forty-six, a "happy, successful man devoted to his family." He spoke in a slow, laconic, relaxed way and radiated an inner peace. His commonsensical, studied calm was reassuring rather than irritating. He had resisted the occupational and social doors opened for him by graduating as a star athlete from a prestigious college. Instead, he had returned to his hometown, living the life he could have lived had he simply graduated from his high school. In short, as several subjects in our study who often deployed the defense seemed to have discovered, repression is easier to maintain if you do not take chances.

This subject's use of repression was reflected by the fact that he denied having had any sexual thoughts or feelings until he was sixteen. A little after that time, he alleged that he was shocked and disillusioned to discover—consciously—that his mother and father had a sexual relationship. When the study psychiatrist first asked him about masturbation, he said that he could not hear the question. When the question was repeated, he replied that he was uncertain what the word "masturbation" meant. Finally, he dismissed the question by saying that he never engaged in masturbation—except when he was half asleep and lacked the willpower to prevent it.

In high school, although a star athlete, he said he had had no sexual curiosity and never dated until he was twenty. His incredulous teammates all vied as to who would be the first to fix him up with a date. None succeeded. He told the college interviewers that going out with girls would be boring. Throughout World War II, during which he was stationed in England, he, unlike most American service men, managed never to meet girls. At forty-nine, as the father of four adolescent children, he could not remember his first date, and he had lost all recollection of ever having been shy about girls in high school. Neither his adolescent physical exam nor his ease siring children suggested that a hormonal deficit could have explained his prolonged lack of interest in sex.

He could not remember his dreams; indeed, as he put it, "I can't even remember my daydreams." In college, he had majored in engineering with expressed plans of becoming an architectural engineer. Instead, under paternal pressure, he became a salesman in his father's business. At forty-eight, he told me, "In college I majored in engineering for no special reason, as I had no ambitions in that field."

Although he seemed outwardly calm, he told me, "People just don't know what's going on inside." When I asked him what was going on, he said that he could not describe it. He said that, under stress, "my mind tightens up." However, although he had never seen a psychiatrist, he had learned to free associate to discover the source of his emotions. For example, "People insult me," he told me, "but don't irritate me. . . . Someone else might punch them." When I asked him how, after being insulted, he felt inside, he admitted, "I don't feel right—then I think, 'Why don't I feel right? It's not physical,' so I figure out the reason and then I try to solve it."

He had no idea what medicine he took for his prostate trouble. But it was common for men who used repression as a dominant defensive style to be unable to remember the names of their medicines, although they often remembered to take them. Of the thirty-two men scoring high in repression, only two were among the forty-six doctors. However, nine of the men in sales, advertising, or public relations—virtually the entire sample—scored high in repression as a defensive style.

My third example of repression is also a man in advertising and public relations. He was described in college as "a little languid and sleepy." He was also described as "very pleasant and congenial, . . . extroverted." However, the possibility of a "problem of neurosis in the future" was raised by a study staff member.

At age twenty, he did not know his parents' telephone number. In giving the study his father's age, he was four years off, and he could give no details about his father's nervous breakdown that occurred when the subject was twelve. A psychiatrist wrote, "He gave a very poor description of his father and mother. His memory is very poor for early events." All his life his mother had felt him to be uninquisitive about sex. At age twenty-six, an interviewer remarked, "The efforts to get definite information out of him can best be compared with attempting to withdraw a wooden stick with a bulbous lower end out of a pot of rapidly boiling molasses." Yet, at age thirty-three, he was able to document quite clearly that his family life as a child had been painful. Without benefit of psychotherapy, he had recovered his memory for painful childhood events.

The subject was a procrastinator par excellence and wrote at twenty-five, "I am naturally lazy and so have a splendid chance to develop that characteristic in the Service." However, his forgetting seemed genuine and defensive rather than a means of expressing passive aggression.

"He had no sense of stress when in danger during the war," a postwar interviewer wrote. "I was amazed at his lack of memory and his utter vagueness about dates." (Yet this man became a success as a newspaper reporter.) At age thirty, he could not remember the first name of the roommate who had been assigned to him in his junior year. At age forty-six, after taking two and a half years to respond to a questionnaire, he wrote, "I suppose my tardiness . . . is a factor in your study, but despite my foot dragging my interest in the study does continue." He was almost unique in leaving blank the entire page on which he was asked to note if and when seventeen serious life events had occurred. He noted only the years that his parents died and then wrote, "I don't understand this whole section!" Again, this remark came from a former newspaper reporter. When interviewed at forty-nine, he could not remember when his mother died, although it had only been eighteen months prior to the interview. "Funny thing," he said, "I can't remember." But, as was the case with my second case example, he could associate. He rummaged through his desk to find a news clipping and then used this to provide me with the date.

Comparing himself to his wife, he said that, if a problem came up, "she wants to talk and I want to sweep it under the rug . . . I don't want to talk about it." He would then lose his temper and be unable to think about the argument until the following morning. The affect was present; the ideational content was absent. I asked him what caused his angry outbursts at his wife. He could not remember, but he let himself associate. He wondered aloud whether all his advertising man's success (into which he had been pushed by his wife) was irritating him.

Conclusion

Let me make two final points. First, how we finally choose to define "repression" will be as arbitrary as how we define any technical term. But consensual definition is perfectly feasible and will be facilitated by the fact that DMS-III-R (American Psychiatric Association 1987) finally offers psychiatry a uniform glossary of defenses.

Second, whether we choose to view repression as altered cognition or evidence for a dynamic unconscious is at present a matter of intellectual taste and style. But, in the future, ingenious experimental paradigms cannot help but bring the cognitive styles of the psychoanalyst and of the cognitive psychologist closer together. Catalyzing such experimentation must surely be one of the goals of this volume.

References

American Psychiatric Association. 1987. *Diagnostic and statistical manual of mental disorders*. 3d ed., rev. Washington, D.C.: American Psychiatric Press.

Freeman, L. 1972. *The story of Anna O*. New York: Walker.

Freud, A. 1937. *Ego and the mechanisms of defense*. London: Hogarth.

Freud, S. [1894] 1962. The neuro-psychoses of defence. In *The standard edition of the complete psychological works of Sigmund Freud*, ed. J. Strachey, vol. 3, pp. 41–68. London: Hogarth.

———. [1900] 1953. *The interpretation of dreams.* In *The standard edition of the complete psychological works of Sigmund Freud,* ed. J. Strachey, vol. 5. London: Hogarth.

———. [1906] 1953. My views on the part played by sexuality in the aetiology of the neuroses. In *The standard edition of the complete psychological works of Sigmund Freud,* ed. J. Strachey, vol. 7, pp. 269–79. London: Hogarth.

———. [1914] 1957. On the history of the psycho-analytic movement. In *The standard edition of the complete psychological works of Sigmund Freud,* ed. J. Strachey, vol. 14, pp. 1–66. London: Hogarth.

———. [1926] 1959. Inhibitions, symptoms and anxiety. In *The standard edition of the complete psychological works of Sigmund Freud,* ed. J. Strachey, vol. 20, pp. 75–175. London: Hogarth.

Loevinger, J. 1976. *Ego development.* San Francisco: Jossey-Bass.

Vaillant, G. E. 1976. Natural history of male psychological health. v. The relation of choice of ego mechanisms of defense to adult adjustment. *Archives of General Psychiatry* 33:535–45.

———. 1977. *Adaptation to life.* Boston: Little, Brown.

———. 1986. *Empirical studies of ego mechanisms of defense.* Washington, D.C.: American Psychiatric Press.

Vaillant, G E., M. Bond and C. O. Vaillant. 1986. An empirically validated hierarchy of defense mechanisms. *Archives of General Psychiatry* 43:786–94.

Vaillant, G. E., and L. McCullough. 1987. A comparison of the Washington University Sentence Completion Test (SCT) with other measures of adult ego development. *American Journal of Psychiatry* 144:1189–94.

12 Repressive Style and Relationship Patterns—Three Samples Inspected

LESTER LUBORSKY, PAUL CRITS-CHRISTOPH AND
KEITH J. ALEXANDER

Chronic use of a particular defensive style leaves pervasive imprints on successive levels of information processing, including inspectional style and recall style. In Luborsky, Blinder, and Schimek (1965), a person classed as a repressor, when shown a photograph of a woman with her breasts exposed (see fig. 1 below), looked around but not at the breasts; another person classed as an isolator looked around but at the breasts as well. The repressor remembered the picture's contents sketchily; the isolator recalled the contents well. This example illustrates that "repressors" (to be defined by the measures to be described) not only forget more but may not even have taken in information because of selective inattention. Such defensive styles must also interact with the patterns of conscious and unconscious knowledge about self and others that are referred to as either "person schemas" or "relationship schemas" (M. Horowitz, in press). It is not a big step to suppose that there is an interaction between the defensive styles and the relationship patterns.

The purpose of this chapter is to examine measures of one kind of defensive style, that is, repressive style, and to find its relation to measures of relationship patterns. More specifically, this examination should move us closer to two goals. (1) The first goal is to review data that will reveal the reliability and the basic nature of three measures of repressive style: the Levine and Spivak (1964) Rorschach Index of Repressive Style (RIRS), the Holzman Rorschach Measure of Repression and Isolation (Gardner et al. 1959; and Holzman, 1962), and the Weinberger Questionnaire Measure of Repression (see chap. 14 in this volume). We will examine their intercorrelations and their correlates with other measures as a way to uncover more about what is tapped by each measure. (2) The second is to include measures of relationship patterns among the correlates of the repressive styles. We expect to find that different defensive styles are associated with different components of relationship patterns. However, it is hard to make specific predictions about such interrelations since this is not an area that has been much investigated.

275

Table 1. Items Composing Two Measures of Repression

RIRS	Holzman Repression
− Specificity	− Specificity
− Elaboration	− Variety of content
− Impulse responses	− Emphasis on color
− Primary process thinking	− Symbolic content without awareness
− Self-references	− Movement < 3
− Movement	− Integrative efforts
− Organization	+ Expressive and phobic
	− Failures < 25 responses
	+ Childlike material

A Three-Study Plan

We will pursue these goals within the samples from three studies, selected because they each contain measures of repressive styles and measures of central relationship patterns. Study 1, "Looking and Early Memories," is an extension of the "Looking as a Function of Defense" study (Luborsky, Blinder, and Schimek 1965), to which we have added relationship pattern measures based on early memories and an expanded sample size. It is a laboratory study on an unselected sample of normal college students who volunteered to be part of the research. Study 2, "Narratives from Therapy," explores the relation of defensive style and relationship patterns on the basis of narratives told by forty-three outpatients during their psychotherapy (Luborsky et al. 1980). Study 3, "RAP Narratives," is a sample of sixteen outpatients in psychotherapy whose narratives are elicited by a "RAP" interview (Luborsky and Crits-Christoph, in press).

Measures of Defensive Style

Each of the three measures of repressive style is described in this section, including the scoring criteria (summarized in table 1 and 2) and the validity correlates (summarized in tables 3 and 4).

Rorschach Index of Repressive Style

The main measure of repressive style in all three studies is the RIRS (Levine and Spivak 1963, 1964). It uses a weighted sum of points for each response in the Rorschach test according to certain characteristics of the response (divided by the number of responses). A high score indicates less reliance on repressive style. Seven scores make up the total: (1) specificity, (2) elaboration, (3) impulse responses, (4) primary process thinking, (5) self-references, (6) movement, and (7) organization. A specific response is op-

Table 2. Items Composing the Weinberger Adjustment Inventory Repressive Restraint Scales

1. Once in a while, I don't do things that people ask me to do.	F
2. I can remember a time when I was so angry at someone that I felt like hurting them.	F
3. I have done some things that weren't right and felt sorry about it later.	F
4. There have been times when I said I would do one thing but did something else.	F
5. Once in a while, I act like I know more about something than I really do.	F
6. Once in a while, I say bad things about people that I would not say in front of them.	F
7. At times I am a little unkind to people I don't like.	F
8. There have been times when I did not finish something because I spent too much time "goofing off."	F
9. I never have trouble getting myself to do what I should.	T
10. Once in a while, I say things that are not completely true.	F
11. There have been times when I didn't let people know about something I did wrong.	F
12. Once in a while, I break a promise I've made.	F

posed to a general or vague one; for example, "animal" reflects more repression than "bear." Elaboration refers to adjectives and adverbs. Reference to the impulses of sexuality, hostility, anality, or dependence is taken to mean less reliance on repression. Self-references are mostly to feeling states and indicate a lesser degree of repression. All movement responses are taken to mean lessened repression. Less organization implies greater repression.

Reliability

For the Levine and Spivak (1964) method, scorer reliability is high (above .90 in several tests), and test-retest reliability after one week is .91. For periods up to ten years, retest reliability coefficients average .60 for children.

Because the reliability of scoring this measure is high, only one judge did our scoring. For study 1, the scorer was one of the originators of the measures, M. Levine; for studies 2 and 3, the scorer was K. Alexander. A check of ten cases by an independent judge confirmed that Alexander's reliability was high (.97).

Validity

1. The RIRS correlates moderately with transcendence-type measures from the Thematic Apperception Test (TAT) ($r = .35$, with "level of interpretation" that ranges from "rejection" of the picture with no story told to "complete narrative with interpretation of feelings, attitudes, and/or thoughts of characters").

2. There is a low but relatively consistent correlation of RIRS with measures of intelligence in both sexes (median $r = .21$ across twenty-one samples) and with need for achievement in males ($r = .36$).

3. Several studies reported by Levine and Spivak (1964) address validity in

Table 3. Correlates of Each Measure of Repression

RIRS	Repression and Isolation	Weinberger Repression
Prior results:	Prior results:	Prior results from marlowe-crown:
Lower level of interpretation (TAT), .35*	Greater leveling and lesser sharpening	Greater reaction times
Lower IQ (.21), 21 studies		Less expression of sexual and aggressive content
Anxiety[a]		More increase in spontaneous GSR
Questionnaires:[a]		More increases in heart rate
Welch's R		More EMG
Welch's Internal		Less self-report of anxiety
K Scale		Greater recognition of negative affect
Hy Denial		Greater use of stereotyped cues
Hanley's defensiveness		
F scale		
Bryne's R-S		
Greater field dependence		
Greater repression for hysterics		
Greater repression for psychosomatics		
Our results:	Our results:	
Less looking study 1:	Holzman Repression:	
Less scatter, −.73**	Lower anxiety, study 1a, −.33*	
Less recall sex content, study 1, −.69**	Older age of earliest memory, study 1a, .54**	
Less advancement of recall of sex pictures, study 1a, .34*	Older average age of earliest memories, study 1a, .58**	
Less hostility in session, study 2, .49**	Advancement of neutral pictures, study 1a, .37*	
More severity of first target symptom, study 2, .35*	Fewer embedded pictures, study 1a, −.43*	
Less emotional freedom, study 2, .33*	Fewer Rorschach responses, study 1a, −.52***	
Less in-therapy activity, study 2, .34*		
Lower WAIS IQ, study 2, .47**	Gardner Isolation:	
Lower performance IQ, study 3, .48*	Higher anxiety, study 1a, .33*	
	Advancement of sex pictures, study 1a, .33*	
	More embedded figures, study 1a, .45*	
	More Rorschach responses, study 1a, .39*	

Note: Study 1a is study 1 with cases added ($N = 24$). $N = 40$ for study 2 and 16 for study 3.
[a] Not correlated.
* $p < .05$. ** $p < .01$. *** $p < .001$.

Table 4. Correlates of Each Measure of Repression with Relationship Pattern Measures (CCRT Standard Categories)

RIRS	Holzman Repression and Isolation	Weinberger Repression[a]
	Repression:	Self-interpretation from RAP:
Movement scale with wish 8, to receive affection, study 2, −.34*	Wish 1, to assert, study 1a, −.55**	Wish 2, to dominate, study 3, .58*
Movement scale with negative response from others 5, criticism, study 2, .35*	Wish 17, to hurt others, study 1a, −.47*	Wish 10, to please others, study 3, −.49*
	Negative response from others 1, domination, study 1a, −.50*	Factor 2, to be competitive, study 3, .57*
	Positive response from others 9, affection, study 1a, .43*	
	Isolation:	Self-report:
	Negative response from others 1, domination, study 1a, .42*	Wish 2, to dominate, study 3, .67**
	Positive response from others 8, closeness, study 1a, −.48*	Wish 4, to win in competition, study 3, .51*
	Negative response from others 10, depression, study 1a, −.40	Wish 8, to receive affection, study 3, .52*
		Wish 14, to be treated fairly, study 3, .61*
		Wish 17, to hurt others, study 3, .63**
		Factor 2, to be competitive, study 3, .85***

[a]*The lower the Weinberger score, the more repressive.*
*$p < .05$.
**$p < .01$.
***$p < .001$.

terms of the extent to which the RIRS relates to questionnaire measures of anxiety. Levine and Spivak report on the results of data that they obtained from other investigators in which they found that the RIRS is not significantly related to the Taylor Manifest Anxiety Scale (MAS) scale, the Cattell Institute Ability and Personality Testing (IPAT) Anxiety Scale, or the Sarason Test Anxiety Scale.

4. A number of measures from the Minnesota Multiphasis Personality Inventory (MMPI) that purport to assess repression or a similar dimension were

not significantly correlated with the RIRS. Nonsignificant findings were obtained for Welsh's R scale, Welsh's internalization ratio, the K scale, the admission scale of the Hy, the denial scale of the Hy, Hanley's defensiveness scale, the F scale, and the repression-sensitization scale.

5. Positive results were obtained when the relation between the RIRS and cognitive styles was examined and when sex differences were examined. Subjects with a repressive style tended to be field dependent; that is, they depended for their orientation on the "field." The results of a large number of studies on sex differences are interpreted by Levine and Spivak (1964) as follows:

> In general, the most clear-cut sex differences in the correlates of RIRS are observed in the comparison of the high males and the high females. The high RIRS (non-repressive style) female seems to admit to personal problems, worries and concerns. She reveals a large discrepancy between her view of an ideal self and her conscious self image. She readily reports dreams, many of which probably have anxious content. Her interests are not well defined, and in a decision-making situation she is prone to form rapid, extreme opinions.
>
> In contrast, the high RIRS (non-repressive style) male appears to have few personal worries and concerns. His image of an ideal self is more congruent with his image of himself. He apparently dreams less, or at least recalls fewer dreams, and this may relate to the fact that dreams frequently have anxious components. His current interests seem rather well defined, and his opinions or judgements tend to be deliberate. [110]

6. The clinical validity of the RIRS was studied by Levine and Spivak (1964) by examining RIRS scores in a variety of patient populations. As predicted by the investigators, "textbook" hysterics were found to score lower (more repressive) on the RIRS than "textbook" obsessive-compulsives. This comparison, however, was confounded by sex, as all the hysterics were female and all the obsessive-compulsives were male. Some other important findings were that neurotics were more repressed (median RIRS = 2.56) than normals (median RIRS = 3.28) and that psychosomatic patients had particularly low scores. Thus, the RIRS seems to yield information that is consistent with clinical experience.

Holzman Rorschach Measure of Repression

The Holzman method (Gardner et al. 1959) has the advantage over other methods of estimating repressive defenses of being closest to one clinical definition of these defenses. The judge looks for evidence of repression and isolation in the Rorschach and then rates the degree of each defense. These defenses do not appear directly in the Rorschach; however, if a person has depended on a particular defense for many years, certain characterologic and thought-organizational qualities are apt to be present. For example, a person who has utilized repression is apt to show "constriction of ideation, absence of intellectualizing, unreflectiveness, naivete, relatively unmodulated affect" (Gardner et al 1959, 130). The specific ways in which these qualities might appear in a Rorschach are listed in Gardner et al. (1959, 130–36): (*a*) expressive and phobic verbalization, (*b*) lack of specificity, (*c*) failures, (*d*) poor integrative efforts, (*e*) childlike material, (*f*) symbolic content without awareness of its significance, (*g*) little variety of content, (*h*) fewer than twenty-five responses, (*i*) fewer than two M's (movement response), and (*j*) emphasis on color.

The defense of isolation has been given less space in the psychoanalytic literature than repression. "Isolation" is usually taken to mean the tendency to separate affect from idea since the concomitance and interconnection of both in consciousness might create intolerable anxiety. Habitual use of isolation might show up in "excessive emphasis on operations of logic, attentiveness to spatial and temporal attributes of objects . . . ; similar qualities appear in isolators' relationships with people" (Gardner et al. 1959, 133). (Specific criteria listed by Gardner et al. are mainly the opposites of those listed for repression plus rumination about symmetry, intellectualizing, and high F + %.) Repression and isolation are supposed to have opposite effects, awareness being narrowed by repression and broadened by isolation, according to Schafer (1948).

Reliability

Gardner et al. (1959) did not provide the usual data on reliability. Two judges pooled their judgments into a single decision on each subject and then concentrated their analyses on those subjects who, by judges' agreement, showed reliance on repression and isolation. In Luborsky et al. (1965), we obtained for all subjects (rather than only for extreme agreed-on repressors vs. isolators) a rating on a five-point scale for degree of reliance on each defense. Before committing ourselves to this method of judging defense, we borrowed a sample of twenty-six cases from Gardner and had them rated blindly by J. Schimek using the Gardner scoring system. The results showed high agreement between the Schimek and the Gardner et al. ratings. A 4 × 4 table for the Gardner et al. versus the Schimek classification into repressors versus isolators gave a chi-square of 23.8, $p < .01$.

Validity

The main measure tried was the schematizing test that measures leveling-sharpening. "Leveling" refers to the tendency to be influenced in the size estimation task in judgments of relative size by the size of the squares seen earlier; "sharpening" refers to the tendency not to be so influenced (Gardner

et al. 1959). Repressors tend to be levelers—the trend does not reach significance for men, but it does for women.

Weinberger Questionnaire Measure of Repression

We will lead up to the description of the Weinberger measure (table 2) by
tracing the measures on which his were built. The most widely known pencil-
and-paper measure is the Byrne (1961) Repression-Sensitization (R-S) Scale.
However, this measure has been found to correlate highly with trait anxiety
measures such as the Taylor MAS, the Cattell IPAT Anxiety Scale, and the
Eysenck Neuroticism Scale. For example, Golin et al. (1967) report a .87
correlation between the MAS and the Byrne R-S Scale and conclude that these
scales do not measure different attributes. Byrne's scale, as do trait anxiety
scales, correctly identifies high-anxious persons (sensitizers) but fails to discriminate between truly low-anxious persons and persons who do not report
anxiety because of a repressive coping style.

Weinberger, Schwartz, and Davidson (1979) have argued that the Marlowe-
Crowne Social Desirability Scale (Crowne and Marlowe 1964) can be used to
discriminate the truly low-anxious person from the repressor. The Marlowe-
Crowne Scale is a standardized, reliable measure that appears to measure defensiveness (see Crowne and Marlowe 1964; Weinberger, Schwartz, and Davidson 1979) and is unrelated to the construct that it is usually thought to
assess, namely, the tendency to respond to questionnaires in a socially desirable direction. What is important is that the Marlowe-Crowne Scale is fairly
independent from the dimension measured by trait anxiety scales (correlations
range from −.2 to −.45).

Weinberger, Schwartz, and Davidson (1979) proposed that, using the
Marlowe-Crowne Scale and a trait anxiety scale such as the MAS, a 2 × 2
table can be constructed consisting of the following four groups: (1) repressors (low MAS, high defensiveness), (2) low anxious (low MAS, low defensiveness), (3) high anxious (high MAS, low defensiveness), and (4) defensive
high anxious (high MAS, high defensiveness). Using a phrase association
task, Weinberger, Schwartz, and Davidson (1979) found that repressors had
significantly longer reaction times, greater verbal avoidance to affective (sexual, aggressive) material, greater increases in spontaneous skin resistance responses, heart rate, and frontalis electromyographic activity during the task,
and lower self-reports of trait anxiety than a low-anxious group. With all measures, the average responses of the repressors were equal to or greater than a
high-anxious group.

Further research (chap. 14 in this volume) has indicated that the four groups
differ in their pattern of self-report of different emotional responses to norma-

Table 5. Intercorrelations of the RIRS Subscales and the RIRS (Study 2)

	RIRS	Movement	Specificity	Elaboration	Impulse Responses	Primary Process
Movement	.75***					
Specificity	.84***	.69**				
Elaboration	.91***	.61***	.64***			
Impulse response	.57***	.36*	.45**	.37*		
Primary process	.76***	.50***	.58***	.66***	.43**	
Self-references	.50***	.07	.19	.56***	.14	.47**

[a]*The lower the Weinberger score, the more repressive.*
*$p < .05$.
**$p < .01$.
***$p < .001$.

tive situations. In particular, repressors were found to have an overall deficit in the recognition of consensually appropriate negative affect relative to low-anxious subjects, while high-anxious and defensive high-anxious groups were relatively sensitized across emotions (happiness, sadness, depression, anger, fear, and anxiety). Repressors were also found to rely more heavily on stereotyped situational cues in their self-reports and were particularly deficient in the recognition of subtle contributions of non–situationally dominant emotions—for example, they failed to recognize elements of anger and anxiety in overall reactions to predominantly sad or depressing situations.

On the basis of this research, Weinberger subsequently developed a twelve-item measure of repressive style (table 2)—the "Repressive Restraint" Scale of the Weinberger Adjustment Inventory (the scale remains unpublished). This new measure was employed in our study 3 to be described. Note that, the lower the score, the more repressive. (For further details on Weinberger's current approach, see his chapter in this volume.)

Intercorrelations within and across Defensive Style Measures

Intercorrelations among Subscales in the RIRS

The intercorrelations among subscales of defensive style measures will indicate the degree to which the measure demonstrates internal consistency. We have scores on the RIRS subscales in study 2 and in study 3. Table 5 presents the intercorrelations from study 2. In the data from both studies, we see that Levine and Spivak (1964) were successful in making a measure with high intercorrelation among its components, although Levine and Spivak them-

Table 6. Intercorrelations of Different Repressive Style Measures

A. Studies 1 and 1a	RIRS
Holzman Repression	$-.54*$ $(N = 16)$
	$-.23$ $(N = 41)$
Holzman Isolation	$.58*$ $(N = 16)$
	$.48**$ $(N = 41)$

B. Study 3	RIRS
Weinberger	$-.05$ $(N = 19)$

$*p < .05.$
$**p < .01.$

selves do not report such intercorrelations.[1] Furthermore, there is a similar pattern of intercorrelations within each of our two studies. In both, the highest correlations of the subscales with the total RIRS score are for elaboration and specificity, and among the lowest is self-reference.

Intercorrelations across the Repressive Style Measures

Intercorrelations across these measures are to be taken as a sign that they may be measuring the same quality. Since they are referred to by similar labels, we would expect that they would show at least a moderate level of correlation. In fact, the three measures of repressive style are sometimes poorly correlated or uncorrelated with each other (table 6). Although the RIRS in study 1 has a significant correlation with the Holzman Repression measure (.54, $p < .05$), this virtually vanishes (.23) when the study is enlarged (study 1a, $N = 41$). However, the correlations of Holzman Isolaters with RIRS are maintained. In study 3, the RIRS is not correlated with the Weinberger measure ($-.05$).

Measures of Central Relationship Patterns

A relationship schema is a person's abstract knowledge structure about the conduct of his or her relationships. The Core Conflictual Relationship Theme (CCRT) method (Luborsky 1984; Luborsky and Crits-Christoph, in press) was applied within each study as the main measure of relationship schemas.

1. All results that we present are for the standard RIRS after it is corrected for number of responses. Further research should explore the value of number of Rorschach responses to measures of repression because we have some indications that number of responses makes a contribution.

The CCRT is a reliable measure of the central relationship pattern as revealed in a series of narratives (Crits-Christoph et al., 1988). The narratives are scored in three components: (1) the wishes, needs, and intentions of the teller of the narrative; (2) the responses of the other person; and (3) the responses of the teller of the narrative. The CCRT reflects the highest frequencies of each type of component. In its usual tailor-made form, the judge searches for a set of types of components that best fit the person; in the ready-made (or standard) categories format, the judge uses a standard list of categories. The CCRT method began with the use of narratives that are spontaneously told during psychotherapy; more recently, a special Relationship Anecdotes Paradigms (RAP) interview has been constructed for eliciting narratives. In study 1, the CCRT was based on three early memories written by each subject and scored by two independent CCRT judges. In study 2, it was based on ten narratives per patient drawn from psychotherapy sessions 3 and 5 and scored by three independent CCRT judges. In study 3, it was based on ten RAP interview narratives per patient and scored by two independent judges.

In all three studies, after the tailor-made CCRT was done the scores were translated by a judge into a set of standard CCRT categories (Luborsky 1985). Standard categories rather than individual tailor-made ones were used as an aid in determining the judges' agreement with each other. Our small-scale reliability studies (Luborsky, Crits-Christoph, and Mellon 1986) suggest satisfactory reliability, and a larger-scale reliability study has shown good reliability (Crits-Christoph et al., 1988). Examples of categories for the wishes, for the responses from others and for the responses from the self are given in the Appendix, and current lists will be provided on request.

Results, Part 1: Correlates of Repressive Style Measures

The examination of correlates is a necessary way to understand each measure. These results are presented in three main sections; each one gives the correlates of repressive style in one of the three studies. Presentation of the results study by study is necessary since, although the RIRS and the CCRT measures of relationship schemas run through all three studies, the samples of subjects and patients are different and some additional measures are offered in each study.

Our hypotheses, made before the results were available, were general and speculative since very little is known about the correlates of relationship schemas. The most general hypothesis was that, since defensive style has such major implications for personality, it should show up in the larger concept of relationship schemas. One specific speculative hypothesis was that relationship schemas involving wishes for love, closeness, and affection would be characteristic of a repressive style as measured by the RIRS while competi-

Table 7. Correlations of Defense Ratings with Measures of Looking

Measure	Repression		Isolation: Holzman Isolation
	Holzman Repression	RIRS	
"Ground score"	−.23	−.12	.55*
Dispersion from center	.00	−.32	.17
Scatter (cells covered)	−.13	−.70**	.40
Scatter per fixation	−.45	−.62**	.51*
Track length	−.37	−.61**	.51*
Duration per fixation	−.19	−.14	.02

Note: $N = 16$.
*$p < .05$.
**$p < .01$.

tiveness and domination are wishes that would be more characteristic of an isolative style. We also expected that some of the major measures of repression would have some degree of correlation with each other. In the following sections, we present results on the correlates of the repressive style measures.

Correlates of repressive Style in the Study 1

Looking Behavior

In their ten-second inspections of each of the ten pictures, the sixteen subjects showed a style that was related to their defensive style. (1) This relationship is summed up in a main trend (table 7): the more repressive the style, the less looking about; the less repressive (the more isolative) the style, the more looking about. One measure of looking about is the scatter of eye fixations around the picture (cells covered), which correlates $-.70$ ($p < .01$) with RIRS. (2) The trend is stronger for the threatening pictures, but it is not confined to them. Two of the three sexual pictures, numbers 4 (TAT 13MF) and 9, most clearly fit the trend. (3) The time spent looking at specific parts of pictures may be different. For example, the repressors may look less at the specific sexual contents of each picture. The example in figure 1 shows two subjects' looking patterns for a sexual picture.[2] The isolator subject spent considerable time looking at the woman's breast, while the repressor spent no time looking at the breast, except for a very peripheral part of it. The repressor in the example spent more time looking at the person's face. Generally, time spent looking at faces may differ between repressors and isolaters, which is consistent with Witkin et al.'s (1954) findings for field dependents versus field independents.

2. Each circle represents a photograph of an eye fixation. The number in the circle is the number of one-sixteenth-second units for the length of the fixation (each frame of film was one-sixteenth of a second).

Mrs. R.'s fixations
(High Repression)

Miss I.'s fixations
(High Isolation)

	Mrs. R.	Miss I.
"Ground" score (sec.)	0.06	0.62
Dispersion from center	0.07	0.31
Scatter	7.00	19.00
Scatter per fixation	0.41	0.59
Track length (mean in mm.)	29.50	38.10
Duration per fixation (mean in sec.)	0.68	0.28
% Sexual items recalled	picture forgotten	100.00
GSR (Rank within each S's 10 pictures)	2.00	3.00

Fig. 1. Illustration and sample scores of two women's looking behavior on picture 7. The illustration is a sketch of the photograph used as the stimulus. Circled numbers denote position and number of frames of film for each fixation.

Table 8. Correlations of Defense Ratings and Recall Measures

Recall Measures, Number Recalled, Each Type Item	Repression		Isolation: Holzman Isolation
	Holzman Repression	RIRS	
Sexual	−.42 (−.63**)	−.62** (−.69**)	.58* (.70**)
Aggressive	−.25 (.14)	−.04 (.10)	.18 (−.02)
Neutral	−.36 (−.35)	−.27 (−.27)	.34 (.34)
Total	−.42 (−.48*)	−.34 (−.25)	.43 (.40)

Note: $N = 16$.
*$p < .05$.
**$p < .01$.

Memory Behavior

From clinical descriptions of repression and isolation, we expected that the repressors would have a harder time recalling the pictures, especially the sexual pictures. This is exactly what appeared in the results (table 8): (1) amount recalled of all pictures is opposite in direction for repression versus isolation but does not reach significance; (2) sexual items alone correlate significantly positively with isolation and significantly negatively with repression; and (3) when the sexual items are slightly weighted in terms of the degree of sexual emphasis in their content (by independent estimates), all the correlations with defense measures are increased. In addition, not looking around much is correlated with not recalling much. Therefore, repressive style appears to express itself in terms of restriction in recall.

Galvanic Skin Response (GSR) and Heart Rate Behavior

The definition of RIRS includes the restriction of verbal expressions of feelings by repressive defenses. Yet, for these people, the psychophysiological arousal may be larger than for isolators. We expected, therefore, that the repressors might show greater GSR response than the isolators to the sexual pictures and less response to the neutral pictures. The evidence for this, taking all pictures as a whole, is not consistent, but an earlier report (Luborsky et al. 1963) shows differences in looking and recall measures for the two pictures with the highest GSR and the two pictures with the lowest GSR for each person. Our interpretation of these differences was that high GSR is associated with avoidance behavior. Taking the differences for four of these measures and combining them by converting them to z-scores yields a sum that can be correlated with defense scores. The hypothesis is that, the higher the z-score, the greater the repression. What emerges is that repression (RIRS) correlates −.48 (which just misses significance).

Other Variables

The RIRS correlates with few of the additional measures in study 1a (table 3). It correlates only with (1) Holzman Isolation (.48, $p < .01$) in the expected opposite direction and (2) with advancement-postponement of recall of the sexual pictures (.34, $p < .05$) (a higher score means more advancement in order of recall, i.e., recalled earlier than the order in which they had been presented). This means that, the higher the RIRS score, the more the isolation and the more the advancement of sexual pictures in recall order. The RIRS correlates only −.23 with Holzman Repression scores (not significant) and .49 ($p < .01$) with the Holzman Isolation score. (By contrast, the uncorrected RIRS correlates with many more measures.) In study 1, the RIRS correlates .54 ($p < .05$) with the Holzman Repression measure.

By contrast, the Holzman Repression measure does better in number of significant correlates (study 1a; table 3). For example, high Holzman Repression goes with low anxiety (−.33, $p < .05$), older age of the earliest memory (.54, $p < .01$), older age of the average of three early memories (.58, $p < .01$), greater advancement-postponement of recall of neutral pictures (.37, $p < .05$), fewer embedded figures discerned (−.43, $p < .05$), less wish to assert (−.55, $p < .01$), less wish to hurt (−.47, $p < .05$), less negative response from other (domination −.50, $p < .05$), more positive response from other (affection: .43, $p < .05$), and fewer responses in the Rorschach (−.52, $p < .001$).

The finding about the age of earliest memories deserves a note here about a somewhat parallel finding. Davis (1987) found that repressors (defined in terms of response on an anxiety scale and a social desirability scale, in the manner of Weinberger repression) recalled fewer negative childhood experiences. Our measure, in contrast, used all memories rather than only the negative ones.

Correlates of Defensive Style in Study 2

Pretreatment Process and Outcome Measures

A broad range of treatment-related measures was examined to see whether a pattern emerges in the types of correlates with the RIRS. We correlated the RIRS with fifty-six patient and treatment variables. Three of the correlations were significant at the .05 level or better, with one marginal. The three correlations in order from highest to lowest in terms of the size of the correlation (table 3) are as follows. Greater repressive style was associated with lower hostility expressed in sessions (.49, $p < .01$), lower Wechsler Adult Intelligence Scale (WAIS) IQ (.47, $p < .01$), and more self-rated severity of the first target symptom (.35, $p < .05$). Less emotional freedom (.33, $p < .05$) was marginally significant. (Less "activity" of the patient as judged from his or her sessions [.34, $p < .05$], fewer social assets [.33], and lower educational level [.31] were close to but not significant.) The general pattern that emerges is that, the more repressed on the RIRS, the more restricted and less expressive the person is (lower hostility expressed and less emotional freedom). This pattern also involves greater restriction in terms of intelligence as well as a higher level of self-rated severity of symptoms.

RIRS and Subscale Correlations with CCRT Standard Categories

These are correlations between the RIRS subscale scores with presence versus absence in the patient's narratives of several standard categories of wishes, responses from others (ROs), and responses of self (RSs) (table 4).

First, it is of interest that RIRS, either corrected or uncorrected for number of responses, has no significant correlations with standard category wishes or responses from others. Second, a few of the RIRS subscales correlate with the CCRT categories—for example, .35—with response from others of rejection and criticism. Less repression (based on the specificity score and the impulse score) is associated with responses from others of rejection and criticism. In general, although there are only a few significant correlations, their direction is consistent with what we have found in this and other studies.

Correlates of Defensive Style in Study 3

Relationship Patterns from the RAP Narratives

These twenty patients took part in our study comparing the perspective of patients to that of clinicians in the assessment of relationship themes (Crits-Christoph and Luborsky, in press). Three main measures were included in the assessment: (1) a newly developed self-report CCRT questionnaire (SR-CCRT; Crits-Christoph 1986), in which subjects rated (on a five-point scale) how typical each of a number of wishes and responses were in their relationships; (2) a self-interpretation (SI-CCRT) of the RAP interview (Luborsky 1978);[3] and (3) a standard CCRT scored by clinical judges from the RAP interview.

3. In the RAP interview, the subjects tell ten anecdotes of specific interactions with other people. The interaction in each anecdote is with a significant other person such as a parent, a friend, or a lover. For each narrative, subjects are asked to rate a set of wishes and responses on the degree to which the wishes and responses apply to their behavior in the narrative. Subjects are also asked to describe the conflicts, if any, that were present in each narrative.

Results

Only the results for the wishes, and not for the responses, are included. The wishes were rated by sixteen patients as part of their self-interpretation of the RAP narratives. (Note that, when clinicians identified a wish, the patient tended to have included the wish in the patient's self-interpretation.) These ratings were correlated with the two main defense measures available in study 3, the RIRS and the Weinberger measure of repression.

As mentioned earlier, our two main defensive style measures, RIRS and Weinberger in study 3, do not correlate significantly with each other ($-.05$), even though they are labeled in a way that would lead one to expect to find a correlation. Although the Weinberger measure of repression does not correlate with the total RIRS, we decided to explore whether it might correlate with the seven scales of the RIRS. None were significant. Knowing this fact, it is less of a surprise that the correlates of the Weinberger and of the RIRS are somewhat different.

The relationship pattern correlates of the Weinberger were the following (table 4): the more repressive, the less the rated wish (on the self-interpretation) to dominate ($.58, p < .05$) and the more repressive the more the rated wish to please others ($-.49, p < .05$). When the wishes are combined into three higher-order factors (to be close, to be competitive, and to be independent), the only significant correlation was for the Weinberger—the more repressive, the lower the competitive wishes ($.57, p < .05$).

The SR-CCRT measure had some similar correlates with the Weinberger (table 4)—for example, the less repressive, the more the wish to dominate ($.67, p < .01$) and the less repressive, the more the higher-order factor 2, to be competitive ($.85, p < .001$).

The patients' ratings of their own wishes as part of the self-interpretation of the RAP were also correlated with the seven scales of the RIRS. Three of these showed significant correlations: movement responses, specific responses, and elaborated responses. For example, the more repressive style patients had fewer of these specific responses and more of the wish for sexual gratification ($-.51, p < .05$); the fewer of these specific responses, the more the wish to win the affection or attention of another over someone else (i.e., an oedipal wish).

Results, Part 2: Correlates of Repression-related Behaviors

Certain correlates will be further examined because they have a special interest in their own right for offering assistance in validating existing repressive style measures. In addition, these are measures of memory that may be especially sensitive to repression effects. Each of them has an appealing surface

Table 9. Correlations of Advancement-Postponement in Recall Order with Other Variables (Study 1a)

	Advancement of Neutral Pictures	Advancement of Sexual Pictures	Advancement of Aggressive Pictures
Holzman Repression	.37*	. . .	. . .
Holzman Isolation	. . .	.33*	. . .
Later age of early memory	. . .	−.41*	. . .
Average age of earliest memory	. . .	−.40*	. . .
RIRS	. . .	.34*	. . .
Total number of embedded figures	. . .	.37	. . .
Guilford-Z, G	. . .	.43*	. . .
Guilford-Z, O	. . .	. . .	−.52*
Wish 8, to receive affection	.41*	.43*	. . .
Wish 17, to hurt others	−.43*	. . .	. . .
Negative response from others 5, criticism	. . .	. . .	.51*
Negative response from self 6, rejection	. . .	. . .	.48*

*$p < .05$.

appearance of behavioral simplicity, although that does not mean they are really simple. The two to be examined here are (1) advancement-postponement in recall order (the higher the score, the more the picture is advanced, i.e., recalled earlier) for each of the three types of pictures, sexual, aggressive, and neutral, and (2) the age of the earliest memory (and the average age of the three earliest memories).

The "simple" behavioral measure, advancement in recall order, provides another set of repression-consistent correlates (table 9): for example, RIRS (.34, $p < .05$) and Holzman Isolation ($-.33$, $p < .05$). Another of these "simple" behavioral measures (table 10) is the subject's age for the average of the three earliest memories. It correlated .58 ($p < .001$) with the Holzman Repression measure, which implies that, the more Holzman Repression, the later the age of the early memories. Age of earliest memories also correlated $-.40$ ($p < .05$) with the advancement in recall order of the sexual pictures (meaning, the less the sexual pictures are advanced in the recall order, i.e., are postponed, the later the age of the earliest memories), and greater anxiety about the sexual pictures (self-report) is associated with later age of the earliest memories (.44, $p < .05$).

Conclusions and Discussion

1. The repressive style measures we examined, especially the RIRS and the Weinberger Questionnaire method, have been shown by us and by others to

Table 10. Age of Earliest Memories (Study 1a)

	Memories	
	Earliest Age	Average Age
Holzman Repression	.54**	.58**
Awareness of experiment	.56**	.61**
Later average age of earliest memories	.89***	. . .
Advancement of sexual pictures	− .41*	− .40*
More embedded figures	− .48*	− .51*
Anxiety to sexual pictures	.43*	.44*
Anxiety for aggressive pictures	− .47*	− .42*
Wish, to assert	. . .	− .46*
Wish, freedom from domination	− .46*	. . .
Negative response from others, domination	. . .	− .48*
Negative response from self, anxiety	. . .	− .42*

Note: $N = 24$.
*$p < .05$.
**$p < .01$.
***$p < .001$.

be reliably measurable and to have other desirable psychometric properties. But they did not correlate with each other. At least a moderate correlation would have been expected because they are presented as measures of the same defense. In study 1a, the RIRS did not correlate with the Holzman Rorschach Measure of Repression. In study 3, the RIRS did not correlate significantly with the Weinberger repression measure. The necessary caveat, therefore, is to beware of choosing one measure of repression and assuming it to be representative of other measures of repression.

2. Although each of the measures has some meaningful correlates, their correlates differ somewhat. (*a*) The correlates of the RIRS imply that it is estimating a narrowing and a selective restricting of expression, especially of affective expression (tables 3 and 9). Especially noteworthy is the constriction of attention (less scatter of fixations, − .73, $p < .01$; less recall of sexual content, − .69, $p < .01$; and less advancement in recall, i.e., postponement of recall, of sexual pictures). (*b*) For the Holzman Rorschach Measure of repressive style, the items in it and its correlates suggest that it is estimating the continuum from more hysterical to less hysterical (tables 3 and 9). Especially noteworthy for this measure is the correlation of Gardner Isolation with advancement of recall order of the sexual pictures (.33). The novel measure tried with the Holzman Repression was the later age of earliest memories; the average age of these memories correlates .58, ($p < .01$). (*c*) As far as the Weinberger questionnaire method of repressive style is concerned (tables 4 and 9), its correlates suggest that it reflects the inclination to keep threatening ideas

out of awareness. It is a measure of denial of negative ideation or behavior, especially aggressive ideation or behavior, and a denial of not measuring up to very high standards of conduct.

These correlates of each measure appear to be consistent with different aspects of the concept of repression as Freud ([1915] 1957) summarized them in his description of "characteristics of repression." They constitute a variety of perspectives on the concept. A brief summary (from Freud [1915] 1957) of these follows in which at least six aspects within the concept are distinguished.

a) "The essence of repression lies simply in turning something away, and keeping it at a distance, from the conscious" (147). (It is this aspect that may be the takeoff point for the RIRS[4] and Weinberger.) In "primal repression," "psychical representation of the instincts are denied entrance into the conscious" (148). In "repression proper," it is derivatives of the repressed that are kept out of the conscious (148).

b) Ideas are not only forced out of but also drawn into the unconscious: "It is a mistake to emphasize only the repulsion which operates from the direction of the conscious upon what is to be repressed; quite as important is the attraction exercised by what was primarily repressed upon everything with which it can establish a connection" (148).

c) Every derivative of what is not conscious depends on its degree of distortion before it can become conscious: "Repression acts, therefore, in a highly individual manner. Every single derivative of the repressed may have their own special vicissitude; a little more or a little less distortion alters the whole outcome" (150). Other conditions besides distortion can circumvent repression. Freud lists two of these as humor and hypnosis (151).

d) Repression requires constant pressure to be maintained: "It is also exceedingly mobile. The process of repression is not to be regarded as an event which takes place once, the results of which are permanent. . . . the repressed exercises a continuous pressure in the direction of the conscious so that this pressure must be balanced by an unceasing counter-pressure" (151).

e) Two different categories exist for what may be repressed, the idea versus the affect. The first is "an idea or group of ideas." The second is affect, and "describing a case of repression we shall have to follow up separately what, as the result of repression becomes of the idea, and what becomes of the instinctual energy linked to it" (152) "It follows that the vicissitudes of the quota of affect belonging to the representative is far more important than the vicissitude of the idea" (153).

f) Hysterics are prone to repress ideas. Strachey points out "that the form

---

4. For example, in study 1, the correlates include the turning away of attention from aspects of the pictures, which is evident in both looking and recalling. This turning away is probably more than just a cognitive style because it involves turning away from the sexual content in both looking and recalling.

of repression which Freud had chiefly in mind here was that which occurs in hysteria" (144). Freud discusses repression as it applies to anxiety hysteria (155). It is this last aspect that may be the takeoff point for the Holzman measure of repression.

Further research is required to learn more about which measures are better in the sense that they tap into central aspects of the concept of repression or tap into concepts that are not repression.

3. Some progress has been made on the aim of examining the interrelations between measures of repressive style and relationship patterns. The results represent an inroad into a new area made more impassible by the limits of the measures of defenses. Nevertheless, there are a few impressive trends (table 4), although the level of the correlations is not high in general. Among these are the correlations of CCRT wishes in study 3, such as a .67 correlation of the Weinberger measure with "wish: dominance" (from the self-report) and a .85 correlation ($p < .001$) with "wish: to be competitive" (from the self-interpretation). This main trend means that Weinberger repressors tend to be low on wishes for dominance and competitiveness and high on wishes to receive affection. This is a significant trend that is also evident in study 1a for Holzman Repression and also to a limited extent in study 2. The trend is appealingly consistent with the much broader one posited by Bonanno and Singer (in this volume) of a dichotomy between preoccupation with relatedness and intimacy, which are associated with repression, and preoccupation with self-esteem and power, which are associated with sensitization or isolation.

This field of research now needs further work on new measures of repressive style involving the "here and now" operation of repression. In contrast, the RIRS measure and other measures probably reflect the chronic and generalized use of a repressive defense; these do not even come near to measuring a repressive defense at the moment of its operation. It must be admitted, however, that few existing measures can boast of having this capacity and that none of these measures have been included in the work so far. The few measures that may have a faint chance of qualifying as such a measure of the repression concept are (1) special content analysis methods for sessions (e.g., Weintraub and Aronson 1967), (2) the slip induction method (e.g., Baars 1987) combined with a word association method, and (3) the context for momentary forgetting instances during free association sessions (e.g., Luborsky, Sackeim, and Christoph 1979). Measures of this sort come closer to tapping the clinical concepts of current operations of defense, which is one of the virtues (according to Erdelyi 1985) of the clinical-quantitative in contrast with the laboratory approach.

Appendix

Examples of CCRT Standard Categories (Edition 1)

A. Wishes ("I want from the other person . . .")

1. To assert my independence and autonomy.
2. To dominate; to impose my will or control on others.
3. To overcome other's domination; to be free of obligations imposed by others; not to be put down.

B. Responses from Others ("The other person responds by . . .")

Negative	Positive
1. Dominating, controlling, interfering, intimidating, intruding	1. Supportive, reassuring
2. Unfair, exploiting, taking advantage	2. Treats fairly, respectful
3. Resentful, angry, irritated, hostile, violently aggressive	. . .

C. Responses of Self ("I become . . .")

Negative	Positive
1. Passive, submissive, dominated, compliant, deferential, controlled ("I give in to the power of other")	1. Assertive, express self assertively, gain control
2. Dependent	. . .
3. Helpless, less confident, ineffectual ("I do not know how to do things")	3. Gain self-esteem, feel affirmed, self-confident

References

Baars, B. 1987. *A cognitive theory of consciousness.* Cambridge: Cambridge University Press.

Byrne, D. 1961. The repression-sensitization scale: Rationale, reliability, and validity. *Journal of Personality* 29:334–49.

Crits-Christoph, P. 1986. Assessing conscious and unconscious aspects of relationship themes from self-report and naturalistic data. Paper presented at the MacArthur Workshop on Person Schemas, Palo Alto, Calif.

Crits-Christoph, P., and L. Luborsky. In press. The measurement of self-understanding: The congruence of the patient's understanding with the CCRT. In L. Luborsky and P. Crits-Christoph, *Understanding transference—the core conflictual relationship theme CCRT method.* New York: Basic Books.

Crits-Christoph, P., L. Luborsky, L. Dahl, C. Popp, J. Mellon, and D. Mark. 1988. Clinicians can agree in assessing relationship patterns in psychotherapy: The core conflictual relationship theme method. *Archives of General Psychiatry* 45:1001–4.

Crowne, D., and D. Marlow. 1964. *The approval motive: Studies in evaluative dependence.* New York: Wiley.

Davis, P. 1987. Repression and the inaccessibility of affective memories. *Journal of Personality and Social Psychology* 53:585–93.

Erdelyi, M. 1985. *Psychoanalysis: Freud's cognitive psychology.* New York: Freeman.

Freud, S. [1915] 1957. Repression. In *The standard edition of the complete psychological works of Sigmund Freud,* ed. J. Strachey, vol. 14, pp. 141–58. London: Hogarth.

Gardner, R., P. Holzman, G. Klein, H. Linton, and D. Spence. 1959. Cognitive control: A study of individual consistencies in cognitive behavior. *Psychological Issues* 4:1–186.

Golin, S., W. Herron, R. Lakota, and L. Reineck. 1964. Factor analytic study of the manifest anxiety, extraversion and repression-sensitization scales. *Journal of Consulting Psychology* 31:564–69.

Holzman, P. 1962. Repression and cognitive style. *Bulletin of the Menninger Clinic* 26:273–82.

Horowitz, M., ed. In press. Personal schemas and maladaptive interpersonal behavior patterns. Chicago: University Chicago Press.

Levine, M., and G. Spivak. 1963. The Rorschach index of ideational repression: Application to quantitative sequence analysis. *Journal of Projective Techniques* 27:73–78.

———. 1964. *The Rorschach Index of Repressive Style.* Springfield, Ill.: Thomas.

Luborsky, L. 1978. The self-interpretation of the Relationship Anecdotes Paradigms (RAP) interview. Department of Psychiatry, University of Pennsylvania. Typescript.

———. 1984. *Principles of psychoanalytic psychotherapy: A manual for supportive-expressive (SE) treatment.* New York: Basic Books.

———. 1985. A dictionary of standard categories for the CCRT. Department of Psychiatry, University of Pennsylvania. Edition 1. Typescript.

Luborsky, L., B. Blinder, and N. Mackworth. 1963. Eye fixation and recall of pictures as a function of GSR responsivity. Monograph Supplement 5–V16. *Perceptual and Motor Skills* 16:469–83.

Luborsky, L., B. Blinder, and J. Schimek. 1965. Looking, recalling, and GSR as a function of defense. *Journal of Abnormal Psychology* 70:270–80. (Also published in *Personality,* ed. R. S. Lazarus and E. M. Opton, 260–75. Harmondsworth: Penguin, 1967.)

Luborsky, L., and P. Crits-Christoph. In press. Understanding transference—the CCRT (the core conflictual relationship theme) method. New York: Basic Books.

Luborsky, L., P. Crits-Christoph, and J. Mellon. 1986. The advent of objective measures of the transference concept. *Journal of Consulting and Clinical Psychology* 54, no. 1:39–47.

Luborsky, L., J. Mintz, A. Auerbach, P. Christoph, H. Bachrach, T. Todd, M. Johnson, M. Cohen, and C. P. O'Brien. 1980. Predicting the outcomes of psychotherapy: Findings of the Penn psychotherapy project. *Archives of General Psychiatry* 37:471–81.

Luborsky, L., H. Sackeim, and P. Christoph. 1979. The state conducive to momentary forgetting. In *Functional disorders of memory,* ed. J. Kihlstrom and F. Evans, 325–53. Hillsdale, N.J.: Erlbaum.

Schafer, R. 1948. *The clinical application of psychological tests.* New York: International Universities Press.

Weinberger, D., and G. E. Schwartz. In preparation. Interactions of trait anxiety, defensiveness and situational determinants in self-reported patterns of differential emotion. Department of Psychology, Stanford University. Typescript.

Weinberger, D., G. Schwartz, and R. Davidson. 1979. Low-anxious, high-anxious and repressive coping styles: Psychometric patterns and behavioral and physiological responses to stress. *Journal of Abnormal Psychology* 88:369–80.

Weintraub, W., and H. Aronson. 1967. The application of verbal behavior analysis to the study of psychological defense mechanisms. IV. Speech patterns associated with depressive behavior. *Journal of Nervous and Mental Diseases* 144:22–28.

Witkin, H. A., H. B. Lewis, M. Hertzman, K. Machover, P. B. Meissner, and S. Wapner. 1954. *Personality through perception.* New York: Harper.

13 Interpersonal Relatedness and Self-Definition: Two Personality Configurations and Their Implications for Psychopathology and Psychotherapy

SIDNEY J. BLATT

The basic assumption of this chapter is that a relative emphasis on either interpersonal relatedness or self-definition defines two broad character or personality types that in the extreme also define two broad configurations of psychopathology. Psychological defenses are an integral part of character style, and, therefore, defenses can also be differentiated into two broad types. Individuals predominantly invested in interpersonal relatedness at the relative neglect of self-definition utilize primarily avoidant defenses (e.g., denial and repression), while individuals predominantly invested in self-definition at the relative neglect of relatedness utilize counteractive defenses (e.g., projection, intellectualization, reaction formation, and overcompensation). The purpose of this chapter is to discuss these two broad character or personality styles and their inherent modes of defense and to demonstrate how these differentiations have important implications for clinical research—especially for the study of depression and therapeutic change.

Personality development occurs as a consequence of a complex transaction of two fundamental developmental lines: (1) the development of the capacity to establish increasingly mature and satisfying interpersonal relationships and (2) the development of a consolidated, realistic, essentially positive, increasingly differentiated and integrated self-definition and identity. These two developmental lines normally evolve throughout the life cycle in a complex dialectic transaction. An increasingly differentiated, integrated, and mature sense of self is contingent on establishing satisfying interpersonal experiences, and, conversely, the continued development of increasingly mature and satisfying interpersonal relationships is contingent on the development of more mature self-definition and identity. Meaningful and satisfying relationships contribute to the evolving concept of the self, and a new sense of self leads, in turn, to more mature levels of interpersonal relatedness. In normal personality development, these two developmental processes evolve in an interactive, recipro-

The author is indebted to Carrie Schaffer for her comments on an earlier version of this chapter.

cally balanced, mutually facilitating fashion from birth through senescence (Blatt and Shichman 1983).

Numerous personality theorists, using a variety of different terms, have discussed interpersonal relatedness and self-definition (or attachment and individuation) as two central processes in personality development. Angyal (1941, 1951) discussed surrender and autonomy as two basic personality dispositions. For Angyal (1951), surrender is the desire to seek a home, to become part of something greater than oneself, while autonomy represents a "striving basically to assert and to expand . . . self-determination, [to be] an autonomous being, a self-governing entity that asserts itself actively instead of reacting passively. . . . This tendency . . . expresses itself in spontaneity, self-assertiveness, striving for freedom and for mastery" (131–32). Bakan (1966), in a conceptualization similar to Angyal's, defined "communion" and "agency" as two fundamental dimensions in personality development. Communion for Bakan (1966) is a loss of self and self-consciousness in a merging and blending with others and the world. It involves feeling a part of and participating in a larger social entity, of being at one with others, of feeling in contact or union, and of experiencing a sense of openness, cooperation, love, and eros. "Agency," in contrast, defines a pressure toward individuation that Bakan believed permeates all living matter. It emphasizes being a separate individual and being able to tolerate isolation, alienation, and being alone. The predominant themes in agency are self-protection, self-assertion, self-expansion, and an urge to master the environment and make it one's own. The basic issues are separation and mastery.

Bakan's communion and Angyal's surrender both define a fundamental desire for union in which the person seeks to merge or join with other people and with the inanimate environment as well as to achieve a greater sense of integration and synthesis. "Surrender" and "communion" refer to a stable dimension of personality organization directed toward interdependent relationships with other people and things. Themes of dependency, mutuality, and unity define a basic dimension in life.

Bakan's "agency" and Angyal's "autonomy" both define a basic striving toward individuation—a seeking of separation from others and from an attachment to the physical environment as well as of a fuller differentiation within oneself. "Agency" and "autonomy" both refer to a stable dimension of functioning that emphasizes separation, individuation, control, self-definition, and autonomous achievement—the striving for uniqueness and the expression of one's capacities and self-interests (Friedman and Booth-Kewley 1987). Communion (or surrender)—the emphasis on connectedness, attachment, and a movement toward a sense of belongingness to and sharing with others (another person, group, or society)—serves as a counterforce to experiences of loneliness and alienation that can occur in agency and autonomy.

Conversely, uniqueness and self-definition serve as a counterforce to experiences of a loss of individuality that can occur in surrender and communion.

Although there is no known citation for the comment, Freud made a distinction similar to the difference between relatedness and self-definition in his often-quoted statement that the two major tasks of life are "to love and to work." Freud ([1926] 1959) also distinguished between libidinal instincts in the service of attachment and relatedness and aggressive instincts necessary for self-definition, autonomy, and mastery. Bowlby (1969, 1973) explored these two groups of instincts, libido and aggression—how they create the emotional substrate for human personality and are expressed in strivings for attachment and separation. Michael Balint (1959), from an object relations perspective, also discussed the centrality of two fundamental tendencies in personality development—a tendency for clinging or connectedness ("ocnophilic tendencies") and a free-moving tendency toward self-sufficiency ("philobatic tendencies"). Shor and Sanville (1978), on the basis of Balint's formulations, discuss psychological development as oscillating between "necessary connectedness" and "inevitable separations," an oscillation between "intimacy" and "autonomy." Karen Horney (1945, 1950) also characterized personality as either moving toward, moving against, or moving away from contact. Gilligan (1982), in a similar fashion, noted the importance of including an emphasis on interpersonal responsibility in formulations of moral development as well as an emphasis on investment in rights and principles of justice.

Other investigators from a variety of theoretical perspectives have also discussed two similar dimensions in personality development such as the importance of motives for affiliation (or intimacy) (e.g. McAdams 1980) and achievement (e.g., McClelland et al. 1953; McClelland 1980, 1986) or power (Winter 1973). McAdams (1985) discussed extensively the interplay between power and intimacy in personality organization. In a series of studies of life narratives, he found two central themes or dominant clusters in his research: (1) themes of intimacy (such as feeling close, warm, and in communication with others) and (2) themes of power (such as feeling strong and of having a significant effect on one's environment). Individuals high on intimacy motivation spoke frequently of reciprocal harmonious interpersonal interactions and participation in social groups. McAdams defined this intimacy motive as a "recurrent preference or readiness for experiences of warmth, closeness and communicative exchange" (76). Individuals high on this motive often portrayed themselves as a helper, lover, counselor, caregiver, and friend. In contrast, people high on power motivation spoke frequently of self-protection, self-assertion, and self-expansion. They separate themselves from a context and express needs for mastery, achievement, movement, force, and action. McAdams defined this power motive as "a recurrent preference or readiness for experiences of having impact and feeling strong and potent vis-à-vis the environment" (84). Individuals high on the power motive often spoke of themselves as a traveler, master, father, authority, or sage. Spiegel and Spiegel (1978) also discuss the importance of these two fundamental dimensions of intimacy and power (McAdams), communion and agency (Bakan), or surrender and autonomy (Angyal), and they draw a parallel between these two personality dimensions and two fundamental natural forces—fusion and fission or integration and differentiation.

There is considerable consensus, from a number of theoretical perspectives, that normal personality organization involves an integration of two basic dimensions: a capacity for interpersonal relatedness and the development of self-definition (Stewart and Malley 1987). Angyal (1951), like Bakan, stressed that the major task in life is to achieve a compromise and balance between these two autonomous forces in which both are represented fully in one's experiences. Increased autonomy, mastery, and a capacity to govern one's life and environment are best achieved not by force or violence but by understanding and respect for laws and rules of the social matrix, attitudes toward society similar to those involved in forming loving relationships. Similarly, not only does a loving relationship require a capacity for relinquishing one's autonomy and agency to some degree, but it also requires a capacity for mastery of one's environment, resourcefulness, and self-reliance, without which a relationship is in danger of deteriorating into helpless dependency, exploitation, and possessiveness. Both Angyal and Bakan emphasize the simultaneous need for differentiation as well as integration and for establishing a constructive resolution of these opposing polarities. Kobassa (1982) also discusses the importance of a blend of communion and agency, of intimacy and power needs (of surrender and autonomy), as central to the development of psychological well-being and hardiness. McAdams (1985) found that an integration of power and intimacy motivation in Thematic Apperception Test (TAT) stories was correlated with a capacity to portray constructive action scripts that are future oriented and high on generativity. Power and intimacy are integrated by establishing a clear agentic sense of self and also by dedicating and devoting oneself to establishing intimate exchange with others. According to Erikson (1974, 27–28), "A mature sense of identity means a sense of being at one with oneself as one grows and develops; and it means, at the same time, a sense of affinity with a community's sense of being at one with its future as well as its history—or mythology." A mature identity for McAdams (1985, 28) is based on a sense of "sameness and continuity which provides unity and purpose", it requires both individuation and connectedness, an integration of identity formation and interdependence, a continuity, and a separation from one's past and one's environment as well as a sense of the future and the capacity to establish new connections.

Bakan discussed the importance of a dynamic tension between agency and communion, between surrender and autonomy. Shor and Sanville (1978) similarly discuss personality development as "oscillating between the necessary connectedness and the inevitable separateness. The pace and style of oscillation and the transitions between these two axes will vary for each person and map out his particular life history, his individual pattern of growth" (121). Shor and Sanville view personality development "as a dialectical spiral or helix which interweaves the two dimensions of development, intimacy and autonomy." They view the emergence of the capacity for adult intimacy—the capacity to love—as a product of two persistent dimensions and "of an intense search to formulate one's individual identity and, once having formed it, to risk to suspend concern with oneself while focusing on the qualities of a potential mate" (126).

The importance of the interplay of interpersonal relatedness and self-definition in normal development is also seen in the developmental psychoanalytic formulations of Margaret Mahler and her colleagues and in the work of Daniel Stern. Stern (1985) presents a theory of the development of a sense of self but does so through describing the child's emerging relatedness with its caring agents, with whom he or she develops a sense of empathy and intersubjectivity. Mahler, Pine, and Bergman (1975) discuss the development of object relations (e.g., the development of object constancy), but they do so by describing the process of separation-individuation in developmental periods of separation, practicing, and rapprochement. Both Mahler and Stern demonstrate how the sense of self and interpersonal relatedness develop as a complex dialectic process.

Erikson's (1950) epigenetic model of psychosocial development, though presented basically as a linear developmental process, also implicitly provides support for the view that normal personality development involves the simultaneous and mutually facilitating development of interpersonal relatedness and self-definition. If one includes in Erikson's model an additional stage of cooperation versus isolation (occurring around the time of the development of peer play and the initial resolution of the oedipal crisis at the age of about four to six) and places this stage at the appropriate point in the developmental sequence between "initiative versus guilt" and "industry versus inferiority" (Blatt and Shichman 1983), then Erikson's epigenetic model of psychosocial development illustrates the complex transaction between interpersonal relatedness and self-definition throughout the life cycle (see Fig. 1). Erikson initially emphasizes interpersonal relatedness in his discussion of trust versus mistrust, followed by two stages of self definition, autonomy versus shame and initiative versus guilt. This is followed by another stage of interpersonal relatedness, cooperation versus isolation, and then by two stages of self-definition, industry versus inferiority and identity versus role diffusion. The

THE DIALECTIC INTERACTION OF INTERPERSONAL RELATEDNESS AND SELF-DEFINITION IMPLICIT IN E. ERIKSON'S PSYCHOSOCIAL MODEL

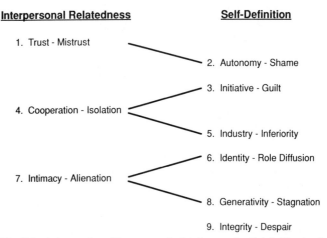

<u>**Interpersonal Relatedness**</u>   <u>**Self-Definition**</u>

1. Trust - Mistrust

2. Autonomy - Shame

3. Initiative - Guilt

4. Cooperation - Isolation

5. Industry - Inferiority

6. Identity - Role Diffusion

7. Intimacy - Alienation

8. Generativity - Stagnation

9. Integrity - Despair

Fig. 1. The dialectic interaction of interpersonal relatedness and self-definition implicit in Erikson's psychosocial model.

following stage, intimacy versus alienation, is again clearly a stage of interpersonal relatedness, followed by two more stages of self-definition, generativity versus stagnation and integrity versus despair (Blatt and Shichman 1983).

This reformulation of Erikson's model (Blatt and Shichman 1983) corrects the deficiency observed by Franz and White (1985), who comment that Erikson's model neglects to some degree the development of intimacy and interpersonal attachment. Franz and White call for the addition of an attachment (or intimacy) developmental line to broaden Erikson's emphasis on individuation and identity. The addition of a stage of cooperation versus isolation to Erikson's model (Blatt and Shichman 1983) enables us to define a relatedness (or an attachment) dimension inherent in Erikson's psychosocial epigenetic formulations and to note more clearly the dialectic developmental transaction between relatedness and self-definition that is implicit in Erikson's formulations.

The inclusion of an attachment, relatedness, and intimacy developmental dimension as an integral aspect of personality development to complement the more usual emphasis on individuation, self-definition, and identity is consistent with the call by feminist theorists (e.g., Chodoroff 1972; Gilligan 1983; Miller [1976] 1986) pointing out the failure to give equal status to the development of interpersonal relatedness in most theories of personality development. This call for recognition of the importance of attachment and relatedness is also consistent with the extensive research and theory of the past two decades that demonstrate the importance of attachment (e.g., Bowlby 1977; Ainsworth 1969), the developmental processes of separation-individuation (e.g., Mahler, Pine, and Bergman 1975), and the development of the capacity for mutuality and empathy (e.g., Stern 1985) in personality development. Figure 2 illustrates this dialectic transactional, hierarchical spirality (Werner 1948) in the developmental integration of interpersonal relatedness and self-definition.

While normality can be defined ideally as an integration of interpersonal relatedness and self-definition, within the normal range individuals can still place relatively greater emphasis on one developmental line over the other. The relative emphasis on either interpersonal relatedness or self-definition delineates two basic personality configurations, each with a particular experiential mode and preferred forms of cognition, defense, and modes of adaptation (Blatt and Shichman 1983). As Bakan noted (1966), individual differences in personality style and motivational disposition can be understood in part according to which of these two tendencies an individual gives priority (Maddi 1980).

Individuals who place a relatively greater emphasis on interpersonal relatedness should generally be more figurative in their thinking and focus primarily on affects and visual images. Their thinking should be characterized more by simultaneous rather than by sequential processing. The emphasis should be on reconciliation, synthesis, and integration of elements into an integrated cohesion rather than on a critical analysis of separate elements and details. In terms of cognitive style, these individuals tend to be repressors and levelers. The predominant tendency is to seek fusion, harmony, integration, and synthesis. The focus is on experiences of feeling, affect, and personal reactions and meaning. These individuals are primarily field dependent and very aware of and influenced by environmental factors. Their thinking is much more intuitive and determined more by feelings, affects, and personal reactions than by facts, figures, and other details. They seek harmony, peace, and satisfaction in interpersonal relationships. Their primary instinctual mode is libidinal rather than aggressive, and they value affectionate feelings and the establishment of close, intimate relationships (Blatt and Shichman 1983).

Thinking in individuals primarily focused in self-definition should be much more literal, sequential, linguistic, and critical. Issues of action, overt behavior, manifest form, logic, consistency, and causality should be attended to rather than feelings and relationships. Emphasis is on analysis rather than synthesis, on the critical dissection of details and part properties rather than on achieving an integration and synthesis. These individuals tend to be sensitizers or sharpeners and field independent (Witkin et al. 1962; Witkin 1965). Their experiences and judgment are determined primarily by internal ap-

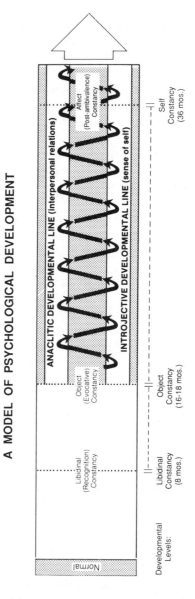

Fig. 2. A model of psychological development.

praisal rather than by environmental events. Their primary goal is self-assertion, control, autonomy, power, and prestige rather than relatedness. Their primary instinctual mode involves assertion and aggression in the service of differentiation and self-definition rather than affection and intimacy (Blatt and Shichman 1983).

Blatt and Shichman (1983), in discussing these two primary personality configurations, utilize the term "anaclitic" to define the personality organization that focuses predominantly on interpersonal relatedness and the term "introjective" to define the personality organization primarily focused on self-definition. Their use of these two terms derives from Freud ([1905] 1953, [1915] 1957), who used the term "anaclitic" (taken from the Greek "anklitas"—to rest or lean on) to characterize all interpersonal relatedness derived from dependency experienced in satisfying nonsexual drives such as hunger or from dependency experienced initially with a pregenital love object such as the mother (Laplanche and Pontalis 1973; *Webster's* 1960). The term "introjective" was used by Freud ([1917] 1957) to describe the processes whereby values, patterns of culture, motives, and restraints are assimilated into the self (e.g., made subjective), consciously or unconsciously, as guiding personal principles, through learning and socialization (*Webster's* 1960).

Spiegel and Spiegel (1978) present a distinction, deriving in part from Immanuel Kant, similar to the anaclitic and introjective personality styles (Blatt and Shichman 1983)—Dionysian and Apollonian personality styles. They describe Dionysians as sensitive to interpersonal issues, more distractable, intuitive, passive and dependent, emotional, naive, and trusting, and focused more on feelings than ideas. They are open to and easily influenced by new ideas and others, place greater value on tactile and kinesthetic experiences, and are more action oriented. They tend to suspend critical judgment, live primarily in the present rather than in the past and the future, and value interpersonal affiliation and relationships.

Apollonians, in contrast, are described as very cognitive, organized, and critical; they value control and reason over emotions. They are very steady, responsible, and reliable, unemotional, highly organized individuals who employ critical reason to plan for the future. Apollonians value their own ideas, use them as a primary reference point, and seek to have others accept and confirm their ideas. They dominate interpersonal relationships, seeking to be in control, and are often very critical about the ideas of others. They are very cautious and methodological, comparing and contrasting alternatives and evaluating ideas and situations piece by piece before they arrive at a final decision and take action. They often pride themselves on being extremely responsible and are hesitant about making commitments, which, once made, they feel obligated by. They are highly reliable and steadfast, often able to stick by a decision, and are relatively uninfluenced by others. They seek to make sure that things are carried out correctly, and they plan logically and systematically. Spiegel and Spiegel (1978) succinctly summarize the differences between these two personality or character styles by noting that Dionysians are oriented to and influenced by the heart whereas Apollonians are organized and influenced by the head.

A similar, but somewhat more limited, distinction was made by Jung (1928) about extroverted and introverted personality styles. Extroverts seek contact with others and derive gratification and meaning from relationships, while introverts give priority to their own thoughts and experiences and maintain a clear sense of self-definition, identity, and uniqueness. Jung, like Spiegel and Spiegel (1978), Blatt (1974), and Blatt and Shichman (1983), saw these character types as independent of, but related to, concepts of psychopathology (e.g., hysteric and obsessive; Shapiro 1965). Eysenck (1960) extended the Jungian topology to discuss neuroticism in terms of both the hysteric and the obsessive. Research with the Myers-Briggs Personality Inventory (e.g., Myers 1962; McCaully 1981) and Eysenck (1960) Neuroticism Scale provides empirical support for the importance of this differentiation of two basic character types and their relations to neurotic psychopathology.

Different types of psychological defenses are integral to these two different basic personality types. Psychological defenses are the cognitive-affective processes through which individuals avoid recognizing and acknowledging conflict and through which they attempt to deal with conflictual aspects within themselves and in reality. These cognitive-affective processes are an integral part of the individual's personality or character style (Shapiro 1965). The cognitive-affective processes inherent in the psychological defenses used to deal with conflict are often the very same cognitive-affective styles individuals use in general adaptation. People rely on the same basic cognitive-affective processes to cope with important situations whether they are relatively neutral and impersonal or difficult, even conflict-laden, personal situations. Psychological defenses are modes of adaptation and therefore involve the individual's preferred cognitive styles. These cognitive styles are an integral part of personality (or character) structure.

Defenses can be discussed as specific mechanisms (e.g., denial, repression, isolation, intellectualization, reaction formation, and overcompensation), or individual defenses can be considered as specific examples of several broad generic types of defense. It may be more productive to establish a generic classification of defenses such as the differentiation of avoidant versus counteractive defenses (Blatt and Shichman 1983). Both avoidant and counteractive defenses attempt to keep aspects of painful and conflict-laden issues out of awareness, but they do so in very different ways. Denial and repression are avoidant defenses; they seek to avoid recognizing and acknowledging the existence of conflictual issues. Conflict and anxiety are denied access to consciousness. In contrast, counteractive defenses such as projection, intellectualization, reaction formation and overcompensation convert and/or transform conflictual impulses in ways that still permit partial but disguised expression. Counteractive defenses do not avoid conflicts but rather disguise the conflictual issues by transforming them into alternative acceptable form, thereby achieving partial expression and/or discharge of the underlying wish or impulse. Reaction formation and overcompensation are examples of counteractive defenses in which an impulse, often aggressive, is transformed into its opposite. The earlier research by Bryne and his colleagues (e.g., Bryne, Barry, and Nelson 1963) on repression and sensitization is an approximation of the distinction between avoidant and counteractive defenses.

These two broad generic types of defense processes, avoidant and counteractive defenses, express particular modes of thinking, feeling, and behaving and are each an integral part of an individual's personality or character style. Avoidant defenses, such as denial and repression, are typical of the character style that emphasizes interpersonal relatedness, while counteractive defenses, such as intellectualization, reaction formation, and overcompensation, are typical of the character style that emphasizes self-definition and identity. In normal development, more mature dimensions of these two personality styles are integrated as the individual develops personally meaningful interpersonal relationships, evolves a reasonably positive and consolidated self-image, and is capable of utilizing sublimation, which is an integration of higher-level avoidant (displacement and repression) and counteractive (overcompensation) defenses.

The two predominant modes of relatedness and self-definition (communion and autonomy, anaclitic and introjective) evolve in normal development in an integrated form so that the individual develops an active commitment to interpersonal relatedness and a viable sense of self. Biological predispositions and disruptive environmental events, however, can disturb this integrated developmental process in complex ways and lead to exaggerated emphasis on one mode at the expense of the other. Mild deviations result in unique character styles that are within the normal range. More extensive deviations, markedly exaggerated emphasis on one developmental line at the expense of the other, however, occur in psychopathology. Exaggerated distortion of one developmental line to the relative neglect of the other occurs as a compensatory response to developmental disruptions. Thus, the differentiation of anaclitic and introjective personality configurations provides a basis for considering the relations among different types of psychopathology. In the extreme, the two generic types of defenses, avoidant and counteractive, become an integral part of two different configurations of psychopathology.

On occasion, severe and repeated untoward events disrupt the complex, normal, dialectic developmental process. Some individuals, depending on biological predispositions, cultural factors, gender, basic capacities and vulnerabilities, and cultural and family patterns, attempt to compensate for serious developmental disruptions by exaggerating one developmental line at the expense of the other. In distorted ways, individuals fixate either on relatedness or on an excessive preoccupation with the sense of self at the expense of the other developmental line. The normal developmental process is disrupted somewhere in the life cycle, and, if there are no subsequent ameliorating circumstances and experiences, these difficulties can be repeated over and over again, becoming consolidated as distorted modes of adaptation. The earlier in the developmental process these disruptions occur and the more extreme the distortions, the more severe the psychopathology. Thus, as a consequence of developmental deviations, individuals can develop particular character types that emphasize one developmental line over the other, some becoming increasingly more concerned about relatedness, others increasingly more concerned about their self-image and their prerogatives. In the extreme, an exaggerated preoccupation with interpersonal relatedness at the expense of developing important aspects of the sense of self—or, conversely, preoccupations about preserving and protecting the sense of self at the expense of developing adequate forms of interpersonal relatedness—defines two primary configurations of psychopathology.

As a consequence of major disruption of the normal developmental processes of relatedness and self-definition, some individuals, most often women, become excessively preoccupied with relatedness at the expense of development of the sense of self. If this developmental disruption occurs early in the life cycle, it can lead to the development of an infantile character, someone exclusively preoccupied with concerns for need gratification—constantly wanting to be held, cared for, fed, and attended to. If this disruption of the dialectic developmental process occurs later in the life cycle, a more organized kind of hysterical disorder can develop in which the person is concerned not only with being held, cared for, and loved but also with being able to express as well as receive love. Some patients more often function at the infantile level, using denial as their primary defense; their concerns are primarily dyadic in structure, and they strive to be accepted and cared for, like the young child with its mother. Other patients are at a developmentally higher hysterical level, using repression as their primary defense; their primary concerns involve triadic configurations and oedipal themes, striving for the attention and love of one parent in competition with the other, But, at both the infantile level and the developmentally more advanced hysterical level, the issues are focused primarily on libidinal attachment—concerns about being loved, intimate, and close. Infantile and hysteric disorders can occur in relatively pure form, but they are not isolated disorders or diseases. Rather, they represent relative end points on a continuum of a configuration of anaclitic psychopathology.

Some individuals, more often men, deal with severe disruption of the normal dialectic developmental process by exaggerated attempts to consolidate a sense of self. In the extreme, this is expressed in disorders of paranoia, obsession-compulsion, guilt-ridden (introjective) depression, and phallic narcissism. These disorders all express preoccupations about the self ranging from primitive concerns in paranoia to more integrated concerns about the self in introjective depression and phallic narcissism. The paranoid patient is preoccupied with maintaining a rigid definition of self as distinct and separate from others. Paranoid patients struggle to prove that they exist as a separate entity and that they are not merged and fused in a symbiotic relationship with another (Blatt and Wild 1976); they struggle to establish a sense of self in a primitive form. All bad is placed onto the other, all good is attributed to the self, and an isolated and embattled distance is maintained from others. Obsessive-compulsive disorders express somewhat higher concerns about the self—concerns about mastery, autonomy, control, prerogatives, and possessions. At a still somewhat higher developmental level, individuals are more concerned about self-worth than about mastery. In introjective depression, the predominant concerns are about one's intent and one's value in comparison to an idealized value system with the belief and feeling that one is a failure or that one has transgressed. Phallic narcissism is the reversal of introjective depression in which through counteraction the individual seeks to exhibit himself or herself and win endless accolades and approval to defend against intense feelings of guilt and shame, worthlessness, and humiliation.

The dynamics, conflicts, defenses, and cognitive-affective and interpersonal style of the various forms of psychopathology of the introjective configuration share a fundamental similarity. Paranoia, obsession-compulsion, introjective depression, and phallic narcissism all involve issues of self-reproach, guilt, and preoccupations with self-definition and self-control. Interest is directed primarily toward things rather than people, and there is a heightened emphasis on thoughts and accomplishments (deeds) rather than on feelings and interpersonal relations. In all the forms of psychopathology of the introjective configuration, defenses are essentially counteractive rather than avoidant. Projection, reversal, intellectualization, doing and undoing, reaction formation, introjection (or identification with the aggressor), and overcompensation all, with varying degrees of effectiveness, attempt to alter or transform impulses and conflicts rather than to avoid (deny and/or repress) them. While each of the disorders in the introjective configuration can be viewed as independent and separate, they are interrelated disorders, and most often individual patients present a complex admixture of these various disorders.

Different types of psychopathology can be considered as distorted exaggerations of either the anaclitic or the introjective developmental line. Thus, there are two primary configurations of psychopathology, each defined primarily by exaggerations of the tasks of each of the two fundamental developmental lines. Anaclitic psychopathologies are distorted and exaggerated attempts to maintain satisfying interpersonal experiences; introjective psychopathologies are distorted and exaggerated attempts to establish an effective concept of the self. As illustrated in figure 3, exaggerated and distorted preoccupation about satisfying interpersonal relations, to the neglect of the development of concepts of self, defines the psychopathologies of the anaclitic configuration—the infantile and hysterical syndromes. Exaggerated and distorted concerns about the definition of the self, at the expense of establishing meaningful interpersonal relations, defines the psychopathologies of the introjective configuration—paranoid, obsessive-compulsive, introjective depressive, and phallic narcissistic disorders.

In each of these two configurations of psychopathology, there are several evolving levels of organization ranging from more primitive to more integrated attempts to establish meaningful interpersonal relations and a consolidated self-concept. The various levels of psychopathology within the anaclitic and the introjective configurations define lines along which patients progress or regress. Thus, an individual's difficulties can be specified as being predominantly in one or the other personality configuration, at a particular developmental level, and with a differential potential to regress or progress to other developmental levels within the configuration. In this conceptualization, the various forms of psychopathology are considered no longer as isolated, independent disease entities but rather as interrelated modes of adaptation, organized at different developmental levels within two basic configurations that focus on either interpersonal relations or self-definition. Psychopathologies within the anaclitic configuration share a basic preoccupation with libidinal issues such as closeness and intimacy. There is a better capacity for affective bonding and a greater potential for the development of meaningful interpersonal relationships. Psychopathologies within the anaclitic configuration also have a similar defensive style with a predominant use of avoidant defenses such as denial, repression, and displacement. Psychopathologies in the introjective configuration share a basic focus on anger, aggression, and themes of self-definition, self-control, and self-worth. They also share a similarity in defensive style with the use of counteractive defenses such as isolation, doing and undoing, intellectualization, reaction formation, introjection, identification with the aggressor, and overcompensation. Cognitive processes are more fully developed, and there is greater potential for the development of logical, abstract thought. Although most forms of psychopathology are organized primarily around one configuration or the other, there also may be some patients who have features from both the anaclitic and the introjective dimensions and whose psychopathology derives from both configurations. (A fuller discussion of the various forms of psychopathology and their interrelationships in

A MODEL OF NORMAL AND PSYCHOPATHOLOGICAL DEVELOPMENT

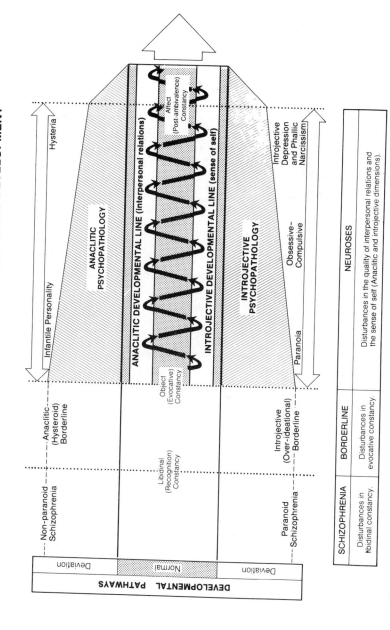

Fig. 3. A model of normal and psychopathological development (Blatt and Shichman 1983).

the anaclitic and introjective configuration is available in Blatt and Shichman [1983].)

Some Research Implications

The importance of the distinction between anaclitic and introjective configurations in the study of personality development and psychopathology is supported by recent research on depression and psychotherapeutic change.

Studies of depression

In the early 1970s, my colleagues and I initiated a series of studies on depression (e.g., Blatt 1974; Blatt, D'Afflitti, and Quinlan 1976; Blatt et al. 1982) based on the premise that psychopathology, especially depression, could be studied most effectively as deviations from normal development rather than as independent disease entities. On the basis of a review of major clinical case reports of depression (e.g., Bibring 1953; Cohen et al. 1954), a list of statements was developed that described details of the quality of the lives of depressed patients (e.g., how they relate to people, how they feel about themselves, the ways they conduct their lives). This list included not symptoms of depression but rather items that reflected how depressed individuals feel about themselves and others and the everyday issues that concern and preoccupy them. A questionnaire of sixty-six items was eventually constructed on which individuals rate, on a seven-point Likert-type scale, how important each of the items is for them. This Depressive Experiences Questionnaire (DEQ) was given to a large number of normal young adults. Three factors emerged from a principal components factor analysis with a varimax rotation. The three factors have good internal consistency and test-retest reliability, and the factor structure is unusually stable, having since been replicated with other samples. The three factors that emerged were labeled "dependency," "self-criticism," and "efficacy" (Blatt, D'Afflitti, and Quinlan 1976).

Table 1 presents the five items that load most heavily on each of the three factors. The items on the dependency factor include concerns about losing people and being rejected, feeling lonely, and worrying about offending or hurting someone who is close. The five items loading most heavily on the self-criticism factor include concerns about differences between self and ideal, feelings of guilt and worthlessness, and feelings that one has disappointed others and has failed to live up to standards or ideals. These data suggest that experiences of depressed individuals focus around two basic dimensions. One dimension involves concerns about dependency and relatedness, and the other involves concerns about self-definition, self-criticism, and self-worth.

A third factor, efficacy, accounts for about 5 percent of the variance and

Table 1. Factors of the Depressive Experiences Questionnaire

DEQ factor	Percentage Variance	α	DEQ Items with Highest Loading on Factor
1. Dependency	10.44	.81	23. I often think about the danger of losing someone who is close to me.
			55. After an argument, I feel very lonely.
			28. I am very sensitive to others for signs for rejection.
			65. Being alone doesn't bother me at all.[a]
			45. I worry a lot about offending or hurting someone who is close to me.
2. Self-criticism	9.65	.80	13. There is a considerable difference between how I am now and how I would like to be.
			43. I often feel guilty.
			36. The way I feel about myself frequently varies: there are times when I feel extremely good about myself and other times when I see only the bad in me and feel like a total failure.
			30. Often, I feel I have disappointed others.
			7. I often find that I don't live up to my own standards or ideals.
3. Efficacy	5.34	.72	33. I have many inner resources (abilities, strengths).
			24. Other people have high expectations of me.
			4. I set my personal goals and standards as high as possible.
			42. I am a very independent person.
			59. What I do and say have a very strong impact on those around me.

Source: Blatt et al. (1982).

[a] Negative loading.

involves feelings of self-confidence, importance, and high standards and performance. In college students, this factor measures a sense of efficacy. In hospitalized patients, however, this scale is an indication of denial and is significantly correlated with the mania scale of the Minnesota Multiphasic Personality Inventory (MMPI) (Blatt et al. 1982).

The two factors of depression—dependency and self-criticism—but especially the self-criticism factor, correlate significantly with standard measures of depression such as the Beck and Zung depression scales, suggesting that the usual measures of depression assess primarily the self-critical rather than the dependent type of depression. The dependency dimension of depression, on the other hand, seems to be a relatively ignored dimension of depression. While the DEQ dependency factor correlates only marginally with traditional measures of depression, an item analysis of each of the twenty items of the Zung Depression Scale with the DEQ factors (Blatt, D'Afflitti, and Quinlan 1976) provided clarification. Fourteen of the twenty items of the Zung are considered to assess psychological concerns such as personal dissatisfaction, self-criticism, and hopelessness (Zung 1972), and each of these fourteen items correlated significantly ($p < .05$) with the DEQ self-criticism factor. Six Zung items concern physical well-being such as digestive functions, fatigue, psychomotor retardation, and irritability, and these correlated significantly ($p < .05$) with the DEQ dependency factor. These data suggest that dependent depressive concerns are often expressed in masked form (Lesse 1974) or as depressive equivalents in physical concerns and complaints. Individuals high on dependency tend not to be concerned about psychological issues but rather to express their depression through somatic complaints and seeking medical care. These findings, which suggest that dependency is a relatively neglected but important dimension of depression, are consistent with the work of Seligman and his colleagues (Seligman 1975; Abramson, Seligman, and Teasdale 1978; Abramson and Sackheim 1977; Peterson, Schwartz, and Seligman 1981) on "learned helplessness" (the generalized expectation of being unable to control one's life) as a central etiological issue in depression as well as with the discussion by Hirschfeld and his colleagues (Hirschfeld, Klerman, Chodoff, et al. 1976; Hirschfeld, Klerman, Gough, et al. 1977) about the importance of dependency in depression. Generally, dependency has not been explored as fully as self-criticism, self-esteem, and guilt in the research on depression.

Despite the stability of the factor structure of the DEQ in nonclinical samples, factor analyses of the DEQ in psychiatric clinical samples do not yield a coherent factor structure. In patients, the two dimensions of depression merge into a single global measure of depression. But the two factors of depression, dependency and self-criticism, defined in nonclinical samples, yield variables that differentially relate to important clinical dimensions in psychiatric patients. On the basis of a median split of each of the three DEQ scales in a clinical sample of one hundred inpatients, patients were identified who were high on dependency but low on self-criticism and efficacy (HLL), high on self-criticism but low on dependency and efficacy (LHL), or high on dependency and self-criticism but low on efficacy (HHL). In addition, a fourth group was identified, patients who were low on dependency and self-criticism but high on efficacy (LLH). A group of four clinicians reviewed brief case reports prepared on these patients at admission, uninformed as to their DEQ groupings, and attempted to identify in which of the four groups the patient had been assigned. The clinical team correctly identified the group membership of 56 percent of the patients, a highly significant ($p . < 001$) differentiation. The clinical team also specified the dimensions of the patient's case record that enabled them to make this differentiation (Blatt et al. 1982).

Patients in the dependency group (HLL) had frequent notes in their clinical case records about early experiences of object loss, rejection, and/or abandonment. The records also contained themes of feeling unwanted and unloved, frequent physical complaints, and excesses in oral behavior (alcohol, food, and drugs). The patients also often made suicidal gestures by taking an overdose of their prescribed antidepressant medication.

The case records of self-critical patients (LHL) often contained themes of striving, feeling a failure, concerns about transgression and guilt, impaired self-esteem, self-blame, and being hypercritical of themselves and others. They often made serious suicide risks, resorting to violent forms of suicide. They often had obsessive and paranoid features.

The clinical team had its most difficulty identifying patients that were high on both dependency and self-criticism—the mixed group (HHL). Most often the clinical team identified these patients as being high on one of the scales but not on the other. The mixed dependency and self-criticism group was characterized by features common to each of the two "pure" types and, in addition, by feelings of guilt, sexual inhibition (impotence, frigidity), and phobias.

In contrast to the difficulty the clinical team had in identifying the mixed group, they had little difficulty identifying the "nondepressed" patients, those low on dependency and self-criticism but high on efficacy (LLH). These patients often denied having serious difficulty, had subtle manic behavior (like going on spending sprees or making a large number of long-distance telephone calls), and were usually occupationally quite successful. They were often employed in helping professions (nursing, social work, teaching, psychology, and medicine). On the inpatient unit, these patients were often the head of the patient government or identified themselves with the hospital staff. Staff often overestimated their progress, and they were frequently discharged prematurely. The patients in the "nondepressed" group also had frequent expression of dependent behavior, similar to the high-dependency group (HLL), but in a context of denial. They provided care and affection, much in the way they unconsciously wanted to be cared for themselves.

Other clinical investigators have also discussed two types of depression similar to dependency and self-criticism identified on the DEQ (Blatt 1974; Blatt et al. 1976). Bowlby (1969, 1973, 1977, 1980, 1988) discussed how "compulsively self-reliant" and "anxiously attached" individuals are both predisposed toward depression. "Compulsively self-reliant" individuals avoid relationships and are scornful of people who seek close, intimate interpersonal relationships. "Anxiously detached" individuals, in contrast, eagerly seek interpersonal contacts and are excessively dependent on others. Arieti and Bemporad (1978, 1980), from a Sullivanian tradition, have discussed a "dominant other" and a "dominant goal" type of depression in which depression can focus on issues of being passively gratified by a dominant other or of being reassured of one's worth and being free of guilt. In the "dominant other" type of depression, the child reacts to the experience of a sudden withdrawal of love and approval by developing a clinging, demanding, dependent, infantile relationship with the dominant other. In the "dominant goal" type of depression, the child reacts to the experience of sudden withdrawal of love and approval by feeling that he or she must submit to the parents' expectations. The child seeks to regain love and approval not only by being compliant but also by directing one's entire effort toward a dominant goal that becomes an end in itself. When the dominant other is lost or the dominant goal is not achieved, depression results. The person feels dependent on others for support, direction, and a sense of well-being and feels that he or she lacks the resources to establish a sense of meaning and purpose of life. Arieti and Bemporad (1978, 167) discuss two intense wishes in depression: "to be passively gratified by the dominant other" and "to be reassured of one's own worth, and to be free of the burden of guilt."

Beck (1983), from a cognitive-behavioral orientation, has recently also begun to discuss a socially dependent (sociotropic) and an autonomous type of depression and has developed a scale—the Sociotropy and Autonomy Scale (SAS)—to assess these two types of depression. Sociotropy (social dependency) "refers to the person's investment in positive interchange with other people. This cluster includes passive-receptive wishes (acceptance, intimacy, understanding, support, guidance); "narcissistic wishes" (admiration, prestige, status). . . . Individuality (autonomy) refers to the person's investment in preserving and increasing his independence, mobility, and personal rights; freedom of choice, action, and expression; protection of his domain;—and attaining meaningful goals" (272). Beck postulates that disruption of personal relationships in socially dependent individuals and a failure to meet personal goals or standards in autonomous individuals can precipitate a depression. In addition, factor-analytic study of the Dysfunctional Attitude Scale developed by Weissman and Beck (1978) to assess attitudes presumed to predispose an individual to depression reveals two major factors labeled concerns about "approval by others" and "performance evaluation" (or self-worth) (Cane et al. 1986) or "a need for approval" and "perfectionism" (Oliver and Baumgart 1985). Thus, several groups, from very different theoretical orientations, have found that issues of interpersonal relatedness and self-definition serve to differentiate two central, independent foci in depression.

A number of research groups (e.g., Hammen et al. 1985; Robins and Block 1987; Segal, Shaw, and Vella 1987; Smith, O'Keeffe, and Jenkins, 1989; Zuroff et al. 1983), using the DEQ and the Beck SAS, have experimentally explored differences between individuals who emphasize either interpersonal relatedness or self-definition. The results indicate that individuals (patients and nonpatients) high on dependency or high on self-criticism are differentially sensitive to issues of loss/abandonment or feelings of failure and criticism. A number of studies have demonstrated that both anaclitic and introjective personalities are vulnerable to depressive affect and that this vulnerability is determined by different types of environmental experiences.

A series of studies (e.g., Mongrain and Zuroff 1988; Zuroff and de Lorimier, in press; Zuroff and Fitzpatrick 1988; Zuroff and Franko 1986; Zuroff et al. 1983) have also examined differences in the quality of interpersonal relationships of anaclitic and introjective individuals. College women high on DEQ dependency (anaclitic individuals) describe their ideal boyfriend as high on needs for intimacy rather than on needs for masculinity and achievement (Zuroff and de Lorimier, in press). Women high on self-criticism (introjective individuals) describe their ideal boyfriends as high on needs for achievement and masculinity (Zuroff and de Lorimier, in press), and they see romantic relationships as a way of attaining social status and esteem (Zuroff and Fitzpatrick 1988). They also describe their boyfriends as responding to conflict by attack or avoidance rather than compromise (Zuroff and Fitzpatrick 1988). Women high on DEQ dependency perceive same-sex friends as friendlier, whereas self-critical women perceive their friends as less supportive and less submissive (Zuroff and Franko 1986).

Another series of studies (e.g., Dauber 1980, 1984; Koufopoulos 1986; Schmidt 1981; Schmidt, Fallot, and Dickson 1985; Fernandez 1986; Brennan 1984; Fonseca 1987) used the subliminal activation method (Silverman 1966, 1983, 1985) to investigate differential sensitivity of highly dependent and self-critical subjects to subliminal stimuli of conflicts about dependency and guilt. While most of the research to date using this method has studied the responses of self-critical women to stimuli designed to provoke guilt, the data consistently indicate a significant increase in depressive affect following subliminal stimulation that is specific to the particular personality type. Subliminal stimulation of dependency results in an elevation of dysphoric affect in individuals high on the DEQ dependency scale, and subliminal stimulation of guilt results in an increase in dysphoric affect of individuals high on the DEQ self-criticism scale.

In summary, a wide range of research with both clinical and nonclinical samples indicates that the distinction between an exaggerated preoccupation with relatedness and one with self-definition identifies two major types of depression that transcend more traditional diagnostic categories. Not only has this distinction been important in the study of depression, but it has also contributed to studies of the therapeutic process. Data from two studies of change during the treatment process indicate that patients excessively preoccupied with issues of interpersonal relatedness (anaclitic patients) and those excessively preoccupied with self-definition, individual autonomy, prerogatives, and control (introjective patients) change in different ways in the treatment process and are differentially responsive to different forms of therapy.

Studies of the Therapeutic Process

Ninety seriously disturbed adolescent and young adult patients, aged eighteen to twenty-nine, hospitalized in a long-term, private, intensive, open, inpatient treatment facility with an active therapeutic community, were selected for study. These patients were selected from among 250 patients who had remained in treatment for longer than one year and had been given a set of psychological tests both early in treatment and again at least one year later during their hospitalization. All patients were included if they were between the ages of eighteen and twenty-nine at admission and had been given a Rorschach, TAT, and intelligence test both at admission and at least one year later and if these psychological test protocols were in a sufficiently legible form so that they could be used in research (Blatt et al. 1988).

No one in this sample was mentally defective (IQ < 80) or had definite indications of central nervous system disturbance. All ninety patients had two hundred or more sessions of individual, psychoanalytically oriented psychotherapy four times per week between the two testings. In terms of traditional diagnostic nomenclature, approximately 30 percent of the sample were considered psychotic, 60 percent severe character disorders or borderline personality disorders, and 10 percent severely neurotic or depressed. Most of the patients came from families of at least the middle socioeconomic class, were reasonably well educated, and were of at least average intelligence. There were forty-five women and forty-five men in the sample, ranging in age from eighteen to twenty-nine, with an average age at intake of 20.94 years. They were hospitalized on average for twenty-three months, with an average of fifteen months between the initial evaluation and the second assessment. The first assessment was conducted after the first six weeks of hospitalization and the second assessment on average fifteen months later, on average 10.9 months prior to discharge; the second assessment was usually not viewed by staff or patient as part of the discharge process.

On the basis of an extensive and intensive admission evaluation conducted with each patient and his or her family during the first six weeks of hospitalization, a detailed case report was prepared that included family history, the developmental history of the patient, a description of the present illness and its onset, any previous therapy, current and past medical evaluations, a description by nurses and activities staff of the patient's initial behavior in the hospital, and a detailed account of the first six weeks of the psychotherapy.

After approximately one year (15 months on the average), another evaluative case report, similar to the initial case report, was prepared on the basis of accounts of experiences with the patient in the various treatment modalities. These two documents, the clinical case reports at admission and about a year later, provided the data on which ratings were made of clinical symptoms, interpersonal behavior, and social adjustment.

In addition, patients were administered an extensive battery of psychological tests, including the Rorschach, the TAT, the Wechsler Intelligence Test, and, in some cases, figure drawings after six weeks of hospitalization and approximately one year later. The responses to the various psychological tests were scored utilizing newly developed conceptual schemes for evaluating various aspects of psychological test protocols that, in previous cross-sectional research, had demonstrated reliability and validity (Blatt and Berman 1984).

Thus, the research data consisted of two independent sets of observations, case records and psychological test protocols, each gathered at two points in the treatment process—after the first six weeks of hospitalization and once again in the treatment process, a year or so later. Using patients as their own control, the nature of change was examined in two types of seriously disturbed patients: those with primarily anaclitic psychopathology and those with introjective psychopathology. Two judges reviewing intake clinical case histories made this diagnostic distinction with high reliability. The judges reported that, in making this differentiation, they were particularly attentive to whether the patient's predominant defenses were avoidant or counteractive and whether the patient's emphasis was on issues of attachment or on aggression and individuation.

On the basis of the rating of initial case records, forty-two patients were considered as primarily anaclitic and forty-eight as having primarily an introjective personality organization. These two groups were not significantly different from one another on a larger number of demographic variables, except for sex. As expected, women constituted two-thirds of the anaclitic subjects but only one-third of the introjective subjects. Other than for sex, however, there were no significant differences between anaclitic and introjective patients in age, socioeconomic class, the number of years of experience of their therapist, and the amount or type of medication they received.

Patients in both groups were, on average, twenty-one years of age at time of admission. Six patients in each group received antipsychotic medications at the time of the first evaluation (after the first six weeks of hospitalization). The two groups did not differ in educational level and occupational status or the occupational status of their parents, except for a trend for the mothers of anaclitic patients to be employed in higher-level (professional) positions than the mothers of introjective patients (28 vs. 14 percent).

There were no significant differences between the two groups of patients in level of premorbid adjustment as assessed by the Phillips-Zigler and the Goldstein Scales of Premorbid Adjustment. The therapists of both groups of patients had, on average, seven to eight years of postdoctoral training and/or experience (range was one to thirty-four years). At the time of the second testing, virtually none of the patients was receiving antipsychotic medication (none of the forty-two anaclitic patients was receiving medication, and only two of the forty-eight introjective patients were still receiving medication— the therapeutic equivalent of 120 to 150 milligrams of thorazine per day).

The clinical case records were rated using procedures developed by Strauss and Harder (1981) for rating case records for symptoms of neurosis, psychosis, labile affect, and flattened affect.[1] Considerable previous statistical analysis (Strauss and Harder 1981; Strauss et al. 1978) indicated that the neurotic and psychotic scales were particularly stable and robust. In addition, the case records were also rated for aspects of social behavior using several scales developed at the Menninger Foundation that are more interpersonally oriented (Harty et al. 1981), including an assessment of the patient's motivation for treatment, the capacity for sublimatory activity, the quality of object relations, the degree of superego integration, and the ability to contain impulsivity. These variables are rated on a one-hundred–point scale, with a number of well-specified and clearly defined points for each scale. The case records were also rated for the extent of interpersonal communication using the Fairweather Scale for Social Adjustment (Fairweather et al. 1960). Judges had achieved acceptable levels of reliability (item alpha $>$ .65) in a prior sample of eighteen case records for all these case record ratings except for Menninger Impulsivity Scale (item alpha $>$ .62).

The ninety case records were randomly split in half, and each half was rated at time 1 by a separate judge. After rating half the ninety case records at time 1, each judge rated the other half at time 2, without knowledge of the other judge's rating at time 1.

Evaluation of Psychological Test Protocols

The analysis of the independently administered psychological test protocols focused on the Rorschach and the Wechsler Intelligence tests. These psychological test protocols were scored by a second set of judges who had no knowledge about the rating of the clinical case records or of any details of the patient, including age, sex, or diagnosis. The judges also did not know which set of test records went together or whether a particular test protocol was administered early or late in the treatment process.

Prior research with the Rorschach (Blatt and Berman 1984) identified seven primary variables that emerged in a factor analysis of Rorschach scores, each of which defined a crucial psychological dimension. These included the de-

---

1. Straus and Harder (1981) originally labeled the labile affect and flattened affect scales as "bizarre disorganized" and "bizarre retarded," respectively. Because very few of our patients exhibited bizarre behavior, we changed the names of these two factors to indicate that the difference between these last two factors was primarily in affect tone.

gree of adherence to reality (F + %; Korchin and Larson 1977); the extent of thought disorder, particularly involving disturbances in boundary articulation (Blatt and Berman 1984; Blatt and Ritzler 1974); the degree of affective lability (the weighted sum of color responses; Blatt and Feirstein 1977; Shapiro 1977); and the amount of differentiated, articulated, and integrated human forms that are accurately or inaccurately perceived (Blatt et al. 1976). The extent of the differentiation, articulation, and integration of accurately perceived human forms (OR +) assesses the capacity for investing in appropriate and satisfying interpersonal relationships; the extent of differentiated, articulated, and integrated inaccurately perceived human forms (OR −) assesses the degree of investment in inappropriate, unrealistic, possibly autistic fantasies rather than realistic relationships. When necessary, analysis of covariance (ANCOVA) was used to control for the effects of the total number of Rorschach responses on a particular Rorschach score.

There were relatively few significant differences between anaclitic and introjective patients on the ratings of the clinical records and the psychological test protocols gathered early in the treatment process. Introjective patients had significantly more psychotic symptoms ($p < .05$) on the Strauss-Harder and somewhat greater investment ($p < .10$) in fantasies of unrealistic relationships (OR −), but they also had greater sublimatory capacity on the Menninger ($p < .04$) and somewhat higher verbal IQ ($p < .10$).

Two-way analyses of variance (ANOVAs) in a repeated-methods design, supplemented by matched *t*-tests, were used to evaluate therapeutic change on the variables derived from the clinical case reports and the independent psychological test protocols gathered early and late in the treatment process. Comparison of anaclitic and introjective patients at time 1 and time 2 indicated highly significant changes in the total sample of patients, including a reduction in clinical symptoms and an improvement in the quality of interpersonal reactions as assessed from clinical case reports. Interpersonal relations improved significantly in both groups of patients, but symptom reduction occurred primarily in introjective patients. The improved social behavior and decreased clinical symptoms in the clinical case records were paralleled by significant changes in the independently administered and scored psychological tests, including a reduction in thought disorder on the Rorschach and an increase in the intelligence, particularly the Performance IQ.

Two-way ANCOVAs were used to assess possible confounding effects of external variables (e.g., the patient's level of premorbid adjustment and severity of psychopathology, the level of therapist's experience, the use of medication, and gender) on the changes noted in the variables derived from the clinical case records and the psychological test protocols. The main effect and interactions of these potentially confounding variables with the anaclitic-introjective distinction were evaluated for all case record and psychological test variables at time 2, covaried for initial level of each of these variables at time 1. The results of these two-way ANCOVAs indicate that the changes noted in anaclitic and introjective patients from time 1 to time 2 were relatively independent of the level of the therapist's experience, the use of antipsychotic medication, severity of the patients' psychopathology or their level of premorbid adjustment, or the gender differences in the two groups of patients.

The evaluation of change in different variables from time 1 to time 2, utilizing repeated-measures ANOVAS and matched t-tests, examined overall group effects. Different subjects in each group, however, may change to varying degrees in different directions on separate variables. These differential effects may cancel each other out in ANOVAs and t-tests. In order to examine possible patterns of change within individuals, change on psychological test variables was correlated with change on the ratings derived from the clinical case records. Despite the caution that needs to be exercised in the interpretation of correlated change scores, correlation of change scores provided an opportunity to assess patterns of change within different groups of individuals as they progress and regress during treatment. Independent of the changes noted for the patients as a total group or as subgroups, there were particular configurations of variables that indicated change in different types of patients. Change in introjective patients was most systematically noted in the correlations between clinical symptoms in the case record and changes in cognitive functioning as independently assessed on the intelligence test and on the Rorschach. Decrease in a wide range of clinical symptoms was significantly related to a decrease in thought disorder on the Rorschach in both anaclitic and introjective patients, but this relation was most apparent with introjective patients. In addition, a decrease in clinical symptoms correlated highly with an increase in intelligence test scores, again primarily for introjective patients. Thus, there appears to be a significant relation between changes in manifest clinical symptoms and different aspects of cognitive functioning (e.g., thought disorder and intelligence), primarily with introjective patients.

Change in anaclitic patients, in contrast, was most consistently noted in the correlations between ratings of interpersonal behavior as reported in the case records (motivation for treatment, capacity for sublimatory activity, the level of superego integration, and the quality of object relations) and the concept of the human object on the Rorschach. Improvement in the quality of interpersonal relationships noted in the clinical case records of anaclitic patients correlated significantly with decreased elaboration of inaccurately perceived human responses on the Rorschach (OR −)—that is, in the investment in inappropriate or autistic fantasies about interpersonal relationships.

The lack of significant correlations between changes in accurately perceived human forms (OR +) and change in the various ratings based on the clinical records is consistent with earlier findings (Blatt et al. 1976) that indicated that it is primarily the extent of the elaboration of inaccurately perceived human form (OR −) that has a significant relation to measures of psychopathology with seriously disturbed patients. Here, too, in this study it was only decreased investment in inaccurately perceived human forms (OR −) (decreased investment in inappropriate or autistic fantasies of human relationships) that was significantly correlated with increases in the quality of the patient's interpersonal behavior.

Thus, anaclitic and introjective patients appear to change in different ways, at least initially, in psychotherapy. Clinical change in anaclitic patients appears primarily in the quality of their interpersonal relationships, paralleled by changes in the quality of their representation of the human figure on the Rorschach. Introjective patients change primarily in the degree to which they demonstrate manifest symptoms of psychosis, neurosis, and affect disturbances, paralleled by changes in the quality of their cognitive processes, as measured by thought disorder on the Rorschach and the Wechsler Intelligence tests. Changes in manifest symptoms and aspects of cognitive functioning appear to be consistent measures of therapeutic change in introjective patients.

It seems quite consistent that anaclitic patients, with their preoccupations about the quality of their interpersonal relationships, should demonstrate therapeutic change primarily in interpersonal behavior as reported in the clinical case record and in changes in their conception of the human figure on the Rorschach. Likewise, it seems quite consistent that the more ideational introjective patients, with their preoccupations about self-definition, should demonstrate change primarily in the reports of manifest symptoms in their case record and on psychological test measures of cognitive functioning and thought disorder.

Thus, the data indicate that seriously disturbed anaclitic and introjective patients change in different ways, at least initially in the treatment process. In assessing change in anaclitic patients, one must be attentive to change in the quality of the interpersonal behavior and their conception of people rather than clinical symptoms and cognitive functioning. Quite to the contrary with introjective patients, manifest symptoms and ideational processes are the primary dimensions along which progression or regression are likely to occur. Change in introjective patients seems to occur more rapidly and in more manifest form. Change in anaclitic patients seems to occur more slowly and subtly. These findings indicate the importance of distinguishing between anaclitic and introjective patients and of expecting change in each of these two types of patients to occur, at least initially, along different dimensions. Patients appear to change primarily along the dimensions most salient to their personality organization.

Although these data provide valuable information about the differential nature of change in two groups of patients, they do not provide information about the nature of the treatment process and what aspects of the treatment process contributed to the degree of change noted in these patients. Another study of psychotherapy change, however, provided the opportunity to examine the differential effect of two forms of treatment, supportive-expressive psychotherapy and psychoanalysis, on anaclitic and introjective patients.

The Menninger Psychotherapy Research Project (e.g., Appelbaum 1977; Wallerstein 1986) is a well-known, carefully designed study that evaluated forty-two patients prior to the start of treatment and then subsequently at the end of treatment. Experienced clinicians conducted the treatment and the independent clinical assessments both at the initiation of treatment and at termination. Thirty-three of the forty-two patients had been given a battery of psychological tests, including the Rorschach, as part of the initial evaluation and again at termination. These data have been extensively examined in prior studies, with little indication of a differential advantage for either supportive-expressive psychotherapy or psychoanalysis.

Access to the basic data from the Menninger Psychotherapy Research Group provided the opportunity to conduct an analysis similar to the design reported in the prior study of psychotherapy change. It is important to note, however, that, in contrast to the prior study, all the patients in the Menninger Psychotherapy were outpatients. Of the thirty-three outpatients assessed with psychological test both prior and subsequent to treatment, nine males and nine females were seen in supportive-expressive psychotherapy, and six males and nine females were seen in psychoanalysis. There were no significant differences between the two treatment groups in terms of age or IQ. Patients in psychoanalysis were on average thirty-one years of age and have a Full Scale IQ of 127, whereas the patients in psychotherapy were on average 32.67 years of age and had a Full Scale IQ of 123. Patients in psychoanalysis were seen on average 4.67 times per week for an average total of 734 sessions, whereas patients in psychotherapy were seen on average 2.72 times per week for an average total of 453 sessions.

On the basis of case-history summaries of the presenting symptoms and life history of each of the patients, two experienced clinicians rated whether the patients were predominantly anaclitic or introjective. The judges agreed on twenty-six of the thirty-three cases (79 percent), and the final decision on the remaining seven cases was made by a third judge, also an experienced clinician, who agreed with one judge on four of the cases and with the other judge on three of the cases. The Rorschach protocols were scored by an independent, experienced clinical psychologist who had participated in the prior research and had previously established acceptable levels of reliability for the various measures derived from the Rorschach. The judge was uninformed about any details of the patients and of the test material; for example, he did not know which two Rorschach protocols were from the same patient or whether a particular Rorschach protocol had been obtained at the start or at the termination of treatment.

These psychological test protocols from the Menninger Psychotherapy Research Project have been studied extensively, and the results have generally failed to demonstrate any differential effect for either support-expressive psychotherapy or psychoanalysis. In the present analysis of the Menninger data, the Rorschach protocols were scored for five of the primary dimensions of Rorschach scores identified by Blatt and Berman (1984) (F + %, thought disorder, sum color, and object representation plus and minus). Based on prior cross-sectional research with the object representation measures (Blatt et al. 1976; Fibel 1979), we expected the OR + measure to be particularly effective in evaluating change in the outpatients of the Menninger Study in contrast to the OR − measure, which was effective for evaluating change in the more seriously disturbed inpatients of the prior study. In addition, the Rorschach protocols were scored for the degree of mutuality and cooperation attributed to the interactions of people, animals, and things (Urist 1977; Urist and Shill 1982). All these Rorschach variables were scored with acceptable levels of reliability (item alpha > .65) and have demonstrated validity in prior research. When necessary, analysis of covariance (ANCOVA) was used to control for the effects of the total number of Rorschach responses on a particular Rorschach score.

On the basis of the judges' ratings of the case history records, twenty-one of the patients were considered to be predominantly anaclitic (eight males and thirteen females) and twelve predominantly introjective (six males and six females). Of the twenty-one anaclitic patients, nine were treated in psychoanalysis and twelve in psychotherapy. Of the twelve introjective patients, six were seen in psychoanalysis and six in psychotherapy. Two-way ANOVAs comparing the age, sex, and IQ at the beginning of treatment of anaclitic and introjective males and females in psychoanalysis and psychotherapy yielded a significant main effect for IQ, indicating that introjective patients had higher IQ scores than anaclitic patients. But no other significant differences were found between anaclitic and introjective patients or between patients seen in the two forms of treatment. There was, of course, a significant main effect between the two treatment groups in terms of the number of treatment sessions per week, but the difference between the two treatment groups in terms of the total amount of treatment sessions was not statistically significant. Two-way ANOVAs of the various psychological test variables derived from the Rorschach at the outset of treatment indicated no significant difference between the two treatment groups, but there were several indications that the introjective group were more disturbed than the anaclitic group in that they had significantly ($p < .05$) higher scores on thought disorder and OR − at the outset of treatment.

Two-way analyses of covariance (ANCOVA), covarying Rorschach scores at termination for the level of each of these scores at the outset of treatment, provided a comparison of the effects of the two different types of treatment (psychoanalysis and psychotherapy) for the two groups of patients (anaclitic and introjective). The data clearly indicated a significant patient by treatment interaction. As expected, there were no significant main effects for type of treatment or interaction effects with type of patient on Rorschach variables designed to assess dimensions relevant to more psychotic levels of functioning such as degree of reality testing (F + %), the extent of thought disorder, or the degree of differentiation, articulation, and integration of inaccurately perceived human forms (OR −). There were also no significant main or interaction effects for total number of Rorschach responses or affective lability (sum color responses). But there were highly significant main effects and interaction terms for the degree of differentiation, articulation, and integration of accurately perceived human forms (OR +) and for the measure of the mutuality of autonomy (Urist 1977), which assesses in part the degree of benevolence-malevolence attributed to interactions between people, animals, or objects. On the two measures used to assess the investment in realistic and appropriate interpersonal interactions (OR +), the patients in psychoanalysis had significantly ($p < .05$) greater improvement at termination, controlling for level at the beginning of treatment, than did those patients seen in psychotherapy. This greater improvement on the OR + measure for patients in psychoanalysis as compared to those in psychotherapy was significant in introjective patients ($p < .02$) but did not reach statistical significance for anaclitic patients. There was, however, a highly significant ($p < .001$) interaction between type of treatment and type of patient on the measure of mutuality of autonomy (MOA) (Urist 1977). In terms of both the average MOA score and the level of the single most maladaptive response, introjective patients attributed significantly ($p < .05$) less malevolence to interactions on the Rorschach at termination (controlling for initial level) if they were in psychoanalysis rather than psychotherapy. The reverse was true for anaclitic patients, who had significantly ($p < .01$) fewer malevolent interactions on the Rorschach at termination (controlling for initial level) if they were in psychotherapy than in psychoanalysis. It seems consistent that anaclitic patients predominantly concerned about issues of interpersonal relatedness should be more constructively responsive to face-to-face supportive-expressive psychotherapy rather psychoanalysis, while introjective patients, predominantly concerned with issues of self-definition, power, and autonomy, should be more responsive in psychoanalysis than in psychotherapy.

Summary

In this chapter, I have presented a theoretical model of personality development and of psychopathology. Personality development was discussed as involving a complex, dialectic transaction between the development of the capacity to establish increasingly mature and satisfying interpersonal relationships and the development of a consolidated, realistic, essentially positive, differentiated, and integrated self-definition and identity. Normal variations in character or personality style occur as a consequence of a relative emphasis on one or the other of these two developmental lines. In the extreme, however, defensive exaggerated emphasis on one developmental line at the neglect of the other defines two major configurations of psychopathology. Psychological defenses are an integral aspect of these two primary configurations of psycho-pathology—one that focuses primarily on desperate attempts to establish and maintain satisfying interpersonal relations at the relative neglect of self-definition and identify (anaclitic pathology) or exaggerated attempts to estab-lish and maintain a consolidated sense of self at the expense of relatedness (introjective pathology). Individuals who place exaggerated emphasis on re-latedness utilize primarily avoidant defenses (e.g., denial and repression) in order to try to maintain peace and harmony. Individuals who place exagger-ated emphasis on self-definition utilize primarily counteractive defenses (e.g., projection, intellectualization, reaction formation, and overcompensation) in order to maintain a sense of control and mastery.

Research on depression and on psychotherapy change clearly indicates the importance of differentiating anaclitic and introjective character styles and types of psychopathology. Specifically in terms of defenses, these data sug-gest that it is advantageous to evaluate defenses in terms of two broad clusters of defenses, avoidant as compared to counteractive defenses, rather than at-tempting to identify a large number of separate, individual defense mecha-nisms. In studying defenses, it is also useful to consider defenses, not in iso-lation, but as an integral part of an overall character style. It is important to evaluate defenses as part of a general cognitive style that is expressed both in ways of coping with conflictual and painful issues as well as in ways of coping and responding to more neutral situations and in general adaptation.

In subsequent research, it may be useful to go beyond the broad differentia-tion of two basic or generic types of defenses (avoidant and counteractive) that are a part of two different character styles (anaclitic and introjective) and also to differentiate the general developmental level of these broad types of defenses and character styles. Both avoidant and counteractive defenses have developmentally lower and higher forms, and it may be quite useful in subse-quent research to specify these various levels of functioning within the broad generic distinction of two types of defense processes that are an integral part of two basic character styles. While the research discussed here demonstrated the value of differentiating between the broad character styles (anaclitic and introjective) and their respective types of defense (avoidant and counter-active), it may prove to be equally valuable to differentiate more and less adaptive levels of these character styles and types of defense. The differences between denial and repression, as two levels of anaclitic defenses, and be-tween splitting and isolation versus intellectualization and overcompensation as two levels within introjective defenses may provide a way for making more subtle differentiation within the two broad types of defenses, and this may be productive in subsequent clinical research.

References

Abramson, L. Y., and H. A. Sackheim. A paradox in depression: Uncontrollability and self-blame. *Psychological Bulletin* 84:838–51.

Abramson, L. Y., M. E. P. Seligman and J. D. Teasdale. Learned helplessness in humans: Critique and reformulation. *Journal of Abnormal Psychology* 87:49–74.

Ainsworth, M. D. S. 1969. Object relations, dependency, and attachment: A theoretical review of the mother-infant relationship. *Child Development* 40:969–1025.

Angyal, A. 1941. *Foundations for a science of personality.* New York: Viking.

———. 1951. *Neuroses and treatment: A holistic theory.* Ed. E. Hanfmann and R. M. Jones. New York: Wiley.

Appelbaum, S. 1977. *Anatomy of change.* New York: Plenum.

Arieti, S., and J. Bemporad. 1978. *Severe and mild depression: The psychotherapeutic approach.* New York: Basic.

———. 1980. The psychological organization of depression. *American Journal of Psychiatry* 136:1365–69.

Bakan, D. 1966. *The duality of human existence: An essay on psychology and religion.* Chicago: Rand McNally.

Balint, M. 1959. *Thrills and regressions.* New York: International Universities Press.

Beck, A. T. 1983. Cognitive therapy of depression: New Perspectives. In *Treatment of depression: Old controversies and new approaches,* ed. P. J. Clayton and J. E. Barrett, 265–90. New York: Raven.

Bibring, E. 1953. The mechanism of depression. In *Affective disorders,* ed. P. Greenacre. New York: International Universities Press.

Blatt, S. J. 1974. Levels of object representation in anaclitic and introjective depression. *Psychoanalytic Study of the Child* 24:107–57.

Blatt, S. J., and W. H. Berman. 1984. A methodology for the use of the Rorschach in clinical research. *Journal of Personality Assessment* 48:226–39.

Blatt, S. J., C. B. Brenneis, J. Schimek, and M. Glick. 1976. Normal development and psychopathological impairment of the concept of the object on the Rorschach. *Journal of Abnormal Psychology* 86:364–73.

Blatt, S. J., J. P. D'Afflitti, and D. M. Quinlan. 1976. Experiences of depression in normal young adults. *Journal of Abnormal Psychology* 85:383–89.

Blatt, S. J., and A. Feirstein. 1977. Cardiac responses and personality organization. *Journal of Consulting and Clinical Psychology* 45:115–23.

Blatt, S. J., R. Q. Ford, W. Berman, B. Cook and R. Meyer. 1988. The assessment of therapeutic change in schizophrenic and borderline young adults. *Psychoanalytic Psychology* 5:127–58.

Blatt, S. J., D. M. Quinlan, E. S. Chevron, C. McDonald, and D. Zuroff. 1982. Dependency and self-criticism: Psychological dimensions of depression. *Journal of Consulting and Clinical Psychology* 150:113–24.

Blatt, S. J., and B. A. Ritzler. 1974. Thought disorder and boundary disturbances in psychosis. *Journal of Consulting and Clinical Psychology* 42:370–81.

Blatt, S. J., and S. Shichman. 1983. Two primary configurations of psychopathology. *Psychoanalysis and Contemporary Thought* 6:187–254.

Blatt, S. J., and C. M. Wild. 1976. *Schizophrenia: A developmental analysis.* New York: Academic.

Bowlby, J. 1969. *Attachment and loss,* vol. 1. New York: Basic.

———. 1973. *Attachment and loss.* vol. 2, *Separation, anxiety, and anger.* New York: Basic.

———. 1977. The making and breaking of affectional bonds. I. Etiology and psychopathology in light of attachment theory. *British Journal of Psychiatry* 130:201–10.

———. 1980. *Attachment and loss.* vol. 3, *Loss, separation, and depression.* New York: Basic.

———. 1988. Developmental psychology comes of age. *American Journal of Psychiatry* 145:1–10.

Brennan, S. 1984. The effect of subliminal separation-individuation schemas on moral reasoning and mood in depressed and nondepressed women. Ph.D. diss., New York University.

Bryne, D., J. Barry, and D. Nelson. 1963. Relation of the revised repression-sensitization scale to measures of self-description. *Psychological Reports* 13:323–34.

Cane, D. B., C. J. Olinger, I. H. Gotlib, and N. A. Kuiper. 1986. Factor structure of the Dysfunctional Attitude Scale in a student sample. *Journal of Clinical Psychology* 42:307–9.

Chodoroff, P. 1972. The depressive personality: A critical review. *Archives of General Psychiatry* 27:666–73.

Cohen, M. B., G. Baker, R. A. Cohen, F. Fromm-Reichman, E. V. Weigert. 1954. An intensive study of twelve cases of manic-depressive psychosis. *Psychiatry* 17:103–37.

Dauber, R. B. 1980. An investigation of guilt, loss and the separation-individuation process in depression. Ph.D. diss., Loyola University of Chicago.

———. 1984. Subliminal psychodynamic activation in depression. *Journal of Abnormal Psychology* 93:9–18.

Erikson, E. H. 1950. *Childhood and society.* New York: Norton.

———. 1974. *Dimensions of a new identity: 1973 Jefferson lectures in the humanities.* New York: Norton.

Eysenck, H. 1960. *The structure of human personality.* Rev. ed. London: Methuen.

Fairweather, G., R. Simon, M. Beghard, E. Weingarten, J. Holland, R. Sanders, C. Stone, and J. Reahl. 1960. Relative effectiveness of psychotherapeutic programs: A multicriteria comparison of four programs for three different patient groups. *Psychology Monographs* 74:171–85.

Fernandez, C. 1986. The effects of subliminal activated guilt versus object loss on anaclitic and introjective depression. M.A. thesis, Ohio University.

Fibel, B. 1979. Toward a developmental model of depression: Object representation and object loss in adolescent and adult psychiatric patients. Ph.D. diss., University of Massachusetts at Amherst.

Fonseca, E. 1987. A study of anaclitic depression using the subliminal psychodynamic activation method. M.A. thesis, New York University.

Franz, C. E., and K. M. White. 1985. Individuation and attachment in personality development: Extending Erikson's theory. *Journal of Personality* 53:224–56.

Freud, S. [1905] 1953. Three essays on the theory of sexuality. In *The standard edition of the complete psychological works of Sigmund Freud*, ed. J. Strachey, vol. 7. London: Hogarth.

———. [1915] 1957. Repression. In *The standard edition of the complete psychological works of Sigmund Freud*, ed. Strachey, vol. 14. London: Hogarth.

———. [1917] 1957. Mourning and melancholia. In *The standard edition of the complete psychological works of Sigmund Freud*, ed. J. Strachey, vol. 14. London: Hogarth.

———. [1926] 1959. Inhibitions, symptoms, and anxiety. In *The standard edition of the complete psychological works of Sigmund Freud*, ed. J. Strachey, vol. 20. London: Hogarth.

Friedman, H. S. and S. Booth-Kewley. 1987. The disease-prone personality: A meta-analytic view of the construct. *American Psychologist* 42:539–55.

Gilligan, C. 1982. *In a different voice.* Cambridge, Mass.: Harvard University Press.

———. 1983. Do the social sciences have an adequate theory of moral development? In *Social sciences: Moral inquiry,* ed. N. Haan, P. Bellak, M. Robins, and P. Sullivan. Berkeley: University of California Press.

Hammen, C. L., T. Marks, A. Mayol, and R. deMayo. 1985. Depressive self-schemas, life stress, and vulnerability to depression. *Journal of Abnormal Psychology* 94:308–19.

Harty, M., M. Cerney, D. Colson, L. Coyne, S Freiswyk, S. Johnston, and R. Mortimer. 1981. Correlates of change and long-term outcome for intensively treated hospital patients: An exploratory study. *Bulletin of the Menninger Clinic* 45:209–28.

Hirschfeld, R. M. A., G. L. Klerman, P. Chodoff, S. Korchin, and J. Barrett. 1976. Dependency, self-esteem—clinical depression. *Journal of the American Academy of Psychoanalysis* 4:373–88.

Hirschfeld, R. M. A., G. L. Klerman, H. G. Gough, et al. 1977. A measure of interpersonal dependency. *Journal of Personality Assessment* 41:610–18.

Horney, K. 1945. *Our inner conflicts.* New York: Norton.

———. 1950. *Neurosis and human growth.* New York: Norton.

Jung, C. G. 1928. *Contributions to analytic psychology.* London: Routledge & Kegan Paul.

Kobassa, S. C. 1982. The hardy personality: Toward a social psychology of stress and health. In *Social psychology of health and illness,* ed. J. Suls and G. Sanders. Hillsdale, N.J.: Erlbaum.

Korchin, S. J., and D. G. Larson. 1977. Form perception and ego functioning. In *Rorschach psychology,* ed. M. Rickers-Ovsiankina. Huntington, N.Y.: Krieger.

Koufopoulos, R. M. 1986. A study of introjective depression using the subliminal psychodynamic activation method. Ph.D. diss., New York University.

Laplanche, J., and J. B. Pontalis. 1973. *The language of psychoanalysis.* New York: Norton.

Lesse, S. 1974. *Masked depression.* New York: Aronson.

McAdams, D. P. 1980. A thematic coding system for the intimacy motive. *Journal of Research in Personality* 14:413–32.

———. 1985. *Power, intimacy, and the life story: Personological inquiries into identity.* Homewood, Ill.: Dorsey.

McCaully, M. H. 1981. Jung's theory of psychological types and the Myers-Briggs Indicator. In *Advances in psychological assessment,* ed. P. McReynolds, vol. 5, pp. 294–352. San Francisco: Jossey-Bass.

McClelland, D. C. 1980. Motive dispositions: The merits of operant and respondent measures. In *Review of personality and social psychology,* ed. L. Wheeler. Beverly Hills, Calif.: Sage.

———. 1984. *Human motivation.* Glenview, Ill.: Scott Foresman.

———. 1986. Some reflections on the two psychologies of love. *Journal of Personality* 54:334–53.

McClelland, D. C., J. W. Atkinson, R. A. Clark, and E. L. Lowell. 1953. *The achievement motive.* New York: Appleton-Century-Crofts.

Maddi, S. 1980. *Personality theories: A comparative analysis.* 4th ed. Homewood, Ill.: Dorsey.

Mahler, M. S., F. Pine, and A. Bergman. 1975. *The psychological birth of the human infant.* New York: Basic.

Miller, J. B. [1976] 1986. *Toward a new psychology of women.* 2d ed. Boston: Beacon.

Mongrain, M., and D. C. Zuroff. 1988. Cognitive vulnerability to depression: An aspect of dependent and self-critical personality styles. Typescript.

Myers, I. B. 1962. *Manual: The Myers-Briggs Type Indicator.* Palo Alto, Calif.: Consulting Psychologists Press.

Oliver, J. M., and B. P. Baumgart. 1985. The Dysfunctional Attitude Scale: Psychometric properties in an unselected adult population. *Cognitive Theory and Research* 19:161–69.

Peterson, G., S. M. Schwartz, and M. E. P. Seligman. 1981. Self-blame and depressive symptoms. *Journal of personality and social psychology* 41:253–59.

Robins, C. J., and P. Block. Sociotropy, autonomy, depressive vulnerability. Paper presented at the meeting of the American Psychological Association, New York, August.

Schmidt, J. 1981. The effects of subliminally presented anaclitic and introjective stimuli on normal young adults. Ph.D. diss., University of South Mississippi.

Schmidt, J., R. D. Fallot, and A. L. Dickson. 1985. The effect of subliminally presented loss and guilt related stimuli on college students. Paper presented at the meeting of the American Psychological Association, Los Angeles, August.

Segal, Z. V., B. F. Shaw, and D. B. Vella. 1987. Life stress and depression: A test of the congruence hypothesis for life event content and depressive subtypes. Paper presented at the meeting of the American Psychological Association, August.

Seligman, M. E. P. 1975. *Helplessness: On depression, development, and death.* San Francisco: Freeman.

Shapiro, D. 1965. *Neurotic styles.* New York: Basic.

———. 1977. A perceptual understanding of color responses. In *Rorschach psychology,* ed. M. Rickers-Ovsiankina. Huntington, N.Y.: Krieger.

Shor, J., and J. Sanville. 1978. *Illusion in loving: A psychoanalytic approach to intimacy and autonomy.* Los Angeles: Double Helix.

Silverman, L. H. 1966. A technique for the study of psychodynamic relationships: The effects of subliminally presented aggressive stimuli on the production of pathological thinking in a schizophrenic population. *Journal of Consulting and Clinical Psychology* 30:103–11.

———. 1983. The subliminal psychodynamic activation method: Overview and comprehensive listing of studies. In *Empirical studies of psychoanalytic theories,* ed. J. Masling, vol. 1. Hillsdale, N.J.: Erlbaum.

———. 1985. Research on psychoanalytic psychodynamic propositions. *Clinical Psychology Review* 5:247–57.

Smith, T. W., J. L. O'Keeffe, M. Jenkins. In press. Dependency and self-criticism: Correlates of depression of moderators of the effects of stressful events. *Journal of Personality Disorders.*

Spiegel, H., and D. Spiegel. 1978. *Trance and treatment: Clinical uses of hypnosis.* New York: Basic.

Stern, D. N. 1985. *The psychological world of the infant.* New York: Basic.

Stewart, A. S., and J. E. Malley. 1987. Role combination in women in early adult years: Mitigating agency and communion. In *Spouse, parent, worker: On gender and multiple roles,* ed. F. Crosby. New Haven, Conn.: Yale University Press.

Strauss, J. C., and D. W. Harder. 1981. The Case Record Rating Scale: A method for rating symptom and social function data from case records. *Psychiatry Research* 4:333–45.

Strauss, J. C., R. F. Kokes, B. A. Ritzler, D. W. Harder, and A. Van Ord. 1978. Patterns of disorder in first admission psychiatric patients. *Journal of Nervous and Mental Disease* 166:611–25.

Urist, J. 1977. The Rorschach test and the assessment of object relations. *Journal of Personality Assessment* 41:3–9.

Urist, J., and M. Shill. 1982. Validity of the Rorschach Mutuality of Autonomy Scale: A replication using excerpted responses. *Journal of Personality Assessment* 46:451–54.

Wallerstein, R. 1986. *Forty-two lives.* San Francisco: Jossey-Bass.

Webster's third new international dictionary. 1960. Springfield, Mass.: Merriam-Webster.

Weissman, A. N., and A. T. Beck. 1978. Development and validation of the Dysfunctional Attitudes Scale: A preliminary investigation. Paper presented at the meeting of the American Psychological Association, Toronto, August.

Werner, H. 1948. *Comparative psychology of mental development.* New York: International Universities Press.

Winter, D. 1973. *The power motive.* New York: Free Press.

Witkin, H. A. 1965. Psychological differentiation and forms of pathology. *Journal of Abnormal Psychology* 70:317–36.

Witkin, H. A., R. B. Dyk, H. I. Faterson, D. R. Goodenough, and S. A. Karp. 1962. *Psychological differentiation.* New York: Wiley.

Zung, W. W. 1972. How normal is depression? *Psychosomatics* 13:174–78.

Zuroff, D. C., and S. de Lorimier. In press. Dependency and self-criticism as predictors of the personality characteristics of women's ideal boyfriends and their satisfaction with actual boyfriends. *Journal of Personality.*

Zuroff, D. C., and D. Fitzpatrick. 1988. Romantic relationships of dependent and self-critical women. McGill University. Typescript.

Zuroff, D., and D. L. Franko. 1986. Depressed and test anxious students' interactions with friends: Effects of dependency and self-criticism. Paper presented at meeting of the Eastern Psychological Association, New York, April.

Zuroff, D., and M. Mongrain. 1987a. Attributions of dependent and self-critical women for interpersonal rejection and achievement failure. McGill University. Typescript.

Zuroff, D. C., and M. Mongrain. 1987b. Dependency and self-criticism: Vulnerability factors for depressive affective states. *Journal of Abnormal Psychology* 96:114–22.

Zuroff, D. C., D. S. Moskowitz, M. S. Wieglus, T. A. Powers, and D. L. Franko. 1983. Construct validation of the dependency and self-criticism scales of the Depressive Experiences Questionnaire. *Journal of Research in Personality* 17:226–41.

14 The Construct Validity of the Repressive Coping Style

*If the "Know thyself" of the oracle were an easy thing for
every person, it would not be held to be a divine injunction.*

Plutarch

In recent years, both psychoanalytic (e.g., Kernberg 1982; Kohut 1971) and
social-cognitive (e.g., Bandura 1986; Mischel 1979) theories have assigned
increasing importance to the concept of the "self." Although terminologies
differ, most current formulations of personality attempt to understand how
individuals' self-perceptions, goals, and values influence their behavior. For
example, it is no longer considered solely a psychodynamic perspective to
suggest that individuals often evaluate their interactions in ways that protect
their self-esteem (e.g., Greenwald 1980; Lewinsohn et al. 1980; Swann
1983).

Beyond this common ground, some fundamental schisms remain between
social-cognitive (including cognitive-behavioral) theories and insight-
oriented approaches (e.g., Messer and Winokur 1980). The former tend to
emphasize the role of the self in regulating and evaluating interchanges with
the outside world (Bandura 1986; Cantor and Kihlstrom 1987). Most cognitive interventions are designed to facilitate these interactions by decreasing
dysfunctional negative affects. For example, Beck (1976, 214) stated that the
goal of cognitive therapy is to "alleviate psychological distress." The other
major set of difficulties targeted by cognitive-behavioral treatments relates to
inadequate impulse control (e.g., Kendall and Bemis 1983). Within a cognitive framework, well-adjusted individuals might be defined as efficacious social problem solvers who experience little dysphoric affect or problems with
self-control (e.g., Rosenbaum 1980).

Psychoanalytic, neoanalytic, and humanistic-experiential theorists would
consider this definition of adjustment at best incomplete. They emphasize that
the self must struggle to understand and integrate internal realities as well as
cope successfully with external ones. Within this tradition, some individuals

The author would like to thank Kim Bartholomew, Chris Beck, Richard Davidson, Matthew
Erdelyi, Martin Ford, Steve Houseworth, Jack Mayer, Craig Smith, and Steve Tublin for their
comments on earlier drafts of this chapter.

337

who seem superficially well adjusted are viewed as having an "idealized self" (Horney 1950, 158) that maladaptively fails to acknowledge some fundamental aspects of human nature. Freud ([1930] 1961) described this phenomenon in terms of the harsh superego's attempts to exclude unsavory affects and impulses from subjective experience as well as from overt expression. Neoanalytic and humanistic theorists provided more enobling descriptions of this type of intrapsychic conflict. One of their hallmarks is the conclusion that some individuals develop an illusory sense of high self-esteem by faithfully meeting the actual or internalized expectations of others in a way that disavowed their "true inner nature" (Maslow 1970, 46), "genuine reactions" (Rogers 1961, 110), or *real self* (Horney 1950, 17).

These formulations remain highly controversial because they postulate mechanisms that are genuinely self-deceptive and therefore partly *unconscious*. Although specifics differ, most humanistic and neoanalytic theorists endorse Freud's general concept of repressive defenses. For example, Rogers (1951, 510) believed that "psychological maladjustment exists when the organism denies to awareness significant sensory and visceral experiences" that are not compatible with "the self-structure." Similarly, Maslow (1962, 57) speculated that we "protect ourselves and our ideal image of ourselves by repression," by which "we avoid becoming conscious of unpleasant or dangerous truths."

According to these views, some highly socialized individuals are so invested in maintaining certain self-perceptions that they regularly misread their own affective reactions. Whereas cognitive interventions stress the importance of controlling negative affects, psychodynamic and phenomenological approaches emphasize the need to become more aware of them. For example, Perls, Hefferline, and Goodman (1951, 432) wrote that a major goal of Gestalt therapy is "to make anxiety tolerable."

This chapter will examine whether individuals operationally defined as having a repressive coping style actually fail to recognize their own affective responses. It is written from the perspective that individuals who consider maintaining low levels of negative affect central to their self-concepts are likely to employ a variety of strategies to avoid conscious knowledge of their "genuine reactions." Before this hypothesis can be evaluated, certain assumptions about the nature of both the emotion system and unconscious defenses must be articulated, and psychometric issues related to identifying individuals prone to a repressive style must be considered. Next, research will be discussed that indicates that repressors, as a group, seem actively engaged in keeping themselves (rather than just other people) convinced that they are *not* prone to negative affect. However, their strongly held beliefs are contradicted by objective assessments of behavior and physiology that indicate that repressors have levels of anxiety equal to or greater than those of individuals reporting chronic distress. Several associated social-cognitive and affective deficits are described that would be expected if repressors' defensiveness is more than a superficial behavior. Finally, potential mechanisms underlying these defensive processes and their effects on psychological and physical health are outlined. As in any investigation of construct validity (Cronbach and Meehl, 1955), these issues will be pursued by investigating the plausibility of alternative hypotheses and evaluating the convergence of the evidence.

A Framework for Conceptualizing Repressive Defenses

The Semiautonomous Functioning of the Emotion System

Freud's early formulations of unconscious defenses focused on the repression of specific memories. At the time, he was interested in explaining hysterical phenomena in which dissociated affects remained in consciousness.[1] However, in his later writings, there was a "centering of the repression concept on the inhibition of the capacity for emotional experience" (Madison 1956, 79). Subsequent psychoanalytic, neoanalytic, and humanistic theorists have also generally emphasized that representations of affects and impulses per se are the primary targets of defense. For example, Anna Freud (1966, 3) defined psychoanalysis as "the study of repressed instinctual impulses, affects, and fantasies." In a similar vein, Karen Horney (1950, 23) emphasized that defenses are designed to exclude "painful and unbearable feelings" by removing the "borderline between what we *should* feel and *do* feel" (Horney 1950, 82).

Hypothesizing that some individuals often do not recognize their own affective reactions only becomes tenable within certain perspectives on the nature of emotion. Gazzaniga (1985), among others, has noted that much of two thousand years of Western thought has urged us to view the brain as creating a unified cognitive process. The dominant view of emotions in the 1960s and 1970s (e.g., Schachter and Singer 1962; Mandler 1975) rested firmly within this tradition. Emotions were formulated as the "interactions between the arousal system and the cognitive-interpretive system" (Mandler 1975, 65), the cognitive system both inciting the affective arousal and determining its meaning. This model leaves little room for self-deception about one's emotional states (cf. Sarbin 1981; Szabados 1985). If the emotion system is considered incapable of independent assessment of sensory information, one's emotional

---

1. The tradition associated with psychoanalytically oriented psychological testing highlighted Freud's early descriptions of hysterical amnesia and hypothesized that repression is associated with histrionic "unreflectiveness, naivete," and "relatively unmodulated affect" (Gardner et al. 1959; cf. Bonanno and Singer and Luborsky, Crits-Christoph, and Alexander, both in this volume). In my lexicon, this phenomenon is more dissociative than repressive (cf. Erdelyi, Kihlstrom, and Spiegel, all in this volume).

state becomes whatever the "cognitive-interpretive system" decides that it is (Schachter and Singer 1962).

However, recent work on the modular, hierarchical, and parallel nature of human information-processing and brain subsystems (e.g., Fodor 1983; Gazzaniga 1985; Hilgard 1986; McClelland and Rumelhart 1986) provides a very different understanding of human nature. A psychobiological perspective suggests that emotions emanate, at least in part, from subcortical centers that are semiautonomous from verbal information processing (e.g., MacLean 1975; Panksepp 1982). MacLean (1975) has summarized that our "paleomammalian brain," which includes the limbic system, has its "own special kind of intelligence" and can function somewhat independently from more recently developed neocortical centers. He noted that this phenomenon "may partly account for conflicts between what we affectively 'feel' and what we 'know'" (75, 81).

Affective specialization within the neocortex has also been demonstrated. For example, the frontal region of the right cerebral hemisphere, which is highly interconnected with the limbic system, seems to be particularly activated during the processing and generation of many negative emotions (Davidson 1984). The judgments of this nonverbal center may at times be functionally dissociated from those represented by the language centers in the left hemisphere (e.g., Davidson 1983; Schwartz, 1986, in this volume).

The current practice (e.g., Lazarus 1984) of using the term "cognitive" to include all human information processing makes it difficult to describe the emotion system as engaging its own form of "thinking" without it seeming a contradiction in terms. Nonetheless, there is growing evidence that this system, though interactive with other subsystems, is capable of conducting its own assessments of sensory information (e.g., Izard 1984; Leventhal 1984). LeDoux (in press) has recently reviewed neurological findings that sensory messages are transmitted directly to regions of the limbic system without initially being relayed through the neocortex. In accord with MacLean (1975) and others, LeDoux concludes that "processes which encode the adaptive value or affective significance" of stimuli occur in subcortical regions outside of conscious awareness. The emotion system, in part, specializes in anticipating whether situations may require significant psychophysiological preparation, such as for flight (experienced as fear), physical combat (i.e., anger), or loss and deprivation (i.e., sadness; Schwartz, Weinberger, and Singer 1981).

Recent research (Leventhal 1984; Roseman 1984; Scherer 1984; Smith and Ellsworth 1985) has begun to model the kinds of information that the emotion system evaluates to determine what specific patterns of emotion seem warranted. For example, sadness seems to reflect an assessment that an unpleasant situation is due to uncontrollable circumstances and that nothing can be done to change it (Smith and Ellsworth 1985). We often have no direct introspective access to how the emotion system itself derives these appraisals; instead, we must rely on our subjective experiences of resulting emotions (Schwartz and Weinberger 1980) and on inferences based on implicit theories about what it must be doing (cf. Nisbett and Wilson 1977). From observations of split-brain patients, Gazzaniga (1985) actually claims to have identified an interpretive subsystem within the left hemisphere that specializes in constructing explanations for behaviors and emotional responses generated by other modules within the brain.

Although we have only a preliminary understanding of how the cognitive-interpretive and emotion systems influence each other, we do know that they can respond very differently to the same event. One obvious example is how they react to inputs from another brain subsystem, the one that produces visual imagery (e.g., Kosslyn 1987). Having individuals imagine a threatening scene or watch a disturbing motion picture reliably incites specific patterns of emotion, including differentiated autonomic changes and facial expressions, even though individuals clearly "know" that these images pose no real threat (e.g., Lang 1979; Schwartz, Weinberger, and Singer 1981). Similarly, Wolpe (1978), representing a behavioral perspective, noted that neurotic individuals are often afraid in situations that they acknowledge are not objectively dangerous. These observations are consistent with the data suggesting that conditioning of emotional responses can occur without any involvement of the higher cortex (LeDoux, in press). Thus, emotional responses to some degree have their own integrity, even when the cognitive-interpretive system considers them irrational or inappropriate (cf. Ellis 1987).

On the Nature of Unconscious Defenses

Current psychobiological research suggests that our cognitive-interpretive and emotion systems can generate quite discrepant assessments of the same stimuli. Therefore, commonplace self-perceptions such as "I am really feeling anxious even though I know there is no reason to be" may validly reflect the modular nature of human information processing. Insight-oriented psychotherapists fairly uniformly assert that not all individuals readily tolerate these types of discrepancies. They suggest that some invoke repressive defenses and self-deceptively reach false conclusions such as "I am not feeling anxious because there is no reason to be."

In this chapter, repressive individuals are hypothesized to be persons who often believe that they are not upset despite objective evidence to the contrary. However, it is no easy task to define when someone is employing this type of unconscious defense. Despite widely held clinical belief, many researchers would conclude that no form of unconscious defense has been adequately demonstrated (e.g., Holmes, in this volume).

For our purposes, a first step may be to define the essential properties of the concept without including auxiliary tenets (e.g., the role of childhood experience). Bower (in this volume) recently highlighted Dennett's (1969) distinction between two types of awareness. In the first sense, people are aware of a proposition if they can talk about it. In psychoanalytic terms, the proposition is either conscious or preconscious. In the second sense, people are aware of a proposition if an observer can claim with justification that they are "taking account of" that belief (proposition) in their behavior (Bower, in this volume). Unconscious awareness might be defined as the condition in which there is awareness according to the second definition but not according to the first. Therefore, individuals would have only unconscious knowledge of those affective states that they sincerely cannot recognize but that observers can reliably infer. Methodological advances now provide a variety of techniques for inferring emotional states independent of verbal reports (e.g., Schwartz 1986).

Evidence that repressive individuals' perceptions of their emotional states may be contradicted by objective assessments is central to claiming the existence of unconscious influences. However, certainly not all unconscious phenomena are the product of motivated defenses (e.g., Bowers and Meichenbaum 1984). Many, if not most, can be interpreted in terms of the limits of our introspective capacities (e.g., Nisbett and Ross 1980). For example, we are often unaware that certain environmental events are influencing our behavior simply because we have not attended to the appropriate cues (e.g., Bower, in this volume).

Two additional criteria are necessary to conclude that information excluded from consciousness involves a defensive process. First, the information must be potentially accessible. Second, there must be clear motivation for keeping it out of awareness.

It is often very difficult to determine the accessibility of mental contents such as specific memories (Erdelyi, in this volume) or interpretations of particular behaviors (Nisbett and Ross 1980). In contrast, it is not an inherently difficult task to know you are upset at times when others are able to infer it. Freud's ([1915] 1957) description of repression requiring an effortful struggle *not* to know seems particularly apt in this regard. Emotions are, by definition, psychophysiological responses that are difficult to ignore. Very young children, who have not yet developed inhibitory controls, have no trouble expressing the fact that they are upset despite difficulties articulating why. Therefore, it is reasonable to conclude that, if an emotional state is unconscious, it is not because we lack the capacity to know what we are feeling.

The second criterion requires specification of why individuals with a repressive style would be motivated to avoid awareness of negative emotion. In psychoanalytic theory, information is not repressed solely because it is unpleasant. Reality testing remains intact such that people do not forget that they have experienced a divorce or been fired from their jobs. Within Gur and Sackeim's (1979) framework, unconscious defenses entail active self-deception in that one is motivated to keep something out of awareness specifically because it is incompatible with a conscious belief. Freud, from the beginning, felt that a person repressed an idea when he (or she) felt an "incompatibility between the unbearable idea and his ego" ([1894] 1940, 62). This formulation suggests that internal or external percepts become the target of defenses when they directly or indirectly contradict strongly held beliefs about the self. Failure, however unpleasant, that confirms an already established self-perception would not ordinarily invoke repression.

Freud clarified his view of this mechanism when he wrote, "Repression . . . proceeds from the self-respect of the ego. The very impressions, experiences, impulses and desires that one man indulges . . . will be rejected with the utmost indignation by another or stifled at once even before they enter consciousness. . . . this formation of an ideal would be the condition of repression" ([1914] 1957, 93). Freud postulated that, as we mature, we develop standards of how we would like to be (our "ego ideal") and how we believe we ought to be (our "conscience"). Experiences of discrepancies between these ideals and perceptions of our actual behavior are themselves major sources of negative affects (Higgins 1987; Higgins, Klein, and Strauman 1985). One strategy for reducing this discomfort is to fail to recognize the discrepancies. For example, if one's self-concept (i.e., "the self-respect of the ego") incorporates an idealized image that one is not prone to certain threatening affects and impulses, defensive maneuvers may be undertaken to exclude them from awareness (Freud 1966).

In summary, individuals with repressive coping styles are likely to use a variety of strategies to avoid awareness of affects and impulses that are incompatible with their self-images. They should not only repress threatening memories (Davis, in this volume) but also recruit several related neurotic-level defenses (Vaillant 1977, in this volume) such as intellectualization and denial. Paradoxically, repressors' preoccupation with avoiding awareness of anxiety may interfere with effective coping and actually heighten behavioral and physiological indications of distress.

Within the framework outlined above, it is possible to evaluate whether repressive individuals actually employ unconscious defenses against negative affect. Postulating this form of self-deception requires a convergence of evidence that repressors *(1) are motivated to maintain self-perceptions of little subjective experience of negative emotion despite (2) tendencies to respond physiologically and behaviorally in a manner indicative of high levels of perceived threat.*

Close examination of data relevant to this formulation is essential for establishing the construct validity of a repressive style. An assessment of repressors' subjective reality, including ways of distinguishing their self-evaluations from impression management, must be juxtaposed with the evidence concerning their nonverbal and physiological behavior.

Psychometric Issues in Defining a Repressive Style

Measuring Repressive Defensiveness as an Individual Difference Dimension

Before these criteria can be evaluated, a reliable and valid procedure is required to identify individuals prone to a repressive style. An individual differences strategy is essential in this case because the phenomenon is not defined as a universal tendency that can be created in the laboratory using unselected subjects (cf. Holmes, in this volume). Rather than idiographically assuming that everyone is different or nomothetically assuming that everyone is the same, this approach highlights the prototypical features of different types of persons (cf. Cantor and Mischel 1979; Weinberger and Schwartz, in press).

As outlined earlier, Freud and other insight-oriented theorists suggested that some individuals are very repressive and that others are not. However, since none of these writers defined their terms operationally, researchers are inevitably testing their own derivative constructs rather than the original theories. Therefore, it is especially important to define these measures clearly in order to facilitate comparisons with alternative formulations.

For the past quarter century, most laboratory studies attempting to identify a repressive style have employed the Byrne Repression-Sensitization scale (see Bell and Byrne 1978). This measure evolved from the perceptual defense literature (e.g., Eriksen 1966), in which repressors were defined as individuals who have heightened recognition thresholds for anxiety-provoking stimuli. However, the Byrne scale has limited discriminant validity, despite its widespread use. It correlates as highly as $-.91$ with the Taylor (1953) Manifest Anxiety Scale (MAS) and almost as high with several other measures of distress (e.g., Golin et al. 1967; Sullivan and Roberts 1969).

At one end of the scales, this is not particularly a problem. It is consistent that someone who reports habitual high anxiety would report being sensitized to negative emotions. However, among those who report low levels of negative affect, the scale does not distinguish between repressors, who maladaptively avoid the perception or experience of negative affect, and truly low-anxious individuals (cf. Spielberger 1972), who accurately report being well adjusted and not prone to excessive distress. Weinberger, Schwartz, and Davidson (1979) hypothesized that the widespread disillusionment (e.g., Hodges 1976) in the 1960s and 1970s that self-reports of anxiety do not correlate with more objective behavioral and physiological indices resulted in part from the repressors' confounding influence.

Beginning in the late 1960s (e.g., Boor and Schill 1967), a small body of research used the Marlowe-Crowne Social Desirability Scale (Crowne and Marlowe 1960) to discriminate defensive versus nondefensive individuals reporting low distress. For example, Holroyd (1972) found that only individuals who scored high on the Marlowe-Crowne as well as low on the Byrne scale

Table 1. Definitions of the Three-Group Typology

Subjective Experience of Anxiety (e.g., MAS)	Defensiveness (Marlowe-Crowne)		
	Low	Moderate	High
High	High anxious	High anxious	High anxious
Low	Low anxious	Low anxious	Repressive

had heightened recognition thresholds for stimuli associated with sexual versus nonsexual pictures. These literatures developed confusing labels such as "nondefensive repressors." Therefore, Weinberger, Schwartz, and Davidson (1979) redefined repressors as those individuals who score low on a measure of trait anxiety (or the Byrne scale) but high (at least in the upper third) on a measure of defensiveness such as the Marlowe-Crowne (see table 1). "Truly" low-anxious subjects were defined as those low in defensiveness as well as anxiety.[2]

The Nature of the Marlowe-Crowne

The use of the Marlowe-Crowne as a measure of defensiveness is notable given the ongoing practice of using the scale to measure response style rather than a substantive dimension (e.g., Tanaka-Matsumi and Kameoka 1986). Crowne and Marlowe (1960) developed their scale because the widely used Edwards (1957) Social Desirability Scale, in essence, reinterpreted reports on the Minnesota Multiphasic Personality Inventory (MMPI) based on desirability ratings of the items. For example, twenty-two of the thirty-nine items on Edward's measure are merely Taylor Manifest Anxiety Scale items scored in the reverse direction (Edwards 1957). Although Edwards demonstrated that individuals consider it more desirable to report low rather than high distress, he did not present evidence of individual differences in response biases.

Crowne and Marlowe (1960) recognized that a low score on items such as "I have diarrhea . . . once a month or more" (Crowne 1979, 154) may at least sometimes reflect reality rather than attempts to "look good." Therefore, they designed their scale to be independent of psychopathology by measuring "behaviors which are culturally sanctioned and approved but which are improbable of occurrence" (Crowne and Marlowe 1960, 350). A prototypic item is "I never hesitate to go out of my way to help someone in trouble."

Within four years, Crowne and Marlowe (1964) recognized that their scale, like Edwards's, was primarily measuring a substantive individual difference dimension rather than a response bias. Since that time, a formidable body of research (e.g., Arkin and Lake 1983; Nordholm 1974; McCrae and Costa

2. To integrate various findings, studies using the Marlowe-Crowne in addition to a measure of distress such as the Byrne scale will be presented using this terminology.

1983; Wiesenthal 1974) has developed, suggesting the scale does *not* identify individuals "who are most likely to distort their responses to survey questions." Rather, the scale largely taps individual differences that are "part of the real variance in the data" (Bradburn and Sudman 1980, 106, 105).

The current evidence is most consistent with the interpretation that high scorers on the Marlowe-Crowne generally believe what they are reporting and attempt to behave accordingly. For example, close friends of high scorers corroborated that these subjects actually try to conform to the rigid standards of self-control reflected in the items (Strahan and Strahan 1972). Although I will return to issues of self-presentation versus self-deception later in this chapter, it is of interest to speculate why the Marlowe-Crowne seems in large part to measure "defensiveness and protection of self-esteem" (Crowne and Marlowe 1964, 206).

For low scorers on the Marlowe-Crowne, "socially desirable" responding may be agreeing that certain perceived universals about human nature also apply to them. They, like the authors of the scale, may simply consider it untenable to deny statements such as "I sometimes feel resentful when I don't get my way." It is common knowledge that individuals who make implausible claims are often suspected of lying (cf. Kraut 1978), and blatant lying is hardly considered "socially desirable." Therefore, high scorers must believe they are at least capable of the kind of extraordinary self-control reflected in the items. Otherwise, they too would consider it folly to make such claims.

Assessing Repressors' Subjective Reality

Consistencies in Reports of Negative Emotion

Once a psychometric definition of a repressive style has been established, it is possible to evaluate its construct validity in relation to the criteria outlined above. Repressors are, in part, defined as individuals who claim, on self-report measures, little tendency to experience distress. There is abundant evidence that individuals who report low distress are typically consistent in these judgments across a large variety of measures and across decades (e.g., Watson and Clark 1984). For example, Costa, McCrae, and Arenberg (1980) found adults' reports of their emotionality on the Guilford-Zimmerman Temperament Survey had average twelve-year test-retest correlations of .70 (without correcting for attenuation). Moreover, a longitudinal study of the MMPI scores of a sample of middle-aged men found, for example, that reports of depression correlated .47 over a thirty-year period (Leon et al. 1979). Thus, individuals who report perceiving themselves as especially low in negative affect are reasonably likely to maintain some semblance of that view throughout much of their adult lives. Although there is considerable intraindividual variation in mood, there is also a notable degree of interindividual stability in terms of the "set points" around which this variation occurs (cf. Ford 1987).

Like aggregated reports of negative affect, defensiveness scores on the Marlowe-Crowne are quite stable over time. Strickland and Crowne (1963) found that the test-retest correlation for clinic outpatients over a five-month period was .68, even though they all participated in twenty to twenty-five hours of psychotherapy. Swann (1983), among others, has emphasized how difficult it is to influence global self-perceptions permanently.

Repressors generally report even less tendency to experience negative affect than nondefensive, low-anxious subjects (Kahn and Schill 1971; Weinberger, Schwartz, and Davidson 1979). Thus, very low scorers on an anxiety measure or on the Byrne scale are likely to have relatively high Marlowe-Crowne scores and be identified as repressors in the Weinberger, Schwartz, and Davidson (1979) typology. Repressors also tend to report lower levels of state anxiety or tension than low-anxious subjects when participating in stressful tasks (Asendorpf and Scherer 1983; Kiecolt-Glaser and Greenberg 1983). These findings are consistent with the hypothesis that repressors find even normative experiences of negative affect to be threatening (cf. Schwartz and Weinberger 1980).

Weinberger and Schwartz (1982) investigated this hypothesis more directly using an emotional situations questionnaire that included events that normatively evoke one of six emotions: happiness, sadness, depression, anger, fear, or anxiety. In this study, repressors and low-anxious subjects were selected to be in the lower third of the Taylor Manifest Anxiety scale distribution and the high-anxious groups to be in the upper third. Repressors were similar to the other groups in the level of happiness that they imagined they would experience in the happiness situations. However, they reported significantly *less* negative emotion than the low-anxious subjects across all six types of situations. In turn, the high-anxious subjects as well as the less prevalent defensive high-anxious ones (i.e., high anxiety–high Marlowe-Crowne) reported significantly more negative affect than the low-anxious group. In response to situations in which negative affect was consensually defined as appropriate (e.g., "Your girlfriend/boyfriend leaves you for another"), the nondefensive, low-anxious group did not differ from a moderately anxious control group. However, the repressors were relatively further below this norm than the high-anxious groups were above it.

The repressors' patterns of emotional responses were also relatively stereotyped, with a particular lack of recognition of nondominant emotions. For example, in rating situations that prototypically involved the loss of a loved one, repressors "knew" as well as the other subjects did that high sadness is a universal response. However, they were less sensitive than the other groups to the less propositional knowledge that these situations are likely to evoke significant anger and anxiety as well.

Repressors' Self-Images and Avoidance of
Disconfirming Evidence

Particular self-images are unlikely to initiate defensive processes unless they are rigidly defined and one is highly invested in their maintenance. An important index of this investment is how central these beliefs are to one's identity or sense of self (cf. Kihlstrom and Cantor 1984; Markus 1977). Weinberger, Schwartz, and Davidson (1979) addressed this question by asking preselected subjects to describe in a few words the most "outstanding or important characteristics" of their personality. Thus, subjects were asked to encapsulate what they saw as the most central features of their self-concepts.

The use of an open-ended format (cf. Higgins, Klein, and Strauman 1985) allowed subjects maximal freedom in responding to the question. If repressors tend to be invested in maintaining control over negative affects and egoistic impulses, we hypothesized that this orientation should be reflected in their self-statements. If, on the other hand, their reports of low perceived anxiety were not made in good faith, they could either attempt to mimic the responses of the low-anxious group or avoid the awkwardness of dissimulation by focusing on unrelated dimensions such as creativity.

Nine of the fourteen repressors emphasized the importance of a rational, nonemotional approach to life. The separate self-descriptions of these nine individuals included (1) "rational (subjugate emotion)"; (2) "I do not get upset very easily"; (3) "I like to deal with people and objects on a nontrivial level"; (4) "I usually plan whatever I do (setting priorities)"; (5) "utilitarian"; (6) "I don't get discouraged very easily"; (7) "tolerant as well as tolerable"; (8) "not overly worried; I reason rationally"; and (9) "I can make an important contribution to humanity" (Weinberger, Schwartz, and Davidson 1979, 378). None of the fourteen repressors painted a picture of themselves as light hearted or spontaneous; rather, they almost always emphasized effortful self-control or some articulated standard of appropriate behavior.

In contrast, the nondefensive, low-anxious subjects emphasized their flexibility, vitality, and enjoyment of interpersonal relationships. Their self-descriptions included (1) "enjoying life"; (2) "versatility, flexibility"; (3) "like being with people"; (4) "interact with people easily and naturally"; (5) "fairly outgoing"; (6) "diversity, adaptability, friendliness"; (7) "open, happy, active"; (8) "outgoing, friendly person"; and (9) "a diverse person who enjoys doing active things" (Weinberger, Schwartz, and Davidson 1979, 379). Although both sets of descriptions are congruent with self-perceptions of low anxiety, the tone is quite different. The repressors often defined themselves as individuals who do *not* become upset rather than as individuals who enjoy themselves and adjust to life as it unfolds. Thus, the experience of negative affect was often explicitly excluded from what they defined as their central self-concept.

These data provide the clearest information to date that repressors see themselves as maintaining firm control over their negative affects and egoistic impulses. There is also considerable evidence using the Byrne scale and similar indices that repressors report very little discrepancy between ratings of their actual and ideal selves (e.g., Altrocchi, Parsons, and Dickoff 1960; cf. Block and Thomas 1955).

Given that repressors seem to have rather consistent self-images and tend to report not wanting to change much about themselves, it is not surprising that they avoid attending to information that might be discrepant with their self-concept. For example, Olson and Zanna (1979) found that repressors, but not sensitizers, on the Byrne scale engaged in "selective exposure" (e.g., Festinger 1957) in terms of inspecting paintings that were consonant with their choices and avoiding those that were not. They were also more likely to re-evaluate the paintings to make their judgments more compatible with their prior beliefs. Mischel, Ebbesen, and Zeiss (1973) obtained analogous results in a study more directly investigating selective attention to the self. After induced failure or under normal circumstances, repressors on the Byrne scale were much more likely than sensitizers to focus on their positive rather than on their negative personality attributes. In essence, the repressors responded as if they were always in the induced-success condition, whereas sensitizers comparably focused on their positive attributes only after actual success feedback. Thus, the repressors collectively demonstrated an investment in maintaining a positive self-image. In both these studies, the participants were unaware that they were being monitored, suggesting that they were engaging in a self-regulatory rather than self-presentational strategy.

Findings concerning high scorers on the Marlowe-Crowne provide complementary evidence that defensive individuals are especially unlikely to attend to information that might alter their positive self-images. For example, in a study of an assertiveness training program, Kiecolt-Glaser and Murray (1980) found that defensive individuals set fewer assertion-related goals, submitted fewer self-monitoring diaries with fewer entries, and reported their internal self-statements during their episodes to be significantly more positive than negative. In other words, they were behaving *as if* they had relatively little difficulty with self-assertion. However, they did not convince their group leaders, who rated them significantly *less* effective during the training sessions (also see Kiecolt and McGrath 1979). The authors concluded that high Marlowe-Crowne scorers have "difficulty in consistently and accurately self-monitoring their own behavior" and may require "preliminary training oriented toward shaping greater awareness of their internal dialogue" (Kiecolt-Glaser and Murray 1980, 246).

Other findings also indicate that high Marlowe-Crowne scorers are unusually resistant to information that might influence their self-images. For example, in a psychotherapy analogue study, Kanfer and Marston (1964)

found that high scorers differentially preferred a "low-risk," reflective therapist to a more speculative and interpretive one. Mosher (1965) approached the
question in a different manner by having a confident, high-status psychologist
ask subjects to confirm or disconfirm his unfavorable projective test interpretations. High Marlowe-Crowne scorers were especially likely to risk offending the authority in order to deny the unflattering assessments. Although
Crowne and Marlowe (1964) labeled high scorers "approval dependent," they
attempt to avoid situations that might lead to disapproval rather than actively
seek approval (Millham and Jacobson 1978).

Repressors, who constitute the majority of high Marlowe-Crowne scorers,
may have little to gain and much to lose by external evaluation (cf. Mischel,
Ebbesen, and Zeiss 1973). They behave as if to say, "I already know that I'm
fine, so you don't have to tell me, and I prefer not to hear information to the
contrary." Crowne (1979), in reviewing the literature on the scale he co-
authored, reached a very similar conclusion. Although it was not his original
formulation, he gradually became convinced that high Marlowe-Crowne scorers "not only *present* themselves as adjusted, self-controlled, responsible, and
self-content, but *think* of themselves that way. When this image is threatened,
they recoil in an avoidant retreat to protect it" (Crowne 1979, 173).

Distinguishing Self-Evaluation from Self-Presentation in Reports of Conscious Beliefs

To summarize the evidence presented thus far, repressors habitually report
experiencing lower than normative levels of negative affect, see maintaining
these low levels of negative affect as central to their self-concept, and attend
poorly to information to the contrary. This constellation suggests that repressors are likely both to find negative emotion threatening and to engage in self-
deceptive strategies to avoid altering their rigidly maintained self-concepts.
However, to conclude that there is a consistent discrepancy between repressors' self-perceptions and the perceptions of objective observers, special attention must be given to assessing whether repressors' self-reports actually
reflect their conscious beliefs. The data mentioned thus far suggest that they
do. Nonetheless, because we cannot directly monitor ongoing thought, a diverse set of strategies is necessary to evaluate adequately the alternative hypothesis that repressors are masters of impression management. Within this
view, repressors' regular and emphatic denial of negative affect would be a
deliberate attempt to keep others from discovering their secret truth: namely,
that they experience considerable negative affect but do not want the added
burden of others' negative evaluations.

There is little doubt that individuals often attempt to behave according to
external as well as internal standards of what seems situationally appropriate
(Bandura 1986). In addition, the same behaviors can serve to create a positive

impression on others as well as a positive evaluation of oneself (Tesser and Paulhus 1983; Tetlock and Manstead 1985). Some evidence suggests that repressors on the Byrne scale (e.g., Graziano, Brothen, and Berscheid 1980) and high Marlowe-Crowne scorers (e.g., Berger et al. 1977) may be particularly likely to change their behavior to make a good impression on others only when the behaviors also serve to protect them from negative self-evaluations. Under these circumstances, self-deceptive mechanisms and impression-managing strategies can operate concurrently. However, repressive defenses as delineated earlier would not be tenable if repressors knowingly present self-concepts that differ markedly from what they believe to be true. Impression management, defined in this circumscribed way, requires close inspection as an alternative hypothesis.

Are repressors responding to self-report questionnaires by simply telling researchers what they want to hear rather than providing genuine self-assessments? One approach to answering this question is to ask subjects about their self-perceptions when they are convinced that their responses will be absolutely anonymous. These conditions were most fully met by Weinberger and Schwartz (1982). In this study, subjects were asked no identifying information other than their age and gender, they were assured (and it was actually true) that the experimenters had no way to match their signatures on the consent form with their unmarked questionnaires. They did not complete the questionnaires in the presence of the experimenter and were allowed to take the forms wherever they wanted; moreover, they were explicitly instructed not to show their answers to anyone. As mentioned earlier, under these circumstances, the repressors reported significantly less negative affect than the low-anxious group when rating their likely responses to specific affective situations. This design maximized the contextual demands for private self-evaluations. If subjects were responding to create a particular social image, it would seem to be one that they maintain without reference to an identifiable audience. Under these circumstances, social role and self-concept become difficult to distinguish (cf. Sarbin 1952).

A direct assessment of the role of impression management versus self-deception in Marlowe-Crowne scores was undertaken by Millham and Kellogg (1980). They used the "bogus pipeline" technique developed by Jones and Sigall (1971). The method controls for social desirability by convincing subjects that a monitoring device (e.g., voice or physiology) can assess when they are lying. They administered the Marlowe-Crowne and the similar Jacobson-Kellogg Social Desirability Scale under neutral conditions and readministered the latter scale one week later under bogus pipeline conditions. Millham and Kellogg defined "self-deception" as scores under the bogus pipeline condition and "other deception" as changes in scores between the two assessments. Although the pipeline procedure produced some general reduction in social desirability scores, answers under these conditions correlated

.68 with Marlowe-Crowne scores during normal administration. The other-deception measure (changes in scores between conditions) correlated .37 with the Marlowe-Crowne but correlated $-.06$ with self-deception scores. Therefore, one can conclude that, by these criteria, most high scorers on the Marlowe-Crowne are primarily self-deceivers whereas a minority may be primarily other deceivers.

Through an additional procedure, Millham and Kellogg (1980) demonstrated that self-deceivers, subjects who did not tend to change their answers, were likely to have a repressive style of dealing with negative evaluations. The laboratory paradigm involved an assessment of memories for positive versus negative self-descriptors. Subjects were grouped into those who were highly self-deceptive and those who were highly other deceptive. High self-deceivers recalled significantly more positive than negative self-descriptors, whereas high other deceivers actually showed the reverse pattern. One can infer from these data that high Marlowe-Crowne scorers who selectively tend to recall their positive attributes (i.e., repressive subjects) are particularly unlikely to change their responses under bogus pipeline conditions. Thus, these subjects continued to stand by statements such as "I never feel resentful when I don't get my way" even when they believed the experimenter could assess when false claims were made. In contrast, individuals high on impression management in their self-reports tend to remember negative evaluations. Presumably, self-enhancement on questionnaires may serve to preclude external confirmation of an already negative self-image (cf. Schlenker and Leary 1982). If one construes one's behavior in positive terms, there is less reason to hide that evaluation from others. The high other deceivers in this study seem to correspond to the defensive high-anxious group, which reports being sensitized to negative affect in addition to having high Marlowe-Crowne scores.

A third method for assessing whether repressors' self-reports represent primarily self-presentation rather than actual self-perception is to establish demand characteristics that specifically request the expression of negative affect and vulnerabilities. Millimet and Cohen (1973), using a measure similar to the Byrne scale, found that individuals who were told that the scale was measuring openness and honesty did not have significantly different scores from those told that it assessed mental illness. Thus, subjects reporting low distress did not tend to alter their responses when the situational demand was for negative self-disclosures.

Doster (1975) elegantly designed a situation in which the admission of vulnerabilities was highly socially desirable. Role-induction techniques were employed to prepare subjects for the kind of honest self-disclosure required in individual psychotherapy sessions. In a group setting, subjects were prepared for individual interviews by explicit instruction in the importance of "self-exploration," including expression of genuine self-perceptions on predetermined topics such as "anxiety and fear" and "self-esteem and self-degradation." In the individual sessions, subjects were instructed to cover each of the six topics sequentially, and the interviewer was trained to provide minimal social cuing. Consistent with Millham and Kellogg's (1980) findings, the repressors were the least likely to inquire about appropriate role behavior. The more impression-managing, defensive high-anxious group were the most likely to inquire. In addition, even when the demand characteristics for disclosure were highly explicit, the repressors were judged to be significantly less disclosing than either the low-anxious or the defensive high-anxious group.

A fourth strategy for assessing an impression-management interpretation of repressors' behavior is to examine the discriminant validity of relevant individual difference dimensions. Snyder (1974) developed the widely used Self-Monitoring Scale to identify individuals who are likely to "observe, monitor, and manage their self-presentation" (530). In his initial validation study, he systematically compared his measure to the Marlowe-Crowne. The two scales correlated $-.19$ ($p < .01$), suggesting that defensive subjects do not claim to be high self-monitors. Various validation data that Snyder reported suggest that high self-monitors tend to manage and be good at managing their self-presentations whereas high Marlowe-Crowne scorers tend to be average or below average in these characteristics. For example, Marlowe-Crowne scores were unrelated both to peer assessments of subjects' ability to control and monitor their self-presentations and to subjects' consultation of normative information when completing self-descriptive personality items. In contrast to high self-monitors, high scorers on the Marlowe-Crowne were significantly worse than low ones in voluntarily communicating emotion both vocally and facially.

These sets of data, taken as a whole, make it quite difficult to purport that repressors consciously believe and can verbalize self-perceptions of being relatively prone to distress. To the contrary, they seem singularly motivated to maintain self-perceptions of being low in negative affect, even when there are countervailing situational demands. The evidence contradicts the notion that repressors are adroit social chameleons who are good at testing the winds and telling people what they want to hear. If anything, the repressors' rigid attempts to avoid the experience of negative affect are associated with specific deficits in this type of social-cognitive and affective information processing (see subsequent discussion).

There have been literally hundreds of studies employing the Byrne Repression-Sensitization or Marlowe-Crowne scales. To my knowledge, in these studies and in newer research differentiating repressors from low-anxious subjects, under no circumstances (e.g., psychotherapy, anonymous questionnaire, lie detection, disclosures to intimates) have repressors as a group remotely indicated conscious beliefs that they experience relatively high levels of negative affect. In addition, their behavior is distinct from that of individuals' reporting high anxiety and suggests that they are quite invested in perceiving themselves as low in negative affect. Therefore, if, by Dennett's (1969) second definition of "awareness," objective observers can infer that repressors' behavior and physiology indicate "taking account of" or reacting with high levels of perceived threat and anxiety, the pattern would be consistent with the outlined criteria for inferring unconscious defenses. Although repressors seem to defend against a variety of specific negative affects (e.g., Weinberger and Schwartz 1982), the physiological and behavioral evidence is largely limited to assessments of anxiety because this state is so readily induced in the laboratory (cf. Schwartz, Weinberger, and Singer 1981).

Objective Assessment of Repressors' Physiological and Behavioral Responses to Stress

Physiological Reactivity

Bell and Byrne (1978) noted that it would seem reasonable to assume that sensitizers on the Byrne scale, who report high levels of distress, would manifest more autonomic reactivity than those subjects who report being relatively calm. Nonetheless, possibly a majority of psychophysiological studies using this scale have found repressors to be *more* reactive than their consciously distressed counterparts (e.g., Hare 1966; Lazarus and Alfert 1964; Parsons, Fulgenzi, and Edelberg 1969; Scarpetti 1973). Even if all low scorers were actually sensitizers who fabricated a more desirable image, one would expect no relation rather than a reciprocal one.

Weinberger, Schwartz, and Davidson (1979) suggested that this paradox may result from confounding repressive subjects with nondefensive subjects, who accurately perceive their affective functioning. We hypothesized that the low-anxious subjects' physiological response would be consonant with their self-reports whereas the repressors would be as reactive or more reactive than a high-anxious comparison group. The subjects were presented with a phrase association task; the only instruction was to complete the phrase as quickly as possible with whatever came to mind. Five neutral, five sexual, and five aggressive phrase stems were counterbalanced, and changes in psychophysiological indices during the sixty seconds following each presentation were calculated from each individual's resting baseline.

As noted earlier, the preselected low-anxious subjects were in the twenty-fifth percentile in self-reported anxiety, compared to the tenth percentile for the repressors and the seventy-fifth percentile for the high-anxious group. In contrast to this pattern of self-reports, the repressors' physiological reactivity was consistently equal to or greater than that of the high-anxious subjects. The repressors responded with significantly greater increases in forehead muscle tension (i.e., EMG) than either the high-anxious or the low-anxious groups. In addition, their increases in palmar sweat gland activity (i.e., spontaneous skin resistance responses) and heart rate (prior to habituation) were equal to those of the high-anxious subjects and significantly greater than those of the low-anxious subjects (Weinberger, Schwartz, and Davidson 1979).

Asendorpf and Scherer (1983) replicated and extended these findings using a German translation of the phrase association task. Once again, the repressors' heart rate changes were significantly greater than those of the low-anxious group. They did not significantly differ from a very high-anxious group in which all subjects were above the seventy-fourth percentile in self-reported anxiety. There also was some evidence that the repressors' and high-anxious subjects' autonomic arousal recovered more slowly after the task according to changes in finger pulse-volume amplitude. Despite these changes, the repressors, unlike the other groups, reported no increase in state anxiety above baseline during the task.

Asendorpf and Scherer (1983) also included a defensive high-anxious group in their study: that is, individuals who report both high anxiety and high defensiveness. In general, these individuals had physiological changes in between those of the repressors and the low-anxious subjects. Thus, high defensiveness scores in conjunction with low rather than high anxiety scores were especially related to high physiological reactivity. Schwartz (in this volume) also reports cardiovascular data consonant with this conclusion.

Levenson and Mades (1980) used a videotape of "industrial accidents" to investigate repressors' versus low-anxious subjects' responses to stress. Although no differences in skin conductance level were reported, the repressors did react with significantly shorter heart-rate interbeat intervals and pulse transmission times. Gudjonsson (1981) reversed the usual individual differences paradigm by asking if personality style could be predicted from discrepancies between self-reports of subjective disturbance and relative changes in skin conductance responses. Subjects were asked a series of questions such as "Do you ever steal things?" and rated their discomfort on a visual analogue scale. When electrodermal responses were assessed both before and after the questions were asked, those with the greatest discrepancy between subjective experience and physiological response had the highest Marlowe-Crowne scores and the lowest Eysenck Neuroticism scores. Skin conductance responses elicited by the questions correlated .42 ($p < .01$) with Marlowe-Crowne scores and $-.39$ ($p < .05$) with Neuroticism scores.

Without the concept of repressive defenses, these findings involving an unselected sample of thirty-six males would be quite perplexing. It is difficult to construct alternative explanations. For example, either high levels of sweating must be interpreted as a correlate of genuine calmness, or *most* individuals with high levels of conscious anxiety must routinely remember to report being unusually content on questionnaires and during laboratory procedures that they know they find disturbing. Gudjonsson's design is particularly interesting from an impression-management perspective in that the procedure mirrors a "lie detection" paradigm. Because subjects knew their physiology was being recorded, there would seem to be little self-presentational value in consciously underreporting given the likelihood of being caught.

Although all four of these studies included only male subjects, other research suggests that repressors' physiological reactivity to stress generalizes to females. Cook (1985), using only female students, came to similar conclusions using a different psychometric technique. He classified subjects on the Byrne scale and then identified those who rigidly chose one coping strategy (i.e., approach or avoidance) on a measure that asked about likely behavior in thirteen different situations. Among the "consistent" subjects, repressors evidenced significantly greater increases in skin conductance levels than sensitizers during both anticipation of and participation in a stressful task. Strikingly, among subjects with more flexible, less defensive coping patterns, the finding was exactly reversed. The "nondefensive" low scorers on the Byrne had significantly less increase in skin conductance than the sensitizers during these conditions, especially when presented with irrelevant or distracting information. Cook's (1985) data, like the self-descriptions presented in an earlier section of this chapter, suggest that adaptability may be a central feature of a low-anxious, well-adjusted group and inflexible adherence to a predetermined self-image and coping strategy a sine qua non of the repressor.

The repressors' discrepancy between self-report and physiological responses has now been demonstrated across a variety of tasks and psychophysiological indices. Although differences are not always found on each measure in each condition, the repressors generally respond with greater physiological activation than low-anxious subjects. Kiecolt-Glaser and Greenberg (1983) assessed male and female subjects' reactions to scenes requiring assertiveness. When the subjects were asked to imagine responding to the scenes, the repressors had significantly higher increases in diastolic blood pressure than the high-anxious or low-anxious groups. During the most provocative of these scenes, those requiring multiple responses, the nondefensive, low-anxious group reported as much subjective tension as the high-anxious group, while the repressors reported significantly less. There were no physiological differences when the subjects responded to a taped prompt; however, the repressors had significantly greater heart-rate changes than the low-anxious group when interacting in a multiple-response scene with a confederate.

King et al. (1986) have documented that the group differences of interest extend well beyond the university campus. In a sample of ninety-nine middle-aged, sedentary men and women, repressors had significantly higher resting and submaximal systolic blood-pressure levels than either the low- or the high-anxious subjects. In addition, distinguishing repressors from nonrepressors accounted for more variance in systolic blood pressure changes during an arithmetic task than assessments of Type A behavior using the Structured Interview (Rosenman 1978). For women, the repressors' mean changes were almost double those of the high-anxious group. In addition, the repressors as a whole had significantly higher total and low-density lipoprotein (LDL) cholesterol levels than the low-anxious group. Schwartz (in this volume) reviews a number of recent studies that further document repressors' heightened physiological response to stress. These data demonstrate reduced levels of resting alpha-band EEG activity and show an association with chronic hypertension. To date, studies comparing repressive versus low-anxious subjects' cardiovascular, muscular, electrodermal, and cortical responses to laboratory stresses have consistently found the repressors to be more reactive. In fact, physiological measures typically suggest that repressors are as anxious or more anxious than subjects who report chronic distress.

Inferring differences in perceived threat from measures of physiological reactivity is based on the assumption that there are no group differences in how individuals' autonomic nervous systems are calibrated. In other words, it is possible that repressors simply have very reactive peripheral nervous systems, so less perception of threat is necessary to produce a given intensity of response. Weinberger, Schwartz, and Davidson (1979) addressed this issue through a biofeedback task that was counterbalanced with the phrase association task described earlier. During nonrest trials, subjects heard a tone corresponding to the R spike of their heart beat. On respective trials, they were asked to make the tones go faster or slower using any imagery or self-instructional strategy they wished. A comparison of rest trials and increase trials revealed that all groups significantly increased their heart rate, spontaneous skin resistance responses, and forehead muscle tension. Furthermore, there were no significant group differences on any of the measures. For example, all groups increased their heart rates approximately eight beats per minute, the same level of change observed in the high-anxious and repressive groups during the phrase association task. Therefore, there was no evidence in this study that the repressors differed from the other groups in terms of the innate reactivity of their peripheral physiology.

Behavioral Measures of Anxiety

Several methods other than physiological measures have been derived to infer whether subjects are responding in ways indicative of high anxiety. One well-established finding is that paralinguistic signs of speech disruption increase under stress (e.g., Kasl and Mahl 1965). Using a composite index, Weinberger, Schwartz, and Davidson (1979) found that the repressors, in responding to the phrase associations, had significantly more verbal interference than the low-anxious group, with the high-anxious group falling in between. This measure, based on the work of Mandler et al. (1961), included such items as changing one's response in mid-course and the stuttering repetition of more than one word (e.g., "He was—he was really angry"). Kiecolt and McGrath (1979) also found that high Marlowe-Crowne scorers were less likely than low scorers to have a decrease in speech disturbances following assertiveness training.

Tolkmitt and Scherer (1986) investigated a number of vocal acoustic parameters that seem sensitive to changes in affective state in a design that crossed two levels of induced stress with two types of tasks. The cognitive task involved responding to easy versus difficult logical problems, and the emotional task entailed judging the chances of healing of mild skin diseases versus severe injuries presented in slides. The repressors judged the tasks to be significantly less difficult than the other groups. However, one of the phonatory measures, fundamental frequency floor values, revealed significant interactions for both males and females in which the repressors as well as the high-anxious subjects responded under high stress with relatively greater increases than the low-anxious group. In addition, the precision of the female repressors' articulation differentially decreased during the high-stress emotional task relative to the cognitive one.

Analysis of facial expressions has served as another important strategy for assessing perceived threat. Expressions associated with several emotions including fear/anxiety are universal across cultures and can be reliably scored by observers (e.g., Ekman 1984). In Asendorpf and Scherer's (1983) study described earlier, repressors, relative to low-anxious subjects, were rated as having significantly greater increases in facial anxiety during the affective phrase association trials. Because of the task demands for quick responses to randomized phrases, there was reduced likelihood that subjects would focus their attention on regulating their facial expressions (cf. Ekman 1984). Levenson and Mades (1980) reported a very different pattern of results when subjects were asked merely to watch a stressful videotape. While viewing the third of a series of industrial accidents, the repressors in this study tended to have greater cardiovascular changes than the low-anxious group at the time the accident occurred. However, the low-anxious group was significantly more likely to respond facially. Under these circumstances, when a discrete affective event could clearly be anticipated with no competing task demands, dampening a normatively expectable facial expression might have been a straightforward strategy for maintaining overt composure. The repressors' overt composure, however, was discrepant with their physiological responses.

A number of studies have also investigated group differences on tasks where negative affects including anxiety might impair actual performance. In the Weinberger, Schwartz, and Davidson (1979) study, reaction time to the phrase stems was included as an additional measure of perceived threat. Recall that the only explicit instruction to subjects was to respond as quickly as possible with whatever came to mind. The repressors responded significantly more slowly than the low-anxious subjects overall and were especially slow in responding to sexual and aggressive phrases. There also was a significant group by trial interaction in which the sensitizing, high-anxious subjects adjusted to the task and responded more quickly over time. In contrast, the repressors did increasingly poorly. Thus, experience with the task made them less rather than more able to report their spontaneous associations.

Boor and Schill (1967, 1968) investigated group differences on the Wechsler Adult Intelligence Scale (WAIS) subscales that seem most sensitive to the disruptive effects of anxiety and other negative affects. In their first study, they found that low-anxious but not repressive subjects did better than high-anxious ones in terms of copying speed on the Digit Symbol task (Boor and Schill 1967). In a second study, they found the same pattern for the Block Design subscale and discovered that both the high-anxious and the low-anxious subjects performed better than the repressors on Digit Span (Boor and Schill 1968).

Martens and Landers (1970) provided some additional findings using a motor tracking task. They found that adolescents scoring below the tenth percentile in manifest anxiety performed significantly worse than moderately anxious ones and as poorly as those scoring above the ninetieth percentile. There also was a group by trial interaction in which the presumably repressive group had the least improvement over time. Not only were the effects consistent across three different levels of induced stress, but this very low-anxious group also had higher mean heart-rate changes than the moderately anxious group. Therefore, underarousal is an unlikely alternative explanation of the presumably repressive group's relatively poor performance.

This latter set of studies supports the conclusion that repressors' performances are often impaired on cognitive and perceptual-motor tasks that seem sensitive to the effects of anxiety. These data, along with the studies measuring paralinguistic, vocal, and facial indices, all corroborate the psychophysiological evidence that repressors consistently respond in a manner indicative of high anxiety despite ostensibly sincere reports to the contrary.

Associated Social-Cognitive and Affective Deficits

Several findings already mentioned (e.g., Kiecolt-Glaser and Murray 1980; Snyder 1974; Weinberger and Schwartz 1982) suggest that repressors' defensiveness may also be associated with deficits in emotional experience, self-knowledge, and social cognition. For example, repressors' attempts to avoid negative affect may in some ways impede their experience of positive affect as well. Repressors relative to low-anxious subjects have been found to report fewer positive as well as negative specific memories of childhood (Davis and Schwartz 1987). Furthermore, individuals with particularly low humor appreciation tend to be repressive on the Byrne scale (O'Connell and Peterson 1964).

Consistent with Kiecolt-Glaser and Murray's (1980) data on assertiveness, repressors seem to lack social competence in interpersonal communication as well as self-knowledge in terms of being able to predict and accurately evaluate their own behavior. Doster (1975) addressed these phenomena in a task that explicitly demanded intimate self-disclosure. For the low-anxious subjects, both their predictions of how much they would disclose and subsequent evaluations of how much they did disclose on the various topics correlated significantly with observers' ratings of their disclosure, with the length of discussion of the topic, and with fewer pauses during their presentation. None of these six correlations were significant for the repressors. Low anxious subjects' ratings of subjective comfort when talking about a topic also correlated significantly with judges' ratings of their level of self-disclosure and with the length of their discussion. In contrast, the repressors' ratings of subjective comfort did not correlate at all with judges' ratings of self-disclosure and correlated significantly *negatively* with how much they spoke about the topic. These results consistently suggest that the repressors had little insight into their ongoing behavior and that their self-presentation was strikingly poor given the explicit requirements of the procedure.

Most psychotherapies function, in part, by providing an interpersonal context that facilitates individuals' articulating and clarifying their self-concepts—their thoughts, feelings, and values. Repressors' defensiveness seems to make it quite difficult for them to make use of this type of social support. Axtell and Cole (1971), in a factorial design, asked subjects to describe their positive or negative attributes in a monologue or with standardized encouraging feedback such as "mm-hmms" and "I wonder if you could give me an example or two." For the moderate or high scorers on the Byrne scale, feedback resulted in nearly doubling their rates of self-disclosure. In contrast, the repressors were basically unaffected, disclosing no more than they and the other groups did in the monologue condition. This phenomenon did not interact with whether they were talking about their positive or negative attributes. Axtell and Cole (1971, 136) concluded that the repressors behaved "as if there were no verbal interaction" and that facilitators' comments did "not provoke further discussion of the self." Thus, they were unwilling or unable to use the interpersonal context to enrich their understanding of the elements of their self-concept.

Strickland and Crowne (1963) presented a very similar picture of high Marlowe-Crowne scorers' inability to engage effectively in psychotherapy. In this study, trained psychotherapists' ratings of defensiveness correlated .67 with Marlowe-Crowne scores in a sample of eighty-five clinic patients. High scorers were also significantly more likely to terminate psychotherapy prematurely. Even with number of sessions partialed out, there were trends in the direction of high scorers being rated less improved at termination and less liked and respected by their therapists. Within the psychotherapeutic context, repressors' defensiveness was palpable and was associated with behaviors that by no means gained approval or created a good impression.

Repressors' deficits in self-knowledge and self-expression seem to be mirrored by a somewhat limited understanding of others' experience. Nielsen and Fleck (1981) investigated this phenomenon by placing repressors and low-anxious subjects in the role of therapist. The task was to be as understanding and helpful as possible. With other students in the role of counselees, there was a trend ($p < .10$) for judges to rate the repressive counselors as less empathic. Those in the role of counselor also listened to tapes that presented difficulties involving more sexual and aggressive themes. The repressors' written responses to these scenarios were judged significantly less empathic.

Both self-knowledge and social inference may be related more to processing relevant cognitive/affective information rather than to simply observing objective behavior (Andersen 1984). Thus, repressors' limited introspective knowledge of their own affective reactions may curtail their understanding the nuances of the reactions of others. Wilkins, Epting, and van de Riet (1972) found that those scoring below the twenty-fifth percentile on the Byrne scale exhibited significantly less interpersonal cognitive complexity than moderate or high scorers. The authors concluded that the repressive group was "generally less discriminating of their social environment" (Wilkins, Epting, and van de Riet 1972, 449). Similarly, Matney, and McManis (1977), using Guilford's measure of social intelligence, concluded that repressors had highly developed induction skills in terms of abstracting common attributes but were lacking in "drawing social implications or predicting social consequences" (837). Repressors' preoccupation with regulating negative affect may also interfere with general cognitive flexibility in terms of the spontaneous, playful aspects of concept formation (e.g., Bergquist, Lloyd, and Johansson 1973).

Especially in the light of the work of Zigler and colleagues (e.g., Katz and Zigler 1967), one might hypothesize that repressors are simply less intelligent or articulate than the comparison groups. However, Clark and Neuringer (1971) found that scorers below the twentieth percentile on the Byrne scale did significantly better than moderate or high scorers on the verbal portion of the Cooperative School and College Ability Tests administered as part of a university placement exam. Repressors having particularly well-developed verbal abilities is consistent with their valuing a rational, nonemotional approach to problems. Our recent data from the Early Adolescence Project (see below) also suggest that repressive twelve-year-old boys are not deficient on standardized achievement test scores or classroom grades (Wentzel et al., in press).

Mechanisms Underlying Repressive Defenses

Strategies for Not Knowing

The specific difficulties that repressors exhibit across affective, social, and cognitive tasks suggest that their habitual style of coping may have broad implications for their overall functioning. These findings also suggest that the psychology of the repressor may be quite distinct from that of high-anxious individuals, who may or may not choose to censor their verbal reports. Therefore, one would expect more process-oriented analyses to reveal that repressors differ strikingly from high-anxious subjects in terms of the specific coping strategies that they employ.

During the 1950s, repressors were operationally defined, without the use of self-report measures, as individuals who avoided disturbing cognitions on experimental tasks (see Brown 1961). In contrast, more rumination-prone sensitizers were defined by their heightened attunement to threatening stimuli. Eriksen (1966, 343) concluded that the early literature revealed that repressors, who "show cognitive avoidance through poorer recall of failure-associated tasks also take longer to learn anxiety-related words and require longer exposure durations for perceptual recognition of these words." Thus, repressors are motivated to distance themselves from negative affect across a diverse set of tasks.

Several authors (e.g., Haley 1974; Holmes 1974, in this volume; Mischel, Ebbesen, and Zeiss 1973) have concluded that repressors' avoidant behavior can be explained by selective attentional processes without the need to invoke the concept of unconscious defenses. As Erdelyi (in this volume) has emphasized, Freud repeatedly noted that repression often begins as conscious suppression. However, the fact that repressors consciously try to control and avoid negative emotion does not contradict the hypothesis that unconscious defenses play an additional role. In part, repressors' defensiveness concerns their beliefs about the *success* of their efforts to avoid the development of negative affect.

One of repressors' primary self-deceptions is convincing themselves that, if they do not attend to internal cues of distress, the distress ceases to exist. In psychoanalytic terms, the distress becomes unconscious in that the person strongly resists acknowledging that the affect is unattended to rather than nonexistent. Similarly, Perls, Hefferline, and Goodman (1951, 431) suggested that repression involves a failure to recognize "deliberate inhibiting that has become habitual." Unfortunately, the psychoanalytic terminology and metapsychology developed to describe repressive defenses have tended to make the process seem much more mysterious than it need be. Freud's original descriptions can be seen as quite compatible with mechanisms outlined in the cognitive literature (cf. Erdelyi, in this volume).

Selective attention seems to be only one of several processes maintaining repressive self-deception. Clearly related ones are perceptual defense per se (e.g., Schill and Althoff 1968) and selective memory (Davis, in this volume; Davis and Schwartz 1987). Repressors also seem to employ a cluster of strategies that clinicians might refer to as intellectualizing defenses such as rationalization, isolation of affect, and denial of the personal meaning of an event. One can reformulate many of these concepts into the kinds of attributional or construal processes described in the social cognition literature (e.g., Ross 1987).

Weinberger, Schwartz, and Davidson (1979) found that repressive subjects were significantly more likely to distance themselves from the content of the phrase stems than either the low-anxious or the high-anxious subjects. Because subjects had to provide a response, this task did not allow them simply to avert their attention. To defend against the perception of threat, the repressors most often reinterpreted the task using evaluative replies such as "That's absurd" rather than elaborating the phrase content as requested in the instructions. The second most popular strategy, labelled "recoding," entailed attempting to neutralize the threatening content per se by interpreting it as either unintentional or unimportant. As an illustration, one repressor responded to the aggressive phrase "He kicked his roommate in the stomach . . ." by adding "but he meant to turn on the light."

There was other evidence in this study that repressors attempt to construe threatening information in a way that negates its potential effect. In response to the phrase association task, repressors did not report less awareness of somatic reactions such as increased heart rate. Furthermore, the Cognitive-Somatic Anxiety Questionnaire (Schwartz, Davidson, and Goleman 1978) was used to inquire about how subjects respond *when* they become anxious. The repressors and low-anxious subjects did not differ in reports of somatic anxiety (e.g., "I feel tense in my stomach"). However, repressors' reports of cognitive anxiety were significantly lower than would be expected relative to that of the low-anxious group and relative to their own level of somatic anxiety. It was as if the repressors were reporting, "When I'm in an anxiety-provoking situation, my physiology reacts, but I don't worry about the situation or interpret my bodily cues as signs that I am an anxious person."

These findings are consistent with more recent work which indicates that repressors may typically maintain a variety of attributional biases as a means of avoiding negative affect. Seligman, Abramson, Peterson, and colleagues (e.g., Abramson, Seligman, and Teasdale 1978; Peterson and Seligman 1984) have documented that depressed individuals tend to attribute negative events to internal, stable, global causes (e.g., lack of ability). Gomes and Weinberger (1986) suggested that repressors are likely to have the opposite bias, tending to deny both the significance and the self-relevance of negative events. In contrast, the nondefensive, nondepressed subjects were expected to have a more balanced style. The repressors did, in fact, rate hypothetical negative events on the Attributional Styles Questionnaire (ASQ) as significantly more likely to be caused by a composite of external, unstable, and specific factors compared to both the sensitized, depression-prone and the nondefensive, low-distress groups. On the subscales of the ASQ, the nondefensive group was similar to the depression-prone group on the internal-external dimension but fell in between on the other two. An exemplary item that discriminated the three styles was "You have been looking for a job unsuccessfully for some time." The depression-prone group most frequently reported reasons concerning a lack of adequate skills, whereas the nondefensive, nondepressed group tended to refer to an internal cause under their control, a lack of sufficient effort. In contrast, the repressors externalized the blame, most often suggesting simply a lack of jobs. Thus, their responses were oriented toward protecting their self-esteem instead of taking the kind of internal responsibility that might facilitate problem-focused coping.

The growing literature (e.g., Alloy and Abramson 1979; Lewinsohn et al. 1980; Taylor and Brown 1988) suggesting that it is normal to make self-enhancing distortions of consensual reality may result partly from the inclusion of repressors in the nondepressed samples. However, teasing apart the distinction between normal, healthy optimism and defensive avoidance of threatening information remains a significant question for future research.

Several investigators (e.g., Lazarus and Folkman 1984) have noted that individuals' general or hypothetical descriptions of their coping strategies need to be supplemented with a more microanalytic analysis of the coping process. Tublin and Weinberger (1987) employed a thought-sampling methodology (e.g., Singer and Klos 1981) to investigate the processing of affect embedded in an interpersonal context. Subjects listened to a neutral audiotape and to a stressful tape of a man expressing intense anger toward his spouse. At random intervals averaging forty-five seconds apart, subjects heard a tone that signaled them to report what thoughts, images, or feelings were on their mind at the time.

Preliminary analyses suggest that, as expected, repressors are more likely than the nondefensive groups to engage in cognitive-interpretive analysis (judging the tape or the actors) or distraction (e.g., focusing on a positive image) to distance themselves from the affective content. On the other hand, the nondefensive groups are more likely than the repressors to integrate interpretive analysis and affect by assessing the relevance of the stimulus to their own lives. This content category, referred to as assimilation, included thoughts such as "I was thinking about my parents arguing" or "I don't know what I'd do in a situation like that." From the neutral tape to the stressful tape, there was also an increase in what Freud would have categorized as primary process thinking. Specifically, after the affective tape, the distress-prone group and the repressors were more likely to report considerable unintegrated imagery such as "I was imagining little green men shooting at people" or "I was thinking about some weird images: a pile of sand and a crane trying to lift it in a boathouse." Thus, the repressors were relatively high on intellectualized as well as nonpropositional, fanciful thought, both modalities in which affective experience is unlikely to become integrated into the self-concept.

Defenses and the Adaptive Use of Cognitive Appraisals

A growing body of literature suggests that cognitive appraisals or interpretations of situations can alter one's level of stress in constructive ways. Many of the mechanisms shown to have a positive effect are at first glance similar to the ones just described as components of repressors' defensive processes. Lazarus (1985), among others, has wrestled with the question of the "costs and benefits" of mechanisms such as denial. One partial resolution has been suggested by Haan (1977), who proposes that the same general processes can be employed as flexible and adaptive coping strategies or as rigid and distorting defenses.

The stress and coping theory developed by Lazarus and colleagues (Lazarus and Folkman 1984) may provide a framework to begin to identify more precisely the distinction between successful coping and maladaptive repressive defenses. In the theory, primary appraisals of what is at stake in an encounter and secondary appraisals of what might or can be done to manage it are hypothesized to be critical mediators of stressful interactions. These evaluative perceptions are often characterized by affective responses and do not necessarily entail "deliberate reflection, rationality or awareness" (Lazarus 1984, 252). As mentioned earlier, there is now considerable evidence that largely nonverbal centers such as the frontal region of the right cerebral hemisphere may be particularly involved in certain negative affective appraisals (Davidson 1984).

Once a situation is appraised as taxing, individuals typically engage in emotion-focused (as well as problem-focused) coping strategies to manage the demands (Lazarus and Folkman 1984). Although affective reactions are rich sources of subjective information (Schwartz and Weinberger 1980), few would question the notion that nonaffective information processing often adaptively guides, alters, or simply overrides one's initial affective reactions (cf. Bandura 1986; Kendall and Bemis 1983). For example, an important form of emotion-focused coping entails reappraising a situation's meaning in a way that reduces its negative effect. Lazarus and Folkman (1984) provide examples of such cognitive maneuvers as " 'I considered how much worse things could be' " (150). Taylor (1983) describes similar adaptive mechanisms in terms of "illusions," in which facts are not necessarily negated but are interpreted in certain lights to enhance a sense of mastery and meaning.

Adaptive forms of emotion-focused coping have been highlighted from a variety of different perspectives. For instance, Vaillant (1977) illustrated the successful use of such mechanisms as humor, anticipation, and suppression of affect. Houston (1977), among others, has found that analytical processing of stressful encounters (e.g., "reasoning why the situation should not be upsetting") may at times be a quite effective coping strategy. Appropriate use of cognitive self-management strategies might produce a hypothetical internal monologue such as "I am feeling anxious; what, if anything, can I think about or actually do to convince my emotion system that the situation is really not that bad?" For example, Bandura (1982) outlined several relevant strategies, including enactive attainment, vicarious experience, and verbal persuasion.

However, the literature reviewed in this chapter suggests that a repressive process attempts to preempt emotion-focused coping by altering the initial appraisal. Because of self-evaluative mechanisms, the affective appraisal itself becomes as much a threat as the external situation. Under these circumstances, nonaffective interpretive centers block or misinterpret affective judgments. An appropriate metaphor is that the dialogue between interpretive cognition and emotion is "functionally disconnected" (Galin 1974) with the result that the affective response systems (e.g., autonomic activity) become dissociated rather than influenced (Schwartz, in this volume).

A repressive mechanism entails ignoring the emotion system rather than informing it. Some experimental research has provided a partial analogue to this process in the form of "avoidant thinking." For example, Houston and Holmes (1974) found that subjects required to read a story had greater physiological reactions to impending shocks than subjects who were not provided with a distraction. Hare (1966) found similar results assessing subjects' spontaneous thoughts; he also found that repressors tended to use an avoidant strategy. Whistling in the dark or various cognitive equivalents are not very effective in convincing the emotion system that its reactions are unwarranted. As Schwartz (1983a) has described, this strategy can lead to disregulated subsystems functioning without the stabilizing effects of appropriate feedback.

Galin (1974), Schwartz (1983a, in this volume), and Davidson (1983) all hypothesize that the discrepancy between repressors' verbal beliefs and their nonverbal and physiological reactions is related to differential processing of the cerebral hemispheres. More specifically, it is proposed that "negative affective information processed in the right hemisphere does not get complete access to verbal centers in the left" (Davidson 1983, 130). A series of studies have now provided evidence that is consistent with this formulation. Schwartz (in this volume) and colleagues have found that repressors' processing of emotion is highly lateralized relative to that of comparison subjects. The findings include differential hemispheric activation as well as lateralized facial muscle and autonomic activity (e.g., skin temperature). It is quite literally as if the side of the body controlled by the right hemisphere expresses greater responsivity than that controlled by the left. Low-anxious subjects tend to exhibit less lateralization and, therefore, more integrated response patterns.

Davidson (1983) and colleagues, using two different paradigms to assess interhemispheric transfer time, have found evidence that repressors have specific deficits in transferring affective (but not nonaffective) information from the right hemisphere to the left.

Lazarus and Folkman (1984), among others, have emphasized that coping with stress is ordinarily a very dynamic and complex process. A variety of strategies are invoked both simultaneously as well as sequentially. Although a repressive style may protect individuals from some of the maladaptive consequences of a sensitizing style, it seems associated with it own set of difficulties. The repressors' attempts to convince themselves that they are not upset, when their emotional centers are responding as if they are, may interfere with problem-focused as well as integrative emotion–focused coping.

The Intensification of Defenses under Stress

Theoretically, psychological defenses contrast with effective coping strategies in terms of being both inflexible and reactive. Within a certain range, they are conceptualized as having an antagonistic quality: the more one is threatened, the more rigidly one adheres to one's defended beliefs. There is evidence that repressors' defensiveness has this property. Weinberger, Schwartz, and Davidson (1979) assessed subjects' self-perceived trait anxiety both under relaxed conditions during the initial preselection and immediately after they observed their behavior in the stressful phrase association task approximately seven weeks later. The sensitizing, high-anxious group, after observing their anxious reactions, reported significantly higher trait anxiety, whereas the nondefensive, low-anxious group maintained a stable self-concept. In contrast, the repressors reported significantly lower trait anxiety after participating in an objectively stressful experience. Not a single repressor responded to the situation by reporting higher proneness to anxiety than had been indicated under relaxed conditions several weeks earlier. Their mean score dropped from 2.5 to 1.6 on a twenty-point scale. Thus, participating in a task that they found stressful, according to objective criteria, led them to proclaim more rigidly that it was out of character for them to become upset.

Schneider and Turkat (1975) reported a similar phenomenon in comparing two groups of subjects who both reported high self-esteem (i.e., a correlate of low distress). Half the subjects were given success feedback and half failure feedback. Compared to the nondefensive subjects, the high Marlowe-Crowne, repressive group that was given failure feedback had a heightened denial of negative self-descriptors both on a checklist and in an essay in which they described their positive and negative attributes. Thus, negative affective experience often tends to heighten repressors' defensiveness, paradoxically resulting in a measurable boosting of reported self-esteem and equanimity.

Repressive Control of Egoistic Desires

Repressors seem to use a variety of strategies to keep themselves convinced that they are not distressed even when behavioral and physiological measures suggest otherwise. Although this phenomenon seems clearly defensive, it needs to be placed within a broader theoretical framework. In the empirical literature, the terms "denier" and "repressor" are used fairly interchangeably to refer to individuals who avoid recognizing distress. However, repressors, as described in this chapter, share characteristics other than simply denial of negative affect. Most notably, repressors tend to see themselves and be viewed by others as unusually responsible and unimpulsive. Most Marlowe-Crowne items have little to do with denying distress; rather, they primarily refer to extreme inhibition of one's own needs when they are in conflict with the needs of others. As mentioned earlier, prototypical items include "I never hesitate to go out of my way to help someone in trouble" and "I have almost never felt the urge to tell someone off."

In this chapter, the generic concept of repressive defenses has been used to describe processes that block conscious recognition of extant but unacceptable affects *and* impulses. Although it is virtually never reflected in the research literature, Freud did not develop a theory primarily of affect regulation but rather one of the struggle between egoistic impulses and internalized prohibitions against them (e.g., Leavy 1980; Lewis 1981). Freud, particularly in his later years, and Anna Freud (1966) emphatically viewed repressive defenses as the result of the overzealous mastery of a developmental achievement—the acquisition of internal standards of acceptable behavior. Freud formulated the "superego" as the internalization of functions that were previously "performed by people in the external world: It observes the ego, gives it orders, judges it and threatens it with punishments" ([1940] 1969, 62). He noted that "its main function remains the limitation of satisfactions" ([1940] 1969, 5) and that "repression is the work of this super-ego" ([1933] 1964, 69).

It would be most consistent with the theory to hypothesize that repressors originally become invested in the control of negative emotion as a strategy for maintaining control over unacceptable impulses. Davis (in this volume) has demonstrated that repressors have particular difficulty remembering emotions such as anger and embarrassment that imply an interpersonal conflict or transgression. In addition, there is considerable evidence that negative affective states do, in fact, often lead to a breakdown of self-control (e.g., Schwartz and Pollack 1977). Therefore, repressors, who maximally value "rational" behavior in accordance with their internal standards, are likely to find dysphoric emotions quite threatening. This view of the repressor as someone with a rigid "superego" is also consonant with developmental theories that contrast a repressive cluster of defenses including neurotic denial with the

Table 2. Definitions of the Six-Group Typology

Subjective Experience of Distress	Suppression of Egoistic Desires (or Restraint)		
	Low	Moderate	High
High	Reactive	Sensitized	Oversocialized
Low	Undersocialized	Self-Assured (Low Defensive)	Repressive (High Defensive)

more immature, externalizing defenses and forms of denial used by individuals with poor impulse control (e.g., Kernberg 1975; Vaillant 1977).

In accordance with these perspectives, Weinberger and Schwartz (in press) reformulated the repressive style within a broader view of social-emotional adjustment. A new six-group typology was developed that was based on the intersection of two superordinate dimensions. One, a self-control dimension, is conceptualized as the Suppression of Egoistic Desires (or Restraint). The other, an affective dimension, is formulated as the Subjective Experience of Distress. Table 2 illustrates that repressors were redefined as those individuals who report low distress but high levels of self-restraint. Thus, as a group, they highly suppress egoistic desires but report little distress about their style of adaptation. Weinberger and Schwartz (in press) found that repressors defined in this way were high on the Marlowe-Crowne and on Rosenbaum's (1980) measure of self-control and low in self-reported aggression, delinquency, alcohol use, and sexual activity. In contrast to formulations that associate a repressive style with hysterical features (cf. Bonnano and Singer and Luborsky, Crits-Christoph, and Alexander, both in this volume), repressors were significantly low on Lazare, Klerman, and Armor's (1966) measure of hysteria but high on their measure of compulsiveness. They were also high on a measure of alexithymia (Kleiger and Kinsman 1980), the emotionally-constricted style prevalent among patients with psychosomatic illnesses. In this new typology, the nondefensive, low-anxious group is split into a relatively well-adjusted, self-assured group that is moderate in restraint and an impulsive, delinquency-prone, undersocialized group that is low in restraint.

The Weinberger Adjustment Inventory (WAI) was recently validated for use with adults and older children (Weinberger 1989), including revised subscales for measuring distress (i.e., anxiety, depression, low self-esteem, and low well-being) and restraint (i.e., suppression of aggression, impulse control, consideration of others, and responsibility). To further refine the distinction between repressive versus self-assured, low-distress subjects, two defensiveness scales were also created for the inventory. The denial of distress scale includes items in which not even occasional negative affect states are acknowledged (e.g., "I never feel sad about things that happen to me"). In addition, a repressive defensiveness scale was developed that includes items in which virtually all lapses in restraint are denied (e.g., "I am never unkind to people I don't like").

A validation study was undertaken to determine what combinations of restraint and defensiveness scores among individuals reporting low distress best discriminated repressors from low-anxious subjects according to the Marlowe-Crowne and Taylor Manifest Anxiety criteria used in prior studies (e.g., Weinberger and Schwartz 1982). With a 75 percent correct classification rate in a discriminant analysis, equal weighting of restraint and repressive defensiveness scores provided the best differentiation. Thus, the designations of between the self-assured and the repressive subject in table 2 represent the use of a restraint/repressive defensiveness composite in identifying the two groups. Defined in this way, both the repressors and the undersocialized group were found to be higher in denial of distress than the self-assured group.

Unlike the Marlowe-Crowne, which was not designed to measure the construct of interest, the new scales allow the various components of a repressive style to be validated separately. Within the new framework, repressors should actually be relatively high in self-restraint in addition to being defensive about not being as high as their idealized self-image would suggest. This hypothesis is consistent with the weak form of Bem's (1972) theory that self-perception is at least partly based on observing one's own behavior. Defensive self-deception, in order to be successful, should require some active attempt to behave in accordance with one's beliefs. Gilbert and Cooper (1985, 76) noted that "knowledge of our own capacity for duplicity means that self-deceptive strategies must do more than merely produce inflated self-assessments; they must produce these outcomes in ways that seem reasonable, accurate, and fair." In other words, repressors could not maintain a belief that they are living by high standards of appropriate behavior if their actions belied them at every turn. By analogy, it is fairly hard to convince yourself or anybody else that you are a liberal if you regularly vote for archconservatives.

There is now considerable evidence that repressors are, in fact, attempting to live by high internalized standards of appropriate behavior. Tublin, Bartholomew, and Weinberger (1987) compared repressors versus nonrepressors in a sample of 298 preadolescent boys. Classmates were significantly *more* likely to nominate repressors relative to other students for high-restraint items (e.g., "Follows the rules, does what he's supposed to") and significantly *less* likely to nominate them as prone to misconduct (e.g., "Often acts selfish, does not help others"). The repressors' teachers also rated them as less prone to misconduct than the other sixth graders.

In terms of affect, teachers could not distinguish between repressors and nonrepressors. In the peer nominations, repressors were significantly less likely to be chosen as high in negative affect (e.g., "Often seems sad, unhappy, or in a bad mood"). However, they were not differentially nominated for being high in positive affect ("Often enjoys himself, usually seems happy"). The peers saw the repressors very much the way the repressors saw themselves in the self-descriptions reported in Weinberger, Schwartz, and Davidson (1979) and in the affect ratings reported in Weinberger and Schwartz (1982). They were judged to be high in self-control and low in the expression of negative affect without being particularly high in positive affect.

The accuracy of repressors' reports of high levels of self-restraint has also been corroborated in studies of adults using both laboratory observations and knowledgeable informants (e.g., Strahan and Strahan 1972). In the laboratory, for example, high Marlowe-Crowne scorers generally inhibit aggressive impulses (Conn and Crowne 1964; Fishman 1965; cf. Hetherington and Wray 1964). Marlowe-Crowne scores have also been found to correlate significantly negatively with spouses' ratings of proneness to hostility and impulsiveness as well as to anxiety and depression (McCrae and Costa 1983). Thus, repressors are to some extent successful in convincing even intimate observers that their self-concepts are veridical (cf. Swann 1983).

If repressors are attempting to maintain firm control over affects and impulses, one would not expect them to seek the kind of disinhibition induced by psychoactive substances. In two diverse samples of college students, Bartholomew and Weinberger (1986) found that repressors on the WAI were low relative to other groups in quantity and frequency of alcohol use and were especially low in using alcohol to facilitate a positive mood. In a third sample, self-reports and independent reports of knowledgeable peers were completely consonant in describing the repressors as low in both drug and alcohol use. For example, according to both self and peer reports, the repressors, on average, had tried approximately one-fifth as many illegal drugs as the low-resistant, high-distress subjects.

Repressors' high levels of restraint and selective inattention to negative affect should also correlate with high tolerance for noxious stimuli. Jamner and Schwartz (1986) investigated pain tolerance using the L-scale of the Eysenck Personality Inventory as the measure of defensiveness. Although there were no differences in sensation thresholds, the high scorers tolerated about twice the milliamps of electrically induced pain. This difference emerged even though subjects were explicitly told that the procedure was to assess subjective judgments and was not an "endurance test." Merbaum and Badia (1967) found similar results using the Byrne scale. These results are of theoretical importance because they run counter to the hypothesis that repressors avoid attending to aversive stimuli because of a lower tolerance for emotional arousal. Rather, the data are more consistent with the hypothesis that being able to remain restrained and unreactive under aversive circumstances is part of the repressors' self-concept, and their ability to ignore their affective appraisals can be used effectively to this end.

The findings that repressors actually are high in restraint and are viewed by knowledgeable informants as low in negative affect are not inconsistent with their use of self-deceptive defenses. Repressors usually do remain overtly calm and self-controlled. The question is, at what cost? Their style seems analogous to a car that maintains a low speed because the driver is leaning heavily on both the brakes and the accelerator. The self-deception is in viewing this mode of functioning as unstressful.

Conclusions

The evidence reviewed in this chapter suggests that at least two very different types of individuals report generally low levels of subjective distress. As a group, low-anxious or self-assured individuals, who also score low on measures of defensiveness such as the Marlowe-Crowne, genuinely seem to respond well to stressful situations. In Collier's (1956) terms, they cope effectively by allowing stressful stimuli into active awareness and assimilating them constructively. They are neither repressors nor sensitizers in that they do not rigidly avoid or maladaptively become preoccupied with negative experiences. Their verbal reports, nonverbal behaviors, and physiological responses are basically congruent.

Repressors, who report low distress but high defensiveness, manifest a very different pattern. They generally claim even less experience of negative affect than the low-anxious group. However, numerous assessments of stress reactivity, including multiple psychophysiological indices as well as vocal, facial, paralinguistic, and objective task performance measures, all suggest that they are as anxious or more anxious than individuals who report chronic distress.

Reliable discrepancies between repressors' self-reports and their objective behavior in stressful situations have been well documented. However, the construct validity of the concept of repressive defenses requires an assessment of the degree to which these discrepancies are consciously recognized. Although to some extent this question stretches the limits of our methodologies, several differentiations seem warranted.

Since the emergence of cognitive psychology, there has been widespread interest in conceptualizing levels of knowing (e.g., Bowers and Meichenbaum 1984). One developing consensus is that conscious versus unconscious mental processes must be viewed as a complex continuum rather than a simple dichotomy. At one end of the continuum, repressors might be thought of as "liars" who consciously create the observed discrepancy by manufacturing self-reports that hide their dysphoria. Within this view, their subjective experience and coping strategies would be very similar to those of chronically distressed individuals; the only difference would be their lack of honest self-disclosure. Although the use of the Marlowe-Crowne scale makes this seem a very plausible hypothesis, it is inconsistent with the evidence. Repressors and highly distressed individuals consistently differ in their strategies for coping with stress.

Work beginning in the 1950s (e.g., Eriksen 1966) has clearly established that repressors suppress and avoid thinking about information associated with negative affect. Thus, repressors have also been conceptualized as "suppressors" who can access the preconscious knowledge that they are experiencing considerable distress; they just do not like thinking about it. Several sources of information are also inconsistent with this view. Repressors do not behave like Vaillant's (1977) well-adjusted suppressors, who, when appropriate, deliberately decide to postpone but not avoid dealing with conflictual issues. Using Haan's (1977) criteria, the rigid and distorting quality of repressors' avoidance suggests that it functions as an unconscious defense as well as a conscious coping style. The crucial transformation from suppression to repression comes when "I prefer not to think about it" becomes "There is nothing to think about." In experimental situations in which repressors are asked about their emotional state, they typically report a relative lack of negative emotion. They do not report that they are upset but prefer not to think about it. Rather, viewing themselves as the kind of persons who do *not* experience much subjective distress seems central to their self-concepts, and they use a variety of active strategies to avoid acknowledging interpersonal and intrapsychic information to the contrary.

No contexts have been found in which repressors "let down their defenses" and recognize that their self-reports are idealized rather than realistic. Moreover, a repressive style does not have the quality of conscious suppression in that the process is by no means easily reversed (cf. Dollard and Miller 1950). For example, Davis (in this volume) has found in a series of studies that repressors seem to have notable difficulty retrieving specific types of emotional memories even when they are explicitly trying. More broadly, repressors cannot readily overcome the discrepancy between their self-perceptions and objective indices. A vivid example is Jamner and Schwartz's (1985) finding that it was not until the ninth month of treatment that a repressive client began to have positive correlations between his subjective experience and his physiological responses as assessed on a daily basis.

Some psychoanalytic formulations would suggest that repressors engage in "successful repression" because they avoid experiencing subjective distress and infrequently develop the kind of psychiatric symptoms that bring individuals to psychotherapy. However, this strategy does take its toll. First, there is growing evidence that repressive individuals are at greater risk than either distressed or nondefensive ones for a variety of specific illnesses including hypertension (e.g., Davies 1970; Schwartz, in this volume), asthma (e.g., Mathe and Knapp 1971), and cancer (e.g., Jensen 1987; Watson, Pettingale, and Greer 1984). We recently found that the association between a repressive style and proneness to physical illness is not limited to adult populations. According to mothers' reports on a physical health checklist, repressive sixth graders, compared to nondefensive, self-assured ones, were higher in somatic symptoms, including asthma and "aches and pains of unknown origin" (Weinberger et al. 1987).

A repressive style of handling affect may directly potentiate the development of certain diseases (Schwartz 1983b). Although the mediating mechanisms are just beginning to be identified, there is evidence that repressive coping may be associated with heightened release of stress-related hormones such as cortisol (e.g., Tennes and Kreye 1985) and norepinephrine (e.g., Esler et al. 1977) and with suppression of the immune system (Jamner, Schwartz & Leigh 1988). This style may also more indirectly contribute to disease by interfering with appropriate health behavior. Repressors' tendency to avoid potential threats is associated with delays in seeking diagnostic information and appropriate medical treatment (e.g., Hill and Gardner 1980; Willett and Heilbronn 1972). This general tendency may also interfere with the monitoring of specific symptoms. For example, Steiner et al. (1987) found that repressive asthmatics were notably poor in sensing changes in the severity of their bronchial asthma.

Repressors' defensive style may often be associated with relatively high levels of psychosocial functioning. However, they do have identifiable interpersonal difficulties related to self-assertion, empathy, and the accurate perception of their own and others' behaviors. They also have performance deficits on tasks that evoke anxiety or require conceptual flexibility.

As Freud ([1930] 1961) emphasized, a repressive style is often "socially desirable" and, therefore, in some sense adaptive in many contexts in modern society. However, there is considerable evidence that repressors' "what you don't know can't hurt you" approach leaves them ill-equipped to cope effectively with psychological difficulties that do emerge. They are likely to avoid seeking help until their problems are severe, to attribute their difficulties to external, nonthreatening causes, and to have little ability to make use of a therapeutic relationship. For example, clients rated as having the most severe presenting problems at a university counseling center averaged in the tenth percentile on the Byrne scale and tended to deny that their problems were personal/social rather than merely educational (Pellegrine 1971). Repressors were judged by intake interviewers to require the most skilled psychotherapists at the clinic because they tended to "be minimally productive" and "shy away from deep interpersonal involvement" (Pellegrine 1971, 335).

The repressors' rigid control of affects and impulses can lead to very poor self-regulation once their defensive structure is broached. Megargee and colleagues (e.g., Megargee, Cook, and Mendelsohn 1967) found in a series of studies that the majority of individuals imprisoned for sudden, extremely violent acts of aggression are repressive rather than undercontrolled. These individuals scored higher than both nonviolent prisoners and college students on a self-report measure of overcontrolled hostility. Violent offenders with little or no prior criminal history also scored higher than those with a record of earlier delinquency. In a less extreme sample, Blackburn (1965) found that, although most psychiatric patients were sensitizers on the Byrne scale, the repressors were more likely to have been referred because of temper outbursts or somatic symptoms (e.g., paralysis or back pain).

Shaw et al.'s (1985) study of myocardial infarction patients also emphasizes the fragility of the repressors' defensive system. High Marlowe-Crowne, high Byrne scale repressors retained less information about life-style risk factors than did those scoring low on the Marlowe-Crowne. More important, the subgroup of repressors who achieved high information levels actually had lower rehabilitation success and psychomedical functioning on six-month follow-up compared to the other groups. Thus, a psychoeducational intervention, when successful in penetrating the repressors' defenses against threatening information, led to *less* rather than more successful coping. This pattern of results has been replicated and extended using patients undergoing coronary angioplasty (Shaw et al. 1987). These types of behaviors further stretch the credibility of construing repressors as simply "liars" or conscious "suppressors."

In sum, the convergent and discriminant validity of the repressive coping style now seems well established. Although our current methodologies allow us to draw only indirect inferences about conscious experience, it is clear that repressors behave as if they do not know and do not want to know that they often have much stronger emotional reactions than their self-reports indicate. Although considerable work remains to be done in order to better understand the nature and implications of this style, the establishment of the basic integrity of the construct opens the doors for more attention to related domains of research.

For example, there has been little investigation of how repressive defenses develop. We have preliminary evidence that preadolescent repressors come from very socially appropriate, highly connected families (Weinberger et al. 1987). Maintaining this sophisticated form of self-deception may require fairly advanced cognitive development (Fischer and Pipp 1984) in addition to extensive socialization. Repressive individuals are likely to establish relatively consistent self-concepts during late childhood (cf. Harter 1983). However, it may be only during adolescence that they fully develop the capacity to convince themselves that they are not upset at times when objective indices suggest otherwise.

It is important to note that the individual differences approach highlights prototypical cases and in some ways disguises the individuality of each person's adaptation. Certainly, those designated repressive on questionnaires are actually defensive only some of the time and in certain domains. In addition, many "nonrepressors" are likely to engage in some repressive behavior that is theoretically or clinically of interest. Contrasting repressors with nondefensive comparison groups was not designed to deny this complexity. Rather, the method served to corroborate psychodynamic and humanistic theorists' assumption that not all paths to low subjective distress are equally adaptive.

More generally, this research area provides an example of the possibility of empirically investigating unconscious defenses by creating operational definitions and exploring alternative hypotheses. Because these mechanisms are so difficult to verify, they should not be assumed when simpler explanations are tenable. On the other hand, the oracle seemed to know something about intrapsychic complexity that modern research is just beginning to heed.

References

Abramson, L. Y., M. E. P. Seligman, and J. D. Teasdale. 1978. Learned helplessness in humans: Critique and reformulation. *Journal of Abnormal Psychology* 87:49–74.

Alloy, L. B., and L. Y. Abramson. 1979. Judgment of contingency in depressed and nondepressed students: Sadder but wiser? *Journal of Experimental Psychology: General* 108:441–85.

Altrocchi, J., O. A. Parsons, and H. Dickoff. 1960. Changes in self-ideal discrepancy in repressors and sensitizers. *Journal of Abnormal and Social Psychology* 61:67–72.

Andersen, S. M. 1984. Self-knowledge and social inference. II. The diagnosticity of cognitive/affective and behavioral data. *Journal of Personality and Social Psychology* 46:294–307.

Arkin, R. M., and E. A. Lake. 1983. Plumbing the depths of the bogus pipeline: A reprise. *Journal of Research in Personality* 17:81–88.

Asendorpf, J. B., and K. R. Scherer. 1983. The discrepant repressor: Differentiation between low anxiety, high anxiety, and repression of anxiety by autonomic-facial-verbal patterns of behavior. *Journal of Personality and Social Psychology* 45:1334–46.

Axtell, B., and C. W. Cole. 1971. Repression-sensitization response mode and verbal avoidance. *Journal of Personality and Social Psychology* 18:133–37.

Bandura, A. 1982. Self-efficacy mechanism in human agency. *American Psychologist* 37:122–47.

———. 1986. *Social foundations of thought and action.* Englewood Cliffs, N.J.: Prentice-Hall.

Bartholomew, K., and D. A. Weinberger. 1986. Adjustment styles and patterns of substance use among college students. Paper presented at the annual meeting of the American Psychological Association, Washington, D.C., August.

Basch, M. F. 1982. The perception of reality and the disavowal of meaning. In *The annual of psychoanalysis,* vol. 9, pp. 125–53. New York: International Universities Press.

Beck, A. T. 1976. *Cognitive therapy and the emotional disorders.* New York: New American Library.

Bell, P. A., and D. Byrne. 1978. Repression-sensitization. In *Dimensions of personality,* ed. H. London and J. E. Exner, Jr., 449–85. New York: Wiley.

Bem, D. 1972. Self-perception theory. In *Advances in experimental social psychology,* ed. L. Berkowitz, vol. 6. New York: Academic.

Berger, S. E., P. Levin, L. I. Jacobson and J. Millham. 1977. Gain approval or avoid disapproval: Comparison of motive strengths in high need for approval scorers. *Journal of Personality* 45:458–68.

Bergquist, W. H., J. T. Lloyd, and S. L. Johansson. 1973. Individual differences among repressor and sensitizers in conceptual skills. *Social Behavior and Personality* 1:144–52.

Blackburn, R. 1965. Emotionality, repression-sensitization, and maladjustment. *British Journal of Psychiatry* 111:399–404.

Block, J., and H. Thomas. 1955. Is satisfaction with self a measure of adjustment? *Journal of Abnormal and Social Psychology* 51:254–59.

Boor, M., and T. Schill. 1967. Digit symbol performance of subjects varying in anxiety and defensiveness. *Journal of Consulting Psychology* 31:600–603.

———. 1968. Subtest performance on the Wechsler Adult Intelligence Scale as a function of anxiety and defensiveness. *Perceptual and Motor Skills* 27:33–34.

Bowers, K. S., and D. Meichenbaum, eds. 1984. *The unconscious reconsidered.* New York: Wiley.

Bradburn, N. M., and S. Sudman. 1980. *Improving interview method and questionnaire design.* San Francisco: Jossey-Bass.

Brown, W. P. 1961. Conceptions of perceptual defense. *British Journal of Psychology Monograph Supplement* no. 35, 1–107.

Cantor, N., and J. F. Kihlstrom. 1987. *Personality and social intelligence.* Englewood Cliffs, N.J.: Prentice-Hall.

Cantor, N., and W. Mischel. 1979. Prototypes in person perception. In *Advances in experimental social psychology,* ed. L. Berkowitz, vol. 12. New York: Academic.

Clark, L. F., and C. Neuringer. 1971. Repressor-sensitizer personality styles and associated levels of verbal ability, social intelligence, sex knowledge, and quantitative ability. *Journal of Consulting and Clinical Psychology* 36:183–88.

Collier, R. 1956. Consciousness as a regulating field: Theory of psychopathology. *Psychological Review* 63:360–69.

Conn, L. K., and D. P. Crowne. 1964. Instigation to aggression, emotional arousal, and defensive emulation. *Journal of Personality* 32:163–79.

Cook, J. R. 1985. Repression-sensitization and approach-avoidance as predictors of response to a laboratory stressor. *Journal of Personality and Social Psychology* 49:759–73.

Costa, P. T., Jr., R. R. McCrae, and D. Arenberg. 1980. Enduring dispositions in adult males. *Journal of Personality and Social Psychology* 38:793–800.

Cronbach, L. J., and P. E. Meehl. 1955. Construct validity in psychological tests. *Psychological Bulletin* 52:281–302.

Crowne, D. P. 1979. *The experimental study of personality.* Hillsdale, N.J.: Erlbaum.

Crowne, D. P., and D. A. Marlowe. 1960. A new scale of social desirability independent of psychopathology. *Journal of Consulting Psychology* 24:349–54.

————. 1964. *The approval motive: Studies in evaluative dependence.* New York: Wiley.

Davidson, R. J. 1983. Affect, repression, and cerebral asymmetry. In *Emotions in health and illness,* ed. L. Temoshok, C. Van Dyke, and L. S. Zegans, 123–35. New York: Grune & Stratton.

————. 1984. Affect, cognition, and hemispheric specialization. In *Emotions, cognition, and behavior,* ed. C. E. Izard, J. Kagan, and R. B. Zajonc, 320–65. Cambridge: Cambridge University Press.

Davies, M. 1970. Blood pressure and personality. *Journal of Psychosomatic Research* 14:89–104.

Davis, P. J., and G. E. Schwartz. 1987. Repression and the inaccessibility of affective memories. *Journal of Personality and Social Psychology* 52:155–62.

Dennett, D. C. 1969. *Content and consciousness.* London: Routledge & Kegan Paul.

Dollard, J., and N. E. Miller. 1950. *Personality and psychotherapy: An analysis in terms of learning, thinking, and culture.* New York: McGraw-Hill.

Doster, J. A. 1975. Individual differences affecting interviewee expectancies and perceptions of self-disclosure. *Journal of Counseling Psychology* 22:192–98.

Edwards, A. L. 1957. *The social desirability variable in personality assessment and research.* New York: Dryden.

Ekman, P. 1984. Expression and nature of emotion. In *Approaches to emotion,* ed. K. R. Scherer and P. Ekman, 319–43. Hillsdale, N.J.: Erlbaum.

Ellis, A. 1987. The impossibility of achieving consistently good mental health. *American Psychologist* 42:364–75.

Eriksen, C. W. 1966. Cognitive responses to internally cued anxiety. In *Anxiety and behavior,* ed. C. D. Spielberger. New York: Academic.

Esler, M., S. Julius, A. Zweifler, O. Randell, E. Harburg, H. Gardiner, and V. DeQuattro. 1977. Mild high-renin essential hypertension: Neurogenic human hypertension? *New England Journal of Medicine* 296:405–11.

Festinger, L. 1957. *A theory of cognitive dissonance.* Evanston, Ill.: Row, Peterson.

Fischer, K. W., and S. L. Pipp. 1984. Development of the structures of unconscious thought. In *The unconscious reconsidered,* ed. K. Bowers, and D. Meichenbaum, 88–148. New York: Wiley.

Fishman, C. G. 1965. Need for approval and the expression of aggression under varying conditions of frustration. *Journal of Personality and Social Psychology* 2:809–16.

Fodor, J. A. 1983. *The modularity of mind.* Cambridge, Mass.: MIT Press.

Ford, D. H. 1987. *Humans as self-constructing living systems.* Hillsdale, N.J.: Erlbaum.

Freud, A. 1966. *The ego and the mechanisms of defense.* Rev. ed. New York: International Universities Press.

Freud, S. [1894] 1940. The defence neuro-psychoses. In *Collected Papers,* ed. J. Riviere, vol. 1, 2d ed. London: Hogarth.

————. [1914] 1957. On narcissism: An introduction. In *The standard edition of the complete psychological works of Sigmund Freud,* ed. J. Strachey, vol. 14, pp. 67–102. London: Hogarth.

————. [1915] 1957. Repression. In *The standard edition of the complete psycholog-*

ical works of Sigmund Freud, ed. J. Strachey, vol. 14, pp. 141–58.) London: Hogarth.

———. [1930] 1961. *Civilization and its discontents.* Ed. and trans. J. Strachey. New York: Norton.

———. [1933] 1964. New introductory lectures on psycho-analysis. In *The standard edition of the complete psychological works of Sigmund Freud,* ed. J. Strachey, vol. 22, pp. 1–182). London: Hogarth.

———. [1940] 1969. *An outline of psycho-analysis.* Trans. J. Strachey. New York: Norton.

Galin, D. 1974. Implications of left-right cerebral lateralization for psychiatry: A neurophysiological context for unconscious processes. *Archives of General Psychiatry* 9:412–18.

Gardner, R. W., P. S. Holzman, G. S. Klein, H. B. Linton, and D. P. Spence. 1959. Cognitive control: A study of individual consistencies in cognitive behavior. In *Psychological Issues, no. 4.* New York: International Universities Press.

Gazzaniga, M. S. 1985. *The social brain: Discovering the networks of the mind.* New York: Basic.

Gilbert, D. T., and J. Cooper. 1985. Social psychological strategies of self-deception. In *Self-deception and self-understanding,* ed. M. W. Martin, 75–94. Lawrence: University Press of Kansas.

Golin, S., E. W. Herron, R. Lakota, and L. Reineck. 1967. Factor analytic study of the Manifest Anxiety, Extraversion, and Repression-Sensitization Scales. *Journal of Consulting Psychology* 31:564–69.

Gomes, M. E., and D. A. Weinberger. 1986. Attributional biases: Distinctions among depressive, defensive, and efficacious styles. Paper presented at the annual meeting of the American Psychological Association, Washington, D.C., August.

Graziano, W. G., T. Brothen, and E. Berscheid. 1980. Attention, attraction, and individual differences in reaction to criticism. *Journal of Personality and Social Psychology* 38:193–202.

Greenwald, A. G. 1980. The totalitarian ego: Fabrication and revision of personal history. *American Psychologist* 35:603–18.

Gudjonsson, G. H. 1981. Self-reported emotional disturbance and its relation to electrodermal reactivity, defensiveness and trait anxiety. *Personality and Individual Differences* 2:47–52.

Gur, R. C., and H. A. Sackeim. 1979. Self-deception: A concept in search of a phenomenon. *Journal of Personality and Social Psychology* 37:147–69.

Haan, N. 1977. *Coping and defending.* New York: Academic Press.

Haley, G. A. 1974. Eye movement responses of repressors and sensitizers to a stressful film. *Journal of Research in Personality* 8:88–94.

Hare, R. D. 1966. Denial of threat and emotional response to impending painful stimulation. *Journal of Consulting Psychology* 30:359–61.

Harter, S. H. 1983. Developmental perspectives on the self system. In *Handbook of child psychology,* ed. P. H. Mussen, 4th ed., vol. 4, *Socialization, personality, and social behavior,* ed. E. M. Hetherington. New York: Wiley.

Hetherington, E. M., and M. P. Wray. 1964. Aggression, need for social approval, and humor preferences. *Journal of Abnormal and Social Psychology* 68:685–89.

Higgins, E. T. 1987. Self-discrepancy: A theory relating self and affect. *Psychological Review* 94:319–40.

Higgins, E. T., R. Klein, and T. Strauman. 1985. Self-concept discrepancy theory: A psychological model for distinguishing among different aspects of depression and anxiety. *Social Cognition* 3:51–76.

Hilgard, E. R. 1986. *Divided consciousness: Multiple controls in human thought and action.* Expanded ed. New York: Wiley.

Hill, D., and G. Gardner. 1980. Repression-sensitization and yielding to threatening health communications. *Australian Journal of Psychology* 32:183–93.

Hodges, W. F. 1976. The psychophysiology of anxiety. In *Emotions and anxiety: New concepts, methods, and applications,* ed. M. Zuckerman and C. D. Spielberger. New York: Halsted.

Holmes, D. S. 1974. Investigations of repression: Differential recall of material experimentally or naturally associated with ego threat. *Psychological Bulletin* 81:632–53.

Holroyd, K. 1972. Repression-sensitization, Marlowe-Crowne defensiveness, and perceptual defense. *Proceedings of the 80th Annual Convention of the American Psychological Association* 7:401–02.

Horney, K. 1950. *Neurosis and human growth.* New York: Norton.

Houston, B. K. 1977. Dispositional anxiety and the effectiveness of cognitive coping strategies in stressful laboratory and classroom situations. In *Stress and anxiety,* ed. C. D. Spielberger and I. G. Sarason, vol. 4. Washington, D.C.: Hemisphere/Halsted.

Houston, B. K., and D. S. Holmes. 1974. Effect of avoidant thinking and reappraisal for coping with threat involving temporal uncertainty. *Journal of Personality and Social Psychology* 30:382–88.

Izard, C. E. 1984. Emotion-cognition relationships and human development. In *Emotions, cognition, and behavior,* ed. C. E. Izard, J. Kagan, and R. B. Zajonc, 17–37. Cambridge: Cambridge University Press.

Jamner, L. D., and G. E. Schwartz. 1985. Self-regulation and the integration of self-report and physiological indices of affect. *Psychophysiology* 22:596.

————. 1986. Self-deception predicts self-report and endurance of pain. *Psychosomatic Medicine* 48:211–23.

Jamner, L. D., G. E. Schwartz, and H. Leigh. 1988. The relationship between repressive and defensive coping styles and monocyte, eosinophile and serum glucose levels: Support for the opioid-peptide hypothesis of repression. *Psychosomatic Medicine* 50:567–75.

Jensen, M. R. 1987. Psychobiological factors predicting the course of breast cancer. *Journal of Personality* 55:317–42.

Jones, E. E., and H. Sigall. 1971. The bogus pipeline: A new paradigm for measuring affect and attitude. *Psychological Bulletin* 76:349–64.

Kahn, M., and T. Schill. 1971. Anxiety report in defensive and nondefensive repressors. *Journal of Consulting and Clinical Psychology* 36:300.

Kanfer, F. H., and A. R. Marston. 1964. Characteristics of interactional behavior in a psychotherapy analogue. *Journal of Consulting Psychology* 28:456–67.

Kasl, S. J., and G. F. Mahl. 1965. The relationship of disturbances and hesitations in spontaneous speech to anxiety. *Journal of Personality and Social Psychology* 1:425–33.

Katz, P., and E. Zigler. 1967. Self-image disparity: A development approach. *Journal of Personality and Social Psychology* 5:186–95.

Kendall, P., and K. Bemis. 1983. Thought and action in psychotherapy: The cognitive-behavioral approaches. In *The clinical psychology handbook,* ed. M. Hersen, A. E. Kazdin, and A. S. Bellack, 565–92. New York: Pergamon.

Kernberg, O. F. 1975. *Borderline conditions and pathological narcissism.* New York: Aronson.

———. 1982. Self, ego, affects and drives. *Journal of the American Psychoanalytic Association* 30:893–918.

Kiecolt, J., and E. McGrath. 1979. Social desirability responding in the measurement of assertive behavior. *Journal of Consulting and Clinical Psychology* 47:640–42.

Kiecolt-Glaser, J. K., and B. Greenberg. 1983. On the use of physiological measures in assertion research. *Journal of Behavioral Assessment* 5:97–109.

Kiecolt-Glaser, J. K., and J. A. Murray. 1980. Social desirability bias in self-monitoring data. *Journal of Behavioral Assessment* 2:239–47.

Kihlstrom, J. F., and N. Cantor. 1984. Mental representations of the self. In *Advances in experimental social psychology,* ed. L. Berkowitz, vol. 17, pp. 1–47. Orlando, Fla.: Academic.

King, A. C., C. L. Albright, C. B. Taylor, W. L. Haskell, and R. F. DeBusk. 1986. The repressive coping style: A predictor of cardiovascular reactivity and risk. Paper presented at the annual meeting of the Society of Behavioral Medicine, San Francisco, October.

Kleiger, J. H., and R. A. Kinsman. 1980. The development of an MMPI alexithymia scale. *Psychotherapy and Psychosomatics* 34:17–24.

Kohut, H. 1971. *Analysis of the self.* New York: International Universities Press.

Kosslyn, S. M. 1987. Seeing and imagining in the cerebral hemispheres: A computational approach. *Psychological Review* 94:148–75.

Kraut, R. E. 1978. Verbal and nonverbal cues in the perception of lying. *Journal of Personality and Social Psychology* 36:380–91.

Lang, P. J. 1979. A bio-informational theory of emotional imagery. *Psychophysiology* 16:495–512.

Lazare, A., G. L. Klerman, and D. J. Armor. 1966. Oral, obsessive and hysterical personality patterns. *Archives of General Psychiatry* 14:624.

Lazarus, R. S. 1984. Thoughts on the relations between emotion and cognition. In *Approaches to emotion,* ed. K. R. Scherer and P. Ekman, 247–57. Hillsdale, N.J.: Erlbaum.

———. 1985. The costs and benefits of denial. In *Stress and coping: An anthology,* ed. A. Monat and R. S. Lazarus, 2d ed., 154–73. New York: Columbia University Press.

Lazarus, R. S., and E. Alfert. 1964. The short-circuiting of threat by experimentally altering cognitive appraisal. *Journal of Abnormal and Social Psychology* 69:195–205.

Lazarus, R. S., and S. Folkman. 1984. *Stress, appraisal, and coping.* New York: Springer.

Leavy, S. A. 1980. *The psychoanalytic dialogue.* New Haven, Conn.: Yale University Press.

LeDoux, J. E. In press. Sensory systems and emotion: A model of affective processing. *Integrative Psychiatry.*

Leon, G. R., B. Gillum, R. Gillum, and M. Gouze. 1979. Personality stability and change over a 30-year period—middle age to old age. *Journal of Consulting and Clinical Psychology* 47:517–24.

Levenson, R. W., and L. L. Mades. 1980. Physiological response, facial expression, and trait anxiety: Two methods for improving consistency. Paper presented at the Society for Psychophysiological Research, Vancouver, British Columbia, October.

Leventhal, H. 1984. A perceptual-motor theory of emotion. In *Advances in experimental social psychology,* vol. 17. Orlando, Fla.: Academic.

Lewinsohn, P. M., W. Mischel, W. Chaplin, and R. Barton. 1980. Social competence and depression: The role of illusory self-perceptions. *Journal of Abnormal Psychology* 89:203–12.

Lewis, H. B. 1981. *Freud and modern psychology.* Vol. 1, *The Emotional Basis of Mental Illness.* New York: Plenum.

McClelland, J. L., and D. E. Rumelhart. 1986. *Parallel distributed processing.* Vol. 2, *Psychological and biological models.* Cambridge, Mass.: MIT Press.

McCrae, R. R., and P. T. Costa. Jr. 1983. Social desirability scales: More substance than style. *Journal of Consulting and Clinical Psychology* 51:882–88.

MacLean, P. D. 1975. Sensory and perceptive factors in emotional functions in the triune brain. In *Emotions: Their parameters and measurements,* ed. L. Levi. New York: Raven.

Madison, P. 1956. Freud's repression concept: A survey and attempted clarification. *International Journal of Psycho-Analysis* 37:75–81.

Mandler, G. 1975. *Mind and emotion.* New York: Wiley.

Mandler, G. M., J. M. Mandler, I. Kremen, and R. D. Sholiton. 1961. The response to threat: Relations among verbal and physiological indices. *Psychological Monographs* 75, no. 9, whole no. 513.

Markus, H. 1977. Self-schemata and processing information about the self. *Journal of Personality and Social Psychology* 35:63–78.

Martens, R., and M. Landers. 1970. Motor performance under stress: A test of the inverted-U hypothesis. *Journal of Personality and Social Psychology* 16:29–37.

Maslow, A. H. 1962. *Toward a psychology of being.* Princeton, N.J.: Van Nostrand.

———. 1970. *Motivation and personality.* 2d ed. New York: Harper & Row.

Mathe, A. A., and P. H. Knapp. 1971. Emotional and adrenal reactions to stress in bronchial asthma. *Psychosomatic Medicine* 33:323–40.

Matney, D. C., and D. I. McManis. 1977. Repression-sensitization status and social intelligence characteristics. *Psychological Reports* 41:837–38.

Megargee, E. I., P. E. Cook, and G. A. Mendelsohn. 1967. Development and validation of an MMPI scale of assaultiveness in overcontrolled individuals. *Journal of Abnormal Psychology* 72:519–28.

Merbaum, J., and P. Badia. 1967. Tolerance of repressors and sensitizers to noxious stimulation. *Journal of Abnormal Psychology* 72:349–53.

Messer, S. B., and M. Winokur. 1980. Some limits to the integration of psychoanalytic and behavior therapy. *American Psychologist* 35:818–27.

Millham, J., and L. I. Jacobson. 1978. The need for approval. In *Dimensions of personality,* ed. H. London and J. E. Exner, Jr., 365–90. New York: Wiley.

Millham, J., and R. W. Kellogg. 1980. Need for social approval: Impression management or self-deception? *Journal of Research in Personality* 14:445–57.

Millimet, C. R., and H. J. Cohen. 1973. Repression-sensitization: A reflection of test-taking set or personal adjustment. *Journal of Personality Assessment* 37:255–59.

Mischel, W. 1979. On the interface of cognition and personality. *American Psychologist* 34:740–41.

Mischel, W., E. B. Ebbesen, and A. R. Zeiss. 1973. Selective attention to the self: Situational and dispositional determinants. *Journal of Personality and Social Psychology* 27:129–42.

Mosher, D. L. 1965. Approval motive and acceptance of "fake" personality test interpretations which differ in favorability. *Psychological Reports* 17:395–402.

Nielsen, L. E., and J. R. Fleck. 1981. Defensive repressors and empathic impairment. *Psychological Reports* 48:615–24.

Nisbett, R. E., and L. Ross. 1980. *Human inference: Strategies and shortcomings of social judgment.* Englewood Cliffs, N.J.: Prentice-Hall.

Nisbett, R. E., and T. Wilson. 1977. Telling more than we can know: Verbal reports on mental processes. *Psychological Review* 84:231–59.

Nordholm, D. A. 1974. A note on the reliability and validity of the Marlowe-Crowne Scale of social desirability. *Journal of Social Psychology* 93:139–40.

O'Connell, W., and P. Peterson. 1964. Humor and repression. *Journal of Existential Psychiatry* 4:309–16.

Olson, J. M., and M. P. Zanna. 1979. A new look at selective exposure. *Journal of Experimental Social Psychology* 15:1–15.

Panksepp, J. 1982. Toward a general psychobiological theory of emotions. *Behavioral and Brain Sciences* 5:407–67.

Parsons, O. A., L. B. Fulgenzi, and R. Edelberg. 1969. Aggressiveness and psychophysiological responsivity in groups of repressors and sensitizers. *Journal of Personality and Social Psychology* 12:235–44.

Pellegrine, R. J. 1971. Repression-sensitization and perceived severity of presenting problem of four hundred and forty-four counseling center clients. *Journal of Counseling Psychology* 18:332–36.

Perls, F., R. F. Hefferline, and P. Goodman. 1951. *Gestalt therapy.* New York: Dell.

Peterson, C., and M. E. P. Seligman. 1984. Causal explanations as a risk factor for depression. *Psychological Review* 91:347–74.

Rogers, C. R. 1951. *Client-centered therapy.* Boston: Houghton Mifflin.

———. 1961. *On becoming a person.* Boston: Houghton Mifflin.

Roseman, I. J. 1984. Cognitive determinants of emotions: A structural theory. In *Review of personality and social psychology,* vol. 5, *Emotions, relationships, and health,* ed. P. Shaver, 11–36. Beverly Hills, Calif.: Sage.

Rosenbaum, M. 1980. A schedule for assessing self-control behaviors: Preliminary findings. *Behavior Therapy* 11:109–21.

Rosenman, R. 1978. The interview method of assessment of the coronary-prone behavior pattern. In *Coronary-prone behavior,* ed. T. Dembroski, S. Weiss, J. Shields, S. Haynes, and M. Feinleib, 55–70. New York: Springer.

Ross, L. 1987. The problem of construal in social inference and social psychology. In *A distinctive approach to psychological research: The influence of Stanley Schacter,* ed. N. E. Grunberg, R. E. Nisbett, J. Rodin, and J. E. Singer, 118–50. Hillsdale, N.J.: Erlbaum.

Sarbin, T. R. 1952. A preface to a psychological analysis of the self. *Psychological Review* 59:11–22.

————. 1981. On self-deception. *Annals of the New York Academy of Science* 364:220–35.

Scarpetti, W. L. 1973. The repression-sensitization dimension in relation to impending painful stimulation. *Journal of Consulting and Clinical Psychology* 40:377–82.

Schachter, S., and J. E. Singer. 1962. Cognitive, social and physiological determinants of emotional state. *Psychological Review* 69:379–99.

Scherer, K. R. 1984. On the nature and function of emotion: A component process approach. In *Approaches to emotion,* ed. K. R. Scherer and P. Ekman, 243–318. Hillsdale, N.J.: Erlbaum.

Schill, T., and M. Althoff. 1968. Auditory perceptual thresholds for sensitizers, defensive and non-defensive repressors. *Perceptual and Motor Skills* 27:935–38.

Schlenker, B. R., and M. R. Leary. 1982. Social anxiety and self-presentation: A conceptualization and model. *Psychological Bulletin* 92:641–69.

Schneider, D. J., and D. Turkat. 1975. Self-presentation following success or failure: Defensive self-esteem models. *Journal of Personality* 43:127–35.

Schwartz, G. E. 1983a. Disregulation theory and disease: Applications to the repression/cerebral disconnection/cardiovascular disorder hypothesis. *International Review of Applied Psychology* 32:95–118.

————. 1983b. Psychobiology of health: A new synthesis. In *Psychology and health: The master lecture series,* ed. B. L. Hammonds and C. J. Scheirer, vol. 3. Washington, D.C.: American Psychological Association.

————. 1986. Emotion and psychophysiological organization: A systems approach. in *Psychophysiology: Systems, processes, and applications,* ed. M. G. H. Coles, E. Donchin, and S. W. Porges. 354–77. New York: Guilford.

Schwartz, G. E., R. J. Davidson, and D. J. Goleman. 1978. Patterning of cognitive and somatic processes in the self-regulation of anxiety: Effects of meditation versus exercise. *Psychosomatic Medicine* 40:321–28.

Schwartz, G. E., and D. A. Weinberger. 1980. Patterns of emotional responses to affective situations: Relations among happiness, sadness, anger, fear, depression, and anxiety. *Motivation and Emotion* 4:175–91.

Schwartz, G. E., D. A. Weinberger, and J. A. Singer. 1981. Cardiovascular differentiation of happiness, sadness, anger, and fear following imagery and exercise. *Psychosomatic Medicine* 43:343–63.

Schwartz, J. C., and P. R. Pollack. 1977. Affect and delay of gratification. *Journal of Research in Personality* 11:147–64.

Shaw, R. E., F. Cohen, B. Doyle, and J. Palesky. 1985. The impact of denial and repressive style on information gain and rehabilitation outcomes in myocardial infarction patients. *Psychosomatic Medicine* 47:262–73.

Shaw, R. E., F. Cohen, J. Fishman-Rosen, M. C. Murphy, S. H. Stertzer, D. A. Clark, and R. K. Myler. 1986. Psychologic predictors of psychosocial and medical outcomes in patients undergoing coronary angioplasty. *Psychosomatic Medicine* 48:582–97.

Singer, J. L., and D. S. Klos. 1981. Determinants of the adolescent's ongoing thought following simulated parental confrontations. *Journal of Personality and Social Psychology* 41:975–87.

Smith, C. A., and P. C. Ellsworth. 1985. Patterns of cognitive appraisal in emotion. *Journal of Personality and Social Psychology* 48:813–38.

Snyder, M. 1974. Self-monitoring of expressive behavior. *Journal of Personality and Social Psychology* 30:526–37.

Spielberger, C. D. 1972. Anxiety as an emotional state. In *Anxiety: Current trends in theory and research,* ed. C. D. Spielberger, vol. 1. New York: Academic.

Steiner, H., C. M. B. Higgs, G. K. Fritz, G. Laszlo, and J. E. Harvey. 1987. Defense style and the perception of asthma. *Psychosomatic Medicine* 49:35–44.

Strahan, R., and C. Strahan. 1972. Nature of the Marlowe-Crowne social desirability variable. *Proceedings of the 80th Annual Convention of the American Psychological Association* 7:67–68.

Strickland, B. R., and D. P. Crowne. 1963. Need for approval and the premature termination of psychotherapy. *Journal of Consulting Psychology* 27:95–101.

Sullivan, P. F., and L. K. Roberts. 1969. The relationship of manifest anxiety to repression-sensitization on the MMPI. *Journal of Consulting and Clinical Psychology* 33:763–64.

Swann, W. B., Jr. 1983. Self-verification: Bringing social reality into harmony with the self. In *Psychological perspectives on the self,* ed. J. Suls and A. G. Greenwald, vol. 2, 33–66. Hillsdale, N.J.: Erlbaum.

Szabados, B. 1985. The self, its passions and self-deception. In *Self-deception and self-understanding,* ed. M. W. Martin, 143–68. Lawrence: University Press of Kansas.

Tanaka-Matsumi, J., and V. A. Kameoka. 1986. Reliabilities and concurrent validities of popular self-report measures of depression, anxiety, and social desirability. *Journal of Consulting and Clinical Psychology* 54:328–33.

Taylor, J. A. 1953. A personality scale of manifest anxiety. *Journal of Abnormal and Social Psychology* 48:285–90.

Taylor, S. E. 1983. Adjustment to threatening events. *American Psychologist* 38:1161–73.

Taylor, S. E., and J. D. Brown. 1988. Illusion and well-being: A social psychological perspective on mental health. *Psychological Bulletin* 103:193–210.

Tennes, K., and M. Kreye. 1985. Children's adrenocortical responses to classroom activities and tests in elementary school. *Psychosomatic Medicine* 47:451–60.

Tesser, A., and D. Paulhus. 1983. The definition of self: Private and public self-evaluation management strategies. *Journal of Personality and Social Psychology* 44:672–82.

Tetlock, P. E., and A. S. R. Manstead. 1985. Impression management versus intrapsychic explanations in social psychology: A useful dichotomy? *Psychological Review* 92:59–77.

Tolkmitt, F. J., and K. R. Scherer. 1986. Effect of experimentally induced stress on vocal parameters. *Journal of Experimental Psychology: Human Perception and Performance* 12:302–13.

Tublin, S. K., K. Bartholomew, and D. A. Weinberger. 1987. Peer perceptions of preadolescent boys with repressive coping styles. Paper presented at the meeting of the American Psychological Association, New York, August.

Tublin, S. K., and D. A. Weinberger. 1987. Individual differences in coping processes: A thought sampling approach. Paper presented at the annual meeting of the Western Psychological Association, Long Beach, California, April.

Vaillant, G. E. 1977. *Adaptation to life.* Boston: Little, Brown.

Watson, D., and L. A. Clark. 1984. Negative affectivity: The disposition to experience aversive emotional states. *Psychological Bulletin* 96:465–90.

Watson, M., K. W., Pettingale, and S. Greer. 1984. Emotional control and autonomic arousal in breast cancer patients. *Journal of Psychosomatic Research* 28:467–74.

Weinberger, D. A. 1989. Social-emotional adjustment in older children and adults. I. Psychometric properties of the Weinberger Adjustment Inventory. Department of Psychology, Stanford University. Typescript.

Weinberger, D. A., D. E. Gordon, S. S. Feldman, and M. E. Ford. 1987. The relationship between family patterns and restraint in preadolescent boys. Paper presented at the annual meeting of the American Psychological Association, New York, August.

Weinberger, D. A., and G. E. Schwartz. 1982. Patterns of emotional responses to affective situations: II. Interactions of anxious and repressive coping styles. Department of Psychology, Stanford University. Typescript.

————. In press. Distress and restraint as superordinate dimensions of self-reported adjustment: A typological perspective. *Journal of Personality.*

Weinberger, D. A., G. E. Schwartz, and R. J. Davidson. 1979. Low-anxious, high-anxious, and repressive coping styles: Psychometric patterns and behavioral and physiological responses to stress. *Journal of Abnormal Psychology* 88:369–80.

Wentzel, K. R., D. A. Weinberger, M. E. Ford, and S. S. Feldman. In press. Academic achievement in preadolescence: The role of motivational, affective, and self-regulatory processes. *Journal of Applied Developmental Psychology.*

Wiesenthal, D. L. 1974. Some effects of the confirmation and disconfirmation of an unexpected monetary reward on compliance. *Journal of Social Psychology* 92:39–52.

Wilkins, G., F. Epting, and H. van de Riet. 1972. Relationship between repression-sensitization and interpersonal cognitive complexity. *Journal of Consulting and Clinical Psychology* 39:448–50.

Willett, E. A., and M. Heilbronn. 1972. Repression-sensitization and discrepancy between self-report and official report of illness. *Journal of Psychology* 81:161–66.

Wolpe, J. 1978. Cognition and causation in human behavior and its therapy. *American Psychologist* 33:437–46.

15 Repression and the Inaccessibility of Emotional Memories

PENELOPE J. DAVIS

The research that I am going to talk about is concerned with the effects of repression on the recall of personal, real-life emotional experiences. At the outset, I would like to say that my own interest in repressive processes, and in the accessibility of emotional memories in particular, grew out of observations—or hunches, to be more accurate—made while working in an acute psychiatric setting. There, it often seemed that some individuals had difficulty not only in recalling distressing experiences from their past but also in perceiving connections between previous experiences and current life situations. Despite this, past events often seemed to have a substantial effect on affective and cognitive reactions to events in the present.

Such ideas have clear implications for understanding current distress and also for therapy; it is equally clear, however, that these ideas are inferences that go far beyond the information available to an external observer. This latter point creates a major difficulty, for inference and intuition abound in acute psychiatric settings, but consensus among clinicians often seems rare. With this very much in mind, I turned to the psychological literature on repression to see if there was any empirical basis for my own ideas. I found that the clinical literature seemed to support the validity of the concept of repression virtually without question, yet had little to offer in the way of hard data. Reviews of the experimental literature, on the other hand, conclude that there is no evidence that repression exists, and hence "the continued use of repression as an explanation for behavior does not seem justifiable" (Holmes 1974, 651). Faced with this impasse, what does one do? To borrow from Erdelyi and Goldberg (1979), does one hold the phenomenon or the methodology accountable?

Clearly, my own intuitions suggested that repression was real, but if so,

This research was supported by a grant from the National Science Foundation to Gary E. Schwartz (experiment 1) and by a grant from the Australian Research Grants Scheme to Penelope J. Davis (experiments 2–7).

then it must be possible to demonstrate predictable phenomena associated with repression, within an experimental framework. And so my own research venture into repression began. Unlike many contributors to this volume, and doubtless many readers as well, I was not particularly familiar with Freud and, indeed, did not read Freud's ([1915] 1957) seminal paper on repression until the completion of the first study presented here. It turns out, however, that the conceptualization of repression underlying the present research is very much akin to that of Freud. According to Freud, "the essence of repression lies simply in turning something away, and keeping it at a distance from the conscious" ([1915] 1957, 147), and the purpose of repression is simply the avoidance of psychological pain or, to use his own words, the avoidance of unpleasure.

One of the major difficulties in repression research is that repression is an elusive process to capture in the laboratory. Experimental manipulations designed to induce repression have been viewed critically by clinicians and experimentalists alike, albeit for different reasons. Clinicians argue that laboratory, analogue studies of repression are so far removed from clinical phenomena and theoretical conceptions of repression that they are essentially irrelevant (cf. Rapaport 1942). Experimentalists, in turn, argue that other processes, such as attention, can be more parsimoniously invoked to account for experimental findings (cf. Holmes 1974). Because of problems in operationalizing repression as a process, researchers began to direct their attention toward studying repression as a trait, and a number of measures designed to identify individuals who characteristically adopt a repressive mode of coping with unpleasant, stressful situations were constructed. The best-known and most widely used of these is the Byrne Repression-Sensitization Scale (Byrne, Barry, and Nelson 1963). The Byrne scale, however, turns out to be very highly correlated with measures of anxiety, and it was to overcome this confound that Weinberger, Schwartz, and Davidson (1979) proposed an alternative measure of repression (see Weinberger, in this volume). A trait approach to the study of repression, using the Weinberger, Schwartz, and Davidson measure, has been adopted in the research presented here. With that brief background, I now move on to the research itself.

Repression and the Recall of Affective Memories

The present research derives from the fundamental proposition that repression serves to keep painful, unpleasant experiences out of consciousness or awareness. If this is indeed the case, individuals who characteristically employ a repressive mode of defense should be less able than others to recall personal, real-life experiences associated with negative affect. I would like to present four studies that were specifically designed to address this proposition. In each study, repression was defined in accord with the approach proposed by Weinberger, Schwartz, and Davidson (1979). To be more specific, repressors were operationally defined as those individuals who report low levels of anxiety in conjunction with high levels of defensiveness. Anxiety and defensiveness were measured using the short form of the Taylor Manifest Anxiety Scale (Bendig 1956) and the Marlowe-Crowne Social Desirability Scale (Crowne and Marlowe 1964), respectively.

The initial study, conducted by Gary Schwartz and me (Davis and Schwartz 1987), employed three groups of female subjects: a low-anxious group, a high-anxious group, and a group of repressors. Subjects were asked to recall and briefly describe childhood memories, and there were six recall conditions. The first recall condition was a general one in which subjects were simply asked to recall childhood experiences and no mention whatsoever was made of affect. In the other five conditions, subjects were asked to recall happy, sad, anger, fear, and wonder experiences from childhood. Each recall period lasted for four minutes, and bilateral facial muscle activity and facial skin temperature were monitored throughout. At the end of each recall period, subjects were asked to rate the original and present intensity of the affect associated with each experience and to indicate which was the earliest experience and their age at that time. What did we find? We found that repressors recalled significantly fewer negative affective memories than low-anxious and high-anxious subjects and, furthermore, that they were substantially older at the time of the earliest negative experience recalled. Somewhat unexpectedly, repressors also recalled fewer positive experiences than low-anxious subjects did, although no group differences in the age of the earliest positive memories were apparent. The data for the number of memories recalled and the age of the earliest memory in each recall condition are presented in figures 1 and 2, respectively.

The major focus of the present paper is repression and memory, but I will briefly describe the physiological results because they, too, are consistent with theoretical conceptualizations of repression. First of all, group differences in skin temperature revealed that repressors were physiologically more aroused than low-anxious subjects across all recall conditions and more aroused than high-anxious subjects in the happy, sad, fear, and wonder conditions (Davis and Schwartz 1986). These physiological differences occurred despite the fact that there were no group differences in subjective ratings of the intensity of affect associated with the various experiences recalled. For repressors, then, there appears to be a lack of congruence or a dissociation between subjective and physiological indices of emotion (see also Asendorpf and Scherer 1983; Gudjonsson 1981; Weinberger, Schwartz, and Davidson 1979). Second, repressors showed a greater difference between physiological responses on the two sides of the body during the recall of negative affective memories. In other words, they were more lateralized during the recall of negative experi-

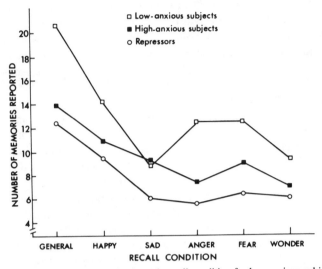

Figure 1. Mean number of memories in each recall condition for low-anxious subjects, high-anxious subjects, and repressors in experiment 1.

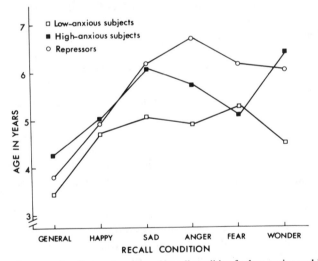

Figure 2. Mean age of earliest memory in each recall condition for low-anxious subjects, high-anxious subjects, and repressors in experiment 1.

ences, a finding that is consistent with Galin's (1974) proposition that the biological mechanism underlying or subserving repression is a functional disconnection between the right and the left cerebral hemispheres.

To return to the memory data, the overall pattern of results obtained in the Davis and Schwartz study suggests that repression is associated with a limited accessibility to affective memories, especially those involving unpleasant, negative emotions. This interpretation needs to be clarified, however, and there are two major reasons for this. The first pertains to the experimental design employed, and the second relates to the nature of the memory task used.

Because measures of anxiety and defensiveness are negatively correlated (see Bell and Byrne 1978), individuals with high scores on both dimensions are somewhat difficult to find. For this reason, a defensive high-anxious group was not included in the initial study. The omission of this group does, however, leave open the possibility that the pattern of results obtained could simply reflect high levels of defensiveness per se. To address this possibility, a defensive high-anxious group was employed in the next three studies. In each study, female subjects with extreme scores on the anxiety and defensiveness scales were selected for each group.

A second issue concerns the nature of the memory task used. The task in the Davis and Schwartz (1987) study was a free recall one in which subjects were asked to describe briefly the emotional experiences they remembered. It is therefore possible that repressors actually recalled as many experiences as others but that for some reason they chose to report fewer. To reduce this potential report bias, a latency-to-retrieve paradigm was used on two subsequent studies. In this paradigm, subjects are asked to recall experiences in response to a series of stimulus words presented and simply to indicate, by pressing a button, when an experience comes to mind. The dependent measure is latency, and the procedure is based on the assumption that the time taken to retrieve memories provides an index of their accessibility (Lloyd and Lishman 1975; Teasdale and Fogarty 1979).

In brief, a major purpose of subsequent research was to sharpen interpretation of the Davis and Schwartz results by including a defensive high-anxious group and a memory task uncontaminated by any possible reluctance to talk about personal, emotional experiences, however briefly. A second purpose was to explore the specificity of the effects of repression on affective memories. The initial finding that repressors appeared to recall fewer childhood experiences in which they themselves felt a range of different emotions raises a number of questions. First, are the effects of repression specific to emotional experiences of the self, or do they extend to all real-life emotional experiences, including those in which it is the feelings of others that are most salient? Second, do the effects of repression extend beyond childhood emotional experiences? Finally, are the effects evident across the broad domain of nega-

Table 1. Mean Number of Memories Recalled by Each Group in Experiment 2

	Experimental Group			
Condition	Low Anxious	High Anxious	Repressor	Defensive High Anxious
Self	8.47	8.55	6.32	7.02
Other	4.25	4.30	6.87	6.72

Note: Numbers in each cell refer to the mean number of memories, collapsed over the happy, sad, anger, and fear recall conditions.

tive emotions, or are some negative emotions more susceptible to repressive processes than others? These questions were also addressed in subsequent research.

The next experiment was specifically designed to investigate the accessibility to memory of emotional experiences of self versus other (see Davis 1987). In this study, half the subjects in each group were asked to recall and briefly describe childhood events in which they themselves felt happy, sad, angry, or fearful, and the other half were asked to recall events in which the various emotions were experienced by another, irrespective of how the subjects themselves felt.

The major finding to emerge from this study was a reliable group by self-other interaction, the means of which are given in table 1. Compared with low-anxious and high-anxious subjects, repressors recalled fewer experiences in which they themselves felt happy, sad, angry, and fearful. This finding replicates the results of the initial study, although differences between repressors and high-anxious subjects are more pronounced here. Difficulty in recalling emotional memories was not evident, however, when repressors were asked to remember experiences in which someone else felt happy, sad, angry, or fearful. Indeed, in this instance, they recalled substantially more experiences than the low-anxious and high-anxious groups did. Evidently, the repressors' apparent difficulty in accessing affective memories does not extend to all emotional experiences but rather is specific to memories of events in which the focus of attention is on the emotions experienced by the self.

Defensive high-anxious individuals also recalled more emotional experiences of others. For some reason, then, the feelings of others around them seem to be particularly salient to both groups of high-defensive individuals.[1]

1. An alternative interpretation of the heightened memory for affective experiences of others is that repressors and defensive high-anxious individuals are better able to perceive and recognize expressions of emotion in other people. Two studies (Davis 1985) have addressed this possibility, and no group differences in the ability to recognize affect were apparent in either study. It thus appears that repressors and defensive high-anxious individuals recall more affective experiences of the other, not because they are better able to discriminate affect in others, but because the feelings of others are more salient to them for some reason.

Unlike repressors, however, defensive high-anxious subjects did not recall significantly fewer emotional experiences of the self than the low-anxious and high-anxious groups did. Nor did they differ appreciably from the repressors in the self condition, a finding that leaves unresolved the important question of whether limited access to affective memories involving the self is specific to repressors or simply reflects high levels of defensiveness per se. The next two experiments (see Davis 1987) further explore the recall of emotional experiences of the self and help clarify this issue.

The third experiment employed the latency-to-retrieve paradigm, in which subjects were asked to recall experiences from anytime in their lives that were in some way associated with a series of stimulus words presented. They were not required to describe the experiences at all but merely to indicate when an experience came to mind. There were five recall conditions. The first was a general one in which subjects were asked to recall personal experiences associated with each word presented, and no mention was made of affect. In the other four conditions, they were asked to recall happy, sad, anger, and fear experiences. The stimuli used were concrete nouns with high ratings on such dimensions as concreteness, familiarity, and imagery. For instance, subjects were asked to recall a happy experience associated with a street or flowers, a sad experience associated with a chair or a bird, and an anger experience associated with a dog or rain. Five different word lists were constructed so that each stimulus word was associated with a different recall condition on each list. Subjects were asked to recall a different experience associated with each retrieval cue, and, in line with previous research using this paradigm, subjects were given a time limit (twenty seconds) in which to recall an experience. If no experience was forthcoming within that time, a latency of twenty seconds was recorded.

Using this memory task, repressors recalled happy and sad experiences just as quickly as others, but they were slower in retrieving anger and fear experiences than subjects in the other three groups (see table 2). At first glance, then, it appears that repressors take longer to recall anger and fear experiences. However, not all stimulus words triggered a relevant experience, so the data for only those trials on which a memory was actually recalled were also analyzed. No group differences emerged. This suggests that the overall longer latency of repressors was due to a higher incidence of stimulus words that failed to elicit a relevant anger and fear experience. Subsequent analysis confirmed this. It seems, then, that repression operates as an all-or-none phenomenon: anger and fear memories that are accessible to repressors are retrieved just as quickly as everyone else's; it is simply that they do not retrieve as many.

The fourth experiment also used the latency-to-retrieve paradigm, but the range of negative emotions was extended to include guilt and self-consciousness, the time period was lengthened to sixty seconds, and the ecological validity of the memory task was increased by using retrieval cues more

Table 2. Results for the Latency-to-Retrieve Task in Experiment 3

Recall Condition	Experimental Group			
	Low Anxious	High Anxious	Repressor	Defensive High Anxious
Mean latency in seconds based on all 10 primes:				
General	3.03	3.76	2.87	2.85
Happy	4.31	6.05	4.67	3.91
Sad	7.76	8.41	8.37	7.36
Anger	5.79	6.59	8.43	7.13
Fear	6.81	6.63	8.69	6.86
Mean number of primes that failed to elicit a memory:				
General	.11	.50	.25	.19
Happy	.78	1.50	.95	.36
Sad	2.11	2.50	2.55	2.14
Anger	1.44	1.35	2.70	1.90
Fear	1.83	1.80	2.85	2.19

meaningfully and prototypically associated with the various emotions. For instance, subjects were now asked to recall a sad experience associated with crying or feeling rejected, a happy experience associated with a birthday or being with someone you love, an anger experience associated with disapproval or being told what to do, a guilt experience associated with sex or hurting someone, and a fear experience associated with failure or doing something wrong. There were ten retrieval cues associated with each of the six emotions, and the order of presentation was randomized with the constraint that no more than two primes associated with the same emotion could occur consecutively. As a brief aside here, self-consciousness experiences were described to subjects as "experiences in which you yourself felt self-conscious, embarrassed, shy." The word "ashamed" was not included here, but the domain of emotional experiences tapped by the retrieval cues used in this condition (e.g., feeling exposed, feeling about two inches tall) is very similar to theoretical descriptions of shame (see Izard 1977; Lewis 1979b; Miller 1985).

The results of this study (see table 3) revealed that latency to retrieve happy, sad, and guilt memories was similar for all four groups, but this was not the case for anger, fear, and self-conscious memories. Repressors took longer to recall fear and self-consciousness experiences than the other three groups. Somewhat unexpectedly, both high-anxious subjects ($p < .05$) and repressors ($p < .10$) took longer to retrieve anger experiences than low-anxious subjects did. Once again, however, further analysis revealed that the overall longer latency of repressors in the fear condition was due to the fact that they actually recalled fewer experiences. A similar trend was apparent for self-consciousness experiences. In the anger condition, virtually all subjects

Table 3. Results for the Latency-to-Retrieve Task in Experiment 4

Emotion	Experimental Group			
	Low Anxious	High Anxious	Repressor	Defensive High Anxious
Mean latency in seconds based on all 10 primes:				
Happy	2.59	4.63	4.74	5.54
Sad	4.38	6.18	6.65	4.70
Anger	4.49	7.88	7.62	5.77
Fear	5.68	5.74	14.38	6.45
Guilt	9.95	8.97	10.55	8.51
Self-consciousness	8.78	9.25	12.93	8.55
Mean number of primes that failed to elicit a memory:				
Happy	.00	.00	.00	.00
Sad	.18	.09	.27	.00
Anger	.09	.18	.09	.00
Fear	.18	.00	1.09	.14
Guilt	.82	.45	.45	.29
Self-consciousness	.36	.36	.73	.29

across the four groups were able to recall an anger experience associated with each retrieval cue provided, indicating that repressors and high-anxious subjects must have taken somewhat longer to do so than the low-anxious group did.

The results of experiments 3 and 4 extend and clarify previous findings in two important respects. First, repressors but not defensive high-anxious subjects had difficulty in retrieving anger, fear, and self-consciousness experiences associated with various retrieval cues. Difficulty in recalling certain kinds of negative affective memories thus appears to be specific to individuals characterized by the conjunction of low anxiety and high defensiveness and cannot simply be attributed to high levels of defensiveness per se. Second, it is clear that the apparent effects of repression on memory do not just reflect a report bias due to reluctance to disclose the content of memories actually recalled. Other kinds of response biases are possible, though, so we subsequently conducted a signal detection study to explore the response bias issue further (Davis et al. 1988). In this study, we presented four groups of subjects (low-anxious, high-anxious, repressor, and defensive high-anxious subjects) with a recognition memory task involving positive and negative affective material. No reliable group differences in response bias (beta) were apparent, indicating that repressors do not adopt a more conservative or stringent criterion when responding to affective memory tasks.

In summary, the major findings of the research presented here indicate that repression is indeed associated with difficulty in recalling personal, real-life emotional experiences, especially those involving negative emotions. The results obtained are thus consistent with theoretical conceptualizations of repression as a process that serves to keep painful, unpleasant experiences out of consciousness or awareness. Interestingly, however, it seems that not all unpleasant, negative emotions are equally vulnerable to the effects of repression.

What Motivates Repression?

To date, little is known about the specific nature of the affect that motivates repression. In his seminal paper in 1915, Freud wrote that "the motive and purpose of repression was nothing else than the avoidance of unpleasure" ([1915] 1957, 153). Although a number of theorists subsequently considered repression to be restricted to ego-threatening situations (see Holmes 1974), there is little direct empirical support for this proposition, and Freud himself remained uncertain about the specific nature of the unpleasure associated with repression. For instance, Strachey, editor of the authorized translation of Freud's works, comments that "the special problem of the motive force which puts repression into operation was one which was a constant source of concern to Freud" (1957, 144). The present research may shed some light on this issue for it appears that feelings of fear, self-consciousness, and possibly also anger are particularly potent motivators of repressive processes.

Is there any commonality among these three emotions that could perhaps account for their shared susceptibility to the effects of repression? A close look suggests one recurrent theme; namely, that all three emotions frequently occur in situations in which attention is focused on the self in a threatening, evaluative way. Fear, for instance, is activated by threat to the self, at either a physical or a psychological level. In self-consciousness, the self feels exposed. The essence of self-consciousness is heightened awareness of the self; it is an experience of the self by the self, activated in situations that focus attention on the self, generally in a negative evaluative manner that results in a sense of the self as small or diminished (Izard 1977; Miller 1985). It is, according to Lewis (1974b), the self's vicarious experience of the other's negative evaluation. These two emotions motivate the threatened or exposed self to escape or withdraw. At first glance, anger seems very different, for it generally is directed toward others and motivates confrontation or conflict. But instigations to anger involve potentially harmful events, especially those appraised as unjustified or avoidable, and, of particular relevance here, anger is very often provoked by situations that violate the self and threaten self-esteem (Averill 1979, 1982).

The proposition that repression is motivated by events that focus attention on the self in a threatening, evaluative way can perhaps account for the finding that sad and guilt experiences seem to be largely exempt from the effects of repression. Feelings of sadness and guilt are painful and unpleasant, but neither emotion is intimately connected with events that direct the attention of others toward the self in a threatening, evaluative way. The major cause of sadness is loss and separation from those we care about, although less frequent causes can involve such events as failure experiences (Izard 1977). Guilt is more complex for it is associated with transgressions against the internalized standards of the self, but in guilt "the self is not the *direct* object of negative evaluation; rather, the *thing* done (or not done) is the focus of experience" (Lewis 1979b, 380). Furthermore, guilt is a private emotion—the external expression of guilt is the least distinctive of all the negative emotions, the instigation is internal, and it is a reaction of the self, independent of the judgment of others (Izard 1977; Lewis 1979a). In brief, the present pattern of results suggests that it is affect associated with threat or evaluation of the self, rather than negative affect or unpleasure per se, that motivates repression. The results thus support theoretical conceptions of repression as a defensive process specifically invoked by ego-threatening situations.

Accessibility versus Availability of Affective Memories

I would like to move on now to consider a fundamental issue that is inherent yet unresolved in the research presented so far. The issue is, How do we know that the fewer affective experiences recalled by repressors reflect a limited accessibility to memory rather than, more simply, the limited availability of affective memories? The final series of studies presented here was designed to explore this question.

The task of separating limited accessibility to memories from a limited availability of experiences actually stored in memory is a particularly difficult one in naturalistic, autobiographical memory research for obviously an experimenter has no prior knowledge of the events of an individual's life. I would therefore like to explain briefly the conceptual and methodological approach adopted. Very simply, I reasoned that an increase in the number of emotional memories recalled by repressors during repeated recall of emotional memories would provide presumptive evidence of experiences that are stored in the memory system but difficult to access and retrieve. In this series of studies, then, repressors were asked to free recall emotional experiences on several occasions. Subsequently, they were tested on the cued recall task used in experiment 4 on which, as previously mentioned, they displayed particular difficulty in recalling fear, self-consciousness, and, to a lesser extent, anger experiences. Would repressors display hypermnesic effects associated with the repeated free recall of emotional memories, and would their performance on the fear, self-consciousness, and anger items on the cued recall task improve to become comparable to that of other subjects? These were the primary research questions of interest.

Three experiments were conducted. In one study, subjects engaged in the repeated recall of childhood anger and fear experiences; in the second study, they recalled anger and self-consciousness experiences from any time in their lives; in the third study, subjects engaged in the repeated recall of childhood anger and self-consciousness memories. In each experiment, the performance of repressors was compared with that of three comparison groups. Subjects for each group were selected from a large subject pool on the basis of the number of affective memories recalled during a free recall task. In experiment 1, selection was based on the number of childhood anger and fear memories recalled; in experiment 2, subject selection was based on the number of anger and self-consciousness memories from any time period; in experiment 3, childhood anger and self-consciousness memories were used as the basis for subject selection.

One of the three comparison groups comprised subjects who recalled the highest number of memories. This group, designated the high-memory group, was included to control for possible regression-to-the-mean effects. The second comparison group, designated the average-memory group, consisted of subjects who recalled an average number of memories. These subjects were included as a normative comparison group to provide an index of the performance of the average subject across repeated recall trials. Finally, a group of subjects who recalled few memories was also selected. Within this latter group, some subjects displayed a repressive pattern of scores on measures of anxiety and defensiveness, and some did not. The low-memory group was therefore subdivided into a low-memory-repressor group and a low-memory-nonrepressor group. The low-memory-repressor group included subjects whose anxiety scores fell below the sample mean on an anxiety scale and whose defensiveness scores fell above the sample mean; subjects with anxiety scores above the mean or with low anxiety scores in conjunction with low defensiveness scores were assigned to the low-memory-nonrepressor group.

Several months after the initial recall task, subjects returned to the laboratory for a second session, in which they completed a series of affective memory tasks that entailed the repeated recall of memories associated with the particular emotions used as the basis for subjective selection (namely, anger and fear in experiment 5 and anger and self-consciousness in experiment 6 and 7). In all three experiments, subjects first engaged in a free recall task identical to that presented several months previously. Second, they engaged in a free recall task that immediately followed a mood-induction procedure designed to induce the particular emotion of interest. A substantial body of evidence reveals that people are more likely to recall experiences that are affectively congruent with their mood at the time of recall (see Blaney 1986; Bower 1981). Mood induction was therefore included in the present research to prime or facilitate the retrieval of affective memories. Finally, subjects were presented with the cued recall task, in which they were asked to recall six different kinds of emotional experiences (including anger, fear, and self-consciousness experiences) in response to a series of retrieval cues provided.

Analysis of the free recall data demonstrated that all subjects, including repressors, increased the number of memories recalled between the initial and the second free recall trials. The hypermnesic effects displayed by subjects in the low-memory-repressor group were not sufficiently large, however, to enable them to catch up to subjects in the normative, average-memory group. Further research with a larger number of free recall trials is needed to see if repressors ultimately would catch up.

Of particular interest are the results on the cued recall task. Providing retrieval cues generally facilitates access to material stored in memory (e.g., Tulving and Pearlstone 1966). A cued recall task following repeated free recall trials should therefore be particularly sensitive to hypermnesic effects. Results revealed that repressors, who initially could remember very few anger, fear, and self-consciousness experiences, were now able to recall these experiences almost as readily as subjects in the other three groups. Specifically, they recalled anger memories as quickly as all other subjects, fear memories as readily as all subjects except those in the high-memory group, and in experiment 7, as many self-consciousness memories as other subjects, though they took somewhat longer to do so. In brief, marked hypermnesic effects were apparent for repressors on the cued recall task.

Interestingly, however, these marked hypermnesic effects were evident only in experiments 5 and 7. These two studies had in common the repeated free recall of childhood emotional memories. Experiment 6, on the other hand, involved the repeated recall of anger and self-consciousness memories from any time period. Furthermore, a postexperimental inquiry revealed that few (20 percent) of the experiences remembered by subjects were childhood memories. In this experiment, in contrast to experiments 5 and 7, repressors had greater difficulty in the cued recall of anger, fear, and self-consciousness memories than did subjects in the other three groups. Substantial increases in the accessibility of emotional memories in repressors thus seem to require the activation of memories laid down in childhood.

To summarize briefly, the repeated recall of emotional memories by repressors resulted in some increase in the number of anger, fear, and self-consciousness experiences remembered during a free recall task and a marked increase in performance on a cued recall task when preceded by the repeated recall of childhood memories. The overall pattern of results observed here clearly indicated that the repressors' initial difficulty in remembering certain kinds of negative affective experiences reflects a limited accessibility to these experiences in the memory system rather than simply their limited availability. It is important to point out, however, that this conclusion by no means precludes the possibility that repressive processes may also have an effect during the encoding and storage stages of memory. The research described here sheds little light on this issue. Across sessions, repressors increased the number of memories they recalled, which indicates a greater availability of memories than was initially apparent, but in general they did not catch up to subjects in a normative comparison group. Whether repressors would ultimately catch up across multiple sessions is unknown and poses an important question for future research. In the meantime, the pattern of results observed here clearly indicates that at least some of the memory deficits apparent in repressors reflect difficulty in accessing certain kinds of experiences stored in the memory system, not just their limited availability.

Concluding Remarks

The results of the present program of research clearly reveal that individuals who characteristically adopt a repressive mode of defense have difficulty recalling certain kinds of negative unpleasant experiences from their lives. Of particular importance, it appears that at least some of the apparently missing memories of repressors are available but relatively inaccessible to memory. Within the context of Gordon Bower's (in this volume) comments on repression, memory, and failures to retrieve, what precisely does the statement "available but relatively inaccessible" mean?

A particularly puzzling—and intriguing—aspect of the present research concerns the discrepant pattern of results obtained during the free recall of childhood memories (experiments 1 and 2) and the latency-to-retrieve task (experiments 3 and 4). In the former studies, repression was associated with limited accessibility to memories across the broad domain of emotional experiences of the self, whereas, in the latter, the effects of repression were far more specific. How can we account for this discrepancy?

The studies themselves differ in terms of the time frame involved, the need to describe experiences, and the free versus cued recall nature of the memory task. Thus, several explanations are possible. It may be that the effects of repression on childhood emotional memories are pervasive or that repressors are reluctant to report the occurrence of some negative experiences even when the need to describe the content of the experiences is removed. Finally, it may be that many emotional experiences of repressors that are not easily accessed during free recall become readily accessible when retrieval cues are provided. The implications of this third possibility are intriguing for it suggests that the processing or organization of affective material in memory may be very different for repressors than for nonrepressors.

In a free recall task, the richness (number and/or strength) of associative connections within and between related categories or event nodes seems to be particularly important. Once initial access to a relevant event node is achieved, retrieval of items should vary as a function of the associative structure within affect-related event nodes (Bower 1981; Bower and Cohen 1982; Clark and Isen 1982; Simon 1982). As Bower comments, "Memory for life events is like a sausage chain. If you retrieve one, its linkages prompt you to retrieve another, and so you pull one memory after another out of your biographical storehouse" (chap. 9 in this volume). The difficulty that repressors have in accessing affective memories in a free recall task thus suggests that the associative pathways or linkages within affect-related event nodes are weaker and less complex in repressors. This, in turn, suggests that repressors engage in less elaborative processing of their own affective experiences than do nonrepressors. One important implication of this analysis of the repressors' apparent failure to remember during a free recall task is that some of the effects of repression on memory may originate during the encoding stage. Limited rehearsal or processing of self-referent affective information in the encoding stage undoubtedly leads to fewer and weaker associative connections, so the subsequent retrieval of a series of affect-related events during free recall is difficult.

A different picture emerges when we turn to consider the results of the cued recall tasks in experiments 3 and 4. These two experiments employed a latency-to-retrieve paradigm in which subjects were presented with specific retrieval cues and asked to recall an affective experience associated with each cue. In this cued recall task, then, it is the connections or access routes among the affect node, the retrieval cue, and the related event node (rather than connections among specific affect-related events themselves) that seem most salient. The pattern of results obtained for repressors suggests that these access routes are intact for happy, sad, and guilt experiences but are weak or obstructed in some way for certain anger, fear, and self-consciousness experiences.

Alternatively, one can conceptualize each retrieval cue as part of the index used to provide access to material stored in memory (see Bower, in this volume; Simon 1979, 1982). Viewed within this framework, the failure of some retrieval cues to elicit a relevant memory suggests that repressors may use a different indexing system in the storage of certain categories of affective experiences. This explanation seems unlikely, however. Following the repeated recall of childhood memories (in experiments 5 and 7), repressors were able to retrieve anger, fear, and self-consciousness experiences associated with the cues presented almost as readily as other subjects. This finding indicates that the particular cues used *can* serve as index prompts for repressors. The locus of their difficulty thus seems to lie in gaining access either to the categories themselves or to the material stored within given categories.

In concluding, the essence of my argument here is that individuals identified as repressors have personal, real-life emotional experiences available and stored in memory that are more difficult to retrieve than are those of nonrepressors. During free recall memory tasks, repressors have more retrieval failures across the broad domain of emotional experiences in general. It thus appears that repressors may be individuals with a propensity to engage in less elaborative processing of their own emotional experiences, with a consequent reduction in the richness of associative pathways among affect-related experiences stored in memory. During cued recall tasks, on the other hand, the effects of repression are specific to certain kinds of negative memories, suggesting that some access routes associated with the indexing system used to organize negative affective material stored in memory may be disrupted in some way. The presence of marked hypermnesic effects when cued recall follows the activation of childhood memories does, however, tell us that at least some of the disruptive effects of repression on memory processes are reversible.

References

Asendorpf, J. B., and K. R. Scherer. 1983. The discrepant repressor: Differentiation between low anxiety, high anxiety, and repression of anxiety by autonomic-facial-verbal patterns of behavior. *Journal of Personality and Social Psychology* 45:1334–46.

Averill, J. R. 1979. Anger. In *Nebraska Symposium on Motivation, 1978*, ed. H. E. Howe and R. A. Dienstbier, vol. 26, pp. 1–80. Lincoln: University of Nebraska Press.

———. 1982. *Anger and aggression.* New York: Springer.

Bell, P. A., and D. Byrne. 1978. Repression-sensitization. In *Dimensions of personality,* ed. H. London and J. E. Exner, 449–85. New York: Wiley.

Bendig, A. W. 1956. The development of a short form of the Manifest Anxiety Scale. *Journal of Consulting Psychology* 20:384.

Blaney, P. H. 1986. Affect and memory: A review. *Psychological Bulletin* 99:229–46.

Bower, G. H. 1981. Mood and memory. *American Psychologist* 36:129–48.

Bower, G. H., and P. R. Cohen. 1982. Emotional influences in memory and thinking: Data and theory. In *Affect and cognition,* ed. M. S. Clark and S. T. Fiske, 291–331. Hillsdale, N.J.: Erlbaum.

Byrne, D., J. Barry, and D. Nelson. 1963. Relations of the revised Repression-Sensitization scale to measures of self-description. *Psychological Reports* 13:323–34.

Clark, M. S., and A. M Isen. 1982. Toward understanding the relationship between feeling states and social behavior. In *Cognitive social psychology,* ed. A. H. Hastorf and A. M. Isen, 73–108. New York: Elsevier/North-Holland.

Crowne, D. P., and D. Marlowe. 1964. *The approval motive: Studies in evaluative dependence.* New York: Wiley.

Davis, P. J. 1985. Repression and sensitivity to affect in others. University of Sydney. Typescript.

———. 1987. Repression and the inaccessibility of affective memories. *Journal of Personality and Social Psychology* 53:585–93.

————. 1988. Repression and the limited recall of affective memories: Are the missing memories unavailable or inaccessible? University of Sydney. Typescript.

Davis, P. J., and G. E. Schwartz. 1986. Repression and the inaccessibility of affective memories: Relationship to temperature laterality and muscle activity of the face. Yale University. Typescript.

————. 1987. Repression and the inaccessibility of affective memories. *Journal of Personality and Social Psychology* 52:155–63.

Davis, P. J., J. L. Singer, G. A. Bonanno, and G. E. Schwartz. 1988. Repression and response bias during an affective memory recognition task. *Australian Journal of Psychology* 40:147–57.

Erdelyi, M. H., and B. Goldberg. 1979. Let's not sweep repression under the rug: Toward a cognitive psychology of repression. In *Functional disorders of memory,* ed. J. Kihlstrom and F. Evans, 355–402. Hillsdale, N.J.: Erlbaum.

Freud, S. [1915] 1957. Repression. In *The standard edition of the complete psychological works of Sigmund Freud,* ed. J. Strachey, vol. 14. London: Hogarth.

Galin, D. 1974. Implications for psychiatry of left and right cerebral specialization: A neurobiological context for unconscious processes. *Archives of General Psychiatry* 31:572–83.

Gudjonsson, G. H. 1981. Self-reported emotional disturbance and its relation to electrodermal reactivity, defensiveness, and trait anxiety. *Personality and Individual Differences* 2:47–52.

Holmes, D. S. 1974. Investigation of repression: Differential recall of material experimentally or naturally associated with ego threat. *Psychological Bulletin* 81:632–53.

Izard, C. E. 1977. *Human emotions.* New York: Plenum.

Lewis, H. B. 1979a. Guilt in obsession and paranoia. In *Emotions in personality and psychopathology,* ed. C. E. Izard, 399–414. New York: Plenum.

————. 1979b. Shame in depression and hysteria. In *Emotions in personality and psychopathology,* ed. C. E. Izard, 371–96. New York: Plenum.

Lloyd, G. G., and W. A. Lishman. 1975. Effect of depression on the speed of recall of pleasant and unpleasant experiences. *Psychological Medicine* 5:173–80.

Miller, S. 1985. *The shame experience.* Hillsdale, N.J.: Analytic.

Rapaport, D. 1942. *Emotions and memory.* New York: International Universities Press.

Simon, H. A. 1979. *Models of thought.* New Haven, Conn.: Yale University Press.

————. 1982. Comments. In *Affect and cognition,* ed. M. S. Clark and S. T. Fiske, 333–42. Hillsdale, N.J.: Erlbaum.

Strachey, J., ed. 1957. *The standard edition of the complete psychological works of Sigmund Freud,* vol. 14. London: Hogarth.

Teasdale, J. D., and S. J. Fogarty. 1979. Differential effects of induced mood on retrieval of pleasant and unpleasant events from episodic memory. *Journal of Abnormal Psychology* 88:248–57.

Tulving, E., and Z. Pearlstone. 1966. Availability versus accessibility of information in memory for words. *Journal of Verbal Learning and Behavior* 5:381–91.

Weinberger, D. A., G. E. Schwartz, and R. J. Davidson. 1979. Low-anxious, high-anxious, and repressive coping styles: Psychometric patterns and behavioral and physiological responses to stress. *Journal of Abnormal Psychology* 88:369–80.

16 Psychobiology of Repression and Health: A Systems Approach

GARY E. SCHWARTZ

This chapter is concerned with the psychobiology of repression and health from a systems perspective. The first section provides an introduction to systems thinking as applied to repression and health. The second section not only reviews new data that provide empirical support for the existence of repression but also suggests specific psychobiological mechanisms whereby repression can lead to a demonstrable disconnection between verbal report of conscious experience and physiological responses of anxiety, anger, and/or depression. Also included in the second section are new data linking subjective/physiological dissociation with compromised immune functioning and physical illness. The opiate-peptide hypothesis of repressive coping is introduced in this context. The third section considers some clinical intervention implications of the psychobiology of repression, including the hypothesis that flexible repression is a prerequisite for health.

A Systems Approach to Repression and Health

What Do We Mean by the Words "Repression" and "Health"?

The words "repression" and "health" are used differently by researchers and clinicians in different contexts, by different disciplines, and from different professional perspectives. Before we can have a useful generic as well as context-specific discussion of the available data regarding the psychobiology of repression and health, it is essential to understand how systems theory can help us to uncover the explicit (typically level-specific) meanings of the terms

This chapter was begun at Yale University and completed at the University of Arizona. I wish to thank Louise Leader and the staff, students, and faculty affiliated with the Yale Psychophysiology Center for their contributions to the theory and data described here. Preparation of the chapter was supported by a grant from the National Science Foundation and a gift from the International Fragrance and Flavors Corp.

405

"repression" and "health" and to discover the implicit (typically more generic) meanings of these terms.

Systems of Meaning and the Meaning of Systems: Introduction to Levels of Meaning of "Repression" and "Health"

From a systems perspective (Bertalanffy 1968; Miller 1978), various meanings of a given word or term can reflect different levels of meaning within a semantic conceptual system. The various levels of meaning of a given word can be organized from the microscopic levels (i.e., specific meanings), through the macroscopic levels (i.e., specific levels), to the "metascopic" level (i.e., the generic level). Differences in the way people use words are individually as well as contextually specific. It follows that there is a system of meanings for all words that varies from the specific to the generic.

In other words, words function as systems. The functioning of a system can be described by taking a "bottom up" approach, or the interaction of the component parts (conceptual subsystems) composing the system (the set of meanings and uses of the word), combined with a "top down" approach, or the system's interaction with its environment (the conceptual suprasystems of which the word is a part).

When we apply a systems perspective to the meanings of the words "repress," "repressing," and "repression," some important implications emerge. From organisms consisting of single cells to organisms consisting of trillions of cells, the ability to repress information is not only a prerequisite for their survival. The ability to repress information is a prerequisite for the emergence of life itself.

Repression and Health as Systems Concepts:

Meanings of terms can be level- and context-specific as well as trans-level and trans-context generic (termed the Cross Level Meta Similarity Hypothesis; Schwartz 1987). From a systems perspective, level- and context-specific meanings of a word can be viewed as reflecting special cases of the generic meaning of the word. It follows that the generic meanings of the words "repression" and "health" should apply to all systems at all levels whereas the context-specific meanings of "repression" and "health" should be limited to certain systems at certain levels in certain contexts. This is illustrated in table 1.

Concerning repression, the potential to check, keep down, hold down, or restrain information is not only present in all systems. Within certain limits, the potential to restrain information is essential for a system to be able to engage in pattern recognition and interpretation, which in turn enables the system to generate adaptive, organized responses to stimuli generated externally and internally.

Table 1. Generic and Specific Meanings of Repression and Health

	Repression	Health
Root	From "repremere" (to check, hold back), from "re" (back) and "premere" "to press"	From "hal" (whole); "heal" is from "haelan" (to make whole), from "hal" (whole).
Generic meaning	To check, keep down, hold down, restrain	To be free from defect, hale, wholesome, sound
Context-specific meaning	To force and keep (ideas, impulses, etc.) painful to the conscious mind in the unconscious, where they still modify behavior	Physical and mental well-being; freedom from defect, pain, disease; normality of mental and physical function

Source: Webster's New Twentieth Century Dictionary (1977).

Concerning health, the potential to be whole and to function as an organized unit is not only mandatory for a system to exist and to self-regulate. The potential to function as an organized whole underlies the concept of a system.

Notice that the specific meanings of the word "repression" used in psychology and psychiatry (such as to force and keep painful beliefs, memories, and feelings out of consciousness) reflect special cases of the generic meaning of the word "repression." Similarly, the specific meanings of "health" used in psychology and psychiatry (such as to be free of defects, discomfort, pain, and disease) reflect special cases of the generic meaning of the word "health."

It is possible to examine the definitions of "repression" and "health" used by each of the authors in this volume and organize these definitions in terms of their intra- and interlevels of meaning. A coherent organization capturing all the definitions of "repression" and "health" should emerge.

The Disattention to Disconnection to Disregulation to Disorder to Disease Hypothesis: Micro, Macro, Meta

There are at least two basic requirements for a system to exist and function: the components (subsystems) must be connected, and information between components must be transmitted and processed accurately.

The concept of self-regulation via feedback requires that the feedback must be connected to the system and that the feedback information must be transmitted and processed accurately. If, for whatever reason, the information is diminished, delayed, or distorted, the system's ability to self-regulate will be impaired. In the extreme case, if the information is not processed at all (i.e., disconnected), the system will be unable to self-regulate. Therefore, some of the systemic (whole) properties will be attenuated, if not lost altogether, as a result of the impaired connections.

This effect is quite general and may well be universal. It is observed in the smallest (micro) systems to the largest (macro) systems.

It is important to appreciate that negative feedback involves subtraction (counteraction) that will return a system to some "mean" value (termed the "set point") while positive feedback involves addition (action) that will advance a system to some extreme value. Negative feedback functions to facilitate homeostasis (Cannon 1932), whereas positive feedback functions to facilitate antihomeostasis.

It is not often appreciated that negative and positive feedback both engender self-regulation. Both negative and positive feedback serve to interconnect components so that the system can function (behave) in a self-regulating (self-moderating or self-amplifying), and therefore predictable, manner. If the information is distorted or misperceived, or, in extreme cases, disconnected altogether, the self-regulation engendered by the negative and/or positive feedback will be impaired or cease altogether.

It is also not often appreciated that, when the feedback is connected, the system will begin self-regulating automatically and will behave with a sense of purpose. For example, when a thermostat and furnace are connected, a systemic interaction occurs immediately. The purpose occurs automatically. When a thermostat-furnace system is connected in a negative feedback (homeostatic) fashion, the system works to maintain a stable temperature around the set point. Moreover, of particular importance is that, in a negative feedback system, if the environmental conditions are relatively stable, the system will rise and fall around the set point in an orderly fashion over time. What emerges is cyclic behavior, and that behavior is rhythmic.

It appears that all healthy biological systems show rhythmic behavior that reflects the operation of automatic negative feedback connections whose purpose is to maintain a stable "internal mileau" (Bernard 1878). Of course, in complex systems, learning through experience can alter these fundamental processes. Learning can alter the degree of connection of the component processes through variations in the direction of attention and the way in which the information is interpreted, not only to enhance or distort the self-regulation, but even to reverse it (i.e., convert negative feedback into positive feedback, and vice versa, through emotional and cognitive interpretations of the feedback). As a result, psychophysiological systems will vary in the combinations (patterns) of normally involuntary self-regulation (automatic, rhythmic, purposeful regulation) and voluntary self-regulation (motivation and interpretation of learned information) occurring in a given situation.

When these various observations and concepts are integrated, the following generic hypothesis emerges: connection (in the case of negative feedback) leads to self-regulation, which is expressed as order (i.e., rhythmic behavior) that occurs with a relative degree of ease (i.e., automaticity) (Schwartz 1977, 1979, 1983, 1984, 1987).

One (but by no means the only) psychological mechanism for enhancing connectivity is self-attention and the voluntary control of awareness. The progression of processes over time is as follows: attention to connection to self-regulation to order to ease. For this progression to be true, the negation of this progression must also be true. If the connection is impaired or, in extreme cases, disconnected, self-regulation will be impaired (i.e., less order, hence more disorder), and the system will no longer function with ease (i.e., disease). One (but by no means the only) psychological mechanism for reducing connectivity is disattention. To complete this logic employing parallel linguistics, the term "disregulation" was coined. The progression of processes over time is as follows: disattention to disconnection to disregulation to disorder to disease (Schwartz 1977).

The Repression-Disregulation-Disease Connection: An Integrative Health Science Hypothesis

Integrating all the above, it follows that repression (and self-deception) includes disattention to negative feedback cues that are essential for self-regulation and, therefore, healing. Disattention promotes a state of relative disconnection (e.g., a functional disconnection of the left and right hemispheres as proposed by Galin 1974). This state of neuropsychological disconnection induces a state of psychophysiological disregulation, which is expressed as disorder in biological, psychological, and social functioning. This disordered biopsychosocial functioning is hypothesized to contribute to physical, mental, and social diseases (viewing the term "disease" in this context as a generic concept).

Recent Research on Repression and Health

Recent Research on the Repression to Disattention to Disconnection to Disregulation to Disorder to Disease Hypothesis: Step 1, Measuring the Repressive Coping Style

The first requirement for investigating the psychobiology of repression is developing a method to distinguish psychometrically between individuals accurately reporting low levels of negative emotions from individuals misrepresenting or inaccurately reporting low levels of negative emotions. In the preponderance of the published literature in psychology and psychiatry concerned with personality, psychopathology, and health, "healthy" control groups have been composed of all subjects reporting low magnitudes on the variables/scales of interest. The implicit assumption in these studies is that the self-reports of the subjects in these "normal" control groups are accurate. Unfortunately, this implicit assumption is fallacious. Consequently, much of the previous published research is confounded and misinterpreted.

Table 2. Combinations of High and Low Self-Reports of Anxiety with High and Low
Self-Reports of Self-Deception and Impression Management.

	Self-Reports of Self-Deception and Impression Management	
Self-Reports of Anxiety	Low	High
High	High anxious	Defensive high anxious
Low	Low anxious	Repressors

Source: Adapted from Schwartz (1984).

As mentioned briefly by Weinberger (in this volume), the study conducted
by Weinberger, Schwartz, and Davidson (1979) successfully differentiated
subjects accurately reporting low levels of distress (termed "true low anxious") from subjects self-deceptively and/or other deceptively reporting low
levels of distress (termed "repressive"). The conceptual and methodological
breakthrough in this study was the discovery that the Marlowe-Crowne Social
Desirability Scale (Crowne and Marlowe 1964) tapped not only impression
management (other deception) but repressive coping (self-deception) as well.

The correlations between scores on the Marlowe-Crowne and measures of
negative emotion are typically mildly negatively correlated. As a result, it is
possible to split subjects reporting low and high levels of distress (e.g., anxiety as tapped into subgroups of subjects scoring low and high on the Taylor
Manifest Anxiety Scale (MAS; Taylor 1953). The resulting 2 × 2 table is
displayed in table 2.

In the Weinberger, Schwartz, and Davidson (1979) experiment, three
groups of subjects were run: two groups reporting low anxiety (split into low-
anxious [$N = 15$] and repressive coping [$N = 14$] on the basis of low and
high Marlowe-Crowne scores) and the third reporting high anxiety (not split
on Marlowe-Crowne scores [$N = 11$]). All subjects were administered fifteen
sentence completions: five involved relatively neutral content, five involved
aggressive content, and the remaining five involved sexual content. Each set
of three trials contained all three contents, the order of contents randomized
across the five blocks trials. Physiological measures were monitored continuously (heart rate, skin resistance, forearm EMG). In addition, the verbal responses to each trial were scored for response latency and content avoidance.

Using the response latency data as a prototype (since the content-rated data
and the physiological data generally paralleled the response-latency data), it
was found that true low-anxious subjects responded relatively quickly to each
of the three contents while the high-anxious subjects responded relatively
quickly to the neutral content sentences, more slowly to the aggressive content

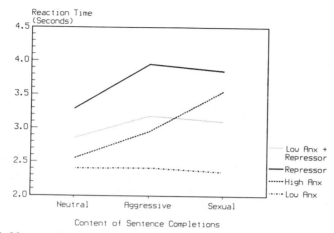

Fig. 1. Mean reaction times to neutral, aggressive and sexual sentence completions by low anxious, high anxious, and repressive subjects. The mean of the low anxious and repressive subjects is also shown.

sentences, and most slowly to the sexually oriented sentences (implying increased stress from neutral through aggressive to sexual content sentences) (see fig. 1).

The repressors, who reported significantly less anxiety than even the low-anxious subjects, showed slow response latencies to the neutral sentences and quite slow response latencies to the aggressive and sexual sentences. We see that, although the repressors reported the least anxiety, they behaved in a more anxious manner, not only more than the true low-anxious subjects, but also more than the high-anxious subjects as well.

Notice in figure 1 that, had the true low-anxious and repressive subjects been combined into a prototypical "low"-anxiety control group, the average of the true low-anxious response times and the repressive response would appear artifactually indistinguishable from the high-anxious group.

It is virtually impossible to determine from the published literature what the ratio of true low-anxious to repressive subjects is in a given control group in a given study. Hence, the published literature is confusing and confounded regarding not only the relation between behavior and self-report but the relation between physiology and self-report as well.

It is illuminating to examine the Weinberger, Schwartz, and Davidson data over the five blocks of three trials (reflecting habituation or sensitization to the sentences over trials, average across content types; see fig. 2). True low-anxious subjects began the experiment with relatively fast response latencies, slowed down a bit in the middle of the experiment, and were faster again by the end of the experiment. The high-anxious subjects, as one might expect,

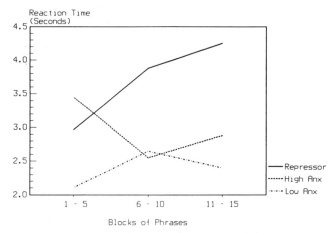

Fig. 2. Mean reaction times over three blocks of sentence completions, 5 sentences per block, by low anxious, high anxious, and repressive subjects.

began the experiment responding with quite slow response latencies, but over the course of the experiment became faster and approached by the end of the experiment the quick response latencies of the true low-anxious subjects.

The repressive subjects were strikingly different. They began the experiment with quite slow response latencies and over the course of the experiment responded slower and slower. Again, had the true low-anxious and repressive subjects been combined and analyzed as a single "control," differences between low and high anxiety would virtually disappear if not appear paradoxical. In figure 2, high-anxious subjects showed habituation/adaptation over the experiment, whereas repressive subjects showed substantial sensitization over the experiment. What would have appeared paradoxical is that, if the prototypic "control" group of all subjects reporting "low" anxiety had been calculated, this "low"-anxious group would appear to show moderate sensitization over the course of the experiment rather than the relatively quick response latencies over the course of the experiment found for the "true" low-anxious subjects.

Validation of the Marlowe-Crowne: Between-Subjects Cardiovascular Measures

These fundamental findings have been replicated and extended in other laboratories (reviewed in Weinberger, in this volume). Presently, the interpretation of high scores on the Marlowe-Crowne are open to at least two interpretations: impression management/social desirability/other deception or defensiveness/repressive coping/self-deception. Research in press and in progress examines these two different (though not necessarily alternative) hypotheses, and the question is far from settled. What is settled is that low self-reports of emotion do not all mean the same thing. For example, the importance of defensiveness, particularly repressive defensiveness, has been replicated and extended in studies examining the recall of personal memories and physiological patterns comparing true low-anxious and repressive subjects (e.g., Davis and Schwartz 1987, discussed in detail in Davis, in this volume).

The robustness of the physiology/self-report dissociation among defensive high-anxious and repressive subjects has been found in a recent study by Jamner and Schwartz (1986a). Drawing on data collected in the Research Division of the International Flavors and Fragrance Corporation (kindly made available to us by Dr. Craig Warren), it was possible to examine systolic, diastolic, and pulse-rate data during a resting period, a moderately stressful sentence completion task, and a timed numeric calculation test. The data set contains a sample of approximately two thousand paid volunteers participating in aroma science research. Marlowe-Crowne and Taylor MAS data were collected, as were self-reports following each of the components of the experiments.

The data reported by Jamner and Schwartz (1986a) represent analyses of the pretest stress reactivity data in the total sample, before any experimental between-subject treatments were initiated. The results were highly stable, significant, and clear cut. When subjects were divided into the four subgroups depicted in table 2, self-reports of anxiety, anger, and embarrassment were lowest in the repressive subjects and true low-anxious subjects and highest in the true high-anxious and defensive high-anxious subjects.

As predicted, the cardiovascular measures were remarkably dissimilar from the self-reports. The highest cardiovascular resting levels and the highest cardiovascular responses to the two laboratory stresses were found in the repressive subjects. Lower levels and stress responsivity were found in the defensive high-anxious subjects, even lower levels and responsivity in the high-anxious subjects, and the lowest levels and responsivity in the true low-anxious subjects. The discrepancy between the true low-anxious subjects (whose physiology mirrored their self-perceptions) and the repressive subjects (whose physiology was substantially at odds with their self-perceptions) is striking.

Validation of the Marlowe-Crowne: Within-Subject Respiratory Measures

What might be considered a critical test of the self-report/physiology disconnection hypothesis as a function of the Marlowe-Crowne is to examine within-subject correlations between an individual's physiological responses to various tasks and his or her own self-reports of emotion to the various tasks.

Schwartz and Jamner (1986) examined this question in a data set collected at Yale University concerned with the relation between respiratory parameters and self-reports following baseline, relaxation tasks, math stress tasks, and various fragrances differing in hedonic and aroma characteristics. Thirty-eight subjects received twenty-six trials, order of trials counterbalanced across subjects. Each subject made twenty-six sets of ratings of emotions, one set per trial. Within-subject self-report/physiological response correlations were calculated between each of the self-reports over the twenty-six trials and each of the respiratory parameters over the twenty-six trials.

As a prototype, consider the within-subject correlations between reports of feeling calm and degrees of respiratory inspiration amplitude (i.e., depth of breath). The predicted relation would be a positive correlation (i.e., the calmer one feels at a given moment, the deeper should be one's respiration). Since the total sample consisted of thirty-eight subjects, it was possible to compute thirty-eight individual calmness/respiratory amplitude correlations (each correlation based on twenty-six pairs of ratings of calmness and inspiration amplitude).

Twenty-six percent of the subjects generated the predicted positive correlations, which were of moderate size and significance (r's of .4N.6). These subjects rated themselves as "calm" at times when their respiratory amplitudes were deep. Another fifty percent of the subjects generated small positive, zero, or small negative correlations. The remaining twenty-four percent of the subjects generated moderate-sized negative correlations, which were the reverse of the predicted hypothesis. These subjects rated themselves as "calm" when their respiratory amplitudes were shallow.

The critical question is, using the Marlowe-Crowne, can we predict which subjects will be perceptually and physiologically integrated (i.e., show the predicted positive correlation) and which subjects will be dissociated, if not counterassociated? A scatterplot placing the thirty-eight individual values from -1.0 N 1.0 on the Y-axis and Marlowe-Crowne values on the X-axis revealed a negative slope with a shift from positive within-subject r's to negative within-subject r's as Marlowe-Crowne values increased. When the individual calmness/respiratory amplitude correlations were correlated with subjects' Marlowe-Crowne (the between-subject r was based on thirty-eight pairs of data), the calculated correlation was a significant negative r.

Taken together, this set of findings provides strong evidence that high scores on the Marlowe-Crowne, especially in combination with low scores on the Taylor MAS, are predictive of dissociations between self-reports and physiological activity. The findings are sufficiently strong and robust to propose that future researchers and clinicians should routinely administer the Marlowe-Crowne to examine evidence of repression within their subjects and patients.

Recent Research on the Repression to Disattention to
Disconnection to Disregulation to Disorder to Disease
Hypothesis: Step 2, Cognitive Strategies of Repressive
Disconnection

One psychological mechanism for "re-pressing" information (pushing the information out of awareness) is to engage in various types of disattention. A simple example is the use of distraction. It is possible to focus one's attention to the external environment (or to one's internal environment) in a selective manner, paying closer attention to "safe" stimuli and avoiding (or reinterpreting/relabeling) stimuli considered "unsafe." Another strategy for increasing disattention to external stimuli is to view the stimuli in a more diffuse and disconnected manner.

Each of these cognitive procedures results in shifting one's attention from the whole of a situation to its parts, especially the safer parts (i.e., from the system to the subsystems). Metaphorically, one's attention is focused more on the trees than on the forest. Also, one's attention may be deployed to view the forest as a diffuse, disconnected, disorganized set of different trees.

Research on these and other cognitive/affective mechanisms is discussed in detail elsewhere in this volume. The important point to highlight here is that, in the original Weinberger, Schwartz, and Davidson (1979) experiment, subjects scoring high in repressive coping (the subjects who showed the large discrepancy between their self-reports and their physiological responses to moderately stressful sentence completion) also showed evidence of significant disattention to (e.g., avoidance of) the stressful content in their verbal responses to the sentence completions. Moreover, they showed significant evidence of producing more global, diffuse responses to the phrases.

On the Cognitive-Somatic Anxiety Scale developed by Schwartz, Davidson, and Goleman (1978), it was found that the repressive and true low-anxious subjects reported comparable degrees of somatic anxiety whereas repressors reported significantly less cognitive anxiety.

Behavioral Strategies of Repressive Disconnection

Analyses in progress (Plante and Schwartz 1988) on a large exercise psychophysiology study conducted by Plante and Karpowitz (1987) have focused on the relation between patterns of Marlowe-Crowne and anxiety scores and involvement in sports and hobbies. They found that repressors reported engaging in significantly more individual and solitary sports (e.g., running) and in significantly more individual and solitary hobbies (e.g., such as listening to music and reading). These same subjects show evidence of significantly higher heart-rate responses to laboratory stressors and significantly slower heart-rate recovery to baseline following the stressors (a physiological indication of an impaired negative feedback loop).

Clearly, more basic research is needed to assess the cognitive processes in repressive individuals in response to content that is personally threatening to the subjects as well as more personality and clinical studies examining life-style preferences and subjective/physiological relations in naturalistic settings. At present, the findings are consistent with the hypothesis that repression is related to disattention and dissociations between self-reports of emotional experience and physiological expressions of emotion.

Recent Research on the Repression to Disattention to Disconnection to Disregulation to Disorder to Disease Hypothesis: Step 3

As discussed previously, one possible neuropsychological mechanism for generating a dissociation between self-reports of feelings and physiological expressions of emotion is to produce a relative, functional disconnection between the left and the right hemispheres (original proposed by Galin 1974). The core of the hypothesis is that parallel process, emotional responses (especially negative/avoidance responses) involve more of the right hemisphere (in right-handed persons) whereas serial process, verbal (especially positive/approach) responses involve more of the left hemisphere.

When the generic concept of disregulation is applied to this specific case, it follows that, if information flow from the right to the left hemisphere is attenuated or blocked altogether, an essential neurocognitive feedback mechanism connecting the two hemispheres will be functionally attenuated or disconnected. The more this feedback is impaired, the more the relation between the two hemispheres will be disregulated.

One way that disregulation between the two hemispheres can be deduced is to look for evidence of more consistent lateralization differences in responding over time in defensive subjects. Basic research on cerebral laterality for cognitive and emotional processes has consistently discovered large individual differences in the degree of lateralization shown between subjects (see Schwartz 1987). The question arises, Can measures of repression account for at least part of these individual differences in lateralization for emotion? A series of recent studies have reported evidence consistent with this hypothesis. These studies are reviewed in Wexler et al. (1986).

The Dichotic Emotional Word Pair Paradigm

In the Wexler et al. (1986) experiment, a dichotic listening paradigm was developed. Pairs of negative-neutral, positive-negative, negative-positive, and positive-negative words were presented to subjects in a counterbalanced order. Each type of word pair was presented both left-right and right-left through stereo earphones. The pairs of words were computer synchronized so that subjects experienced and reported hearing only of the two words of each pair. Using this paradigm, repressive subjects were found to report hearing the least negative words, especially when the negative words in the word pairs were presented to the left ear (right hemisphere).

Following the results of Polonski and Schwartz (1988) and Warrenburg et al. (in press) (finding greater laterality in measures of facial muscle patterns, particularly in the corrugator region [facial muscles that pull down the brows in concentration or anger], in repressive subjects), Davis and Schwartz (1988) (finding greater laterality in measures of facial temperature, particularly in the cheek region overlying the zygomatic muscles [facial muscles that pull up the corners of the lips in happiness], in repressive subjects), and Singer and Schwartz (1986) (finding greater laterality in measures of lateral eye movements while subjects recalled positive and negative memories, especially memories of positive and negative smells [the olfactory bulbs have direct connections to the limbic system]), Wexler et al. (1986) obtained measures of facial laterality, skin conductance, and heart rate while subjects performed the dichotic emotional word pair task. Facial laterality (especially between the left and the right corrugator muscle regions) was greatest in repressors during the negative emotion pairs (especially when the negative word was presented to the left ear/right hemisphere).

More intriguing was the finding that, during those negative-positive or negative-neutral pairs when the repressors reported hearing the positive or neutral word (and not the negative word), the magnitude of the corrugator laterality was significantly greater than when the negative words were actually reported by the repressors. In other words, on those word pair trials where repressors "repressed" the negative emotions "out of awareness," their upper faces revealed an even greater negative emotion laterality response. This finding is consistent with the idea that disattention involving disconnection takes effort (i.e., effort and energy is required to keep "re-pressing" the information that is "pressing" to be processed).

In summary, one neuropsychological mechanism (or expression) of the repressive coping style and the repressing of information is relative functional disconnection between the right and the left hemispheres. The word "functional" should be emphasized since the prediction follows that, when therapy is successful in repressive subjects and repression is no longer a major, automatic response to personally threatening information (from the external environment or from subjects' own internal environments), then accompanying the reduction of repression should be a reduction in the functional cerebral disconnection.

The potential clinical applications of the methods and findings should be self-evident. Data supporting this hypothesis in a single case study was recently reported by Davis (1988).

Recent Research on the Repression to Disattention to
Disconnection to Disregulation to Disorder to Disease
Hypothesis: Step 4

In the light of the evidence linking repression, disattention, disconnection, and physiological "disorder" (i.e., enhanced reactivity plus slower recovery, the latter being a key element of disregulated negative feedback), a critical test of the complete hypothesis would measure and link all the components in one study, with a particular focus on the disconnection to disorder relation.

Cardiovascular Rigid and Flexible Responders

Bowen and Schwartz (1988a, 1988b) addressed these questions in research that contained an important accidental finding. The first study examined the relation between instructions to control heart rate voluntarily (generate increases and deceases in heart rate without biofeedback) and instructions to induce voluntarily different emotional states (happiness, sadness, anger, and fear) previously found to elicit different patterns of cardiovascular response (Schwartz, Weinberger, and Singer, 1981).

While examining the data, Bowen discovered that he could split the subjects into two subgroups on the basis of their performance during the voluntary heart-rate control task. "Undifferentiated, rigid responders" were those subjects who generated global increases and decreases in heart rate, systolic blood pressure, diastolic blood pressure, and pulse transit times. "Differentiated, flexible responders" were those subjects who generated selective patterns of increases and decreases in heart rate, systolic blood pressure, diastolic blood pressure, and transit times; one prototypical pattern was heart-rate increase to systolic increase to diastolic decrease to pulse transit times no change during a trial instructing subjects to increase their heart rate voluntarily.

When subjects were split into rigid (undifferentiated) and flexible (differentiated) cardiovascular responders on the basis of their performance during instructed heart-rate control in part 1 of the study, marked differences were found in cardiovascular patterning during the different instructed emotions in part 2 of the study. Undifferentiated, rigid responders showed no cardiovascular patterning during the different emotional imagery trials, whereas the differentiated, flexible responders showed striking cardiovascular patterns that differed as a function of the different emotions induced by imagery.

To replicate and extend these findings, in the second study (Bowen and Schwartz 1988b) left- and right-sided EMG recordings from the corrugator and zygomatic regions were taken during voluntary heart-rate control (part 1) and imagery-induced emotion (part 2). In addition, the Marlowe-Crowne, the Taylor MAS, the World Hypothesis Scale (WHS; Harris, Fontana, and Dowds, 1977), and a scale gathering information on prior illnesses and the use of the university health service during the previous year were administered.

The rigid/flexible distinction was replicated for cardiovascular patterning. Rigid heart-rate voluntary control patterns predicted cardiovascular arousal (i.e., undifferentiation) to emotions elicited by imagery. In addition, it was found that the undifferentiated, rigid subjects evidenced significantly greater facial laterality during the emotional imagery tasks; higher scores on the Marlowe-Crowne; higher scores on the WHS, reflecting a preference to use a categorical (yes-no) style of information processing; and significantly more reported illness during the previous year.

Hence, individuals who score high on the Marlowe-Crowne and in particular score low on the Taylor MAS evidence an association between repression to disattention strategies to disconnection (disconnection between self-report and physiology within the individual as well as functional disconnect between the two hemispheres) to disregulation (a process inferred by) to evidence of increased physiological disorder (particularly reflected in recovery processes) to disease (self-reports of illness being higher in subjects emphasizing a more dichotomous-categorical style of thinking).

The links between CNS (central nervous system) and ANS (autonomic nervous system) laterality need to be established, but not only through future neuroanatomical and psychobiological research. Research already published can be reinterpreted and integrated across levels.

Cerebral Laterality, Cardiac Laterality, and Cardiac Disease

Lane and Schwartz (1987) have recently integrated two relatively disconnected yet parallel literatures. One literature concerns animal studies on lateralization ANS control of the heart and predisposition to ventricular tachycardia, ventricular fibrillation, and sudden cardiac death during emotional high-stress conditions. The other concerns human studies on lateralization CNS during different cognitive and emotional states and the role of emotion in predisposing or triggering different kinds of cardiac arrhythmias that can lead to sudden death.

When these two bodies of literature are integrated into a single body of knowledge, a set of specific hypotheses emerges that more precisely tests the links between repression, CNS-ANS laterality, cardiovascular disorder, and disease. The Lane and Schwartz model predicts that different cardiac diseases will emerge as a function of different CNS lateral dominances. Persons who characteristically (stylistically) emphasis left- versus right-hemispheric processing of information should be predisposed to develop one set of cardiac diseases (e.g., ventricular tachycardia). Persons who characteristically (stylistically) emphasis right- versus left-hemispheric processing of information should be predisposed to develop another set of cardiac disease (e.g., supraventricular tachycardia).

From a systems perspective, the following picture emerges: to the extent that a system expresses one particular pattern (set) of subsystem regulations versus another, specific disconnections should lead to specific disregulations that are selective, differential, and therefore measurable.

Right-sided Strokes and Supraventricular Tachycardia

Lane et al. (1987) have obtained preliminary evidence supporting the cardiac laterality hypothesis. Among forty-one patients who had suffered lateralization strokes, all five cases of supraventricular tachycardia were found in patients with right-sided strokes (presumably caused by the disinhibition—disregulation—of right sided sympathetic to the atria). Research in progress by Lane and colleagues includes measurement of EKG changes in patients with left- and right-sided strokes during the Wada test (which functionally and selectively "puts to sleep" the left and right hemispheres) and measurement of EEG-EKG changes in normal, true high-anxious, defensive high-anxious, and repressive college students while exposed to various degrees of personally relevant stress.

Recent Research on the Repression to Disattention to Disconnection to Disregulation to Disorder to Disease Hypothesis: Step 5

Ultimately, if a systems approach to repression and health is useful and valid, then scores on the Marlowe-Crowne and the Taylor MAS should predict not only clinical outcome in specific diseases but also the status of the underlying restorative/healing/self-regulatory mechanisms (e.g., the immune system) in true low-anxious versus repressive individuals. A set of recent studies conducted at Yale and Boston universities has discovered evidence consistent with this hypothesis.

Repressive Coping, Dysregulation, and Cancer

In a comprehensive prospective study drawing on a carefully controlled sample of fifty-two women with a history of breast carcinoma and thirty-four health-matched controls, association between psychological factors and the progression of neoplastic disorder were examined on follow up averaging 624 days (Jensen 1987). Multiple regression was employed to control for disease stage at original diagnosis, age, total length of disease course, hematological factors, and blood chemistries measured at study onset. Using the Marlowe-Crowne and the Taylor MAS to classify repressors and the other three subtypes, Jensen found that repressors reported significantly less negative emotion, yet their rate of remission was 46 percent greater than nonrepressors (1,755 days for nonrepressors vs. 1,204 days for repressors).

Of the eleven patients who died during follow-up, ten had no history of maternal breast cancer. However, eight of the patients who died were repressors. Drawing on predictions from disregulation theory (Schwartz 1979, 1988), Jensen hypothesized that those repressors who used positive imagery that focused on the external environment (e.g., sunny beaches) rather than on the internal environment (thoughts, emotions, and bodily sensations and feelings in the region of the cancer) would be engaged in even further disattention to self, resulting in greater disregulation and worse clinical outcome. Using a set of items from the positive daydream subscale on the Imaginal Processes Inventory (Huba, Aneshensel, and Singer 1981), Jensen's prediction was confirmed. Jensen concluded that "the daydreaming findings, in particular, cautions strongly against 'intuitive' psychological approaches. . . . What may appear to be helpful or harmless psychologically may not necessarily be so in a broader psychobiological context" (1987, 340).

Jensen emphasizes that future research is necessary to "identify the physiological mediation and subcortical pathways which may be involved in the processes of psychobiological regulation and disregulation." Identifying the neuroendocrine and immunological processes associated with CNS-ANS dysregulations is also a challenge for future research.

Repressive Coping, Dysregulation, Asthma, and Immune Function

In a comprehensive study of imagery and immune function in asthma, Polonski et al. (1988a) studied thirty-four asthmatic patients who were not taking steroids. Psychological tests, measures of pulmonary function, and measures of immunoglobulin G (IgG) tested at three histamine levels were obtained at the beginning and the end of the six-week study. In one set of analyses, the relation between shift in imagery (from external and avoidance to internal and approach) and change in IgG functioning over the six weeks was examined. It was found that, the greater the shift in imagery from external/avoidance to internal/approach, the greater the increase in IgG levels indicative of improved immune functioning. This finding is consistent with Jensen's hypothesis that positive imagery directed toward self and one's illness can have positive effects in terms of enhanced self-regulation and associated healing.

In the light of the imagery/immune relation found by Polonski, could individual differences in asthmatics' openness to change their imagery from external/avoidance to internal/approach be predicted by their overall coping styles as measured by the Marlowe-Crowne and the Taylor MAS? Disregulation theory would predict that subjects high in repressive-defensiveness should be less likely (and may be resistant) to changing their imagery in a way that would enhance immune functioning relevant to the healing of asthma (e.g.,

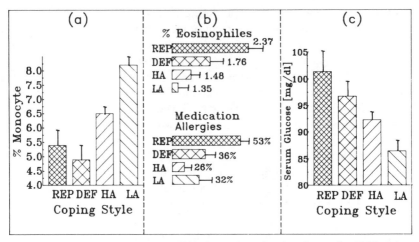

Fig. 3. (a) Mean monocyte count (per 100 leukocytes) as a function of repression (REP), defensive high anxious (DEF), high anxious (HA) and low anxious (LA) coping styles. (b) Mean eosinophile count (per 100 leukocytes) and group percent of patients reporting allergies to medication as a function of coping style. (c) Mean serum glucose levels (mg/dl) for REP, DEF, HA, and LA groups.

levels of IgG). This hypothesis was tested by Polonski et al. (1988b). They reported that pretreatment scores on the Marlowe-Crowne and the Taylor MAS predicted both the healthy change in imagery and the associated healthy change in IgG levels over six weeks. The combination of findings in Jensen (1987) and Polonski et al. (1988a, 1988b) provide strong suggestive evidence linking repression to immune function to disease.

Repressive Coping, Dysregulation, Behavioral Medicine Patients, and Immune Function

Jamner, Schwartz, and Leigh (1988) recently examined the relation between repressive coping style and measures of monocyte, eosinophile, and serum glucose levels in a random sample of 312 patients seen at the Yale Behavioral Medicine Clinic over a five-year period. The findings are displayed in figure 3. Not only was repressive coping related to immune function as measured by monocyte counts, but the increased eosinophile counts and self-reports of allergic reactions to medication, coupled with the increased serum glucose levels, also provide support consistent the Jamner and Schwartz's (1986b) opiate-peptide hypothesis of repression.

The Opiate-Peptide Hypothesis of Repression: An Example of Integrative Health Science Theory

The opiate-peptide hypothesis of repression predicts that repressive coping is associated with increased functional endorphin levels in the brain, which can result in decreased immunocompetence and hyperglycemia. From a systems perspective, the hypothesis emerges that there should exist integrative psychoneuroendocrine/psychoneuroimmunologic/psychoneurophysiological mechanisms whereby repressive coping involves attenuated emotional experiences of pain and distress (including memory of these experiences) coupled with compromised resistance to infectious and neoplastic disease. Increased endorphin levels and/or increased opiate receptors are hypothesized to function as an integrative, yet disregulatory, mechanism that would be expressed at multiple levels (i.e., within and across multiple systems/subsystem). The emergence of this theory occurred through the confluence of two bodies of literature that until recently had existed in a relatively disconnected yet parallel fashion.

Self-Deception, Pain Tolerance, and the Opiate-Peptide Hypothesis

Jamner and Schwartz (1986b) examined the relations among individual differences in the perception and coping with physical pain, endorphin theories of pain, individual differences in repressive coping, disregulation theory of repression and disease, and theories of endorphin/immune system/CNS interactions.

In his doctoral thesis, Jamner (1987) examined the relation between coping with levels of electric shock, physiological response, and measures of neuroticism and extroversion from the Eysenck Personality Inventory (EPI; Eysenck and Eysenck 1968). Although levels of pain and physiological response showed some relation when evaluated using multivariate statistics, the classic measures of extraversion and neuroticism showed little relation to perception and coping with pain.

Jamner had used the Lie scale (LS) of the EPI for its traditional presumed purpose, to remove subjects with high scores who were supposedly engaged in "lying." However, an item analysis of the Marlowe-Crowne and the LS (table 3) revealed sufficient overlap to explore use of the LS as a possible measure of defensiveness (i.e., self-deception). When the total sample of subjects was split on low/medium/high scores on the LS, striking differences in coping with levels of electric shock emerged. Not only were the differences between subgroups highly significant, but the magnitude of the actual differences was also substantial (shown in fig. 4).

Notice that the amount of electric current judged by the low-LS subjects to be at their tolerance level (the highest level of shock subjects were willing to take—level 4) was judged by the high-LS subjects to be only moderately painful (level 2). In terms of actual milliamps of electric current tolerated by the groups, the high-LS subjects accepted twice as much electric current before judging it to be at their tolerance level as the low-LS subjects did. The

Table 3. Sample Items from the Marlowe-Crowne Social Desirability Scale and the Eysenck Personality Lie Scale

Marlowe-Crowne Items	Eysenck Items
1. I am always courteous even to people who are disagreeable.	1. Are all your habits good and desirable ones?
2. I never resent being asked to return a favor.	2. If you say you will do something do you always keep your promise no matter how inconvenient it might be to you?
3. I almost never felt the urge to tell someone off.	3. Of all the people you know there are some whom you definitely do not like?
4. I don't find it particularly difficult to get along with loud-mouthed obnoxious people.	4. Once in a while do you lose your temper and get angry?
5. When I don't know something I don't at all mind admitting it.	5. Do you sometimes talk about things you know nothing about?
6. I like to gossip at times.	6. Do you sometimes gossip?
7. I have never been irked when people expressed ideas very different from my own.	7. Do you occasionally have thoughts and ideas that you would not like other people to know about?

Source: Adapted from Jamner and Schwartz (1986b).

moderate-LS subjects fell virtually in the middle of the low- and high-LS subjects.

The strength of these findings called for an interpretation that included psychobiological theories of pain, psychobiological theories of repression, and psychobiological models of disease in general. This led to the opiate-peptide theory of repression. Space precludes further discussion of this theory here. What is important to remember is that integrative health science theory encourages a number of integrative hypotheses that are amenable to direct empirical test.

Levels of Systems: Levels of "Re-pression," Levels of Disregulation, Levels of Defense, and Levels of Emotional Awareness

Approaching repression and health from a systems perspective has the qualities of being both a gift and a curse. The gift side of the systems perspective is the extent to which it fosters continued openness to new information, connecting the information within and across levels, thereby stimulating new insights regarding the organization and functioning of a given system as a whole system. The curse side reflects the extent to which it fosters information overload, the negative consequences of receiving too much information too soon, which leads to specific information overload and generic information over-

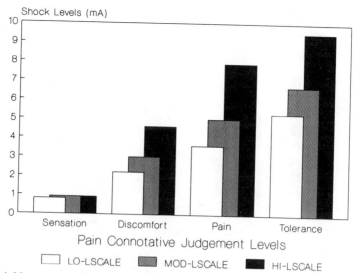

Fig. 4. Mean intensity of electric shock required to elicit the sensation threshold and the 3 pain connotative judgements as a function of High, Moderate, and Low Deception.

load. The skillful application of the systems perspective depends on our ability through practice to develop the cognitive tools not only for visualizing generic information across levels but also to restrict our vision by "repressing" the conscious processing of selective external and internal information.

Disconnecting information (relatively speaking) can take place within and across levels of a system. It follows that, to the extent that higher levels in a system represent more complex integrations and emergents of lower levels of information in a system, different types of "re-pression", and hence different types of defense, should vary as a function of the particular levels involved in a system. This leads to the hypothesis that, although different psychological defenses may reflect a common (generic) "re-pressing" process, defenses will vary in their levels of complexity and therefore vary in the levels of consequence for the person.

Differentiated Denial and Repression

For example, Levine et al. (1987) recently reported that cardiac patients scoring high on the Levine Denial of Illness Scale (LDIS; denial is typically interpreted from a psychoanalytic perspective as being a more primitive defense than repression) do better (e.g., are more likely to survive) during the acute phase of inpatient intensive care following a heart attack but do worse on follow-up after leaving the hospital. It appears that repressing of information can be so basic and effective that it reduces or removes awareness of one's

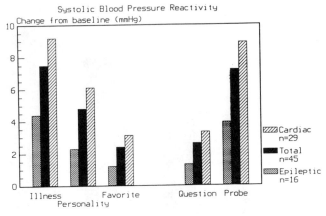

Fig. 5. Mean systolic blood pressure reactivity (change from baseline in mmHg) to illness, personality and favorite questions in cardiac and epileptic patients. Also shown is mean systolic blood pressure reactivity to the questions and to probes of the questions in cardiac and epileptive patients. The means of the total sample are displayed as well.

physical state and people's labels of their physical state (e.g., "I didn't have a heart attack"). Strong denial of illness (or denial of stress in general) can enable a person to interpret his or her internal and external environment as "safe," which in turn should reduce central and peripheral reactions to the stress in the short term. However, if this same denial mechanism continues after leaving the hospital, these patients will continue to distort or disattend to physical and emotional feedback. Lacking the feedback, they will be less likely to engage in disease-preventing and health-promoting behaviors. Denial of illness becomes a gift in the short term and a curse in the long term.

Warrenburg et al. (in press) conducted a laboratory study of cardiac and epileptic patients, examining multiple physiological responses to one set of personally positive questions (favorite activities) and two sets of personally negative questions (Marlowe-Crowne and LDIS questions). In addition, after subjects gave their answers to the questions, they were probed further about each of their answers (thus potentially challenging their selective repression of information). As shown in figure 5, systolic blood-pressure responses in general were larger in cardiac patients than epileptic patients, illness questions in general were associated with the largest systolic blood-pressure changes and favorite questions with the smallest systolic blood-pressure changes, and the probe condition in general engendered larger systolic blood-pressure responses than the question condition.

The LDIS was only mildly correlated with the Marlowe-Crowne. Hence, LDIS and Marlowe-Crowne scores could be evaluated relatively independently. As shown in figure 6, Warrenburg et al. (in press) found that, as pre-

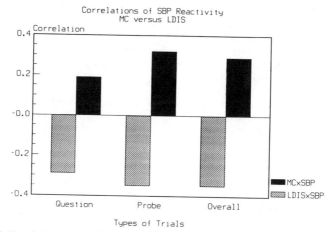

Fig. 6. Correlations of systolic blood pressure reactivity to the questions, the probes of the questions, and overall, separately with the Marlowe-Crowne (MC) and Levine Denial of Illness Scale (LDIS).

dicted, the correlation between scores on the LDIS and systolic blood-pressure reactivity was negative (i.e., the greater the denial, the smaller the cardiovascular response to the stress). This is contrasted by the correlation between scores on the Marlowe-Crowne and systolic blood-pressure reactivity. The Marlowe-Crowne was correlated positively not only with systolic blood-pressure reactivity but also with increases in levels of physiological activity during the baselines as the experiment progressed (i.e., high Marlowe-Crowne patients became more sympathetically aroused and/or less parasympathetically aroused as the experiment progressed). Notice that the reactivity and baseline findings of Warrenburg et al. (in press) replicate the reactivity and baseline findings of Weinberger, Schwartz, and Davidson (1979).[1]

Levels of Emotional Awareness and Levels of Defense

How are differences between the LDIS and the Marlowe-Crowne to be explained? The recent analysis by Lane and Schwartz (1988) concerning levels of emotional awareness provides a generic strategy for specifying the concept of levels of defense. Lane and Schwartz's central hypothesis is that levels of cognitive processing of the external environment are paralleled by levels of cognitive processing of the internal environment. The five levels described by

1. Plante and Schwartz (1988) have found that, although the Marlowe-Crowne and the LS show a significant correlation, the Marlowe-Crowne is a more reliable differentiator of perceived emotion distress and skin conductance and the LS is a more reliable differentiator of perceived pain (from electric shock) and pulse volume. The LS, like the LDIS, may tap a more elemental level of defense than the Marlowe-Crowne.

Table 4. Levels of Emotional Awareness and Levels of Theories of Emotion

	Emotional Awareness	Theories of Emotion
Level 5	Blends of emotion (e.g., feeling "Sorry-Grateful Regretful-Happy"[a]	Blends of emotion theories (e.g., Lane and Schwartz)
Level 4	Blends of emotions (e.g., feeling happy and sad)	Blends of emotion theories (e.g., Tompkins, Izard, Ekman)
Level 3	Single, differentiated emotions (e.g., feeling happy vs. feeling sad)	Specific emotions theories (e.g., Darwin, James-Lange)
Level 2	Behavior reaction and undifferentiated emotion (e.g., feeling upset)	Approach/avoidance theories (e.g., Miller)
Level 1	Somatic awareness	Arousal theories (e.g., Duffy, Malmo)

Source: Adapted from Lane and Schwartz (1988).
[a]The title of a song from Stephen Sondheim's *Company.*

Lane and Schwartz are shown in table 4.[2] Notice in table 4 that theories of emotion themselves can be organized using the same generic framework. Also notice that each higher level of emotional awareness and each higher-level theory of emotion implicitly if not explicitly incorporates concepts and findings from the lower levels.

Individuals may vary not only in their characteristic (e.g., trait, style) level of emotional awareness but also in particular areas ("islands of defense") in which lower-level emotional processing and expressing occur. Notice that lower levels of emotional awareness are neither necessarily nor intrinsically "worse" than higher levels. For example, if an automobile suddenly swerves in front of you while you are driving, it is highly adaptive to respond in a relatively reflex-like manner (e.g., brake and/or turn, levels 1 and 2) and subsequently bring higher levels of emotional awareness to bear on the situation after the potential danger has been averted successfully. In certain contexts, the repressing of higher-order perceptions is not only essential. It is a prerequisite for health.

Healthy "Re-pression" as a Prerequisite to Health: Theory and Clinical Examples

From a systems perspective, the possibility arises that repression is not only sometimes adaptive but may also actually function as a prerequisite for the

2. Research on the reliability and validity of the new Levels of Emotional Awareness Questionnaire is in progress (Quinlan, Lane, and Schwartz 1988).

health of any system. The hypothesis that the development of repression under certain circumstances is healthy was stimulated not only from a systems perspective but also by direct clinical observations made over a seven-year period (1981–88) in the Yale Behavioral Medicine Clinic.

I was fortunate to have treated a number of highly intelligent, successful teenagers and adults whose biological, psychological, and social functioning was compromised as a consequence of pervasive repression. The physical diseases of these patients included tension and migraine headaches, Crohn's disease, ulcers, allergies, hypertension, impotence, and vaginal herpes.

These particular patients came to the clinic ostensibly for stress management. However, stress management relatively quickly turned into psychotherapy (combining dynamic, behavioral, and humanistic/philosophic perspectives). These patients had, to varying degrees, difficulties in experiencing specific negative emotions as well as specific positive emotions, thinking about certain issues in a nonthreatened, nondefensive manner, and developing effective, close, loving relationships with family and friends. In addition, their childhood memories were remarkably impoverished. These patients were biased toward seeing their parents and siblings in an excessively positive light.

This pattern of behavior fits the general style of repressive defensiveness. For these patients, their current problems tended to mirror certain key experiences in childhood that could not be recalled initially or were dismissed as being unimportant, if not irrelevant, to their current problems. However, as each therapeutic relationship developed, it became clear that the patients' family situations involved significant cognitive, emotional, and/or physical abuse and destructiveness. Of particular significance is that these patients had managed to cope with this abuse in what proved to be a remarkably adaptive and typically highly creative fashion.

Some striking qualities of these people were that they had elected (in some cases, consciously chosen) to suppress (at least verbally) their needs for love and affection; to push out of their minds feelings of loneliness, depression, anger, and fear; and to become overachieving children. By and large, they were obedient, well-behaved, responsible children who were actively involved with their schoolwork (although they had few friends in school). They managed to do extremely well in grade school and high school despite living in the presence of serious problems at home. They managed to leave their homes and go on to college with relatively few memories, especially negative memories, of their past. Although they accumulated some physical unhealed scars along the way (e.g., severe migraines, Crohn's disease, and sleep disorders), they otherwise claimed, at least initially, to be okay.

Typically, their siblings tended to be more assertive, acting out against their parents or themselves (i.e., the younger siblings were more likely to cope by resorting to drugs or alcohol, becoming sexually promiscuous, or doing poorly in school). Whereas the repressors inhibited thoughts, feelings, and actions that might cause problems in the family, their siblings were a source of problems for their parents, for their teachers, and for themselves.

How did these patients end up using repression as a major means of coping with their highly stressful, unhealthy families? Was it because of their superior intelligence? Was it due to some psychophysiological differences that were genetically endowed (e.g., these patients turned out to be extra sensitive and easily aroused as children—did this encourage them to push and repush their feelings of pain, anxiety, and fury away)? Did one or more of their relatives or friends serve as a model of successful repressive defensiveness when the patients were young? The answers to these questions are not known. The development of personality and its relation to health needs to be addressed in future research.

The patients I saw in treatment were veritable masters of repression. My approach in therapy was to help them discover this "talent" (rather than "sickness") and to help them relabel their repressiveness as a highly mastered tool of the mind that they should be proud of rather than ashamed of. Instead of feeling guilty for being mentally and physically sick, the patients were encouraged to reinterpret their prior coping styles as being remarkably adaptive, creative, and highly effective in helping them not only survive their childhood and adolescence but also reach their current levels of professional success.

However, they were helped to discover that what was once a necessary and highly adaptive general coping strategy was no longer necessary and adaptive. They were helped to discover that it was now safe for them no longer to rely primarily on this overlearned mental tool and learn new, more flexible coping tools.

The process of coming to trust the therapist and unlearn some of the automatic repression is, of course, easier said than done. However, with time, the strategy outlined above helped these patients become more hopeful, more realistic, and more open minded, to see therapy as a positive challenge that in a safe context could help free them.

At certain points in therapy, it became useful and appropriate to help these repressed patients think about the general process of selective attention. Patients can come to discover that, if their present thoughts and previous memories had not been successfully repressed, mental confusion if not mental chaos (e.g., schizophrenia) would have resulted.

An individual's ability to push things out of awareness automatically is essential if he or she is to be well, be in good health and have the potential to heal, and be able to engage in effective interpersonal and social communication. This applies to patients and therapists alike. If a therapist had to worry that various traumas from his or her past might emerge as unpredictable and uncontrollable flashbacks during therapy, the effectiveness of the therapist would be in serious question. Theoretically, as therapy progresses and patients become more flexible in perceiving their past and envisioning possible futures, greater ease in making new connections should occur at multiple levels (biological, psychological, and social).

Flexible Repression, Disease, and Health: A Paradigm Shift?

If repression is viewed as a special case of "re-pression," and if defenses are viewed as varying in terms of levels of repression, and if flexible "re-pression" is viewed as a prerequisite for both becoming and being a healthy system, then it is possible that the existence of disease plays an adaptive feedback role in the promotion of health and well-being, not only for the individual, but also for the species and the world as a whole ecological system. The implications that unfold from this hypothesis are inherently far reaching. They may be indicative of an evolving paradigm shift (Kuhn 1962), not only in the basic and applied sciences related to personal and public health care, but also in the very way we view health and illness at all levels in nature (Schwartz 1984, 1988). They also may be misguided and prove to be mistaken. Future research will tell.

References

Bertalanffy, L. von. 1968. *General systems theory.* New York: Braziller.

Bowen, W., and G. E. Schwartz. 1988a. Cardiovascular flexibility and rigidity: Relationship to repression, disregulation, and facial laterality in expressions of emotion. Department of Psychology, University of Arizona. Typescript.

Bowen, W., and G. E. Schwartz. 1988b. Individual differences in cardiovascular flexibility and rigidity: Effects on cardiovascular differentiation to emotion. Department of Psychology, University of Arizona. Typescript.

Buchsbaum, M. S., G. C. Davis, and W. E. Bunney. 1977. Nalaxone alters pain perception and somatosensory evoked potentials in normal subjects. *Nature* 270:620–22.

Cannon, W. B. 1932. *The wisdom of the body.* New York: Norton.

Crowne, D. P., and D. Marlowe. 1964. *The approval motive: Studies in evaluative dependence.* New York: Wiley.

Davidson, R. J. 1984. Affect, cognition and hemispheric specialization. In *Emotion, cognition and behavior,* ed. C. E. Izard, J. Kagan, and R. Zajonc. New York: Cambridge University Press.

Davis, P. J. 1988. Physiological and subjective effects of catharsis: A case report. *Cognition and Emotion* 2:19–29.

Davis, P. J., and G. E. Schwartz. 1987. Repression and the inaccessibility of affective memories. *Journal of Personality and Social Psychology* 52:155–62.

———. 1988. Repression and the inaccessibility of affective memories: Relationship to skin temperature and muscle activity of the face. Harvard University. Typescript.

Eysenck, H. J., and S. B. G. Eysenck. 1968. *Eysenck personality inventory.* San Diego: Educational and Industrial Testing Service.

Galin, D. 1974. Implications of left-right cerebral lateralization for psychiatry: A neurophysiological context for unconscious processes. *Archives of General Psychiatry* 9:412–18.

Harris, M., A. F. Fontana, and B. N. Dowds. 1977. The World Hypothesis Scale: Rationale, reliability, and validity. *Journal of Personality Assessment* 41:337–47.

Huba, G. J., C. S. Aneshensel, and J. L. Singer. 1981. Development of scales for three second-order factors of inner experience. *Multivariate Behavioral Research* 16:181–206.

Jamner, L. D., and G. E. Schwartz. 1986a. Integration of self-report and physiological indices of affect: Interactions with repressive coping strategies. *Psychophysiology* 23:444.

———. 1986b. Self-deception predicts self-report and endurance of pain. *Psychosomatic Medicine* 48:211–23.

Jamner, L. D., G. E. Schwartz, and H. Leigh. 1988. Repressive coping predicts monocyte, eosinophile and serum glucose levels: Support for the opioid-peptide hypothesis. *Psychosomatic Medicine* 50:567–77.

Jensen, M. R. 1987. Psychobiological factors predicting the course of breast cancer. *Journal of Personality* 55:317–42.

Kuhn, T. S. 1962. *The structure of scientific revolutions.* Chicago: University of Chicago Press.

Lane, R., J. Wallace, G. E. Schwartz, P. Pangan, and A. Gradman. 1987. Supraventricular tachycardia in patients with right-sided strokes. Paper presented at the annual meeting of the American Psychosomatic Society, Philadelphia, March.

Lane, R. D., and G. E. Schwartz. 1987. Induction of lateralized sympathetic input to the heart by the CNS during emotional arousal: A possible neurophysiologic trigger of sudden cardiac death. *Psychosomatic Medicine* 49:274–84.

———. 1988. Levels of emotional awareness: A cognitive-development theory and its application to psychopathology. *American Journal of Psychiatry* 144:33–43.

Levine, J., S. Warrenburg, R. Kerns, G. E. Schwartz, R. Delaney, A. Fontana, A. Gradman, S. Smith, S. Allen, and R. Cascione. 1987. The role of denial in recovery from coronary heart disease. *Psychosomatic Medicine* 49:109–17.

Miller, J. G. 1978. *Living systems.* New York: McGraw-Hill.

Plante, T. G., and D. Karpowitz. 1987. The influence of aerobic exercise on physiological stress responsivity. *Psychophysiology* 24:670–77.

Plante, T. G., and G. E. Schwartz. 1988. The influence of defensive and repressive coping styles on physiological stress responsivity. *Psychophysiology* 25:475.

Polonski, W. H., P. H. Knapp, E. L. Brown, G. E. Schwartz, M. E. Osband, and E. Cohen. 1988a. Psychological factors, immunologic function, and bronchial asthma. I. Mental imagery and immunologic change. Department of Psychiatry, Boston University. Typescript.

———. 1986. Psychological factors, immunologic function, and bronchial asthma. II. Emotional defensiveness and immune function. Department of Psychiatry, Boston University. Typescript.

Polonsky, W. H., and G. E. Schwartz. 1988. Facial electromyography and the self-deceptive coping style: Individual differences in the hemispheric lateralization of affect. Department of Psychiatry, Boston University. Typescript.

Quinlan, D. M., R. D. Lane, and G. E. Schwartz. 1988. The levels of emotion scale: A cognitive-developmental measure of emotion. Paper presented at the annual meeting of the Society for Personality Assessment, New Orleans, March.

Schwartz, G. E. 1977. Psychosomatic disorders and biofeedback: A psychobiological model of disregulation. In *Psychopathology: Experimental models*, ed. J. D. Maser and M. E. P. Seligman. San Francisco: Freeman.

———. 1979. Disregulation and systems theory: A biobehavioral framework for biofeedback and behavioral medicine. In *Biofeedback and self-regulation*, ed. N. Birbaumer and H. D. Kimmel. Hillsdale, N.J.: Erlbaum.

———. 1983. Disregulation theory and disease: Applications to the repression/cerebral disconnection/cardiovascular disorder hypothesis. *International Review of Applied Psychology* 32:95–118.

———. 1984. Psychobiology of health: A new synthesis. In *Psychology and health: Master lecture series*, ed. B. L. Hammonds and C. J. Scheirer, vol. 3, pp. 145–95. Washington, D.C.: American Psychological Association.

———. 1987. Personality and health: An integrative health science approach. In *The G. Stanley Hall Lecture Series*, ed. V. P. Makosky, vol. 7, pp. 121–57. Washington, D.C.: American Psychological Association.

———. 1988. From behavior therapy to cognitive therapy to systems therapy: Toward an integrative health science. In *Paradigms in behavior therapy: Present and promise*, ed. D. B. Fishman, F. Rotgers, and C. M. Franks, 294–320. New York: Springer.

Schwartz, G. E., R. J. Davidson, and D. J. Goleman. 1978. Patterning of cognitive and somatic processes in the self-regulation of anxiety: Effects of meditation versus exercise. *Psychosomatic Medicine* 40:321–28.

Schwartz, G. E., and L. D. Jamner. 1986. Subjective/respiratory dissociation and the repressive coping style. *Psychophysiology* 23:459–60.

Schwartz, G. E., D. A. Weinberger, and J. A. Singer. 1981. Cardiovascular differentiation of happiness, sadness, anger and fear following imagery and exercise. *Psychosomatic Medicine* 43:343–46.

Singer, J. A., and G. E. Schwartz. 1986. Lateral eye movements to the recall of positive and negative aromas: Effects of repressive coping. Department of Psychology, Connecticut College. Typescript.

Taylor, J. A. 1953. A personality scale of manifest anxiety. *Journal of Abnormal Psychology* 48:285–90.

Warrenburg, S., J. Levine, G. E. Schwartz, A. F. Fontana, R. D. Kerns, R. Delaney, and R. Mattson. In press. Defensive coping and blood pressure reactivity in medical patients. *Journal of Behavioral Medicine*.

Warrenburg, S., and G. E. Schwartz. 1987. Relationship of blood pressure reactivity to facial laterality and repression in medical patients. Department of Psychology, University of Arizona. Typescript.

Webster's new twentieth century dictionary of the English language: Unabridged. 1977. 2d ed. Reprint. New York: Collins World.

Weinberger, D. A., G. E. Schwartz, and R. J. Davidson. 1979. Low-anxious, high-anxious, and repressive coping styles: Psychometric patterns and behavioral and physiological responses to stress. *Journal of Abnormal Psychology* 88:369–80.

Wexler, B. E., G. E. Schwartz, S. Warrenburg, and M. Servis. 1986. Effects of emotion on perceptual asymmetry: Interactions with personality. *Neuropsychologia* 24:699–710.

17 Repressive Personality Style: Theoretical and Methodological Implications for Health and Pathology

GEORGE A. BONANNO AND JEROME L. SINGER

A recent confluence of intriguing empirical findings from the emergent field of health psychology suggests the value of a fresh review and appraisal of the notion of a repressive personality style. In the field of cancer research, for example, clinical and prospective studies consistently suggest that persons characterized as repressors, that is, individuals whose self-reports reflect a combination of high defensiveness and low anxiety, are at greater risk for obtaining a diagnosis of cancer or, if diagnosed, for showing a poor course of treatment (Kneier and Temoshok 1984: Jensen 1984). Psychophysiological measurements indicate that a subgroup of individuals who show low scores on anxiety questionnaires but high scores on defensiveness or impression management are distinguishable in terms of their high rates of bodily arousal or blood pressure patterns from nondefensive low-anxious test responders (Bowen 1984; Weinberger, Schwartz, and Davidson 1979). This accumulating body of data suggests the value of a reexamination of the insights and observations of clinicians like Harry Stack Sullivan, David Rapaport, and David Shapiro, who proposed that certain of the basic defense mechanisms postulated by Freud can become crystallized into stylistic patterns of recurrent response that may characterize individual personalities.

The history of the concept of defense mechanisms is too well known and extensively reviewed to require special attention at this point (Erdelyi and Goldberg 1979; Erdelyi 1985). The linking of recurrent defenses to neurotic or more general personality styles derives from Freud's "The Neuropsychoses of Defence" and "Character and Anal Erotism" (Freud [1894] 1962, [1908] 1959). During the 1940s, David Rapaport, working through the test batteries of cognitive and projective methods, began to formulate sets of

Preparation of this chapter was supported by the Network on Health and Health-Promoting Behaviors and by the program on Conscious and Unconscious Mental Processes, John D. and Catherine T. MacArthur Foundation.

operations for defining repressive or obsessive personality styles (Rapaport 1942; Rapaport, Gill, and Schafer [1945] 1968). During that same period, Harry Stack Sullivan proposed similar crystallized neurotic styles definable from interpersonal communications patterns (Sullivan 1940, 1956). In approaching the more recent proposals about a repressive personality style, we shall begin with the accounts of Sullivan and of David Shapiro (whose work concisely extends Rapaport's approach) and then move to more recent and suggestive formulations by Helen Block Lewis, Sidney Blatt, and Mardi Horowitz. Next, we will review the efforts to develop questionnaire measurement procedures for the repressive style and then examine recent empirical research reports bearing on this pattern of behavior. The recent findings in the health area implicating a repressive style in disease course will also be considered. Finally, we will attempt a formulation of health and psychopathology related to the two major polarities of the human condition, agency and communion.

The Hysterical-Obsessional Continuum in Psychopathology

Sullivan (1956) characterized hysteria as a disorder of disturbed interpersonal relations and described a competitive "contempt for other people" (209), stemming from a "disturbance of the clarity of connection between other people" (211). The behavioral pattern generally associated with hysteria—extreme exaggeration or lying to conceal shortcomings and overtly positive self-presentation—was viewed by Sullivan as evidence for a lack of subjective awareness and for repression: the symptoms of the disorder serve the function of limiting information about the self.

Obsessionalism is regarded, in contrast to the interpersonal difficulties related to hysteria, as a disorder characterized by an inadequate "self-function" and by serious doubts about personal worth. Rather than the limited elaboration or the shallowness of processing that characterizes hysteria, in Sullivan's (1940) view the obsessive is typified by "obscure power operations" that serve the function of control of the environment and of keeping "other people busy so that they are not apt to attack" (252). The complexity and interweaving of themes and qualifiers that characterize the obsessional patient's communications avoids direct confrontation with feelings of guilt or powerlessness.

Shapiro (1965) echoed Sullivan's emphasis on the polar quality of hysteria and obsessionalism while expanding his analysis to include the modes of general information processing or cognitive styles involved in each disorder. He advanced the notion that hysteria can be characterized by a lack of subjective awareness and by simplified processing. He described "hysterical cognition" as "impressionistic, relatively immediate, and global." Shapiro, like Sullivan, contrasted the hysteric's passive lack of subjective awareness with the obsessional individual's active self-awareness and focused manipulation to the environment. Obsessional cognition is viewed as sharp and intense but also as narrowly focused and inflexible. Hysterical cognition is characterized by a global and impressionistic quality, while the obsessional experience is viewed in terms of a deliberate, but emotionally anesthetized, absorption of mental activity—what is commonly known as obsessive rumination. The obsessive is also haunted by an internalized punitive figure, that is, the harsh superego. In Shapiro's words, "If . . . we chose to characterize the obsessive-compulsive's activity as driven, then we must also characterize him as the driver. . . . [He] functions like his own overseer" (34) and reveals thought processes that are predominantly characterized by the phrase "I should" (Shapiro 1965, 41).

The adaptive quality of the various modes or styles, as well as their defensive function to avoid conflict, is also emphasized in terms of developmental organizing principles and the human need for consistency. In this context, Shapiro cautioned against the application of a dynamic interpretation, concluding that the stable patterns of cognition associated with a particular style are in a sense independent matrices around which dynamic forces are organized. This distinction is crucial for the comparison of related styles and to the thrust of this chapter. Shapiro viewed the paranoid style as "in every instance" a more primitive and extreme "transformation" of the general style that links it with obsessionalism. Thus, paranoia may reflect more pathological dynamic factors in development.

Hysteria could be linked to other forms of symptomatology. Shapiro (1965, 133) concluded,

> Hysterical people are by no means the only ones whose cognition and subjective experience are characterized by impressionistic, quickly and insufficiently organized mental contents, nor by any means the most severely or conspicuously so. . . . Those individuals who are described as passive or impulsive characters exhibit these features in even more marked degree without, however, being characterized by great emotionality in the usual sense of the word. They are inclined, rather, to impulsive action, that is, action that seems to others, and feels to them not entirely deliberate, not wholly participated in or decided upon.

Included in this latter group are the so-called psychopathic and narcissistic characters. Again, the implication is for a range of disorders within a general style, varying in extremity and initiating dynamic influences, but structured into repetitive patterns.

Helen Lewis (1971, 1976, 1985) advanced a model of personality that clearly places psychopathological disorders and nonpathological character styles in a single bipolar relation. She related these poles to dual facets of superego structure; the field-independent/guilt style, which includes obsessionalism and paranoia, and the field-dependent/shame style, which includes hysteria and major affective disorders. Like Shapiro, Lewis considered the nonpathological manifestations of these poles as personality styles. Furthermore, she proposed specific dynamic factors that influence the development and maintenance of each style and related these factors to the gender differences in personality that have traditionally been ascribed to men and women.

The reference to field dependence and field independence as the two poles of a cognitive style continuum reflects Lewis's long association with the research program directed by the late Herman Witkin (Witkin and Goodenough 1981). In scores of studies, these investigators have explored the correlates of an information-processing style in which (in perceptual experiments or psychometric procedures) individuals showed a tendency either to depend heavily on external cues or social information (field dependent) or to rely primarily on self-generated responses or materials drawn from bodily cues or long-term memory (field independent). In a seminal paper, Witkin (1965) reviewed a very large range of studies that showed that various forms of psychopathology as well as normal personality styles were systematically correlated with field dependence/independence. Thus, hysterical patterns were linked to the former style, obsessional patterns to the latter. The many subsequent studies generally supporting these and related linkages are reviewed in Witkin's final work (Witkin and Goodenough 1981).

Lewis had also engaged in empirical evaluation of these styles by analyzing psychotherapy transcripts of patients categorized as field dependent or field independent (Lewis 1971). As predicted, field-independent patients made more references to guilt than to shame and were characterized by a therapist as employing "distancing" and manipulation of control of the therapy situation. The patient's voice in therapy was paraphrased as saying, "Sit there and shut up and I will tell you what the whole thing is about."

In contrast, field-dependent patients made more references in their psychotherapy sessions to shame than to guilt and were characterized by a therapist as forming a "clinging transference—He [patient] would come and live with me if I would let him." A pervasive sense of shame, fear of public humiliation, characterizes the field-dependent, hysterical patient, masking a long suppressed rage over presumed early experiences of embarrassment. By tying hysteria and repression to the mention of shame and to a global, field-dependent cognitive style, Lewis has advanced the earlier formulations into the more modern period of cognitive-affective research.

Blatt (Blatt and Shichman 1983) has recently proposed a model in which personality development is viewed in terms of two primary and fundamental developmental tasks: the development of intimate and mutually satisfying interpersonal relationships and the establishment of a stable and differentiated sense of identity. These two developmental lines are viewed as evolving, under normal circumstances, as part of a complex "dialectical" process: "The development of concepts of the self is dependent upon establishing satisfying interpersonal experiences, and the continuation of satisfying interpersonal experiences is contingent upon the development of more mature concepts of the self" (Blatt and Shichman 1983, 188). Blatt's model allows for the possibility that one developmental task may be emphasized over the other, with the result being personality styles related in a polar fashion and, in the extreme cases, psychopathology.

In a similar fashion, Franz and White (1985) have proposed an extension of Erik Erikson's epigenetic stage model, which parallels Blatt's emphasis on two primary developmental pathways. They criticized Erikson's account for its neglect of the development of intimacy and interpersonal attachment. Franz and White proposed a revision of Erikson's well-known table of epigenetic stages by adding an attachment pathway and its appropriate stage-specific tasks to the individuation pathway of the original model. Blatt and Shichman (1983) took a more moderate stance on Erikson's model and proposed the inclusion of one additional stage to complete what they viewed as the oscillation of interpersonal relatedness (attachment) and self-definition (individuation) already inherent in Erikson's theory.

Two primary configurations of psychopathology are postulated by Blatt that are highly consistent with those described above. Yet Blatt's model goes beyond the simple linking together of a few disorders, for he proposes that many forms of psychopathology may be viewed as distortions or exaggerations of one of the two developmental lines. Psychopathological disorders that are typified by the exaggeration of the task of establishing satisfying interpersonal relations, the anaclitic configuration, are viewed as interrelated and sharing a preoccupation with intimacy, cooperation, trust, and mutuality, with dependency and dependability, with the capacity to give and to receive love. Disorders within the anaclitic configuration include hysteria, the more pathological and immature narcissistic personality, the form of depression focused around dependency and feelings of not being loved (anaclitic depression; Blatt 1974) psychosomatic disorders, eating disorders, and substance abuse.

Defenses within the anclitic configuration are described as primarily avoidant maneuvers: denial and repression. Blatt's description of the cognitive style of an anaclitic individual as "figurative and focused primarily on affects and visual images," as characterized by parallel, global processing rather than by sequential thinking, and as field dependent in cognitive style is consistent with the descriptions we have reviewed thus far of hysteria and other related disorders.

Psychopathological disorders that are typified by the exaggeration of the task of establishing a stable and differentiated identity, the introspective configuration, are viewed as interrelated and sharing a preoccupation with self-definition, self-worth, and impulse control. Disorders within the introjective configuration include obsessionalism and paranoia as well as the form of depression focused around self-criticism and self-worth—introjective depression (Blatt 1974)—and phallic or exhibitionistic narcissism. Again consistent with descriptions of obsessionalism, paranoia, and related disorders, the defenses within the introjective configuration are described as counteractive and include projection, reaction formation, rationalization, and intellectualization, and the cognitive style is described as "analytic, critical, precise, linear and sequential," with concerns centering around "cause and effect, responsibility and blame." There is "little spontaneity and feeling" and an "emphasis on power and control" (Blatt and Shichman 1983, 189).

Blatt, like Lewis, extends his definition of personality styles to include the dynamic factors that influence development and variation within each style. These are not simply achieved or failed in childhood but are viewed as continuous throughout the life cycle. In cases of pathology, however, specific and temporally located traumas may be involved, with the resulting disorder representing an exaggeration of one or the other developmental task in the service of potentially adaptive coping behavior. Difficulties with relatedness resulting in anaclitic pathologies can occur in early infancy, during the formulation of the basic trust bond or during a later period, when the beginnings of gender identity are formed. Difficulties with self-definition and self-worth resulting in introjective pathologies can accompany the infant's earliest attempts to separate from the mother or struggles with autonomy that can occur during toilet training or later childhood. Less serious disturbances may occur at various points in the life cycle, but it is assumed that traumas during early childhood development are the primary causal agents in the development of psychopathology.

Blatt's and Lewis's analyses and characterizations of the hysterical-obsessional dimension extend Sullivan and Shapiro's proposals by introducing the role of specific emotions (shame and guilt). They also point to specific patterns of early and continuing life experiences that sustain and crystallize the behavioral and cognitive styles of hysterics or obsessionals. Of even greater importance is their increased reliance on systematic data collection and empirical research findings that support their positions. Thus, a recent study of the links in a normal young adult sample between gender role and identity, daydream patterns, and depressive style (anaclitic vs. introjective) revealed configurations supportive of both Blatt's and Lewis's formulations (Golding and Singer 1983).

On the basis of a series of carefully studied, videotaped cases of short-term therapy with patients suffering from posttraumatic reactions or aggravated grief responses, Horowitz (1977) has formulated a view of the hysterical personality that meshes well with the descriptions just cited. He adds to the cognitive analysis a greater attention to the hysteric's "loss of reflective self-awareness" as a presumably unconscious means of reducing the "intensity of unpleasant emotions." The failure to attend to one's ongoing thought, to stay with an idea and elaborate on it, leads to a transient form of learning. This presumably occurs because the failure to rehearse an experience mentally and to explore more fully its associative links to other stored material may make for less "deep processing" and reduced retrieval capacity at a later time. Geller (1984) has also emphasized the lack of elaborative processing in hysteria, in terms of the failure to translate imagistic representation into conceptual/lexical representation. We shall return later to some of the implications of this repressive defensive pattern and the inattention of self-generated material or the "unwillingness" to explore one's own thoughts (Singer 1974).

We have begun with a review of several major clinicians' groupings of cognitive patterns, defenses, personality traits, and symptomatology associated with a hysterical versus obsessive dimension. Sullivan and Shapiro's work chiefly reflects their own observations, some of the psychological test work of Rapaport, and a careful reading of the clinical literature to the time of their writing. The very similar formulations of Lewis and Blatt reflect not only comparable personal clinical observation and reviews of published anecdotal case reports but also an accumulating empirical literature involving psychometric studies and experiments. Let us next consider more carefully some of the systematic research that bears on the intriguing link between global, externally oriented cognitive style, a defensive system built around repression and denial, a dynamic involvement with avoidance of shame or coping with dependency, and a hysterical symptom complex. To what extent is such a personality configuration regularly identifiable when we review the psychological research with larger normal groups using a variety of relatively objective psychometric procedures?

The Repressive Personality Style

In 1915, Freud wrote that "the essence of repression lies simply in turning something away, and keeping it at a distance, from the conscious" (Freud [1915] 1957, 147). Evidence that a relatively distinctive personality style characterized by such a continuing emphasis on avoidance of (1) potentially psychologically threatening social encounters or (2) extended lines of associative thought that might lead to conscious awareness of conflict or embarrassing experience has emerged in almost thirty years of psychometric and laboratory studies. Such a repressive orientation may be a precursor of a later development of a hysterical neurosis or may remain merely as a preclinical, relatively "normal" life-style in which the secondary form of a repressive defense mechanism or the related mechanism of denial dominates in daily adaptation. This repressor style has been extensively explored in the studies of repression-sensitization initiated by Byrne, Barry, and Nelson (1963) and has more recently been revived with greater emphasis on its psychophysiological components by Weinberger, Schwartz and their collaborators (Weinberger,

Schwartz, and Davidson 1979; Weinberger, in this volume). Before turning to a review of available research studies, let us consider how repressive or obsessional personality styles may fit into a framework based on the inherent polarities of human experience already hinted at above in our citation of Blatt's "dialectical" view of development, the "life tasks" of interpersonal attachment and individuation.

Some Intrinsic Polarities, Tensions, or Information-processing Contrasts in the Human Condition

If we take a broader perspective on the nature of the human experience, we can identify again and again two kinds of contrasting tensions that reflect the individual's motivations, emotions, and style of information processing. Although Freud is best known for proposing the dichotomy of life and loving versus death and aggression (eros and thanatos), he also identified humankind's major tasks as "to love and to work." It is this latter polarity, the yearning for intimacy and also the desire to express one's individual skills or capacities, that has proven to mesh well with many other theorists' proposals. Adler's (1979) emphasis on striving for power or superiority as opposed to social interest, Rank's (1945) repeated emphasis on the inherent need for uniqueness versus blending and surrendering of one's will, Schachtel's (1959) theory of two major affects, activity and embeddedness, all show a commonality of thought. This polarity is perhaps best summarized in Bakan's (1966) extremely thoughtful and integrative review, in which he suggests as two fundamental modalities of all living forms the striving for agency and communion. Agency reflects the striving for uniqueness, expression of capabilities, and self-protection, while communion represents a struggle against the inherent loneliness of agency and a positive movement toward identification, sharing with others, and a sense of belonging to at least one other person, group, society, or, indeed, species.

Such polarities need not (in contrast with eros and thanatos) be considered mystical or even metaphysical. They can be operationalized into quantifiable variables, as McAdams (1985) has demonstrated; they can be labeled as power and intimacy motivation and can be assessed for each individual as a basis for estimating personality variation (Maddi 1980) and response to relationships over the life course (McAdams and Constantian 1983).

At the level of cognitive processing, one can see such polarities reflected in the classic personality dimension of thinking introversion-extraversion (Jung 1971; Guilford 1959) or in Eysenck's (1960) more social measure of introversion-extraversion (which, when linked to neuroticism, identifies the obsessive vs. hysteric psychometrically). Thus, introverts give relatively higher priority to examining and developing their own thoughts—the ultimate in uniqueness—while extroverts seek their information and gratification in social conduct and communion (Singer 1984b). Such a polarity is also apparent, as we noted earlier, in field independence and field dependence as cognitive styles. At even more reductionist levels of information processing, one can see the processes by which such differences in agency and communion operate in the cognitive styles of long sampling and short sampling identified by Broadbent (1958). He specifically related these styles to introversion-extraversion. Klein's (1970) sharpeners and levelers in perception, Paul's (1959) importers versus nonimporters in story memory, and Miller's (1981; Miller, Brody, and Summerton 1988) blunting and monitoring in information utilization are additional styles. The various factors analyses of daydreaming that regularly point to individual differences in relative enjoyment or elaboration of private imagery and fantasy in contrast to assignment of low priority to processing or inability to attend to one's ongoing thought stream (Singer 1978; 1981; 1984b) also suggest internalized consistent processing patterns.

If we examine the descriptions of the hysterical personality provided in the clinical literature, we see a connection at once to an overemphasis on communion (dependency and attachment conflicts) at the neglect of agency motives or processing priorities. The repressive defense mechanism that is regularly linked to the hysterical neurotic style may be manifested through hasty and superficial processing (short sampling) and through greater dependence on external information than on attention to one's meandering thoughts. In depth processing or attention to the subjective, thoughts are avoided presumably because of their links to the awareness of one's unfulfilled wishes, conflicts, fears, or earlier experiences of shame and humiliation. What evidence is there for identifying a crystallized use of repressive defenses (in contrast with obsessive or sensitized ones) that forms a measurable personality dimension?

Repression Sensitization

As estimated from questionnaires, the repression-sensitization dimension has been intensely researched for nearly a quarter decade. The resulting portrait of the repressor and the sensitizer closely matches the bipolar scheme outlined above. It is remarkably consistent with the descriptions of the hysteric-obsessive continuum and Blatt's anaclitic-introjective theory of psychopathology (Blatt 1983; Blatt and Shichman 1983).

Research on the repression-sensitization dimension began with the work of Byrne and his colleagues and their development of the Byrne Repression-Sensitization Scale (cf. Byrne, Barry, and Nelson 1963). Empirical investigations using the Byrne scale produced a large and compelling body of data. The validity of the Byrne scale was seriously questioned, however, in the late 1970s, and, for a brief period, research on psychometric approaches to repression-sensitization was dormant. Weinberger (Weinberger, Schwartz, and Davidson 1979) then developed an alternative measure, concentrated primarily on the distinction of the repressor pole, that has stimulated a new and burgeoning research interest. In the following sections, we will first review the evidence garnered from the Byrne scale, next discuss the methodological criticisms of the scale in greater detail, and, then review the evidence, particularly in the health area, obtained with the Weinberger measure (see also Weinberger, in this volume).

The parallels between the repression dimension, as measured on the Byrne scale, and the anaclitic configuration or hysterical style are pointed up by abundant research findings. Repressors consistently present an overly positive report of their inner processes. Repression, relative to sensitization, has been associated with a positive self-description and less reported self/ideal self discrepancy (Byrne, Barry, and Nelson 1963; Shavit and Shouval 1977), less reported anxiety (Scarpetti 1973; Beutler et al. 1977; Slough, Klenknecht, and Thorndike 1984; Schmitt and Kurdek 1984), less reported conflict (Tempone and Lamb 1967) or illness (Feder 1967), less reported vulnerability to disease (Dziokonski and Weber 1977), and fewer reports of horrible, sexual, or aggressive dreams (Rofe, Lewin, and Padeh 1977). In a sample of pregnant women, repressors reported less anxiety (Rofe and Lewin 1982), pain, and fear concerning labor and delivery (Rofe, Lewin, and Padeh 1981). Despite this generally positive self-presentation, repressors consistently exhibit the highest levels of physiological arousal in response to experimentally manipulated stress (Scarpetti 1973; Hill and Gardner 1976; Shipley et al. 1978).

There are two possible explanations for this characteristic discrepancy, both consistent with the anaclitic style. One explanation is that repressors, like hysterics, have very little awareness of their inner processes. White and Wilkins (1973), for example, found that, when given bogus feedback suggesting high physiological arousal during a perceptual recognition task for Thematic Apperception (TAT) slides, repressors exhibited higher response thresholds. The sensitizer style, which we will discuss shortly, was associated with lower response thresholds. It appears that subjects had assumed that the arousal feedback that they were given was accurately related to their subjective responses to the TAT and that they had unknowingly raised or lowered their perceptual responsivity thresholds in accordance with some type of schematicized process. In other words, repressors appear to respond to the bogus high-arousal feedback with the activation of a perceptual avoidance schema and, as hysterics are presumed to do, store less information about the environment. The possibility of such a schema has been discussed elsewhere (e.g., Hamilton 1983; Schwartz 1983; Singer 1984a; Kihlstrom 1984) and suggests a circular system in which the paucity of information taken in results in simplified perceptions of the self and the external world, which in turn leads to the failure to develop complex representations of the self and the external world in memory and in response to questionnaires or projective tests. A simple representational set then continues the circular system by disposing the individual to further simplified perceptions.

Epstein and Fenz (1967) obtained similar findings. They also used a perceptual recognition task and found that repressors took longer to perceive emotional words and also exhibited less arousal for these words. Again, this finding suggests that the presentation of an emotional word to a repressor results in the activation of an avoidance schema. The longer response latency would serve the function of lessening the threat of emotional engagement and, thus, result in lessened arousal. Epstein and Fenz also found that repressors had longer response times for associations to emotional words, but in this case displayed greater physiological arousal. By the same explanation, a perceptual avoidance schema may have been activated that again slowed response latency for emotional stimuli but, owing to the unavoidably greater processing requirement of the association task, was ineffective in reducing physiological arousal. Extensive data from studies with the Rorschach inkblots suggest that individuals who otherwise display hysterical or repressive-like characteristics tend to respond to inkblots by reacting to the most obvious forms or to color rather than introducing more original elements or perceiving humans in action (M responses), a sign of imaginative richness (Singer and Brown 1977). An extensive series of studies by Levine and Spivak (1964) developed a Rorschach Index of Repressive Style based on poverty of associations, use of stereotyped phrasing, lack of human movement responses, and choice of percepts based only on the most "popular" or clearly representational forms. Repressive respondents showed more links to hysterical symptomatology, psychosomatic illness, and behavior patterns consistent with the clinical descriptions of consistent use of repressive defenses.

Despite its theoretical consistency and appeal, the evidence for perceptual blockage and lack of subjective awareness in the repressor style must be considered with caution. There are obvious methodological concerns within this paradigm. The notion of perceptual defense in general has caused great controversy and is yet unresolved (Erdelyi and Goldberg 1979; Erdelyi 1985). Specifically, it is not altogether clear whether the studies mentioned above are not merely evidence for report and response patterns that mimic specific subjective states. Further, related evidence of a differential perceptual reactivity in repression-sensitization has been inconclusive. For example, Byrne's repression—sensitization has not been found to interact with eye movements (Woods 1977) or field articulation (Ihilevich et al. 1977). This latter finding is puzzling in the light of the Lewis's (1971) and Witkin's (1965) conclusions based on the field-articulation cognitive style measures but may be accounted for by inadequacies in the use of the Byrne scale as a measure of repression-sensitization (see below). On the other hand, McGrath and Cohen (1980) found that, when repressors attempted unsolvable and presumably stressful anagrams prior to sleep, they had shorter REM onset latencies and intervals than sensitizers. Shorter REM onset latencies and shorter intervals between REM periods are generally assumed to reveal a greater need to process day residues (Fiss and Ellman 1973; Fiss 1979). This would suggest a daytime processing overload in relation, perhaps, to the difficulties involved in assimilating complex material to simple schematic representations. This finding is also important because it links the repressive style to depression, a disorder that has also been associated with short REM onset latencies (Hartmann 1973, 1981).

An alternative but consistent explanation for the dissociation between repressor's reports of subjective processes and the actual physiological measurement of these processes is that repressors are overly concerned with the manner in which they are perceived by others; that is, they have a defensive need for positive self-presentation and impression management. They seem to perceive the external world as peopled by powerful, unpredictable, and unreliable others. Spring and Khanna (1982), for example, found that repressors attributed control of their destinies to powerful others and to chance. Ambivalence in the perception of others is suggested by findings that repression correlates with high levels of dispositional jealousy (Bringle and Williams 1979) and with unwillingness to voice favorable attitudes toward political enemies (Rofe and Weller 1981) or criticism of an interview process (Davis and Sloan 1974). Repressors tend to be less willing to disclose personal information and viewpoints (Carroll 1972; Davis and Sloan 1974; Miller and Nuessle 1978) or to report perceptions of hostility on the TAT (O'Gorman and Stair 1977).

Graziano, Brothen, and Berscheid (1980) provided evidence that clearly associates an ambivalent and conflictual interpersonal response with the repressor style. They found that repressors rated a fictitious negative evaluator less favorably than other subjects. However, when they thought that they would be required to meet with the evaluator at a future date for further evaluation, they rated the fictitious negative evaluator more positively than did other subjects. Similarly, Varca and Levy (1984) found that repressors reported greater interest and enjoyment in a test situation and accepted greater responsibility for their performance on the test when performance feedback was given for the group as a whole instead of individually.

This evidence is consistent with the type of difficulties in interpersonal relatedness that has been postulated to underlie hysteria and, in general, the anaclitic type of psychopathologies. The most logical explanation for the observed characteristics of the repressor style may be a combination of the two factor discussed above. In other words, the repressor style may be characterized by dependent and ambivalent interpersonal relations and by a lack of subjective awareness related to simple representations of self and other. Support for the interaction of both these factors comes from evidence that links the repressor style with low levels of cognitive complexity (Starbird and Biller 1976) and with poor ability to draw implications and inferences from cartoon portrayals of social interactions (Matney and McManis 1977). The investigation of the potential contribution of each factor to the repression style is currently underway in our laboratory.

Additional evidence concerning the effects of repression-sensitization on the forgetting and recovery of hypnotic events also suggests the importance of both impression-management and defense components. Kunzedorf and Benoit (1985–1986) recorded subjects' reports of posthypnotic forgetting and recovery as they occurred spontaneously and, alternatively, as they occurred in response to posthypnotic suggestions. They found that repressors spontaneously forgot more after hypnosis and spontaneously recovered more through rehypnosis but recovered fewer hypnotic events following the posthypnotic suggestion to do so than did sensitizers. Kunzendorf and Benoit conclude that the posthypnotic suggestions introduce "social demand characteristics" while the spontaneous tasks seemed to be more "pure" or "true" forms of hypnosis. When viewed in the context of such an interpretation, their findings are consistent with the evidence reviewed thus far and suggest that the spontaneous forgetting exhibited by repressors reflects a lack of subjective awareness or field dependence, and that their greater recovery during rehypnosis occurs because of a compensatory amelioration of the self-awareness deficit. Similarly, Kunzendorf (1985–1986) found that repressors reported less vivid waking imagery than sensitizers but also that their imagery rose in vividness to the level of sensitizers when the repressors were hypnotized. The vividness of sensitizers' imagery was not affected by hypnosis. In addition to the self-awareness deficit, Kunzendorf and Benoit's (1985–1986) findings also reflect the overly positive self-presentation and difficulties with relatedness component in the lesser response exhibited by repressors to the demand characteristics of the posthypnotic recovery suggestion.

Conversely, the sensitizer style, as measured on the Byrne scale, closely parallels the obsessional style and the introjective personality configuration, which Blatt described as focusing on primary concerns of "self-control, self-worth, and identity" (Blatt and Shichman 1983, 203). Consistent with the preoccupation with self-worth, and in contrast to the positive self-presentation of the repressor, the sensitizer style is associated with an overly confessional self-report. In the same studies cited above for positive self-report in repressors, sensitizers reported greater self/ideal self discrepancy, anxiety, conflict, illness, vulnerability to disease, disturbing dreams, and fears, yet they did not exhibit the high levels of arousal associated with the repressor style.

Zanna and Aziza (1976) examined repression-sensitization in terms of the resolution of cognitive dissonance. They followed up on an earlier study by Zanna (1975), who demonstrated a normal tendency in subjects to change their opinions on a controversial issue to a contrary opinion if, when instructed to write an essay in support of the contrary opinion, they were allowed to choose participation and were allowed to sit quietly following the essay task. Zanna and Aziza (experiment 2) found that sensitizers demonstrated the least attitude change in a condition that forced attention to the essay task and the most attitude change in a distraction condition. They concluded, consistently with the patterns we have outlined thus far, that the sensitizer style is characterized by an obsessional "rumination." Their findings concerning repressors, also consistent, showed the opposite pattern, that is, least attitude change in the distraction condition and the most in the forced-attention condition.

Another characteristic of the obsessional style and the anaclitic configuration that may also characterize the sensitizer style is the presence of an extremely punitive internal figure, the harsh superego. Recall Varca and Levy's (1984) findings discussed earlier in terms of the repressor style. Whereas repressors presumably preferred group feedback because it minimized public evaluation and the influence of their perceptions of interpersonal unreliability, sensitizers preferred individual written feedback, perhaps because it allowed self-evaluation but also was of a benign enough nature as to minimize the activation of a harsh internal judgment.

Repressor Personality Style as a Combination of Low Self-reported Anxiety and Defensiveness

The evidence discussed thus far was garnered from studies using the Byrne Repression-Sensitization Scale (Byrne, Barry, and Nelson 1963). Yet this scale has been criticized for its high correlation with other measures, most notably reported anxiety (Sullivan and Roberts 1969; Slough, Klenknecht, and Thorndike 1984). Even if the measures do not overlap perfectly, they may be measuring a common variable (Lazarus et al. 1985). Repressors tend to provide low self-reports of anxiety while exhibiting high levels of physiological arousal. Yet subjects who actually experience low levels of physiological arousal also report low anxiety and are indistinguishable from repressors on the Byrne scale. Weinberger, Schwartz, and Davidson (1979), as a solution to this problem, used a combination of measures: the Taylor Manifest Anxiety Scale (the Bendig short form) and the Marlowe-Crowne Social Desirability Scale. The latter is considered a measure of defensiveness (Crowne and Marlowe 1964; Weinberger, in this volume). Repressors on this combined measure are those subjects who report low anxiety while scoring high on defensiveness. True low-anxious subjects, then, are those who report low anxiety yet also score low on defensiveness. Finally, high-anxious subjects are those who report high anxiety and score low on defensiveness. High-anxious subjects may be considered sensitizers.

Since the development of the new repressor style measure is presented in detail by Weinberger (in this volume), we shall focus primarily on some of the research findings bearing on this measure that have emerged in very recent experimental studies. Then we will examine the use of variants of this measure in the area of physical health.

A particular concern that can be raised with reference to identifying a repressor personality style by a combination of low-anxiety scale and high Marlowe-Crowne scores is whether repressors are essentially impression managers if not outright liars. That issue was never fully resolved in the earlier empirical literature using the Byrne measures. From the standpoint of a systematic theory of avoidant defense mechanisms, it is useful to establish the extent to which repressors may actually respond in relatively automatized fashion (an overlearned script reaction) by avoiding potentially negative affective situations, potentially unpleasant implications of a social situation, or even personal lines of thought that might evoke conflictual or self-esteem-threatening content. One line of investigation involves experiments from which evidence of conscious impression management can be adduced or through which we can observe behavioral consequences of a repressor style in circumstances in which a conscious "putting one's best foot forward" is irrelevant to the processes measured.

The data produced by recent studies using the combined anxiety and defensiveness measures provides strong support for a relatively automatized avoidant processing pattern. Consistent with the earlier findings, repressors reported low anxiety while exhibiting high levels of physiological arousal (Weinberger, Schwartz, and Davidson 1979; Gudjonsson 1981; Asendorpf and Scherer 1983; Davis and Schwartz 1986). In addition, Weinberger, Schwartz, and Davidson (1979) investigated performance in a phrase association task using neutral and emotionally charged phrases and found repressors to have slower response times, higher levels of content avoidance, and higher levels of verbal disturbance than other participants. In a similar study, Tublin and Weinberger (1987) collected reports of ongoing thought as participants listened to either neutral or stressful audio tapes. Content analysis showed repressors to rely more heavily on distancing procedures, such as focusing on the actors in the tape or the actual quality of the tape, and distraction procedures, such as focusing on a positive image.

Bonanno et al. (1988) investigated avoidant processing directly using a dichotic-listening paradigm. Repressors and nonrepressors were required to repeat aloud any words they heard in a designated ear, the shadowed channel, and deliberately to ignore any words in the other ear, the nonshadowed channel. In this paradigm, the number of errors in shadowing the words in the assigned channel is considered an index of processing resources directed away from the shadowed channel and toward the unshadowed channel. While repressors did not show a specific response to the type of words in the non-shadowed channel, neutral or threatening words, they did make the fewest shadowing errors overall. Repressors also reported high levels of anxiety, frustration, and task difficulty and reported the greatest influence of task-related interfering thoughts on a postexperiment questionnaire. Together, these findings suggest that repressors responded to the presence of threatening stimuli by rigidly adhering to the instructions of the experiment and by minimizing attention to peripheral input. The rewards of such a strategy are good performance but, apparently, at the cost of a high level of subjective distress.

We suggested earlier that an avoidant processing style should be accompanied by a simplified representational system and by limited encoding and/or access to elaborate memories. Davis and Schwartz (1987) used the combined measure and found that repressors recalled fewer negative childhood experiences than other respondents. The presumed age level of recalled childhood events was also later for repressors. In another recent study (Loring et al., in preparation), when repressors were asked to search for distant negative memories, they showed an increase in alpha brain waves. Alpha waves are typically associated with cerebral inactivity. Thus, repressors may have avoided the task and not searched for negative memories or may have simply shown minimal activity because they had so few and poorly organized memories to search for in the first place.

The recent findings of Wexler et al. (1988) are interesting in this context. They employed a dichotic-listening paradigm in which participants were presented with word pairs differing in only the beginning consonant (e.g., "gill" and "dill"). Some of the word pairs included negatively toned words. Since both words were presented simultaneously, participants could consciously perceive or "hear" and report only one word from a pair. Wexler et al. found that low-anxious participants (low anxiety, low defensiveness) showed the greatest corrugator muscle activity (negative emotion) when they reported a negative word. Repressors, interestingly, showed the opposite pattern. They showed the greatest corrugator response when they were presented with a negative-neutral word pair and reported the neutral word. In other words, repressors showed greater signs of negative emotion when they were exposed to, but did not consciously perceive, negative stimuli. In addition, this finding was significant only when the negative word was presented to the left hemisphere. Davis and Schwartz (1986) also found laterality differences in repressors. They proposed that repressors can be characterized, not only by poor access to memory for affective experiences, but also by a "functional disconnection" between the sequential and the parallel processing functions of the brain hemispheres (Galin 1974). It may be that repressors process negative stimuli sequentially, rather than in parallel, and in a manner that is "split off" from channels leading to conscious awareness.

In contrast to the evidence for avoidant processing, no evidence has emerged, using the combination of anxiety and defensiveness scales, to support the impression-management hypothesis. This is particularly striking since several studies have specifically addressed the issue in their experimental design. The dichotic-listening studies mentioned above (Bonanno et al.

1988; Wexler et al. 1988) could rule out a reporting bias explanation with a reasonable degree of certainty because avoidant processing was measured directly as performance. Similarly, Davis (1987) replicated Davis and Schwartz's (1987) finding, that repressors recalled fewer negative childhood memories, by using a latency-to-retriever task in which participants merely signaled the recall of a distant memory by button press and were not required to report the memory.

Davis et al. (1988) specifically addressed the question of reporting biases by performing a signal detection analysis on the data from an incidental recognition task. Repressors exhibited the poorest adjusted recall ($\underline{d}'$) and also, consistently with previous studies, the highest confidence in their performance. No differences were found, however, between repressors and other participants in decision criterion (β). Bonanno (1988–89) also considered the potential influence of ongoing thought under two separate conditions. Content analyses showed that a condition designed to suggest a greater risk of public disclosure and evaluation resulted in thoughts that were more concerned about others, were more emotional, involved less fantasy, and were reported as more difficult to control than thoughts in a condition designed to suggest anonymity. Despite these effects, the thought reports of repressors were not influenced by the reporting conditions.

While the high-anxious respondents (high anxiety, low defensiveness) can be considered to parallel the sensitizer style, most of the studies employing the anxiety and defensiveness measures have focused primarily on the repressive respondents. In contrast to the repressors, the high-anxious group in Bonnano's (1988–89) study were influenced by the threatening disclosure condition, producing thoughts that were more emotional and difficult to control. This finding is consistent with the evidence from the Byrne scale suggesting that sensitizers may be overly disclosive or confessional in their self-reports. The high-anxious participants in the Weinberger, Schwartz, and Davidson (1979) study, also in contrast to the repressors, did not show evidence of content avoidance or verbal disturbance but also exhibited intermediate levels of physiological arousal that were greater than the low-anxious respondents and less than repressors. The high-anxious respondents in this study also exhibited a decrease in physiological arousal over trials, suggesting the struggle with impulse control associated with obsessionalism and the introjective style. On the other hand, the high-anxious respondents in the dichotic-listening study of Bonanno et al. (1988) did not show performance patterns in the opposite direction of repressors (i.e., vigilance to threatening peripheral input), as these investigators predicted. Rather, the vigilant pattern was exhibited by an additional group of participants, the defensive high-anxious group (high anxiety, high defensiveness). Even less is known about these individuals, however, because they are relatively rare in normal populations.

To summarize, considerable research data collected using the Byrne

Repression-Sensitization Scale indicated a personality continuum that clearly parallels the hysteric-obsessive continuum in psychopathology that we outlined in the earlier sections of the chapter. This evidence suggested a repressive style, characterized by a superficial or avoidant style of information processing, limited self-awareness, and, possibly, an excessive concern with positive self-presentation. Although less attention was paid to the sensitizer style, these individuals appeared to contrast repressors by showing a vigilant or obsessive style of information processing and an overly disclosive pattern of self-presentation. Following a brief loss of interest by researchers, investigation of repression-sensitization was revived by Weinberger, Schwartz, and Davidson's (1979) development of a more exact measurement of repressive individuals. Recent empirical work with the new measure has focused primarily on the repressor group. To further clarify the apparent contradiction that repressors avoid threatening information and show limited self-awareness, on the one hand, and present themselves in an overly favorable manner, on the other, many of these studies employed direct performance measures or specifically addressed the question of reporting biases. Virtually no evidence was produced to suggest that repressors consciously bias their self-reports. Compelling evidence has emerged, however, that repressors employ an avoidant and superficial style of information processing. Further, some of this evidence suggests that, as a consequence, repressors show deficits in their abilities to store and retrieve information in memory and exhibit an unusually high level of physiological arousal in response to threatening or stressful situations. We will now examine the possible negative consequences of such an avoidant processing style by turning to empirical studies that investigate more precisely the links between personality and the consequences for physical health.

Repression-Sensitization and Physiological Health

The repression-sensitization character styles have taken on added significance in light of recent associations with disease proneness. The repressor personality style, in particular, has been frequently linked to the development and course of cancer. Sensitization has been associated with cardiovascular disease, but the evidence there is not as clear.

There are seemingly intractable problems with empirical attempts to associate specific psychological dispositions with disease course. Two confounding factors related to disease course, and partially independent of character style, are most notable: the psychological changes that occur in response to physiological changes brought about by disease and the psychological changes that result from the stressful experience of confronting the implications of suffering from a major illness (Fox 1978). The earliest attempts to examine psychological factors in disease course used a retrospective paradigm but fell prey to the confounding influence of the factors mentioned above. An alternative paradigm, prospective investigation, offered a solution to one of these factors, the psychological stress of contracting a major illness, by assessing the psychological characteristics of subjects who shared a biopsy diagnosis of potential cancer but had not yet received a conclusive diagnosis. In such studies (Greer 1979; Greer, Morris, and Pettingale 1979; Mastrovito et al. 1979; Wirsching et al. 1982), repression-like characteristics have proved to be a major predictor of a later conclusive diagnosis of cancer. The prospective paradigm, however, is still unable to account for the second confound, the possible psychological influence of the physiological changes brought about by the disease.

More reliable results have recently been obtained using longitudinal studies and premorbid prospective strategies, that is, the analyses of psychological records prior to any signs of physiological illness. Several studies of the latter type have demonstrated a link between repression-like characteristics and the eventual development of cancer (Grossarth-Maticek, Siegrist, and Vetter 1982; Grossarth-Maticek, Bastiaans, and Kanazir 1985). Of particular importance was a study by Dattore, Shontz, and Coyne (1980), who examined the premorbid Minnesota Multiphasic Personality Inventory (MMPI) scores of patients at a Veterans Administration hospital. The MMPI was routinely administered to all patients admitted to the hospital. Dattore, Shontz, and Coyne screened thousands of medical histories in order to obtain records with a clear absence of any significant medical or psychological diagnosis at least a year after the administration of the MMPI. The mean interval between MMPI administration and the first noted disease of any kind was three to five years. The patients who eventually developed cancer reported less depression and responded with significant scores as repressors on the Byrne scale. These patients also scored significantly higher on the Denial or Hysteria Scale, a measure indicating low insight and an anti-interoceptive attitude as well as a posture of moral virtuousness.

An important paper by Temoshok (1987) reviewed an extensive body of literature on psychosocial predictors of the occurrence and course of cancer (see also our discussion of Kneier and Temoshok below). She concluded that there was reasonable evidence for delineating a Type C or cancer prone personality characterized by a "stoic" adjustment (Greer, Morris, and Pettingale 1979) and by an "accepting, self-sacrificing" orientation in a person "who struggles to maintain a strong and happy facade" (Temoshok et al. 1985). Temoshok (1987) identified a seeming contradiction in the data on cancer; patients at risk for occurrence of poor outcomes also showed a helpless-hopeless orientation or evidence of depression, fatigue, and inertia (Herberman, Levy, and Maluish 1985).

In an effort to resolve the differences between indications of a repressor trait cluster, on the one hand, and evidence of self-reported feelings of depression or helplessness, Temoshok proposed a distinction between self-reported moods and attitudes and physiological evidence of stress and tension, the distinction observed also by Weinberger, Schwartz, and Davidson (1979; see Weinberger in this volume) in identifying the repressor personality. She proposed also that the Type C or repressor was characterized by a struggle to maintain a facade of adjustment in the light of an underlying experience of distress and hopelessness or helplessness. Such a facade might give way at times, and, depending on when patients were psychologically examined, they might show either a repressor style or a helpless-hopeless self-report pattern. Indeed, in one study (Temoshok and Heller 1984), it was the defensive high-anxious responders (using the Weinberger, Schwartz, and Davidson 1979 scoring), the group that might be termed the "failed would-be repressors," who showed significantly thicker tumors.

Temoshok has speculated that the Type C coping style may develop out of a genetic or early socially learned disposition to suppress negative emotion, to abrogate important needs in the interests of appearing cooperative, unassuming, appeasing, and accepting. Such behavior can be adaptive and "win friends" but, she suggests, often at the cost of a conscious suppression of physical needs ("I won't bother Mommy by telling her I'm hungry"). Such a habitual suppression may, by repetition, become automatic and unconscious and may also lead to thinking or saying only "good things" out of a chronic but repressed sense of helplessness or hopelessness.

While the data on a Type C coping or personality style may not be sufficiently developed, there seems considerable value in regarding the cluster of traits described by Temoshok as forming an important research link to the repressor style we have so far been emphasizing. We next turn to another prognostic study of cancer outcome, unusually carefully executed in terms of psychological measurement and matching of patients, and observe how repressor measures, helplessness-hopelessness, and personal daydreaming patterns interact in prediction of outcome.

Jensen (1987) has recently demonstrated a strong association between repression and cancer using a longitudinal strategy. He carefully controlled for several classes of variables, including those suspected of influencing the development of cancer (e.g., age and personal and familial medical histories), the initial diagnosis and treatment (e.g., cancer site, weight), and disease course prior to testing (e.g., length of remission period following treatment), and then statistically accounted for the influence of these variables on the progress of disease. Jensen studied three groups of women, a nondiseased control and two groups with diagnosed malignant breast cancer. One cancer group had been in remission for some time, while the other group bore a much more recent diagnosis and was still under active treatment. There were significantly more repressors as measured by low anxiety and high defensiveness among the two groups of cancer patients, one currently in remission and one currently grossly ill. These findings suggest that the repressor style reflected not only current disease state but possibly also proneness to development of the disease since it characterized a sizable number in the remitted group as well.

Jensen also collected data at a follow-up period that on the average exceeded six hundred days. Subjects high in repression from both cancer groups had a shorter remission period following initial treatment and a greater mortality rate at follow-up. A single follow-up variable, clinical and vital status (FS), was computed, and, as expected, a high score suggestive of a poor outcome was most common for repressors. Multiple regression analysis of all psychological, physiological, and control variables indicated that FS was significantly predicted by the repressor style, the use of comforting, future-oriented daydreaming, and two physiological variables: initial hematocrit and alkaline phosphate levels. Analysis of the partial correlations indicated that the repressor style influenced FS independently of all other factors. Interestingly, repression and the use of comforting daydreaming each predicted a worse outcome but were statistically independent. Further analysis revealed that high levels of comforting daydreaming in nonrepressors resulted in a significantly worse outcome and that repressors, who in general had the worse outcome, were not differentiated by daydreaming style.

Jensen's findings are understandable in terms of the lack of subjective awareness that we had earlier associated with the repression style. Presumably comforting, future-oriented daydreaming directs attention away from subjective awareness of the dangers of one's disease. Since a lack of subjective awareness is in some way associated with both variables, it may be presumed to play a role in poor outcome. The fact that outcome status for repressors was not affected by daydreaming is logical if a lack of subjective awareness is a stable style associated with repression. Similarly, since a lack of subjective awareness is not a general characteristic of nonrepressors, the utilization of comforting daydreaming as a temporary strategy, a form of escape, perhaps, results in a poor outcome. This is indeed an important finding in terms of its implications for treatment interventions with cancer patients. What may be viewed by some therapists as helpful pleasant imagery in the form of a distraction from the process of confronting and actively seeking to cope with one's disease might actually have harmful effects.

Jensen's findings are important because they reflect a major attempt to embrace the alternative explanations for psychological dispositions in disease proneness, that is, the influence of physiological changes and stress factors. Although complete negation of these factors would be nearly impossible, Jensen demonstrates at lease some gross control over genetic, hormonal, and treatment factors. Although it is still possible that other factors not known to be crucial in cancer development may have influenced psychological responding, the two cancer groups used in this study, advanced and recurrence free, did not differ from each other or the control group on any of the psychological measures other than repression.

A longitudinal study by Visintainer and Casey (1984) provides some indications of how denial of problems in self-presentation (another component typical of the repressive style) may be linked not only to a poor course for malignant disease but also to an underlying immune system process. Studying thirty eight patients with malignant melanoma followed over nine months, they found that those patients who showed a denial pattern in their questionnaire responses (SCL-90 revised) also showed less anxiety, anger, or symptoms at the time of diagnosis. After nine months, however, these patients had clinically worsened, were more upset, and showed a lower level of "natural killer" (NK) cell activity in their immune essays. Thus, one might surmise that denial, however initially comforting, may inhibit the development of greater immune NK activity, a finding in keeping with animal studies that suggest that endorphin activity (presumably self-comforting) actually enhances tumor growth in animals (Shavit et al. 1984). By contrast, the patients who seemed initially overtly more distressed and hostile at the time of diagnosis were actually doing better nine months later and showed higher NK cell activity.

One cannot avoid the thought that, at least for malignant disease, the self-soothing or psychic pain-avoidant effects of shifting attention to extraneous activities or pleasant fantasies may be counterproductive and that the release of endorphin occasioned by such behavior might impede the development of NK activity. Additional support for this hypothesis comes from recent studies by Levy and her colleagues (Levy, Herberman, and Maluish 1985; Levy et al. 1987) that demonstrate the association of low levels of NK activity in breast cancer patients with greater tumor burden. Surprisingly, the interim administration of chemotherapy and/or radiotherapy did not significantly influence changes in NK levels at three-month follow-up. Regression analyses, however, revealed that from 30 to 50 percent of the variance in NK levels could be accounted for by psychological factors, such as fatigue/depression, lack of social support, and objective ratings of adjustment, that is, the "appearance" of a lack of distress. Goleman (1985) has elaborated on the special role of what he calls "vital lies" or avoidant mechanisms that reduce suffering in some circumstances and thus sustain life but that, in situations of certain cancers, might actually be inappropriate psychologically and physiologically (for additional recent data on this issue, see Levine et al. 1987).

Sensitization and Cardiovascular Disease

In keeping with the polar thrust of these styles, the sensitization style has sometimes been considered in terms of a predisposition to cardiovascular diseases. Grossarth-Maticek (Grossarth-Maticek, Siegrist, and Vetter 1982;

Grossarth-Maticek, Bastiaans, and Kanazir 1985) attempted to assess the long-term influence of personality on the development of disease. They undertook an extensive ten-year prospective study of 1,353 inhabitants of a small Yugoslavian town. The oldest disease-free individuals in selected houses and their spouses were interviewed. Responses were categorized along dimensions similar to the repression-sensitization styles. The development of cancer at ten-year follow-up was associated with a categorization of passive repression, long-lasting hopelessness, a lack of relevant positive emotion, ignoring illness, and rationality/antiemotionality. In short, their cancer-prone participants showed typical characteristics of the repressor style.

The development of cardiovascular disease, on the other hand, was associated with characteristics typical of the sensitizer style. These subjects showed behavior of the type that evokes a repressive response from others and might be described as aggressive or as likely to be perceived as interpersonally unreliable. The overt expression of anger, low levels of hopelessness, and low levels of the need for harmony and acquiescence were also apparent. Subjects developing cardiovascular disorders, in other words, show an approach to the environment that might be characterized as active, focused on the self, and socially provocative.

Kneier and Temoshok (1984) have provided more direct evidence for the bipolar quality of cancer and cardiovascular disorders in relation to repression-sensitization. They employed the Byrne scale and a repressive coping measure that they had developed. To score repressive coping, subjects were shown slides of stress-inducing statements, for example, "You deserve to be ill." Each slide was shown for five seconds and was then rated by subjects for the degree of distress they had experienced. Physiological measurements of arousal were also obtained. For each subject, the degree of distress reported and the amount of physiological arousal recorded was averaged. A repressive coping score was assigned when, for a specific slide, the subject's reported distress was lower than their average reported distress and when the subject's level of physiological arousal was above their average level of physiological arousal. Kneier and Temoshok (1984) found that cancer patients scored higher as repressors on both the Byrne scale and the repressive coping measure. Cardiovascular patients, in turn, had a more sensitized response on those measures and also reported more anxiety and more difficulty in adjusting to disease.

This is not the place to review the extensive literature attempting to establish links between personality patterns such as the presumed Type A and cardiovascular disease (cf. Wright 1988). What is relevant for our purposes is that the problem of coping with anger, hostility, and guilt, which is more characteristic of the obsessive neurotic or sensitizer, does show some ties to cardiovascular activity. Crits-Christoph (1984) sought to test whether it was the habitual suppression of anger (as measured by questionnaires) or its overt expression that was associated in normal individuals with hypertensive reactivity. He used overt anxiety or habitual suppression of anxiety as a control for the expressive versus suppressive dimension in more general affective responses. Crits-Christoph's data clearly indicated that both habitual expression of anger and persistent hostile, aggressive fantasies were most predictive of hypertensive responses; suppression of anger and suppression of overt anxiety were much less significant factors in hypertensive reaction. These data from the laboratory seem consistent with the longitudinal findings of Williams et al. (1980) that indicate that MMPI items indicative of attitudes of hostility and cynicism (crystallized in the Cook-Medley scales) are strong predictors of significant cardiovascular pathology by the forty to fifty decade of the life span. Wright (1988) has added a variable of experienced time urgency to these trait clusters and has shown that expressed anger and time urgency combined define a strong path toward cardiovascular disease.

Short-Term Denial versus Long-Term Repressive Style

The repressive style is best measured, as we have suggested, by evidence that there is no conscious report or awareness of anxiety or general distress even when the physiological measures of arousal taken from such respondents are higher than others. We have reviewed evidence linking this pattern to a proneness toward the development and recurrence of cancer. A recent paper, however, indicates that such a repressive pattern may also be linked to cardiovascular risk (King et al. 1985). These investigators studied ninety nine sedentary repressors by the Bendig Manifest Anxiety scale (low scores) and the Marlowe-Crowne Social Desirability Scale (high scores). Repressors showed significantly higher resting levels of systolic blood pressure, greater changes in blood pressure during mental arithmetic, and higher levels of cholesterol. Results were strongest for female repressors. The repressor measures were more predictive of variability in systolic blood pressure than measures of Type A, hostility or frustration.

In order to understand these data on repressors, we need to consider the evidence of how denial and repression occur over time. Work at the West Haven Veterans Administration Center directed by Levine (Levine et al. 1987) has employed a measure called denial of illness designed to assess specific reactions to an immediate illness. Levine et al.'s findings (similar to those of Levinson et al. 1984) lead them to propose that denial may be adaptive in the acute phase of cardiovascular disease, in effect reducing additional stress on the heart that may be occasioned by thoughts about death, leaving loved ones behind or uncared for, and so on. Once disease is stabilized, such continued denial (more like a habitual repressive style) may prove to be harmful.

Different types of information may be involved (or ignored) in the denial of illness and in the repressive style. Shaw et al. (1985) examined the effects of repression-sensitization and denial in terms of the efficacy of a cardiovascular education program. They used patients chosen as candidates for rehabilitation, controlled for age and intelligence, and measured pre- and postrehabilitation cardiac knowledge. Both denial and repression were related to less information gain, but in different areas of cardiac knowledge. Patients scoring high in denial gained less information concerning anatomy and physiology and may be engaging in the potentially healthy practice of denying the fact that physical damage had occurred. Repressors, on the other hand, gained less information concerning risk factors and, one might assume, suffer from the failure to acknowledge the type of life-style changes necessary for successful recovery. Yet the level of information gain was not related to six-month outcome. Interestingly, however, repressors with high risk-factor information gain had a greater incidence of complications and poorer psychomedical functioning. Thus, only those repressors who did learn about risk factors related to their disease exhibited a poor recovery.

A clue as to the process by which cardiovascular response and repressive style operates comes from studies by Bowen (1984) and Bowen and Schwartz (1985). They were able to show that defensive responders on the Marlowe-Crowne are also characterized by less differentiated cardiovascular response patterns when following imagery-related attempts to express different emotions. Subjects with relatively small change in pressure or with less variability as a function of different aroused emotions also gave simpler affective reports, reacting in the "global," "all-or-none" fashion that we have seen earlier as characteristic of hysterics, repressors, or field-dependent personality patterns.

The evidence for a simple relation between the sensitization style and cardiovascular disease is theoretically appealing since it fits the bipolar quality of our scheme neatly. The association of the repressor style with cardiovascular disease, however, suggests that the influence of personality may be more complex. Further research is needed to clarify the role of short-term denial of illness, of risk factors, of long-term repressive responses, of the complexity of expressed emotion, and of other personality factors that may contribute to the development or maintenance of cardiovascular disorders. Further, the evidence for the role of sensitization in cardiovascular disease is vulnerable to some of the same confounding factors that surfaced in the early studies of the repression style and cancer. The Grossarth-Maticek studies, for instance, were based on interview ratings. This practice is potentially problematic since the interviewers or raters are usually medically sophisticated and their ratings of subjects may be influenced by personal theories concerning physiological or psychological symptoms. Thus, the possibility that raters may actually and unknowingly predict disease on the basis of their personal theories cannot be ruled out. The Kneier and Temoshok study involved a patient population that had already developed diseases and was, thus, confounded by the possible psychological effects of disease-related stress or physiological changes occasioned by the illness. The Jensen cancer study illustrated a methodology that controlled for these factors by using a non-disease matched group for some comparisons, by comparing remitted with overtly ill patients, and by measuring several illness and treatment variables over time.

Alexithymia: A Concept in Search of Data

The term "alexithymia" was introduced into the psychiatric literature by Sifneos (1983) in the early 1970s and crystallized more formally at the Heidelberg Conference of the European Psychometric Research Society (Taylor 1984). It denotes a disturbance characterized by inadequacy in describing one's feelings or thoughts or in discriminating emotional states from bodily reactions. The alexithymic lacks a rich and varied imaginative life, self-presents as well adapted, and shows "pseudonormality" and a high degree of social conformity. Alexithymics are presumably especially prone to developing psychosomatic illnesses. Clearly, the description of alexithymics bears a close resemblance to the repressor or to a considerable body of earlier literature on individuals whose performance on projective tests like the Rorschach inkblots shows evidence of very limited imagination and who have been characterized as repressive or constricted (Singer and Brown 1977; Levine and Spivak 1964). Levine and Spivak, for example, reported that psychosomatic patients and hysterical neurotics showed significantly more evidence of repression on their Rorschach Index of Repressive Style.

Despite a considerable body of clinical reports and theoretical papers, including at least one recent effort (Martin 1985) to distinguish repressors from alexithymics (the latter presumably show less affective awareness), there is a paucity of satisfactory research data demonstrating the syndrome as unique and predictive (Lesser and Lesser 1984). An MMPI alexithymia scale developed by Kleiger and Kinsman (1980) yielded items that seem to hold together statistically in predicting another measure, the Beth-Israel score, but lacks conceptual clarity or face validity. Taylor (1984) found that these items, while correlating with measures of social conformity, did not correlate either with other measures of ability to express feelings verbally or with fantasizing capacity, presumably the two capstones of the construct. We are left wondering if, despite dozens of speculative articles, the concept has any independence or whether it may be reflecting a facet of the better-measured repressive style.

Conclusions: Personality Style, Psychological Health, and Physiological Health

In the preceding sections, we have seen that several theorists have observed a logical consistency between two types of psychopathological disorders and that, historically, this consistency has resulted in an increasingly more encompassing theoretical organization of these disorders along a single bipolar con-

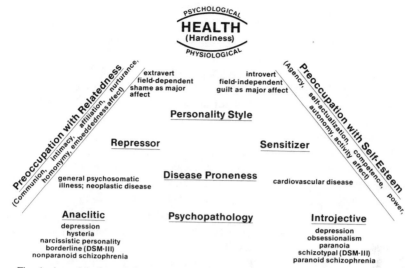

Fig. 1. A model of psychological and physiological health as a function of the balance of interpersonal relatedness and self esteem.

tinuum. We have also seen that various theoretical formulations of nonpathological character styles are generally consistent with this continuum. Particular attention was paid to the repression-sensitization styles, and we found that the empirical evidence concerning these styles formed a comparable pattern with the hypothesized relation between psychopathological disorders such as hysteria and obsessionalism. Finally, we saw that the repression-sensitization styles show at lease some association with proneness to disease, sensitization (or at least the overt expression of hostility) to cardiovascular disorders, and repression to cancer. Stronger evidence exists for the latter association.

Up to this point, we have not discussed psychological or, for that matter, physiological health. The relation of psychopathological styles to mental illness and the relation of character styles to disease proneness, however, suggests a hierarchical ordering of psychological and physiological health along a comparable continuum. This grand polar continuum might be termed anaclitic-introjective, after Blatt, or repression-sensitization. The most appropriate term, however, would be one based on the prominent characteristics of each pole. Thus, we will refer to the overall dimension as interpersonal relatedness versus self-esteem. Such a hierarchy would extend from the most extreme exaggerations of each polar style, the psychopathologies, at the bottom to equilibrium and the integration of the two styles at the top.

Nonpathological character styles, because of their association with disease, would lie somewhere in between (see fig. 1). In postulating such a hierarchy, we must assume fluidity; that is, an individual may be characterized by a certain location in the hierarchy but may also regress to a lower and more exaggerated station or improve to a more healthy state as a function of situational variability or changes over the life course. Further, such a hierarchy includes the inherent assumption that psychological and physiological health are characterized by the complex interplay between the need for communion or relatedness, on the one hand, and that for agency, power, or self-esteem, on the other. Since this interplay varies in normal development, with further distance from health being a more extreme and exaggerated emphasis on one horizontal side of the pole, the hierarchy takes on a triangular shape. This shape is portrayed in figure 1. In other words, the emphasis on relatedness in the repressor style and self-esteem in the sensitization style would be less fixed and less encompassing than the polar dichotomy between anaclitic and introjective styles of psychopathology. Further, developmentally more advanced and consolidated disorders within each configuration of psychopathology, such as depression or paranoia, would exhibit less fixed and less encompassing exaggerations of relatedness or self-esteem than developmentally less advanced and less consolidated disorders within the same configuration, such as paranoid schizophrenia or the more socially disorganized forms of schizophrenia.

The assumption that the ideal of psychological health rests on the interplay between the need for relatedness and the need for self-esteem is basic to this model. This assumption, however, is not uncommon to the literature. Rollo May (1984) reflects on this idea and describes the healthy person as one who can experience creativity and beauty, the fusion of inner vision and objective facts, "in their work and in their love." Similarly, Kohut (1971, 1984) described the psychological health as a "sectorial functional continuum from one pole of the self to the other" (Kohut 1984, 96). He elaborated on this polar continuum in an earlier work (1971, 9), defining "normalcy" as consisting of mature forms of admiration for others at one pole and positive self-esteem at the other.

The ideal of physiological health is a more complex and controversial matter. Although more readily observable in most cases, and perhaps easier to define, the manner in which physiological health is influenced by psychological states has only recently become the object of investigation. The existence of such an influence is, however, no longer doubted (see Monat and Lazarus 1985). The effects of character style on disease proneness has gained wide acceptance as a mediator between stress and illness (Holroyd and Lazarus 1982). The possibility that including physiological health in a bipolar scheme of psychological styles may be premature is countered by urgent need and the heuristic value of such a conceptualization in guiding further theoretical and empirical study. For example, the research of Kobasa and Maddi and their group on hardiness, a tendency for generally good health, supports the importance of the capacity for commitment, for cognitive restructuring of danger into challenge, and for personal flexibility. Hardiness is, in turn, suggestive of a blending of the agency-communion, autonomy-homonomy, or power-intimacy needs of the individual (Kobasa, Maddi and Kahn 1982). Jasnoski and Schwartz (1985) have proposed a definition of health as the "potential to heal." The assessment of this potential, they propose, would be based on the sytems analysis of the many synchronous layers of personality, physiology, and environment. The bipolar scheme outlined in this chapter provides a clear and parsimonious framework that is compatible with such a view.

Perhaps none of us can ever resolve the tension between our inherent struggle for individuality, for unique expression of our skills, for power and competence, on the one hand, and our basic desire to blend with another person, to lose ourselves in the warmth of family, friends, the comfort of religion, nationalistic or professional affiliation, or the excitement of life, on the other hand. Our review suggests that psychological and physical maladaptive behavior emerges as one moves too far toward one extreme at the sacrifice of the other needs. When the field-dependent extravert uses these stylistic trends to focus on mechanisms of repression and denial, on resolving issues of intimacy or dependency at the cost of self-esteem and individuality, the balance may be tipped toward psychopathology or physical illness.

References

Adler, A. 1979. *Superiority and social interest.* Edited by H. Ansbacher and R. Ansbacher. 3d ed. New York: Norton.

Angyal, A. 1965. *Neurosis and treatment: A holistic theory.* New York: Wiley.

Asendorpf, J. B., and K. R. Scherer. 1983. The discrepant repressor: Differentiation between loss anxiety, and repression of anxiety by autonomic-facial-verbal patterns of behavior. *Journal of Personality and Social Psychology* 45:1334–46.

Bakan, D. 1966. *The duality of human existence.* Chicago: Rand McNally.

Beutler, L. E., D. T. Johnson, K. Morris, and C. W. Neville, Jr. 1977. Effect of time-specific sets and patients' personality style on state and trait anxiety. *Psychological Reports* 40:1003–10.

Blatt, S. J. 1974. Levels of object representation in anaclitic and introjective depression. *Psychoanalytic Study of the Child* 24:107–57.

Blatt, S. J., and S. Shichman. 1983. Two primary configurations of psychopathology. *Psychoanalysis and Contemporary Thought* 6:187–254.

Bonanno, G. A. 1988–89. Sampling conscious thought: Influences of personality style and reporting conditons. *Imagination, Cognition, and Personality* 8:293–306.

Bonanno, G. A., J. L. Singer, P. J. Davis, and G. E. Schwartz. 1988. Repression-sensitization and the avoidance of threatening auditory stimuli. Department of Psychology, Yale University. Typescript.

Bowen, W. 1984. Individual differences in cardiovascular functioning, emotional blends and cognition: Rigid and flexible response patterns. Ph.D. diss., Yale University.

Bowen, W., and G. E. Schwartz. 1985. Self-regulated differentiated and undifferentiated cardiovascular responding: Relationship to emotion. Department of Psychology, Yale University. Typescript.

Broadbent, D. 1958. *Perception and communication.* London: Pergamon.

Bringle, R. G., and L. J. Williams. 1979. Parental-offspring similarity on jealousy and related personality dimensions. *Motivation and Emotion* 3:265–86.

Byrne, D., J. Barry, and D. Nelson. 1963. Relation of the revised repression-sensitization scale to measures of self-description. *Psychological Reports* 13:323–34.

Byrne, D. G., H. M. Whyte, and G. N. Lance. 1978–79. A typology of responses of illness in survivors of myocardial infarction. *International Journal of Psychiatry in Medicine* 9:135–45.

Carroll, D. 1972. Repression-sensitization and the verbal elaborations of experience. *Journal of Consulting and Clinical Psychology* 38:147.

Chodorow, N. 1971. Being and doing: A cross-cultural examination of the socialization of males and females. In *Women in sexist society,* ed. V. Gornick and B. K. Moran. New York: New American Library.

Crits-Christoph, P. 1984. The role of anger in high blood pressure. Ph.D. diss. Yale University.

Crowne, D. P. and D. Marlowe. 1964. *The approval motive.* New York: Wiley.

Dattore, P. J., F. C. Shontz, and L. Coyne. 1980. Premorbid personality differentiation of cancer and non-cancer groups: A test of the hypothesis of cancer proneness. *Journal of Clinical Psychology* 48:388–94.

Davis, J. D., and M. Sloan. 1974. The basis of interviewee matching of interviewer self-disclosure. *British Journal of Social and Clinical Psychology* 13:359–67.

Davis, P. J. 1987. Repression and the inaccessibility of emotional memories. *Journal of Personality and Social Psychology* 53:585–93.

Davis, P. J., and G. Schwartz. 1987. Repression and the inaccessibility of affective memories. *Journal of Personality and Social Psychology* 52:155–62.

———. 1986. Repression and the inaccessibility of emotional memories: Relationship of skin temperature and muscle activity of the face. Department of Psychology, Yale University. Typescript.

Davis, P. J., J. L. Singer, G. A. Bonanno, and G. E. Schwartz. 1988. Repression and response bias during an affective memory recogniton task: A signal detection analysis. *Australian Journal of Psychology* 40:147–57.

Dziokonski, W., and S. J. Weber. 1977. Repression-sensitization, perceived vulnerability, and the fear appeal communication. *Journal of Social Psychology* 102:105–12.

Epstein, S., and W. Fenz. 1967. The detection of areas of emotional stress through variations in perceptual threshold and physiological arousal. *Journal of Experimental Research in Personality* 2:191–99.

Erdelyi, M. H. 1985. *Psychoanalysis: Freud's cognitive psychology.* New York: Freeman.

Erdelyi, M. H., and B. Goldberg. 1979. "Let's not sweep repression under the rug": Toward a cognitive psychology of repression. In *Functional disorders of memory,* ed. J. F. Kihlstrom and F. J. Evans. Hillsdale, N.J.: Erlbaum.

Eysenck, H. 1960. *The structure of human personality.* Rev. ed. London: Methuen.

Feder, C. Z. 1967. Relationship of repression-sensitization to adjustment status, social desirability, and acquiescence response set. *Journal of Consulting Psychology* 31:401–6.

Fiss, H. 1979. Current dream research: A psychobiological perspective. In *Handbook of dreams*, ed. B. J. Wolman. New York: Van Nostrad Reinhold.

Fiss. H., and S. J. Ellman. 1973. REM sleep interruption: Experimental shortening of REM period duration. *Psychophysiology* 10:510–16.

Fox, B. 1978. Premorbid psychological factors as related to cancer incidence. *Journal of Behavioral Medicine* 1:45–133.

Franz, C. E., and K. M. White. 1985. Individuation and attachment in personality development: Extending Erikson's theory. *Journal of Personality* 53:224–56.

Freud, S. [1892–93] 1966. A case of successful treatment by hypnotism: With some remarks on the origin of hysterical symptoms through "counter-will." In *The complete psychological works of Sigmund Freud*, ed. J. Strachey, vol. 1. London: Hogarth.

———. [1894] 1962. The neuro-psychoses of defence. In *The complete psychological works of Sigmund Freud*, ed. J. Strachey, vol. 3. London: Hogarth.

———. [1908] 1959. Character and analerotism. In *The complete psychological works of Sigmund Freud*, ed. J. Strachey, vol. 9. London: Hogarth.

———. [1915] 1957. Repression. In *The complete psychological works of Sigmund Freud*, ed. J. Strachey, vol. 14. London: Hogarth.

———. [1926] 1959. Inhibitions, symptoms and anxiety. In *The complete psychological works of Sigmund Freud*, ed. J. Strachey, vol. 20. London: Hogarth.

Galin, D. 1974. Implications for psychiatry of left and right cerebral specialization. *Archives of General Psychiatry* 31:572–83.

Geller, J. D. 1984. Moods, feelings, and the processing of affect information. In *Emotions in health and illness: Applications to clinical practice*, ed. C. VanDyke, L. Temoshok, and L. S. Zegans. New York: Grune & Stratton.

Golding, J. M., and J. L. Singer. 1983. Patterns of inner experience: Daydreaming style, depressive moods, and sex roles. *Journal of Personality and Social Psychology* 45:663–75.

Goleman, D. 1985. *Vital lies, simple truths*. New York: Simon & Schuster.

Graziano, W. G., T. Brothen, and E. Berscheid. 1980. Attention, attraction, and individual differences in reaction to criticism. *Journal of Personality and Social Psychology* 38:193–202.

Greer, S. 1979. Psychological attributes of women with breast cancer. *Cancer Detection and Prevention* 2:289–94.

Greer, S., T. Morris, and K. W. Pettingale. 1979. Psychological response to breast cancer: Effect on outcome. *Lancet* 2:785–87.

Grossarth-Maticek, R. 1980. Psychological predictors of cancer and internal diseases: An overview. *Psychotherapy and Psychosomatics* 33:122–28.

Grossarth-Maticek, R., J. Bastiaans, and D. T. Kanazir. 1985. Psychosocial factors as strong predictors of mortality from cancer, ischaemic heart disease and stroke: The Yugoslav prospective study. *Journal of Psychosomatic Research* 29:167–76.

Grossarth-Maticek, R., T. Siegrist, and H. Vetter. 1982. Interpersonal repression as a predictor of cancer. *Social Science in Medicine* 16:493–98.

Gudjonsson, G. H. 1981. Self-reported emotional disturbance and its relation to electrodermal reactivity, defensiveness, and tract anxiety. *Personality and Individual Differences* 2:47–52.

Guilford, J. P. 1959. *Personality*. New York: McGraw-Hill.

Haan, N. 1985. Conceptualizations of ego: Processes, functions, regulations. In *Stress and coping: An anthology*, ed. A. Monat and R. S. Lazarus. New York: Columbia.

Hamilton, V. 1983. Information-processing aspects of denial: Some tentative formulations. In *The denial of stress*, ed. S. Brenitz. New York: International Universities Press.

Hartmann, E. 1973. *The functions of sleep*. New Haven, Conn.: Yale University Press.

———. 1981. The functions of sleep and memory processing. In *Sleep, dreams, and memory*, ed. W. Fishbein. New York: SP Medical and Scientific.

Hill, D., and G. Gardner. 1976. Repression-sensitization and cardiac responses to threat. *Australian Journal of Psychology* 28:149–54.

Holroyd, K. A., and R. S. Lazarus. 1982. Stress, coping and somatic adaption. In *Handbook of stress: Theoretical and clinical aspects*, ed. L. Goldberg and S. Breznitz. New York: Free Press/Macmillan.

Horowitz, M. 1977. *Hysterical personality*. New York: Aronson.

Ihilevich, D., and G. D. Gleser. 1971. Relationship of defense mechanisms to field dependence-independence. *Journal of Abnormal Psychology* 77:296–302.

Jasnoski, M. L., and G. E. Schwartz. 1985. A synchronous systems model for health. *American Behavioral Scientist* 28:468–85.

Jensen, M. R. 1987. Psychobiological factors predicting the course of breast cancer. *Journal of Personality* 55:317–42.

Jung, C. G. 1971. *Psychological types*. In *Collected works*, vol 6. New York: Pantheon.

Kihlstrom, J. F. 1984. Conscious, subconscious, unconscious: A cognitive perspective. In *The unconscoius reconsidered*, ed. K. S. Bowers and D. Meichenbaum. New York: Wiley.

King, A., C. Albright, C. B. Taylor, W. Hadkell, and R. DeBusk. The repressive coping style: A predictor of cardiovascular reactivity and risk. Paper presented at the meeting of the Society for Behavioral Medicine, San Francisco.

Kleiger, J. H., and R. A. Kinsman. 1980. The development of an MMPI alexithymia scale. *Psychotherapy and Psychosomatics* 34:17–24.

Klein, G. S. 1970. *Perception, motives, and personality*. New York: Knopf.

Kneier, A. W., and L. Temoshok. 1984. Repressive coping reactions in patients with malignant melanoma as compared to cardiovascular disease patients. *Journal of Psychosomatic Research* 28:368–78.

Kobasa, S. C., S. R. Maddi, and S. Kahn. 1982. Hardiness and health: A prospective study. *Journal of Personality and Social Psychology* 42:168–77.

Kohut, H. 1971. *The analysis of the self*. New York: International Universities Press.

———. 1984. *How does analysis cure*. Edited by A. Goldberg. New York: International Universities Press.

Kunzendorf, R. G. 1985–86. Repression as the monitoring and censoring of images: An empirical study. *Imagination, Cognition, and Personality* 5:303–10.

Kunzendorf, R. G., and M. Benoit. 1985–86. Spontaneous posthypnotic amnesia and spontaneous rehypnotic recovery in repressors. *Imagination, Cognition, and Personality* 5:303–10.

Lazarus, R. S., A. Delongis, S. Fokman, and R. Gruen. 1985. Stress and adaptational outcomes: The problem of confounded measures. *American Psychologist* 40: 770–79.

Lesser, I. M., and B. Z. Lesser. 1984. Alexithymia: Examining the development of a psychological concept. *American Journal of Psychiatry* 140: 1305–8.

Levine, J., and G. Spivak. 1964. *The Rorschach index of repressive style.* New York: Thomas.

Levine, J., S. Warrenburg, R. Kerns, G. Schwartz, R. Delaney, A. Fontana, A. Gradman, S. Smith, S. Allen, and R. Cascione. 1987. The relation of denial to the course of recovery in coronary heart disease. *Psychosomatic Medicine* 49:109–17.

Levinson, G., R. Kay, J. Monteferrante, and M. Herman. 1984. Denial predicts favorable outcome in unstable angina pectoris. *Psychosomatic Medicine* 46: 25–32.

Levy, S., R. Herberman, M. Lippman, and T. d'Angelo. 1987. Correlation of stress factors with sustained depression of natural killer cell activity and predicted prognosis in patients with breast cancer. *Journal of Clinical Oncology* 5:348–53.

Levy, S., R. Herberman, and A. Maluish. 1985. Prognostic risk assessment in primary breast cancer by behavioral and immunological parameters. *Health Psychology* 4:99–113.

Lewis, H. B. 1971. *Shame and guilt in neurosis.* New York: International Universities Press.

———. 1976. *Psychic war in men and women.* New York: International Universities Press.

———. 1985. Depression vs. paranoia: Why are there sex differences in mental illness? *Journal of Personality* 53:150–78.

Lorig, T. S., J. L. Singer, G. A. Bonanno, and G. E. Schwartz. In preparation. Personality style and EEG during retrieval of affective memories. Department of Psychology, Yale University. Typescript.

McAdams, D. P. 1985. *Power, intimacy and the life story.* Homewood, Ill.: Densey.

McAdams, D. P., and C. A. Constantian. Intimacy and affiliation daily living: An experience sampling analysis. *Journal of Personality and Social Psychology* 45:851–61.

McGrath, M. J., and D. Cohen. REM drive and function: A study of the interactive effects of personality and presleep condition. *Journal of Abnormal Psychology* 89:737–43.

Maddi, S. 1980. *Personality theories: A comparative analysis.* 4th ed. Homewood, Ill.: Densey.

Martin, J. B. 1985. The stress-alexithymia hypothesis: Theoretical and empirical considerations. *Psychotherapy and Psychosomatics* 43: 169–76.

Mastrovito, R. C., K. S. DeGuire, J. Clarkin, T. Thaler, J. T. Lewis, and E. Cooper. 1979. Personality characteristics of women with gynecological cancer. *Cancer Detection and Prevention* 2:281–87.

Matney, D. C., and D. L. McManis. 1977. Repression-sensitization status and social intelligence characteristics. *Psychological Reports* 41: 873–38.

May, R. 1985. *My quest for beauty.* Dallas, Tex.: Saybrook.

Miller, G. A., and W. Neussle. 1978. Characteristics of the emotional responsiveness of sensitizers and repressors to social stimuli. *Journal of Consulting and Clinical Psychology* 46: 339–40.

Miller, S. M. 1981. Predictability and human stress: Toward a clarification of evidence and theory. In *Advances in experimental social psychology*, ed. L. Berkowitz, vol. 14. New York: Academic.

Miller, S. M., D. S. Brody, and J. Summerton. 1988. Styles of coping with threat: Implications for health. *Journal of Personality and Social Psychology* 54:142–48.

Miller, S. M., and C. E. Mangan. 1983. Interacting effects of information and coping style in adapting to gynecologic stress: Should the doctor tell all? *Journal of Personality and Social Psychology* 45:223–36.

Monat, A., and R. S. Lazarus. 1985. *Stress and coping: An anthology*. 2d ed. New York: Columbia University Press.

O'Gorman, J. G., and L. H. Stair. 1977. Perception of hostility in the TAT as a function of defensive style. *Journal of Personality Assessment* 41:591–94.

Parsons, T., and R. F. Bales. 1955. *Family socialization and interaction process*. New York: Free Press.

Paul, I. H. 1959. *Studies in remembering: The reproduction of connected and extended verbal material*. New York: International Universities Press.

Paulhus, D. L. 1984. Two component models of socially desirable responding. *Journal of Personality and Social Psychology* 46:598–609.

Rank, O. 1945. Will therapy and truth and reality. New York: Knopf.

Rapaport, D. 1942. *Emotions and memory.* New York: International Universities Press.

Rapaport, D., M. Gill, and R. Schafer. [1945] 1968. *Diagnostic psychological testing.* Edited by R. R. Holt. Rev. ed. New York: International Universities Press.

Rofe, Y., and I. Lewin. 1982. Psychological factors and blood pressure during pregnancy and delivery. *Psychophysiology* 19:7–12.

Rofe, Y., I. Lewin, and B. Padeh. 1977. Affiliation before and after child delivery as a function of repression-sensitization. *British Journal of Social and Clinical Psychology* 16:311–15.

———. Emotion during pregnancy and delivery as a function of repression-sensitization and number of childbirths. *Psychology of Women Quarterly* 6: 163–73.

Rofe, Y., and L. Weller. 1981. Attitudes toward the enemy as a function of level of threat. *British Journal of Social Psychology* 20:217–18.

Scarpetti, W. 1973. The repression-sensitization dimension in relation to impending painful stimulation. *Journal of Consulting and Clinical Psychology* 70:377–82.

Schachtel, E. 1959. *Metamorphosis*. New York: Basic.

Schmitt, J. P., and L. A. Kurdek. 1984. Correlates of social anxiety in college students and homosexuals. *Journal of Personality Assessment* 48:403–9.

Schwartz, G. E. 1983. Disregulation theory and disease: Applications to the repression/cerebral disconnection/cardiovascular disorder hypothesis. *International Review of Applied Psychology* 32:95–118.

Shapiro, D. 1965. *Neurotic styles*. New York: Basic.

Shavit, H., and R. Shouval. 1977. Repression-sensitization and processing of favorable and adverse information. *Journal of Consulting and Clinical Psychology* 33:1041—44.

Shavit, Y., J. W. Lewis, G. W. Turman, R. P. Gale, and J. C. Liebeskind. 1984. Opiod peptides mediate the suppressive effect of stress on natural killer cell cytotoxicity. *Science* 223:188–90.

Shaw, R. E., F. Cohen, B. Doyle, and J. Palesky. 1985. The impact of denial and repressive style on information gain and rehabilitation outcomes in myocardial infarction patients. *Psychosomatic Medicine* 47: 262–73.

Shipley, R. H., J. H. Burt, B. Horowitz, and J. E. Farbry. 1978. Preparation for a stressful medical procedure: Effect of amount of stimulus pre-exposure and coping style. *Journal of Consulting and Clinical Psychology* 46:499–507.

Sifneos, P. E. 1983. Psychotherapies for psychosomatic and alexithymic patients. *Psychotherapy and Psychosomatics* 40: 66–73.

Singer, J. L. 1974. *Imagery and daydreaming methods in psychotherapy and behavior modification.* New York: Academic.

———. 1978. The constructive potential of imagery and fantasy processes. In *Interpersonal psychoanalysis: New directions,* ed. E. Witenberg. New York: Gardner.

———. 1981. Research implications of projective methods. In *Assessment with projective techniques,* ed. A. I. Rabin. New York: Springer.

———. 1984. *The human personality.* San Diego, Calif.: Harcourt Brace Jovanovich.

———. 1984b. The private personality. *Personality and Social Psychology Bulletin* 10: 7–29.

———. 1988. Sampling ongoing consciousness and emotional experience: Implications for health. In *Psychodynamics and Cognition,* ed. M. J. Horowitz, 297–346. Chicago: University of Chicago Press.

Singer, J. L., and S. Brown. 1977. The experience balance. In *Rorschach psychology,* ed. M. R. Ricker-Dvsiankina. New York: Krieger.

Slough, N., R. A. Kleinknecht, and R. M. Thorndike. 1984. The relationship of the repression-sensitization scales to anxiety. *Journal of Personality Assessment* 48:378–79.

Spring, R., and P. Khanna. 1982. Locus of control, repression-sensitization, and interpersonal causality. *Psychological Reports* 50:175–97.

Starbird, D. H., and H. B. Biller. 1976. An exploratory study of the interaction of cognitive complexity, dogmatism, and repression-sensitization among college students. *Journal of Genetic Psychology* 128: 277–32.

Sullivan, H. S. 1940. *Conceptions of modern psychiatry.* New York: Norton.

———. 1956. *Clinical studies in psychiatry.* New York: Norton.

Sullivan, P. F., and L. K. Roberts. 1969. The relationship of manifest anxiety to repression-sensitization on the MMPI. *Journal of Consulting and Clinical Psychology* 33: 763–64.

Taylor, G. J. 1984. Alexithymia: Concept, measurement, and implications for treatment. *American Journal of Psychiatry* 141: 727–32.

Temoshok, L. 1987. Personality, coping style, emotion and cancer: Towards an integrative model. *Cancer Surveys* 6: 545–67.

Temoshok, L., and B. W. Heller. 1984. On comparing apples, oranges, and fruit salad: A methodological overview of medical outcome studies in psychosocial oncology. In *Psychosocial stress and cancer,* ed. C. L. Cooper. Chichester, N.Y.: Wiley.

Temoshok, L., B. W. Heller, R. W. Sagebiel, M. S. Blois, D. M. Sweet, R. J. Clemente, and M. L. Gold. 1985. The relationship of psychosocial factors to prognostic indicators in cutaneous malignant melanoma. *Journal of Psychosomatic Research* 29: 139–54.

Tempone, U. J., and W. Lamb. 1967. Repression-sensitizationand its relation to measures of adjustment and conflict. *Journal of Consulting Psychology* 31: 131–36.

Tublin, S. K., and D. A. Weinberger. 1987. Individual differences in coping processes: A thought-sampling approach. Paper presented at the annual meeting of the Western Psychological Association, Long Beach, Calif.

VanBaeyer, C. 1982. Repression-sensitization, stress, and perception of pain in others. *Perception and Motor Skills* 55: 315–20.

Varca, P. E., and J. C. Levy. 1984. Individual differences in response to unfavorable group feedback. *Organizational Behavior and Human Performance* 33: 100–111.

Visintainer, M., and R. N. Casey. 1984. Adjustment and outcome in melanoma patients. Paper presented at the meeting of the American Psychological Association, Toronto. August.

Weinberger, D. A., G. E. Schwartz, and J. R. Davidson. 1979. Low-anxious, high-anxious, and repressive coping styles: Psychometric patterns and behavioral and physiological responses to stress. *Journal of Abnormal Psychology* 88: 369–80.

Wexler, B. E., G. E. Schwartz, S. Warrenburg, and L. D. Jamner. 1988. Corrugator muscle response to unconsciously processed negative emotion-evoking stimuli: Differences between repressors and true low anxious subjects. Department of Psychiatry, Yale University. Typescript.

White, M. D., and W. Wilkins. 1973. Bogus physiological feedback and response thresholds of repressors and sensitizers. *Journal of Research in Personality* 7: 78–87.

Williams, R., T. Haney, K. Lee, Y. Kong, J. Blumenthal, and R. Whallen. 1980. Type A behavior, hostility and atherosclerosis. *Psychotherapy and Psychosomatics* 42: 539–49.

Wirsching, M., H. Stierlin, F. Hoffman, G. Weber, and B. Wirsching. 1982. Psychological identification of breast cancer patients before biopsy. *Journal of Psychosomatic research* 26: 1–10.

Witkin, H. 1965. Psychological differentiation and forms of pathology. *Journal of Abnormal Psychology* 70: 317–36.

Witkin, H. A., and D. R. Goodenough. 1981. *Cognitive styles, essence and origins: Field Dependence and field independence.* New York: International Universities Press.

Woods, D. J. 1977. Conjugate lateral eye movements, repression-sensitization, and emotional style: Sex interactions. *Journal of Clinical Psychology* 33: 839–41.

Wright, L. 1988. The type A behavior pattern and coronary artery disease: Quest for the active ingredients and the elusive mechanism. *American Psychologist* 43: 2–14.

Zann, M. P. 1975. The effect of distraction on resolving cognitive dilemmas. Paper presented at the annual meeting of the American Psychological Association, Chicago.

Zanna, M. P. and C. Aziza. 1976. On the interaction of repression-sensitization and attention in resolving cognitive dissonance. *Journal of Personality* 44: 577–93.

18 Summary Chapter: Beyond Repression and the Defenses

JEROME L. SINGER AND JULIE B. SINCOFF

The reader who has remained with us to reach this concluding chapter may well hope for some assistance in organizing, integrating, and summarizing the mass of theory and research characterizing this volume. Such a task may be beyond our powers, at least in any elegant, succinct form. We shall, however, attempt several brief, concluding sections to provide our readers with cognitive schemas that enable them to keep the serious efforts of so many passionate contributors memorable. Perhaps we can do even more, arousing the affect of curiosity and stimulating at least some readers toward further investigations, encouraging the scientific enterprise to continue on its ever-hopeful task of exploring the unbounded areas of human behavior.

If we look back over these chapters, we discover a number of different subtexts embedded in the material. These reflect variations in approaches to science, in intentions, in systematic orientation, and in language use and terminological definitions. Let us review some of these variations to see if this effort can help us, first, generate some adaptive schemas or categories from the material, and second, discern new opportunities for integrative theorizing and creative research approaches.

The "Politics" of Studying Repression and the Defenses

One source of variation among our contributors concerns professionalism and the values assigned to the kinds of evidence of interest to the investigators. Put most boldly, the chapters by Edelson, Horowitz and his colleagues, Vaillant, and, to a lesser extent, Spiegel, all of whom are physicians and psychiatrists, reflect a different attitude from the other authors toward (*a*) the kinds of data that need to be explored to provide the basis for a theory and (*b*) the relative importance of studies of pathological processes or individual clinical patients. All our contributors are empirically oriented; all are committed to science versus mysticism and intuition. However, the chapters we have cited

471

place considerable weight on data derived from case studies, from anecdotes, and from analyses of pathological behavior. At the other extreme of this dimension, we find Bower, Bowers, Davis, Holmes, Kihlstrom and Hoyt, and Weinberger, with Blatt, Bonanno and Singer, Erdelyi, Lewis, Luborsky and his colleagues, Schwartz, and Shevrin occupying a more intermediate position on the dimension. The group composed of physicians and psychiatrists, while respecting the laboratory, seems more comfortable with the data that can be obtained from clinical interviews, whereas Holmes and the psychologists proclaim the critical role of systematic experimentation and quantitative analysis. To the extent that phenomena such as repression were first identified through the clinical observations of Sigmund Freud and continue to be apparent in their current work with patients, the physicians cannot easily be dissuaded from proposing theoretical structures or definitions of defenses; as Vaillant notes, the defenses are now enshrined in DSM-III-R (American Psychiatric Association 1987), despite contradictory laboratory evidence. Nor are the psychologists likely to be persuaded by dramatic videotapes or anecdotal accounts of the behavior of hysterical neurotics in therapy.

Lest we turn this issue into a professional turf war, we must quickly point to another, related source of professional variation that has epistemological implications. Blatt, Lewis, Luborsky, Shevrin, and Singer—all of whom occupied the middle ground on the above dimension—were trained formally in psychoanalysis along with Edelson, Horowitz, Spiegel, and Vaillant. Erdelyi, too, has a history of involvement with the psychoanalytic literature in addition to his long-term research interests in memory and cognition. Bower, Bowers, Davis, Holmes, Kihlstrom, and Schwartz represent contributors who may be less personally oriented toward psychoanalytic conceptions, with Weinberger in a more intermediate position. Toward the psychoanalytic pole of this dimension, we find contributors who take the data derived from psychoanalysis or a related long-term psychodynamic psychotherapy as informative, as potentially theoretically significant, and as insightful about ongoing behavior in a manner that is more intriguing than that which can emerge from even the most elegant cross-sectional laboratory experiment. At the other pole are contributors who may concede some observational genius to Freud but who are ready to forge ahead with new conceptions or models of behavior. For this latter group, much of what happens in a given psychoanalysis is tendentious theoretically, unverifiable, and likely to yield unreliable evidence.

The subtext one can discern at the psychoanalytic pole of this dimension may be heard in the question, How can we save psychoanalysis? Edelson's chapter presents this position most clearly, for its tenor seems to be one in which it criticizes most psychoanalysts who seek quantitative behavioral manifestations of repression or who see psychoanalysis as a general personality theory (as Horowitz and Singer apparently do). If we recognize that psychoanalytic theory is primarily a model of the vicissitudes of human fantasies and wishes, especially in their more unconscious form, then repression and the defenses are fantasies themselves or are operations performed on fantasies. We can find out about such subtle human behaviors chiefly through psychoanalysis, and, if we wish to engage in legitimate scientific tests of hypotheses about defenses, we should direct our research efforts to psychoanalyses or to other idiographic methods rather than to the laboratory. Closest theoretically to Edelson is Shevrin, although it is clear that he feels it necessary to perform laboratory tests of the concepts of repression and the defenses derived from psychoanalysis. Vaillant, too, seems near this pole, emphasizing longitudinal, idiographic studies but clearly not shunning quantitative analyses. Horowitz and his collaborators, while proposing formal definitions of defenses, seek to forge links between these defenses and established cognitive processes, thus viewing repression (in contrast to Edelson) as more like overt behavioral processes. Blatt and Bonnano and Singer also adopt a broader view of defenses and link them more closely with general personality dimensions that reflect patterns of object relations and interpersonal interactions. At the information-processing pole of this dimension, the contributors imply that current cognitive science has the concepts and methods to forge ahead with studies of selective perception, thought, and memory and that they are ready—cheerfully and nonconflictually—to forget about repression.

A subgroup of our contributors, Bower, Bowers, Kihlstrom and Hoyt, and Spiegel, shows a special concern with the phenomenon of hypnosis because it dramatically manifests dissociation, a process Freud did not distinguish from repression. In these chapters, we see a most encouraging congruence of conceptions and a movement toward a model of cognitive processes that can clarify the peculiarities of dissociation observed originally in clinical studies of hysterics and multiple personalities. Perhaps the kinds of blends between clinical observation and experimental study that characterize the best hypnotic research can become a model for future research on other defensive operations or even on defenses as fantasies.

The Problem of Terminology

A major concern that emerged at the original conference was one of agreement on terminology. It was felt that an examination of the semantics of our discussions would be useful as a section of this volume. We have therefore attempted such an effort based on the diversity of ideas contained in the chapters in this book.

Psychological terms often reveal evolutionary changes in meaning, especially as their use spreads from one area of psychological inquiry to another. Terms that begin with a narrow definition as used by one theorist or researcher often grow more ambiguous and inclusive as more is learned about the phenomenon in question. Certainly, this is the case with the term "repression." In an effort to clarify the meaning of repression and related terms, we will trace and summarize the ways in which the authors of the chapters in this book use and define the terms "repression," "dissociation," "defense," and "consciousness."

Repression and the Repressive Personality Style

Given the almost fifty-year evolution of the term "repression" in Freud's writing, modern writers have had a head start in expanding the meaning of an extremely important psychoanalytic concept. Freud began by describing repression as motivated forgetting, as an intentional failure to access information stored in memory. As his theory of the defenses developed, the concept of repression absorbed these developments so that it came to represent the defense mechanisms in general rather than forgetting in particular. In the introductory chapter to this book, Singer observes that "repression" eventually came to denote the systematic avoidance, through any variety of mechanisms, of potentially threatening material in thought or social experience. Recognizing the value for clinical practice of specifying the various types of defense mechanisms, of which repression is but one example, Anna Freud and other writers have broken down the defense mechanisms into specific defenses and into categories of similar defenses. The authors of the chapters in this book generally use the term at one of these two levels—as a specific defense or as a class of related defenses.

Table 1 contains this dimension, the generality of the authors' use of the term "repression," along with four other dimensions that explicate each author's working definition of the term. The second dimension addresses the nature of the authors' definitions of repression. Are their definitions theoretical or operational? The third dimension questions whether the contributors differentiate repression from either dissociation or suppression. The fourth dimension concerns the underlying purpose of the mechanism. That is, is repression a defensive strategy that is potentially maladaptive, a neutral mechanism, or a coping strategy that is predominantly adaptive? Finally, what stance do the contributors take regarding the individual's awareness of repression? Is repression a conscious or an unconscious process? The table indicates the positions of each author on all these dimensions. The authors' positions on each of the dimensions reflect their predominant usage of the term "repression" in their respective chapters in this book; their positions may be explicitly stated or implied. Although the authors' definitions may seem arbitrary in some ways, as they are influenced by individual differences in both theoretical orientation and personal preference, the table does reveal some consensual trends in the use of the term "repression" by modern psychologists and psy-

Table 1. Dimensions of Repression Selected to Indicate Each Author's Working Definition of the Term

Author	Generality		Definition		Differentiation			Mechanism		Awareness	
	Specific Defense	Class of Related Defenses	Theoretical	Operational	Dissociation	Suppression	Defense	Neutral[a]	Coping	Conscious	Unconscious
Blatt	•		•				•				•
Bonanno and Singer		•	•				•				•
Bower	•		•	•	•	•		•	•	•	•
Bowers[b]		•	•	•	•			•			•
Davis		•		•	•						•
Edelson	•		•				•				•
Erdelyi	•		•		•		•				•
Holmes	•						•		•	•	•
Horowitz et al.	•				•	•	•				•
Kihlstom and Hoyt	•					•	•				•
Lewis	•		•				•	•			•
Luborsky, Crits-Christoph, and Alexander		•					•				
Schwartz		•	•	•			•		•		•
Shevrin	•		•	•						•	•
Spiegel[b]	•		•		•					•	
Vaillant	•	•			•	•	•		•		•
Weinberger	•		•	•			•				•

[a] Authors conceptualizing repression as a neutral mechanism characterize it as motivated, but they do not address whether the motivation or outcome is adaptive or maladaptive.

[b] These authors, who address dissociation rather than repression in their chapters, tend to adopt a traditional view of repression.

Most authors treat repression as a specific, unconscious, defensive strategy for dealing with ego-threatening material. Their definitions are guided largely by theory, although the necessity for operational definitions is felt by many of the authors of this book.

Repression

The authors who use the term "repression" as a specific defense tend to adopt either information-processing or psychoanalytic paradigms. Representing the information-processing paradigm, Bower describes repression in operational terms, as the motivated forgetting of wishes and events. He uses theory on memory development to show that such forgetting may occur during the initial learning or encoding of the event or wish, during storage over the retention interval, and during the retrieval phase of memory. Thus, he decomposes the concept of motivated forgetting into its subcomponents—motivated nonlearning, motivated nonrehearsal, and motivated nonretrieval or nonreporting of memories. Shevrin also describes repression as the motivated inhibition of recall. He breaks the process down into an initial, conscious withdrawal of attention from a given event or wish and a subsequent, involuntary pull of the avoided material from the dynamic unconscious. The pull serves to mesh the repressed material more deeply into a web of repressed contents. Edelson, reflecting a psychoanalytic viewpoint, also emphasizes such a spreading effect or activation; he notes that repression is a continually active process that unconsciously extends its sphere of influence. Certainly, although the information-processing and psychoanalytic paradigms are vastly different, some blending is inevitable. Shevrin represents only one of several authors who attempt to merge some of the features of cognitive psychology with the features of psychoanalytic psychology. Horowitz and his collaborators, more than the other psychoanalytically oriented authors, approach a cognitive description of repression. They define repression as a potentially maladaptive outcome or process of inhibiting conscious representation of a theme or of parts of a theme. Erdelyi, although he emphasizes that repression is a process and not an outcome, also takes an intermediate position. He believes repression is manifested as a defensive use of schematic or reconstructive recall of memories.

Two trends are apparent among the authors who define "repression" as a specific defense. First, the operationalizations of repression tend to be cognitive, based on theories of information-processing and memory. Second, the term "repression" tends to be differentiated from other terms, particularly from "dissociation" and "suppression." Horowitz and his collaborators, Kihlstrom and Hoyt, and Vaillant, for example, all emphasize that the major difference between repression and suppression is that the former is unconscious, whereas the latter is conscious or semiconscious and is thus usually intentional. Vaillant suggests that suppression is more temporary than repression, and Horowitz and his collaborators assert that suppression is more adaptive than repression. There remains a question, perhaps for future research to address, as to whether repeated efforts at conscious suppression may lead to a gradual automatization of the process. Thus, repression may develop after a series of conscious suppressions, and the two processes may not be that different after all. The distinctions between repression and dissociation are more complex and will be discussed below.

For several authors, the term "repression" tends to be further differentiated in terms of the content of the repressed material. A major distinction is that between repressed ideas and repressed affect. Although not all authors make this distinction, some draw special attention to it. According to Vaillant, repression involves forgetting ideas but retaining affects associated with those ideas in consciousness. The defense mechanism of isolation, conversely, allows the ideas to remain in consciousness, although they are not accompanied by emotional responsiveness. Horowitz and his collaborators note that this splitting of ideas and feelings leads to flatness of affect in individuals using isolation as a defense mechanism. Erdelyi asserts that repression is characteristic of hysteric patients, whereas isolation (he does not use this term but rather describes repressed affect) is characteristic of obsessional patients. In addition to the distinction between repressed ideas (i.e., repression) and repressed affect (i.e., isolation), some authors, although certainly not all, distinguish between primary repression and secondary repression. Edelson considers only primary repression—the means of expelling material from awareness—as an instance of repression. He considers secondary repression—the means of ensuring that repressed material is permanently prevented from returning to awareness—as an instance of countercathexis. Many defense mechanisms, such as projection and reaction formation, alter repressed material and thus prevent the individual from consciously experiencing it.

The splitting off of affect from ideation is too important a clinical notion to permit it to be passed over as simply a matter of definition. The notion derived from Freud's view that every wish or drive has an ideational and an affective component and that one or another of these facets can be suppressed or repressed. Much theorizing about the differences between hysterics and obsessional neurotics is built on this notion. The chapters by Blatt and Bonanno and Singer make much of this clinical difference. However, what solid evidence do we have that these clinical groups really differ in recurrent reliance on isolation or repression? What evidence is there from either clinical material or from the laboratory that (*a*) wishes and impulses do take both forms and (*b*) separation of idea and affect can actually take place during suppression or repression? Here we confront a fertile area for further investigation.

Edelson and Shevrin make much of the belief that repression is an active process. They use the term "countercathexis," implying an expenditure of energy. The image of a jack-in-the-box impulse popping up unless one keeps one's hand on the box's cover suggests that a research study should be able to estimate the effort involved in sustaining such forgetfulness. To anticipate our discussion of the repressive style, is it possible that, despite reporting no anxiety, repressive individuals are indeed demonstrating high physiological arousal (using the Weinberger paradigm) because of the continuous effort at sustaining avoidance? A study by Lorig, Singer, Bonanno, Davis, and Schwartz (in preparation) sought to measure conscious efforts at retrieval, elaboration, and suppression of positive and negative affective memories while measuring EEG patterns. There were suggestions that repressive personalities showed less evidence of physical strain when asked to retrieve negative memories, indicating that they did not try very hard. On the other hand, they showed more evidence of an EEG response associated with strain for all behaviors, suggesting that they were actually more distressed than were the other subjects. Clearly, we need considerably more work along these lines to support the countercathexis notion.

Repressive (or Repressor) Personality Style

The authors treating repression as a class of related defenses tend to be personality theorists. They adopt a trait approach toward the study of repression (e.g., Davis). In his introductory chapter, Singer describes a personality style as a recurrent and habitual reliance on particular defenses; this reliance is reflected in lifelong mannerisms and, particularly in personality research, in the identification of personality types. The nonpathological manifestations of personality types form personality styles (e.g., Blatt; Bonanno and Singer), whereas extreme manifestations of personality types form configurations of psychopathology (e.g., Blatt).

Blatt distinguishes avoidant defenses from counteractive defenses. Avoidant defenses, specifically denial and repression, allow the individual to avoid recognizing and acknowledging the existence of conflictual issues. Counteractive defenses, such as projection, reaction formation, and intellectualization, transform conflictual issues in ways that permit disguised expressions of those issues. Although Blatt classifies both repression and denial as avoidant defenses, he asserts that repression represents a developmentally higher level of organization than denial. Bonanno and Singer, as well as Luborsky, Crits-Christoph, and Alexander, use the terms "repressive defenses" and "repressive styles" in the same sense as Blatt uses "avoidant defenses." Blatt's distinction between avoidant and counteractive defenses is similar in some respects to Edelson's distinction between repression and countercathexis.

The authors studying repressive personality styles (e.g., Bonanno and Singer; Weinberger), anaclitic configurations of psychopathology (e.g., Blatt), and field-dependent, shame-oriented personalities (e.g., Lewis) are less concerned with the formal properties of repression than they are with describing individuals who typify the personality styles. Bonanno and Singer describe repressive individuals as continually avoiding potentially threatening social encounters or streams of associative thoughts that may create awareness of conflictual issues or embarrassing experiences. These individuals provide overly positive self-descriptions of their inner processes. Weinberger adds that repressive personalities are motivated to avoid awareness of affects and impulses that are incompatible with their self-images. This last point opens the way for a very fertile research area now that we have more precise methods for measuring schemas of self and others.

As was true for authors who define repression as a specific defense, two trends also characterize the chapters of authors emphasizing the identification of a personality style marked by habitual use of denial and repression. First, their operationalizations of repression, designed to identify individuals with repressive personality styles, are usually self-report measures that have been validated through psychiatric records and physiological assessments. Bonanno and Singer argue that repressive styles are best measured by evidence that an individual displays no awareness of anxiety or distress, even though physiological assessments of arousal indicate that such individuals are more aroused or anxious than are people who consciously report these feelings. Weinberger states this simply—repressive personalities often believe that they are not upset despite objective evidence to the contrary. Weinberger's early formulation of the repressive personality style was operationalized as low reported anxiety and high defensiveness. His recent operationalization requires low reported distress and high restraint against aggressive impulses. Are aggressive wishes the only ones involved? Should further work examine this restraint in relation to other desires or fantasies incompatible with one's predominant schemas about the self in various domains?

Second, authors who study repressive personality styles are more likely than writers who define "repression" as a specific defense to acknowledge the potentially adaptive functions of denial and repression. Bonanno and Singer, for example, argue that a repressive personality style may be a precursor to the later development of psychopathological disorders (e.g., hysteria) or that it may remain a preclinical style that permits adaptation to distressful daily events. Weinberger emphasizes that individuals who are classified as repressive personalities on the basis of questionnaires are defensive only some of the time in certain circumstances; at other times, they are coping adaptively with daily stress. If so, then we need more research on the matches between person, wish or intention, self-schema, and situational demands to determine when a style is transformed into a neurotic defense.

Dissociation

Although repression was equivalent to dissociation for Freud, the two terms are not equivalent for most of the authors of this book, especially for those authors concerned with the classification of defense mechanisms and with research and theory on hypnosis. Indeed, Bowers and Spiegel, who write primarily about hypnotic phenomena, emphasize the distinction between repression and dissociation by addressing dissociation rather than repression; repression is associated with psychopathology, whereas dissociation is linked to hypnosis.

Several authors (e.g., Davis; Horowitz et al.; Spiegel) use the term "dissociation" to indicate a lack of connection, or a severing of ties, between two linked processes. Spiegel adds that the severed parts of a system may communicate with one another, although they are not experienced as a whole. Kihlstrom and Hoyt indicate that this may result because dissociated contents are fully activated yet are not linked with active mental representations of self, context, or both. Kihlstrom and Hoyt operationally define dissociation as the differential effects of an experimental manipulation on two dependent variables assessing different aspects of memory. One dependent variable may be influenced by the manipulation, whereas the other may not show any effect of the manipulation.

Depending on the author, dissociation may or may not be a defensive strategy. Kihlstrom and Hoyt, for example, do not view dissociation as defensive; like Janet, they treat repression as a defensive variant of dissociation. Spiegel views dissociation as neutral in some cases but as defensive in others. During hypnosis, dissociation is a consequence of intense absorption; the hypnotized individual processes more information than his or her absorbed state allows into awareness. Indeed, Spiegel views both dissociation and absorption as defining characteristics of hypnosis. In clinical settings, however, Spiegel asserts that dissociation involves the fragmentation of consciousness primarily for defensive purposes. Horowitz and his collaborators view dissociation as a strategy for dealing with emotional conflict and stress. Dissociation alters the integrative functions of consciousness or identity. Vaillant takes this even further by defining "dissociation" as a temporary but drastic modification of one's character or identity to avoid emotional distress.

Here again we can point to some intriguing questions and research possibilities. Is it possible that our shifts in thought to other fantasy roles may provide practice in dissociation? Is it likely that persons who can become absorbed in rich fantasies of alternative behaviors or life-styles are learning and automatizing methods for coping with unmanageable wishes or situational demands as well as for simply increasing the scope of their cognitive capacities? Acting out different roles can be adaptive socially or can lead to the skills of a performer in addition to increasing the risks of fugue states or multiple personalities. Research avenues beckon when we explore the implications of a concept rather than simply accepting it as a given.

In general, repression is best imagined as a pushing (or pulling) of ideas deep into the unconscious where they cannot be accessed. Alternatively, it involves systematic patterns of "selective inattention," as Sullivan (1956) termed it and as Luborsky demonstrated in his eye-tracking studies of repressive individuals. Dissociation is best imagined as a severing of the connections between various ideas and emotions. Even in the chapters of authors who do not attempt to distinguish repression from dissociation, its different usage is implied. Erdelyi, for example, noting that Freud treated "repression" and "dissociation" synonymously, generally does not discriminate between the two terms. However, he implies differences in meaning when he defines the defense mechanism of isolation as a two-step process that involves the prior "dissociation" of fact and affect and the subsequent, selective "repression" of the affective component of the material. Given the complexity of unconscious phenomena and of the various defense mechanisms, differentiation between repression and dissociation seems necessary simply for descriptive purposes as well as for the development of a formal taxonomy of defense mechanisms.

Defense

Although none of the authors of this book use repression and defense interchangeably, most agree that repression serves defensive purposes for the individuals who use it in research settings and particularly in clinical settings. The authors' use of the term "defense" reveals four defining characteristics of defense mechanisms. By consensus among those authors who discuss the concept of defense (not all authors address the topic), defense mechanisms are (*a*) maladaptive, (*b*) unconscious, (*c*) motivated, and (*d*) creative.

Weinberger, as well as Horowitz et al., point out that defenses, compared to the coping strategies studied in stress research, generally yield outcomes that are less adaptive and that are often even maladaptive. Weinberger adds that defenses are less effective than coping strategies because they are inflexible and reactive. Blatt describes defenses and modes of adaptation as different sides of the same coin; the mechanisms themselves may be potentially adaptive or maladaptive, but their defensive use renders them maladaptive in practice. Empirical data may eventually demonstrate when coping strategies become maladaptive. Perhaps we need studies or clinical observations that show under what conditions an avoidant response is socially effective and when it leads to self-defeating behavior.

Furthermore, defenses operate unconsciously. Horowitz et al. describe a two-part process involving the unconscious assessment of threat and also the unconscious selection of control operations designed to reduce the threat. It is clear that, although the defenses are unconscious, they are motivated and thus may be thought of as unconscious strategies. Blatt defines "defense mechanisms" as cognitive-affective processes that allow individuals to avoid recognizing and acknowledging their difficulties. He also indicates that defenses serve as strategies for helping individuals deal with their conflictual issues. Edelson clearly believes that defenses are motivated strategies. According to Edelson, the motivation behind the use of defense mechanisms is the quest for pleasure. The defenses attempt to solve the problem of achieving gratification under conditions of threat. Edelson notes that the motivation underlying the use of defense mechanisms is apparent in the individual's resistance to his or her therapist's interpretations of expelled material and their significance to the individual.

Once more we must raise a question that merits possible research exploration. Why are defenses by definition unconscious? It may be that, when they are overlearned, they operate automatically in the same way that well-established motor and linguistic habits do. Is it not possible that they sometimes represent strategies we learn in order to deal with interpersonal dilemmas? Confronted with a much bigger bully whom one would like to pummel, is it not often a conscious act to behave with extreme politeness? Reaction formations are often well practiced and are used quite frequently as tactics by lawyers with hostile witnesses. Displacements or rationalizations may be clearly thought-out means for deceiving others about one's conscious motives. Perhaps we need more studies of the evolution across time of defenses and of how they move from conscious tactics to automatized reactions that may then be inappropriately or excessively employed.

Finally, the defense mechanisms—or a given individual's uses of defense mechanisms—are creative. Although attempts have been made to classify defenses according to transformational rules and computational formulas, Edelson argues that defense mechanisms are not computational or calculated but are improvisatory and inventive. Erdelyi highlights the creativity inherent in defenses when he characterizes them as frequent types of schematic reconstructions of memories. Schematic memory can be quite imaginative. The setting in which the reconstructions occur—the clinic—and the purpose they serve—defense—do not render them less creative. As was suggested when talking about dissociation, it may be that imaginative role playing not only generates temporary distraction or escape but also trains new mental skills for dealing with psychological pain.

Consciousness

Given that the use of defense mechanisms, including repression, is typically unconscious and that one of the goals of therapy is to make both the use of such mechanisms and the expelled material conscious, several authors grapple with the definition of consciousness. Throughout this book, the terms "consciousness" and "awareness" are used interchangeably. Two different definitions of "awareness," however, permit a distinction between awareness and consciousness.

Following Dennet, Bower distinguishes awareness in the sense that the individual is able to talk about or intentionally communicate some proposition from awareness in the sense that the individual behaves as though he or she is taking a proposition into consideration even though he or she cannot talk about it or acknowledge it. In the clinic, the first type of awareness demonstrates consciousness of a proposition, whereas the second type of awareness would be considered unconscious. The same is true in studies of subliminal perception (e.g., Shevrin); subjects are unconsciously influenced by subliminal messages. Indeed, Bower defines unconscious processes as those psychological and bodily states that the individual cannot talk about or directly address even though the individual incorporates such states, and changes in state, into his or her daily functioning. Bower suggests, although he notes that there is little experimental evidence to support the suggestion, that repression may operate unconsciously in repressive individuals because the process of repression has become automatic in those individuals. Kihlstrom and Hoyt claim that automatic mental processes (and bodily processes) are unconscious in that the person does not have introspective access to their functioning. Thus, automatic, unconscious material may be represented in the second type of awareness but not in the first.

Bowers expands this distinction by referring to the second type of awareness as perception without noticing (i.e., unconscious perception). The function of "first-order consciousness," according to Bowers, is to transform something perceived (the second type of awareness) into something noticed (the first type of awareness). Once something is noticed, it may become part of "second-order consciousness," which represents the individual's beliefs and theories about the noticed information. Kihlstrom and Hoyt discuss concepts similar to Bowers's first- and second-order consciousness when they note that conscious material is both activated or noticed (first-order consciousness) and linked to activated representations of the self and one's environment (second-order consciousness). According to Kihlstrom and Hoyt, it is the link between first- and second-order consciousness that is severed during dissociation.

The Problem of Denial

It is intriguing that most of our contributors do not systematically address the distinction between repression and denial. Eidelberg (1968, 92–93) states, "In ranking the defense mechanisms, unsuccessful repression and denial appear to be basic [primary] and, in this consideration, are employed to defend against the conscious awareness of infantile wishes; the other defense mechanisms [secondary] appear to deal with the derivatives of these [primary] instinctual defenses." Denial (disavowal) is "aimed at the elimination of traumatic sense organ perceptions, the offensive perceptions mobilized by it being kept from consciousness. It specifically relates to the defense against the claims of external reality. For example, the impotent male patient denies the presence of an attractive woman" (93–94).

In their chapter, Horowitz and his colleagues propose a broader definition of "denial" in which the mechanism is not so clearly linked to a libidinal stimulus. They link it with information processing so that the individual withholds, or refuses to take in, the meaning and implications of perceived material. In normal individuals, denial avoids the necessity for responding to bad news. Horowitz et al. go on to associate denial with persons with myocardial infarctions who insist that their pains are caused by "indigestion." The study by Levine et al. (1987) is fairly specific in indicating that denial may be beneficial for cardiovascular patients in an acute stage of their illness but that continued denial predicts a more serious outcome later. Levine et al. found that a specific measure of denial of illness was more useful than measures of the general repressive personality style in predicting cardiovascular response. Holmes is especially explicit in arguing that studies of the repressive style are really talking about denial; the Weinberger measure involving the reporting of low anxiety and high defensiveness is one of denial more than repression. Additional studies may reveal whether such terminological distinctions are scientifically useful.

Vaillant makes distinctions among psychotic denial (a man weeping in a cemetery who denies the existence of tears), neurotic denial or dissociation (getting the giggles and getting drunk at the wake), repression (weeping at the cemetery but later forgetting the cause of the weeping), and suppression (postponing grief until a more opportune moment). While Vaillant's distinctions may seem arbitrary to some readers, he provides empirical data indicating that people classified from initial data as neurotic deniers do less well over their life span. In contrast, his definition of "suppression" reliably predicts a positive life course, both emotionally and physically. His specific use of "repression" seems uncorrelated with most later behavioral and adjustment measures, although the patterns are similar to those for neurotic denial. These are intriguing findings. However, we cannot avoid raising the question of whether his measure of suppression may not simply be an estimate of good ego functioning. The goal of the ego is postponement or delay of gratifying reactions in the interests of self-preservation and the reduction of anxiety, and "suppression" as Vaillant defines it seems to be just that. His linkage of dissociation with neurotic denial raises some problems; it may be that, as the contributors to the section on hypnosis suggest, dissociation is a fundamental capacity or skill, a neutral ability. It is when it is used to deny important issues that require sustained attention or action that we see it become crystallized as a potentially maladaptive behavioral or cognitive strategy.

Edelson's position that the defenses are themselves fantasies leads to a terse definition of "denial" as an imagined assault on another, on the self, or on the relation between the two. Repression is more of a fantasy about swallowing ideas; gaps in memory may be a fantasy about "female genitalia," a concept sure to drive feminist readers into a fury. Edelson's conception, in some ways a reversion to the psychoanalysis of the "libido" days and comparable to what is found in Fenichel's (1945) text, is also an effort at creating a more precise conception of the nature of psychoanalysis and its data. These are not so much the "vicissitudes of the instincts (or drives)" but the vicissitudes of the largely unconscious fantasies one has about one's wishes, especially those related to sexuality in its infantile and genital forms. It remains to be seen if Edelson, committed to a scientific rather than a hermeneutic model, can eventually provide some kinds of replicable operational methods for establishing how one can identify the defense fantasies within an analysis or in other kinds of relevant situations.

Conclusions

Although this brief discussion of the ways in which the authors of this book define and use the terms "repression," "dissociation," "defense," and "consciousness" highlights the progress that has been made in the evolution of these concepts, the tone of the authors' chapters communicates that we can look forward to continued progress toward their clarification and specification. The quest for such progress is tremendously challenging and exciting. We are certainly aware (the second type) of the importance of these concepts for understanding human cognition and personality and for working with people in clinical settings, yet we are continually striving to be more aware (the first type) of the meanings of "repression," "dissociation," "defense," and "consciousness" in science and practice.

The Repressive Personality Style: Problems and Possibilities

It seems clear that precise definitions of "repression" in specific instances in terms of the motivated forgetting of conflictual material continue to be difficult to demonstrate in the laboratory and to identify within psychoanalytic sessions, at least in forms that can convince outside observers as well as they convince the participating psychoanalyst. Considering all the effort that has gone into identifying repression, it appears that demonstrations of each separate defense under laboratory conditions (a task scarcely attempted as yet) will be unrewarding. Reexamining the repression process in relation to the nature of selective attention, selective rehearsal, and various general cognitive filtering functions may be a more useful direction to follow, and here Bower, Erdelyi, Holmes, Horowitz et al., and most of the other contributors (except

Edelson) are in agreement. Especially effective are the redefinitions of the dissociation process, which are cast in cognitive terms by Bowers, Kihlstrom and Hoyt, and Spiegel.

The group of investigators who discuss on-going personality styles seem to be finessing the problem by measuring a more fuzzy prototype of repression– a pattern of systematic avoidant behaviors. Such behaviors may involve inattentiveness to stimuli that are potentially threatening to one's self-esteem or that arouse conflictual wishes (as Luborsky's studies of eye-tracking by repressive personalities suggest), or they may even involve some failures of basic processing at the preattentive levels (as Shevrin's laboratory procedures suggest). They may be manifested as oversimplifications and as global responses, as Lewis's work on field dependence and the Rorschach inkblot literature point toward. Davis's studies point most closely to poor recall, but without being able to specify how much of this is occasioned by initial encoding failure, inadequate rehearsal, use of distractions, a generally high level of anxiety (despite denial of the experience), or a more active "pushing down" of the material–the countercathexis cited by Edelson and Shevrin. As Holmes suggests, the use of the term "repressive personality" for so many different scoring systems and for a set of presumed operations that lead to dependent variables as diverse as poor recall, impulsiveness, some kinds of psychopathology, and proneness to physical illness may be grossly misleading.

On the other hand, one cannot brush aside a general commonality of findings in the past decade, as reviewed in the chapters by Blatt, Bonanno and Singer, Davis, Schwartz, and Weinberger. The results in the health domain are especially intriguing. A number of different methods seem to identify individuals or groups who deny personal weaknesses, frailties, or fears, who regularly avoid extended examination of new information that arouses conflicts or threats to one's self-esteem, and who generally show an avoidant cognitive or behavioral pattern, even when confronted with life-threatening situations that call for action, sustained thought, worry, or consideration of remedies and consequences. Blatt and Weinberger pose some hypotheses about the origins of such styles, but the developmental problem beckons for much more extensive research. The links between the styles and life-span patterns of psychopathology, psychophysiology, and health are pointed to by Blatt, Bonanno and Singer, Lewis, Schwartz, Vaillant, and Weinberger. However, as the work of Luborsky and his colleagues suggests, we may not be able to set up effective, replicable studies in these areas unless we can develop psychometrically confluent, reliable, and reasonably valid scales or procedures. Weinberger has made a start, but he clearly sees a difference between his current measures and the earlier approach he developed with Schwartz and Davidson, which still has yielded effective results.

If there is one clear conclusion that we can draw from this accumulation of empirical data, it may be that we ought finally to give up the term "repressive personality." The term bears too heavy a load of implied meanings, theoretical loyalties, and confused operational definitions to serve personality theory in the future. Blatt's proposed "avoidant personality" may be more useful, provided we specify that avoidant behavior is addressed toward fantasies or information rather than toward social intercourse. The heretofore repressive or hysterical neurotic is often gregarious and socially extroverted, presumably to distract him or her from confronting lines of threatening thoughts. Developing a fruitful new terminology is a challenge for the future; would Miller's (Miller, Brody, and Summerton 1988) monitoring or blunting style be a better concept?

The chapters on dissociation do not focus on style as much as on process. However, we would like to propose that their convergence and cognitive clarity afford a fascinating opportunity for future personality research. If dissociation is a basic skill or capacity, then it is possible that some persons use it more adaptively or effectively, whereas others use it for avoidant purposes. Once crystallized into a habitual pattern, a dissociative trend may lead to acting skill, to the ability for self-distraction or self-entertainment, and to absorption skills that permit one to become deeply engaged in the enjoyment of reading, films, music, or other aesthetic experiences. Conversely, if certain long-standing conditions exist, then dissociative ability may develop into the classic hysterical symptoms of amnesia, fugue, multiple personality, or less dramatic but generally maladaptive states of confusion in self-schemas and alterations in consciousness as well as in excessive reactivity to drugs or alcohol. The origins of such dissociative trends in early socialization should be explored. Indeed, we propose that we may eventually move beyond the hypnosis paradigm of dissociative phenomena, finding other conditions under which dissociative personality trends can be studied. We propose that we give up the term "hypnotic susceptibility," which suggests weakness, in favor of hypnotic ability, a manifestation of the human capacity for functioning with the split awareness described by Bowers, Kihlstrom and Hoyt, and Spiegel.

Beyond Repression

Toward the end of the three-day conference from which this volume arose, one of us (JLS) ventured the seemingly blasphemous proposal that any future conferences on thoughts and behaviors related to warding off conflictual cognitive contents ban any references to Sigmund Freud. Let historians of science or scholars of epistemology devote themselves to the endless task of ferreting out what the old sage really meant. We, as cognitive and personality researchers or as clinicians, have new paradigms, new models of how experience is organized, new methods, and new skills for devising replicable psychometric or clinical tools for engendering and testing hypotheses. Perhaps we need to start where the cutting edge of our scientific enterprise lies and not fret about whether it is consistent with a body of presumed psychoanalytic theory, for which there is really no general agreement. We are speaking here not of psychoanalytic practice or of the clinical observations that have emerged from its practice–for example, transferences, self-defeating behaviors or resistances, and the informational value of free associations and of reports of fantasies and dreams. Instead, we are emphasizing the necessity for concentrating on our current experiments, clinical observations, and empirical models. Let us start by proposing models of the human condition that reflect the tremendously rich cognitive literature, the increasingly heuristic work on differentiated emotions, and the new approaches to studying patterns of thought and behavior across the life span.

Suggestive possibilities abound in the present volume. Although to some readers Edelson's chapter may seem offbeat, it does contain a proposal about the human being as a scripting organism that (pace Edelson) bears many similarities to current cognitive psychology and to social-cognitive researchers' emphases on ways of conceptualizing human thought. Silvan Tomkins (1962, 1:13), a pioneer of this development and still active in trying to systematize a notion of nuclear or commitment scripts as the basic material of personality research, wrote,

> Afferent sensory information is not directly transformed into a
> conscious report. What is consciously perceived is imagery
> which is created by the organism itself . . . the world we per-
> ceive is a dream we learn to have from a script we have not writ-
> ten. It is neither our capricious construction nor a gift we inherit
> without work. Before any sensory message becomes conscious it
> must be matched by a centrally innervated feedback mechanism.
> This is a central efferent process which attempts to duplicate the
> set of afferent messages at the central receiving station . . . .
> matching the constantly changing sensory input is a skill that one
> learns as any skill. It is this skill which eventually supports the
> dream and the hallucination, and which central sending produces
> as the conscious image in the absence of afferent support.

Long before Tomkins or Freud, Francis Bacon, in *The Advancement of Learning,* wrote, "For sense sendeth over to imagination before reason have judged; and reason sendeth over to imagination before the decree can be acted; for imagination ever precedeth voluntary motion." Edelson's proposal that we devote scientific effort to exploring the changing patterns of human ongoing wishful thought and examining how conflictual or vexing fantasies or wishes are modified by further fantasy offers a challenge to a fully rounded model of human cognition and information processing. Perhaps the psychoanalytic procedure remains the premier avenue for such an exploration, or at least some more controlled modification of it is possible that is not so heavily burdened with clinical constraints. New approaches in sequential imagery or in thought sampling may also be useful here (Singer and Kolligian 1987).

Most of the other contributors to this volume seem in general agreement that the old concept of defenses needs reformulation in terms of information processing and the connections between cognition and emotion. Kihlstrom and Hoyt have sketched a conception of a cognitive unconscious (elaborated also in Kihlstrom 1987) that seems to us to open an exciting new direction for formulating hypotheses about how potentially distressing or conflictual wishes may be addressed or avoided and how some of this avoidance may operate outside awareness. Bower and Bowers have both moved us farther along in identifying the structures and functions of experiences in various states of awareness. Horowitz and his coauthors acknowledge the usefulness of such a direction. Spiegel takes a daring leap in trying to link multiple personality disorder to the new and challenging parallel distributed processing (PDP) models.

Future conceptual and empirical work is necessary to see if one can still maintain a distinction between a notion of a dynamic unconscious as separate from a cognitive unconscious. What special properties would be necessary to sustain a model in which a set of wishes, fantasies, or powerful impulses can persist out of awareness and generate new and complex organizations that are reflected in our day and night dreams? Can current cognitive models such as Bower's or Kihlstrom's encompass such a system, or do we require the complexity seemingly introduced by the PDP group (Rumelhart and McClelland 1987; see Spiegel's chapter)? None of these approaches has fully integrated the important motivational role of the emotions, as illustrated in Lewis's chapter or in works by Buck (1985), Mandler (1984), Tomkins (1962–63), and Zajonc (1980). The challenges to one's beliefs about the self or to one's self-oriented memories that Kihlstrom emphasizes as a key to how motivated forgetting or dissociation is set in motion must also involve experiences of fear, anger, or sadness. What roles will these emotions play in the cognitive models cited or in the PDP system? Schwartz hints at some of the physiological links among emotion, inattention to thought content, and physical health, but he does not provide a systematic view of the cognitive processes involved.

We can discern a consensus emerging in many of these chapters, suggesting that we can begin to move beyond the earlier notions of specific defenses and the ambiguities of the concept of repression. Bower, Bowers, Erdelyi, Holmes, Horowitz et al., Kihlstrom and Hoyt, Schwartz, Spiegel, and most of the contributors who address personality styles seem to view what psychoanalysis has labeled "defenses" as facets of more general, adaptive cognitive strategies or as interpersonal communication patterns. Perhaps we can summarize this trend in a simplified form and close this volume with the hope that it will whet readers' appetites to re-read and rethink the very thoughtful contributions assembled herein.

The human being can be regarded as an information-seeking, information-processing organism. We need to assign meanings to the ambiguities we confront in each new physical or social setting. Our emotional system is closely linked to the rate, ambiguity, and complexity of the new information we must process from moment to moment. Our established schemas or scripts, along with our wishes and fantasies, lead us to anticipate what we may confront in the next room or in the next social encounter. We rarely get it exactly right, but we seem to be wired up so that moderate degrees of incongruity arouse interest and curiosity, motivating further exploration until we can match the new data with some array or prior schemas. Then we laugh, smile, or experience relief. More extreme degrees of incongruity or disconfirmation of expectancies evoke fear, and the persistence over time of such unexpected information that cannot readily be assimilated evokes anger, distress, or sadness (Mandler 1984; Singer 1974, 1984; Tomkins 1962–63, vol. 1). As Kihlstrom and Hoyt suggest in their chapter (and in keeping with much research on the self-concept), a special role is played by the relevance of information or beliefs about the self or of memories defined as autobiographical.

We can propose that there are three major sources of stimulation that serve as settings for our encounters with new information. These include the physical or social environment outside our skins, although this real world takes on a personal meaning based on our experiences and the complexity of our differentiated schemas, scripts, and prototypes for defining it. A second source of stimulation is from the ongoing activity of our memory system—our stream of consciousness, which provides us with fleeting associations, elaborate and sometimes frightening fantasies, and odd but generally intriguing night dreams. This is the domain that Edelson proposes is the special area for psychoanalytic exploration. Finally, the ongoing machinery of our bodies presents us with a continuing series of signals, some fairly readily interpretable as in alimentary, digestive, or excretory functions or reactive pains, but many mere twitchings or, in the case of autonomic or central nervous system functions (such as brain waves), largely outside an awareness level that permits effective communication to others (see Bower's chapter). Evidence of conditioning of bodily activities or of voluntary control through biofeedback (often still without verbal labeling or descriptive awareness) suggests that such signals can be discriminated but not interpreted into a lexical or imagery system that permits the formation of schemas.

In effect, part of the human dilemma is that we must maneuver our way through life from moment to moment choosing which stimuli we wish to attend to at both the first and the second types of awareness. Generally, we give highest priority to our own physical and social milieu (what Neisser [1988] has termed the "ecological self") because survival necessitates, for example, that we look before crossing city streets. We must, of course, slip back into the private self of memory or fantasy in order to help us interpret new experiences, but this is often an overlearned, automatized process. We can, however, give more attention to our memories, wishes, and fantasies when our external demands are reduced by redundant settings and overlearned situations such as routine chores, solitary environments, and waiting rooms. Centrally generated stimuli can divert our attention from the physical environment, as when we pass a flower shop while riding on a bus and suddenly remember that it is Mother's Day, or even without external cues, as when the face of one's most recent romantic flame stares up at one from a pile of data analyses. Body signals generally receive lowest priority except when a persistent urge to urinate leaves one wiggling and twisting while trying to conduct a serious conversation or when a pang of muscle pain suddenly interrupts a pleasant reverie about a future victory in tennis.

Growing up involves learning a variety of strategies for choosing where to focus attention, for determining under what circumstances we can give higher priority to private thoughts and wishes, for gaining control over bodily functions, and so on. We also begin to develop metastrategies (presumably through early socialization by family and culture as well as through management of constitutional temperamental proclivities) for determining the relative emphasis to place on internal and external signals–the origins of an introversion-extroversion dimension of personality. We need a metastrategy that can become automatized for limiting the complexity and levels of inputs from all sources so that what Baars (1989; see Spiegel's chapter) has called the global workspace of consciousness does not become too cluttered.

The notion of selective filtering thus becomes a critical human task and almost certainly the basis for what later emerges as avoidant strategies. Gradually, we learn not to divert too much attention to what experience proves to be nonconsequential features of the environment in the interest of greater focus on matters of special importance. We also learn avoidant strategies for reducing clutter even when the issue is not threatening, as in the case of turning away from the television set during the commercials. The array of procedures for voluntarily avoiding attention (and hence encoding or storage) includes the ways we learn to skim a newspaper, making judgments from headlines or sections of the paper, so that we spend no time reading and later remembering material in which we have little interest. Luborsky's clever demonstration of repressive people's avoidance of sexually provocative material in a picture is a special case of such a skimming strategy. The chapters by Bower, Bowers, Erdelyi, and Kihlstrom and Hoyt outline a variety of ways in which the forgetting feature of repression is constructed out of a series of cognitive processes from attention through encoding, rehearsal, and various retrieval strategies. How such avoidant strategies can become automatized is also suggested in the chapters by Bower and Kihlstrom and Hoyt.

We would like to propose that suppression of unwanted thought can also be produced by shifts of attention to avoid spontaneous mental rehearsal. The pain or distress one might experience if one thinks for a while about a lost opportunity or lover can be quickly avoided by busying oneself with making a drink, lighting a cigarette, flicking on the television, or trying to engage one's neighbor at a cocktail party in light chatter. Such failures of rehearsal may to some extent reduce the probability of later spontaneous retrieval of the thought.

Conscious suppression of thought may indeed be quite adaptive, as Erdelyi, Schwartz, Vaillant, and other contributors suggest, in the interest of more effective timing or consideration of one's issues. We all confront the reality that, if we think too much about desired pleasures or about the dangers to human existence posed by nuclear armaments, pollution, population density, and chemical hazards in food and at the workplace, then we can barely make it through the day, let alone get work done. To suppress such thought about potential dangers, however, does not mean to minimize its importance. That would be the most primitive and usually more pathological defense of denial. Instead, one decides when one can fruitfully think of these issues and what practical actions one can take, whether by joining organizations, contributing money, changing dietary habits, or otherwise engaging in activities that ensure that others are actively thinking and working on such issues and that one's government is not denying or repressing the dangers.

The same principle applies to more private yearnings, pains, and sorrows. We can temporarily suppress dwelling on them in the interest of completing certain urgent tasks or obligations, but we must allow ourselves some opportunities to confront our recurrent wishes in order to discover whether at least some are attainable, to ponder over failures in order to do better, to mourn for people who have died, and to recognize through physical pain the possibility that we may require some form of medical attention.

With respect to bodily functions, we go through a phase of first noticing them a great deal in infancy, gradually differentiating those most important for survival or for avoiding the embarrassment of soiling. We automatize control of our bodily functions; then we turn our attention away from them for many years of our lives until the aches and pains of the later years become more insistent. Again, there may be interesting individual differences in awareness of some kinds of bodily functions or organ systems–for example, athletes and their muscular and skeletal systems and individuals with more deviant narcissistic body fixations. It remains an interesting, developing area of study to ascertain whether the denial or repression discussed in the health psychology areas (see Bonanno and Singer's and Schwartz's chapters) reflects a form of selective inattention to cardiovascular system signals or even to certain messages from the immune system.

One emerging implication from the chapters of this volume appears to be that, although a search to trap repression in a classical sense as it happens may be a dubious approach, there is an heuristic opportunity for studying individuals who differ systematically in their reliance on avoidant processes. We need to know more about how such processes develop–in what kinds of families, under what social constraints, and in what domains of activity or around what kinds of problems. Blatt suggests that exaggerated avoidant strategies are more closely associated with early experiences emphasizing social concerns, fear of loss of love, abandonment or rejection, and experiences of shame (see also Lewis's chapter). Strategies that involve what he calls counteraction (e.g., isolation, reaction formation, and obsessive-compulsive rituals) are more likely to emerge from problems of self-esteem, guilt, and fear of failure. Of course, we cannot avoid noticing that even so-called counteractive strategies may essentially be avoidant. Sullivan (1956) used the term "obsessional substitution" to suggest that ritualistic behavior, preoccupation with petty details, and rumination about trivial thought may be in the service of avoiding confrontation with an idea, environmental cue, or needed action that either would be incapable of fulfillment or would involve social risk or inner conflict. Indeed, it might be arguable that many of the so-called defenses may be forms of systematic self-distraction to preclude attention or to prevent learning and rehearsal of conflictual ideas and communications, thereby deceiving oneself and possibly other people about one's desires and intentions. As these become overlearned, they may indeed function outside awareness, but they may be identifiable fairly readily (sometimes with the help of a therapist-observer) in the same way that we can reconstruct the sequences in an overlearned motor act once we find it necessary to explain the process to someone else. As our chapters on dissociation suggest, the human capacity for compartmentalizing complex sets of differentiated social, emotional, and motor behaviors is greater than we generally realize.

The special role of avoidant strategies in the health or psychophysiological area beckons for greater exploration. Why should denial of illness or systematic avoidance of thought about one's worries or interpersonal skills be so often associated with physical problems? Schwartz's chapter uses the notion of system disregulation to suggest an approach to linking avoidant thought and behavior to body organ malfunction. Recently, there has been increasing finger pointing at the immune system. A recent study by Pennebaker, Kiecolt-Glaser, and Glaser (1988) demonstrated that simply asking undergraduates to write about the major traumas in their lives for four consecutive days led to significantly lower subsequent visits to health services and was also associated with changes in immune system functioning (compared to control subjects). Although the specifics of the immune system results are subject to question on various technical grounds and cannot be shown directly to account for subsequent perceived good health, the sizable reduction in visits to the doctor's office after "confession" has now been replicated several times. This opposite effect of the avoidant strategy used by the repressive personality clearly encourages further research. Indeed, in one of the studies cited by Schwartz (1987), repressive individuals showed more frequent visits to the college health service, despite the denial of problems reported on questionnaires. Just what links there may be between the immune system and the central nervous system may be a study not only for immunobiology but also for careful psychophysiological work. There may be ways in which some individuals have overlearned a cluster of avoidant strategies designed to maintain a constricted sense of well-being; these strategies may, however, yield a failure to identify subtle bodily signals of malaise or to engage in appropriate self-care behaviors.

It is probably best that we consider using other terminology than "repression" to describe persons who show systematic styles of avoiding thought or self-awareness of potentially troublesome life issues or who actively avoid situations that might remind them of such issues. If this book achieves its scientific purposes, it may turn out to be the last book on repression or on the repressive personality style. We need to move toward newer constructs, newer models, and better integration of cognitive laboratory research with the observations by clinicians of their patients' self-defeating and pathological behaviors. We can acknowledge that all thought involves selectivity and filtering processes, that we may in given situations consciously assign differential priorities to processing material from the environment, from our memories and wishes, or from our bodies. We gradually develop strategies that permit us to perform many of these tasks so smoothly that they occur without perceptual awareness. Selective inattention, avoidance of labeling, avoidance of reminiscence and rehearsal, distraction through physical or social activity, and ruminative thoughts about trivialities all may interfere with the subsequent retrievability of troublesome experiences. Rather than invoke the concepts of defense and repression to close this book, we propose that individual differences in reliance on various types of selective, cognitive-affective strategies under certain circumstances and in particular domains of human concern may become the basis for differences in self-presentation, psychopathology, and physical health.

Appendix

Although most of the chapters contained in this volume offer suggestions for future research, we have assembled a list of research suggestions here. It is our hope that this volume has motivated theorists and researchers to begin examining the questions raised by the contributors to the book.

1. What are the relations between repressed memories (presumably incompatible with one's self-image) and one's schemas of the self and others?

2. Does the separation of ideas and affects take place during repression or dissociation?

3. Do clinical populations differ in their repeated reliance on isolation or repression?

4. Do repeated efforts at conscious suppression lead to a gradual automatization of the process, resulting in a process that is similar to repression?

5. Is there effort involved in sustaining repression or motivated forgetfulness? That is, does research support the countercathexis notion?

6. What are the links between avoidant thought and behavior and body organ malfunction? Does the immune system serve as an intermediate link?

7. How are conflictual fantasies modified by further fantasy? Are there consistent strategies for modifying conflictual fantasies?

8. Do shifts in thought from one fantasy role to another provide practice in dissociative phenomena?

9. When do coping strategies become maladaptive? Can we specify the conditions under which an avoidant response is socially effective versus when such a response is self-defeating?

10. What is the evolution across time of defensive strategies? How do they move from conscious tactics to automatized reactions that may be inappropriately or excessively employed?

11. Can we specify the links between people, wishes or intentions, self-schemas, and situational demands to determine when a style is transformed to a neurotic impulse?

12. What are the origins of avoidant strategies in infancy?

13. What are the origins of avoidant strategies in childhood?

14. Can we verify the existence of a dynamic unconscious that is different from a cognitive unconscious? What distinguishes the dynamic unconscious from the cognitive unconscious?

References

American Psychiatric Association. 1987. *Diagnostic and statistical manual of mental disorders*. 3d ed. Washington, D.C.: American Psychiatric Press.

Baars, B. J. 1989. *A cognitive theory of consciousness*. New York: Cambridge University Press.

Buck, R. 1985. Prime theory: An integrated theory of motivation and emotion. *Psychological Review* 92:389–413.

Eidelberg, L. 1968. *Encyclopedia of psychoanalysis*. New York: Free Press.

Fenichel, O. 1945. *The psychoanalytic theory of neurosis*. New York: Norton.

Kihlstrom, S. 1987. The cognitive unconscious. *Science* 237:1445–52.

Levine, J., S. Warrenburg, R. Kerns, G. Schwartz, R. Delaney, A. Fontana, A. Gradman, S. Smith, S. Allen, and R. Cascione. 1987. The relation of denial to the course of recovery in coronary heart disease. *Psychosomatic Medicine* 49:109–17.

Lorig, T. S., J. L. Singer, G. A. Bonanno, P. Davis, and G. E. Schwartz. In preparation. Personality and EEG patterns during affective memory and attempted thought suppression. Department of Psychology, Yale University.

Mandler, G. 1984. *Mind and body.* New York: Norton.

Miller, S. M., D. S. Brody, and J. Summerton. 1988. Styles of coping with threat: Implications for health. *Journal of Personality and Social Psychology* 54:142–48.

Neisser, U. 1988. The self: An ecological analysis. Keynote address, presented to the twenty-fourth International Congress of Psychology, Sydney.

Pennebaker, J. W., J. K. Kiecolt-Glaser, and R. Glaser. 1988. Disclosure of traumas and immune function: Health implications for psychotherapy. *Journal of Consulting and Clinical Psychology* 56:239–45.

Rumelhart, D., and J. L. McClelland. 1987. *Parallel distributed processing.* 2 vols. Cambridge, Mass.: MIT Press.

Schwartz, G. 1987. Personality and health: An integrative health science approach. In *The G. Stanley Hall Lecture Series,* vol. 7., ed. V. P. Makosky. Washington, D.C.: American Psychological Association.

Singer, J. L. 1974. *Imagery and daydream methods in psychotherapy and behavior modification.* New York: Academic.

———. 1984. *The human personality: An introductory text.* San Diego, Calif.: Harcourt, Brace, Jovanovich.

Singer, J. L., and J. Kolligian, Jr. 1987. Personality: Developments in the study of private experience. *Annual Review of Psychology* 38:533–74.

Sullivan, H. S. 1956. *Clinical studies in psychiatry.* New York: Norton.

Tomkins, S. 1962–63. *Affect, imagery, and consciousness.* 2 vols. New York: Springer.

Zajonc, R. 1980. Feeling and thinking: Preferences need no inferences. *American Psychologist* 35:151–75.

Index